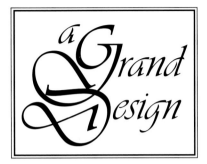

THE ART OF THE VICTORIA AND ALBERT MUSEUM

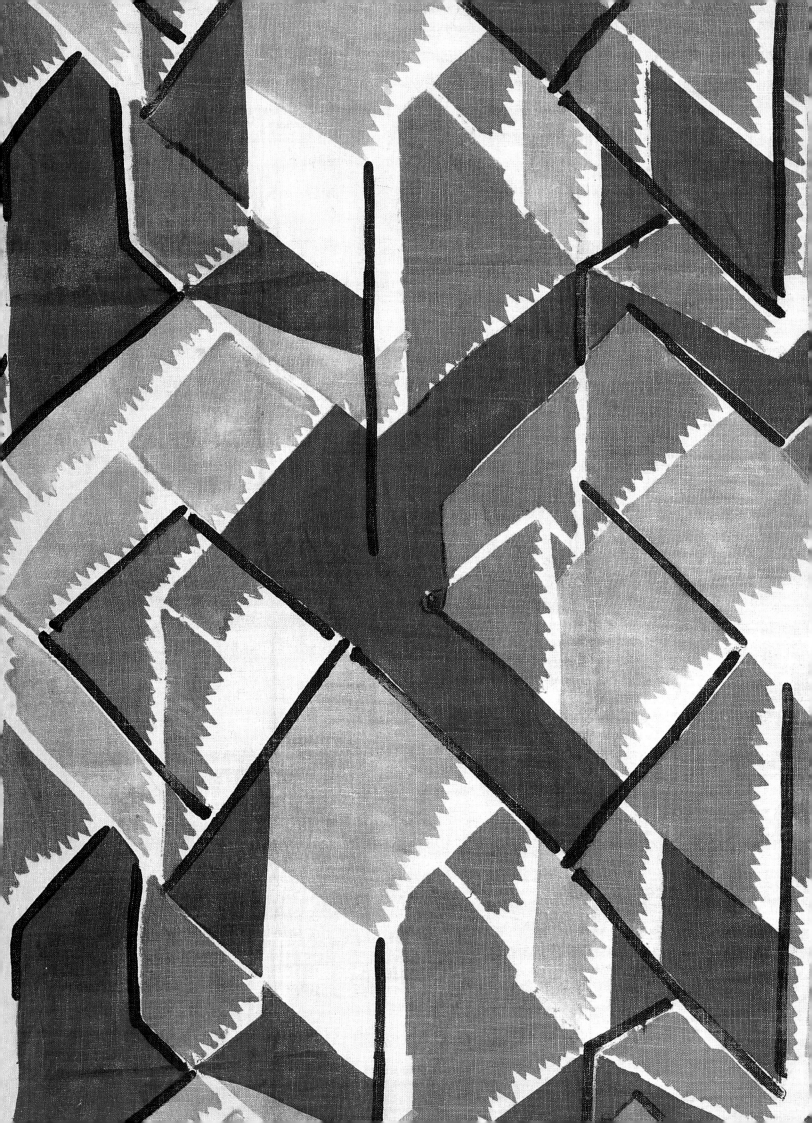

A Grand Design

THE ART OF THE VICTORIA AND ALBERT MUSEUM

MALCOLM BAKER
BRENDA RICHARDSON

General Editors

with research and essays by

ANTHONY BURTON
CRAIG CLUNAS
MICHAEL CONFORTI
RAFAEL CARDOSO DENIS
RICHARD DUNN
PARTHA MITTER
CHARLES SAUMAREZ SMITH
TIMOTHY STEVENS
PETER TRIPPI
CHRISTOPHER WILK

HARRY N. ABRAMS, INC., PUBLISHERS

with

THE BALTIMORE MUSEUM OF ART

Frontispiece: Detail of cat. 171, Vanessa Bell, *Maud,* 1913

For Harry N. Abrams, Inc.:
Editor: Elisa Urbanelli
For The Baltimore Museum of Art:
Editor: Brenda Richardson
Designers: Alex Castro and Ingrid Castro

Published in conjunction with the exhibition

A Grand Design: The Art of the Victoria and Albert Museum

organized and circulated by The Baltimore Museum of Art

in association with the Victoria and Albert Museum

Exhibition brought to North America by
Visa U.S.A. and Lockheed Martin

THE BALTIMORE MUSEUM OF ART
October 12, 1997–January 18, 1998

MUSEUM OF FINE ARTS, BOSTON
February 25–May 17, 1998

ROYAL ONTARIO MUSEUM, TORONTO
June 20–September 13, 1998

THE MUSEUM OF FINE ARTS, HOUSTON
October 18, 1998–January 10, 1999

FINE ARTS MUSEUMS OF SAN FRANCISCO
February 13–May 9, 1999

VICTORIA AND ALBERT MUSEUM, LONDON
October 14, 1999–January 16, 2000

Library of Congress Cataloging-in-Publication Data

Victoria and Albert Museum.
    A Grand design : the art of the Victoria and Albert Museum / edited by Malcolm
Baker and Brenda Richardson.
        p.   cm.
    Catalog of a traveling exhibition shown at the Baltimore Museum of Art, and other
museums Oct. 1997–Oct. 1999.
    Includes bibliographical references and indexes.
    ISBN 0-8109-3399-3 (clothbound)   0-912298-70-7 (paperback)
    1. Art—Exhibitions. 2. Art—England—London—Exhibitions. 3. Victoria and Albert
Museum—Exhibitions. 4. Victoria and Albert Museum. I. Baker, Malcolm. II. Richardson,
Brenda. III. Baltimore Museum of Art. IV. Title.
N1150.A58 1997
707'.4'7526—dc21   97–3644

Published in 1997 by Harry N. Abrams, Incorporated, New York,
and The Baltimore Museum of Art, Baltimore, Maryland

Printed and bound in Italy

Harry N. Abrams, Inc.
100 Fifth Avenue
New York, N.Y. 10011
www.abramsbooks.com

Contents

9 PREFACE
Arnold L. Lehman and Brenda Richardson

15 FOREWORD
Alan Borg

17 MUSEUMS, COLLECTIONS, AND THEIR HISTORIES
Malcolm Baker

23 THE IDEALIST ENTERPRISE AND THE APPLIED ARTS
Michael Conforti

49 THE VICTORIA AND ALBERT MUSEUM: AN ILLUSTRATED CHRONOLOGY
Richard Dunn and Anthony Burton

79 INDUSTRIAL ARTS AND THE EXHIBITION IDEAL
Peter Trippi

89 Catalogue Entries 1–13

107 TEACHING BY EXAMPLE: EDUCATION AND THE FORMATION OF SOUTH
KENSINGTON'S MUSEUMS
Rafael Cardoso Denis

117 Catalogue Entries 14–39

149 AN ENCYCLOPEDIA OF TREASURES: THE IDEA OF THE GREAT COLLECTION
Timothy Stevens and Peter Trippi

161 Catalogue Entries 40–86

221 THE EMPIRE OF THINGS: THE ENGAGEMENT WITH THE ORIENT
Partha Mitter and Craig Clunas

238 Catalogue Entries 87–117

275 NATIONAL CONSCIOUSNESS, NATIONAL HERITAGE, AND THE IDEA OF "ENGLISHNESS"
Charles Saumarez Smith

284 Catalogue Entries 118–163

345 COLLECTING THE TWENTIETH CENTURY
Christopher Wilk

354 Catalogue Entries 164–200

396 NOTES

401 BIBLIOGRAPHY

412 ACKNOWLEDGMENTS

418 INDEX

Contributors

MALCOLM BAKER is Deputy Head of Research at the Victoria and Albert Museum in London.

BRENDA RICHARDSON is Deputy Director for Art and Curator of Modern Painting and Sculpture at The Baltimore Museum of Art in Baltimore, Maryland.

CRAIG CLUNAS is a Reader in the History of Art at the School of Cultural and Community Studies, University of Sussex, Brighton.

MICHAEL CONFORTI is Director of the Sterling and Francine Clark Art Institute in Williamstown, Massachusetts.

RAFAEL CARDOSO DENIS teaches at the Escolo Superior de Desenho Industrial in Rio de Janeiro.

RICHARD DUNN is a curator with the British Galleries Project at the Victoria and Albert Museum.

PARTHA MITTER is a Reader in the History of Art at the School of English and American Studies, University of Sussex, Brighton.

CHARLES SAUMAREZ SMITH is Director of the National Portrait Gallery in London.

TIMOTHY STEVENS is Assistant Director (Collections) at the Victoria and Albert Museum.

PETER TRIPPI is Consultant Curator of Nineteenth-Century British Art at The Baltimore Museum of Art.

CHRISTOPHER WILK is Chief Curator of the Department of Furniture and Woodwork at the Victoria and Albert Museum.

AUTHORS OF CATALOGUE ENTRIES

MICHAEL ARCHER, cat. 45

MALCOLM BAKER, cats. 61, 64, 71, 134, 136–137

DIANE BILBEY, cats. 24, 26–27

CLARE BROWNE, cats. 131, 138

MARIAN CAMPBELL, cats. 46–48

CRAIG CLUNAS, cats. 105, 109

FRANCES COLLARD, cats. 9, 157, 163

KATHERINE COOMBS, cats. 121–122

ROSEMARY CRILL, cats. 4, 93, 98

JUDITH CROUCH, cat. 84

LUCY CULLEN, cat. 32

SUSAN DACKERMAN, cats. 8, 131

AMY DE LA HAYE, cat. 200

CATHIE DINGWALL, cat. 199

RICHARD DUNN, cats. 104, 165–166, 181, 197

ANN EATWELL, cats. 2, 3, 156

RICHARD EDGCUMBE, cat. 153

RUPERT FAULKNER, cats. 114–116

WENDY FISHER, cat. 85

PHILIPPA GLANVILLE, cats. 125–126, 147–148

ALUN GRAVES, cats. 180, 187

JOHN GUY, cats. 87–91

MARK HAWORTH-BOOTH, cats. 33–34, 172, 189, 194

CATHERINE S. HAY, cats. 129, 150

WENDY HEFFORD, cats. 12, 17–19, 79

SORREL HERSHBERG, cat. 195

ROBIN HILDYARD, cats. 13, 75, 127–128

JULIA HUTT, cats. 10, 117

GREG IRVINE, cats. 112–113

ANNA JACKSON, cats. 11, 114–116

ELEANOR JOHN, cat. 68

ANITA JONES, cat. 131

NORBERT JOPEK, cats. 65–66, 69

ROSE KERR, cats. 107, 110

FIONA LESLIE, cat. 16

REINO LIEFKES, cats. 49–50, 53, 72

SARAH MEDLAM, cats. 7, 77, 149

VALERIE MENDES, cats. 171, 178, 190

ELIZABETH A. MILLER, cats. 21, 31

PETA MOTTURE, cats. 23, 54–59

TESSA MURDOCH, cats. 135, 151–152

CHARLES NEWTON, cats. 139, 186, 188

ANTHONY R. E. NORTH, cats. 28, 30, 70, 76, 102, 133, 154

JENNIFER H. OPIE, cats. 5–6, 8, 71, 160, 167, 174, 183–184

RONALD PARKINSON, cats. 1, 51–52, 60, 86, 118–120, 158

LINDA PARRY, cats. 159, 162, 164, 168, 171, 175

CLARE PHILLIPS, cat. 124

BRENDA RICHARDSON, cats. 1, 8, 31, 36–39, 61, 104, 140, 158–159, 165–166, 168, 171, 175, 191

PIPPA SHIRLEY, cats. 22, 67, 73

MICHAEL SNODIN, cat. 29

SUSAN STRONGE, cats. 92, 94–97

CHRISTOPHER TITTERINGTON, cats. 25, 35

MARJORIE TRUSTED, cats. 80–82

ERIC TURNER, cat. 20

OLIVER WATSON, cats. 99–101, 176, 185, 198

ROWAN WATSON, cats. 14–15, 62–63, 155, 161, 192

JENNIFER WEARDEN, cats. 78, 103

CHRISTOPHER WILK, cat. 165

LIZ WILKINSON, cat. 111

GARETH WILLIAMS, cats. 169–170, 173, 177, 179, 181–182, 193, 196

PAUL WILLIAMSON, cats. 40–44

MING WILSON, cat. 108

VERITY WILSON, cat. 106

LINDA WOOLLEY, cats. 130, 132

JAMES YORKE, cats. 74, 83, 123

HILARY YOUNG, cats. 140–146

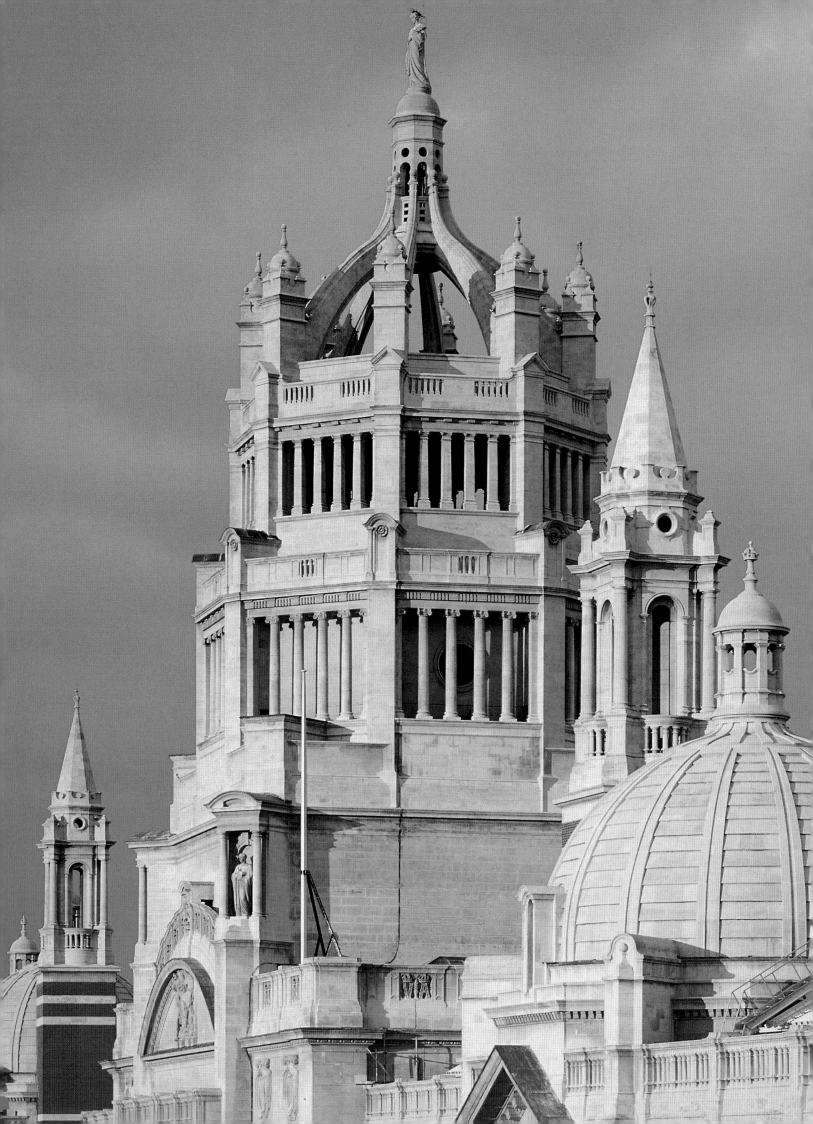

Preface: A Point of View

ARNOLD L. LEHMAN, Director
BRENDA RICHARDSON, Deputy Director for Art
The Baltimore Museum of Art

"THE CHOICE OF A POINT OF VIEW IS THE initial act of a culture. . . . To define is to exclude and negate," wrote Ortega y Gasset (*The Modern Theme,* 1923). England is a nation grounded in tradition, a nation that has defined itself within the boundaries of class, hierarchy, and territory. Inspired by the model of international industrial displays at the Great Exhibition in 1851, the institution that has since 1899 been called the Victoria and Albert Museum was founded in 1852 as the Museum of Manufactures, an institution dedicated to presenting the applied, or decorative, arts. The new museum's mission was spelled out by Henry Cole—the entrepreneur, educator, and civil servant whose initiative and convictions were in large part responsible for the stunningly successful 1851 Crystal Palace exhibition—in his first annual report to the Board of Trade:

> [A] Museum presents probably the only effectual means of educating the adult, who cannot be expected to go to school like the youth, and the necessity for teaching the grown man is quite as great as that of training the child. By proper arrangements a Museum may be made in the highest degree instructional. If it be connected with lectures, and means are taken to point out its uses and applications, it becomes elevated from being a mere unintelligible lounge for idlers into an impressive schoolroom for everyone.[1]

Throughout the intervening century and a half, the V&A (as the Museum came to be called) has struggled with the viability and relevance of its founding mission in relation to its ever-evolving social and cultural context; new technologies; constantly changing audience demographics; iconic collections—now numbering more than 4 million objects spanning two thousand years of art in virtually every medium—that make the V&A one of the greatest and most comprehensive treasure houses in the world; and, not least, the influence of the Museum's own administrative and curatorial staff over the years as it brought to the institution divergent and

Fig. 2. The Dome, Victoria and Albert Museum, South Kensington, London

often conflicting attitudes, expertise, and intellectual points of view. Commenting in the 1990s on Henry Cole's 1850s vision, former Museum director Dame Elizabeth Esteve-Coll wrote that

> it is important to be aware, in understanding the history of the Museum, that its educational and didactic purposes preceded the acquisition of its collections. It was to be a distinctive type of Museum, oriented towards the understanding and interpretation of the principles of design in manufactured goods, educational in the ways that the collections were displayed, and to be enjoyed by as broad an audience as possible.
>
> Since the Museum was established, it has pursued these ideals, not always with equal success....[2]

The Victoria and Albert Museum has been forced to struggle not simply with its frequently splintered vision of itself, but to delineate its place within a national culture and, more specifically, within a sociopolitical system that often seemed to allow little flexibility or innovation. Art and its institutional place in public life were carefully prescribed. For decades in England objects of historical and archaeological significance were designated for the collections of the British Museum, as were objects defined as ethnography; paintings considered to be of universal *art* historical significance were designated for the collections of the National Gallery; modern English paintings and sculptures were directed to the Tate Gallery, initially administratively part of the National Gallery; and objects of applied art went to the V&A. When occasional messy "overlaps" or uncertain definitions were acknowledged, groups of objects would be divided among two or more institutions.

In Britain, "Art" and "Science" manifested themselves in distinct fashion that rarely caused confusion among the civil servants who administered decisions about proper disposition of objects. However, until very recent times, art has been much more narrowly defined than science. Even as England brought home the riches of empire, it discriminated among the spoils available for looting from its colonies. England, reflecting culturally instilled biases, actively collected "refined" Western-style Indian sculpture, for example, while leaving behind the "much maligned monsters" (to borrow scholar Partha Mitter's memorable book title on this subject) of more characteristic Indian art in the Hindu style. Similarly, England saw the material culture of its African colonies as "primitive"—objects of historical or ethnographic interest and thus "Science" rather than "Art"—and consigned those pieces to the British Museum or the Museum of Mankind. It must be reported that in this latter regard American and European museum experience is not unlike that of the V&A and other English art museums. In the United States, too, African artifacts were most often considered within the context of anthropology and accordingly consigned to ethnographic museums. It was not until the 1920s that American art museums incorporated what was then called "primitive art" into their collections as well as their exhibition programs (The Brooklyn Museum of Art became the first in 1923 when it purchased 1,500 works of African art for its collection and put many of them on public display). The difference is that the V&A, even through the twentieth century, never diverged from its prescribed course relative to African art, despite Britain's colonization of much of that continent.

Ironically, certain key aspects of the V&A's character derived more directly from practices typical of museums of history and anthropology than from those of art museums. Founding director Henry Cole adopted education as the overriding mission of the new South Kensington Museum and to the present day the V&A features typological displays adapted from ethnographic paradigms. In an art museum, "even the most disparate and foreign objects become contemporary and accessible"; in an ethnographic or "natural history museum, on the other hand, all is culture-bound, and the subjective words 'quality' and 'beauty' never grace a label. The displays are left the dull task of providing context...."[3]

It is all the more stunning, then, that out of this culture of certainty sprung a museum that has had a greater and more profound impact on museums worldwide than any other in history. At its founding in the mid-nineteenth century, the South Kensington Museum departed radically from everything museums were supposed to be in that era. In doing so, the V&A introduced the concept that museums ought to operate in the public interest and, further, promulgated the conviction that objects within the museum should—and could—convey educational benefit, enjoyment for the populace, and even (by displaying the best industrial design as exemplars of the genre) the means to economic reward. This then revolutionary mission is today shared by nearly every museum in North America and, indeed, by most major museums throughout the world.

The Baltimore Museum of Art was incorporated in 1914 on essentially the same founding principles as those that define "the South Kensington ideal." The BMA's articles of incorporation cite the new museum's five official purposes:

> (a) The establishing and maintaining . . . of a Museum and Library of Art.
> (b) The encouraging and promoting of the study and enjoyment of the fine and industrial arts. (c) The application of art to manufactures and to practical life. (d) The furnishing of instruction to the public in regard to the foregoing subjects by means of exhibitions and lectures. . . . (e) The receiving of gifts or loans of objects of Art . . . to be used for the foregoing purposes. . . .

Though stopping short of citing the Victoria and Albert Museum in its charter—as several other American museum charters in fact do—it is clear that the South Kensington approach was known to and appreciated by the BMA's incorporators. Like those who organized new art museums from Boston to Bombay, Baltimore's founders too looked to the Victoria and Albert Museum as a lodestar of educational innovation and enlightened public interest.

This is a moment in the history of museums when our most fundamental purposes as public institutions are being questioned and occasionally undermined. In the last decade of the twentieth century certain of our greatest museums have seen their missions and integrity compromised by extra-institutional sociopolitical agendas and "community standards." It has become nearly impossible for mainstream American museums, at least, to take on historically sensitive subjects, whether black slavery, gay activism, Japanese internment, or U.S. military initiatives. David Lowenthal, the distinguished English scholar of social sciences, recently commented on cultural critic Louis Menand's representation that "When [subcultures] acquire official patronage, they're on the way to the museum." Lowenthal promptly responded in a published letter, "But museums are not morgues; as the Smithsonian's Enola Gay fracas showed, they are prime foci of partisan action."[4]

It is precisely this reality of the museum as an arena of partisan action that *A Grand Design* addresses. The selection, presentation, and publication of art and artifacts by museums are expressions of specific points of view. Each such expression represents a choice, and each point of view defines one thing while it excludes and negates something (or everything) else. This reality is not commonly understood by the museum-going public, which generally sees the museum's choices as something approaching acts of God or, at the least, as driven by absolute and objective standards.

To make this reality of museums as fields of "partisan action" tangible to a broad audience—to bring the issues into the public arena for thoughtful consideration and lively dialogue—requires an institutional subject prepared to be dissected, with each of its choices, whether historical or contemporary, put under a magnifier. The Victoria and Albert Museum is an ideal subject: home to great collections acquired, for diverse and ever-evolving reasons, over a century and a half; vast archives documenting specific actions over that same period; a commitment to intellectual rigor; a staff eager to advance understanding of the V&A's history as a means to better understand the meanings, influence, and implications of museums worldwide; and a willingness to engage in candid dialogue about the full spectrum of the Museum's actions, whether those actions in retrospect appear to have been foresighted or retrograde, informed or uninformed, benign or malevolent.

Aware of the seminal role played by the V&A in the formation and ideology of museums of fine and applied arts internationally—along with the knowledge that this unique and complex institution had built over its century and a half one of the most exceptional collections in the world—it seemed not just worthwhile but potentially important to present and publish a broad selection from the V&A's collections that might serve to crystallize the central issues that face all art museums today. Such a presentation would also acquaint a much enlarged public in North America about this great museum, its influential history, and its dazzling collections.

The format for *A Grand Design* took shape only over a period of years, ultimately assuming a thematic structure designed to reveal layers of collection development from the mid-nineteenth century to the present. Each of six sections focuses on one thematic aspect of choices made by this uniquely complex Museum: (1) "The Great Exhibition and the Industrial Ideal" addresses the idealistic goals of the V&A's founders—most especially the Museum's first director Henry Cole—to present industrial arts as a means of improving national design standards among manufacturers and working classes; (2) "Teaching by Example" talks about the fundamental—and then revolutionary—concept promulgated at the South

Kensington Museum that art objects can be used to educate a broad public; (3) "An Encyclopedia of Treasures" focuses on the era when the museum's profoundly influential first curator, Superintendent of Art Collections John Charles Robinson, brought great treasures of Italian Renaissance art into the Museum's collections, and the implications of the "encyclopedic schoolroom" becoming a "treasure house"; (4) "The Engagement with the Orient" candidly scrutinizes the politics of empire, colonialism, and racism as it impacted decision making at the Museum; (5) "The Idea of 'Englishness'" looks at the V&A's renewed consideration in the early twentieth century of national heritage and the importance of collecting major works of British art; and (6) "Collecting the Twentieth Century" addresses the delicate matter of engaging with contemporary artists and craftspeople and collecting the art of our own time (art whose significance and merit are as yet untested by the passage of years).

The Victoria and Albert Museum is called "the V&A" or "the Museum" throughout *A Grand Design* even when the nomenclature is anachronistic. The Museum was founded in 1852 as the Museum of Manufactures (at Marlborough House), renamed the Museum of Ornamental Art in 1853, opened as the South Kensington Museum in 1857, and renamed the Victoria and Albert Museum on 17 May 1899 by Queen Victoria (b. 1819; reigned 1837–1901) in her last official public appearance. A tribute to her beloved consort Prince Albert (1819–1861), the name has led to confusion about the Museum's identity among the public, many of whom are said to visit the V&A in the belief that it houses the personal collection of Victoria and Albert. In fact, the V&A's collections of more than 4 million objects are drawn from two thousand years of cultural history, and include ceramics, metalwork, jewelry, furniture and woodwork, sculpture, textiles, paintings, drawings, prints, and rare and illustrated books. The Baltimore Museum of Art is extremely proud to join in partnership with the Victoria and Albert Museum to present *A Grand Design* in North America and, by the year 2000, in the United Kingdom as well.

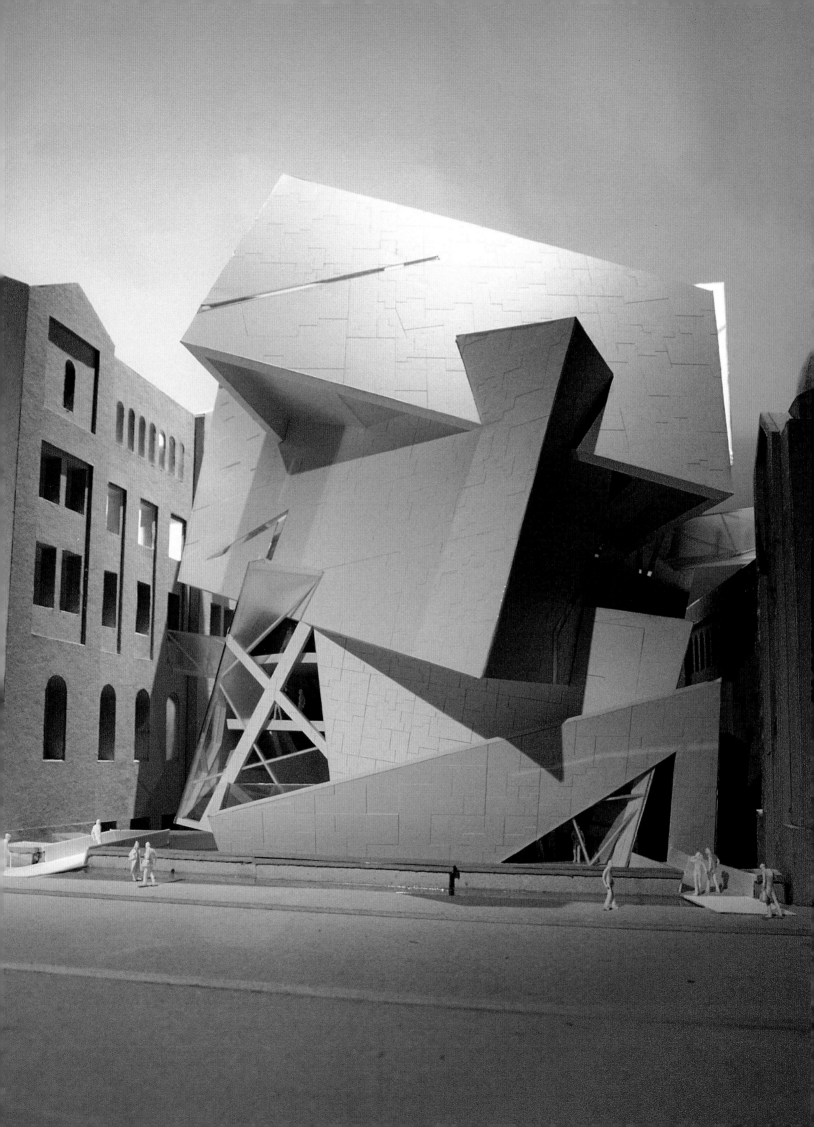

Foreword

ALAN BORG, Director, Victoria and Albert Museum

A GRAND DESIGN REVEALS THE WAY IN WHICH A GREAT MUSEUM came into being and has grown over almost one hundred and fifty years. It is a fascinating story, full of extraordinary characters, great works of art, many triumphs, and some disasters. No institution stands still, and the history of the Victoria and Albert Museum reflects the ways in which society, taste, perception, and scholarship have changed over the years.

That process of growth has not stopped, and indeed this book and the exhibition it celebrates represent just another stage in the Museum's continuing evolution. It is an important stage, however, marking a revival of the V&A's links with some of the great museums of North America. The V&A was influential from its earliest days in promoting the idea that museums are engines of social improvement and education. This was a theme taken up by many American museums, which often looked to the V&A as a model. But this Museum's role as a spiritual and intellectual example for other cultural institutions to follow was to diminish in the twentieth century, and today we are perhaps less well known outside the United Kingdom than we were a hundred years ago. *A Grand Design* will help to change that perception and is therefore especially welcome.

All exhibitions are collaborative ventures, both within and without the museums that present them. In this case a very large number of the staff of the V&A have been involved—far too many to name individually, but I am grateful to them all. (I should like to pay particular tribute, however, to Daniel McGrath, who took many of the photographs for this book—including those for the cover—and who was, tragically, killed in a car accident in December 1996.) I think all those who have worked so hard on this project have succeeded in giving a fair portrayal of a great British institution, but that is really for our viewers and readers to judge. *A Grand Design* was first proposed by Arnold Lehman, Director of the BMA, to my predecessor, Dame Elizabeth Esteve-Coll, and the project was already far advanced when I came to the V&A as director. The preparation of the exhibition has been for us a useful and enjoyable exercise, not least because of the close cooperation with our colleagues at The Baltimore Museum of Art, especially Arnold Lehman and Brenda Richardson, the Deputy Director. Seeing it to fruition has taught me a lot about this Museum and given me a much better appreciation of its amazing character. I believe *A Grand Design* will delight all who see the exhibition or read this book.

Fig. 3. Architect Daniel Libeskind's design for the V&A's Boilerhouse Building, scheduled for completion in 2002 (see pp. 74–5). Working model, built January 1997 by Studio Libeskind, Berlin

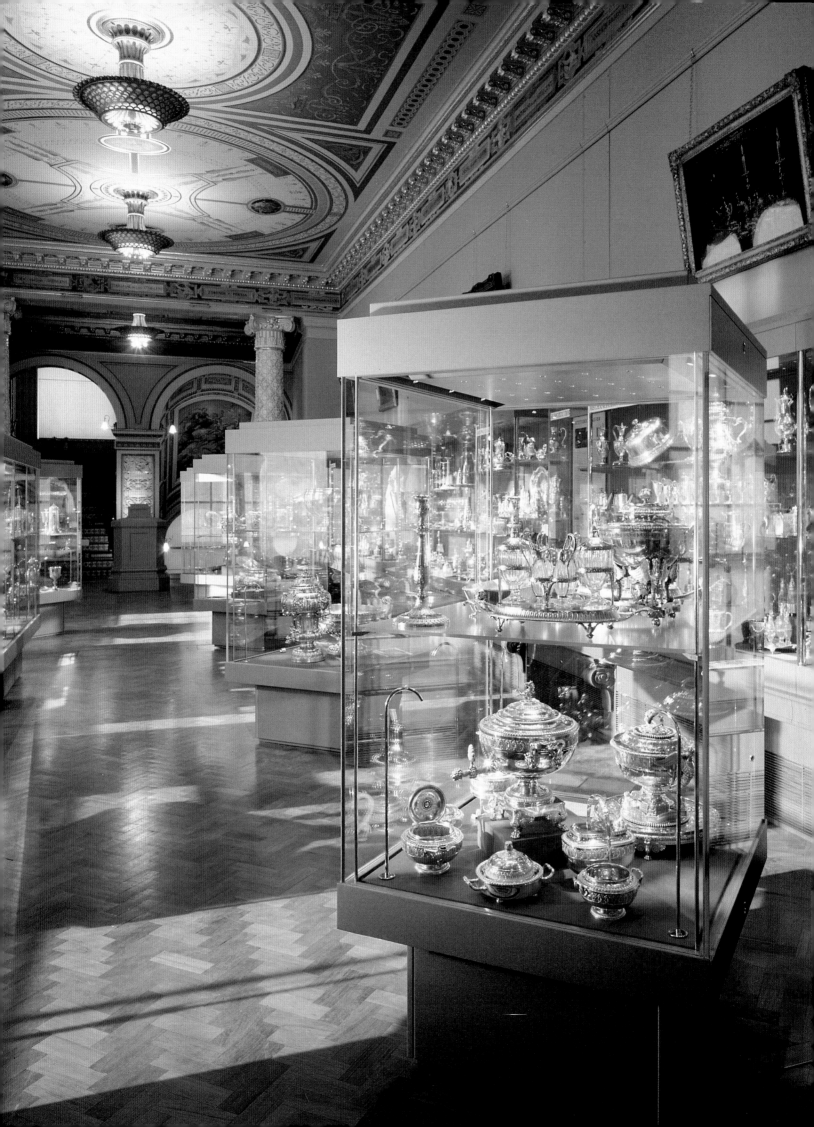

Museums, Collections, and Their Histories

Malcolm Baker

Founded with the aim of preserving the past, museums, their collections, and their architecture have often been seen as presenting authoritative narratives of history to successive generations of visitors. Like the pyramids in the eyes of Renaissance writers, museum collections are expected to endure until the end of time. The individual artifacts and works of art considered worthy of inclusion in museum collections are assumed to be similarly enduring because of their aesthetic or documentary value. But museums can change over time, as can the meanings ascribed to the objects they contain—changes that often reflect shifting cultural and social conditions. Starting from the assumption that art institutions, their collections, and the meanings of those collections evolve, *A Grand Design* presents an account of one of the world's largest and most important museums and how its collections were formed, displayed, and constantly reinterpreted. The book—and the exhibition it documents—deal not only with the institution's origins but also with the ongoing life of the collections and, through the continuing relevance of the subject's themes, even the Museum's future.

The Victoria and Albert Museum was established in 1852. Following its move in 1857 to South Kensington (then on the western edge of central London), it was for more than four decades known as the South Kensington Museum, until its renaming by Queen Victoria in 1899. Founded by the British Government following the Great Exhibition of 1851, the Museum from the start differed markedly in both its aims and the scope of its collections from two other existing national museums: the British Museum and the National Gallery. These institutions had their own governing boards of trustees, and large parts of their collections were assembled by private individuals. By contrast, the South Kensington Museum, though benefiting from some outstandingly generous private bequests, contained collections that either had been purchased with government funds from the Great Exhibition and subsequent international exhibitions, or assembled for the use of the Government Schools of Design. Unlike the British Museum and the National Gallery, the V&A (as the Museum is routinely called) was, until 1983, under the direct control of a government department, initially the Board of Education, and at least in its first half-century, the Museum formed an integral part of a wider system of national art education.

The Victoria and Albert Museum also differs from its sister institutions in the nature of its collections, primarily composed of the applied or decorative arts.

Fig. 4. The V&A's Silver Gallery, opened 1996

Among the earliest institutions to be devoted to this category of material, the V&A served as a model for similar museums throughout Europe, North America, and India, and its collections are the most extensive of all applied arts museums. Like those of both the British Museum and the National Gallery, the V&A's collections are international in scope, while also containing major British works—in the V&A's case, the world's foremost holdings of British silver, ceramics, textiles, and furniture. Although the V&A collections include more paintings than the National Gallery and cover some areas that are also represented at the British Museum, they differ markedly from those collections precisely because of the V&A's primary focus on the applied arts.[1] The V&A's collections, however, are not comprehensive and do not consist solely of works classified as applied arts. Though at first sight the collections as a whole are paradigmatic of a museum of the applied arts, they have a rich ambiguity that merits detailed investigation. Which categories of work are included, and which are excluded, is a significant issue; the Museum's contents are less systematic and coherent than might be assumed. *A Grand Design* therefore sets out not only to present a selection of remarkable works from the V&A's collections, but also to examine the artistic, social, political, and individual forces involved in the formation of the collections, along with the ways in which they have been redefined and used over the century and a half since the Museum's founding. This is not a straightforward narrative. Each section of *A Grand Design* includes objects acquired at different times and deals with a cluster of issues that have relevance in any consideration of the Museum's ongoing purposes and uses. Texts about individual objects document the circumstances leading to, and the thinking that informed, the acquisition of an object, as well as the various meanings that objects have been given by virtue of their subsequent display and publication.

Throughout *A Grand Design,* several histories are intertwined. One concerns the formation of the collections, focusing on an investigation of the sources of particular works, the reasons for acquiring them, and the ways in which acquisitions came about—through a combination of considered policy, chance availability, and the personal tastes and motivations of curators and donors. A second history relates to the periodic reinterpretation of objects and their ongoing life within the Museum.[2] One means of assessing changed interpretations of objects and styles over time is by examining the history of displays, as represented in surviving photographs and guidebooks. Museums present an array of objects in diverse displays intended both to educate and impress the viewer—the notion of spectacle as a means of gripping the imagination of the museum visitor grew in part out of the nineteenth-century international exhibitions. But the Museum also functions as a three-dimensional archive that preserves history, documents the passage of time, and serves as a resource for research and publication. Changing attitudes toward individual artworks, shifting notions as to which periods and categories of material are considered most significant, and a constant reformulation of what is considered worthy of inclusion in the canon can be discerned in these different modes of presentation.

Yet another history—about viewing the collections—is narrated in *A Grand Design,* and it is perhaps the most difficult to document or conceptualize. While guidebooks may suggest what the visitor should look at, and even the route that he or she should follow around the building, the trajectory that any one visitor might follow—and the meanings that this single individual might read into the objects encountered along the way—will only rarely coincide with the strategic thinking of the Museum's planners. How a visitor interacts with artworks and their settings is determined by personal needs, associations, biases, and fantasies rather than by institutional recommendations. In considering this history—that of response to, and reception of, the collections—the issue is not with the Museum as defined by its official aims and aspirations, but with how it is reconstituted in the individual imagination. Inevitably elusive and infinitely various, this history can be suggested only between the lines. All of these various histories of the Museum are interwoven throughout *A Grand Design.*

The notion of addressing the Victoria and Albert Museum's history and the formation and continual reinterpretation of its collections was conceived and developed just as the history of museums in general began to attract unprecedented attention.[3] *A Grand Design* draws on a rapidly growing literature about museums as institutions and about the history of collecting.[4] One strand within this literature has been concerned with the histories of individual museums. The emphasis of most of these studies has been antiquarian, documenting in rich and telling detail the sources, formation, and growth of collections, as well as the institutional structures that govern them and the buildings that house them. Among such publications, usually written by curators of particular museums, are accounts of the Ashmolean Museum in Oxford, the Germanisches Nationalmuseum in Nuremberg, and the Rijksmuseum in Amsterdam.[5] Many recent exhibitions have also focused on the histories of collections in particular institutions, including those of the Princeton Art Museum, and of the Department of Prints and Drawings of the British Museum. A major show at the Musée d'Orsay in Paris examined the development of French museums in the nineteenth century.[6]

Another strand in the literature examines a variety of institutions and collecting practices in terms of their uses as instruments of ideology, the systems of knowledge underlying their classificatory schemes, and the issues of representation involved in their strategies of display.[7] These critiques of the museum, largely by academics working outside museums, have provided a valuable theoretical framework in which questions about the histories of individual institutions can be addressed. While often referring to evidence about specific cases, they nonetheless neither set out to provide a sustained and detailed analysis of single institutions, nor to follow the ways in which these issues are worked and reworked by such institutions over the course of their histories. *A Grand Design* attempts, in a modest and necessarily limited way, to make use of these methods of inquiry by considering the formation and reconfigurations of one major institution's collections in terms of how a museum represents the past and its own and other cultures.

A Grand Design presents, from different viewpoints, a composite and fragmentary history of the V&A's collections, documenting their formation and uses, while raising issues relevant to the Museum's role as a public institution. One of the most sensitive of these issues centers on the dichotomy between stated aims and what is achieved, between the aspirational and the contingent. Another involves the tension between, on the one hand, Museum policy about acquisition and interpretation—

as this has been formulated over time to reflect political or national considerations—and, on the other, the particular influence of individuals, whether administrators, curators, or donors. Notable is the relationship between the parts of the collections assembled by purchase with government funds and those substantial groups of material given by private collectors—the Jones, Ionides, Salting, Schreiber, and Sheepshanks bequests being perhaps the most notable examples.

Also surfacing at many points is uncertainty as to whether the collections should be sweepingly international (as the early claims about the V&A's supposedly encyclopedic aims suggested) or give particular prominence to British material. The development of this schism would seem to be connected with the Museum's growing role in articulating national identity at a time when Britain's imperial powers were beginning to wane. Indeed, the Museum's identity as an institution inextricably linked with the structures of imperialism underlies both approaches to its collecting and the interpretation of the collections once they were assembled. This is most clearly evident in the central, but problematic, position of the Indian collection; the very specific attitudes taken toward collecting the arts of China and Japan; and the almost complete absence of African artifacts, which were seen as constituting ethnography rather than art and design. But such imperialist assumptions may also be glimpsed in how the V&A's displays have so often aspired to present an overarching survey of the applied arts. This imperial basis of the collections not only is an issue lodged in the Museum's past but also has vital implications for the way the institution is perceived in its postcolonial present and future.

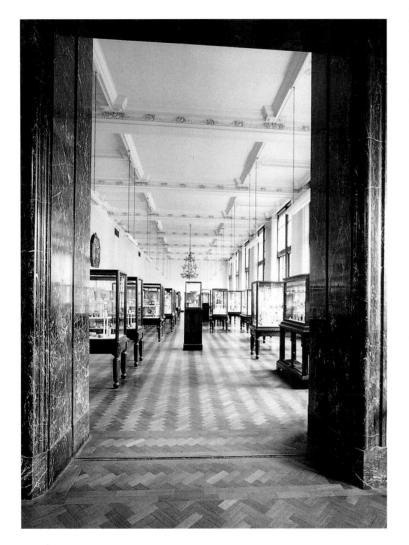

Fig. 5. The V&A's Glass Gallery, c. 1972, with casework as arranged in about 1950

Such tensions and dilemmas are discernible throughout the V&A's history and make up the agenda of the continuing debate over what this Museum—perhaps, indeed, what museums in general—are for. Nowhere is this more strikingly evident than in the arguments concerning what the V&A's collections should include and what might constitute a canon of the applied arts. The notion of a canon of "masterpieces" consisting of great works by major painters and sculptors is a familiar one. Despite a growing awareness that such canons are not absolute but are, rather, subject to historical change and sociopolitical influence, most viewers almost certainly accept the presence of such "masterpieces" in art museums as entirely natural.

In the case of the applied arts, however, it is much more problematic to determine what constitutes a masterpiece and whether it is appropriate for museum display. In part, the problem arises from the question of authorship. Unlike most paintings and sculptures—associated with the name of an artist (and sometimes a very famous name)—many objects of applied art are of unknown origin as to maker. These "useful arts" are often attributed to "anonymous" or "unknown" makers or, if to a specific maker, to someone whose name is relatively unfamiliar. Compounding a certain skepticism about the value of "nameless" works is the prominence of the function of the applied art object. Even if a painting of a saint originally from a Baroque altarpiece was created specifically for purposes of religious devotion, once it has been removed from its context and placed in a museum, it is seen as a work of art, not as an expression of church dogma designed to function in a particular setting. Most ceramics or furniture, on the other hand, prompt questions about what they were for and how they were used; in other words, their function rather than their artistic qualities or historical interest is placed in the foreground. This very ambiguity that underlies how such objects are presented and viewed in museums can lead to a new awareness of the museum itself on the part of the visitor. Usually unconnected with a familiar name and lacking the aura associated with the nonfunctional artwork, objects of applied art on display in museums have the potential to alert the visitor to the artificiality, subjectivity, and seeming arbitrariness of the institutions in which they are placed, as well as to the conventions of representation these institutions employ.

The ambiguity provoked by placing on display—out of reach or locked away in glass cases—objects fundamentally intended to be used, sat upon, and handled, presents a unique challenge to the interpretation of not only the applied arts objects themselves but also the museums that house them. As the largest of all museums of the applied arts and the model for so many other museums, the Victoria and Albert Museum is the ideal subject for critical analysis. *A Grand Design* not only documents the life of a major museum but also raises important questions about how museums represent the past through the formation and interpretation of their collections.

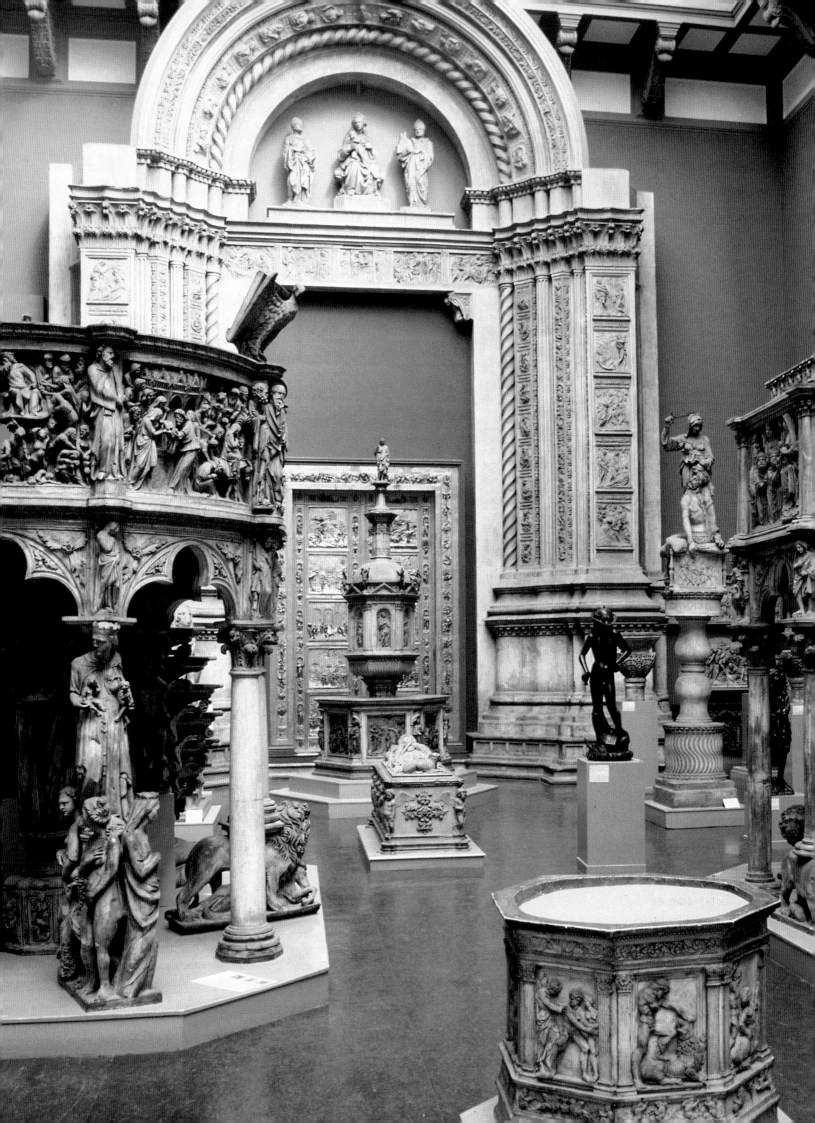

The Idealist Enterprise and the Applied Arts

Michael Conforti

From its origins in the eighteenth century, the art museum has subtly and variously represented the power of nations, the triumph of elites, the ambiguous and contingent manifestation of a culture's social and aesthetic ideals. Of all the explicit and implicit functions of these societally mandated instruments for artistic encounter, however, the most sustained and consistently articulated aspiration has been public service through education. This is particularly true in Britain and America, where the belief in the art museum's civic responsibility had both its origins and its earliest mandated institutional expression.

The first museum to direct its educational objectives toward broad audiences in a systematic and engagingly forceful way was one devoted to the applied arts, the Victoria and Albert Museum. With its historical roots in the liberal political philosophy of the nineteenth century and its early programs evolving from the publicly directed commercial spectacles that were the international exhibitions of the time, the V&A (or the South Kensington Museum, as it was called until 1899) represents a historical paradigm for public engagement through creative educational programming. The model it offered is as relevant to the issues of mission and audience, of social purpose and public responsibility, that face museums at the dawn of the twenty-first century as it was to institutional culture 150 years ago.

It was South Kensington's very lack of aloofness, its amalgamation of audience excitement, educational purpose, aesthetic ambition, and, indeed, commerce-enhancing ends, that energized the nascent American museum movement in the second half of the nineteenth century. Combating decades of national negligence in the study of art reflected in attitudes like that of John Adams, who had seen "not indeed the fine arts which our country requires [but] the useful, the mechanic arts," civic leaders like Charles Taft of Cincinnati grasped in the example of South Kensington an opportunity to generate the start-up funds for something as foreign as an art museum in the pragmatic, still somewhat insular climate of late-nineteenth-century America. When he lectured in 1878 to the Women's Art Museum Association of Cincinnati on the value of establishing a South Kensington–style museum in his city, Taft constantly referenced its potential economic and social value, as many of his fellow civic leaders would throughout the United States.

> Many of us have visited the Dresden Gallery . . . and the Berlin Museum and
> the term museum suggests to us . . . a series of rooms, filled with costly
> paintings of the old masters, antique marbles, coins, jewels . . . etc. The

Fig. 6. A view of the east Cast Court of the V&A. At the far end is the electrotype copy of Lorenzo Ghiberti's (1378–1455) famous bronze doors (nearly eighteen feet high) from the Baptistry in Florence, dwarfed by a plaster cast from Bologna's Basilica of San Petronia, the doorway sculpted by Jacopo della Quercia (c. 1374–1438) rising more than fifty-one feet in the space.

Ladies Association, in establishing such an institution [as South Kensington] is seeking to relieve the present pecuniary distress of our idle population, by opening new industries or enlarging the scope of the already existing.[1]

The Cincinnati Art Museum opened three years later. Its collection and programs, like those of many of America's largest art museums, followed those established at South Kensington.

The respected lawyer Joseph Choate inaugurated the first permanent building of New York's Metropolitan Museum of Art in 1880 with regular references to its potential imitation of South Kensington's program. The writings and speeches of the Boston arts advocate and South Kensington promoter Charles Perkins helped to create that city's Museum of Fine Arts. The faith in the South Kensington example in Philadelphia and Chicago, in Providence and St. Louis, was a product of the international reputation it had established for effectively integrating contemporary aesthetics in design with social and commercial purpose, all directed at the broadest possible public. William T. Walters, the Baltimore railroad magnate and founder of that city's Walters Art Gallery, made special note of South Kensington's widely perceived commercial, social, and artistic achievement:

> The South Kensington Museum . . . has accomplished more for the general diffusion of art knowledge and love of the beautiful among the English people than all the inactive art collections of Great Britain put together. . . . [It] injects its influence into the everyday life of the people; the [other museums] invite the gaze of the lovers of the beautiful and the curious, but are like preachers whose sermons are delivered with folded arms and closed eyes.[2]

In spite of South Kensington's extraordinary achievements, and the widely accepted belief in its unconditional success, the Museum's reputation in England in the 1880s and 1890s had begun to falter. Its first permanent exhibitions had brought together collections of art and science, foodstuffs and animal products, mirroring the informal arrangements of international exhibitions. The fame of these early exhibitions had established the Museum's founding director, Henry Cole, as an international figure. The excitement generated by these pedagogical installations began to evaporate after Cole's retirement in 1873. The question as well as the consequences of confusion of purpose stemming from the Museum's multiplicity of programs was worsened by the issue that still nags at museums committed to social engineering through a gallery experience: How do you effectively educate the public in a room filled with inanimate objects? How, and what, do you teach the uninitiated as you provide pleasure for the frequent, knowledgeable visitor?

One of the legacies of the Victoria and Albert Museum, evident from virtually its moment of inception, was an institutional rhetoric that supported the educational purpose of its art collections and an institutional practice that focused on the collecting of the unusual and the fine. These objects of aesthetic merit continue to attract us today, often for reasons different from those stated at the time of acquisition. From a historical perspective, works of art in the V&A collections document a changing museological value system reflecting national and imperial ambitions, antiquarian fascinations, material and technical concerns, and changing aesthetic ideals, all integrated within the stated purpose of social and economic improvement. They also represent a mid-nineteenth-century mimetic educational philosophy, based on the experience of art, whose compelling and highly influential lesson is still with us. Most importantly, however, the V&A's sculpture, paintings, works on paper, and applied arts collections served in the past and exist today as international standards of art and design, the canonical touchstone for excellence in each of the fields they represent. These collections remain the single greatest legacy of this portentous, extraordinarily influential institution, a Museum still able to garner the passions of its constituencies as it did when it was inaugurated more than a century ago.

SOUTH KENSINGTON: ITS ORIGINS

When the South Kensington Museum opened in the 1850s, public education was a benignly assumed but rarely stated goal of the many organizations that called themselves museums, whether these institutions focused on paintings or objects, and whether the objects were of aesthetic, historic, or scientific interest. The values of the Enlightenment had encouraged royal collections like those in Vienna

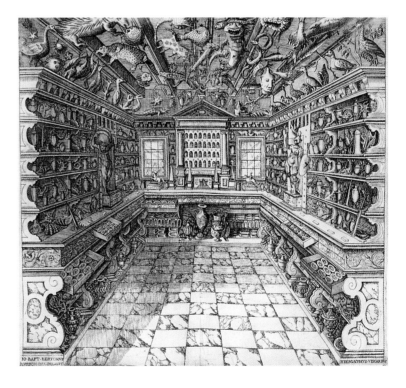

Fig. 7. The "cabinet" of Francesco Calzolari (1522–1609). Sixteenth-century "cabinets of curiosities" such as this were the first recognizable forerunners of the museum movement, which flourished during the Enlightenment. (Engraving from Benedetto Ceruti and Andrea Chocco, *Musæum Francesci Calceolari* [sic], Verona, 1622 [National Art Library, V&A])

and Dresden to be made publicly accessible in the last half of the eighteenth century. Dresden's collection derived from the mid-sixteenth-century *Kunstkammer* of Augustus the Strong. Literally translated from the German as "art room," but understood at the time as a "Cabinet of Curiosities," the *Kunstkammer* was a collection of objects, usually intermingling examples from art, nature, and science, that were seen as novel, extraordinary, or wondrous (fig. 7). Dresden's was one of the first "working" or teaching collections, with areas provided to allow the king's craftsmen to work with its tools or study its holdings.[3] Providing objects to bolster the royal image was the ultimate purpose of this training opportunity. Similarly, in 1708 when the German philosopher G. W. Leibniz advised Russia's Peter the Great to create a public collection "as a means to perfect the arts and sciences," Peter eventually embraced the idea with the words, "I want the people to look and learn." The ultimate goal of the St. Petersburg *Kunstkammer,* however, like that of its earlier Dresden counterpart, was to advance the level of craft production at Peter's ambitiously Westernizing court.[4]

The political value of a public display of art also drove the founding in Paris of the most influential museum of the late eighteenth and early nineteenth centuries, the Louvre. In the spirit of the democratic ideals of the Revolution, the French royal collections were made available to all French citizens. The Louvre displays were not only splendiferous, but, like a handful of German collections of the time, were installed chronologically and by national school, with French painting maintaining a special pride of place.[5] This politically purposeful bow to the pedagogical goals of the Enlightenment was expressed in French attitudes toward the useful arts and trades as well. The government-sponsored Ecole des Arts Décoratifs, an organization that still operates today, was founded in Paris in 1762 to train artists to work in industry. This institution in turn led to a regular series of exhibitions of industrial arts from 1798 on; and, in the wake of the Revolution, the Conservatoire des Arts et Métiers was established, a museum of industrial art that collected objects and explained their construction and use.[6]

By the opening years of the nineteenth century a number of industrial training schools, societies, and collections of the "useful arts" had been established on the Continent. While they would sometimes later be incorporated into a city's South Kensington–style applied arts museum, as often as not they remained separate from the larger effort.[7] England's privately organized study and support group, the Society for the Encouragement of Arts, Manufactures and Commerce, had begun in 1754. Open to both men and women from its founding, it regularly awarded prizes for exceptional work or deeds, and is still in existence today. Prince Albert was elected the Society's president in 1843. He met and was impressed by Henry Cole at Society meetings, some of which were convened to help organize the Great Exhibition of 1851. Albert's presence gave the Society new energy, for it had gone through its weakest period in the early decades of the nineteenth century, a time when Continental countries enjoyed established and sometimes government-supported industrial arts training efforts.

While the success of the future South Kensington Museum was ensured by the positive relationship that developed between Prince Albert and Henry Cole at the Society of Arts in the 1840s, the movement to establish Continental-style education programs in the applied arts had been initiated by a newly elected group of English reform politicians a decade earlier. Wondering how aesthetic education and industrial training might be worked into their own liberal mercantile program, they formed a parliamentary committee to investigate the problem. Gustav Waagen, director of the recently opened Altes Museum in Berlin, was prominent among those who testified in 1835 to this Select Committee. Its members were attracted by the reputation of Waagen's new museum, but they focused more specifically on the school of crafts and industrial arts that he oversaw. When asked about the Committee's primary purpose—what might be "the best mode of extending taste and a knowledge of the fine arts among the people generally"—Waagen replied, "accessible collections." He further suggested that the Renaissance connection between workman and artist could be restored by organized educational efforts within such collections

> . . . by giving the people an opportunity of seeing the most beautiful objects of art in the particular branch which they follow; by having collections of the most beautiful models of furniture and of different objects of manufacture. . . . It is not enough, however, merely to form these collections; there

must also be instruction to teach the people on what principles those models have been formed.[8]

Not only was it was widely recognized that English art and design industries commanded little respect in the world, it was clear, too, that the museums and schools currently operating in England were not equipped to address the issue as Waagen had recommended. The National Gallery, begun in 1824, was still a private preserve for picture connoisseurs. It would not establish its reputation as an art museum until the third quarter of the century under its first formidable director, Charles Locke Eastlake. The British Museum had a decidedly academic orientation, limiting its collections, beyond ancient art, to objects of historical, scholarly, or ethnographic interest. Until reforms linked to increased government subsidies were initiated in the mid-1830s, the public it embraced was primarily "the curious" among the educated classes who had to apply for tickets in order to gain entrance, then only to be led around its disorganized

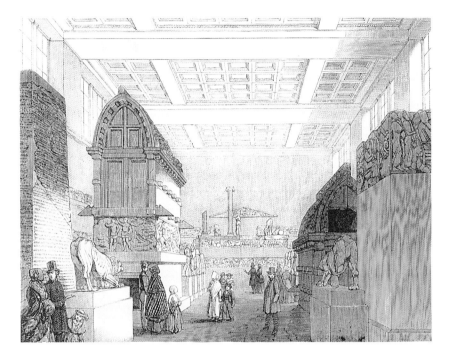

Fig. 8. "The Xanthian Room just opened at the British Museum," from *The Illustrated London News*, 15 January 1848. The British Museum, founded in 1753, was an important antecedent and in many ways a subsequent rival to the South Kensington Museum.

array of specimens at a frantic pace and often in groups of five to ten (fig. 8).

The Select Committee realized that new institutions had to be established to reach its goal. A School of Design was chartered a few months after the Committee adjourned in 1836. While it initiated a collection in the 1840s, its teaching program was never considered a great success. The opportunity to address English design education arose again, however, in 1851 when, in the wake of the Great Exhibition, the School of Design was incorporated into a museum that opened at Marlborough House under the directorship of Henry Cole.[9]

By 1853, with the museum and school incorporated into a newly named Department of Science and Art, an organized program of lectures and classes had begun. A staff also had been appointed, including the artist Richard Redgrave, the designer Owen Jones, the erudite German expatriate architect and theoretician Gottfried Semper, and the young connoisseur John Charles Robinson. The government's charge to Cole and his colleagues was the reform of art and design training in England, a reform that would ultimately improve English goods from an artistic perspective, enabling the country to compete more favorably in foreign markets. What resulted was a museum and associated teaching program brilliantly innovative in adapting that directive to a broader educational purpose, all the while remembering its given audience of artisans, designers, and manufacturers.

From 1857, Cole's Museum at its South Kensington site became the most imitated and programmatically influential museum of the late nineteenth century. During its first twenty-five years of operation, the South Kensington Museum's commercially driven mission came to be inextricably integrated with contemporary social ideals associated with the belief in a practical, even moral, education for the working classes through their collective experience of art. This, in turn, had somewhat surprising results in the collections that were formed during the Museum's earliest years, a period when it virtually cornered the European market on important medieval and Renaissance sculpture and decorative arts.

The scope and ambition of the enterprise created huge audiences of domestic and foreign visitors, resulting in the widely held perception of the Museum's extraordinary success in reaching its goals. Importantly, this perception endured longer abroad than at home. Indeed, the Museum spent much of the last two decades of the nineteenth century extracting itself from charges of confusion of purpose arising, on the one hand, from conflicts between its government-mandated mission and the wide variety of collections it often was forced to display and, on the other hand, the staff's broad and experimental way of articulating the institution's exhibition and training program. It could even be argued that the legacy of this history of divergent expectation and reality affects the Museum to this day.

SOUTH KENSINGTON: ITS PROGRAM

The purpose the government assigned to the new organization became the foundation of its long-term goals: the founding of a London-based museum with "the most perfect illustrations and models" connected with a "school of the highest class." South Kensington through its education program would support a system of local schools of industrial science and art, all institutions being "as much self supporting as possible" and all "calculated . . . to aid [commercial] competition . . . in the great neutral markets of the world."[10] Cole would take this directive and broaden its aims to embrace his own museum ideals. His agenda was driven by attitudes that ranged from his belief in public education through visual instruction, to his commitment to establish a National Gallery of British Art in order to promote the importance of British painting. At the root of Cole's interpretation of his government charge was a more subtly reformative social agenda than the one he was handed. Its foundation lay in Cole's early engagement with the utilitarian philosophy preached by the followers of Jeremy Bentham, who advanced the concept of "the greatest happiness for the greatest number." Their ideas also had convinced Cole that methodical administration, as well as private support of public institutions, would result in social betterment for all.

Cole descended from relatively humble origins. From early in his life, he was given to self-improving pastimes like concerts, lectures, and plays. By the 1840s, while still in his thirties, he had become a manufacturer of modestly priced designer products, a sometime museum critic, and a pamphleteer who eventually came to be trusted by Prince Albert for his special achievements within the thicket of the civil-service bureaucracy. His tenacity and devotion to administrative order had resulted in a complete reform of the Public Record Office early in his career. At the same time, however, Cole had earned a reputation among his civil-service peers as being abrasive, more than slightly impatient, and occasionally opportunistic—a fighter not above a certain deviousness in reaching his goals, no matter how lofty. It seems that he rarely submitted to the role of team player unless he felt he could eventually arrange to be appointed captain.[11] One might at first see these characteristics as sorry qualifications for a museum director, but given the expectations assigned to his Museum and the speed of its growth, his personal attributes of administrative efficiency, political adeptness, and a desire to take control can be seen as uniquely apt to his task. Cole's belief in and commitment to the broad social ideals of his enterprise knew no bounds.

Within five years of taking on the mission of raising design standards in manufacturing for the purpose of advancing national commerce, Cole had expanded the role of the Museum to that of a more public enterprise with a broad educational mandate. In 1852 he had proposed a plan for elementary arts education in cities and towns around the country that would remain in place until the end of the nineteenth century. He also spoke of his institution as being directed to workmen of every vocation. Such educational efforts can be considered commercially purposeful—to indoctrinate the present and future consumer while also training the maker. For a Benthamite idealist like Cole, however, these initiatives also had a more fundamental social benefit. Cole's broadly based public lecture and publication program to "improve public taste" expanded over time, never compromising the rhetoric identifying South Kensington as a training ground for designers and manufacturers.[12] This latter message was driven not only by the Museum's founding mission, but also by the need to preserve the government funding to keep his vast array of programs alive. Dependence on government support became an institutional condition despite Cole's—and the government's—hope that the Museum and school would eventually be self-sustaining.[13]

It may have been the goal of self-sustainability that made South Kensington such a lively, even market-driven, certainly public relations–conscious enterprise. In this way, Cole and his institution—fighting bureaucracy through expediency in this environment of conflicting values—anticipated museum concerns of the late twentieth century more than any other museum of the nineteenth and early twentieth centuries. In South Kensington's earliest years an enthusiastic trial-and-error atmosphere permeated the institution. The confident, pragmatic approach to operations by Cole and his staff was to become an Anglo-American museum tradition. Museums in Britain and the United States enjoy common origins in the liberal, civic-minded social philosophy of the time, museums in both countries being supported by a rising business class, whether functioning through the government, as in London, or through the private sector, as in the United States.

To make the Museum's collections more widely known and understood, catalogues were published that chronicled holdings still in the process of formation. A variety of special exhibitions were arranged that also attracted large audiences. Although a program was developed to circulate some of the Museum's collections to regional institutions, the educational mission to which Cole was most committed—after the lectures and classes of the school itself—was the documentation of Europe's artistic treasures through photographs and plaster reproductions.[14] In the process, South Kensington positioned itself not only as an educational instrument but as a popular entertainment—crowded on weekends, ever responsive to the audience it actively sought. Cole politicked for regular, inexpensive public transportation to then far-off Kensington. He established the first-ever museum restaurant in 1857, the year his department and collections moved to their permanent South Kensington site.

Admission policy for the Museum also set a precedent. While earlier museums were often tentative about how many people and which social classes should be encouraged to visit, Cole embraced the concept of attracting large numbers of visitors, hoping this audience would extend to every strata of society. In 1857, speaking of the easy access of the working classes to South Kensington, he emphasized that his Museum was open free to the public over half the time, a total of three days and an unprecedented two evenings a week, noting that "at the National Gallery and the British Museum the public are excluded on student or private days. Here it cannot be said there are any private days."[15]

South Kensington was a vibrant audience- and education-directed, even populist institution, yet it never tried to veil the narrower economic purpose on which it was founded. It was widely perceived, especially by visiting foreigners and its many advocates abroad, that the Museum was highly successful in reaching its expressed goal of improving manufactured goods. Knowing that its greatest success in public terms today is its extraordinary collections, it could be argued that the educational mission of the Museum became separated from the institution's collecting activity very quickly. Nonetheless, given the optimistic educational philosophy of the time (for Waagen, education was based on "giving people the opportunity of seeing the most beautiful objects") and given, too, the antiquarian spirit for collecting that has driven England's museum endeavors since the seventeenth century, it is clear that Cole and his colleagues believed deeply in the reformative power of the exquisite and the old. In fact, the mimetic value of the beautiful was regularly referenced by both Cole and Robinson.[16]

Working with Robinson's recommendations, Cole devoted considerable effort, and significant diplomatic and bureaucratic skills, to securing collections of older objects for his Museum. Such purchases were often justified on educational grounds: the acquisition of the Soulages collection (cats. 52, 71, 74, 79), for example, was advocated because "models of the highest excellence [need to be] kept before the eyes of artisans, as an inducement and an encouragement to them to attain the highest degree of excellence."[17]

Such mission-enhancing arguments reflect some of the many complicated reasons why vast quantities of old and foreign objects were brought to London. Through such efforts, South Kensington's collections became truly international, deep and nuanced in virtually all the areas the Museum chose to cover. While early purchases concentrated on Western medieval and Renaissance objects, the Museum's pedagogical approach to acquisitions and display embraced non-

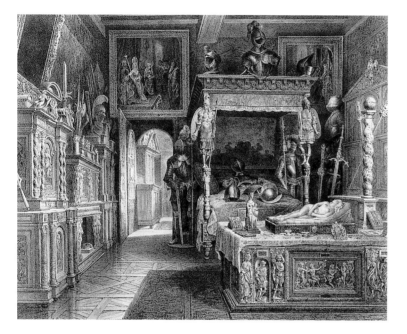

Fig. 9. An interior of the Hôtel de Cluny, Paris, the contents of which were assembled by Alexandre Du Sommerard (1779–1842), an influential connoisseur of medieval and Renaissance objects. The museum's interiors presented objects in a romantically historicizing environment.

Western objects as well, though these were often presented as exotic examples of special techniques and materials. In this way, Cole expanded the scope of the collections as he articulated his enterprise's responsibility to represent the range of artistic expression encompassed by the growing British empire.[18]

The installations, as much as the objects displayed and the lectures presented, were an important component of South Kensington's educational program. Throughout his career Cole was preoccupied with the visitor's experience of the Museum galleries and the didactic effectiveness of installations. While we have only a suggestion of how the earliest rooms at Marlborough House were arranged (to a large degree they were organized by material), we can assume, given Cole's introductory gallery of "Examples of False Principles in Decoration," that they also embraced teaching goals.[19] During Robinson's tenure, the educational function of the displays remained, but their interpretive direction and appearance moved from Cole's perspectives favoring training and rules, to Robinson's primary aim of fostering aesthetic judgment.

Like most connoisseurs of medieval and Renaissance objects, Robinson had been impressed early in his life by the romantically historicizing environments that Alexandre Du Sommerard had created at Cluny, the much-visited and admired Paris house that became an even more influential museum on Du Sommerard's death in 1842 (fig. 9). After Robinson's arrival, Marlborough House maintained some of the materials-specific installations with which it opened in 1852—one display case containing only ceramics, another presenting metalwork (fig. 10). The overriding goal, however, seems to have been the juxtaposition of dissimilar objects for aesthetic effect, much as the Musée de Cluny was arranged. Given Robinson's expressed views on the educational value of the experience of art, these displays also served a didactic purpose, broadly conceived.[20] When an "Art Museum" opened at South Kensington, separate from the other galleries in the Museum, it was installed on aesthetic principles, with objects of different origin, scale, and medium artfully juxtaposed in an attempt to evoke the atmosphere of a grand domestic environment. An early sixteenth-century carved Flemish altarpiece from Ghent was displayed along with a contemporary Minton vase, two seventeenth-century Roman Baroque busts, mirrors, paintings, wall reliefs of various periods, and an eighteenth-century German secretary—all integrated by reproductions of the pilasters and lunettes from Raphael's Loggia at the Vatican. Standing in the center of this eclectic assemblage, surveying its abundance, was a full-scale plaster cast of Michelangelo's *David*.

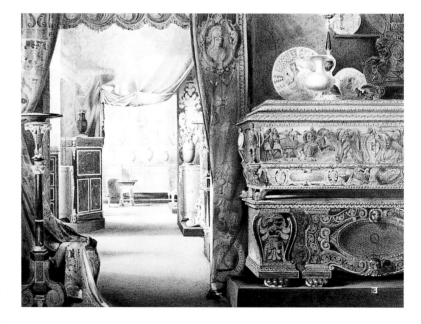

Fig. 10. One of the galleries of the Museum of Ornamental Art at Marlborough House, about 1856

The antiquarian ideals of the second quarter of the nineteenth century, so evocatively articulated in the collections and installations at Cluny, now would be manifested in the larger and more educationally mandated galleries of the early

South Kensington museum. While justified as serving a practical purpose, these collections also represent a special taste for the rare, the old, and the beautiful, an aesthetic antiquarianism that one could argue represents a telling nuance in the character of English culture from the seventeenth century to the present. In no other country has collecting become a national exercise practiced with such persistence and in so many different directions. In no other country is the phrase "national treasure" bandied about so effectively as a rationale to purchase objects created long ago and somewhere else for its public museums. While the extraordinary collections brought together at the early Victoria and Albert Museum were presented as educational models essential for commercial advancement, Robinson's intricate search and negotiation tactics, and Cole's deep-seated belief in collection growth, reflect a cultural aspiration far more complex than would be evident in any government acquisition report.

The origins of England's insistent antiquarianism lay in the desire among its elite, never confident of their own artistic heritage, to gather the material manifestations of admired societies and favored pasts together as a testament to English learning, worldly experience, and power. Young English gentlemen on the grand tour of Europe supported the art of connoisseurship in the seventeenth and eighteenth centuries not only as a learned attribute, but as protection against the many on the Continent anxious to maximize the price of any object, real or imitation, whose context and function were about to change as it traveled north to an English domestic setting. In the industrial era, Britain's home manufacturing and colonial outposts grew, producing extraordinary wealth and a newly rich middle class eager to acquire the trappings of educated gentlemen. An obsession with history deepened, stemming from an aristocratic quest for stability through reverence for the old and an urge to preserve what would never be produced again—to care for it and to pass it on to posterity.

In many countries, particularly in the later nineteenth century, collecting was driven by a nationalist longing to return to the purity of folk traditions being lost through industrialization. England, however, with its strong economy and far-flung colonial outposts, thought more internationally. Beyond the thrill of possession and intellectual attainment, picking and choosing from the chattels of earlier societies enabled Victorians to achieve an educational objective of increasing importance to them: the creation of better things in their own time. This was one of the motives that made England believe that collecting on the vast scale, as initiated at South Kensington, was necessary to overcome the deficiencies of a culture deprived.[21]

During the 1840s and 1850s, medieval and Renaissance objects largely displaced antiquities as the all-consuming collecting passion of the erudite aesthete. For propagandists such as A. W. N. Pugin and Robert and Elizabeth Barrett Browning, who believed in the religious and moral purity of the art of the Middle Ages and early Renaissance, the objects brought together at South Kensington must have been impressive. With collections that countered the British Museum's extensive holdings of Greek and Roman art, with the Museum's commitment to social improvement and commercial advancement, and with its wildly popular programs, it is not surprising that South Kensington's international fame was marked, even among the toughest Continental critics. As the French art historian and Inspector General

Charles Yriarte told an English parliamentary committee: "Today, for all of us foreigners South Kensington is a mecca. England there possesses the entire art of Europe and the East, their spiritual manifestations under all forms, and Europe has been swept into the stream in imitation of England."[22]

SOUTH KENSINGTON: ITS INTERNATIONAL INFLUENCE

As the words of Yriarte attest, the success of the first twenty years of the Victoria and Albert Museum was so acclaimed throughout the world that a number of other institutions were created in its likeness. As we have seen, England's efforts in design education had begun in the 1830s, driven by the British government's competition with European countries that already had schools or associations devoted to the teaching or display of industrial arts. France had taken the lead in these early efforts, although by the second quarter of the nineteenth century many such organizations existed in Austria and Germany as well. By 1860, however, nothing on the scale of South Kensington, nothing with as broad a public scope or as effective an educational program as the English initiative, existed on the Continent.

European fear of England's imminent rise in arts manufacturing began in the aftermath of the Great Exhibition of 1851, when even the French began to worry that their dominance in the field of decorative arts and design might not last forever. Comte Léon de Laborde and others argued for schools of applied arts that would replace the existing schools and the still active apprentice system. Indeed, a private organization was established, L'Union Centrale des Beaux-Arts Appliqués à l'Industrie, to maintain French design superiority through organized classes and regular exhibitions. A museum of decorative arts sponsored by the Union Centrale opened in 1864 and still operates today, as the Musée des Arts Décoratifs, Paris.[23]

By the early 1860s, the fame of South Kensington's Museum and school, as well as the reputation of Henry Cole, was well established in Austria and Germany, but the institution was interpreted somewhat differently there due to the enormous impact of the architect and theorist Gottfried Semper. In London as a refugee from the German uprisings of 1848, Semper was overwhelmed by the Great Exhibition, where the assembled industrial works of modern mechanized societies and the sophisticated ornament and traditional design of non-Western cultures were all displayed with bold and unconditional belief in industrial progress. While working at the Exhibition he wrote a pamphlet, *Science, Industry and Art,* summarizing the importance of the 1851 event. Intrigued by Semper, Cole had earlier recommended him as a Great Exhibition designer and published one of Semper's articles in the December 1851 issue of the *Journal of Design.* In 1852 Cole decided to test the architect's skills further by commissioning him to write a catalogue on the nature and history of metalwork, which resulted in Semper's appointment to a teaching position later that year. After attending Semper's first public lecture in May 1853, Cole described it as "thoughtful and suggestive" in his ordinarily opinion-free diaries.[24]

Like Waagen, Semper brought the theoretical sophistication of German history and aesthetics to decisions that would fundamentally affect the South Kensington enterprise. His *Science, Industry and Art* probably prompted the 1853 renaming of

Cole's enterprise to the Department of Science and Art.[25] The German-born Prince Albert, also impressed by Semper, commissioned him to create a master plan for South Kensington's building complex. It was rejected in 1855 by a government committee, resulting in Prince Albert's endorsement of the infamous Brompton Boilers, the temporary iron structures that in the opinion of many, including Cole, blighted the site until they were substantially removed in 1866. Semper moved to Zurich soon after his building scheme was rejected but he continued to be admired by many in London, including Cole, who hoped the architect would eventually return to teach at South Kensington.[26]

Semper's influence on the Continent has been seen as more wide-ranging than in England, yet it was during his London years that he developed his theories, theories that one might think would have been fundamental to South Kensington's reformative purpose. In *Science, Industry and Art,* Semper had prophetically recognized that the forces of industrialization and capitalism were destroying the historical basis of art. His conclusions, however, were optimistic: ". . . this process of disintegrating existing art types must be completed by industry, by speculation, and by applied science before something good and new can result."[27] Semper went on to formulate a revolutionary and innovative theory that disregarded subject matter, which had been the foundation of academic criticism since the sixteenth century. He focused instead on the symbolic nature of individual motifs in objects and the transformation of their meaning in varying situations of production and cultural environments. Semper saw the artistic manipulation of material, technique, and motif as central to the creation of symbolic form. His system, as published in 1860, effectively resulted in the theoretical marriage of the fine and applied arts.[28]

Semper's ideas were immediately taken up by museums given the task of mimicking the success and addressing the commercial challenge of South Kensington. His perspectives not only elevated the status of the applied art object and the industrial artist, with which these new museums were concerned, they created an ordering system based on materials, a system that museum professionals felt could be applied to both libraries and museum installations. Semper's four main divisions of classification—ceramics and glass, metalwork, textiles, and furniture and woodwork—gave a more purposeful rationale to the materials-based presentations that had occurred haphazardly since the days of the *Kunstkammer,* lending greater seriousness to the mission of the applied arts museum in the process.

It was in Vienna in the mid-1860s, at the newly formed applied arts museum, where Semper's ideas were first utilized. Rudolf von Eitelberger, an art history professor, was sent by the Austrian government to the 1862 International Exhibition in London. The government supported Eitelberger's recommendation that a museum be founded to advance the country's earlier efforts to improve the design of objects for daily use. A permanent building was planned for the new museum in the mid-1860s by Heinrich von Ferstal, an avid admirer of Semper (fig. 11). Eitelberger corresponded with the German architect, eventually receiving from him a copy of the *Practical Metals* catalogue that Cole had commissioned in 1852. In the end, Semper's ideas regarding a scientific ordering by material were adapted to the Viennese museum's library, a system that is maintained to this day. His theories as adapted by

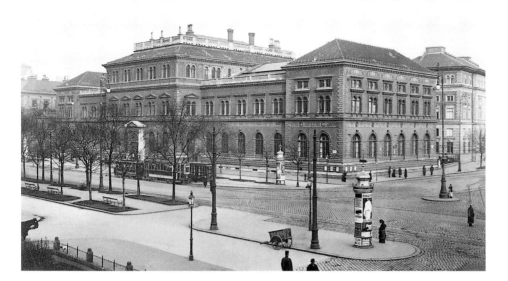

Fig. 11. The Österreichisches Museum für Kunst und Industrie (now the Museum für angewandte Kunst), Vienna, in 1910

Ferstal and Eitelberger also governed the installation of the museum, which was meant to mirror the library in organization and purpose.[29]

From the mid-1850s until the end of the century, museums of applied arts were established throughout the world on South Kensington's model. The Industrial Museum of Scotland (later the Royal Scottish Museum) in Edinburgh was opened in 1860 by Cole's own Department of Science and Art, and South Kensington served as a model, directly or indirectly, for a number of museums within the British Empire, including one in Bombay (1855) and the Royal Ontario Museum in Toronto (1912). Anxious to direct South Kensington's training philosophy to less industrialized populations, civic and national governments as well as local manufacturers and trade associations supported museums with ambitious training programs in Moscow (1868), Budapest (1872), Brno (1873), Zagreb (1880), and Prague (1884).

The applied arts museum movement took root in Scandinavia with the founding of Oslo's applied arts museum in 1876 and the Kunstindustrimuseum in Copenhagen in 1890. Because of Arthur Hazelius's successful and highly influential Nordiska Museet in Stockholm (opened in 1873 as the Scandinavian Ethnographical Collection and renamed in 1880), an applied arts department eventually was integrated in the largely painting- and sculpture-oriented Nationalmuseum. This is one of the few instances in Western Europe in which a broadly focused decorative arts department was combined with departments of painting and sculpture in a national museum, a model that is so common among civic museums of the United States. The Rijksmuseum in Amsterdam, however, represents the most significant European example of this integration. Victor de Stuers, one of the principal planners of the building that still houses the museum, recommended that the new structure not only be a monument to Dutch art and history, but, like South Kensington, also incorporate a training school for artists. The original plans, finished in 1876, included an enormous gallery for the display of both large- and small-scale sculpture and applied arts, a vast navelike space that imitated South Kensington's North and South Courts completed a few years before.

Italy's efforts to advance training in the applied arts led to the establishment of museums in Milan and Bologna, but the most important was Rome's industrial arts museum, founded in 1872 by the city government in part due to an articulate and powerful proponent, Prince Baldassare Odaschalchi. Throughout the 1870s the prince expressed himself eloquently, not only on the sorry state of Italian industrial production, but also on the pillaging of the Italian artistic heritage for the purpose of educating Northern designers at museums like South Kensington.[30]

At the same time, while Japanese art was increasingly referenced by Western aesthetes, the Japanese government asked the administrators of South Kensington to consult on the establishment of an Imperial Museum in Tokyo. The designer Christopher Dresser was sent to Japan by the V&A with a donation of English objects and with the additional directive to advise authorities on their proposed museum installations.

It was in Germany, however, where the teaching and exhibition programs of South Kensington were most imitated. In the twenty-five years following the 1864 inauguration of Vienna's decorative arts museum, thirty such museums were founded in various German cities.[31] Berlin's museum project began at the instigation of Crown Princess Victoria, who followed her father Prince Albert's interest in arts and industry by sending a government official, Hermann Schwabe, to England to examine South Kensington and its programs. His published report led to the establishment of a museum of applied arts in 1867, and a school was begun the following year. The entire collection of the extraordinarily prescient Institut Minutoli was soon absorbed into that of the new museum, and Berlin's Kunstgewerbemuseum became one of the most important applied arts institutions on the Continent.[32] By 1880, under the leadership of its renowned director Julius Lessing, the Berlin museum moved to a building designed by Martin Gropius, which, with its central court and surrounding galleries, mimicked the neo-Renaissance architecture that Captain Francis Fowke had completed in 1869 for South Kensington.

Lessing followed a Semperian system of displaying objects in most of his new museum's galleries, but he was also a leader in establishing a different direction for applied arts installations in Germany, one which sought to arrange objects culturally and historically, mixing mediums in one gallery to simulate domestic environments rather than separating objects by material. Another leading director of a German museum, Justus Brinckmann, later discussed these new objectives in relation to his Museum für Kunst und Gewerbe in Hamburg: "... [A] technological and aesthetic collection of instructional aids ... cannot exist without a socio-historical foundation." His institution's most significant task, he said, would now be directed toward "exhibiting objects according to their natural living context ... [a method] which has long since been recognized by ethnographic museums."[33]

Brinckmann promoted his views on installation, with their contemporary parallels in culturally based art history and in the emerging field of anthropology, both to combat the historical revivalism he felt had been caused by "artists weaned from their own creativity and pushed towards a superficial eclecticism," and to focus his museum on a broader public, one that extended beyond that of artisans and manufacturers. As the modern movement began, applied arts museums throughout Germany began to reorganize their installations along cultural and historical lines. The movement had a parallel development in museums of fine arts through the influential work of Director Wilhelm von Bode, whose Kaiser Friedrich Museum in Berlin opened in 1904 to international acclaim.[34]

Brinckmann began his career as an adamant follower of Semper and his ideas. Recognizing the depth and subtlety of Semper's thinking, he introduced his perspectives endorsing a more cultural and historical direction in installations by quoting from Semper's *Science, Industry and Art.* Brinckmann rightly separated the breadth, range, and cultural understanding of Semper's thought from the materials-based installations that were to become so associated with his reputation, a reputation derived from the practical application of his ideas by his many museum followers: "Collections and public monuments are the true teachers of a free people. They are not merely the teachers of practical exercises, but more importantly the schools of public taste."[35]

SOUTH KENSINGTON: ITS INFLUENCE IN THE UNITED STATES

When the South Kensington Museum opened in the 1850s, only a handful of institutions in America exhibited objects considered to be works of art for public enjoyment and instruction. Some were art schools, like Philadelphia's Pennsylvania Academy and New York's National Academy of Design, while others were libraries or historical societies, like the Boston Athenaeum, the New-York Historical Society, the Peabody Museum in Salem, and the Brooklyn Institute (now the Brooklyn Museum of Art). Only the Wadsworth Atheneum, established in 1842 in Hartford, Connecticut, could have been considered—like art museums today—an organization whose primary public purpose centered on the exhibition of a permanent collection of art objects. The situation was to change completely by the end of the nineteenth century. The international fame of the South Kensington Museum and its schools, and the belief in the success of the English enterprise, were in no small measure responsible for this revolution in the United States. Throughout the late 1860s and 1870s, the South Kensington example was invoked to motivate America's business and education leaders to establish art museums in a number of cities, each with an avowed purpose of public service through education.

While South Kensington was the catalytic agent that motivated civic and business leaders, education was the battle cry. As Charles Perkins wryly observed in 1870, the opening year of Boston's Museum of Fine Arts, which he helped found: "We may safely say that as a nation we should be totally indifferent if all the works of art in the world were to vanish into space." He emphasized, therefore, that the special mission of any art museum movement in the United States had to be "collecting material for the education of a nation in art, not at making collections of objects of art."[36]

Given this perception of the country's deficiencies in art education in the mid-nineteenth century, it is not surprising that a number of teaching institutions were established whose primary purpose was to organize art classes; a somewhat secondary emphasis was placed on museum collections as teaching tools. In 1853, for example, the nine-year-old Philadelphia School of Design for Women became a part of the Franklin Institute, which is still in operation. That same year, iron magnate Peter Cooper laid the cornerstone in Manhattan for the Cooper Union for the Advancement of Science and Art, which to this day maintains the practice of free tuition for all its students. Space for a "museum of history, art and science" was prepared on the top floor of the Cooper Union building, which opened in 1859 to the design of Frederick A. Peterson, but it never reached its potential in the school's early years. Not until 1897, and only because of the efforts of Cooper's devoted granddaughters, the Misses Hewitt, was a museum of decorative arts—primarily for the use of the school's students—established on that site. Today the Cooper-Hewitt Museum is part of the Smithsonian Institution and occupies the former mansion of industrialist Andrew Carnegie on New York's Upper East Side. It has become the National Museum of Design in the United States.

Some of the largest and most effective schools were established in the wake of the highly influential 1876 Centennial Exposition in Philadelphia, where South Kensington's achievements in raising the standards of England's arts industries were touted to the visiting crowds. The purpose of New Haven's Connecticut Museum of Industrial Art, chartered in the months following the Centennial's closing, was "as that upon which the South Kensington is founded." The most prominent teaching institution begun in the wake of Philadelphia's exhibition, however, was the Rhode Island School of Design in Providence, established in 1877 by the Women's Centennial Commission of Rhode Island. The Commission hoped their "good School of Design with a subsidiary Gallery of Art . . . would benefit all classes and both sexes as the experience of English schools had already proved." Already in 1854 the Rhode Island Art Association had been created to establish "a permanent Art Museum and Gallery of the Arts of Design . . . cultivating and promoting the Ornamental and Useful Arts." The Rhode Island School of Design quickly moved to establish a museum, which today remains Providence's principal art gallery.[37]

A nationally supported museum focused on training in the decorative arts did not take root in the United States—as it had in virtually every European country by 1900—largely because the American art museum movement itself sprang from the very motivations that brought about the applied arts museum movement abroad, namely, a concern for better training facilities for "objects of beauty and utility." A pragmatic self-improvement ethic directed at advancing business and commerce had been fostered in the New World long before John Adams, in 1789, recommended the study of "the useful, the mechanic arts." With that ethic came an equally deep-seated skepticism of the fine arts and their capacity for contributing to the self-prescribed task of expanding the country and capitalizing on its natural resources. For these reasons, Charles Perkins and his contemporaries believed that while America's cultural institutions might perform a useful purpose integrating practical art and education, such an effort could never be supported by the government. Museums would have to result from the joint effort and financial commitment of the country's civic leaders. Therefore, the "carrot" of commercial prosperity attained through artistic enterprise prompted the commitment of America's businessmen to the art museum movement. As the movement evolved, it was further driven by a complex set of motivations, ranging from civic duty and personal recognition, to the transfer of the homogeneous values of America's elite to the country's broad, mostly immigrant underclass.

South Kensington was consistently the referenced model in the rhetoric behind virtually every American art museum founded in the 1870s. The references were never more explicit, however, than in the boosterish words accompanying the founding of the Cincinnati Art Museum. Between 1877 and 1880 a well-orchestrated effort inspired by the Centennial Exposition and led by the Women's Art Museum Association of Cincinnati promoted the founding of a permanent art museum, using the appeal of South Kensington's success to support its cause. A number of lectures, including two talks on South Kensington—the first given by one of the city's foremost citizens, Charles P. Taft—focused on the benefits of an art museum to the city's industry. The effort was further enhanced by a regular series of classes offered by the Association and a loan exhibition comprised of more than two thousand objects drawn from local private collections. As a result of this concerted drive, in 1880 Charles W. West announced that he would give $150,000 toward the establishment of a new museum, provided that his gift was equaled by public subscription. Within four weeks his gift was matched and plans for a muse-um building were begun. The Cincinnati Art Museum opened in 1886 on its present site in Eden Park (fig. 12).[38]

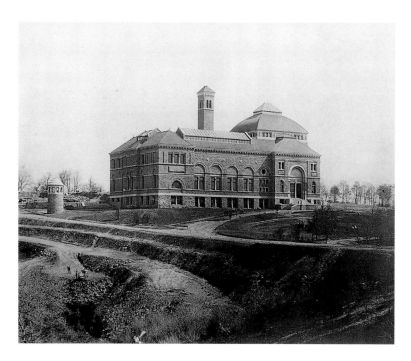

Fig. 12. Cincinnati Art Museum in 1886

It was through such focused efforts on the part of citizen groups that most of the large, urban art museums of the United States were formed. While individual histories vary, the ever-present conditions of the museum building movement included local pride that drove competition of both a civic and commercial kind, as well as a belief among the educated population in the moral and practical value of art education. In certain cities, as in Cincinnati, it was women's groups that served as the organizational catalysts. In 1877, the all-female Chicago Society of Decorative Art was founded. Its effect on the city's male business leaders in establishing the Art Institute of Chicago is demonstrated by the fact that the Society's program was quickly integrated with that of the art museum once that organization was established. In other cities, the educational program of South Kensington was promoted by teachers of art and design who were the primary catalysts to local initiatives in founding museums. Halsey Cooley Ives, a drawing instructor at Washington University in St. Louis, promoted Cole's work after his return from a study trip to England in 1875. In part through his efforts, the Saint Louis Art Museum opened in 1879.[39]

The Corcoran Gallery in Washington, D.C., was founded in 1859 when banker William W. Corcoran made his private collection available to the public. Following the 1876 Centennial Exposition in Philadelphia, with its encouragement of civic initiatives in art education, a school of design connected with the Gallery opened in 1878. That the centennial celebration was an important agent in bringing South Kensington's achievements to public awareness is most clearly demonstrated in Philadelphia itself. The Pennsylvania Museum and School of Industrial Art—later to become the Philadelphia Museum of Art—was chartered on the eve of the Exposition as both a "perpetual" source of "improvement and equipment" and an educational organization "to develop the Art Industries of the State." The museum cited South Kensington specifically in its charter and, almost as a reminder of the English museum's origins in the Great Exhibition, was located in the Exposition's main building, Memorial Hall, for years thereafter.[40]

Philadelphia's Centennial Exposition was not the only means by which the example of South Kensington was transmitted to America's civic community. The two largest art museums in the country—the Museum of Fine Arts, Boston, and The Metropolitan Museum of Art in New York—were each chartered in 1870. When compared to museums founded in the five years following the Philadelphia Exposition, it is apparent that the value of South Kensington's programs and collections was integrated more subtly into the charters of these earlier museums. The South Kensington model still served these large eastern urban centers, however, as a rallying point for civic action.

The Metropolitan Museum was established for the stated purpose of "encouraging and developing the study of the fine arts, and the application of arts to manufacture and practical life." It was chartered one year after a famous dinner at the Union League Club during which a room full of New York's wealthy and powerful listened to a program of speeches following a lengthy address by the renowned American literary figure William Cullen Bryant. Each of the evening's presentations extolled the benefits of an art museum to a city like New York. The rhetoric was geared to an audience of the potentially social-minded and guilt-ridden who, like so many of the rich at the time, believed that an expansion in the number of public high schools, universities, and morally uplifting cultural organizations might be an antidote to the ills perpetrated on the country by industrialization and rapid growth.

Invited speakers included the architect Richard Morris Hunt and Henry Cole's brother, each of whom planted the practical program and potential economic advantage of a South Kensington–style institution in the minds of all present. By 1875 the fledgling museum was exhibiting "reproductions of works of art [from the] South Kensington Museum" on the ground floor of its temporary quarters. The success of the English museum in establishing an effective rationale for the new enterprise is evident in the remarks of Metropolitan Museum trustee Joseph Choate, who referred to South Kensington frequently in his 1880 address opening the first building in Central Park.[41]

The primary advocate for the establishment of a South Kensington–style institution in Boston, Charles C. Perkins, developed his commitment through a personal knowledge of the English museum, making his advocacy the most sophisticated of any founding American museum trustee. Given a project in which the integration of the interests of business, art, and social enterprise was essential, Perkins had

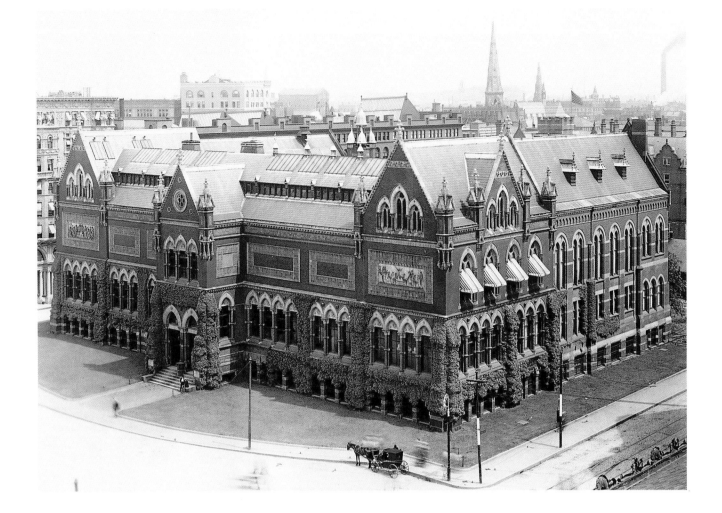

Fig. 13. Museum of Fine Arts, Boston, at its first site in Copley Square, 1902

established links with each constituency. Grandson of a wealthy China trade merchant, he had studied art in Europe and authored books on Italian sculpture. Through his research, Perkins had met several of the South Kensington officials. In 1869, as chairman of a special committee of the American Social Science Association considering art from an educational perspective, he touted the value of appreciating the beautiful in nature and art as a prelude to proposing the establishment of institutions throughout the country based on South Kensington's model.[42]

Boston's museum effort also included the involvement of the city's many institutions of higher education, Harvard University and the Massachusetts Institute of Technology among them. Perkins's views, therefore, had to be integrated with those of his colleague trustees, some of whom favored the British Museum model over that of South Kensington. Due to Perkins's efforts, the Museum of Fine Arts effectively combined both museological perspectives in its earliest years. He made sure, however, that a representative of the Lowell School of Industrial Design was represented on the board. He also personally consulted with Cole in the 1871 hiring of Walter Smith, an English graduate of South Kensington who was picked by the Boston school board to begin a drawing program in the city.[43]

At the inauguration of the museum's first building (fig. 13), whose architecture was closely modeled on South Kensington, Perkins stated his hope that it "would be

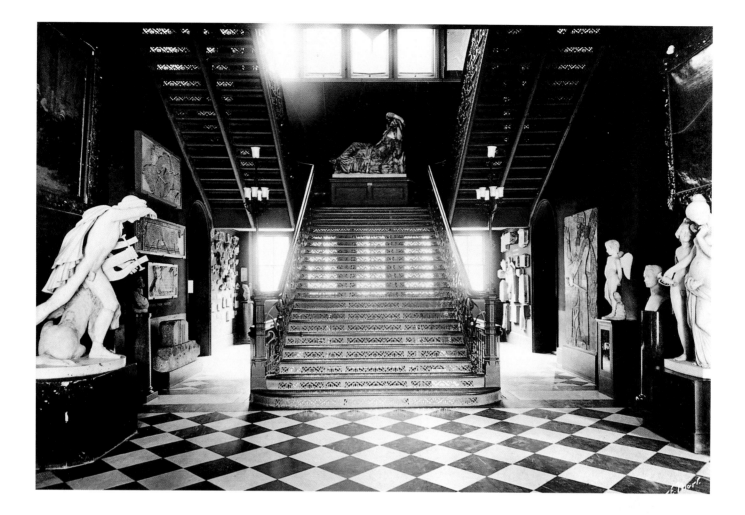

Fig. 14. Entrance to the Copley Square
Building of the Museum of Fine Arts,
Boston

a rival . . . of the great industrial museums at Kensington and Vienna."[44] The museum strived to do so in its installations from the beginning. While its ground-floor galleries were devoted to a few ancient artifacts and numerous casts of sculpture (fig. 14), on its second floor, in the words of a contemporary spokesperson, "the 'South Kensington' aspect develops." A variety of Western and Eastern objects were displayed in these galleries, along with the first period paneling ever mounted in an American museum, a sixteenth-century carved oak surround intended to enhance an installation of furniture, sculpture, and armor (fig. 15). A Boston museum supporter, writing of his city's effort and that of all American art institutions of the time, noted that "the success of the South Kensington Museum is the corner-stone of our art museums."[45]

While a cornerstone it certainly was, by the mid-1880s the South Kensington model had lost much of the power it earlier had demonstrated in galvanizing the American museum movement. This was no doubt due in part to the criticism the institution had begun to receive in England. That criticism reflected more than just the failed leadership of those administrators who came to power in the years after Cole's 1873 retirement. A different intellectual environment, an evolved social and aesthetic value system in both England and the United States, was affecting public expectations of museums. By the turn of the century, American institutions increasingly focused on more culturally centered displays and emphasized the historical and aesthetic importance of the individual works on view, paintings in particular. As in German museums of the time, less emphasis was placed on the material and technical attributes of objects considered so important to the training of designers, artisans, and manufacturers.

In addition, toward the turn of the century the international museum world was ever more distracted by the competitive atmosphere of collection enhancement, symbolized so publicly by the rise of influential art dealers like that of the Duveen firm in London and New York. With museums and their private supporters intent on acquiring expertise, whether through professionals employed by museums, such as Wilhelm von Bode at the Kaiser Friedrich Museum in Berlin, or those outside the museum world, such as the paintings expert Bernard Berenson, an altered museological value system expressed itself through a growing shift in institutional priorities.

When J. P. Morgan became president of the Metropolitan Museum in 1905, he deemphasized the institution's well-established rhetoric of education through design training and began to direct the museum far more toward the aesthetic stan-

Fig. 15. The Lawrence Room, Museum of Fine Arts, Boston, painted by Enrico Meneghelli (American, 1852–after 1912), oil on canvas mounted on masonite, 16 x 20" (40.6 x 50.8 cm). Museum of Fine Arts, Boston, Gift of M. Knoedler & Co.

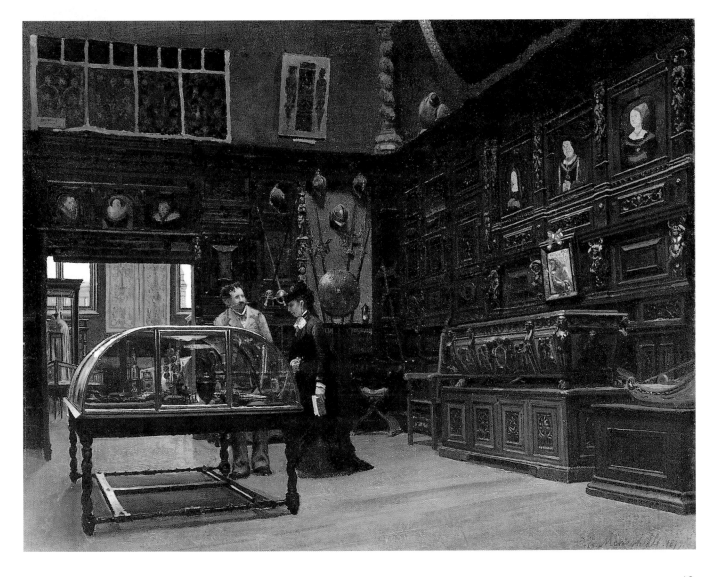

dards of objects on display. While Morgan succeeded in convincing the V&A's director, Sir Caspar Purdon Clarke, to head the Metropolitan in 1905, Clarke's tenure was not considered a great success. The prominent English critic Roger Fry's appointment as paintings curator, in the same year that Clarke arrived in New York, signaled an institutional shift toward collecting masterpieces. In addition, a more historically and culturally centered presentation of applied arts was assured when Bode's assistant, Wilhelm Valentiner, was hired as decorative arts curator in 1907.

In spite of these changes, the purpose of teaching New York's designers and craftsmen was maintained, not only in the Metropolitan Museum's education program, but through the establishment of a Department of Industrial Relations in 1916, a department that began to organize a series of annual exhibitions highlighting the country's most recent industrial products. Those exhibitions continued until World War II, when the function was assumed by the young Museum of Modern Art.[46]

Unlike the Metropolitan Museum, since 1877 Boston's Museum of Fine Arts had advanced its educational role by supporting a separate art school within the museum. Because Boston's art school included the study of industrial art, the museum was able to back away even more easily than the Metropolitan from a dedicated commitment to applied arts training in its galleries. By the opening years of the twentieth century, Boston's ties to its South Kensington roots became very tenuous indeed. The break became imminent when the museum initiated plans to leave its original South Kensington–style building on Copley Square and move to the structure it still occupies along the Fenway. The arrangement of the new building not only incorporated the views of the museum's influential secretary, Benjamin Ives Gilman, who would establish an international reputation for himself promoting the primary aesthetic role of the art museum, it also drew on the principles underlying the highly praised galleries of Bode's Kaiser Friedrich Museum. The Boston museum's building committee visited Berlin soon after its museum opened. The Museum of Fine Arts, Boston, eventually created a two-level program for the presentation of its collections, an approach that came to be recognized around the world. Primary galleries emphasized singular masterpiece objects presented whenever possible in culturally evocative displays, while other rooms were set aside for dense installations intended for a more learned audience of collectors and scholars. This type of organization was to be adopted by a number of museums in the United States and elsewhere in the twentieth century. Leigh Ashton would eventually reinstall the Victoria and Albert Museum on these principles in the late 1940s.[47]

From South Kensington to the V&A

In 1904, the year Wilhelm von Bode's Kaiser Friedrich Museum opened, Caspar Purdon Clarke, then head of the newly renamed Victoria and Albert Museum, visited the Berlin museum and was deeply impressed with what he saw. However, his move that same year to assume the directorship of New York's Metropolitan Museum prevented him from sitting on the 1908 committee focused on the reinstallation of the Museum's collections. The reinstallation was the last of a series of reforms forced on the institution by popular dissatisfaction with the Museum's program of acquisitions and display, a dissatisfaction that had grown during the last two decades of the nineteenth century. The criticisms resulted in a government inquiry overseen by the Select Committee on the Museums of the Science and Art Department. While this committee issued two reports, in 1897 and 1898, critiquing the Museum's aims and methods, the problems it addressed had their roots in decisions made and directions taken during the institution's earliest years.

Henry Cole was a brilliantly innovative, publicly engaged, pragmatic—indeed opportunistic—director working within England's civil service, a complex and restricting bureaucracy even in the nineteenth century. His occasional rigidity with staff, which increased as his tenure stabilized, was countered by an almost too-present willingness to accept an extraneous new program if it might appeal to a political power or advance his institution's public image. Even in his early years, Cole bemoaned the fact that South Kensington had become "a refuge for destitute collections." While Cole accepted the inevitable and tried to improve it, in contemporary terms we might say that he took on too much, too quickly, accepting the bureaucratic directives of a government little conversant with the public expectations and responsibilities of museums with an artistic mission.

Only Cole—the art and education idealist, the civil servant as impresario, the lobbyist without compare—could balance the design and commerce, education and art edification goals of South Kensington and shape them into a program that could be received positively by both the public and its government representatives. When he retired, the house of cards he balanced began to dissolve under the oversight of lesser men. Criticism mounted as the English art world sensed a power vacuum and an institutional loss of direction, but, in truth, ill feeling had already surfaced at Cole's retirement in 1873 with the abortive attempt to have the best of South Kensington's collections taken over by the British Museum. The Department of Science and Art began to look confused, inelegant, ineffective.

Between 1880 and 1910 the Museum slowly reconditioned itself, focusing its objectives on its multifarious collections—collections reflective of its earlier and more diverse, albeit somewhat scattershot, programs. Institutional reconditioning began in 1880 with the move of modern manufactured objects to Bethnal Green, and it ended with the 1909 establishment of a separate Science Museum at South Kensington, the solution finally arrived at to manage the Semperian vision of "Science being reunited with Art" that had helped to spawn the confusion in the first place. The most significant action taken during this period of reform was the creation of materials-based curatorial departments in 1897. A few years later, with complete awareness of the trend toward cultural and historical displays, the Museum opted to reform its installations along lines established during its earliest years. The 1908 committee on display embraced what were then considered to be the founding installation principles of Cole's enterprise, the exhibition of objects by material and technique, in order to better serve the museum's primary designer and craftsman audience (fig. 16).

This reformation, however, eventually resulted in a tradition of scholarship that had little to do with Cole's ideals and was in no way reflective of Semper's. A new generation of young scholars began to work for the museum in the 1890s.

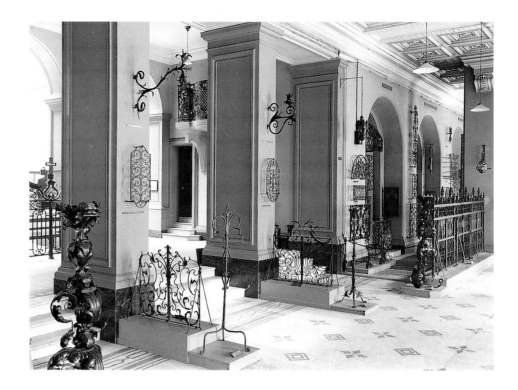

Fig. 16. The Ironwork Gallery at the V&A in 1925

Eventually they deepened as they reformed the scholarly role of the Museum by applying the disciplined historical and aesthetic concerns of turn-of-the-century art criticism to the decorative arts. In the process, the Museum turned further away from contemporary art as well as from the institution's elaborate regional education programs for both beginning and intermediate students. It focused instead on collection care and advancement, with a highly educated audience in mind. The new intellectual direction of the Museum, developed and nurtured over most of the twentieth century, combined contemporary taxonomic concerns with the English national tradition of erudite antiquarian expertise. Together, these commitments fostered a system of connoisseurship based on materials, technique, and the empirical understanding of an object's history that had never been achieved before and probably never will again. Its refinement and accomplishment were such that by the middle decades of the twentieth century, the international stature of the Victoria and Albert Museum as a source of object-specific knowledge in the decorative arts was unparalleled.

As the V&A moved into the late twentieth century, however, the academic rigor given primacy in the institution increasingly appeared to be out of step with the interests and demographics of a dramatically expanding national and international museum audience. It began to occur to some at the V&A that sustaining the narrow world of art scholars who practiced a life of connoisseurship—a word, indeed, which few members of the potential new museum-going public could even define—clearly threatened the viability, perhaps even the survival, of the institution. The Museum's directors in the last quarter of the twentieth century moved to update institutional practices, broaden intellectual perspectives, and to focus again on the designer and craftsman audience to which the Museum was originally directed and from which it had become disengaged.

Confronting, in many ways, that very environment of conflicting values overseen by Cole and Robinson in the nineteenth century, the tug of war between scholarship and accessibility seems to remain unresolved within the institution today, much as it remains unresolved in the museum world as a whole. The schism between these two institutional directions, however, is somehow magnified at the V&A, no doubt because it is this Museum that is so central to our historical comprehension of the elusive educational dream in Western museum culture.

Our continuing respect for the Museum in the final analysis has as much to do with its collecting achievement as with the articulation of its educational mandate so influential to so many subsequent museum enterprises. The collections of the Victoria and Albert Museum comprise more than four million objects—countless works of art of unique significance and aesthetic excellence that have been and will be appreciated by generations past, present, and future. These collections also constitute a priceless archive reflecting a changing canon variously interpreted and displayed over time, a canon that evolved out of the aesthetic, social, and political fabric shaping the Museum over the century and a half of its existence. The V&A's treasures and all that they signify define an institution that remains one of Britain's greatest contributions to the international artistic legacy we all share.

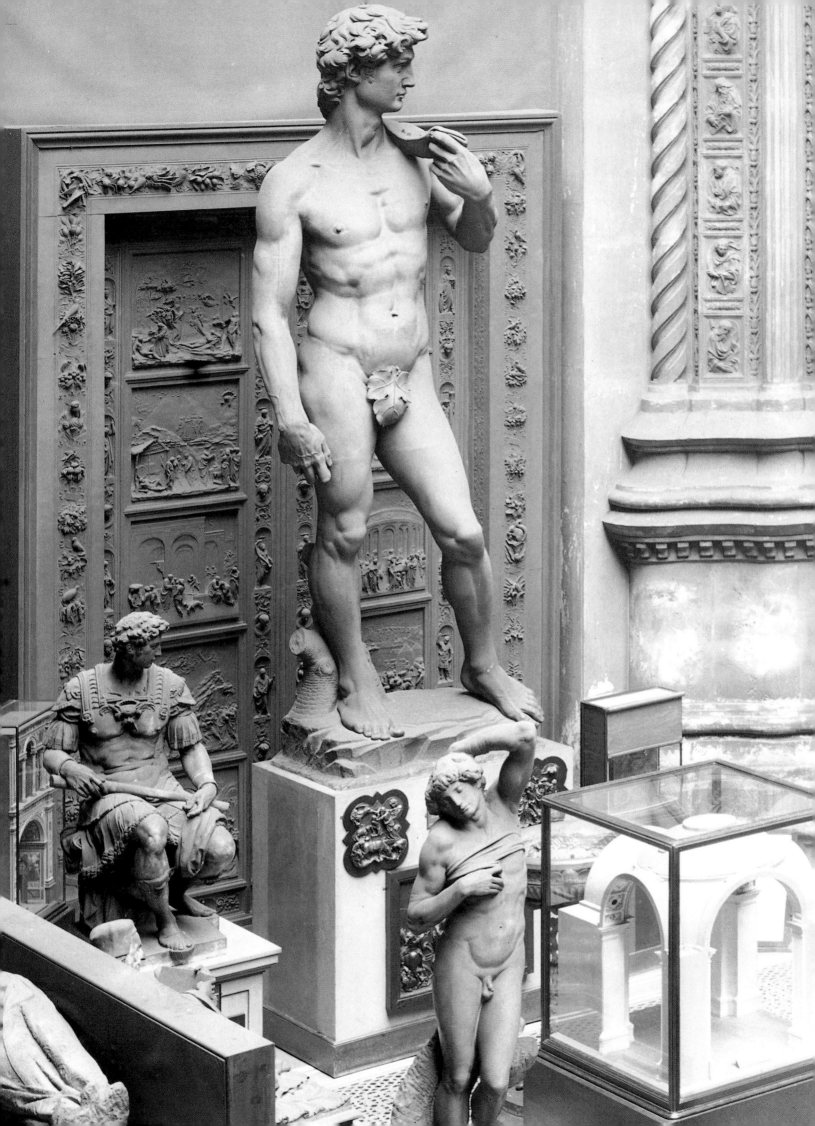

The Victoria and Albert Museum: An Illustrated Chronology

RICHARD DUNN AND ANTHONY BURTON

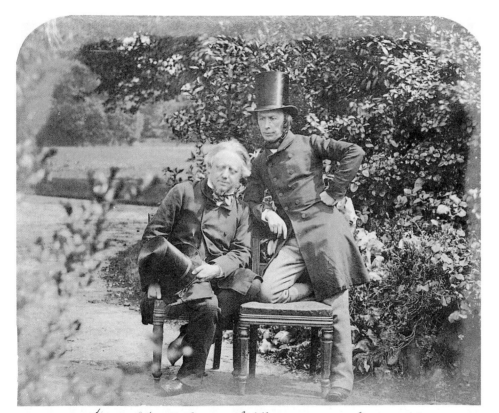

Henry Cole 1857   Mr Redgrave Gardenouse garden

Fig. 17. Henry Cole, left, and Richard Redgrave

Henry Cole (1808–1882) and Richard Redgrave (1804–1888) were central to the foundation of the Museum. Cole was appointed head of the new Department of Practical Art in 1852; Redgrave, an artist in his own right (see cat. 52), became Superintendent for Art. When the Department of Practical Art became the Department of Science and Art in 1853, Cole became its head and held that post until his retirement in 1873.

Opposite: Fig. 18. The east Cast Court, with casts of sculpture (including Michelangelo's *Giuliano de' Medici, David,* and *"The Dying Slave"*) and architecture (Ghiberti's Florentine Baptistry doors) as well as architectural models. The educational mission to which Henry Cole was most committed was the documentation of Europe's artistic treasures through plaster reproductions.

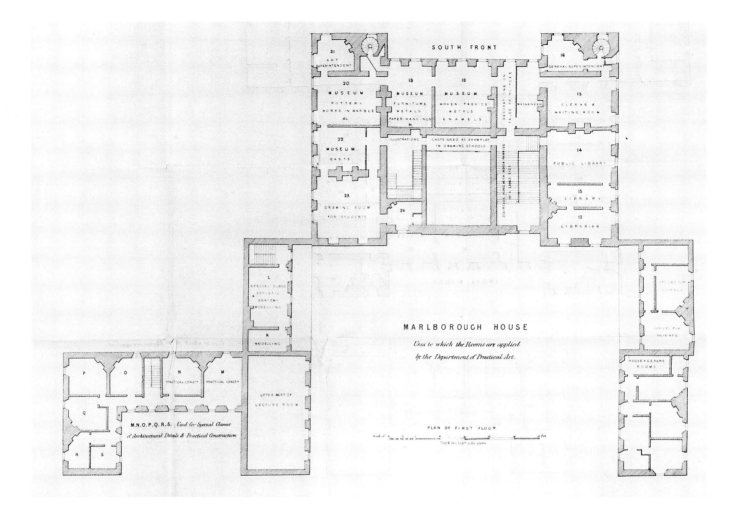

Fig. 19. A plan of Marlborough House, from *First Report of the Department of Practical Art,* London, 1853

Marlborough House was the first home of the Department of Practical Art, which opened a Museum of Manufactures there in 1852. The museum's educational emphasis was clear, with two libraries (one marked "Public Library") and study rooms designated for "Casts Used as Examples in Drawing Schools," "Drawing Room for Students," "Special Class Artistic Anatomy Modeling," and "Special Classes of Architectural Details & Practical Construction." Museum rooms were demarcated by material, with rooms given over to fabrics, metals, enamels, furniture, paper hangings, pottery, works in marble, and casts. Marlborough House also briefly featured the infamous display called on this plan "Decorations on False Principles."

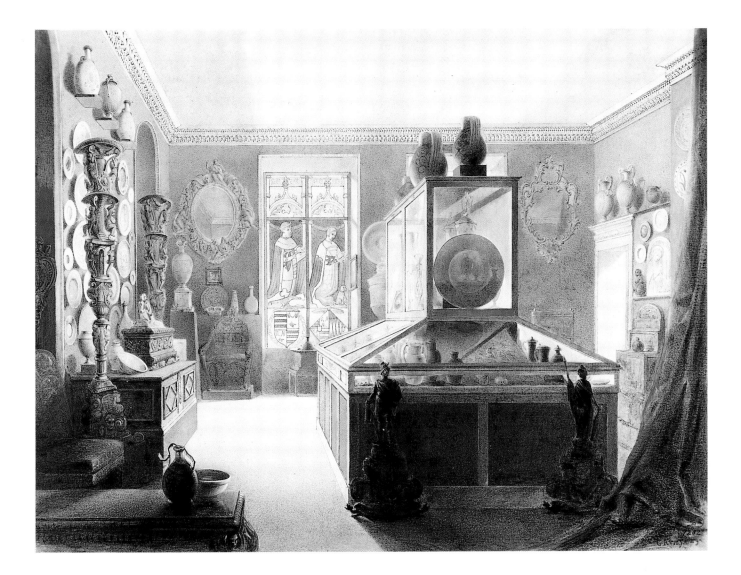

The museum at Marlborough House included contemporary manufactures, as well as objects purchased from collectors such as Ralph Bernal and Jules Soulages. This view, painted in 1856–57, indicates the range of material in the Museum of Ornamental Art (its name since 1853). It also shows that a materials-based arrangement was not rigorously followed. Rather, the room has the feel of an antiquarian interior.

Fig. 20. A gallery at Marlborough House, 1856–57

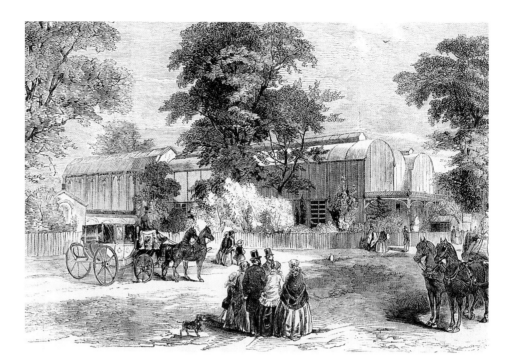

Fig. 21. "The South Kensington Museum: General View," from *The Illustrated London News*, 27 June 1857

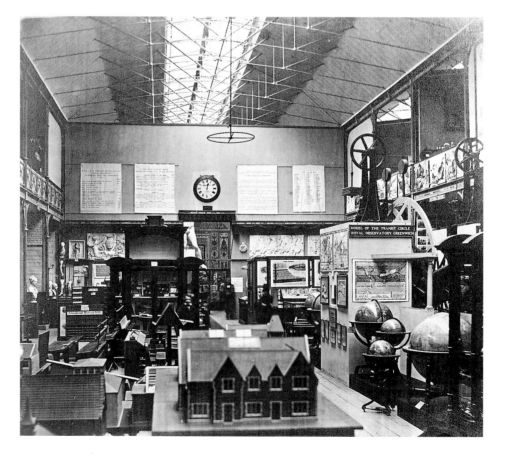

Fig. 22. The Educational Museum in 1859

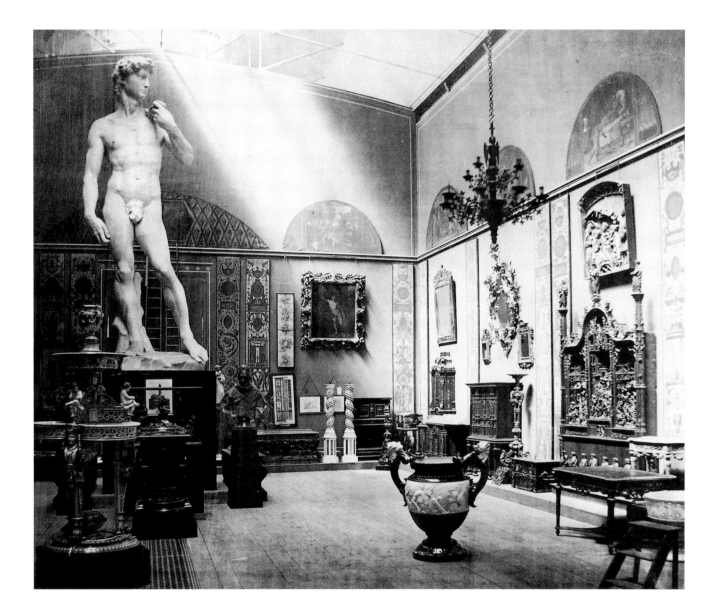

Fig. 23. The interior of the Art Museum, c. 1857–59

Part of the profits of the Great Exhibition of 1851 had gone toward the purchase of land in Brompton where, in 1855, work began on a prefabricated iron structure to house a museum. The buildings were soon christened the "Brompton Boilers," because they looked like steam boilers lying side by side. They opened on 22 June 1857 as the South Kensington Museum (fig. 21).

Inside, the visitor was presented with a more varied collection than seen previously at Marlborough House. In addition to the art and architecture collections, there were displays of Patented Inventions, Products of the Animal Kingdom (see cat. 18), and an Educational Museum (fig. 22). Walking through the latter, the visitor came to the art collections (fig. 23), visible through the doorway in figure 22, where one can see part of the cast of Michelangelo's *David* (with fig leaf attached; see cat. 26). The Art Museum contained many notable objects, including the pilasters and lunettes copied from Raphael's Loggia in the Vatican, a mirror from the Bernal collection, and a Flemish altarpiece previously shown in Marlborough House (fig. 20).

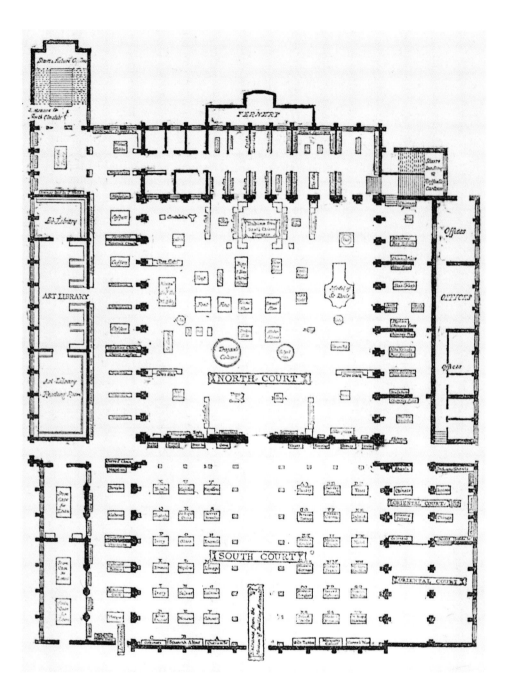

Fig. 24. Ground plan of the North and South Courts, from *A Guide to the South Kensington Museum* (1865)

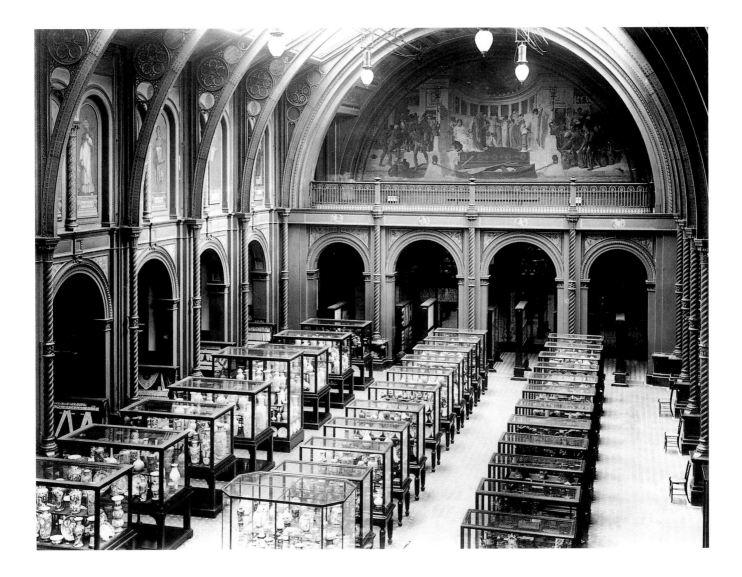

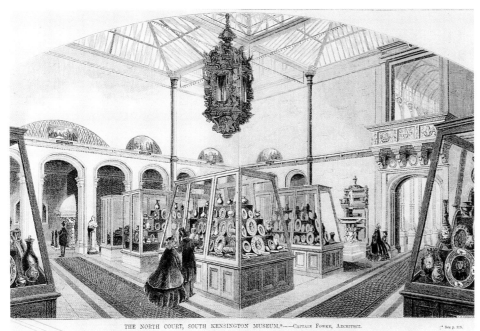

THE NORTH COURT, SOUTH KENSINGTON MUSEUM.*——CAPTAIN FOWKE, ARCHITECT.   * See p. 315.

Fig. 25. The South Court, c. 1886

Fig. 26. The North Court, from *The Builder*, 3 May 1862

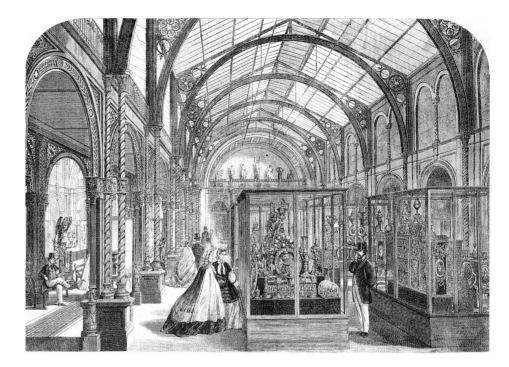

Fig. 27. "The Loan Collection of Works of Art at South Kensington Museum," from *The Illustrated London News*, 6 December 1862

In 1862 two new courts were opened to house the rapidly expanding collection. The interior of the South Court combined decorated ironwork with murals, notably the cycle known as the "Kensington Valhalla" (see cats. 51 and 52). By 1886 two frescoes commissioned by Henry Cole from Frederic, Lord Leighton—*The Industrial Arts of War* and *The Industrial Arts of Peace* (subjects conceived by the late Prince Consort)—enhanced this scheme. Figure 25 shows the "Valhalla" on the left, and Leighton's "Peace" fresco at the back. The South Court was initially used for an exhi-

Fig. 28. "The Sunday Question," from *Punch*, 17 April 1869

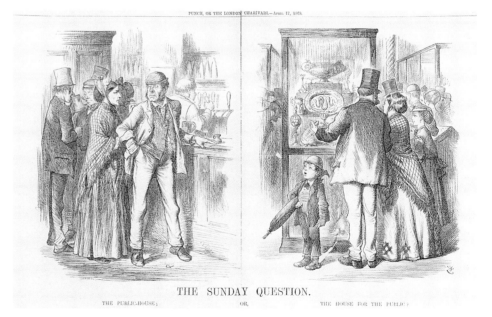

bition of works of art on loan to the Museum and served as a gallery for loans for the next forty-five years.

The North Court (fig. 26) contained ceramics as well as the copies of the lunettes from Raphael's Loggia (see fig. 81). The opening of these courts also allowed for a return to materials-based systematic ordering; the 1865 plan shows each case in the South Court labeled by material. Despite the creation of these new galleries, however, the Museum remained short of space and had a crowded appearance.

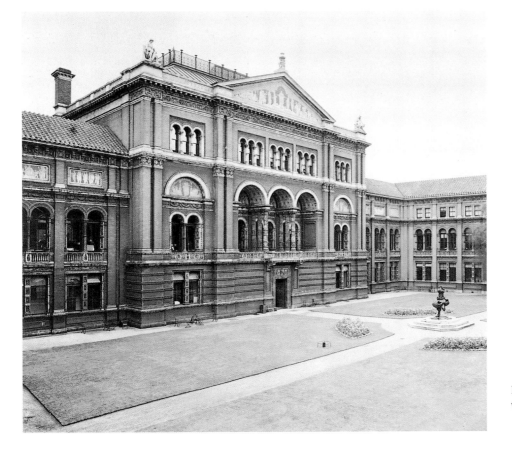

Fig. 29. Facade of the Lecture Theatre wing in 1920

In 1860, Francis Fowke (the architect responsible for many of the South Kensington buildings) proposed an ambitious expansion plan. This included a range of buildings centered on a block incorporating a lecture theater and refreshment rooms, completed in 1869 (fig. 29). This served as the main entrance of the Museum until the opening of the Aston Webb building in 1909.

Cole's intention was that South Kensington should attract the widest possible audience. In particular, following the installation of gas jets, he hoped that "the evening opening of Public Museums may furnish a powerful antidote to the gin palace." Although it is not certain what the breakdown of the Museum's audience was at this time, contemporary illustrations (fig. 28) give the impression that there were visitors of all classes. Also illustrated in the cartoon is the Palissy dish (cat. 71), purchased as part of the Soulages collection.

See fig. 18, p. 48. The Architectural Courts (also called the Cast Courts) in 1920

From its beginnings, the Museum displayed casts as part of its educational role (see figs. 6, 18, 52). The 1860s and 1870s witnessed an ambitious program of acquisitions, including casts of the huge Portico de la Gloria from Santiago de Compostela (see cat. 25) and of Trajan's Column. By the mid-1860s this expanding collection was mostly on display in the North Court (see fig. 26), but space was so tight that the Portico de la Gloria had to be shown in sections. In 1873, therefore, the Architectural Courts, designed by General Henry Scott, were opened. *The Builder* remarked that "the height of the apartments, the magnitude of many of the objects . . . and the beauty of others, all concur to produce a lasting effect." Casts and photographs of European works (as well as original objects) were displayed in the West Court; Indian architecture was displayed in the East Court. The theme begun with the "Kensington Valhalla" was continued in the display around the West Court of the names of cities celebrated in the history of art. A photograph taken in 1920 shows casts of objects from Renaissance Italy, including Michelangelo's *David* (with fig leaf attached; see cat. 26).

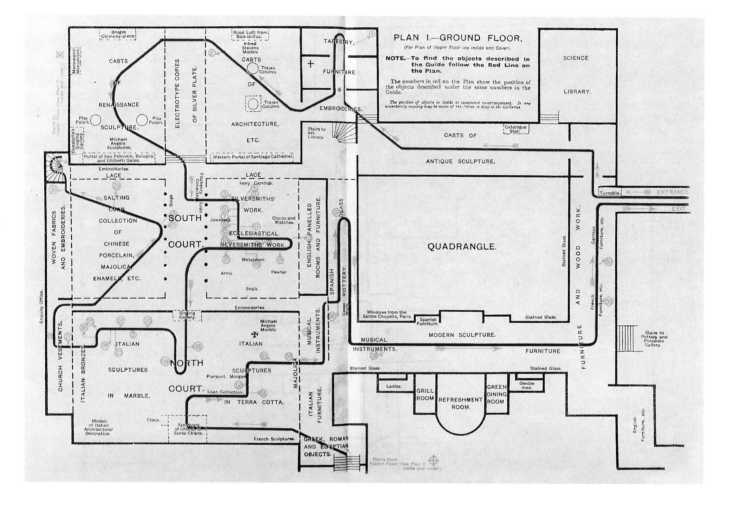

Fig. 30. Plan of the ground floor of the V&A, from *The Red Line Guide to the Victoria and Albert Museum* (1905)

Opposite: Fig. 31. The new facade of the Museum, 1909

By 1905, although the Victoria and Albert Museum (as renamed in 1899) was reorganized into five curatorial departments—ceramics, woodwork, metalwork, textiles, and sculpture—its arrangement remained confusing. One attempt to solve this problem was the provision in Museum guides of a "red line," a suggested route that was intended to turn the chaos into an intelligible narrative.

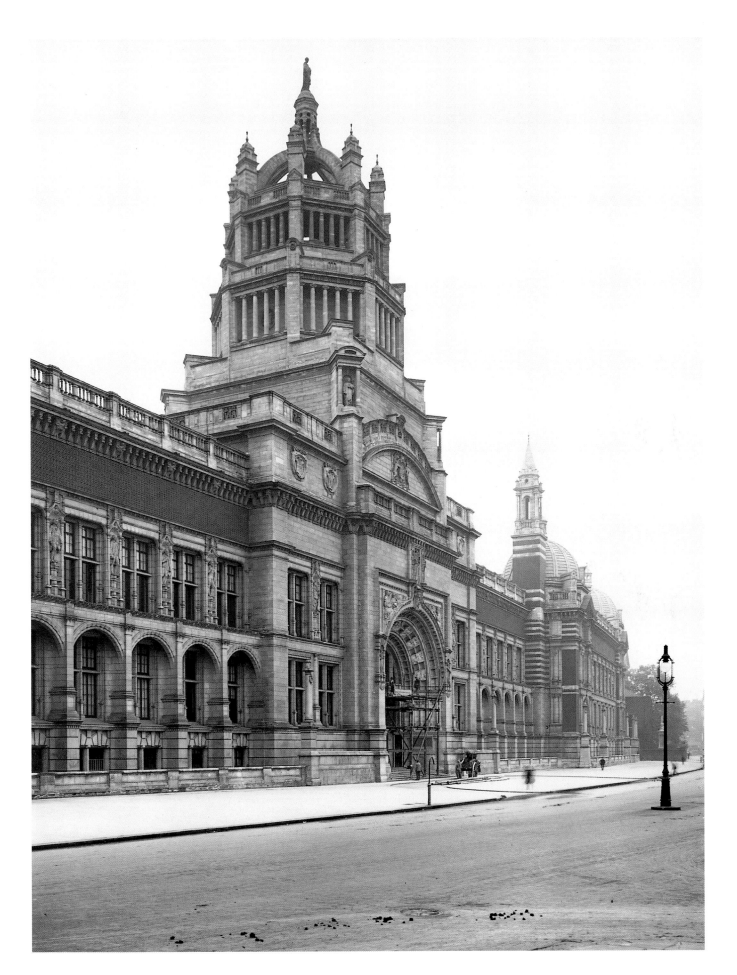

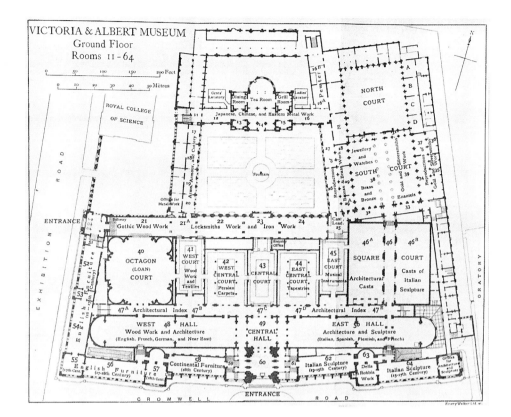

VICTORIA & ALBERT MUSEUM
Ground Floor
Rooms 11-64

Fig. 32. Plan of the ground floor of the V&A, from *Muirhead's Short Guide to London* (1918)

Fig. 33. A Buddha being set up near the Museum's main entrance, from *The Sphere*, 19 March 1910

Filling the Nation's Treasure-house with Costly Gifts.

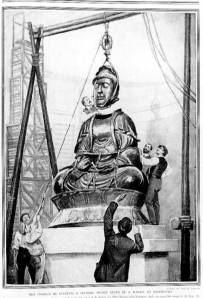

In 1890 the British government decided that the Museum's premises should be properly expanded; the resulting competition was won by Aston Webb. Construction did not begin until 1899, however, and ten years elapsed before the opening in 1909.

One result of the new building was that much-needed space became available. Consequently, a major reorganization of the Museum was possible and in 1908 Robert Morant, secretary of the Board of Education, set up a Committee on Re–arrangement. The Committee considered the possibilities for display in the Museum, notably the choice between a materials-based arrangement and an aesthetic/historical presentation (placing together objects of different mediums but of the same period and style) that many European museums had adopted. The final report opted for materials-based displays, however, and this arrangement (as seen in the 1918 plan) remained for forty years. Although rigidly didactic, this system of classification was in accord with contemporary studies of the decorative arts by material, important contributions to which were made by V&A curators.

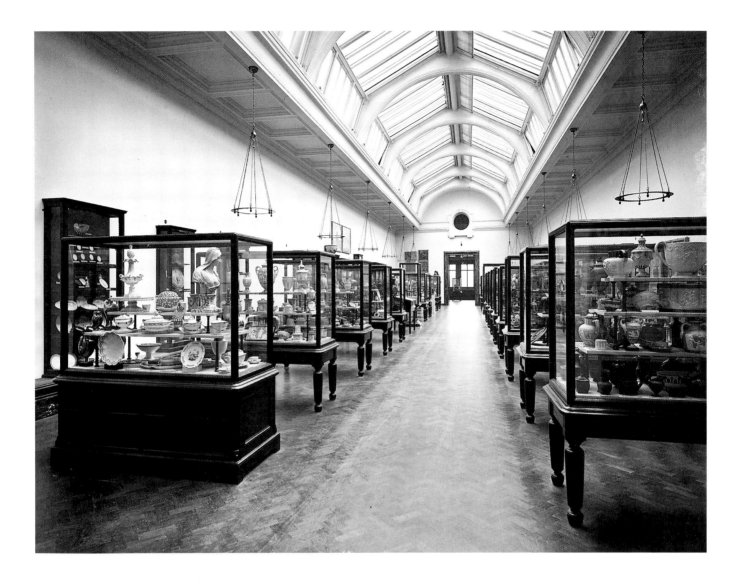

The Museum received much publicity following its rearrangement and expansion, in particular concerning the acquisition of important objects. One of the most impressive of these was a twenty-foot-high bronze statue of Buddha (fig. 33). This object has been displayed in many different galleries in the Museum—even in the courtyard—and has recently gone on long-term loan to a Buddhist temple in Birmingham, England.

The Museum's new galleries alternated long galleries and corridors with lofty courts. The former presented rows of cases containing objects of similar appearance (fig. 34). The displays were set against plain walls, so as not to crowd exhibits. This contrasted dramatically with displays created under Cole, which had elaborate settings in bold colors. The new displays were not universally applauded. The *Daily Telegraph,* for instance, thought that the V&A had taken a retrograde step, complaining, "For one technical student or artificer who will derive instruction . . . a thousand visitors bent on deriving pleasure . . . will be repelled and disconcerted."

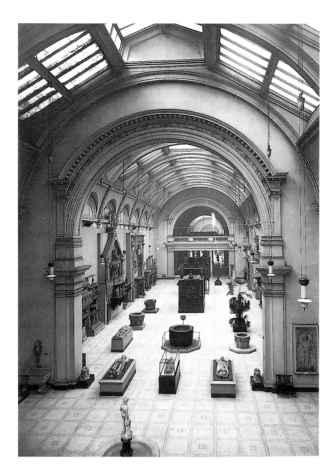

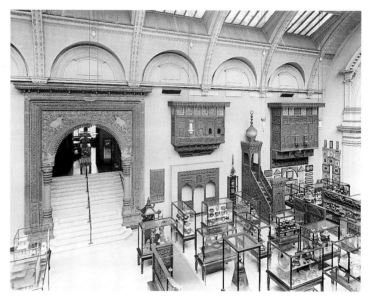

Fig. 35. The East Hall, c. 1920

Fig. 36. The West Hall, c. 1920

The 1909 building provided huge halls on either side of the main entrance. The East Hall (fig. 35) was devoted to European architecture and sculpture. The West Hall (fig. 36) contained examples of architectural woodwork, including a fifteenth-century *minbar* (pulpit) from a Cairo mosque and the Gwalior Gateway, made specifically for the Museum and presented by the Maharaja Scindia in 1883. An Egyptian mosque lamp (cat. 102) can be seen in a case in the foreground of figure 36.

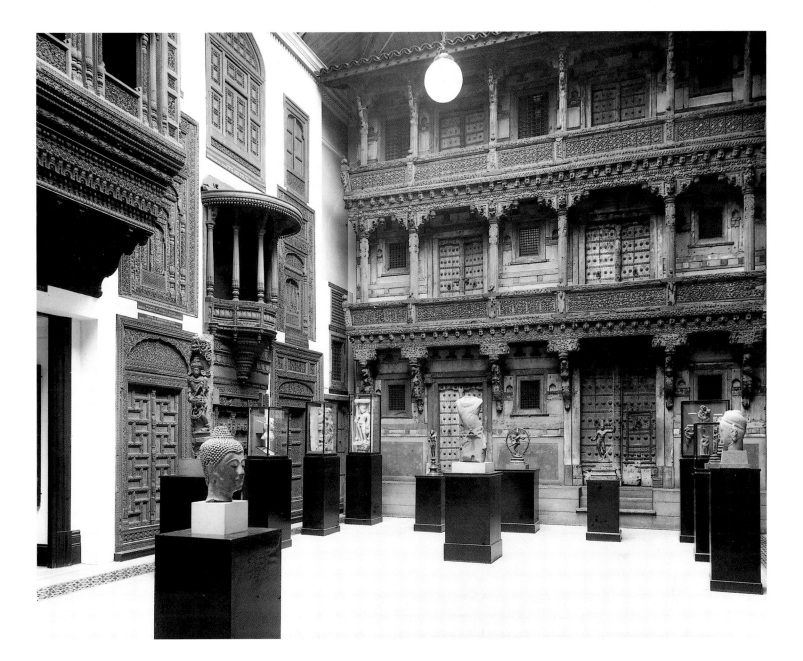

The Museum acquired most of the collection of the East India Company's India Museum in 1879–80 when the company's holdings were divided between the South Kensington Museum and the British Museum. (The South Kensington Museum retained the name India Museum.) The early displays echoed the imperialistic notions that underpinned the India Museum's formation, with weapons and other artifacts displayed as trophies. Following the opening in 1888 of the Imperial Institute and the foundation of the Society for the Encouragement and Preservation of Indian Art around 1890—both institutions on the South Kensington site—a reappraisal of the collections took place, leading to increased emphasis on the representation of traditional life and industries. The Oriental collections remained in these galleries (fig. 37), called the Eastern Galleries, until 1955, when, after the demolition of the Imperial Institute, they were moved to the main Museum building.

Fig. 37. The entrance hall of the India Museum of the South Kensington Museum, 1936, which housed the Museum's Near and Far Eastern art collections

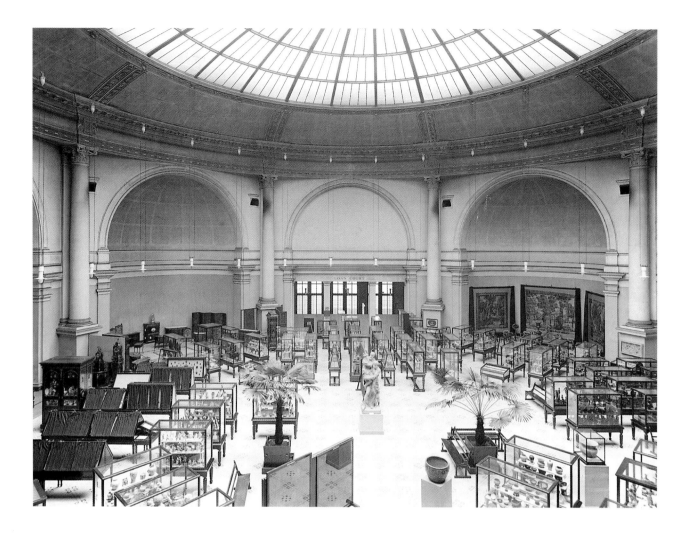

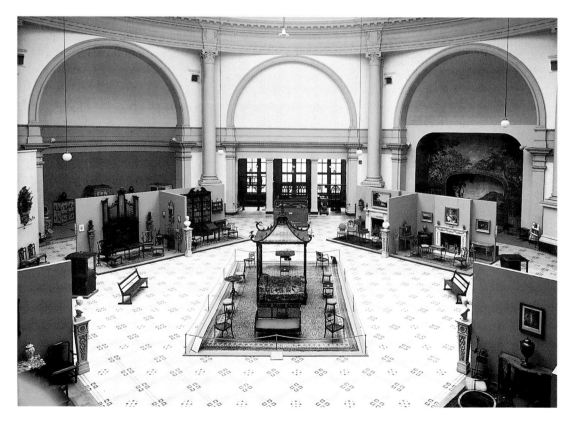

Taking advantage of the increased space in the 1909 building, the large Octagon Court became the new Loan Court (figs. 38 and 39). Loans have been important in the history of the V&A, particularly in its first eighty years, accounting, for instance, for between a quarter and a third of the displays in the 1860s and 1870s.

Subsequently, the Octagon Court has served other purposes. In 1936 it became the stage for an innovative contextual display of eighteenth-century English decorative arts, mixing for the first time objects from different departments (fig. 39). The gallery was hailed as a revolution in the Museum, and set the tone for the changes that were to occur after World War II. Following the success of this move away from materials-based displays, the Octagon Court had an upper gallery added in 1962; the lower space was turned into the Costume Court, which remains its purpose.

George Salting was a prolific collector in a number of areas, including Chinese and Japanese ceramics and European art. By 1874 his collection had outgrown his residence in St. James's Street, prompting him to lend items to the South Kensington Museum. After his death in 1909, the majority of this astonishing collection passed to the V&A, where it was shown in its own galleries. Cats. 70, 75, 107, and 121 came from the Salting bequest.

Opposite, top: Fig. 38. The Octagon Court as the Loan Court in 1920

Opposite, bottom: Fig. 39. A display of English art in the Octagon Court, 1936

Fig. 40. The Salting bequest on display, 1912

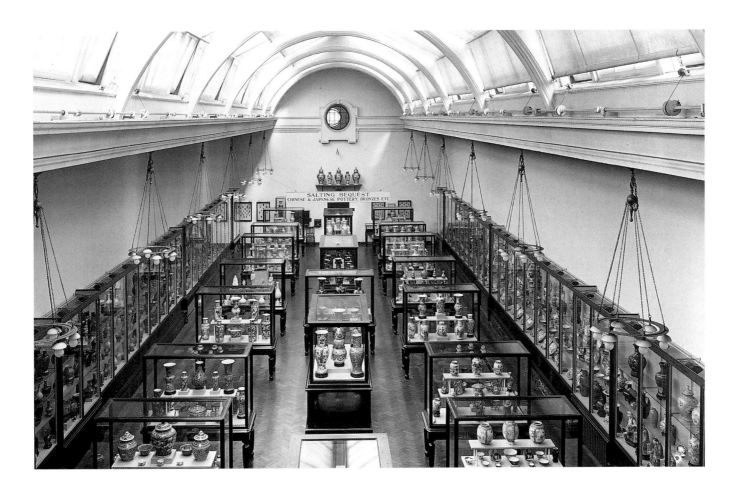

The Jones collection was almost equal in size to Salting's, although more focused in scope. After retiring, John Jones, a former tailor and army clothier, lived at No. 95 Piccadilly, where he amassed his collection (fig. 41). He died in 1882 and left his collection, valued at £250,000, to the Museum. The collection was composed largely of French furniture, porcelain, miniatures, bronzes, paintings, and sculptures of the eighteenth century. Initially it was displayed in the southwest corner on the first floor of the Museum and was hailed as a major addition; an 1883 article in *The Cabinet Maker and Art Furnisher,* for instance, stated: "No wonder that the South Kensington authorities can hardly find words to express their delight, for the Sheepshanks, Dyce, Forster, and Townshend legacies fall far short in value to the Jones Collection."

Following the rearrangement and expansion of the Museum in 1909, the Jones collection was moved to the former ceramics galleries on the first floor (fig. 42). After World War II, it moved again to the ground-floor galleries near the main entrance, where it remains (fig. 44). This photograph shows two Sèvres vases from the collection (cat. 86); these are illustrated in place at No. 95 Piccadilly a century before (fig. 41). Cats. 60, 84, and 85 also come from the Jones collection.

Fig. 41. The dining room at No. 95 Piccadilly, from the Jones collection handbook (1883)

Fig. 42. The Jones collection, c. 1910

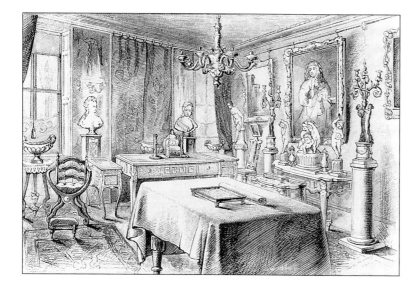

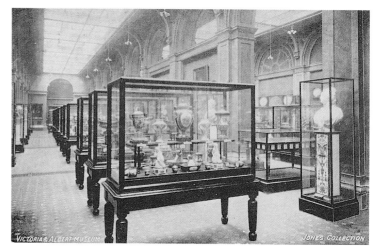

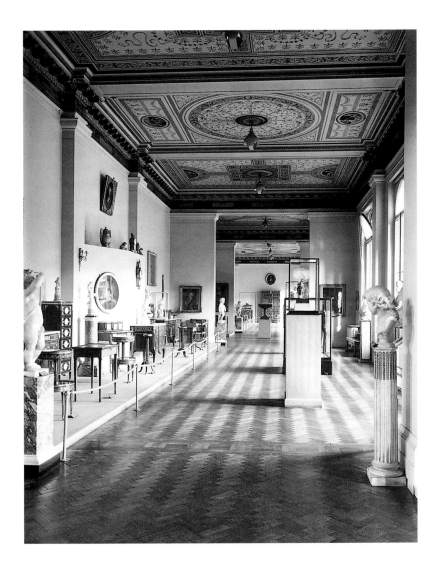

Fig. 43. The Jones collection, 1928

Fig. 44. Part of the Jones collection in Gallery 7, 1971

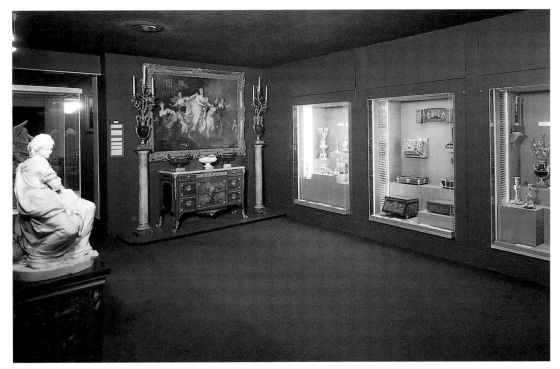

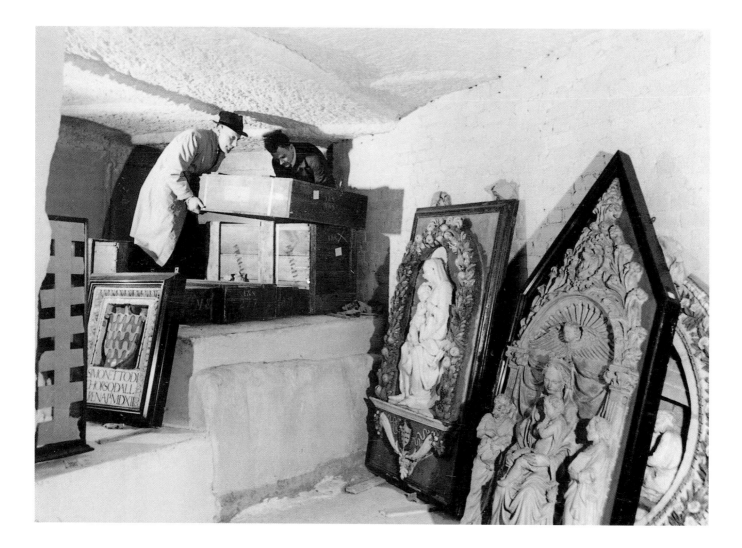

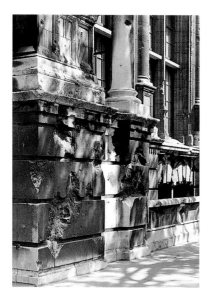

At the outbreak of World War II, the risk of bombing led to the decision in 1939 to evacuate the galleries (fig. 45). In order to encourage public morale, however, the V&A reopened in 1940. Only a limited number of objects were displayed, although according to *The Connoisseur* these were "just sufficient to make an hour's relaxation from our ceaseless vigilance and obsession with war concerns." The Museum also served as a school for evacuees from Gibraltar and as a canteen for the Royal Air Force (fig. 47). The V&A did, however, suffer a bomb blast to its west end (fig. 46), after which the decision was made to leave the damage as "a memorial to the enduring values of this great museum in a time of conflict."

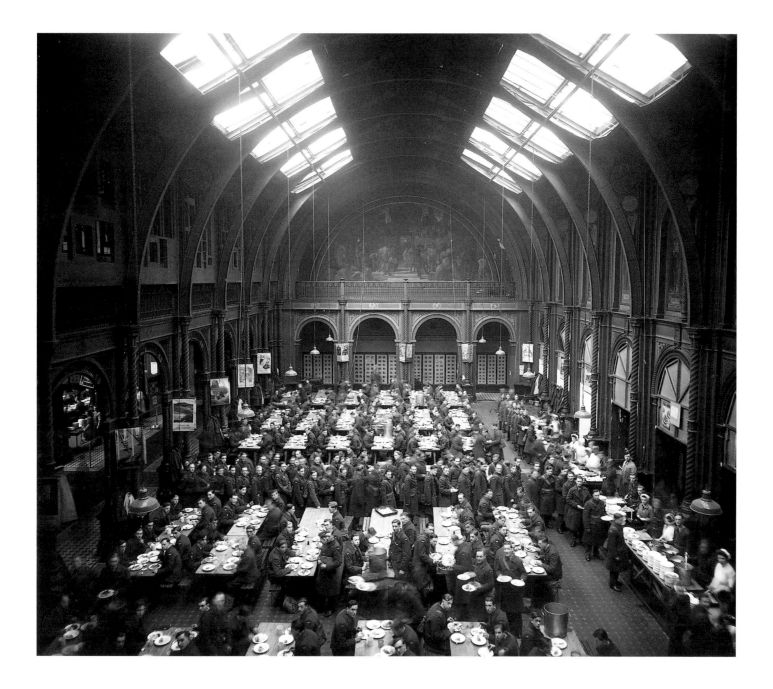

Opposite, top: Fig. 45. Museum objects, including cat. 56, della Robbia's Virgin and Child, being packed up in 1939 for their protection in the face of war

Opposite, bottom: Fig. 46. Bomb damage to west end of the V&A

Fig. 47. The Museum's South Court converted to a wartime canteen for the Royal Air Force

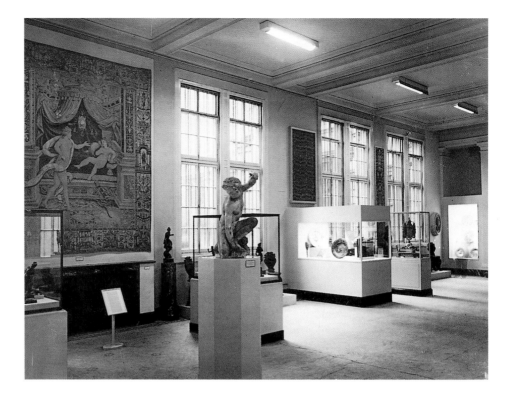

Fig. 48. Display of sixteenth-century Mannerism in Room 21 of the V&A

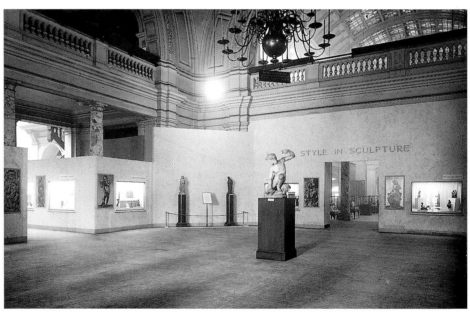

Fig. 49. "Style in Sculpture" exhibition, 1946

Toward the end of the war, the Museum began to consider the options for rearrangement made possible as a result of the evacuation of the galleries. It was decided to break away from a single, materials-based approach. Director Leigh Ashton chose to divide the galleries into two types: the Primary Galleries would contain displays by style, period, or nationality; the Secondary Galleries retained materials-based displays. Figure 48 shows a Primary Gallery of sixteenth-century Mannerism, containing the so-called Michelangelo *Cupid* (cat. 58) alongside other works from the same artistic context. As the architect of this shift in display philosophy, Ashton was hailed as an innovator. Indeed, Ashton took great care over the new displays, experimenting with colors in order to choose those that best complemented particular exhibits. His taste led him toward spacious galleries with walls of pale colors.

Ashton was also conscious of the V&A's public role. Keen to promote it as an exciting place to visit, he instituted a vigorous exhibition program, producing about four exhibitions each year. Indeed, before the rearrangement could begin, the Museum was largely taken over by the Council of Design's massive 1946 exhibition, "Britain Can Make It," whose aim was to promote postwar British industry. The more academically substantial "Style in Sculpture" of the same year (fig. 49) offered a survey of the development of style from the Romanesque to the present day, concentrating on historical context, an indication of the Museum's change of approach. Among the exhibits displayed was the so-called Michelangelo *Cupid*.

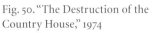

Fig. 50. "The Destruction of the Country House," 1974

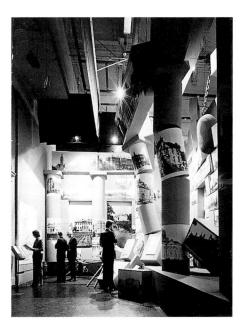

The V&A presented the exhibition "The Destruction of the Country House" in 1974 (fig. 50), signaling the Museum's commitment to preserve intact important country house collections in Britain. In the 1970s V&A curators were heavily involved in a campaign to avert the breakup of the Rothschild collection, for example, which included the Medici Cabinet (see cat. 77).

The need for profile-raising exhibitions remains high on the agenda. The V&A now regularly mounts major exhibitions, intended to be both popular and of high academic quality. The Pugin exhibition (fig. 51) was an important element in the reappraisal of nineteenth-century decorative arts, in which the V&A has played a major role, as well as a rare opportunity to view an extensive representation of work by the extraordinarily influential English designer A. W. N. Pugin.

Fig. 51. "Pugin: A Gothic Passion," 1994

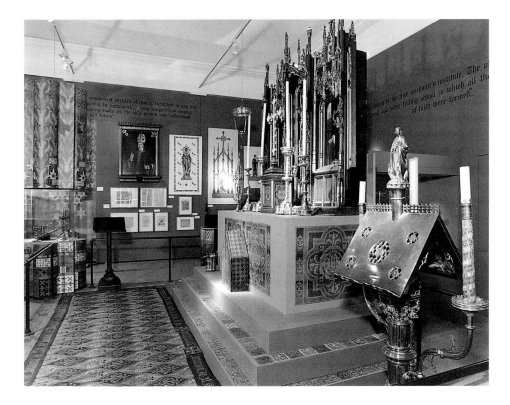

As well as maintaining a program of major exhibitions, the V&A has continued to rethink and refurbish its permanent displays. Recent gallery developments have modified Ashton's guidelines; the division is now between Materials and Techniques Galleries, which focus on the production of objects, and Art and Design Galleries, which examine the uses of objects within the cultures for which they were produced. The year 1994 saw the completion of the Glass Gallery, a reconfiguration of an important Museum collection into a Materials and Techniques Gallery (fig. 53). Conversely, the decision was made to redisplay the Cast Courts in the spirit of their original arrangement. Opened in 1982, the gallery (fig. 52) is a partial recreation of the original displays of the casts, though not the objects or photographs previously shown (see fig. 76).

Fig. 52. The Cast Courts, c. 1982

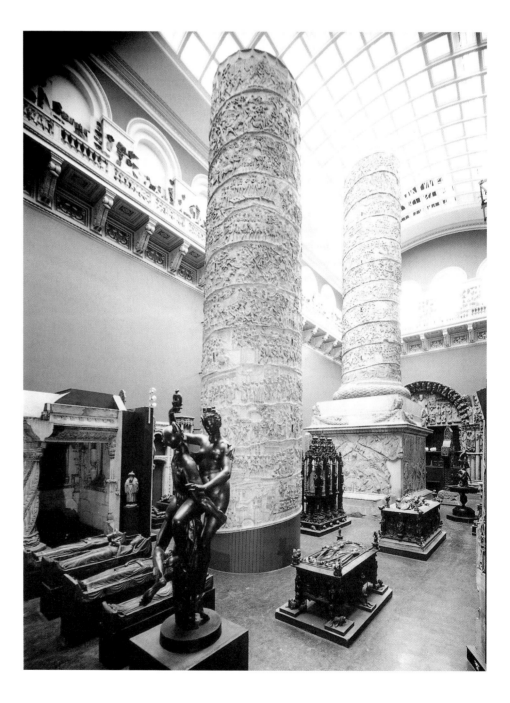

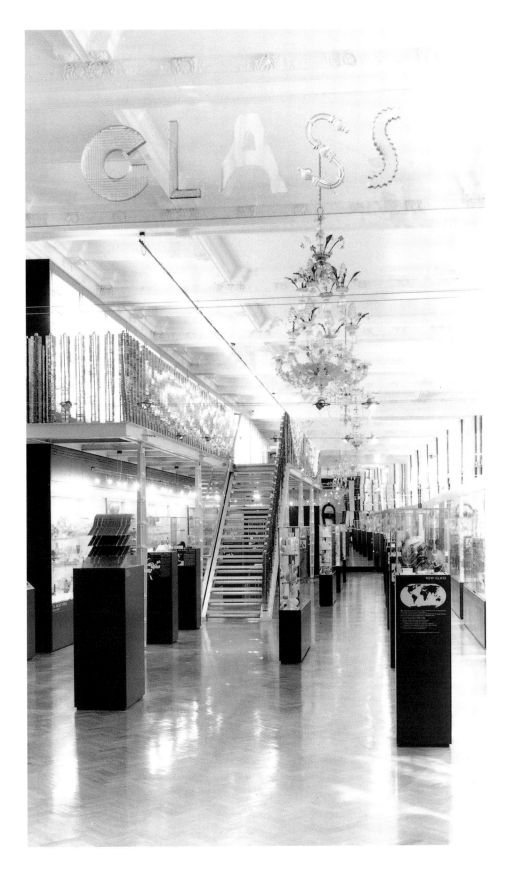

Fig. 53. The Glass Gallery, 1994

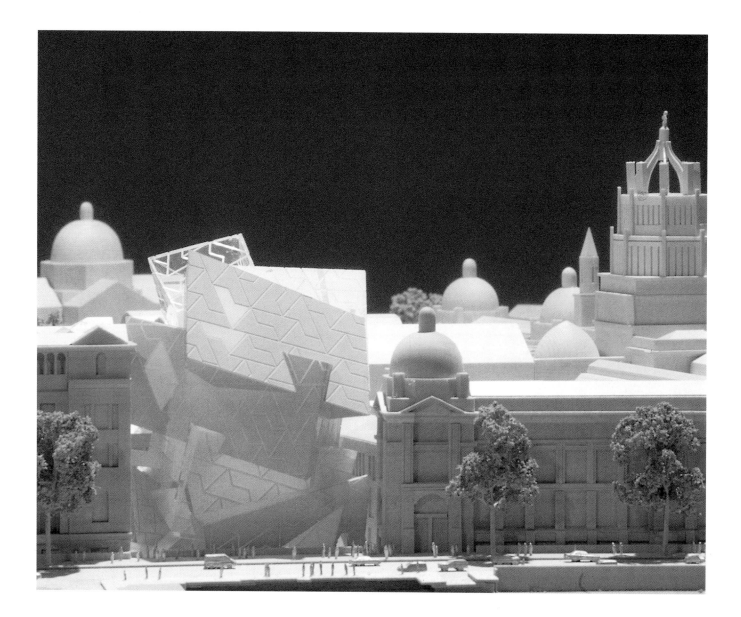

Fig. 54. Architect Daniel Libeskind's design for the V&A's Boilerhouse Project. Detail of the context model, built October 1996 by Ben Taylor and Tim Mason

Opposite: Fig. 55. An early working model of Libeskind's Boilerhouse Project design (see fig. 3 for a more recent working model)

The V&A is looking ahead to the next millennium and toward creating displays that will maintain its profile and emphasize its commitment to the promotion of contemporary design. In 1995–96 a competition was held in order to select an architectural design for a new building (the Boilerhouse Project) to occupy the one remaining undeveloped site at South Kensington. The winning design by Polish-born architect Daniel Libeskind, a startlingly modern seven-story structure in glass and tile with a spiral silhouette, is intended both as an architectural statement and as a center for innovative displays and exhibitions.

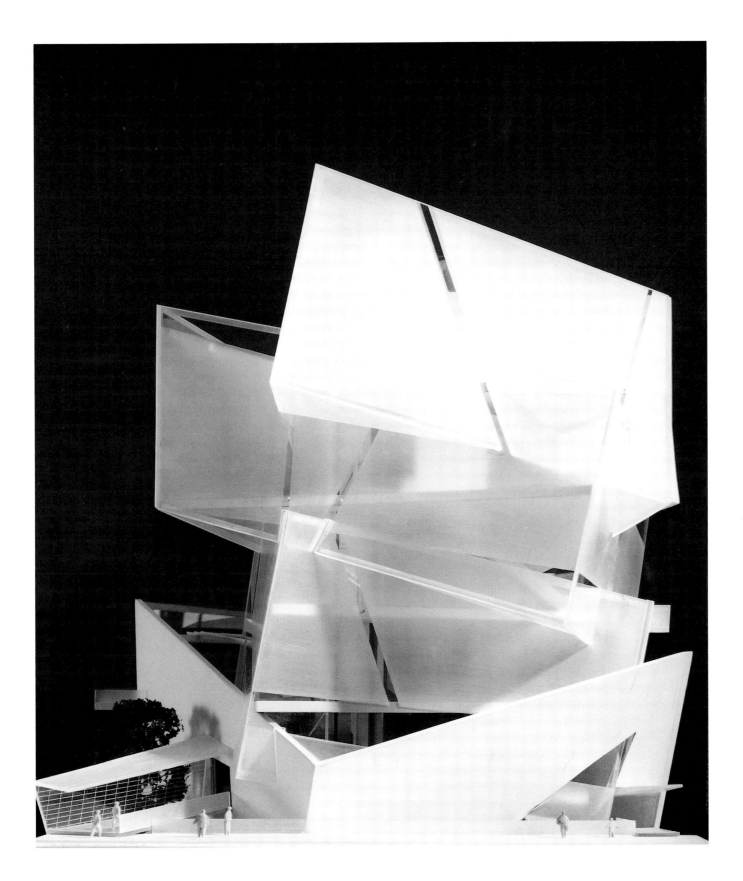

V&A The Victoria and Albert Museum: A Summary Time Line

1835–36	Select Committee of Arts and Manufactures
1837	Foundation of the Government School of Design in Somerset House, London
1851	The Great Exhibition in the Crystal Palace in Hyde Park
1852	Henry Cole appointed general superintendent of the Department of Practical Art
	The Department, including the Museum of Manufactures and the School of Design, moves into Marlborough House
1853	Department of Practical Art becomes Department of Science and Art
	Museum of Manufactures renamed the Museum of Ornamental Art
	Publication of the National Course of Art Instruction
	John Charles Robinson appointed first curator ("Superintendent of Art Collections")
1855	Building work begins on the South Kensington site
1857	South Kensington Museum opens
	Sheepshanks gift
1862	Opening of the North and South Courts
	Loan exhibition takes place in the South Court
1864	Loan of the Raphael Cartoons from the Royal Collection
1869	Central Lecture Theatre block opened
1872	Official opening of the Bethnal Green Museum
1873	Opening of the Architectural Courts
	Retirement of Henry Cole
1874	Science Schools building completed
	Philip Cunliffe Owen appointed director
1876	Forster bequest
1879	Collections of the India Museum largely transferred to the South Kensington Museum
1882	Jones bequest
1884	Art Library building completed
	Schreiber gift
1888	Opening of the Imperial Institute
1893	Art Museum and science collections given separate directors
	John Henry Middleton appointed director of the Museum
1896	Caspar Purdon Clarke appointed director of the Museum
	Division of the Museum into five curatorial departments by material

1897	Government Select Committee set up to investigate the South Kensington Museum	1955	Cross Gallery (housing the Indian collections) closes
1899	Foundation stone for the new Aston Webb building laid by Queen Victoria	1956	Trenchard Cox appointed director
	South Kensington Museum renamed the Victoria and Albert Museum		Hildburgh bequest
1900	Ionides bequest	1967	John Pope-Hennessy appointed director
	Donaldson gift	1974	Roy Strong appointed director
1905	Arthur Banks Skinner appointed director	1975	Bethnal Green Museum relaunched as the Bethnal Green Museum of Childhood
1908	Committee on Re-arrangement formed	1978	Final closure of Regional Services (formerly Circulation Department)
1909	Opening of Aston Webb building	1983	The Henry Cole Wing (previously the Royal College of Science building) opened
	Cecil Harcourt Smith appointed director		V&A accorded trustee status under the National Heritage Act
1910	Salting bequest		
1924	Eric Maclagan appointed director	1987	The Theatre Museum opens in its new premises in Covent Garden
1939	Museum closed at the start of World War II due to fear of bombing	1988	Elizabeth Esteve-Coll appointed director
1940	Museum reopens with limited displays	1989	Reorganization of the Museum's curatorial departments
1945	Leigh Ashton appointed director	1995	Alan Borg appointed director
1947	Apsley House, the nineteenth-century residence of the Duke of Wellington, placed in the care of the V&A		
1948	Division into Primary and Secondary Galleries announced		

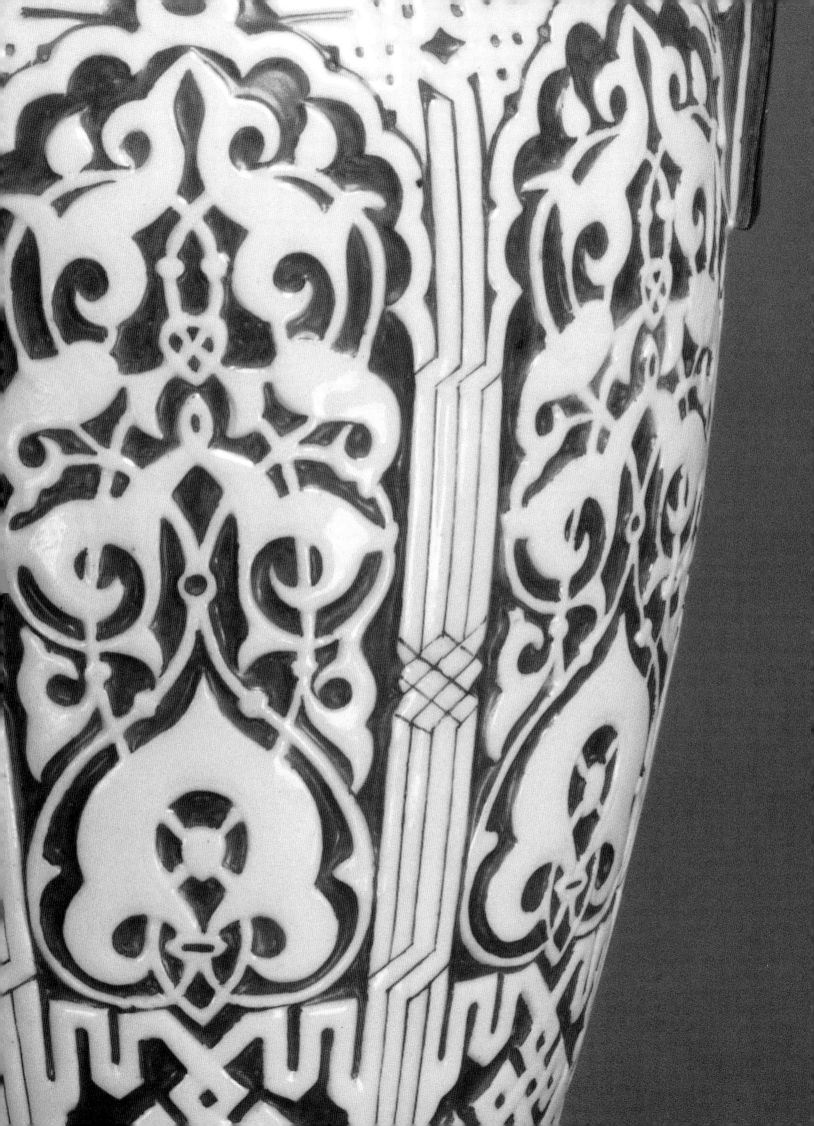

Industrial Arts and the Exhibition Ideal

PETER TRIPPI

THE VICTORIA AND ALBERT MUSEUM IS ROOTED in the extraordinary success of a single public event. Between May 1851, when it was opened in London by Queen Victoria, and October 1851, when it was closed by her consort Prince Albert, the Great Exhibition of the Works of Industry of All Nations attracted more than six million visitors, making it the most heavily attended event known to that date. Forerunner of many international expositions and world's fairs, this Great Exhibition has been imprinted indelibly on the Western consciousness via the "Crystal Palace," the name given immediately to its innovative building by the satirical magazine *Punch*.

Although the Exhibition displayed more than one hundred thousand objects, its most renowned exhibit was the building itself. Erected in less than nine months to the plans of the English horticulturist and conservatory designer Joseph Paxton, the Crystal Palace rose over eighteen acres of London's Hyde Park, enclosing thirty-three million cubic feet and twenty-one acres of exhibiting space. The ironwork and glass for the building were manufactured in Birmingham, more than a hundred miles from London, making it an early—and gigantic—example of prefabricated construction. This innovative technology imparted a geometric precision and functional clarity that has led later architects to identify the Crystal Palace as one of the first truly modern buildings. Though this is a reasonable assertion in some senses, it would be wrong to underestimate the extent to which traditional forms and methods contributed to the building's success. The central core of the Crystal Palace was, in effect, made in wood by skilled artisans, while each of the three hundred thousand sheets of glass was individually cylinder-blown.

Venturing through one of three entrances, visitors were awed by the unprecedented scale of the Crystal Palace: 1,848 feet long and 408 feet wide, the transept soaring 108 feet. The Welsh designer Owen Jones coordinated an interior scheme of alternating blue, yellow, and red pillars and girders that stretched into the distance, accented by dark red banners announcing from the upper floor's galleries the locations of particular exhibits. Browsing among the wares of the nearly fourteen thousand exhibitors, visitors must have felt they were in a giant greenhouse as they encountered tropical plants, a glass fountain, and fully grown elms undamaged by the construction. Visitors could spend the entire day inside enjoying refreshment courts, the first public "comfort" rooms for both men and women, filtered water, the music of twenty-four pipe organs, and splendid vistas from the upper galleries.

Fig. 56. Detail of cat. 5, a porcelain vase, c. 1840, by Edouard-D. Honoré

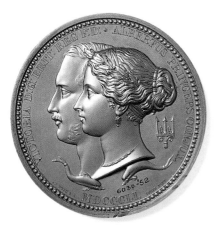

Fig. 57. The 1851 Great Exhibition Prize Medal (V&A 6030–1852) designed by William Wyon (English, 1795–1851)

The event was organized by a Royal Commission whose two most influential leaders were Prince Albert and Henry Cole. The commissioners had a number of interdependent motives, of which commerce was perhaps the most overt. They hoped the Exhibition would increase foreign trade and promote discerning consumption at home through elevation of the taste of producers and consumers alike. The Exhibition also had a strong social and political agenda, in that it was intended to give the nation a sense of cohesion and loyalty in a period of unrest. Planning began in earnest in 1848, a year in which Europe was wracked by revolution and Chartist reformers were active across Britain. The commissioners hoped that their vast essay on the achievements of the nation would encourage loyalty and ensure stability. Connected to these motivations was the desire to present the imperial possessions, which were good for both business and national pride, and which, if shown off effectively, would serve well as propaganda in an international environment. Thus, half of all exhibitors came from Britain and its empire, with the Indian Court at the heart of the imperial exhibits.

The non-British contingent was perhaps the most striking feature of the Great Exhibition, which can be considered the world's first truly international cultural display because half of its total space was given over to foreign exhibitors. Numerically, these were led by France, followed by the states of northern Germany, Austria, Belgium, Russia, Turkey, Switzerland, the Netherlands, Egypt, Spain, Portugal, Brazil, Mexico, China, Arabia, and Persia.

Chosen and arranged on stands by the exhibiting manufacturers themselves, the objects shown were classified by the Commission into four exhibit categories reflecting the cycle of production: Raw Materials, Machinery and Mechanical Invention, Manufactures, and Sculpture and Plastic Art. Throughout the Crystal Palace, the air vibrated with the sounds of machines showing how products were manufactured. The latest work in virtually any medium could be found, including arms, ceramics, clocks, fountains, glass, jewelry, leatherwork, lighting, metalwork, mirrors, musical instruments, sculpture, textiles, and wallpaper. Although visitors could purchase a guide to find particular areas, exhibitors sought to attract attention by displaying what came to be known as "exhibition pieces"—oversized or highly decorated objects that often demonstrated the varied skills of a firm's entire work force.

Coveted by exhibitors as much for advertising purposes as for personal fulfillment, 2,918 Prize Medals (fig. 57) were awarded for a "certain standard of excellence in production or workmanship." In addition, 170 Council Medals were presented in recognition of some "important novelty of invention or application, either in material or process of manufacture, or originality, combined with great beauty of design."[1] Among the recipients of this more prestigious medal was A. W. N. Pugin, who designed the entire Medieval Court in which his objects appeared (fig. 58).

The popularity of the Great Exhibition was extraordinary by standards of the era, welcoming, on average, forty-two thousand visitors a day. On Tuesday, 7 October 1851, almost one hundred ten thousand people came to enjoy the Exhibition over the course of twelve hours; at one point that day ninety-three thousand people were in the building simultaneously.

Although the Crystal Palace was ostensibly open to all, a basic charge of a shilling prevented a considerable section of British society from attending. Fear of the mob also led to a Hyde Park ban on the vendors who were typically associated with festivals and popular events. Alcohol was forbidden on the site, and police had strategic vantage points from which they could monitor the crowds. Nonetheless, the Exhibition enjoyed a richer social mix than any previous event of such a high cultural order. Contemporary reports tell of trains packed with agricultural laborers in quaint attire led to Hyde Park by their clergymen, Midlands factory workers given leave to glimpse the products of their manufacture displayed in glory, and even peasants who walked across the country to visit the Great Exhibition. The entrepreneur Thomas Cook enhanced his reputation by coordinating group visits—an early form of "Cook's tours"—to the Crystal Palace.

After Queen Victoria opened the Great Exhibition with much pomp on 1 May 1851 (cat. 1), she wrote: "The Green Park and Hyde Park were one mass of densely crowded human beings, in the highest good humour. . . ."[2] Later in May the queen reported: "We went up to the Gallery on the south side and stood at the end of the Transept, to watch the people coming in, in streams. . . . all so civil and well behaved, that it was quite a pleasure to see them."[3] Only three years after revolutions had shaken the royal foundations of their Continental counterparts, Victoria and Albert had special reason to be satisfied with the public's decorum.

Fig. 58. The Medieval Court, designed by A. W. N. Pugin, at the Great Exhibition of 1851

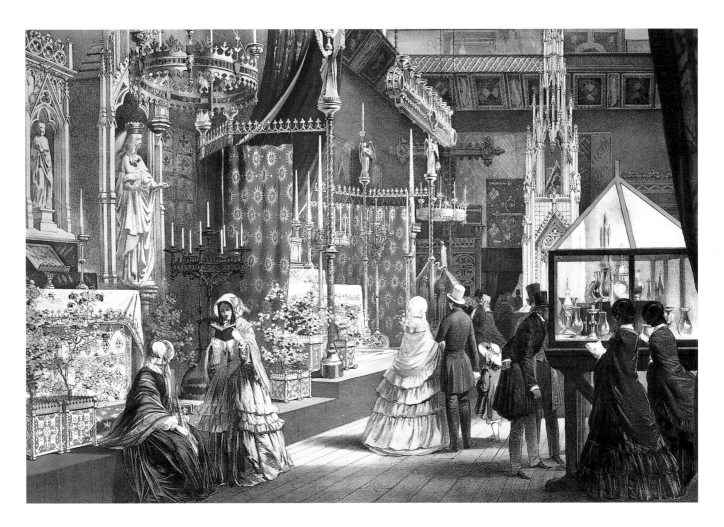

The Great Exhibition was a turning point in the history of public spectacles because it blended an array of presentation techniques borrowed from other media: Britain's few public museums; the for-profit public entertainment of panoramas (theaterlike rooms decorated to evoke other times and places); attractions at London venues such as the Egyptian Hall; the Mechanics Institute exhibitions visited by English artisans; the oversized samples displayed by retailers; commercial art galleries; and the elegant arcades where the well-to-do shopped and socialized. By blending these techniques, the Commission "translated these into exhibitionary forms which, in simultaneously ordering objects for public inspection and ordering the public that inspected, were to have a profound and lasting influence on the subsequent development of museums, art galleries, expositions, and department stores."[4]

The Great Exhibition was the first event in what was to become a spectacular sequence. During the second half of the nineteenth century some forty international exhibitions were staged worldwide, in cities such as Dublin, Paris, New York, Vienna, Philadelphia, Sydney, Atlanta, Amsterdam, Boston, New Orleans, Calcutta, Antwerp, Barcelona, Chicago, Nashville, Stockholm, and Guatemala City. These expositions expanded the scope of the original concept to embrace every aspect of human activity.[5] The successful revival of the Olympic Games in 1896, for example, can be traced to this source. Indeed, the second, third, and fourth Olympiads were all held in conjunction with expositions—in Paris, St. Louis, and London, respectively. The two nations to take up the exhibition idea most competitively were France and the United States, which, between them, staged some fourteen major events before 1900.

The Great Exhibition had several direct forebears. First, and perhaps most important, were the activities of the Society of Arts (later decreed the Royal Society of Arts) which, from its founding in 1754, promoted British industry through the use of artistry and invention. Debates, publications, and awards were among the tactics the Society employed to encourage every aspect of art and manufacture. In 1760, the Society held what one British historian has called "the first *specially organized* exhibition of art in this country."[6] Prince Albert (fig. 59) was later to become the Society's president, while Henry Cole and many other commissioners were members. The Society's exhibitions in 1847, 1848, and 1849 focused on what might be called industrial arts by showing "Specimens of British Manufactures and Decorative Art," particularly in precious metals.

While the Society of Arts developed an intellectual and pragmatic agenda that joined art with industry, the French government provided another model in the form of large-scale National Exhibitions of industrial arts, ten of which were held between 1797 and 1849.[7] Consisting of juried displays by manufacturers of their

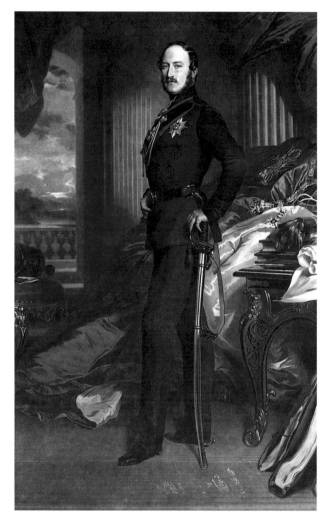

Fig. 59. Francis Xavier Winterhalter (German, 1806-1873). *Prince Albert of Saxe-Coburg-Gotha.* 1867. Oil on canvas. 95 x 61¾" (241.3 x 156.8 cm). National Portrait Gallery, London: Given by Queen Victoria. (This is a replica by the artist of his painting of Prince Albert done in 1859, in the Royal Collection.)

currently available products, the scale, sales-oriented agenda, and cultural ambition of the French events clearly anticipated the Crystal Palace, and all expositions after it. (Cole was tremendously impressed by what he saw at the Paris exhibition in 1849, the same year he launched the *Journal of Design and Manufactures.*)

Until the Great Exhibition, so diverse a public had never before participated in so large a spectacle. Although many visitors paid more attention to the Exhibition's sensuous pleasures than to its intended lessons, the success of this ambitious project validated the commissioners' belief (and that of the government that had commissioned them) in displaying objects as a "means" of "promoting Arts, Manufactures and Industry."[8] In 1852 they acted to continue the teaching of taste to manufacturers, artisans, and consumers by establishing the Museum of Manufactures through Cole's leadership of a new government department under the Board of Trade. Here Cole intended to carry on his lifelong quest for rationalization and classification by creating a systematic collection of manufactures for nationwide reference.

The commissioners used the Exhibition's profits to purchase a large tract of land south of the Crystal Palace. This area of South Kensington, now home to a range of educational and cultural institutions, including the V&A, is still legally

Fig. 60. The Crystal Palace, Sydenham, southeast of London. Moved from Hyde Park in 1853 and enlarged, the structure was open to the public as a museum from 1854 until it was destroyed by fire in 1936. This postcard image, c. 1925, was collected by sisters Dr. Claribel Cone and Miss Etta Cone of Baltimore, Maryland.

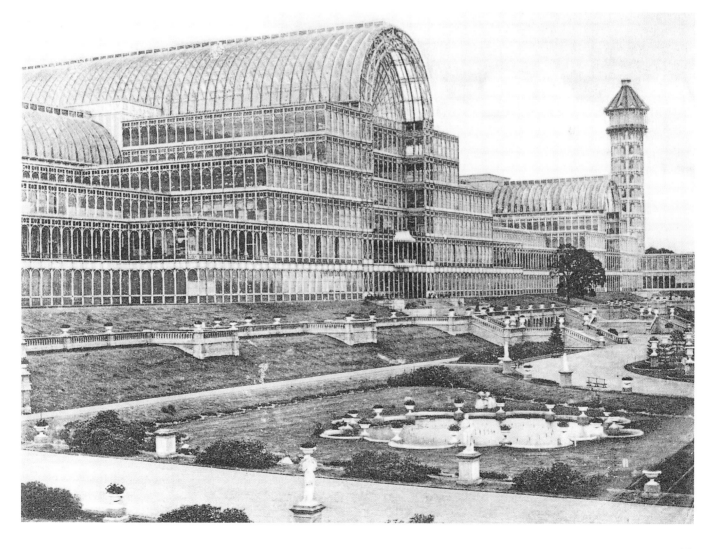

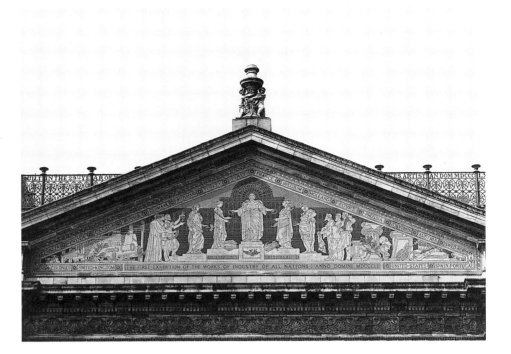

Fig. 61. The mosaic pediment, on the Museum's 1869 facade, featuring Queen Victoria distributing Exhibition medals

owned by the successors to the commissioners of the Great Exhibition. (The Crystal Palace was moved in 1853 to the London suburb of Sydenham, where it was destroyed in a fire in 1936 [fig. 60].)

South Kensington sustained the Crystal Palace spirit of technology and accessibility, becoming the world's first museum with artificial lighting—which made evening visits possible—and with a permanent restaurant situated at the entrance to encourage dining before viewing. More than 6.5 million of the more than 15 million visits to South Kensington between 1857 and 1883 were made in the evenings, when working-class people could come.[9] In contrast to the forbidding, neoclassical porticoes of the British Museum and National Gallery, South Kensington's 1869 facade of warmly colored brick and terra cotta beckoned visitors. Approaching the Museum, no one could ignore the pediment's monochrome mosaic depicting Queen Victoria distributing Exhibition medals, surrounded by a silhouette of the Crystal Palace, the names of participating nations, and a railway locomotive (fig. 61). Attendance at the British Museum—where visitors' credentials were still being inspected as late as the 1830s—soared during and after 1851, another indication that the Great Exhibition had generated a broader arts-aware public. (The British Museum did not, however, inaugurate evening hours until 1883.)[10] The patronizing mistrust of the mob evidenced by the commissioners of the Great Exhibition lived on at South Kensington, too: always aware that he was competing with easier pleasures for workers' attention, Cole hoped that "Perhaps the evening opening of Public Museums may furnish a powerful antidote to the gin palace."[11]

In 1851, French exhibitors advancing the "Louis" styles carried away more medals than any other nation. After two decades of growing anxiety about France's apparent superiority in industrial manufacture, this acknowledgment—pointedly reported and critiqued by British commentators—spurred a determination to compete with the French for dominance in this arena.

A central concern was the perceived gap between technical and aesthetic excellence in native manufactures, particularly luxury goods. The 1857 *Guide to the South Kensington Museum* noted that English products at the Great Exhibition "were fully equal to those sent over to compete with them, as regarded workmanship and material . . . ," but "the public felt that much for the improvement of public taste was still to be accomplished."[12] (Whether *the public* really felt this is debatable, but the argument was convenient to Cole and other Museum administrators.)

Operated under the patronage of Prince Albert and closely associated with his circle of design reformers, the *Art Journal* conveyed the commissioners' optimism late in 1851: "The results of the Great Exhibition are pregnant with incalculable benefits to all classes of the community. . . . [A]mong the eager thousands whose interest was excited and whose curiosity was gratified, were many who obtained profitable suggestions at every visit: the manufacturer and the artisan have thus learned the most valuable of all lessons—the disadvantages under which they had laboured, the deficiencies they had to remedy, and the prejudices they had to overcome."[13]

More than anything else, the Great Exhibition ushered in a new age of art and design criticism. From 1851, design reform grew steadily in Britain as a professionalized activity, with exhibitions and publications on the subject proliferating. After the Great Exhibition, the *Art Journal* predicted that "when His Royal Highness Prince Albert issues his summons to another competition, British supremacy will be manifested in every branch of Industrial Art."[14] In fact, Albert died the year before London's International Exhibition of 1862, but the prediction was correct: the medal count revealed British design standards to have risen to the point where they rivaled those of the French.

It is hardly surprising that among the Museum's early acquisitions were modern manufactures from the Crystal Palace. Of a £5,000 Parliamentary grant allocated to Cole upon the Museum's founding, more than £2,000 was spent on foreign exhibits, £1,500 on objects from the Indian Court, and less than £1,000 on those from the British displays. This allocation and the items to be purchased were determined by a Museum committee of men pivotal in the reform of mid-Victorian design: Henry Cole, John Rogers Herbert, Owen Jones, A. W. N. Pugin, and Richard Redgrave.[15] In their catalogue, the committee members expressed their general disapproval of most exhibits before explaining that "each specimen has been selected for its merits in exemplifying some right principle of construction or of ornament."[16] The moralistic certitude of such phrases as "right principle" reflects the zealousness of these reformers, particularly Pugin, who had published *The True Principles of Pointed or Christian Architecture* in 1841. The committee selected "Elkington electrotypes, china from Minton and Sevres, oriental arms and armour, Belgian gold and silver, and other striking objects, including—perhaps from politeness—a few of Pugin's chalices."[17]

Like the Museum collection that grew from them, the Great Exhibition's displays presented both familiar and exotic lands from a confident Western perspective. Thus the Crystal Palace—and by inference the movement it spawned—has been critiqued as "classically imperialist in conception and construction" and its contents as "the material culture of an industrial, commercial empire, with an emphasis on manufactured goods from colonial raw materials."[18]

Lessons to be taught by at least one colonial people were not ignored by "the Cole group," however: Jones felt that the Indian exhibits provided "most valuable hints for arriving at a true knowledge of those principles both of Ornament and Colour in the Decorative Arts."[19] In his *Supplementary Report on Design* for the commissioners (1852), Redgrave observed that "ornament is merely the decoration of a thing constructed . . . and must not usurp a principal place."[20] Praising the Indian synthesis of utility and beauty through ornament—the making beautiful of useful objects—Jones favorably contrasted Indian art with English abuses of naturalism and historical styles (see cats. 19–20): "There are no carpets worked with flowers whereon the feet would fear to tread, no furniture the hand would fear to grasp, no superfluous and useless ornament which caprice has added and which accident might remove."[21] The point was demonstrated explicitly in the new Museum's short-lived display of "Examples of False Principles in Decoration," and through Jones's enduring *The Grammar of Ornament* (1856).

Between 1852 and 1900, the Museum's curators came to see the international exhibitions as key opportunities for acquiring contemporary manufactures. Items purchased from British and foreign stands at the 1862 exhibition in London included jewelry, cast iron, mosaics, sideboards, carved frames, silver, tapestries, glass, and ceramics (fig. 62). Acquisitions from the London exhibition in 1871 were still more diverse: French curtain fabrics, Moorish ceramics, Portuguese tile panels, Indian furniture and marble pillars, Hungarian and Moravian earthenware vases, Spanish pigskin bottles, and Venetian glass, with many examples of Indian and European jewelry.[22] The collections of ceramics and glass, having grown by seven objects in 1851, were enhanced with seventy-five more from the exhibition of 1862. Curators of ceramics and glass then went on to buy ninety-nine items from the Paris Exposition Universelle of 1867, and a total of one hundred items from the three Paris shows of

Fig. 62. The 1862 International Exhibition held in London

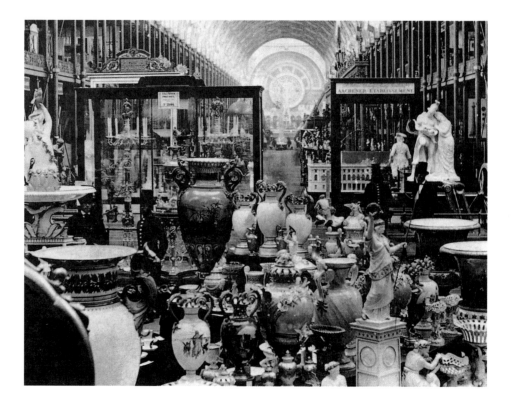

1878, 1889, and 1900.[23] They also satisfied their desire for things Japanese by commissioning the purchase of 216 Japanese ceramics that were then featured in the Philadelphia Centennial Exposition of 1876 (fig. 63 [see cats. 114–116]).[24]

Curators of other collections used the expositions in much the same way, though the motives for purchase could vary dramatically. The Fourdinois cabinet—awarded first prize at the Paris Exposition Universelle of 1867 and widely seen as the era's premier exhibition piece (see cat. 7)—clearly satisfied multiple sets of criteria. Many of the glass objects purchased from the same show, however, were obtained only because of their "cheapness of manufacture."[25] Although these objects were often wonderful in their own right, their acquisition was originally intended to fulfill the commercial objectives Cole had been preaching since the 1840s. While testifying before the 1860 Parliamentary Select Committee, he was asked how "the manufacturer of china is affected by the exhibition of the South Kensington Museum." Cole responded:

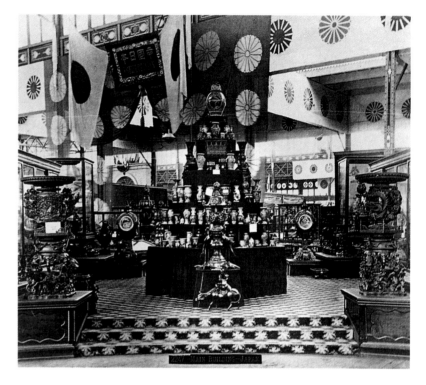

Fig. 63. A view of the Japanese national display at the Philadelphia Centennial Exposition, 1876

> I think that the first result of this kind of exhibition is to make the public hunger after the objects; I think they go to the china shops and say, "We do not like this or that; we have seen something prettier at the South Kensington Museum"; and the shopkeeper, who knows his own interest, repeats that to the manufacturer, and the manufacturer, instigated by that demand, produces the article.[26]

Regardless of which country was hosting, the international exhibitions validated the nineteenth-century progressivist view that the Western way of life was superior to any known by earlier peoples. The Crystal Palace and its dazzling contents were widely perceived by Victorians as triumphant evidence of Britain's apotheosis, reflecting her rapid advances in science and technology, prowess in railroads and navigation, enormous empire, and political stability. In 1851 Cole observed:

> The activity of the present day chiefly develops itself in commercial industry, and it is in accordance with the spirit of the age that the nations of the world have now collected together their choicest productions. It may be said without presumption, that an event like this Exhibition could not have taken place at any earlier period, and perhaps not among any other people than ourselves. The friendly confidence reposed by other nations in our institutions; the perfect security for property; the commercial freedom, and the facility of transport which England pre-eminently possesses, may all be brought forward as causes which have operated in establishing the Exhibition in London.[27]

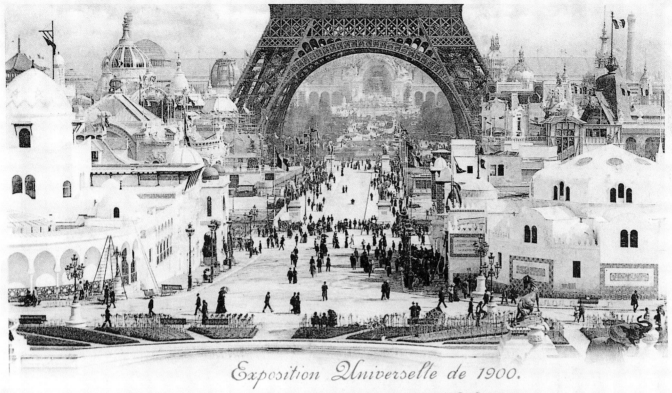

Exposition Universelle de 1900.

Les Colonies et le Champ de Mars. L. L.

Fig. 64. The Exposition Universelle, Paris, 1900. This huge exhibition was characterized by large pavilions erected by each of the participants. The V&A acquired a large number of Art Nouveau objects from this exhibition (cats. 165–167).

Imbued with this optimistic outlook, exhibition organizers of all nations from 1851 onward identified their work with industrial capitalism, conspicuous modernity, and constant growth. From one international exhibition to the next, each nation sought to exceed the scale and impact of its previous displays or pavilions, always with an eye toward boosting national prestige and economic vitality (fig 64).

The ethos of technology and progress fueled the processes of modernization that transformed Britain in the nineteenth century. The Great Exhibition was, in this sense, a microcosm of the society that gave rise to it. By the end of the century, however, new forms of cultural modernity were arousing fear and suspicion. A gift to the Museum of Art Nouveau furniture from the 1900 Paris exhibition (see cats. 165–167) provoked in England an antimodern outcry that undermined the already weakening policy of acquiring objects directly from the exhibit stands. Those of the V&A's modern manufactures that had not already been transferred to the branch facility at Bethnal Green in East London were hastily transferred thereafter. Only beginning in 1952, when the Museum mounted an exhibition of Victorian and Edwardian decorative arts, did these objects (the ones not deaccessioned since 1900) enjoy new attention from staff and scholars. By the 1980s, it became clear that the many pieces acquired by the V&A from the international exhibitions had played a pivotal role in the Museum's original work. These objects have returned to prominence as the Museum continues to reaffirm its relationship with industrial manufacture and design.

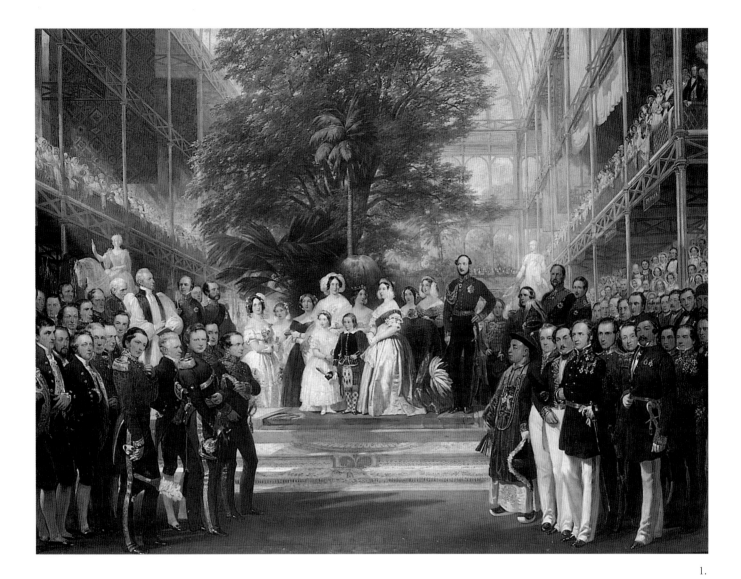

1. HENRY COURTNEY SELOUS (English, 1803–1890).
*The Opening of the Great Exhibition by Queen Victoria
on 1st May 1851.* 1851–52. Oil on canvas, 66¾ x 95¼"
(169.5 x 241.9 cm). Signed and dated "H C Selous 1851/2."
Given by Warren W. De La Rue, 1889. V&A 329–1889

The 1851 Great Exhibition was an event that led in part to the foundation of the Museum in the following year, and purchases of "modern manufactures" from this and later international exhibitions figured prominently among the Museum's early acquisitions. The 1851 Exhibition took place in the vast glass structure of the Crystal Palace, erected in Hyde Park close to the Museum's present site, and included manufactured goods arranged according to nation.

This painting, which commemorates the Exhibition opening by Queen Victoria, was executed as a commercial venture so that prints could be made from it—but the interest shown in the painting by the queen, Prince Albert, Henry Cole, and others gave it a semiofficial status from the start. After it was given to the Museum in 1889 it came to be seen as the authoritative image

of this historic event as well as a symbolic representation of the Museum's origins. The painting was prominently featured in 1951 in the centenary display about the Great Exhibition, around which time a new interest was being shown in Victorian decorative arts and especially in Great Exhibition pieces.

The Exhibition was an extravaganza of mythic proportions. More than twenty-five thousand people attended opening day, even though admission was restricted to invited dignitaries and season ticket holders (the latter from the wealthy upper classes). The inaugural program included speeches by Prince Albert, Queen Victoria, and the archbishop of Canterbury, followed by massed choirs performing Handel's *Hallelujah Chorus.* Selous included in the right foreground a Chinese man, who has been described as being in "official dress" and thus interpreted as having some diplomatic role in the program. Indeed, according to contemporary accounts this Chinese man, Hee Sing, was so moved by the ceremony that he dashed forward and bowed before the queen during the performance of the Handel. (Notably, however—as Craig Clunas points out—"Victoria's own, typically breathless, account of the opening ceremony makes no mention of any such happening.") In fact, no formal embassies were sent abroad from China at this date, and there is no evidence that any Chinese person was present in a formal capacity at the inaugural program. Selous almost certainly appropriated the figure from another exhibition coincidentally in Hyde Park at the same time, where a Chinese man named Hee Sing was on display along with other Chinese men, women, and children to demonstrate the daily habits and manners of foreign races. Such exhibits of humans were common in Britain, Europe, and the United States from the mid-nineteenth century through the early twentieth century.

According to the *Art Journal* in 1852, the "centre of the picture is occupied by the Royal party and their attendants, the right by the foreign commissioners, chairmen of juries, &c, and the left by the ministers of the state, the royal commissioners, and the executive officers." In that group were Warren De La Rue and his wife. De La Rue was a scientist and inventor (he exhibited the first envelope-making machine at the Great Exhibition), a friend of Sir Henry Cole, and a juror on the 1851 "Committee for Class 29: Miscellaneous Manufactures and Small Wares." It was De La Rue who eventually acquired the painting and then presented it as a gift to the South Kensington Museum.

Lit. *Art Journal*, 1852; *Athenaeum*, 1852; Cole and Cole, 1884, vol. I, p. 179; Wood, 1976, frontispiece and pl. 11; Bonython, 1982, pp. 37, 40; Parkinson, 1990, pp. 257–8

RONALD PARKINSON/BRENDA RICHARDSON

2. English (London). *Flagon.* 1850–51. Silver, parcel-gilt, 24⅜" high x 12" diam. (62 x 30.5 cm). London date hallmarks; marks of Charles Thomas and George Fox, made for and exhibited by Lambert and Rawlings at the Great Exhibition of 1851. V&A 2743–1851

This spectacular flagon is typical of the fashionable, historicized decorative arts displayed at the Great Exhibition. As a well-crafted, specially produced, nonfunctional exhibition piece, it exemplifies the objects selected from the 1851 Exhibition for the Museum by a committee that included Owen Jones and A. W. N. Pugin. Its later history within the collection also illustrates the changing attitude toward objects acquired from international exhibitions, once the Museum's early links with manufacturers became less significant.

Lambert and Rawlings of Coventry Street, London, was founded by Francis Lambert in the early nineteenth century and became one of the most important retailers of reproduction as well as genuine antique plate. The Fox family of silversmiths enjoyed a long working relationship with the retailing firm, generally supplying items in period style such as this Gothic Revival flagon.

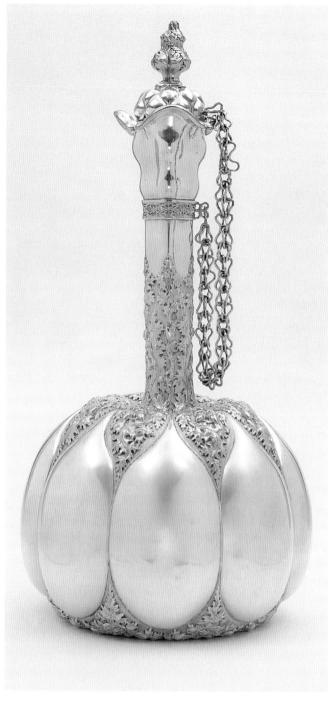

2.

A more elaborately chased example with vine leaf and grape decoration, exhibited as a companion to this flagon, secured an Exhibition Prize Medal for Lambert and Rawlings. But it was the restraint of the design of the present piece that led to its being recommended for purchase by the Museum for £28 8s. According to the Department of Science and Art Report of 1852, the flagon was "remarkable for the elegance and simplicity of the general form, and the delicacy and subordination of the ornamental portions." From the end of the nineteenth century, interest in and enthusiasm for this type of richly decorated display piece was on the wane in the Museum. After many years in storage, it was placed on prominent display in 1965 with the opening of a major gallery dedicated to showing the best of nineteenth-century work.

Lit. Bury, 1966, pp. 218–22; Culme, 1977, pp. 76–7

ANN EATWELL

3. Designed by A. W. N. PUGIN (English, 1812–1852); manufactured by JOHN HARDMAN AND CO. (English [Birmingham]) especially for the Great Exhibition, 1851. *Chalice.* 1850–51. Silver, parcel-gilt, enameled, and set with semiprecious stones, 10¼" high x 7¼" diam. (26 x 18.4 cm). Birmingham hallmarks. V&A 1327–1851

This richly embellished chalice is among the finest pieces produced in the short but influential collaboration between the architect and designer A. W. N. Pugin (who, with Charles Barry, designed the new Houses of Parliament [1836–c. 1860] in the Gothic Revival style) and the manufacturer John Hardman, Jr. As a work in the Gothic Revival style designed by a figure closely linked with the Museum's early history, the chalice represents the interconnections between the Museum's role in encouraging the highest standards of design in modern manufactures and the prevailing concern with styles from earlier periods. Pugin was an influential figure in the formation of the collections and in relation to the room devoted to the seminal didactic display, "Examples of False Principles in Decoration" (cats. 19–21), which was probably conceived as an inversion of Pugin's *True Principles,* published in 1841.

Pugin and Hardman shared a commitment to the reestablishment of the Roman Catholic church in Britain and concentrated on rich church furnishings. Founding their business in 1838, they described themselves as the first "medieval metalworkers," thereby putting into practice Pugin's assertion that Gothic was the only appropriate Christian style. The design of the chalice reflects Pugin's homage to fifteenth-century Italian church plate, of the type that the Museum began to collect in 1844. Although only a small quantity of the firm's production was in precious metal, it could be of very high quality, drawing on both traditional craft skills and the latest industrial techniques.

The chalice was first shown as part of the large display of altar plate and church fittings in the Great Exhibition's Medieval Court, designed by Pugin, which assisted in winning for its designer the highest accolade of a Council Medal. Purchased from the Exhibition for the Museum by a committee of which Pugin was himself a member, the chalice, like other nineteenth-century objects, later fell out of favor among the Museum's staff. Although Pugin had already been celebrated in Kenneth Clark's

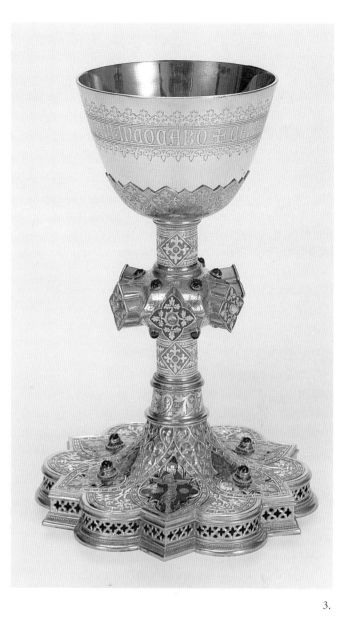

3.

1928 book, *The Gothic Revival,* the artist's significance was emphasized further by the inclusion of this chalice and other pieces in the Museum's groundbreaking exhibition of Victorian and Edwardian decorative arts in 1952.

Lit. Campbell, 1987; Eatwell and North, in Atterbury and Wainwright, 1994

ANN EATWELL

4. Indian (Benares). *Sari.* c. 1850. Silk and gold thread, 146 x 67¼" (371 x 171 cm). V&A 769–1852

The purchase of this sari from the Great Exhibition for the unusually high price of £50—the flagon (cat. 2) purchased at the same time, for example, cost only £28—was an indication of the prominence of Indian material at the Exhibition. It also showed the significance to the Museum of Indian textiles in particular as models of good design. The sari was woven in Benares (modern Varanasi) in northern India, which is still one of the main centers of production for these lavish silk and gold woven textiles called *kimkhab* in the nineteenth century.

The Indian textiles shown at the Great Exhibition greatly impressed the critics of the day, including Richard Redgrave, the Exhibition's official reporter, who praised them not only for the excellence of their designs, which were felt to conform to the "correct principles" of textile design, but also as a source of inspiration for European manufacturers. The widespread admiration for Indian decorative arts, which extended also to metalwork and ceramics, was in marked contrast to the revulsion felt by the British art establishment toward most Indian painting and sculpture, which had to wait until the twentieth century for acceptance (cats. 87–98). Indian and Islamic textile designs were central to the theories of Owen Jones who, in *The Grammar of Ornament* (1856), drew on pieces from the Great Exhibition to illustrate his "rules for the decoration of fabrics," which were, essentially, that decoration should be flat, it should not be strictly representational, and it should take into account the nature of the fabric and its appearance when draped and folded.

Lit. Robinson, 1857, no. 31

ROSEMARY CRILL

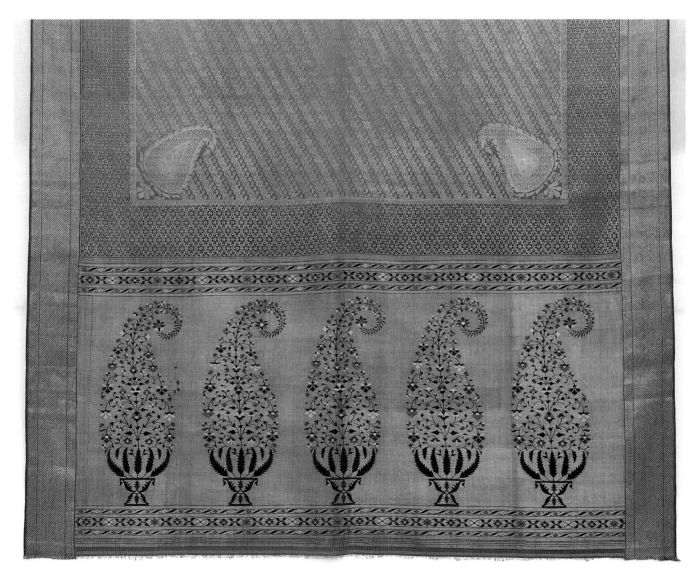

4.

5. Designed and made by EDOUARD-D. HONORÉ (French, died 1855). *Vase.* c. 1840. Porcelain, painted in colors, 18 x 6¾ x 5¾" (46 x 17.5 x 14.6 cm). Marks: "E D HONORÉ BOUL. POISSONNIERE No 6 à PARIS MAN- UFACTURE à CHAMPROUX ALLIER No. Prix" printed. V&A 3101–1846

Shown in the 1844 Paris Exhibition of Industrial Art, this exotic vase colored in bright orange and turquoise was purchased from the maker at that time, along with three of his plates. It was acquired, prior to the founding of the Museum, as a model of contemporary French design for students at the Government Schools of Design.

E.-D. Honoré headed one of the major porcelain manufactories, founded by his father in Paris, with a salesroom on Boulevard Poissonnière, decorating studios in Montparnasse, and a white ware factory in Champroux. A key figure in the French porcelain industry, Honoré regularly won awards, including a silver medal at the 1844 Paris exhibition. His technical innovations were highly regarded; he patented methods for applying high-temperature colored grounds and decorating porcelain by lithographic printing. Table services by Honoré were supplied to the court of Louis XVIII and to three American presidents—Madison, Monroe, and Polk.

The ceramics exhibited by Honoré at the 1844 exhibition were in the "Moorish" as well as the Chinese and Rococo Revival styles. This example was described in the Museum's 1846 acquisitions register as "French modern" in the "Moorish Alhambra" pattern. While the three Honoré plates, which had printed decoration, were of interest because of their technical features, the vase seems to have been purchased primarily because of its style. Its acquisition should therefore be understood in the context of wider interest in "Alhambresque" objects, including Owen Jones's illustrations of ornament from the Alhambra (cat. 15), and plaster reproductions of details from the building itself (cat. 17). In the 1850s the vase was prominently featured at Marlborough House along with ceramics on loan from the Soulages collection (see figs. 20 and 84). At some point it went into storage where it remained for many years; when it went on exhibition at Bethnal Green in 1970, it was shown in the context of nineteenth-century eclecticism as an illustration of the exotic, thus complementing examples of historicist and naturalistic works.

Lit. Plinval de Guillebon, 1972

JENNIFER H. OPIE

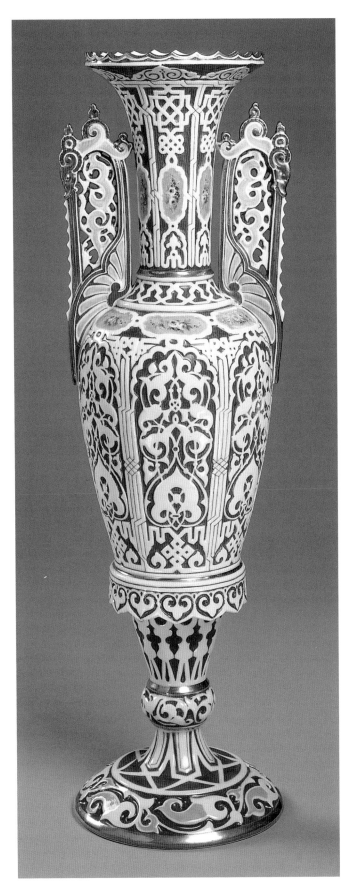

5.

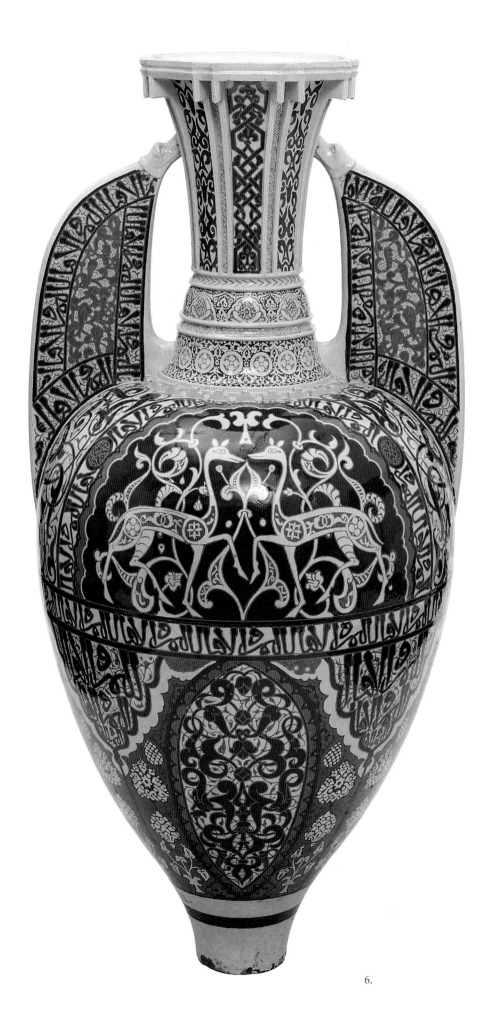

6.

6. JOSEPH-THÉODORE DECK (French [Paris], 1823–1891), in collaboration with BARON JEAN-CHARLES DAVILLIER (French, 1823–1883). *Alhambra Vase*. 1862. Earthenware, inlaid with colored clays and painted, 42 x 20 x 18⅞" (107 x 51 x 48 cm). Marks: "TH.DECK 1862" painted. V&A 18–1865

This full-size copy of a two-handled vase that formed part of the original furnishings for the Alhambra (the thirteenth- to fourteenth-century citadel and palace in Granada, Spain [see cats. 15–16]) was exhibited by J.-T. Deck at the international exhibition held in London in 1862. It was one of many impressive, large-scale works purchased by the Museum from this exhibition with £5,000 provided by the Treasury. Its interest lay in the way it combined the Moorish style, popular since the 1840s, with a variety of sophisticated ceramic techniques derived from earlier periods.

Joseph-Théodore Deck, later the director of artistic and technical development at the Manufacture Nationale at Sèvres, was already an accomplished ceramicist with a voracious interest in the techniques and decorative styles of the past and of the Middle and Far East. For this piece he evidently collaborated with the writer on ceramic history, Baron Davillier, who in 1861 had published his *Histoire des Faïences Hispano-Moresques à reflets métalliques*. But the Alhambresque form is here combined with techniques from other sources—painting in enamel colors (instead of Hispano-Moresque luster glazes) and inlaid decoration based on sixteenth-century French ceramics, known as Henri II ware (cat. 72). When acquired, the vase was described as "A modification of Henri II ware copied from the original by M. le Baron Davillier." J. B. Waring gave a fuller account of Deck's work in his lavishly illustrated publication on the 1862 exhibition. Under the heading "Artistic Earthenware," he describes how Deck was awarded a medal for a display in which the

> . . . decorative ware designed after Oriental or Arabic models was exceedingly pleasing and effective. Some of these pieces are executed like Henri Deux ware, that is, by an inlay of various clays, but all are characterized by refinement, good taste, finish and brilliancy of tone.

According to *Harper's New Monthly Magazine* in 1875, the Alhambra Vase was then in the Ceramics Gallery at the V&A, where beneath each "specimen a card tells when and where it was made and the price paid for it by the museum," below a window "showing the building of the Alhambra and its wonderful vase." The report that "an agent of the museum found it 'going a-begging'" and purchased it for far less than its actual value, suggests that the price of £60 was lower than that originally asked at the exhibition three years earlier. By 1884 the Museum owned no fewer than twenty pieces by Deck, whose work was singled out for praise in the volume entitled *French Pottery* in the series of South Kensington handbooks issued from 1875:

> Since 1859...M. Deck has remained the first ceramic artist of the time and French industry is proud of him as being one of its most justly-honoured representatives.... [T]he numerous works by him in the Museum hardly give an idea of...this skilful ceramicist['s]...perfect workmanship and purity of form.... [T]he faience signed by him can compare and be placed on a par with the finest productions of the ceramic art of all times.

Deck's ceramics were prominently displayed in the Ceramics Gallery until that space was converted to house the Jones collection in 1910. The Alhambra Vase was displayed again only in 1987 when the present gallery dedicated to the nineteenth-century arts of Europe and North America was opened.

Lit. Davillier, 1861; International Exhibition (1862), Reports, 1863; Waring, 1863, vol. III; Marryat, 1866; Burty, 1869; Conway, 1875, pp. 499, 502; Eudel, 1883; Gasnault and Garnier, 1884; Jervis, 1987

JENNIFER H. OPIE

7. Manufactured by HENRI-AUGUSTE FOURDINOIS (French, 1830–1907) to designs by HILAIRE AND PASTI (figures) and NÉVILLÉ (arabesque ornaments). *Cabinet on Stand*. 1861–67. Ebony, partly veneered on oak, with inlay and carved decoration in box, lime, holly, pear, walnut, mahogany, and hard stones, 98 x 61 x 20½" (249 x 155 x 52 cm). Inlaid on the center base panel, "ANNO HENRI FOURDINOIS 1867." V&A 721–1869

This exceptionally elaborate cabinet is a virtuoso example of the cabinetmaking skills of the Fourdinois firm. The family business was founded by the father of Henri Fourdinois in the 1830s and built up a reputation for technical sophistication and fine carving, supplying pieces to the royal and imperial households of France. This particular cabinet was shown at the Exposition Universelle in Paris in 1867 where it won the Grand Prix and was hailed in several publications as the masterpiece of the exhibition. It was immediately alluring as a traditional form, being, in fact, a re-creation of a grand seventeenth-century cabinet on stand (cat. 77). At the same time, it presented an innovative marquetry technique that highlighted the role of the skilled craftsman. The prize also served to reward the acumen of a large furniture manufacturing firm in investing in both design and craft skills. These qualities were characteristic of many objects purchased from international exhibitions.

Praise in 1867 was concentrated on the new technique of inlaying contrasting woods for carving so that, although the fine arabesques appear to be applied to the surface of the ebony, the

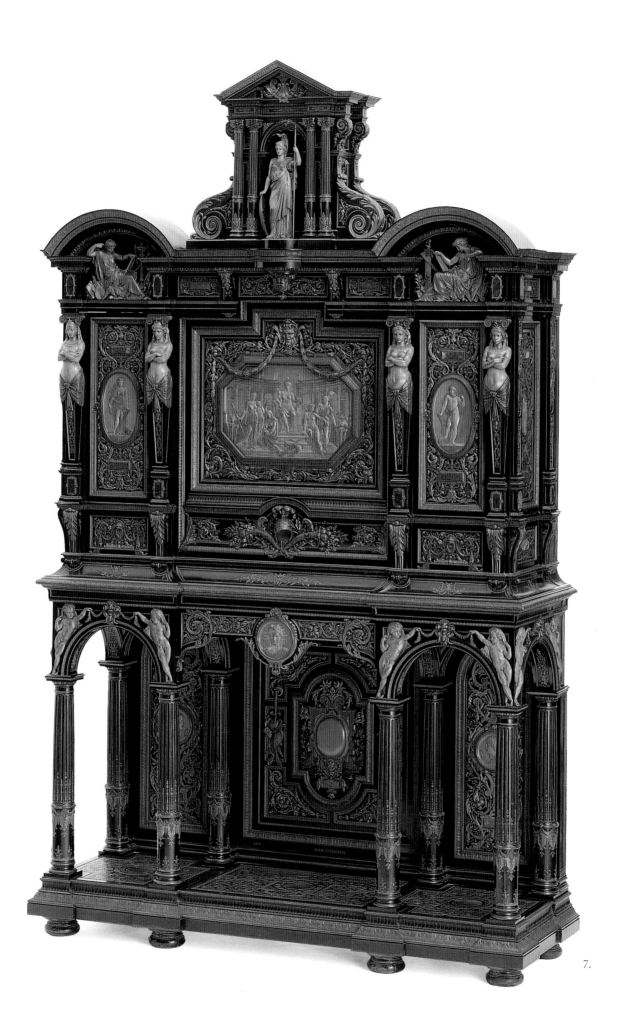

7.

sections of wood from which they are carved are in fact laid into the wood to the depth of three-eighths of an inch, and in some cases right through the thickness of a section, in the manner of *pietre dure* (hard stones). The inlay was left slightly above the surface and finally carved with the detail. This technique, which prevented movement of the inlays, was known as *marqueterie en pleine*. So proud was Fourdinois of this technique that the firm supplied with the cabinet two samples, demonstrating the technique in two stages.

Two years after the exhibition the piece was acquired by the Museum for £2,750, its high price signaling contemporary views about its artistic and technical qualities. This was much more than would have been spent at the time on historic pieces; for example, the Museum's much-admired seventeenth-century French ebony cabinet, richly decorated with episodes from the Endymion story, was bought in 1856 for only £132.

The firm of Fourdinois also showed a second cabinet at the exhibition, in the style of the sixteenth century, in carved walnut. The Museum's representatives in fact preferred that cabinet but purchased the ebony one "on account of the profuse and highly finished character of the ornamentation, which would furnish innumerable details and motives of further use to an art workman than the specimen of purer outline." Such euphoria was short-lived. Evidence of how quickly a work seen as a model of design and technique can fall from esteem, by 1874 John Hungerford Pollen was writing that the cabinet "has not, in all its joints and fitments, the accuracy that may be found in the fine specimens of workmanship both in France and England, amongst modern as well as old examples"; by 1900 the cabinet had been banished to the branch museum at Bethnal Green. It was not until the 1980s, when preparations were in hand for new galleries of nineteenth-century European and North American art and design, that the cabinet was brought back to South Kensington.

Lit. Hungerford Pollen, 1874, II, pp. 61–4; Jervis, 1987, pp. 110–1; Wilk, 1996, p. 162

Sarah Medlam

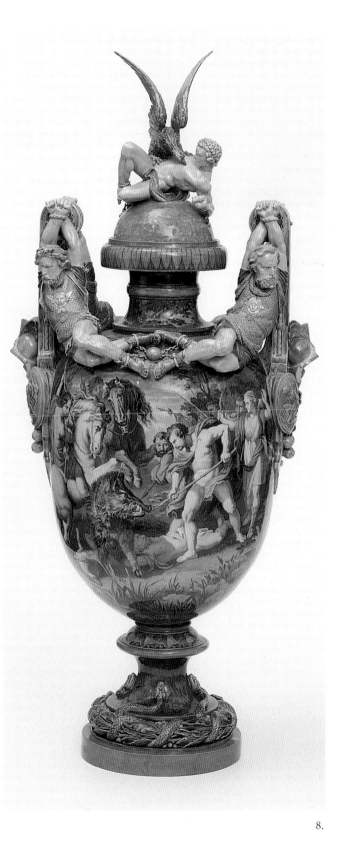

8.

8. Designed by Victor Etienne Simyan (French, 1826–1886 [active England from 1860]), painted by Thomas Allen (English, 1831–1915), and made by Minton & Co. (English [Stoke-on-Trent]). *Prometheus, or Captive, Vase.* 1867. Earthenware painted in colors, 49½ x 24¾ x 11" (126 x 63 x 28 cm). V&A 1047–1871

This vase, acquired from the 1867 Paris Exposition Universelle, though appearing outlandish to many modern eyes, was typical of the richly, sometimes even excessively, decorated exhibition pieces that the Museum was displaying in the 1860s to represent contemporary production and to raise the standard of British industrial arts to rival those of the French.

This vase is one of two versions made for the 1867 exhibition, both of which were bought by the Museum, each for £158. Other versions were shown at the Paris exhibition of 1878, where one was described as "one of the noblest pieces ever produced." This example was modeled by Victor Simyan, a French sculptor who came to England in about 1860 and joined Minton & Co., where his compatriot Léon Arnoux had been art director since 1849. The vase's painter, Thomas Allen, was trained at the Stoke-on-Trent School of Design when already an apprentice at Minton. In 1852 Allen became one of the first students to be awarded a National Art Training Scholarship to the School of Design at Somerset House.

In its form and decoration the vase draws on an eclectic mixture of sources. The captive warriors and trophies that form the handles are based on Florentine sixteenth-century models, but the snakes that decorate the base are in the manner of the sixteenth-century French ceramicist Bernard Palissy. The dramatic figure atop the lid—perhaps derived from a print after a painting (in the collection of the Philadelphia Museum of Art) of the subject by the Flemish Baroque artist Peter Paul Rubens—is Prometheus, one of the Greek Titans of myth, who stole fire from heaven to give it to humankind. (Prometheus would have been a particularly appropriate subject for a virtuoso example of ceramic technique since ceramics were described in the nineteenth century as one of the "arts of fire.") In retribution, Zeus chained him to Mount Caucasus, where an eagle preyed on his liver each day and the liver renewed each night. The highly charged imagery and exuberant style of the vase's painted decoration were based on prints after paintings, also by Rubens, of the Calydonian Boar Hunt, one of which shows Meleager spearing the boar in nearly the same stance as that of Antico's splendid late-fifteenth-century bronze *Meleager* (cat. 59).

The brightly colored lead glazes that so distinguish the Prometheus Vase were perfected by Arnoux and introduced in works presented at the 1851 Great Exhibition. Although known as Minton's "majolica," this piece bears no technical resemblance to Italian Renaissance *maiolica,* after which it was named. Minton & Co. had close links with South Kensington and carried out much of the glazed tile wall and floor decoration of the 1869 Lecture Theatre building.

By 1936 the two vases appeared on a list of similar pieces that were to be returned from Bethnal Green to the Ceramics Department, where, as curator Bernard Rackham suggested, "the question whether they should be kept for reference or disposed of can then be dealt with." This consideration was interrupted by World War II. Although preserved by the happenstance of timing, the vase did not appear in any of the exhibitions or displays of Victorian objects that were mounted from 1952 onward and was placed on view again only in 1990. It was then shown in the ornament gallery and described as a typical nineteenth-century virtuoso piece notable for its command of technique and visual sources.

Lit. *Art Journal,* 1868, p. 93; Atterbury and Batkin, 1990; Jones, 1993

Jennifer H. Opie/Susan Dackerman/Brenda Richardson

9. Designed by Bruce James Talbert (Scottish, 1838–1881); made by Holland and Sons (English [London]). *Cabinet.* 1867. Walnut, carved and inlaid with various woods, and inset with an electrotype panel depicting the story of the Sleeping Beauty from "The Day Dream," a poem by Alfred, Lord Tennyson, and with six enamel plaques, 55¾ x 58½ x 17" (142 x 149 x 44 cm). Given by Paul F. Brandt. V&A Circ.286–1955

Originally trained as a carver, Talbert became a prolific commercial designer of textiles, wallpapers, metalwork, stained glass, and furniture. He worked for various large furniture-making firms, including Holland and Sons, for which he designed this cabinet and other pieces for the 1867 Paris Exposition Universelle. The sturdy construction, geometric inlay, and subtle moldings epitomize Reformed Gothic furniture of the 1860s. This revival style, which also incorporated features such as chamfers and stumpy columns derived from ecclesiastical woodwork, was popularized in Talbert's influential book of designs, *Gothic Forms Applied to Furniture, Metalwork and Decoration for Domestic Purposes* (Birmingham, 1867).

A number of influential designers, including Talbert, were not adequately represented in the V&A's "Victorian and Edwardian Decorative Arts" exhibition of 1952, as examples of their work could not be found. Three years after the exhibition, the acquisition of this cabinet enabled the Museum to acknowledge Talbert's influence as a highly skilled interpreter of Gothic forms in the 1860s.

Lit. Aslin, 1962, pp. 46, 65–6; Burke, 1986, pp. 145–6, 470–1; Jervis, 1989

Frances Collard

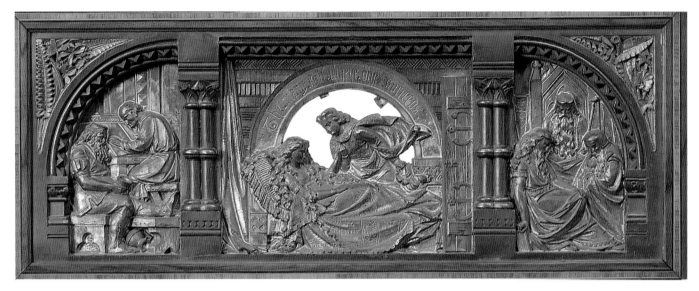

9. (detail)

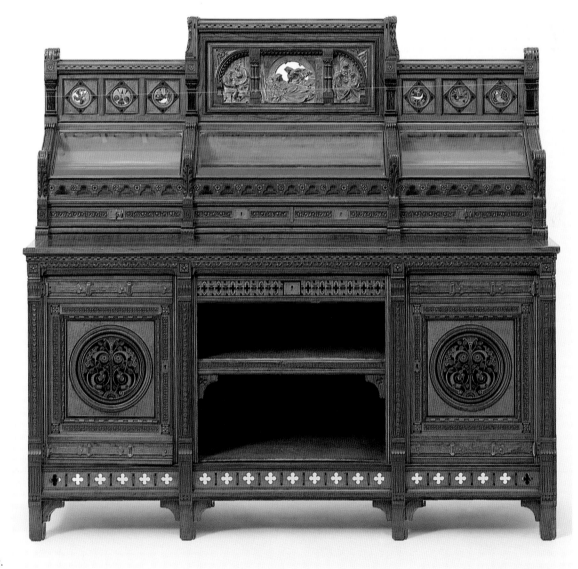

9.

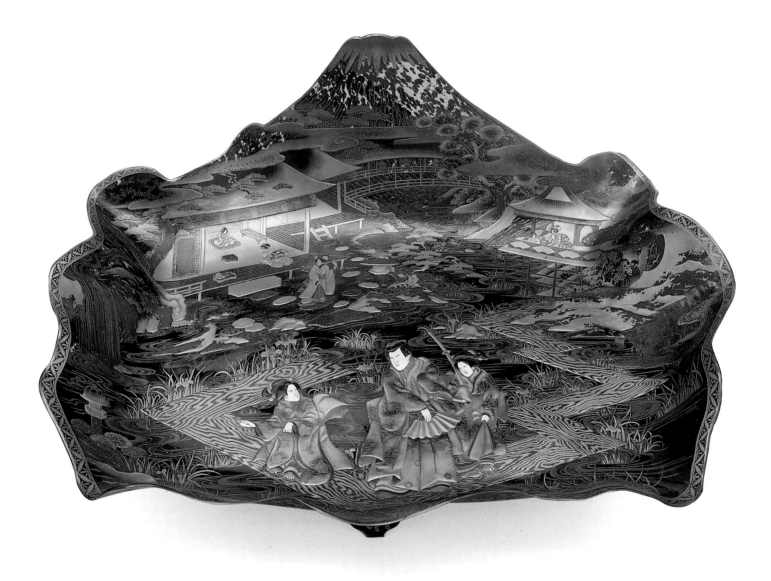

10.

10. Japanese (Nagasaki?). *Tray in the Form of Mount Fuji.* c. 1870. Tortoiseshell with lacquer and ivory appliqué, 16 x 41½ x 31" (41 x 105.8 x 79.2 cm), irreg. V&A 844–1872

Extravagant in scale and luxurious in material, this remarkable tray uses the natural shape of the tortoiseshell to represent Mount Fuji rising to a peak. The elaborate decoration in gold lacquer and ivory that covers the inside of the shell depicts a scene of a bridge, pavilions, and figures below Mount Fuji, taken from the Tales of Ise in classical Japanese literature. Shown at the London international exhibition of 1872, this exotic tray is an impressive example of the lacquerwork that was being produced for the Western market. Although using traditional lacquer techniques, such works were often in a flamboyant style that reflected high Victorian, rather than Japanese, taste. A manifestation of this was the application of lacquer to a base material other than wood, such as tortoiseshell, which was predominantly manufactured at Nagasaki around the 1870s.

The tray was lent to the 1872 exhibition not by the manufacturer but by Sir Rutherford Alcock, who had been appointed British Minister to Japan in 1859. His many purchases in Japan had formed the nucleus of the Japanese section of the 1862 exhibition, which was the first large-scale display of Japanese arts and crafts in the West and played a vital role in bringing such works to a British audience. The 1872 exhibition was altogether a more modest affair, with only a handful of Japanese exhibits.

Lit. Faulkner and Jackson, 1995

JULIA HUTT

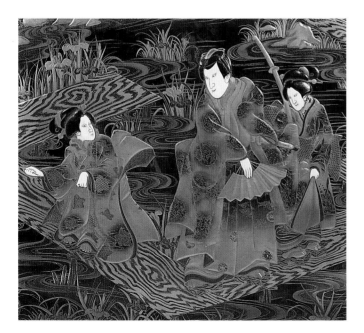

10. (detail)

11. KAJIWARA RIKICHI OF THE KORANSHA COMPANY (Japanese [Arita]). *Dish.* 1875. Porcelain with underglaze blue, 42" (106.7 cm) diam., 11¾" (30 cm) high. V&A 688–1878

A tour de force of porcelain manufacture, this immense dish was made by the Koransha Company of Arita, Saga Prefecture, specifically for the Paris international exhibition of 1878. It is difficult not only to form an object of this size but to fire it without substantial structural warping. The dish is elegantly decorated in deep blue with an abundance of chrysanthemums.

In the Meiji period (1868–1912), ceramic production at Arita, the main porcelain manufacturing center of Japan, underwent major modernization, Koransha being one company that expanded rapidly in response to the increasing overseas demand for Japanese art. During this time Japanese manufacturers took advantage of welcome European interest by participating in international exhibitions, seeing these events as an opportunity to learn of the latest technological advances and to develop export markets. Recognizing that the greatest honors were conferred on highly decorative and technically impressive works, the Japanese were encouraged to exhibit works such as this massive dish, which was bought, with its mate, by the Museum for £100.

During the 1870s and 1880s Japan had an extremely high profile in the Museum, which acquired many contemporary Japanese pieces from international exhibitions. As early as 1878, however, a review of the Paris exhibition criticized the ceramics for "inclining to a style which can only be regarded as a misfortune . . . this [being] due to the almost unnatural velocity with which the Japanese have approximated themselves to European civilization." In response to such views, the Museum's interest in modern Japan waned dramatically in the 1890s. For most of the twentieth century the Meiji period has been ignored by scholars of Japanese art, and it is only in recent years that objects such as this remarkable dish have been rediscovered and acknowledged for their important contribution to our understanding of the arts of Japan at a crucial period in that country's history.

Lit. Schaap, 1987; Impey and Fairley, 1995, vol. 1

ANNA JACKSON

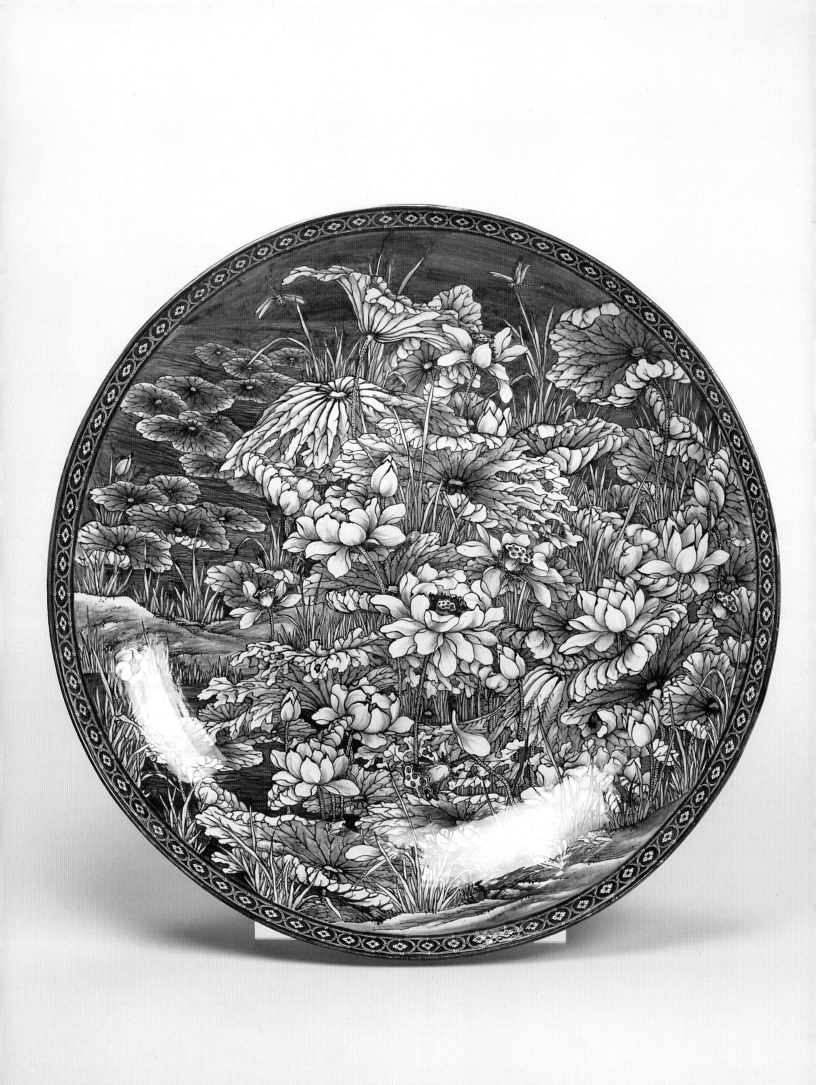

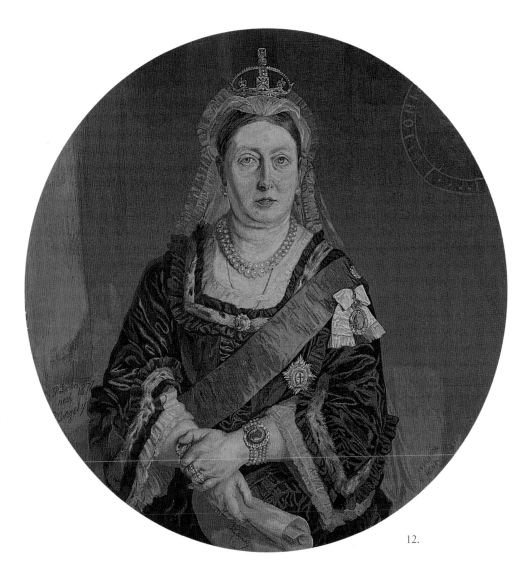

12.

12. English (Windsor). Adapted by PHOEBUS LEVIN (German-born, active London 1855–1878), after an 1875 painting by HEINRICH VON ANGELI (German, 1840–1925); made at the ROYAL WINDSOR TAPESTRY MANUFACTORY. *Portrait of Queen Victoria.* 1877. Tapestry-woven in silk and wool, 37⅜ x 35¼" (95 x 89.6 cm), oval. Inscribed "P. Levin 1877 nach Angely" and "WINDSOR H. Henry M. Brignolas." V&A T.94–1968

Ninety years separate the debut of this tapestry at the Paris exhibition of 1878 and its purchase by the Museum. The Royal Windsor Tapestry Manufactory was established in 1876 with six weavers from Aubusson in France, on the initiative of H. C. J. Henry, artistic advisor to the Lancaster and London furnishing firm of Gillow & Co. The firm's first large commission, from Gillow, was to decorate the Jacobean dining room in the Pavilion of the Prince of Wales at the Paris exhibition. This tapestry portrait of the queen, designed by Levin after a contemporary painting by Angeli, presided above the fireplace.

Scenes from Shakespeare's *Merry Wives of Windsor* were woven for the walls. After the exhibition, at which the tapestries won a gold medal, Sir Albert Sassoon purchased the entire dining room for his house in Kensington.

Although designs of Royal Windsor tapestries were mainly English, their extremely fine weave was based on that of contemporary French tapestry pictures from the Gobelins and Beauvais factories, much admired at the international exhibitions. William Morris considered weaving copies of paintings an "idiotic waste of . . . skill," preferring the textures of Gothic tapestry. This tapestry portrait, however, was Royal Windsor's tour de force, judged by eminent critics to be "faithful to the original, and with perhaps a little more life."

Lit. *The Furniture Gazette,* 1887–88, passim; Hefford, 1969, pp. 30–2; Cullingham, 1979, pp. 4–5, 15

WENDY HEFFORD

13. English (Staffordshire). Made by BOURNE, BAKER & BOURNE OF FENTON, for the retailers Bailey & Neale, London. *Jug.* c. 1830. Lead-glazed earthenware with transfer-printed decoration, 27¾ x 30¼ x 24" (71 x 77 x 61 cm). Given by Mrs. Illidge. V&A 53–1870

Probably the largest blue-and-white jug in existence, this object still has the power to arrest the viewer by its sheer size and astonishing technical perfection. It was produced around 1830 as an advertising piece, a virtuoso example of ceramic technique for display in a London retailer's showroom (at 8 St. Paul's Churchyard), and thus may be regarded as a forerunner of the exhibition pieces acquired by the Museum. Its qualities as a technical tour de force presumably made it especially attractive to the Museum when it was offered as a gift in 1870. More recently it has been discussed in terms of its significance within the history of transfer-printed decoration on English ceramics and the relationship between producers and retailers of pottery in the early nineteenth century.

The sides of the jug are decorated with prints of the "Wild Rose" pattern set in oval "windows" whose shape was probably originally designed for meat dishes. This pattern, extensively used by potteries between 1830 and 1850, derives from a print published in 1811 by W. Cooke, after a drawing by Samuel Owen. The scene depicts Nuneham Courtney, the seat of Lord Harcourt, with its grounds landscaped by Capability Brown between 1779 and 1782. Although the jug is unmarked, the traditional attribution is to Bourne, Baker & Bourne (c. 1818–40), a major blue-and-white ceramics manufacturer with a flourishing export trade. The donor, Mrs. Illidge, whose husband was a descendant of the Bailey of the retailers Bailey & Neale, gave

another huge piece made for the firm's showrooms and lent other pieces made by the Neale factory in Staffordshire. From the late eighteenth century onward successful earthenware manufacturers such as Wedgwood, Spode, and Neale all acquired London showrooms. Bailey & Neale was unusual in selling not only pottery—especially the new blue-and-white printed wares of the type made by this firm as well as by Spode—but also glass and porcelain. By the mid-nineteenth century the retailing of ceramics in London by the manufacturers themselves had been eclipsed by the rise of independent dealers in luxury ceramics who, like Bailey & Neale before them, supplied a range of glass, pottery, and porcelain, thus attracting purchasers away from the factories that produced these wares.

It seems unlikely that V&A curator George Wallis, when he visited the Illidge home in Brixton in February 1870, could have foreseen either the collecting interest in blue-and-white of a century later, or the academic study of ceramics consumption. He merely reported that "The large Earthenware jug . . . would probably hold *30 Gallons*. It is admirably proportioned and a remarkable example of manufacture." Too large for the Circulation Department, it spent its early Museum life at Bethnal Green, but following the publication of W. L. Little's *Staffordshire Blue* in 1969, and the V&A's traveling exhibition "Staffordshire Blue & White," organized by the Circulation Department in 1976, the jug was made a focal point in the Museum's encyclopedic display of British pottery.

Lit. Coysh and Henrywood, 1981, p. 399

ROBIN HILDYARD

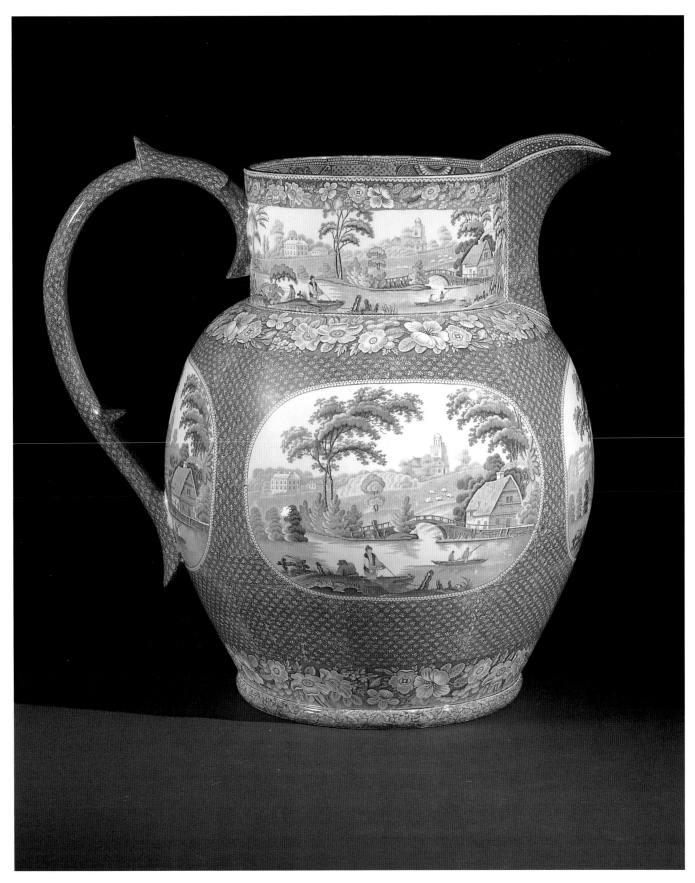

13.

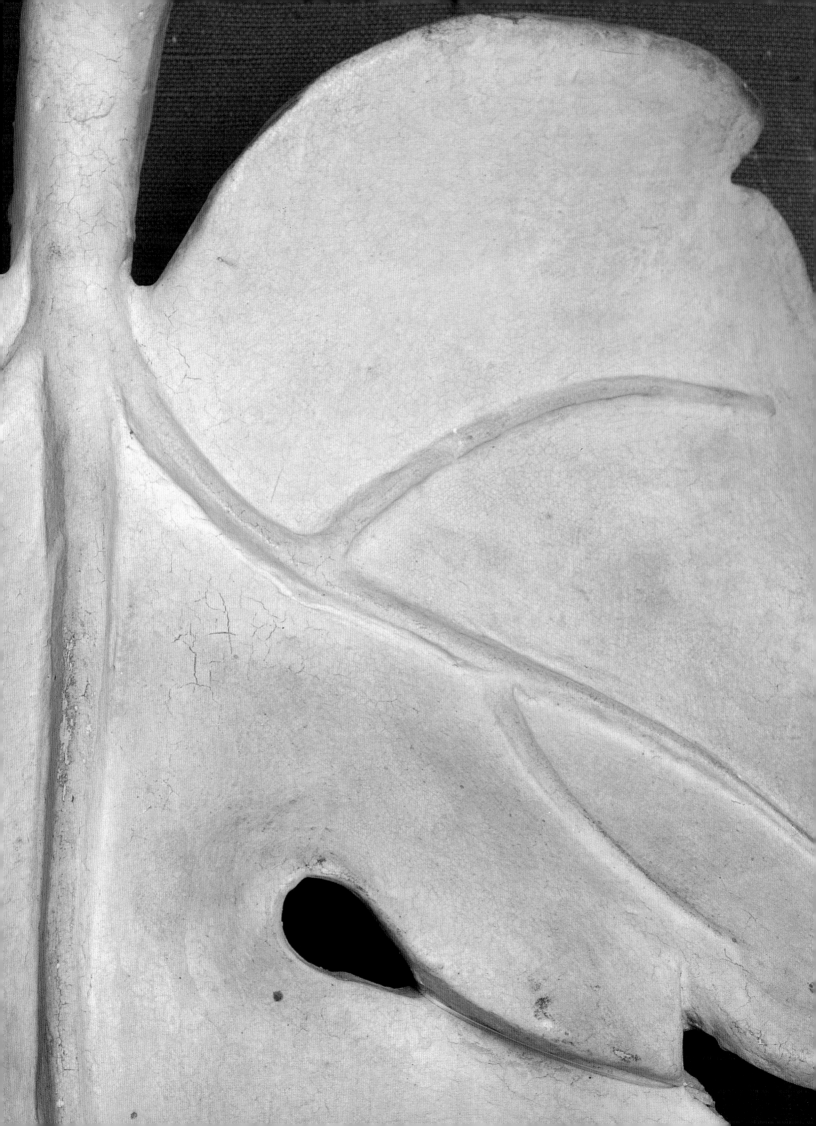

Teaching by Example: Education and the Formation of South Kensington's Museums

Rafael Cardoso Denis

WHEN LOOKING BACK UPON ALL THE MAGNIFICENT ACHIEVEMENTS that make up the history of South Kensington, it is easy to forget that the great institutions it produced are rooted in an instance of resounding failure. Although the collections' origins can be traced to the Great Exhibition of 1851, the British Government's primary purpose in granting public money for the promotion of science and art was not the accumulation and display of objects. Parliamentary frugality was overcome by the argument that the manufacturing population needed training in design, so that Britain would thereby be better equipped to outdistance her international rivals. The nagging fact that this original purpose went largely unfulfilled has been eclipsed by the huge subsequent ascendancy of South Kensington as an emblem of national culture, wealth, power, and prestige. This dichotomy between teaching and collecting, like the nature of the instruction provided, must be understood within the context of its time.

The teaching of art and design changed dramatically throughout Europe during the late eighteenth and early nineteenth centuries. Generally speaking, instruction in fine art and in crafts became increasingly separate, as academies of art sought to distance their members from the world of trades and to cast themselves in the role of guardians of a liberal profession. With the ultimate disintegration of the system of guild apprenticeships, the provision of practical instruction in applied arts and crafts slipped into a state of unprecedented neglect, aggravated by the widespread introduction of new manufacturing techniques and methods of production.[1] In Britain a point of crisis came shortly after 1824 when the lowering of tariffs allowed the market to be flooded by foreign imports, especially French luxury articles that for three decades before had been available only intermittently and at high prices. The somewhat disingenuous argument was made that the success of Continental goods could be attributed to the superiority of their design and, within a few years, the periodical press and other voices were emphasizing the commercial value of taste to manufactures. Out of the ensuing political commotion arose England's first publicly funded system of Schools of Design in 1837, whose mission was to raise the standard of British manufactures by training good designers.[2]

Fig. 65. Detail of cat. 26, the fig leaf for the V&A's plaster cast of Michelangelo's *David*

Despite the innovations of William Dyce, the first headmaster of the Schools of Design, the schools were all but defunct by the early 1850s, when they gave way to a new set of administrative and political priorities. Much of what had been achieved in those first fifteen years was subsequently rejected and even actively undermined, but one particular aspect of the initial project was taken up with remarkable zeal: namely, the collecting of plaster casts (cats. 24, 26–27) and other works of art (see cats. 22–23, 25, 28) for use as examples in teaching. The Schools' original collection, begun as early as 1838, was substantially enlarged by the purchase of objects from the Great Exhibition (cats. 2–4), for which a large grant of public money was made available.[3] Further purchases, as well as numerous gifts, prompted the transformation in 1852 of the erstwhile study collection into a Museum of Manufactures, introducing a public display role which was to endure far longer than the rather sporadic attempts at education in design. The Museum quickly took on a separate didactic function of its own, particularly with the inclusion of a room devoted to the exposition of "False Principles in Decoration" (see cats. 19–20). These events gave a new direction to the educational venture in its broadest sense and signaled a bold decision to use the collections to foster public taste quite apart from the purposes of applied industrial instruction. The evolving character of South Kensington teaching over the latter half of the nineteenth century can be fully understood only in terms of this shift away from the original clamor for design reform in the 1830s.

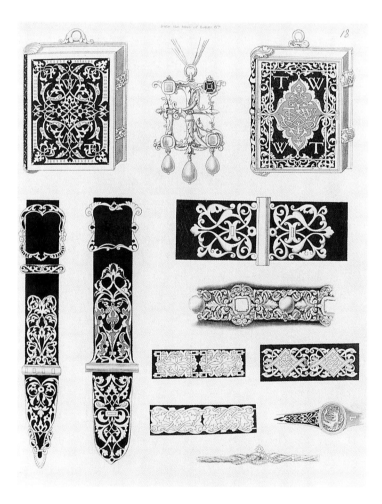

Fig. 66. Goldsmiths' designs by Hans Holbein from Shaw's *Encyclopedia of Ornament* (National Art Library, V&A). Designs of this sort were copied by students at the art schools.

Although the South Kensington system eventually came to encompass not only instruction in art and design but also in science, the original mission of the Department of Science and Art (hereafter, DSA), as set out in the early 1850s, focused more narrowly on what was dubbed "practical art," a term intended to denote a rupture with the outgoing system, which was perceived as not being practical enough. Its earliest years were, therefore, almost exclusively occupied with the concerns of art and design education; and discussion of its later development must begin within that particular context.

The new Department wasted no time in reorganizing the pedagogical system it inherited from the old Schools of Design. Richard Redgrave, Superintendent for Art, was responsible for putting together the National Course of Art Instruction (hereafter, NCAI), which was officially published in 1853, just as the DSA was beginning to take more definite shape.[4] Although the NCAI has become notorious for its "cast-iron" rigidity,[5] little is generally known about its actual operation, and the mistaken assumption that South Kensington's teaching was unchanging and uniform has obscured its significance. From the start, both Henry Cole and Richard Redgrave were keen to establish a national curriculum for art and design education; Redgrave announced the first attempt to devise an appropriate syllabus in 1852. The proposed course of instruction consisted of twenty-two stages: ten of drawing ornament (fig. 66), the figure, and flowers from the flat and from the round (mainly, casts [fig. 67]); seven of painting the same types of examples; three of modeling them; and the last two devoted to "composition in design." The drawing stages were mandatory for all students, who would then split up to do either painting or modeling, and finally meet up again at the end.[6]

By the time the initial course actually came into effect one year later, a few changes had already been made. The ten drawing stages were expanded and the amount of drawing from nature increased; painting continued to occupy seven stages and modeling, three. Stage 21—previously dedicated to "studies from the life"—was fleshed out to include time sketches and compositions from nature and from memory. Stage 22—"elementary design"—was similarly amplified to include the ornamental treatment of natural forms (fig.

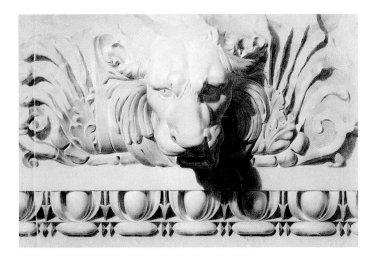

Fig. 67. Student drawing by R. W. Herman, 1840 (V&A E.196–1909A), inscribed: "This drawing obtained the first prize ever offered by the Government School of Design for drawing ornament from the cast"

68), the ornamental arrangement of forms to fill given spaces, and the study of historic ornament. This stage offered a theoretical introduction to abstract principles of design, constituting a sort of classroom version of the ideas Owen Jones would make famous in *The Grammar of Ornament* of 1856 (cat. 14). The main alteration, though, was the addition of a further stage 23 entitled "technical studies." Representing the most unqualified commitment thus far to workshop training and applied design,[7] this new stage promised to cover architectural design; ornamental surface design; ornamental relief design; molding, casting, and chasing; lithography; engraving on wood and metal; and porcelain painting.

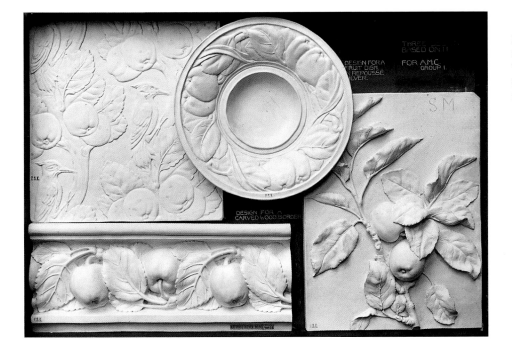

Fig. 68. A series of designs based on a study of apples, by Dorothy E. G. Woollard, a student at the Municipal School of Art, Bristol. Winner of a National Silver Medal

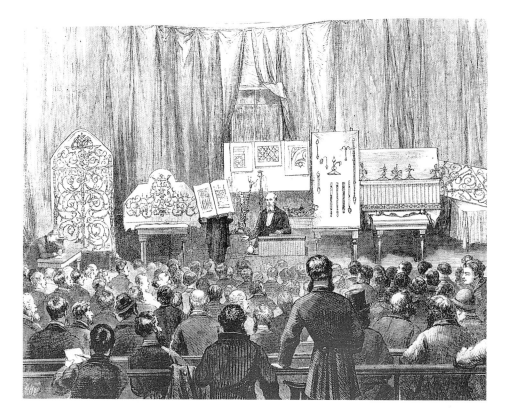

Fig. 69. "Lecture on Ironwork," from *The Illustrated London News*, 5 March 1870. Among the objects being used to illustrate ironworking styles and techniques is a German cresting from a gate of about 1700 (cat. 22).

The subjects covered in stage 23 corresponded to the so-called special classes offered at Marlborough House between the end of 1852 and 1856, which were special not only in nature but also in terms of their limited access. This comparatively advanced level of study, involving actual creative work and not simply the copying of examples, was restricted to the Central Training School for Art and, even among the students in London, only those able to afford the high fees could contemplate the possibility of workshop training. With the move to South Kensington in 1857, the special classes were discontinued and practical training became largely restricted to a number of workshops established to assist in the decoration of the new buildings.[8]

The establishment of the NCAI signaled a further change of much wider significance for the development of art and design education throughout Britain. The full, twenty-three-stage syllabus described above represented only a small part of the DSA's system of teaching. Its complete title was "Course for Designers, Ornamentists, and Those Intending to Be Industrial Artists." As this name implies, it was only made available to those pursuing full-time studies during the daytime at a recognized School of Art (as the Schools of Design were renamed in 1853). All other classes of students were obliged to follow one of three more limited programs, each comprising a different combination of stages from the full course: the "Primary Course for Schools, Principally by Means of Class Teaching," the "Course for General Education," or the "Course for Machinists, Engineers and Foremen of Works" (fig. 69).[9]

In terms of classroom practice, the existence of four distinct syllabuses meant that participants were pigeonholed from the start. Students could not simply pick and choose among courses, as these were offered at different times of day, often in distinct locations and at widely divergent fees.[10] This practical subdivision of efforts into several echelons was further enshrined in the Department's stated policy that it would only subsidize advanced training in the central schools of science and art, mainly in London. Despite protestations from the various branch and provincial schools, from masters, and even from Parliament, the principle of maintaining a multitiered system, with differentiated levels of instruction, was steadfastly preserved even after the administrative reforms of 1863–65.[11] As time wore on, the division between day and evening classes widened into something of a gulf, to the extent that they often had little in common besides sharing the same building. Working artisans entertained virtually no hope of pursuing full-time studies, of following the complete syllabus, of achieving National Medallions (fig. 70), and, therefore, of qualifying for National Scholarships which, after 1863, functioned as the principal route to the advanced study of design at the newly reorganized National Art Training School in South Kensington.

The segregation of studies was further enforced by the DSA's rigorous system of examination and inspection, which effectively prevented individual teachers and schools from deviating too much from the established norms. At the Lambeth School, where John Sparkes introduced a regime of applied technical instruction around 1860, a unique collaboration with Doulton's manufactory for the production of "art-pottery" received no encouragement from the DSA, despite the high level of commercial success achieved by the new Doulton ware, a large proportion of which was designed and executed by Sparkes and his students. In fact, the Department's increasingly vocal opposition to workshop instruction after the late 1860s, on the grounds that it constituted a subsidy to particular trades and industries, hindered the initiation and maintenance of experiments of this type.[12]

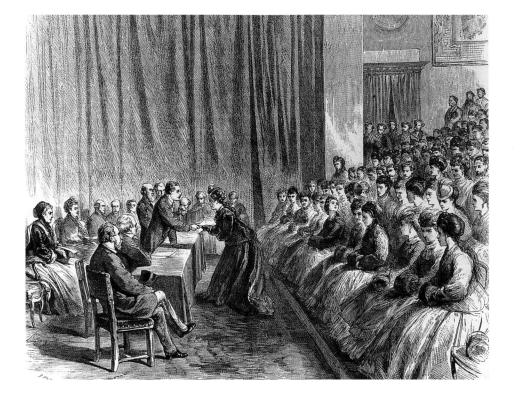

Fig. 70. "Presentation of Prizes by Prince Teck at the South Kensington Museum," from *Graphic,* 26 February 1870

Generally speaking, the teaching in branch and provincial Schools of Art tended to remain at an agonizingly basic level, following a progression which led from a slow and tedious process of copying flat examples to a tightly controlled system of drawing from casts and, in a small minority of cases, on to the higher stages of the NCAI. As Hubert von Herkomer—who attended the Southampton School in 1863—later summarized it, the actual practice consisted of "stipple, stipple, stipple, night after night, for six or perhaps nine months, at one piece of ornament something under fourteen inches long."[13] The strict regulation of examinations and competitions ensured that students could not move up the curricular ladder too quickly. On average, a student with no previous experience took from one to two years to produce a medal drawing in one of the lower stages. In 1864 the Select Committee on Schools of Art was told that a "Mr. Fildes" from the Warrington School of Art took six months on a chalk drawing of apples, thus earning him a National Medallion that qualified him for a scholarship at South Kensington. (Luke Fildes ultimately became one of the Victorian era's most successful painters.) Making it to the National Art Training School was extremely difficult for any single individual, no matter how talented; and even there, at the highest level of studies, the instruction left much to be desired.[14]

The Department's commitment to advanced education had been rather half-hearted from the start, as workshop training and technical instruction involved a comparatively high level of investment in specialized teachers and facilities. From the beginning of his tenure in 1852, Cole made official pronouncements that reflect a discernible reluctance to engage in anything beyond the diffusion of elementary knowledge; and, by 1857, he felt confident enough in his newfound convictions to assert quite categorically that technical education, by its very nature, could not succeed.[15] Those first few years of the Department's existence were marked by a less-than-subtle effort to concentrate funds in London by bleeding the budget previously reserved for branch and provincial schools in order to offset elevated expenditures on the activities of the Central Training School. The DSA's total appropriation was substantially increased at just the time when the special technical classes were abolished and the expenses of the Central Training School thereby radically reduced. Where was all the new money being spent? It is revealing that the demise of organized workshop training under the Department's auspices coincides perfectly with the inception of its new role as custodian of the South Kensington site and with the intensification of the public display role of its collections.[16]

With the royal inauguration of the South Kensington Museum in 1857, the DSA's lukewarm disposition toward advanced instruction began to translate into a concrete shift in investment priorities. Apart from the one-fifth spent on salaries, most of the million pounds or so voted for the DSA between 1853 and 1868 went to noneducational purposes within South Kensington itself, including administration, buildings, and collections.[17] The high level of expenditure on the Museum attracted a great deal of criticism both from the press and in Parliament, including angry accusations that it was "nothing but a great toyshop for the amusement of the residents in the west-end," as one member of Parliament phrased it in 1860.[18] The Department countered such accusations by insisting that the Museum was important as a pedagogical aid and that the main purpose of its collections was to serve

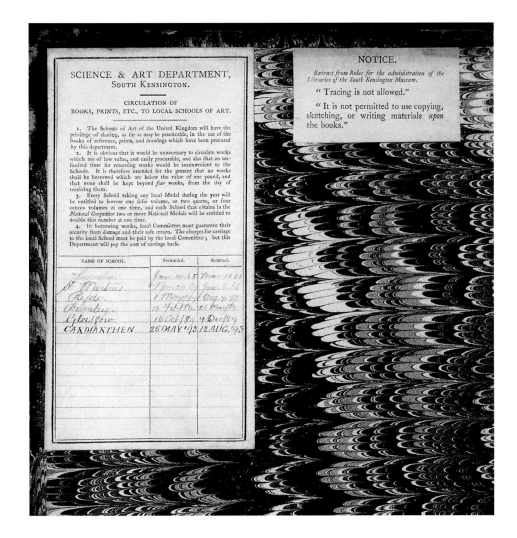

Fig. 71. A circulation log affixed inside
the cover of a book lent by the Science
and Art Department to art schools
around the country, showing where
the volume went. This label is from
Shaw's *Encyclopedia of Ornament* (see
fig. 66).

as examples for the training of students. During the 1860s, however, evidence con-
tradicting this position began to multiply rapidly. Students in local and provincial
schools continually complained that the Museum was inaccessible (fig. 71); and, in
1864, a written statement from the students at South Kensington declared it to be of
extremely limited utility, even to them. As one Lambeth artisan reported to the
Society of Arts, the Museum "might as well be in the moon" for any advantage he
could derive from it.[19]

As the frequency and intensity of these criticisms grew, the DSA felt pressured
to justify its ever-increasing expenditure on collections, particularly the substantial
amounts invested in paintings and other objects of only tangential relevance to
design and decorative art, as opposed to the casts and copies which had been the
mainstay of the old Museum of Manufactures. In a confidential memorandum of
1869, Cole listed a number of reasons why such spending should be allowed and
even encouraged, including, of course, the familiar idea that the examples purchased were essential for study. His strongest argument, however, concerned not
education but the idea that collecting was a positive investment in itself. Since
ancient works of art tended to increase in value, it was profitable to purchase them
whenever possible. If necessary, he surmised, the whole collection could be sold to
the United States government for a handsome profit. Besides, Cole argued, since

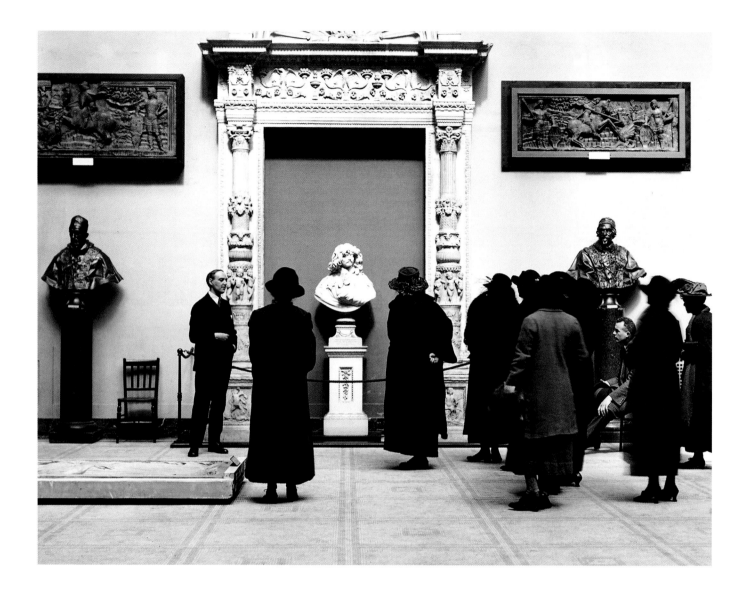

Fig. 72. A lecture to visitors in one of the V&A sculpture galleries in 1923

other countries were busy creating institutions similar to South Kensington, Britain would be exposed to contempt and ridicule for grudging expenditure of this type, adding, rather peevishly, that the British Museum and the National Gallery should be stopped from making purchases first because they were of less direct use to industry.[20] This important memorandum reveals a very significant shift from the idea of collecting for teaching purposes toward the goal of collecting as an end in itself. For the first time in the short history of government-sponsored education in art and design, the suggestion was being made that the physical possession of antique and/or aesthetically desirable objects was a source of national wealth and prestige, quite apart from any potential for positive influence on people and production.

The emerging conflict between the purposes of education and collecting at South Kensington was to remain open and active long after the retirement of Cole and Redgrave in 1873 and 1875, respectively. When the Committee on Rearrangement for the Art Division of the Victoria and Albert Museum was appointed in 1908, its main stated concern was the lack of "a clear definition of function" for the collections. Although the Museum had been founded originally as an instrument for stimulating the improvement of manufactures, crafts, and decorative design, the Committee suggested, the scope of that attribution had been almost insensibly enlarged over the years—dating from the acquisition of paintings under the Sheepshanks bequest of 1857—to a point at which the very purpose of the institution was shrouded in confusion.[21]

Even today, this conflict still raises questions of profound importance in evaluating the historical function of the modern museum. On the one hand, there can be little doubt that the purposeful accumulation of historical objects during the nineteenth century was perceived to contribute directly to the improvement of design standards by providing examples for the producer of manufactured goods. On the other hand, the abundant indications that collections were often funded by diverting investment away from the direct training of artisans and designers might suggest that their primary purpose was not didactic but, rather, ostentation and display (fig. 72). A third hypothesis, advocated ever more stridently by Cole after his retirement, argued that the crucial educational role of museums resided in their ability to "create consumers" by molding and influencing public taste.[22] Whereas the latter function has certainly been fulfilled by the subsequent development of museums—with the ubiquitous museum shop presenting the most familiar face of a vibrant heritage industry—the conflict between the former two roles remains largely unresolved.

The 1908 Committee was perhaps confusing cause and effect in singling out the acquisition of paintings as the point of rupture with the original task of technical instruction. The objets d'art included in the Bernal and Soulages collections (see cats. 50, 53, 71, 74), acquired even earlier, can similarly be subjected to a particular way of looking at objects that is intrinsic to the concept of collecting extraordinary specimens for their beauty, artistry, tastefulness, or superior design. The theory underlying the didactic display of objects of this kind would suggest that to do so incites emulation on the part of the producer and discernment on the part of the consumer or, in other words, that taste is thereby elevated and craftsmanship encouraged. The actual result of displaying objects in a museum setting has often been, however, to endow each of them with an aura of uniqueness and to enhance their claim (and that of their makers) to the status of model, archetype, or "original," in relation to which anything similar is judged a mere imitation, good or bad. Ironically, such attributions of uncommon value tend to defeat the didactic purpose, transforming discernment into snobbery over possession and emulation into what nineteenth-century commentators commonly decried as "slavish copying."

The DSA's educational policymakers could not necessarily control the uses that were made of objects in the Museum, even though they sometimes desired to do so. Designers and manufacturers routinely appropriated historical patterns and shapes, reproducing them integrally or combining them in eclectic variations (see cat. 17). Both procedures violated Owen Jones's sacrosanct rule that the forms of the past were never to be copied but only studied in order that their fundamental principles should be better understood.[23] Display could thus function as a concrete stimulus to design, even if bypassing the formal mechanisms of instruction. The organizers of museums like those of South Kensington were to some degree aware of the contradictions involved in fetishizing individual objects and struggled to guard against them by contextualizing artifacts within broad typological displays, emphasizing not only differences between individual pieces but also their similarities. For them, the notion of "good design" rested implicitly on contrast with the bad and on exhaustive explanation of the principles underlying such distinctions (fig. 73), especially in terms of understanding materials and techniques (see cat. 32). Thus, the labels for tinned peaches (cat. 21) exhibited in the early part of the twentieth century in many ways echo the sort of comparative display made famous by the "chamber of horrors" (as the 1852 "False Principles" installation was colloquially described). By focusing on the mundane and burying individuality in type (see cat. 30), this sort of display avoided the pitfall of subordinating the didactic purpose of collecting to the purely acquisitive one.[24] Perhaps the more irreversible blow to the educational aspirations of South Kensington's collections came when the objects and processes of production were largely split apart into separate museums of science and art.

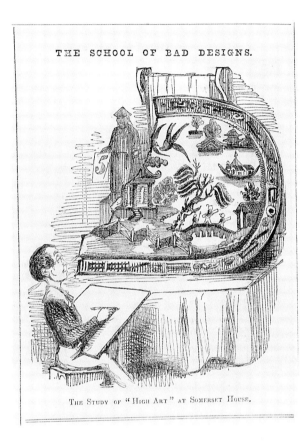

THE SCHOOL OF BAD DESIGNS.

The Study of "High Art" at Somerset House.

Fig. 73. "The School of Bad Designs," from *Punch,* September 1845. A humorous observation on the practices at the Government School of Design at Somerset House

The historical tension between collecting for the purpose of teaching and collecting for the purpose of hoarding treasure lies, fundamentally, in the way that objects are viewed and endowed with value. Although the growth of South Kensington's collections during the latter half of the nineteenth century depended to a great extent on a deliberate erosion of its educational mission, these two aims are certainly not necessarily opposed. The thrust of outside criticism at the time was never that collecting should not be undertaken at all but that it should be made to conform to objectives and guidelines more general than the logic of accumulation for its own sake; and the main complaint on the part of DSA students was not that the displays were useless in themselves but, rather, that the difficulty and expense of gaining access to them negated their inherent value. It would be easy to condemn the accumulation of great collections as an example of how readily public monies are manipulated for more or less private purposes; yet, the objects themselves are not the problem, for they are capable of serving a variety of ends and, as *A Grand Design* demonstrates, are eminently susceptible to reinterpretation. The deeper ethical dilemma appears to lie in the relative value attributed to objects and to people, in the manner that the former are used to exclude a variety of social groupings from that broad set of aspirations encompassed by the word "culture" or, alternatively, to include them within it.[25]

During the early years of South Kensington's existence, the pursuit of advanced popular education was undoubtedly sacrificed to a narrow vision of culture for the privileged few. From the vantage point of today, however, we cannot allow ourselves the luxury of looking back on that past with any sense of smugness. In an age when the noble ideal of public service is increasingly under threat, more than ever the challenge endures to reclaim the museum's original educational mission, not by denying altogether the value of museums but by ensuring that accessibility and outreach continue to be treated as unassailable priorities.

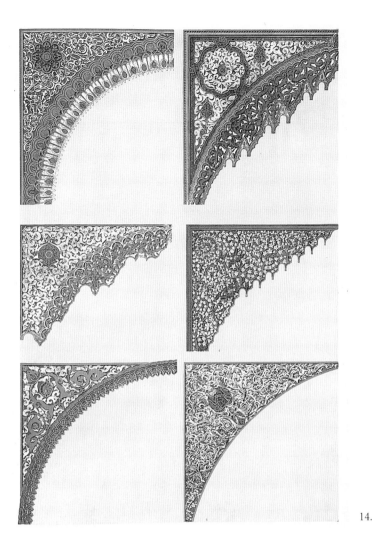

14.

14. OWEN JONES (English, 1809–1874). *The Grammar of Ornament.* 1856. One hundred folio plates, chromolithographed by Day & Son, London, from drawings by F. Bedford, 22 x 14½ x 1⅜" (55 x 37 x 3.5 cm). V&A 4.10.1868/NAL1598. [Illustrated: plate 40]

The Grammar of Ornament was the publication that most clearly exemplified the role and aspirations of the South Kensington Museum in a national program of art and design education. Its author, Owen Jones, along with three other figures closely involved with the Museum (Henry Cole, Richard Redgrave, and Matthew Digby Wyatt), was one of a group of design theorists who directed the establishment of art and design education in Britain after 1851. By this date Jones's famous publication on the Alhambra (cat. 15) was being used by students at the Government Schools of Design, and he was already acclaimed as the designer of the Crystal Palace interiors for the 1851 Great Exhibition.

The Grammar of Ornament adopted an analytical approach in identifying principles that were taken to govern decoration used by cultures all over the world. Jones included, for example, patterns from "savage tribes" in New Zealand and ornament from China; significantly, Japanese ornament was not included at this date. The publication, visually dazzling and erudite in its scope, was intended to establish a universally valid taxonomy of design, to designate what was "correct," and to deduce prescriptive principles from those examples.

Jones's work was part of a movement to provide students with examples of all types of artifacts that could be called art, from plaster casts of sculpture and architectural decoration to drawings of textiles and frescoes. The School of Design in the South Kensington Museum owned several copies of *The Grammar of Ornament,* many of which were loaned to provincial art schools. At the high price of £17 10s., Henry Cole declared that the work would be loaned only to those provincial schools that gained good examination results.

The Grammar of Ornament inspired a whole genre of similar publications in France, Germany, and the United States.

Lit. Macdonald, 1970; Darby, 1974

ROWAN WATSON

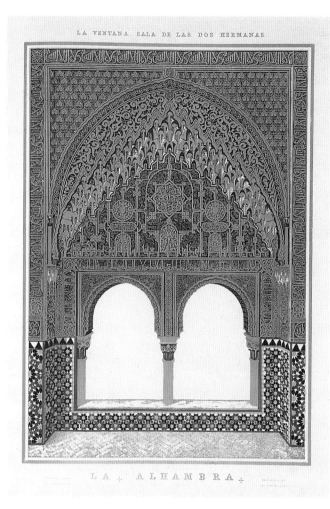

LA VENTANA. SALA DE LAS DOS HERMANAS

LA + ALHAMBRA +

15.

British contemporary, novelist and poet Sir Walter Scott, to seek out romantic sites and folk tales relating to them, Irving published stories about ancient Andalusia that were to make the area a mecca for seekers of "the exotic." Jones became familiar with the Alhambra when he toured Greece, Istanbul, Egypt, and Spain in the early 1830s. The two volumes were eventually sold at £36 10s.

Color was an essential message of Jones's publication. Earlier illustrations, such as those in J. F. Lewis's *Sketches and Drawings of the Alhambra* (1838), were picturesque in style and rendered in monotint. Jones's emphasis on color and decorative detail aimed to provide contemporary architects, students, and historians with models, and to serve as a manifesto for polychromy in architecture. Some 162 copies of Jones's *Alhambra* were sold to subscribers, including the library of the Govern-

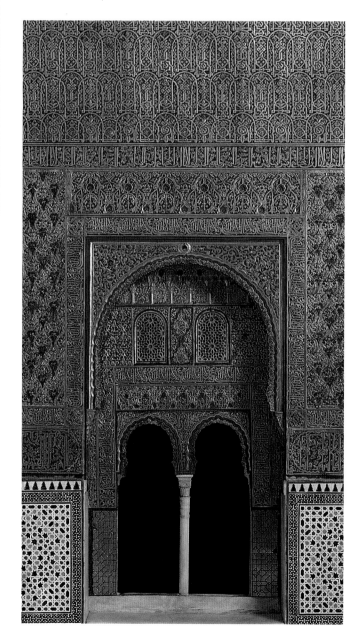

16.

15. OWEN JONES (English, 1809–1874) and JULES GOURY (French, died 1834). *Album Book: Plans, Elevations, Sections, and Details of the Alhambra, from Drawings Made on the Spot in 1834 by the late Jules Goury, and in 1834 and 1837 by Owen Jones.* 1842–45. Printed on paper with chromolithographic plates; later half-leather and board covers, 26⅜ x 19⅞ x 2" (67 x 50.5 x 5 cm). V&A 110.P.36. [Illustrated: page 103]

Owen Jones's spectacular album book on the Alhambra was one of the most influential and widely used sources of design at the South Kensington Museum and beyond during the nineteenth century, as well as being a monument of the early color printing process known as chromolithography. The Moorish palace called the Alhambra (13th–14th century) outside Granada, Spain, was little known among antiquarians and others before the 1820s, but, along with other Spanish monuments, it became more widely known through Richard Ford's accounts of Spain. Its inclusion in the canon of the world's great buildings owes much to the American author Washington Irving (1783–1859) and his 1832 book *The Alhambra.* Inspired by the work of his

ment School of Design at Somerset House, the precursor of the National Art Library at the V&A; other subscribers included the monarchs of Prussia and France. The School of Design cut out plates from the book for students to use; the fate of several such books was justified by the need to provide multiple examples for students to copy from. Despite its high price, the album was also acquired in the mid-1840s for the provincial schools of design then being set up.

Lit. Darby, 1974; White, 1994

<small>ROWAN WATSON</small>

16. Spanish. *Architectural Model of a Large Lateral Arch in the Hall of the Comares, Palace of the Alhambra.* c. 1865. Painted stucco and marble, 32¾ x 20 x 4" (83.5 x 51 x 10.5 cm). Presented by The Countess von Bothmer. V&A 1890-52

Examples of design and decoration were made available not only through illustrated books such as those by Owen Jones (cats. 14–15) but also through models and plaster casts. By 1856 Jones's plates of the palace of the Alhambra (13th–14th century) were supplemented at the South Kensington Museum by no fewer than twenty-six models. This particular model, given to the Museum in 1890, is a duplicate of an example (V&A 1865–462) which is no longer in the collections. Models of this type were readily available in Spain for purchase by visitors as souvenirs, many being produced by the firm of Don Raphael Contreras.

Architectural models were often displayed alongside original objects, fragments, and plaster casts to provide a context for architectural details. In 1883 the Museum acquired, through an exchange program with the Academia de la Historia, Madrid, a large collection of plaster casts of architectural details taken from various parts of the Alhambra. These were probably used for teaching at the Government Schools of Art and Design. However, it was not until early in the twentieth century that more active collecting of Alhambra material took place, when actual fragments of the decorative features of the Alhambra (as opposed to reproductions) were acquired by the Museum.

Lit. Department of Science and Art, 1891a; Darby, 1974

<small>FIONA LESLIE</small>

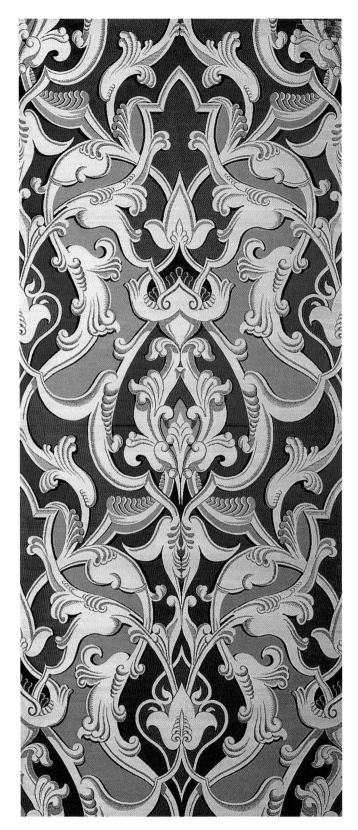

17.

17. English (Spitalfields). *Furnishing Silk known as "Alhambresque".* 1850s. Jacquard-woven silk, 50 x 21⅞" (127 x 55.6 cm). Given by Warner & Sons Ltd. V&A T.132–1972

The published work of Owen Jones was a boon to designers in the mid-nineteenth century. Jones designed silks for the manufacturer Benjamin Warner (the firm that had indirectly taken over that of Daniel Keith & Co., the likely manufacturers of this silk). It is therefore unclear whether this silk was designed by Jones or only inspired by plates in the 1856 edition of his famous work, *The Grammar of Ornament* (cat. 14). Clearly figures 1, 2, and 6, Jones's "Turkish No. 2" (plate XXXVII in *The Grammar of Ornament*), inspired this silk's ground colors of red, blue, and green; and Jones's figure 21, "Turkish No. 1" (plate XXXVI) contains the basic pattern of "Alhambresque," with arabesques of the type found in this silk and described by Jones in a text illustration in *The Grammar of Ornament* as characteristically Turkish. This design, which at some point came to be called "Alhambresque," was not in fact inspired by the Alhambra (ornament that Jones called "Moresque") but by ornament from the late-fifteenth-century "New Mosque" (or Blue Mosque) in Constantinople, illustrated in Jones's plates.

Lit. Jones, 1856, unnumbered text page, pls. XXXVI, XXXVII

WENDY HEFFORD

18. *Samples of Textiles in Silk and Wool Selected (by Condition, Size, and Importance) from more than 800 Surviving Specimens of the "Collection of Animal Products" of the South Kensington Museum.* 43½ x 80½ x ¼" (111 x 205 x 1 cm). All gifts not specified below were made by the manufacturers to the commissioners for the 1851 Great Exhibition or later to the South Kensington Museum.

18.1. English (Spitalfields). *Sample of Jacquard-woven silk* with broad stripes of flowers on a woven ground simulating "watered" patterning—a design "sham" of which Henry Cole would not have approved (see cat. 19). Exhibited (in a different colorway, A.P. 357[3]) in the 1851 Exhibition (Class XIII, No. 31) by Campbell, Harrison & Lloyd, which won a Prize Medal. V&A A.P.357(1)

18.2. English (Spitalfields). *Vest fabric of Jacquard-woven silk* with a design of water lilies. Exhibited (in a different colorway) in the 1851 Exhibition (Class XIII, No. 24) by J[ames] & W[illiam] Robinson & Co. V&A A.P.356(2)

18.3. Prussian (Vierssen). *Two pieces of furnishing brocatelle,* red and green colorways making one repeat of a design based on seventeenth-century velvets. Exhibited by Christian Mengen in the Zollverein section of the 1851 Exhibition (Class VIII, No. 581). V&A A.P.358(1) and A.P.358(4)

18.4. English (Kidderminster). *Sample of three-frame Brussels carpeting,* woven like a velvet with looped pile. This economical design, requiring only three frames of colored pattern warp, would have been approved by Henry Cole for its flat treatment. Manufactured by Worth & Co. V&A A.P.98(3), renumbered V&A T.2–1959

18.5. English (Sutton, Macclesfield). *Two cards with twelve of fifty surviving samples* described in the Animal Products Register as "small wares in silk, bands, braids, trimmings, &c." from James Smith & Son. V&A A.P.340(7–18)

18.6. Irish (Dublin). *Hanks of dyed silk (blue) and worsted (red),* as used respectively for the warp and weft in weaving poplin, presented by W. M. Geogehan. V&A A.P.402(10) and A.P.402(12)

18.7. English (Norwich). *Fragment of poplin with diaper pattern,* in blue, white, and red silk, and blue worsted, presented by Messrs. Middleton and Ainsworth, who exhibited in 1851. V&A A.P.405(4A)

18.8. Irish (Dublin). *Poplin, red silk warp, and worsted weft with silver strip.* This design was exhibited by R. Atkinson & Co. in the 1851 Exhibition (Class XV, No. 256) in blue and gold. It is engraved in *The Illustrated Inventor,* 31 October 1857, as a product of the Dublin School of Design, on the committee of which Mr. Atkinson, "Her Majesty's Poplin Manufacturer," offered premiums for designs. V&A A.P.406(14)

18.9. Irish (Dublin). *Poplin, white silk, and worsted,* with additional pattern wefts of colored silks and metal strip, described in 1851 as "Brocaded and gold-barred Irish Poplin, with rose, thistle and shamrock coloured to nature," one of the fabrics for which R. Atkinson & Co. (Class XV, No. 256) won a Prize Medal. The firm had a Jacquard loom making poplin at the entrance to the Irish court in the Exhibition. V&A A.P.409(17)

18.10. French. *Four "specimens of French Cashmere or silky wool* of Graux de Mauchamp[s] (presented by Her Majesty)" are "in the raw state, washed, carded, spun," according to the Animal Products Register of 1860, though this wool of "increased strength, brilliancy and fineness ... the best quality for combing," as it was described on winning a Council Medal in 1851 (Class IV, No. 245), would have been combed, not carded. Jean Louis Graux's new wool had been used in shawls exhibited in the French Industry Exhibitions of 1839 and 1844. Presented by Queen Victoria. V&A A.P.144(1–4)

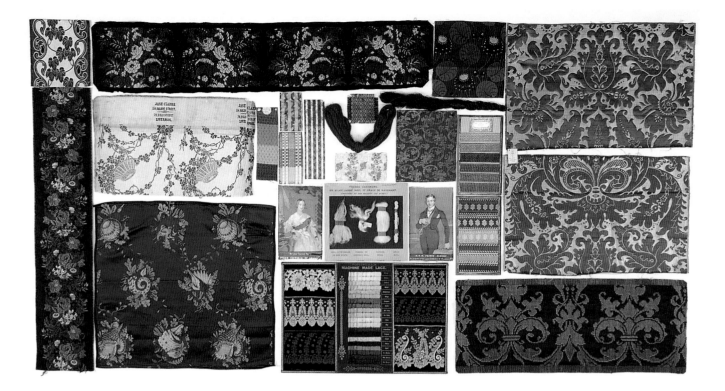

18.

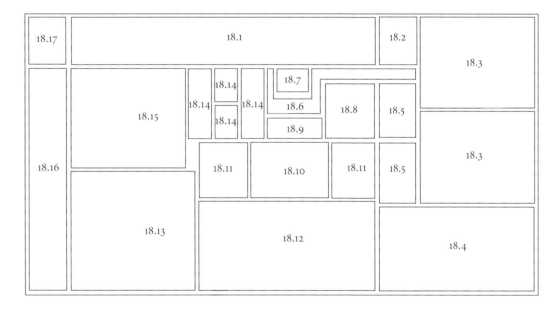

18.11. French (St. Etienne). *Portraits of Queen Victoria and Prince Albert* woven in black and white silk by Barrallon & Brossard, from engravings by F. Bacon, 1841, after paintings by William Charles Ross. The French firm exhibited in the London exhibitions of both 1851 and 1862. V&A A.P.119–1862 and V&A A.P.120–1862

18.12. English (Nottingham). *Frame advertising the machine-woven silk lace* of Rylands & Sons Ltd., showing six designs and twenty colors. "Pink" and "coral" have faded, but "serpent green" is still vivid. V&A A.P.10(1–26)–1889

18.13. English (Spitalfields). *"Conchus," a brocaded figured silk* designed for Daniel Walters & Sons by William Folliott (English, 1835–1925), who studied and taught at the Spitalfields School of Design. Folliott first lent, then gave to the Museum a piece of *Conchus,* entered in the Animal Products Register in 1873 and later numbered Misc.13–1923. Displayed here is an unfaded colorway, a later gift from Warner & Sons, which took over Walters in 1894. Given by Warner & Sons Ltd. V&A T.145–1972

18.14. English (Spitalfields). *Four small-patterned silks of 1794–95* from "91 patterns as illustrating the silk manufacture of Spitalfields between the years 1794 and 1860," lent to the Museum in 1872 and later given by William Folliott, silk designer. These are from pattern books which Folliott possibly acquired for teaching aids in the Spitalfields School of Design. Silks in the Animal Products display of 1860 included a historical section with patterns dating from 1695 to 1800. Given by William Folliott. V&A Misc.23–1923 through V&A Misc.26–1923

18.15. English (Spitalfields). *"Enamelled" silk,* as described in the 1851 catalogue: "A white ground, covered with gold baskets filled with green enamel shamrocks," exhibited by Jane Clarke, "Designer and Manufacturer," but probably designed and manufactured exclusively for her, as she also exhibited Irish lace and was featured in directories as a milliner selling antique lace and fans. V&A A.P.320(5), renumbered V&A T.31–1959

18.16. English (Coventry). *"The Coventry Town Ribbon,"* produced by a committee of Coventry manufacturers for exhibition in 1851, from a design by Thomas Clack of the Coventry School of Design. It won a Prize Medal and the commendation of Ralph Wornum, then lecturer at the Schools of Design, who said, "no ribbon in the Exhibition can compare with the Coventry Ribbon." V&A A.P.394(1), having faded, is represented here by a later acquisition. Given by Miss H. Sanderson Stewart. V&A T.29–1947

18.17. English (Coventry). *Silk ribbon.* Exhibited in 1851 (original label on the back) by R. S. Cox & Co. (Class XIII, No. 66), which won a Prize Medal. V&A A.P.393(9), renumbered V&A T.310–1967

Raw materials in profuse variety were displayed at the South Kensington Museum in 1857 alongside items made from those materials, ranging from the commonplace to the curious. Among the many textiles was a "pair of cuffs handspun and knitted from the hair of French poodle dogs." This encyclopedic cabinet of curiosities formed a didactic display of "animal products" to "instruct and inform the visitor," leading viewers from the animal, bird, fish, or insect through all processes of manufacture (illustrated by samples at various stages with lithographs, drawings, and models), and finally to examples of the finished product.

Originally the commissioners for the 1851 Exhibition intended "to form a museum . . . to remain as a national record of the exhibition," but by 1857 they wished it to be a "growing Collection." After the presentation of this collection to the government in 1859, new acquisitions continued to be made and were recorded in the Animal Products Register with year of entry incorporated in their numbers. The collection, first at South Kensington, then at Bethnal Green, remained distinct until 1917, when the last entries were made of Animal Products.

From the start, the collection of Animal Products, designated by 1860 to the Science Division, was regarded as separate from the Art Division collections. With the renaming of the Museum in 1899 as the Victoria and Albert Museum, and the establishment of the Science Museum as a separate institution, educational displays such as Animal Products were dispersed—orangutan, crocodile, ermine, and vampire bat soon to be moved to the Natural History Museum. Many moth-eaten, faded, or disintegrating items disfigured by long display—particularly the raw materials—were discarded. However, four rare samples of a special wool developed in France to rival cashmere (cat. 18.10) were fortuitously preserved in a gift from Queen Victoria. Some eight hundred Animal Products survive, mainly textiles woven in silk and wool. Most of these are of historical importance because they were shown at the Great Exhibition of 1851 and their manufacturers can be identified (cats. 18.1–.4, 18.7–.9, 18.15–.17). A few are known products of the Schools of Design (18.8, 18.13, 18.16), making it possible to compare them with textiles acquired from the international exhibitions as examples of "ornamental art."

Lit. Simmonds, 1857; South Kensington Museum, 1857a; South Kensington Museum, Animal Products Registers, 1860s–70s; Simmonds, 1880

WENDY HEFFORD

19. English. *Printed Furnishing.* c. 1850. Block-printed cotton, 34½ x 34½" (87.5 x 87.5 cm). V&A T.10–1933

The Museum, created to improve standards of design in Britain, still holds some of the original items shown in 1852 at the Museum of Ornamental Art in Marlborough House to represent what was then considered bad design. This chintz was among the contents of a room set aside for "Examples of False Principles in Decoration." The section on "False Principles" in the Marlborough House guide detailed the faults perceived in the exhibited objects by such arbiters of taste as Henry Cole, Richard Redgrave, and Owen Jones. According to Redgrave, the decoration of chintzes in particular

> seems at present to be of the most extravagant kind. Overlooking the fact that the lightness and thinness of the material will not carry a heavy treatment, and that . . . the use of imitative floral ornament is particularly unsuitable on account of the folds, the taste is to cover the surface almost entirely with large and coarse flowers . . . which are magnified by the designer much beyond the scale of nature.

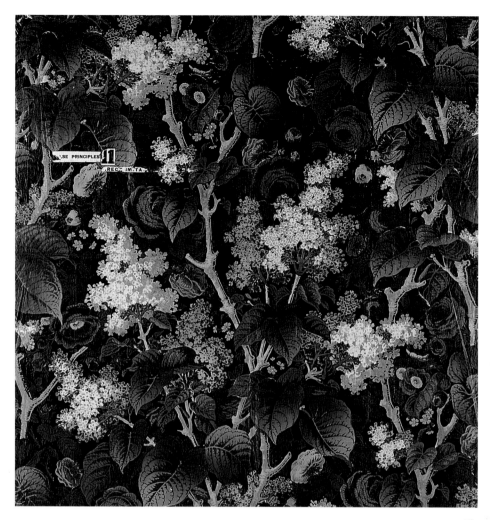

19.

This example, which retains traces of its original label (No. 11), was condemned for "Direct Imitation of Nature" involving "branches of lilac and rose trees made to bend to the forms of sofa cushions and chair arms." Further complaints read, "In No. 11, the ground, which should be light in chintzes, [is] entirely obscured by the pattern. General want of repose."

Other "false principles" decried in the catalogue included "shams"—using one medium or technique to imitate another, like the woven pattern imitating "watering" exhibited in 1851 (cat. 18.1)—and depicting on soft, flat fabrics objects that are in nature hard and three-dimensional, such as shells (cat. 18.13). These precepts were aimed particularly at the pupils of the Schools of Design. Despite the attempts of Cole and his successors to improve public taste (see cat. 21), consumers continued to favor floral chintzes, which remain popular for draperies and upholstery to this day.

Lit. Department of Practical Art, 1853; Wainwright, 1994

WENDY HEFFORD

20. Made by R. W. WINFIELD (English [Birmingham]). *Gas Jet.* c. 1848. Gilt brass and glass, 12½ x 5¼ x 5" (32 x 13.5 x 13.2 cm). Marks: stamped with a Design Registry mark for 15 February 1848 (parcel 3). V&A M20-1974

Like the floral chintz (cat. 19), this fanciful lamp by a manufacturer who exhibited in the 1851 Great Exhibition was among the objects selected for the Marlborough House display, "Examples of False Principles in Decoration." In an appendix to the display's guide, Henry Cole commented:

> There has arisen a new species of ornament of the most objectionable kind, which is desirable at once to deprecate on account of its complete departure from just taste and true principles. This may be called the *natural* or merely imitative style, and is seen in its worst development in some of the articles of form.

This gas jet was dismissed with the remark, "Gas flaming from the petal of a convolvulus!—one of a class of ornaments very popular but entirely indefensible in principle." When the display closed after only two weeks, it was expected to reopen shortly. However, the reopening never happened, and the Winfield gas jet—along with other examples of "false principles"—was consigned to storage and identified only 122 years later as an exhibit from that landmark display.

ERIC TURNER

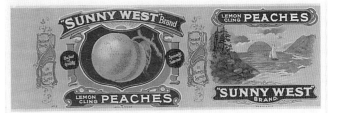

21.1.

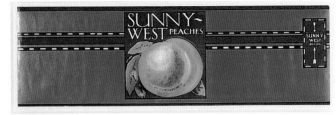

21.2.

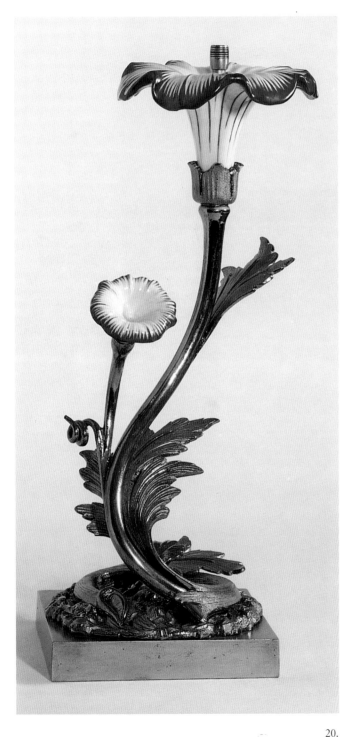

20.

21. English. *Two Labels for "Sunny West" Brand of Tinned Peaches.* Color lithographs, framed, 23 x 31⅛ x 1" (58.5 x 79 x 2.5 cm). Caption by Martin Hardie (English, 1875–1952), c. 1923. Given by Messrs. Morris & Jones Ltd., Liverpool

21.1. (upper). Designer unknown. c. 1910. V&A E.323–1923

21.2. (lower). Frederick Charles Richards (English, 1878–1932). c. 1923. V&A E.314–1923

During the early decades of the twentieth century the Museum continued to instruct its visitors to distinguish between what was considered good design and bad design, even though Henry Cole's systematic attempt in 1852 to single out bad design by exhibiting "Examples of False Principles in Decoration" was short-lived (see cats. 19–20). This framed display, with its original label written by V&A curator and watercolor specialist, Martin Hardie, dates from around 1923. The text favors the revised lower design over the one at the top, but viewers in the 1990s may have difficulty distinguishing between the merits of the two designs.

ELIZABETH A. MILLER

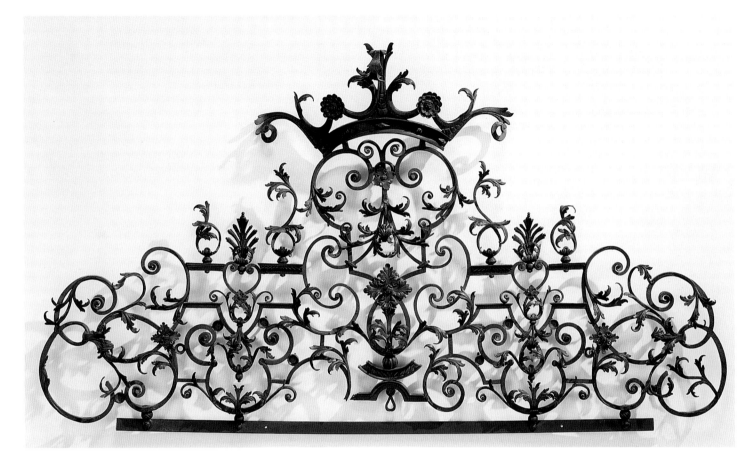

22. German. *Cresting from a Gate.* c. 1700. Wrought iron with applied embossed and engraved foliage scrolls, 30⅜ x 55⅛" (77 x 140 cm). V&A 5979–1856

The explicit educational use of the collection is documented in an engraving published in *The Illustrated London News* for 5 March 1870, showing a "Lecture to working men on ornamental ironwork at the South Kensington Museum," in which this particular cresting is one of the works illustrated (see fig. 69). The cresting formed part of a collection of ornamental ironwork that was already extensive by 1870. The lecture was one of a series of six given in 1870 by a Mr. Capes, of Balliol College, Oxford, and the lecture notes reveal the way in which the Museum's mission to improve design and manufacture was presented. The "unsatisfactory condition" of the ironworking industry is blamed on "the want of a class of highly skilled artisans ... the debasement of public taste, and still more in the substitution of the system of casting iron for the higher process of forging." This prejudice against cast iron (made by pouring molten iron into a mold), which was ideal for mass production, is reflected in the collection, which focused almost exclusively on wrought iron until the 1930s.

Crestings such as this were a common element of ironwork gates and screens and provided an opportunity for an elaborate display of the blacksmith's skill. Ironwork of this type is very rarely dated; once a piece has been removed from its context, the only means of attribution is stylistic. The scrolled foliage has a Baroque exuberance despite its delicacy, which, combined with the quality of the workmanship, make the cresting typical of the ironwork of south Germany.

Lit. Höver, 1961; Baur-Heinhold, 1977; Campbell, 1985

Pippa Shirley

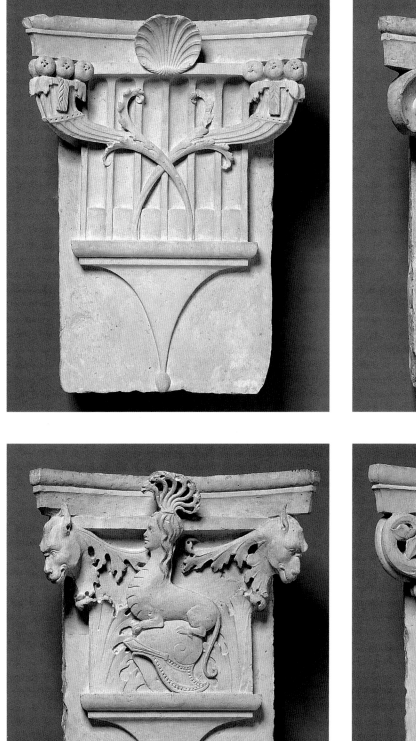
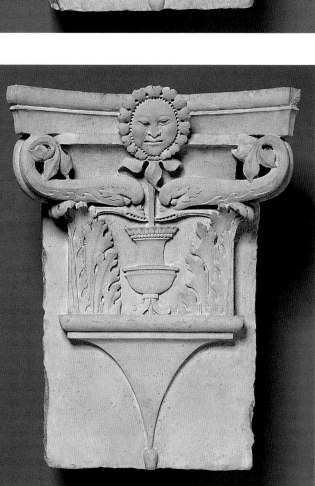

23.

23. Italian. *Four Pilaster Capitals or Brackets.* c. 1483–90. Istrian stone, each approx. 18⅛ x 14⅛ x 9"(46.5 x 36 x 23 cm). V&A 368C-, 368J-, 368O-, and 368P-1878

These crisply carved capitals were among a group of twenty-one acquired as examples of Renaissance ornament. Like the casts from Santa Maria de' Miracoli (cat. 24), they illustrate the way in which the Museum's concern to assemble a repertory of decorative motifs made ornamental, nonfigurative carving a significant element within the collection of sculpture. J. C. Robinson had always advocated "a systematic collection of medieval and renaissance sculpture" in view of its "intimate connection" with the decorative arts. This was to include "auxiliary illustrations," such as prints and photographs, and especially plaster casts. In Robinson's view, however, there was no substitute for original artworks; casts were to be selected only to fill gaps in a series. Since the opening of the Aston Webb extension in 1909, these capitals have been shown in various settings alongside some larger works of architectural sculpture.

The capitals came from the Rocca Roveresca di Mondolfo (destroyed 1864–95) near Sinigallia in the Marches, central Italy. It is thought that this stronghold was built between 1483 and 1490 and designed, at least in part, by the painter, sculptor, architect, and engineer Francesco di Giorgio Martini for Giovanni della Rovere, whose coat of arms appears on one of the capitals. The capitals were bought in London in 1878 from Robinson himself, who had "selected all the fine specimens" of architectural fragments from the Rocca and offered them to the Museum. In 1887 he presented another seventeen to the Birmingham Museum and Art Gallery.

Lit. Robinson, 1862b, pp. x–xi; Pope-Hennessy, 1964, pp. 301–8; Adams, 1993

Peta Motture

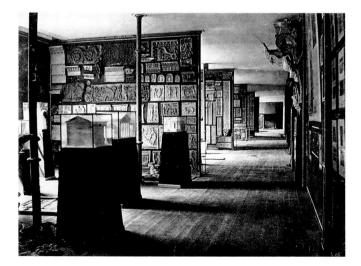

Fig. 74. Plaster casts of fragments of architectural decoration, in a view from about 1900

24. Italian. *Ornamental Panels Cast from Architectural Components of Santa Maria de' Miracoli, Venice, 15th century.* c. 1851. Plaster

24.1. Floral ornament on a pilaster from the Presbytery. Original by Tullio Lombardo, c. 1500. 34 x 8½ x 1¼" (86.5 x 21.5 x 3.5 cm). V&A 1851–16

24.2. Vase with floral ornament surmounted by an eagle from a pilaster. 34 x 8½ x 1¼" (86.5 x 21.5 x 3.5 cm). V&A 1851–465

24.3. Floral ornament with basket of fruit from a pilaster. 34 x 8½ x 1" (86.5 x 21.5 x 3.5 cm). V&A 1851–466

24.4. Floral ornament from a pilaster. 34 x 8½ x 1¼" (86.5 x 21.5 x 3.5 cm). V&A 1851–464

24.5. Scrollwork from a relief with a dolphin's head. Original by Tullio Lombardo, 15th century. 18 x 12 x 2½" (46 x 30.5 x 5.3 cm). V&A 1851–427

24.6. Floral ornament from a relief. 20½ x 12¾ x 2½" (52 x 33 x 5.3 cm). V&A 1851–470

The importance placed on the study of ornament led to the acquisition of both original pieces of architectural decoration (cat. 23) and casts such as these. All six were taken from Santa Maria de' Miracoli, an early Renaissance church in Venice. These casts were part of an extensive assemblage of 487 such fragments purchased in 1851, among the earliest casts acquired by the Museum as "a collection originally made for the use of Schools of Design under the Direction of the Board of Trade." Later in the 1850s, when the collection was moved to South Kensington, the casts were supplemented with composite photographs of other, related pilasters, and around 1900 such casts were being displayed alongside photographs showing fuller views of the buildings from which the details were taken (fig. 74). Some of the casts from Santa Maria de' Miracoli were discussed and illustrated in Ralph Nicholson Wornum's *Catalogue of Ornamental Casts in the Possession of the Department, 3rd Division, The Renaissance Styles,* published in 1854. Wornum described the facade of the church as "one of the most remarkable in Italy as a monument of the florid Cinque-cento arabesque, and is in itself an admirable exponent of the style." Much of this collection of casts was photographed in groups in 1893–94.

Examples of ornament were among the casts that the Government Schools of Design supplied to provincial art schools. The firm of Brucciani & Co., which produced many of the Museum's casts, including that of the Portico de la Gloria (cat. 25), continued to issue these until 1922 when, on the company's failure, the workshop was taken over by the Museum, which continued to issue casts until 1951 (fig. 75). Although modernist reforms to the art school curriculum meant that drawing from casts was no longer considered a necessary part

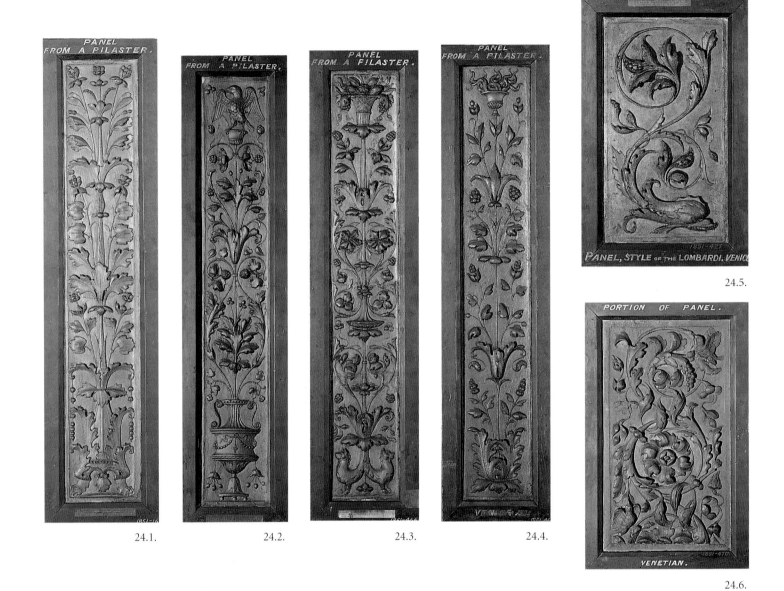

24.1.   24.2.   24.3.   24.4.

24.5.

24.6.

of an artist's training during the 1960s and 1970s, a renewed interest in the casts has developed among both artists and art historians in the past fifteen years. This shift is reflected in the refurbishment of the cast courts (see fig. 52) in the early 1980s and the active use now made of them.

DIANE BILBEY

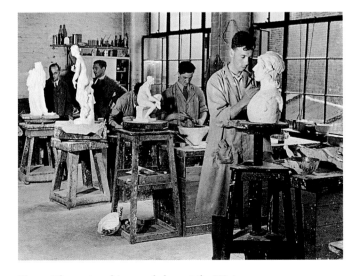

Fig. 75. The cast-making workshop at the V&A, c. 1940s

25. CHARLES THURSTON THOMPSON (English, 1816–1868). *The West Front of Santiago Cathedral.* 1866. Albumen print from wet collodion negative, 17¾ x 14½" (45.5 x 37.5 cm). Received from Cundall & Co., 1868. V&A 62.598

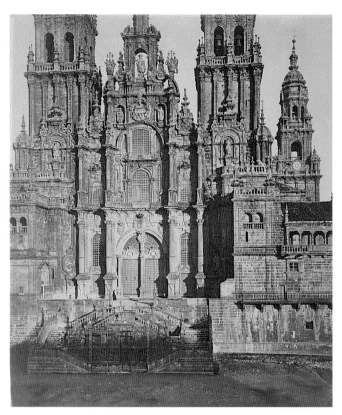

25.

Thurston Thompson, the Museum's photographer, was sent to photograph Santiago Cathedral in order to complement the immense cast of the Cathedral's late-twelfth-century west portico. At the same time as the photographs were taken, the cast was being made by Domenico Brucciani. In 1873 the cast was placed on the north wall of one of the newly erected Architectural Courts (fig. 76). In sending Thompson to Spain to take these views while commissioning the cast from Brucciani, J. C. Robinson used photographs to provide an impression of the context of the original work. Thus, two forms of reproduction were employed in the Museum to establish what was thereafter to be regarded as one of the canonical works of medieval art.

Robinson first saw the portico in 1865, describing it in a letter to Cole as "incomparably the most important monument of sculpture and ornamental detail of its epoch. . . . [I]n abstract relative importance as a work of art this is on a par with the gates of Ghiberti." In his eyes it was "one of those extraordinary and unique works, in which a great artist seems at one bound to have emancipated himself from contemporary mannerism and produced a masterpiece for all time." Following his return to South Kensington, Robinson successfully argued for Brucciani and his team to be sent to Santiago, and for Thurston Thompson to accompany him to record the form and the setting of the doorway. Robinson was exacting in his detailed instructions as to where Thompson should set up his camera, specifying precise viewpoints, such as "General view of the cathedral and its adjoining buildings from betwixt the 9th and 10th tree at the roadside."

The portico is concealed behind the later west front, and Robinson was not confident that Thurston Thompson would be able to photograph the dark interior of the building, which would require exposures of many minutes. Indeed, even this exterior view shows evidence of a long exposure, with a "ghost" figure visible to the right of the steps in the foreground—presumably a person who grew tired of waiting for the picture to be finished and walked off while the exposure was underway. Despite these difficulties, Thurston Thompson succeeded in producing an impressive sequence of views, as well as a remarkable record of other objects previously noted by Robinson in various cathedral treasuries elsewhere in Spain. In addition to complementing the cast at South Kensington, the photographs were given an independent existence as a publication by the Arundel Society in 1868. This Society, which had been established to make known major works of art, had already published Thurston Thompson's photographs of the Raphael Cartoons. Unlike the cartoons, however, the portico had been virtually

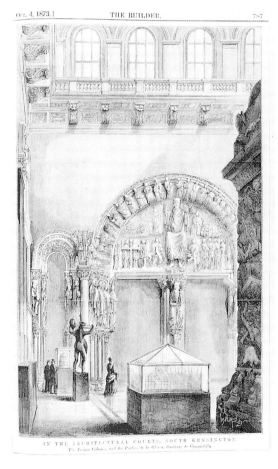

Fig. 76. Illustration from *The Builder,* 4 October 1873, showing the newly installed Santiago Cathedral cast

unknown until the 1860s and this volume, together with the cast and a book about Spanish medieval works by George Edmund Street (one of the Museum's advisors on acquisitions), secured it a prominent place within later histories of medieval art.

Lit. Arundel Society, 1868; Baker, 1988; Fontanella and Kurtz, 1996

CHRISTOPHER TITTERINGTON

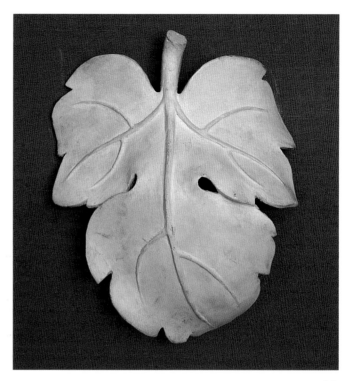

26.

26. English(?), perhaps by the firm of D. BRUCCIANI & Co. *Fig Leaf for "David"*. c. 1857. Plaster, 15½ x 11¾ x 6¾" (40 x 30 x 17 cm). Presented to Queen Victoria by the Grand Duke of Tuscany. V&A 1857–161:A

The Museum's cast collection developed through systematic acquisition as well as by less conventional means. The acquisition of the cast of Michelangelo's *David* is an example of the latter (fig. 77). From the marble original by Michelangelo (1475–1564) in the Accademia di Belle Arti, Florence, the cast—eighteen feet in height—was delivered to South Kensington in February 1857 and was installed in the newly completed "Brompton Boilers," the first permanent buildings on the South Kensington site. Henry Cole noted in his diary on 21 February 1857 that at 4:30 that afternoon the legs of *David* were erected "not without jeopardy" in the Educational Museum housed in the Brompton Boilers (see fig. 22). The enormous cast was thus placed in the center of the Art Museum and appears with its fig leaf in place in a photograph of 1859 (see fig. 23) amid both originals and reproductions of major European art. It was subsequently moved to the Architectural Courts, where in 1920 (see fig. 18) it was shown in front of the electrotype copy of Ghiberti's *Gates of Paradise*, while the cast of the *Bruges Madonna* (cat. 27) was displayed to the side of the Pisano pulpit. In this way some of the key canonical works in the history of Italian Renaissance art could be viewed together.

Inappropriate as it may seem, the cast of *David* was presented to Queen Victoria by the grand duke of Tuscany as a peace offering after he had vetoed the export of a painting by Ghirlandaio, which the National Gallery had sought to acquire. The queen received no advance notification of the gift, and the cast was immediately directed to the Foreign Office and then on to South Kensington. In 1857 the *Art Journal* commented on the arrival of the *David* cast: "The original does not appear to have added to the great master's reputation in his own country, nor will the cast of it in this." That a sketch in wax was also in the Museum's collection suggested "that any deficiencies that may exist in the statue do not arise from want of study." The "sketch" referred to is the wax model bought by the Museum from the Gherardini collection in 1854; although ascribed to Michelangelo at the time of its acquisition, and then thought to

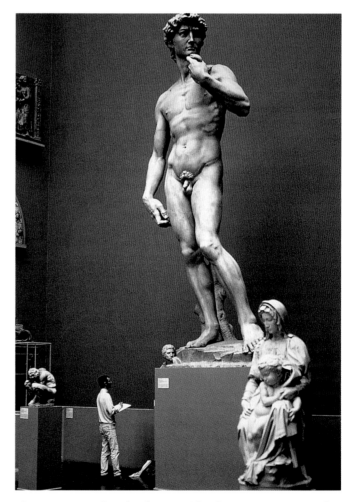

Fig. 77. An art student sketching *David* in the east Cast Court, with the *Bruges Madonna* (cat. 27) in the right foreground, c. 1995

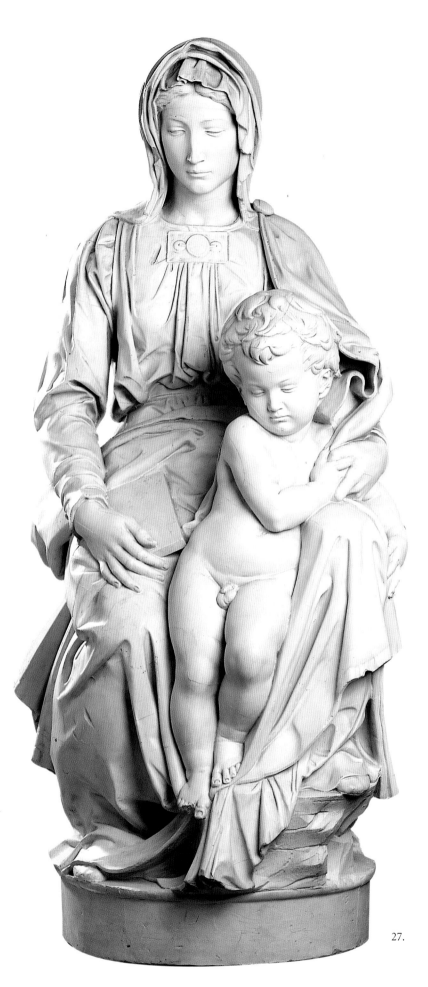

27.

be a preparatory study for *David*, it has since been removed from the sculptor's oeuvre.

According to anecdotal information, on her first encounter with the cast of *David*, Queen Victoria was so shocked by his nudity that a firm suggestion was made that something should be done. Consequently, the correctly proportioned fig leaf was created and stored in readiness for any visit Queen Victoria might make to the Museum, for which occasions it was hung on the figure from two strategically implanted hooks. The fig leaf may have been provided by the plaster casting workshop of D. Brucciani & Co., which had obtained a mold for *David* in the same year as the Museum acquired its cast. Among the many items subsequently available for purchase from Brucciani's gallery was a large fig leaf.

The queen was not alone in her objection to the nudity of *David*. In 1903 a Mr. Dobson protested to the Museum about the nude male statuary displayed: "One can hardly designate these figures as 'art'!; if it is, it is a very objectionable form of art." Tin fig leaves had been used in the early years of the Museum on other nude statuary but, along with the British Museum, the authorities at South Kensington dismissed later objections, noting that "The antique casts gallery has been very much used by private lady teachers for the instruction of young girl students and none of them have ever complained even indirectly." The fig leaf is currently displayed in a case attached to the back of the pedestal for *David* in the east Cast Court and was last used in the time of Queen Mary (1867–1953).

DIANE BILBEY

27. Belgian(?). *Cast of Michelangelo's Madonna and Child (Bruges Madonna)*. Probably late 1871. Painted plaster, approx. 50⅜ x 25¼ x 24¾" (128 x 64 x 63 cm) overall, irreg. V&A 1872–62

This plaster cast after Michelangelo's marble original, 1504–06, in the Church of Notre-Dame, Bruges, Belgium, was acquired from the Belgian government in 1872 through the international exchange scheme initiated by Henry Cole. The agreement—for the "promotion of art"—facilitated exchange between museums across Europe of reproductions of objects in their respective countries. The document concluding this agreement, the International Convention, was signed by the fifteen crowned princes of Europe in 1867 at the Paris exhibition. With the aid of this agreement, the South Kensington Museum was able to amass a collection of casts unrivaled in its international scope and diversity.

In 1863, in his capacity as "Art Referee" (advisor on acquisitions), J. C. Robinson visited Bruges. In his report to Cole, he enthused over the *Madonna and Child* he saw at Notre-Dame

and urged that a cast be made. While not disregarding the question of the "genuineness" of the group as the work of Michelangelo, Robinson nonetheless went on to describe it as "one of the most highly finished, complete and most beautiful works of the great master," concluding, "the great merit of the work and its importance in the history of art, would I think fully justify the outlay attending its reproduction." The cast was not acquired by the Museum until 1872, however, when procedures for acquiring reproductions had been formalized by the International Convention. In its year of acquisition, the cast was lent to the international exhibition held in London, where it was displayed in a gallery devoted to art reproductions. In the exhibition catalogue and in the original Museum register entry, the cast is recorded as being from an original "attributed" to Michelangelo, illustrating once again the shift in thinking as to the authorship of the group.

The cast of the *Bruges Madonna* is today displayed alongside other casts of sculpture by Michelangelo in the east Cast Court, devoted entirely to reproductions of Italian works of art. It is probable that the surface of this cast was left unfinished—showing the casting seams—to illustrate the complex network of piece molds required to make such a reproduction.

DIANE BILBEY

28. Made by ELKINGTON AND CO. (English [Birmingham]). *Electrotype Copies of Two Rosenborg Castle Lions*. c. 1885. Electroplated copper, silvered, V&A 1885–194: 38⅝ x 66⅞ x 25¼" (98 x 170 x 64 cm), V&A 1885–194A: 38⅝ x 65 x 23⅝" (98 x 165 x 60 cm). V&A 1885–194&A

Electrotype copies of metalwork, particularly goldsmiths' work, formed an important part of the Museum's growing collection of reproductions, complementing the plaster casts and photographs of original works. From the 1840s the Elkington firm dominated the English trade in electrotyping—an electrical equivalent of casting—and many of the Museum's electrotypes, including the two life-size lions, were produced by Elkington in the 1870s and 1880s. The firm was particularly successful with large-scale electrotypes, which are technically very difficult to make. Electrotypes—also called Galvanoplastic copies, named for Luigi Galvani (Italian, 1737-1798), whose early experiments stimulated research on electricity—are closely related to electroplating. A mold (initially usually of wax, but later of metal) is taken from the object to be reproduced; copper is deposited on the mold in a plating vat; the mold is then removed, revealing a reproduction in copper of the original work. Ordinarily, the copper reproduction would be gilded or silvered (as with the lions) to imitate the

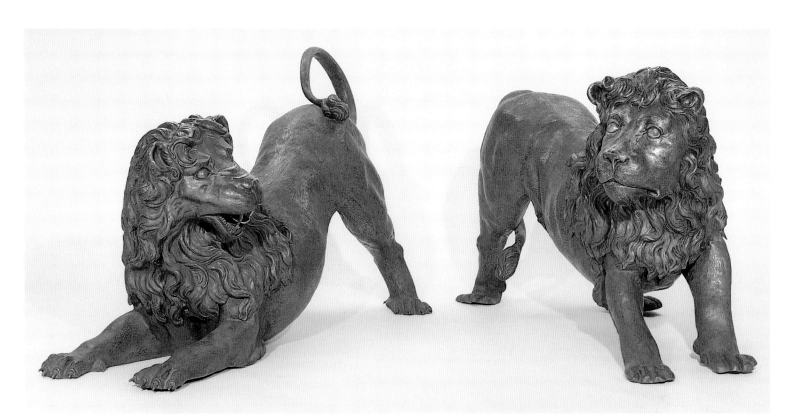

28.

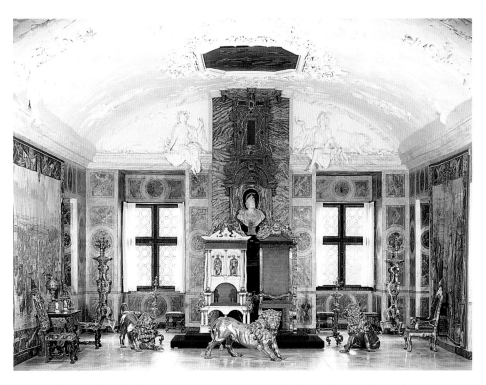

Fig. 78. The royal Danish throne room at Rosenborg Castle, Copenhagen, with its three seventeenth-century silver lions that symbolically protect the sovereignty

material of the original. (The age-tarnished lions were photographed before they were cleaned back to silver.)

These enchanting animal figures reproduce two of the three silver lions—one seated, one standing, and one crouching—made in 1665–70 by the Copenhagen silversmith Ferdinand Kyblich to "protect" the royal Danish thrones at Rosenborg Castle (fig. 78). The lions symbolize the Great Belt, the Little Belt, and the Sound, the three territorial boundaries that then demarcated Scandinavian sovereignty.

ANTHONY R. E. NORTH

29. OCTAVIUS HUDSON (English, died c. 1873?). *Saint Luke.* 1844. Watercolor, 29½ x 21" (75 x 54 cm). V&A 4164.8

This watercolor is a traced copy from an early fourteenth-century stained-glass window at St. Mary's Church, Hitcham, Buckinghamshire. Although acquired in 1873—together with 212 other drawings of stained glass—it was made three decades earlier by Octavius Hudson when he was a teacher at the Government Schools of Design. When these drawings were purchased by the Museum for the comparatively large sum of

£55—an amount then equivalent to a working man's annual wage—they were highly valued as reproductions of medieval glass, being described then as a "series of the highest interest to the students of glass painting" and "an important collection . . . most accurate and artistic." This group was the first major acquisition of copies of English stained glass, and joined the thousands of drawings in the Art Library recording architecture and the applied arts.

Hudson's carefully drawn copies were made at the same moment as the secrets of medieval glassmaking were being rediscovered, leading to the great stained-glass revival of the second half of the century. By the 1870s designers of stained glass would have found such records especially useful in making windows for churches both old and new, and according to Museum records, even in 1908 the Hudson drawings were "still in constant use and . . . highly appreciated." The chancel windows at the Hitcham church were in a "ruinous and jumbled state" in 1906 but were repaired and restored shortly afterward.

Lit. Department of Science and Art, 1873; Strange, 1908, p. 262; Powell, 1915

MICHAEL SNODIN

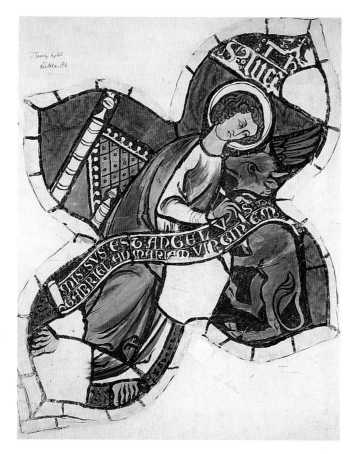

29.

30. *Group of Western and Southeastern European Candlesticks.* Except as noted, candlesticks are brass; height is the only dimension cited.

30.1.   English. c. 1520. 7⅛" (18 cm). V&A M.55–1967

30.2.   Italian (Venice). c. 1600. 7¾" (19.5 cm). V&A M.2&A–1953 (a pair)

30.3.   Danish. c. 1650. 9⅝" (24.5 cm). V&A M.305–1912

30.4.   Dutch. c. 1650. 7⅛" (18.2 cm). V&A 673–1904

30.5.   English. c. 1650. 6" (15 cm). V&A M.389–1906

30.6.   German (Augsburg). c. 1650. 6⅞" (17.5 cm). V&A 2074–1855

30.7.   Danish. c. 1680. 7⅝" (19.5 cm). V&A M.1048–1926

30.8.   Dutch. c. 1680. 17⅛" (43.5 cm). V&A M.73–1913

30.9.   English. c. 1680. 4¾" (12 cm). V&A M.218–1939

30.10. Flemish. 16th century. 13¾" (35 cm). V&A M.117A–1919

30.11. Turkish. 16th century. Bronze, 8" (20.3 cm). V&A 931–1884

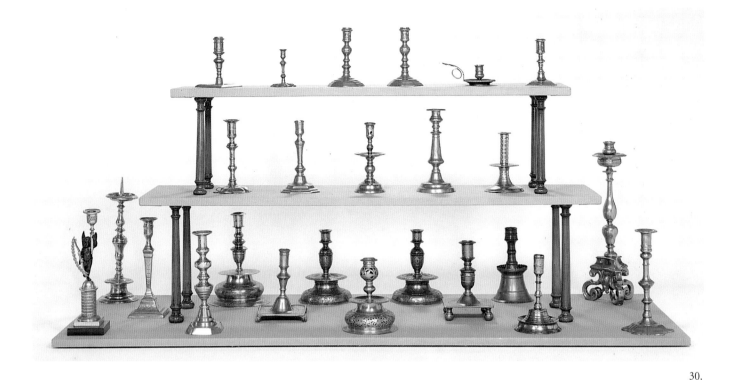

30.

30.12. French. c. 1700. 2⅜" (6 cm). V&A 2177A–1855

30.13. Italian. c. 1700. 5¼" (13.4 cm). V&A M.1099–1926

30.14. Spanish. c. 1700. 6⅞" (17.5 cm). V&A M.313–1923

30.15. Dutch. c. 1730. 6⅛" (15.5 cm). V&A M.176&A–1939 (a pair)

30.16. French. c. 1740. 7¼" (18.5 cm). V&A M.203A–1939

30.17. English. c. 1750. 7½" (19 cm). V&A M.398–1917

30.18. English (Birmingham). c. 1750. 9⅞" (25 cm). V&A M.119–1919

30.19. English. Taper stick. c. 1760. 4" (10 cm). V&A M.144–1939

30.20. English. c. 1780. 10" (25.5 cm). V&A M.455A–1926

30.21. English. c. 1800. 9⅝" (24.5 cm). V&A M.392–1917

30.22. English. c. 1800. 8½" (21.6 cm). V&A M.396–1917

30.23. Austrian. c. 1825. 12" (30.5 cm). V&A M.238A–1912

A number of the large individual private collections bequeathed to the Museum—notably those assembled by John Jones and George Salting—contained many related objects that were already understood as series through which it was possible to trace the development of a particular type of artifact or style. Although the seemingly comprehensive nature of such collec-

tions was of course illusory, the Museum's holdings of vast numbers of like materials nonetheless made it possible to display row after row of similar objects, thus representing visual typologies. These typological displays, which were much indebted to anthropological models of the era, are exemplified by this series of brass candlesticks. Such massed groups of objects that, taken individually, have never been regarded as "masterpieces," form an important facet of the Museum's collections and are still a significant part of its displays (fig. 79).

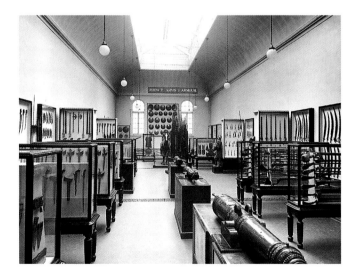

Fig. 79. Part of the Arms and Armour collection as seen at the India Museum, 1936, in a typological display characteristic of many of the V&A's presentations up to the present day

These candlesticks represent but a small fraction of what is one of the most comprehensive collections in existence. They range in style from plain medieval forms found in excavations to finely engraved Venetian candlesticks of the sixteenth century, and present a history of the domestic candlestick from the twelfth to the nineteenth century.

Much of the interest in ordinary domestic brass and copper wares was stimulated by the English Arts and Crafts movement around 1900, and the emergence of candlesticks as a category of collectors' item, with a growing literature, is really a twentieth-century phenomenon, developing after the candlestick was no longer an essential domestic object. The Museum, however, had already begun collecting in this field as early as 1855.

ANTHONY R. E. NORTH

31. French. Various engravers, after JEAN BERAIN I (French, 1640–1711). *Ornemens Inventéz par Jean Berain.* c. 1700–13. Book with pages of etching and engraving, in a binding of gilt-tooled, marbled calf, probably from the Low Countries, 21¼ x 15⅜ x 2⅜" (54 x 39 x 6 cm). V&A E.4123–4259–1906. [Illustrated: page 29]

With each page carrying a red stamp stating that it belonged to the School of Design, Somerset House, this volume of 137 prints after designs by Jean Berain I is characteristic of the sets of ornament prints that would have been considered useful for students. Such a volume would have been among the "large and richly illustrated works of architectural and various other kinds of ornament, published in France, Germany and Italy" that made up the School's reference library as described in 1845. Its condition suggests that it was much used.

Son of a gunsmith, Berain published in 1659 a suite of designs for the decoration of guns and, in 1663, a suite of ironwork. Employed in 1670 to engrave plates depicting the decorations of the Galerie d'Apollon at the Louvre—a project conceived to promulgate the achievements of Louis XIV—Berain went on to further official success and an appointment as royal garden designer in 1677. Ultimately, he designed textiles, metalwork, furniture, carriages (one, in 1696, for the King of Sweden), ship decoration, and palace interiors. Berain's grotesque ornament designs are especially admired for their fantasy and inventive compositions of varied decorative motifs, much influenced by his experience designing decorations and costumes for royal entertainments, including ballet and opera. His highly successful tapestries of *Grotesques,* designed before 1689, were still in production in 1725.

When the Museum of Ornamental Art was established at Marlborough House in 1852, the volume was stamped again with the name of the Department of Practical Art and made available

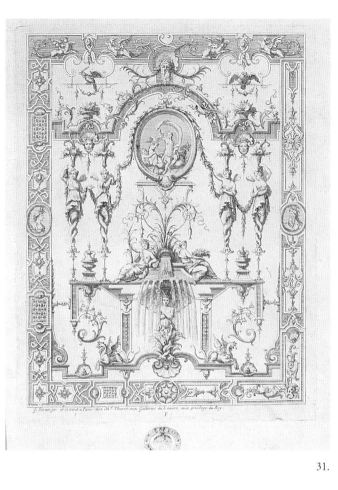

31.

to a wider public as well as to students. This continued to be the case when the volume became part of the Museum's library at South Kensington. Following the Museum's reorganization of 1909 and the creation of the Department of Engraving, Illustration and Design, prints and drawings formerly held by the Library became a distinct curatorial preserve. This book, though still accessible to design students, then became part of a vast archive of ornament prints, which is highly valued as a resource for historians of art and design.

Lit. Government Schools of Design, 1845; Jervis, 1984; White, 1994

ELIZABETH A. MILLER/BRENDA RICHARDSON

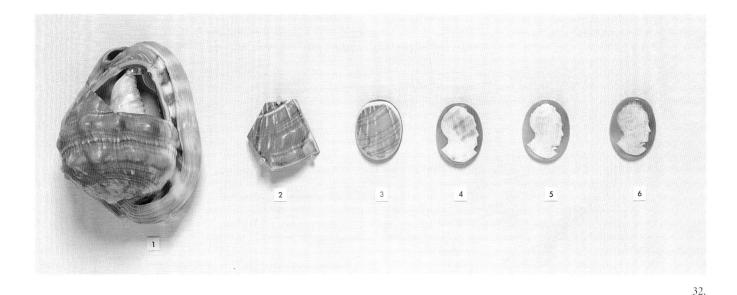

32. JAMES RONCA (English, 1826–after 1908). *Mounted Display Showing the Process of Cutting a Shell Cameo.* Second half of the 19th century. Bull's Mouth shell (*Cassis rufa*), framed, 8⅜ x 19½ x 5⅛" (21.3 x 49.5 x 13 cm). Given by James Ronca. V&A 1386a–to 1386e–1874

An interest in both materials and processes of manufacture motivated many of the Museum's early acquisitions, as with the purchases made from international exhibitions (cats. 2–13). Although the degree of this concern with materials and techniques has varied, it has always been reflected in the collection of models (cats. 16, 87, 136–137), textile designs (cats. 139, 186.1, 190.1), and works that illustrate printing processes (cats. 36–39). This irresistible demonstration of craftsmanship was given in 1874 by the artist James Ronca, a carver of cameos in hard stones and shell, who had for thirty years produced the cameo portraits of Queen Victoria and Prince Albert that were mounted in the Royal Victorian Order, the queen's personal award.

This six-step series was made to illustrate the preparation of a shell-cameo portrait from its earliest state—the shell itself, with a section for the cameo removed—to the finished portrait of Sir John Everett Millais, the Pre-Raphaelite painter. Intermediate stages demonstrate how the carver cut a rough blank and sketched on the shell a pencil outline of the portrait. Outer layers of the shell were then partially stripped away and the profile cleared right down to the ground (the bottom or inside layer of the shell). In the final state, fine details such as hair are silhouetted against the dark polished ground, while portions of the upper layers are retained to give color and relief to the head. As well as being clearly instructive, the series is a virtuoso example of nineteenth-century shell-cameo carving and shows how the more experienced carvers in the medium could produce work of a quality rivaling that of the more costly and prestigious hard-stone cameos.

At the time of its acquisition, the series was sent to Bethnal Green where it was quickly consigned to storage. Rediscovered only in 1991, it was displayed at the V&A in the Sculpture Department's Materials and Techniques galleries. In its new position next to the collection of carved gems and shell cameos the series is accompanied by a panel explaining the cameo-carving process, with an illustration of a nineteenth-century shell cameo–cutter's workbench. The label also quotes a passage from an interview of 1908 with Ronca in which he describes his work and the different processes involved in cutting hard-stone and shell cameos.

Lit. Thompson, 1898; *Evening News*, 1908; Bury, 1991, vol. 1, p. 218

LUCY CULLEN

33. JULIA MARGARET CAMERON (Scottish, born India [of Scottish parents], 1815–1879 [English resident 1848–75]). *Saint Agnes.* 1864. Gold-toned albumen print from wet collodion-on-glass negative, 15⅜ x 11⅝" (39 x 29.5 cm). V&A 44.771

The Museum's purchase of this photograph from Mrs. Cameron herself in 1864 is indicative of Henry Cole's interest in this new medium and its potential usefulness in furthering the institution's didactic aims. The South Kensington Museum was highly responsive to new imaging technologies and indeed actively collected examples of various printing methods, including the nature-printing process by which images could be obtained

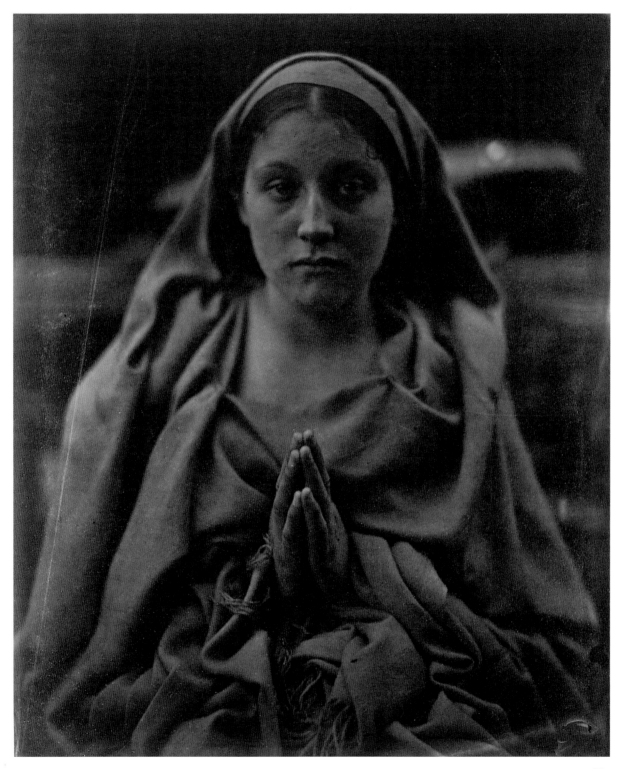

33.

directly from objects by contact printing. Like this process, photography also seemed to offer direct and unmediated imagery and was thus seen as an invaluable tool in communicating visual information about the collections. Cole in 1856 founded the Museum's collection of photographs when he purchased a large group of pictures from the exhibition of the Photographic Society of London in the same year. If Cole was quick to recognize the aesthetic potential of photography, he was also swift to set up a darkroom for official museum use under the guidance of Charles Thurston Thompson (see cat. 25). Photographs of the Museum's collections, produced by the official staff photographers, were circulated to provincial art colleges and offered for sale to the public.

Photographs by Cameron were acquired at a time when the institution's concern with the medium was already well established. According to the Museum's registers, four Cameron photographs were presented by Cole in June 1865 to the Museum's chief designer, Godfrey Sykes, who was at that time busy with the columns that still decorate the south-facing garden facade and the loggias of the Henry Cole Wing, where the Photography Collection is now housed. Could it be that Sykes's idyllic, Italianate women and children in terra cotta owe something to Cameron's photographs? Certainly Cameron saw her photographs, at least at that early stage in her career, as offering inspiration to artists: a note printed in the catalogue to her 1865 Colnaghi Gallery, London, exhibition stated that her photographs were available to artists at half price.

Cameron's ambitious and adventurous approach is vividly evident in her evocation of Saint Agnes (as portrayed by Cameron's maidservant, Mary Hillier), who is represented in prayer, dedicating herself to the "Heavenly Bridegroom." The inspiration was "St. Agnes Eve," a poem by Cameron's friend, Alfred, Lord Tennyson. The model appears in a "day-for-night" setting with a painted moon.

The Museum's acquisition of Cameron's photographs in 1865 was presumably instigated by Cole himself, whose diary records that he visited Mrs. Cameron to be "photographed in her style" on 19 May 1865. This is one of twenty Cameron photographs bought by the Museum on 17 June 1865. Others were acquired by purchase and gift in the same year, including duplicate and triplicate sets for the Museum's national touring program. A selection was shown in the Museum's main galleries that autumn. Cameron also used the Museum's photographic facilities for portraiture in the 1870s. She gave many of her greatest portraits to Sir Henry Cole, and they were presented to the Museum by his son, Alan S. Cole, in 1913.

Lit. Haworth-Booth, 1994a

MARK HAWORTH-BOOTH

34. CAMILLE SILVY (French, 1834–1910). *River Scene.* 1858. Gold-toned albumen print from two wet collodion-on-glass negatives, 12 x 16½" (30.5 x 42 cm). Bequeathed by the Rev. Chauncy Hare Townshend, 1868. V&A 68.012

A technical triumph and one of the most celebrated nineteenth-century photographs, this print of Silvy's *River Scene* was bequeathed to the Museum in 1868 by the Reverend C. H. Townshend along with a collection of paintings, prints and drawings, gems, intaglios, and fine books. Townshend's bequest at a date when photography was not yet routinely collected by museums may point to the awareness among contemporary connoisseurs of photography of the V&A's early interest in this still relatively new medium. The history of Silvy's photograph also exemplifies how the medium was viewed in the 1850s. It was first shown at the annual exhibition of the Photographic Society of Scotland in December 1858, having been sent by the London photographic suppliers and dealers in fine photographs, Murray & Heath. Although it was one of more than a thousand exhibits, Silvy's landscape was frequently commended in the large press coverage of the exhibition. *The Edinburgh Evening Courant* commented on 21 December 1858:

> We cannot pass this picture of a new artist without notice. The water, the foliage, the figures, the distance, the sky are all perfect. But above all, what some perfect photographs want, they are all beautiful. It is the most exquisite landscape we have seen in photography.

Another critic in the *Daily Scotsman* had written more cautiously three days earlier:

> If this photograph is untouched, and taken from nature, it is a triumph of the art, and equal to any picture by Van der Neer [the Dutch seventeenth-century landscape painter Aert van der Neer] or other famous delineator of similar scenery.

Silvy's landscape met with further acclaim in London and Paris in 1859: it appeared, as *Vallée de l'Huisne,* in the first ever Salon treating photography as a fine art, held in Paris in the spring of 1859. Silvy moved to England in the summer of 1859 to open London's first *carte de visite* studio.

Because of the extreme sensitivity of wet collodion-on-glass negatives to the blue parts of the spectrum, it was almost impossible to record cloud detail and the relatively darker landscape beneath on one plate; Silvy, in fact, used separate negatives for the upper and lower parts of the composition, carefully printing them—consecutively—on the same sheet of paper. He worked with fine brushes and inks, too, in order to deceive the eye into reading the image as a seamless whole. He had, of course, positioned the people in the scene exactly as he wanted them—and is known to have drawn compositions in

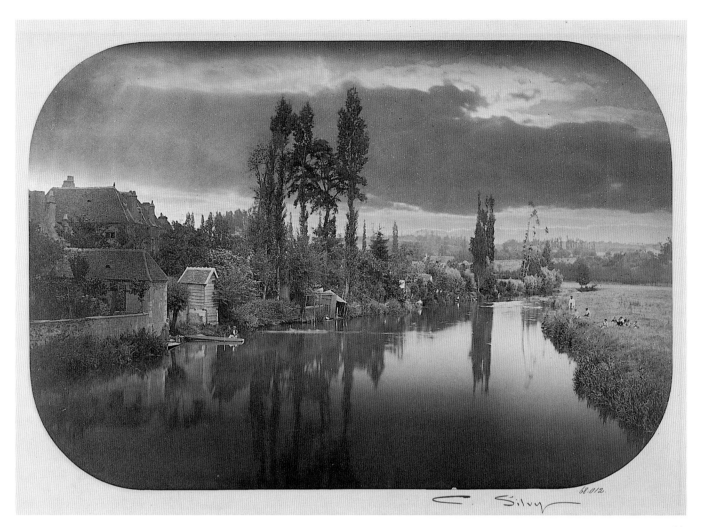

34.

advance for some of his photographs. So cumbersome was the technique of photography in this period—requiring a portable darkroom in which large glass plates were sensitized on the spot and exposed, still moist, in the camera—that choice of subject was highly deliberate.

One of four known examples, this print was purchased (perhaps from Murray & Heath) by Townshend, who owned other remarkable photographs—notably seascapes and forest scenes by Silvy's contemporary Gustave Le Gray—and contemporary paintings by Théodore Rousseau and others. He kept photographs in presses with his other fine prints, and the South Kensington officials who went through his collection after his death marked them for inclusion in the material to be accepted by the Museum.

Lit. Haworth-Booth, 1992

MARK HAWORTH-BOOTH

35. FRANCIS FRITH (English, 1822–1898). *The Great Pyramid, and the Great Sphinx.* 1858. Albumen print from wet collodion negative, 20⅝ x 28⅜" (52.5 x 72 cm). V&A Ph.18–1983

Francis Frith made three journeys to Egypt and Palestine in the late 1850s. Under what must have been extraordinarily strenuous and testing conditions he produced a magnificent series of mammoth-plate negatives by the wet collodion process. Because the plates had to be coated with light-sensitive emulsions immediately before exposure, the process required the transport of many large sheets of glass, water, and dangerous chemicals, as well as a mobile darkroom (which may be the tent visible in the center middle ground of this picture). The resulting book, *Egypt, Sinai, and Jerusalem: Twenty Photographic Views* (1860), with texts by Mr. and Mrs. Reginald Stuart Poole, featured the largest photographs then published in book form. Frith's work is universally admired not only for its exceptional formal and technical achievement but also for its landmark status as eloquent documentation of non-Western cultures and monuments known firsthand to few outsiders.

This photograph was acquired in 1983, some eight years after the Photography Collection was established as a distinct section within the Department of Prints, Drawings and Paintings. Purchased primarily on account of its qualities as a photograph, Frith's significance within the history of photography, and the work's interest as an example of photographic technique, this spectacular image also complements the many images that the Museum purchased, commissioned, and produced at the time Frith took this photograph.

Lit. Naef, 1973; Perez, 1980; van Haften, 1980

CHRISTOPHER TITTERINGTON

36.
VALENTINE GREEN (English, 1739–1813), after
JOSEPH WRIGHT OF DERBY (English, 1734–1797).
A Philosopher Shewing an Experiment on an Air Pump.
1769. Mezzotint (first state), 20⅛ x 24⅜" (51 x 62 cm).
V&A 29445.1

The painter Joseph Wright of Derby established a prestigious reputation for his "candlelight pictures," in which tenebrous effects heightened the drama of portraits and narrative subjects. These effects could be achieved vividly in the medium of mezzotint, a tone engraving process in which the artist works from dark to light. Mezzotint, which had already been used successfully by the Irish engraver Thomas Frye, offers unusual capacity for strong chiaroscuro and deep velvety blacks. After it was introduced into English professional printmaking by Dutch immigrants, mezzotint flourished in England more than

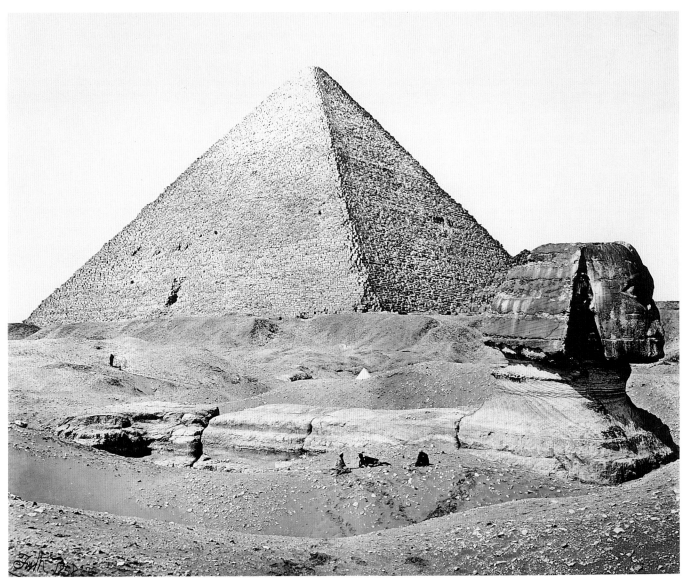

35.

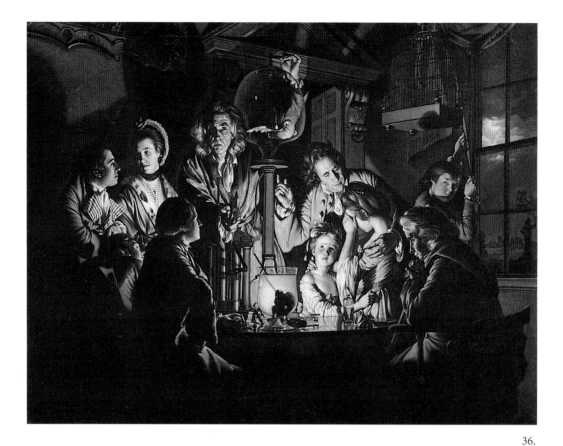

36.

in any other country (indeed, the French call mezzotint "la manière anglaise").

Experiment with the Air Pump, 1768 (National Gallery, London), is perhaps Wright's greatest achievement, a large and complex narrative that addresses the contemporary interest in science while subtly raising issues of ethics and mortality. Recent interpretations—noting the "carious human skull" in the glass jar on the table—suggest that *The Air Pump* is a *vanitas* picture, a reminder that "death is inevitable and its moment unpredictable." Masked as an illustration of the advance of scientific knowledge, the subject is macabre. The air pump was invented in Germany in 1650; by the mid-eighteenth century, the air pump was a common "prop" in science lectures as well as a type of luxury object that would have been in many eighteenth-century homes. A bladder, or less often, a living animal such as a bird or mouse, is placed in the glass container attached to a pumping apparatus. Air is pumped out to demonstrate the animal's reaction (unconsciousness, then death); if the experimenter readmits air in time, the animal is revived. Wright took artistic license in painting a rare white cockatoo as the experiment's subject; in reality, common species like sparrows would have been used. (Wright had previously painted this cockatoo, and knew the dramatic effect its white plumage would make in the shadows.) The experiment is depicted at its most crucial moment: the bird, deprived of air, has fallen to the bottom of the glass receiver; the lecturer can turn the stopcock in time to save the bird, or not.

Wright purposefully exploited prints to create a record of his most important paintings and to make certain that his work was known internationally, which was made possible by the wide dissemination of relatively inexpensive prints (even as mezzotints were generally more costly than other types of prints). *Experiment with the Air Pump* was exhibited in 1768 at the Society of Artists; within a year, Valentine Green's engraved copy, titled *A Philosopher Shewing an Experiment on an Air Pump*, was completed (it is thought that Wright gave Green permission to draw from the original painting at the house of its owner). The print too was then exhibited at the Society of Artists, in 1769, and to great acclaim.

This extraordinary mezzotint was acquired by the Museum in 1883, along with four other mezzotints after works by Wright. A 1903 exhibition at the V&A of British engraving and etching included Green's *Air Pump* as well as plates and tools showing how mezzotints are made. These demonstration pieces became the basis for a permanent display about printmaking techniques and, though subject to many revisions over the years, the educational display remains on view in a dedicated gallery in the Museum.

Lit. V&A, 1903, p. 40; Egerton, 1990, and Clayton, 1990 (in Egerton), cats. 21 and 153, pp. 25–8, 58–61, 235; Solkin, 1992

BRENDA RICHARDSON

37. WILLIAM HOGARTH (English, 1697–1746). *Cruelty in Perfection*, Plate 3 (of 4) from *The Four Stages of Cruelty*. 1751. Etching and engraving, 15⅛ x 12⅜" (38.5 x 31.5 cm). Bequeathed by John Forster, 1876. V&A F.118(90)

The Four Stages of Cruelty is a series of four images described by scholar Ronald Paulson as being "Hogarth's most shocking, most purely expressive prints ... clearly intended both to horrify ... his usual customers and to appeal to a lower, more general audience." Hogarth is much admired as a major history and portrait painter, even as he is most widely known for the sharp satire of the morality tales he narrated through such engraved series as *The Rake's Progress* and *Marriage à la Mode*. Acknowledged as an unusually astute observer of the English national character, Hogarth tailored the medium of his expression to the socioeconomic class he targeted. *The Four Stages of*

Cruelty, according to the artist, was designed "in hopes of preventing in some degree that cruel treatment of poor Animals. . . ." For this purpose, Hogarth reported that the prints needed "neither great correctness of drawing or fine Engraving," which would have "set the price of them out of . . . the reach of those for whome they were cheifly intended." Accordingly, the set of four images was engraved, with some impressions printed on lighter-weight, less expensive paper (and sold more cheaply than those on heavier paper); the last two of the four images were also cut in wood (though the technique proved too expensive to complete the other two images in the series).

The Four Stages of Cruelty tells the story of "Tom Nero," a barbarous character whose inhuman behavior escalates from the killing of small animals (Plate 1, *First Stage of Cruelty*) to his sadistic beating of a disabled dray horse (Plate 2, *Second Stage of Cruelty*) to *Cruelty in Perfection* (Plate 3), in which Tom Nero has murdered his pregnant lover ("Ann Gill") for the valuables

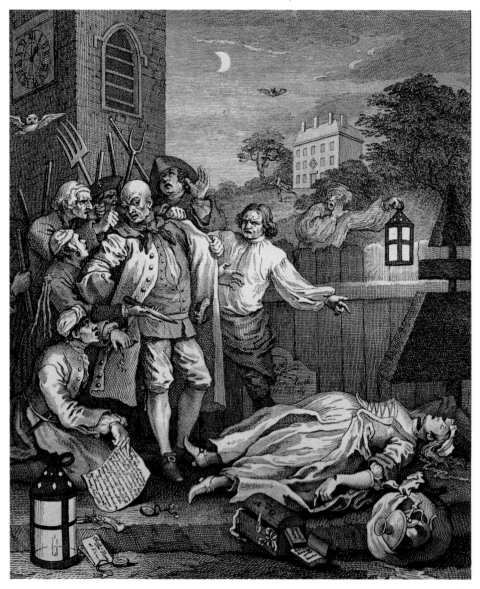

37.

he had cajoled her into stealing from her employer. This graphic horror is but a preamble to the final Plate 4 (*The Reward of Cruelty*), in which the murderer Tom Nero is disemboweled before onlookers in a shockingly grisly scene. In eighteenth-century London, Paulson writes, "cruelty was much more than a source of criminal behavior; it was a way of life. . . . Dissections of malefactors following execution were also often public and were included as part of the sentence imposed on the prisoner."

Hogarth's "popular" prints—including *The Four Stages of Cruelty*—were morality tales for rich and poor alike, for the "respectable" upper classes as for the alleged criminal element trapped in poverty. In each of the four plates, Nero is the center of a scene of communal cruelty; he is surrounded by fellow citizens committing various acts of torture, though only Nero's behavior is noted and condemned as criminal.

Cruelty in Perfection is from a collection of 217 works by, or relating to, Hogarth, all of which came to the Museum as part of the 1876 bequest of John Forster that also included manuscripts by Charles Dickens (cat. 155) and the Leonardo da Vinci notebooks (cat. 62).

Lit. South Kensington Museum, 1893, p. 14; Paulson, 1965; Paulson, 1971

BRENDA RICHARDSON

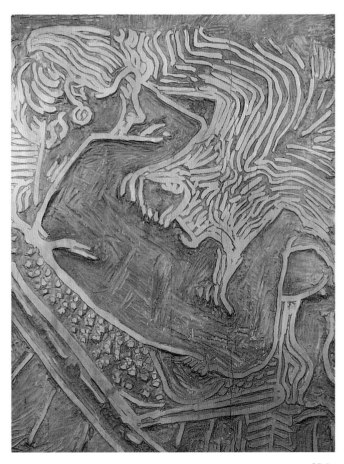

38.1.

38. HENRI MATISSE (French [Paris], 1869–1954). *The Large Woodcut (Le Grand Bois).* 1906

38.1.   Woodblock, with residue of blue and white paint, 19½ x 15¾" (49.5 x 40 cm), irreg. Purchased with the assistance of the National Art Collections Fund. V&A E.409-1975

38.2.   Woodcut on Van Gelder wove paper (numbered 10 from an edition of 50), 22⅝ x 18⅛" (57.6 x 46 cm). Purchased with the assistance of the Lumley Cazelet Gallery in Memory of Frank Perls. V&A E.276-1994

In 1905–06 Henri Matisse did a group of woodcuts and lithographs of a nude model in a deck chair. The woodcuts can be securely dated because they were shown in Paris at the Galerie Druet in March–April 1906. The largest and most powerful of the group is *The Large Woodcut,* in which the model, seemingly asleep, is curled away from the viewer, toward what one writer has described as "a mass of lines that fill the background like magnetic waves." To make the woodcuts, Matisse produced ink drawings, sometimes with a reed pen, of unusual boldness and energy; the ink drawing was then used to transfer the composition onto the wooden block as a "pattern" for the carving. Matisse's fluidity and spontaneity as a draftsman are evident in the abstraction of *The Large Woodcut,* unexpected at such an early date in the artist's work.

The only surviving woodblock for any of the prints in the group was that for *The Large Woodcut.* It went unidentified for many years because it had been painted with blue and white paint and thus was thought to be a material other than wood. The woodblock, an exceptionally rare and precious object and an archival document—most especially in combination with the print itself—was acquired from the heirs of turn-of-the-century French art dealer and publisher Ambroise Vollard (who may have acquired the block to issue an album of woodcuts by Matisse and other artists) by another dealer, the late Frank Perls, who in turn sold it to the V&A in 1975. It was nearly two decades before the Museum was able to locate and acquire an impression of *The Large Woodcut* to complete the story of the woodblock, thus bringing together compellingly tangible evidence of Matisse at work.

BRENDA RICHARDSON

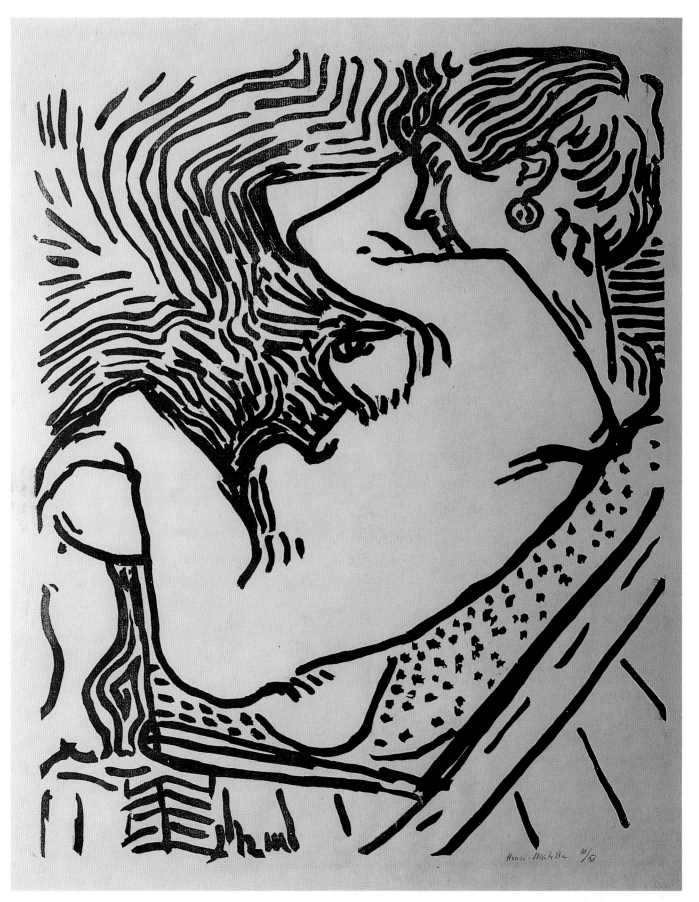

38.2.

39. DAVID HOCKNEY (English, born 1937 [U.S. resident since 1963]). *The Sexton Disguised as a Ghost, from Six Fairy Tales from the Brothers Grimm* (published by Petersburg Press, London). Given by David Hockney and Petersburg Press Ltd. 1969–70

39.1. Cancelled plate, chrome-faced copper, 9½ x 11" (24 x 28 cm). V&A E.870–1973

39.2. Etching and aquatint on handmade white rag paper, 17⅜ x 15¾" (44 x 40 cm). V&A Circ.152–1971

In 1961–62 David Hockney did several etchings that illustrated the story of Rumpelstiltskin from *Grimm's Fairy Tales* (first published in 1812), a collection of Germanic folk tales—some printed and some passed down as oral history—that totaled 210 stories by the book's third edition in 1857, compiled by philologist and folklorist Jakob Ludwig Karl Grimm (1785–1863) and his brother Wilhelm Karl Grimm (1786–1859). Hockney says that he had always enjoyed the stories and had read them all. He had also researched earlier illustrations of the stories, including rare German editions as well as those by Arthur Rackham and Edmund Dulac that were quite well known in England. He even took a trip up the Rhine so that he could incorporate authentic architectural details in his Grimm illustrations. "They're fascinating, the little stories," commented Hockney, "told in a very very simple, direct, straightforward language and style; it was this simplicity that attracted me. They cover quite a strange range of experience, from the magical to the moral."

The illustrations of six Grimm stories that Hockney created in 1969–70 were innovative in both form and technique. Hockney set out to do a book—not the luxury portfolio of prints typical of that moment in art, but a real story book which would have a narrative illustration for every page of text. Wanting spontaneity, the artist often worked directly on the etching plate rather than doing preparatory drawings. Hockney says that he "stumbled on" a way to force exceptionally rich blacks, by building up layers of etched cross-hatching so that the ink got very thick.

The Sexton Disguised as a Ghost is one of eleven illustrations for the story *The Boy Who Left Home to Learn Fear.* The story begins very simply:

> A farmer had two sons. The elder was clever and knew his way around but the younger one was stupid and good for nothing. When people saw him they said: "That boy will give his father trouble." It was always the elder boy who had to help his father; but if he was sent on an errand late at night and on the way he had to cross the churchyard or some other dismal place, he would plead: "No father, I'd rather not go, it makes me shudder."

When the younger brother sat in a corner and heard people telling ghost stories by the fire, he couldn't understand them when they said: "Oh, that makes me shudder!"

"Why do they always say it makes me shudder, it makes me shudder," he asked himself, "I can't shudder—that must be something I have to learn."

One day his father spoke to him: "Listen my boy, you're getting older. It's about time you started to work. Look at your brother, he earns his keep; but what do you have to offer?"

"Father, I'd like to learn something," he answered, "if I had my choice I'd learn to shudder; I don't know the first thing about it."

His brother grinned and thought, "Heavens, what a fool he is! He'll never get anywhere."

The father sighed: "You'll learn soon enough what it is to be afraid; but you won't earn a living that way."

The story then takes the boy through a series of encounters with people who offer to teach him fear. The first is the sexton who sends the boy at midnight to ring the church bell. The sexton drapes himself in a sheet and silently confronts the boy on the bell tower stairs, expecting to be taken for a ghost. The boy shouts at the figure to identify himself and, when the "ghost" stands silent, the boy throws him down the stairs, then rings the bell and goes home. Most of the boy's adventures are gruesome and horrific but, since he knows no fear, he consistently triumphs by responding in a manner which is so simpleminded as to be clever.

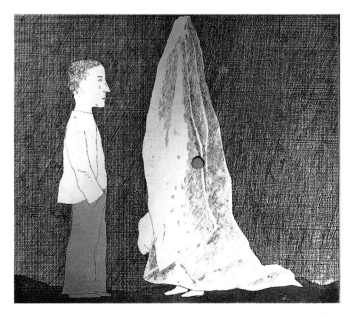

39.1.

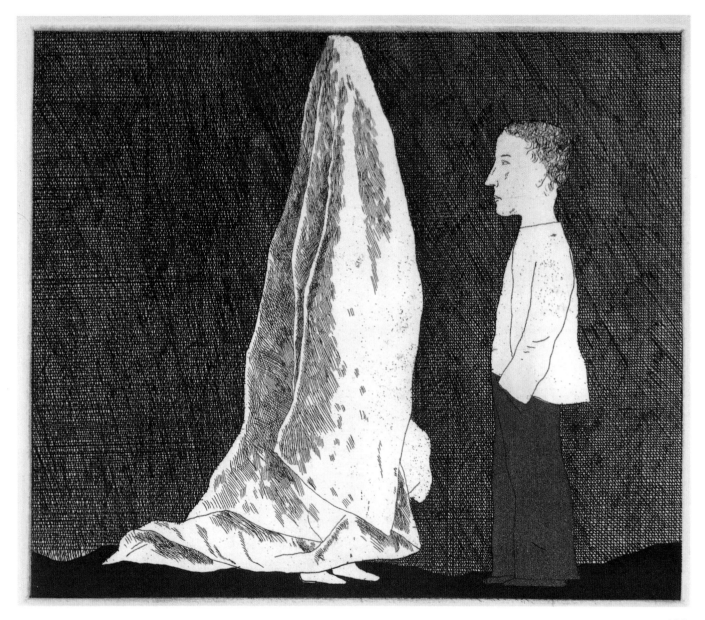

Hockney reported that his rendering of the ghost was "like those [René] Magritte stone paintings" and was inspired by a line in the story which had been translated for him as "The . . . ghost stood still as stone."

The etching plate has had a hole cut through its center to preclude unauthorized printings from the plate subsequent to the original editions. Such purposeful damaging ("cancellation") of the plate is routine in the publication of limited-edition prints.

Even as late as the 1970s, prints were being acquired at the V&A primarily as instructional documents to illustrate various printmaking techniques. Hence, as with the Matisse woodcut and its woodblock (cat. 38), there would have been special significance in having both the Hockney etching and its copper plate as evidence of the etching process. One of England's best-known living artists, Hockney was actively collected by the Museum's Circulation Department until its closure in 1976, so that the artist's work could be included in the traveling displays that were sent throughout Britain.

Lit. Stangos, 1977, pp. 194–6, 201–2, 212–6 (story translation quoted above); Hogben and Watson, 1985, p. 334

BRENDA RICHARDSON

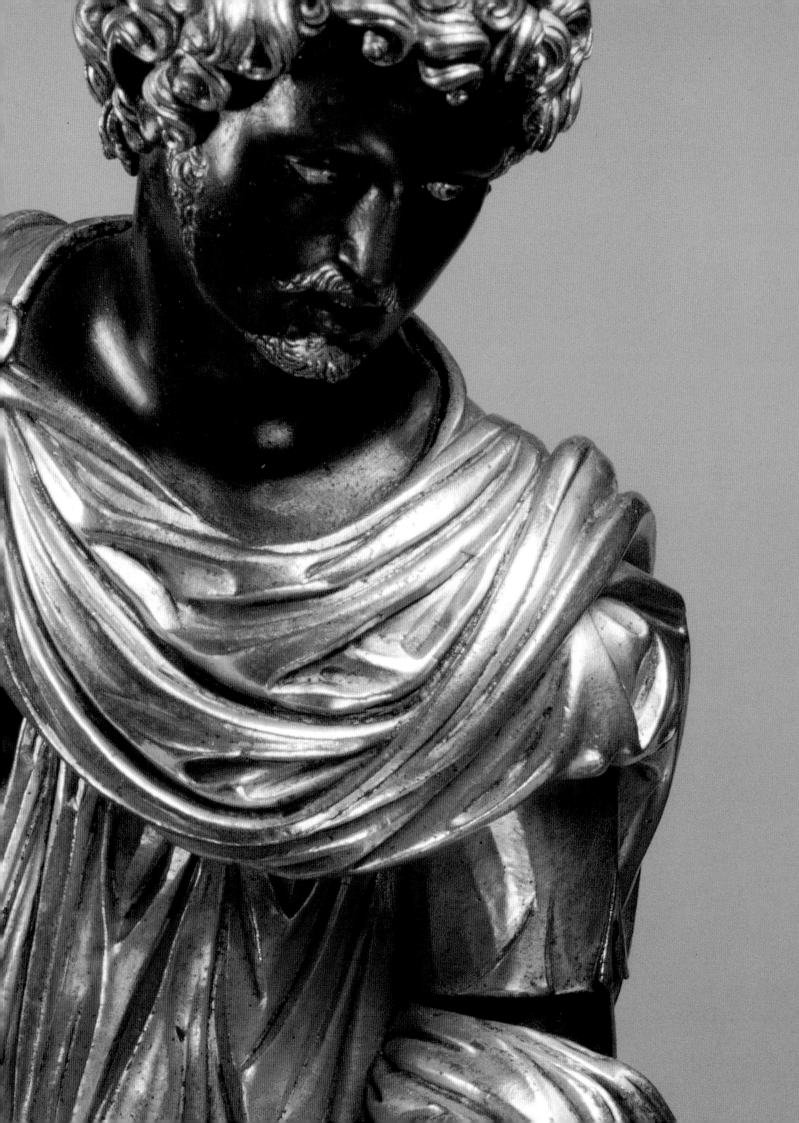

An Encyclopedia of Treasures: The Idea of the Great Collection

Timothy Stevens and Peter Trippi

In assembling, displaying, and interpreting its collections, the Victoria and Albert Museum has constructed a comprehensive canon of Europe's greatest applied arts and their makers. Like other canons, this one has been reconfigured over time to reflect new discoveries and shifting ideas as to what deserves prominence. What makes this canon unique is the fact that it has been shaped almost exclusively within the context of a single institution. Rather than "falling from the sky" fully formed—as visitors often assume of museum collections—the V&A's canon has been considered and reconsidered by Museum curators and administrators who, despite their expertise and methodologies, bring to the enterprise their own predilections. The perspectives of these individuals have been especially relevant at the V&A because this unique institution did not start with a "founding collection," as did the National Gallery and the British Museum.[1]

Unlike European painting, for which a canon was established by Giorgio Vasari in 1550, the applied arts had not inherited by the 1850s a "road map" of excellence for practitioners, connoisseurs, and laymen to consult. Since then, the V&A has grown to universal stature by transforming itself into an encyclopedic "treasure house" of "masterpieces" that illustrate its canon. The visitor absorbs this achievement through countless visual messages, ranging from the shrinelike setting of the Medieval Treasury to the imperial grandeur of the rotunda.

The Museum has built the canon and its collections through four intersecting factors: the connoisseurship of influential curators stretching from Sir John Charles Robinson (1824–1913) to Sir John Pope-Hennessy (1913–1994) to those of today; the emergence of opportunities to acquire objects and collections; the prominence bestowed on particular pieces through Museum installations; and strategic publication of its artworks. The interweaving of these factors is perhaps best demonstrated through the growth of the Museum's medieval and Renaissance holdings, the centrality of which has predicated consideration of all other European material.

A commitment to Italian Renaissance art—long perceived in England as the "highest" period in the history of art—can be traced to two early acquisitions made by the Government School of Design at Somerset House. The School had been encouraged by Parliament in 1836 to collect "casts and paintings, copies of the Arabesques of Raphael . . . every thing, in short, which exhibits in combination the

Fig. 80. Detail of cat. 59, Antico's *Meleager*, c. 1484-90

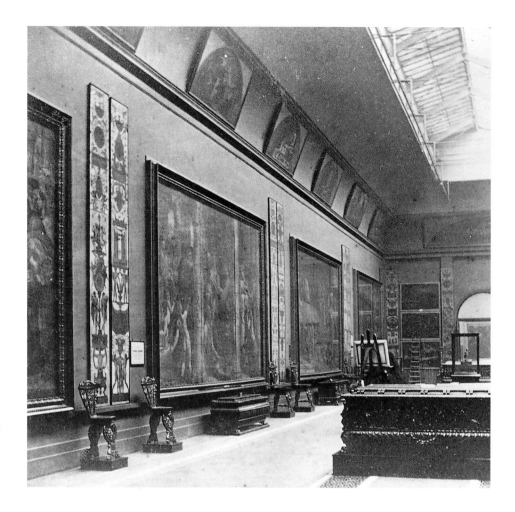

Fig. 81. The Raphael Cartoons as displayed in the South Kensington Museum in 1868, with the copies of the lunettes and pilasters from Raphael's Loggia in the Vatican

efforts of the artist and the workman . . ."[2] Among the gifts made during the School's inaugural year of 1837–38 was a set of engravings of Raphael's pilasters and lunettes from the Vatican Loggia.[3] In 1843, headmaster C. H. Wilson mounted reproductions of these renowned decorations on "quadrangular pillars" for students' reference.[4] (These were subsequently displayed in various ways at South Kensington; fig. 81, and see figs. 23, 26.)

These copies—together with Queen Victoria's loan to the Museum in 1865 of Raphael's cartoons for tapestry from the Sistine Chapel—demonstrate how this artist was put forward as personifying the link between the fine and applied arts. As a "canonical" painter whose compositions were also used in ornament, Raphael helped legitimize the applied arts, extending to them through his stardom the status of masterpiece, even when the objects in question were reproductions or studies. Through the 1840s, the School continued to acquire applied arts from the Renaissance—such as majolica—though its emphasis remained squarely on modern manufactures.

The first builder of the Museum's canon was Henry Cole, whose familiarity with industrial arts was balanced by the expertise in historical artworks he had developed during his celebrated reforms of the Public Record Office. More recently Cole had helped organize the Society of Arts's large 1850 loan exhibition of ancient and medieval art in London.[5] Inspired by French precedents such as the Musée de

Cluny as he set up the Museum at Marlborough House in 1852, Cole opted not to focus exclusively on the numerous modern manufactures at his disposal, but to display applied arts of earlier periods. Thus—*before* the hiring in August 1853 of John Charles Robinson, the Superintendent of Art Collections usually remembered as the Museum's sole advocate of earlier art—Cole was already combining historically diverse objects, enough to make him change the name of the modern-sounding "Museum of Manufactures" to "Museum of Ornamental Art." Indeed, in its first report (1853), the Museum was described as a place where "all classes might be induced to investigate those common principles of taste, which may be traced to the work of all ages."[6]

Initially satisfied to borrow from dealers, Cole soon began to purchase historical objects—among them the Museum's first medieval ivory, from the estate sale of his friend A. W. N. Pugin in February 1853—also before Robinson's arrival.[7] Such acquisitions show Cole moving on a parallel track to that of his friend, the connoisseur A. W. Franks (1826–1897), who had joined the British Museum in 1851 to begin collecting medieval objects.[8]

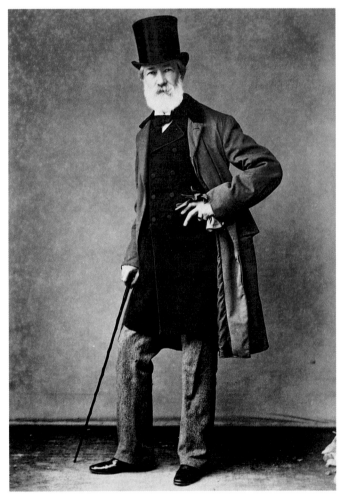

Fig. 82. John Charles Robinson (1824–1913), Superintendent of Art Collections of the South Kensington Museum

Robinson became the canon's second key builder by accelerating the drive to acquire large numbers of older artworks, regardless of their national origin. Sixteen years Cole's junior, Robinson was a native of Nottingham who had trained as a painter in Paris, where visits to the Louvre laid the groundwork for his profound understanding of the Renaissance (fig. 82). He came to the Museum after six years as headmaster of the Government School of Art at Hanley, Staffordshire, the heart of England's ceramics industry. The Hanley school's engagement with "art potteries" such as Minton & Co. helps to explain Robinson's lifelong passion for aesthetic and technical excellence in ceramics and sculpture. It also suggests that Robinson was not entirely hostile—as is often thought—to the Museum's original mission of applying art to industry. In keeping with this mission, Robinson worked with Cole to create in 1854 a system of circulating artworks to provincial institutions, where more students, designers, and laymen could learn from them.

Robinson's early publications at the Museum include such educative titles as *A Manual of Elementary Outline Drawing* (1853), *A Collection of Examples of Coloured Ornament* (1853), *An Introductory Lecture on the Museum of Ornamental Art* (1854), and *The Treasury of Ornamental Art* (1857). The second and fourth of these reveal Robinson's quasi-antiquarian commitment to an eclectic range of contemporary designers inspired (but not constrained) by earlier art—Albert Carrier-Belleuse (who had lectured at Hanley), Owen Jones, Pugin, Henry Shaw, and Antoine Vechte. Citing these and other men, Robinson could legitimately show how modern designers are inspired by historical masterpieces, particularly the sculpture he loved so passionately. In 1862 he highlighted

> . . . the two-fold aspect under which sculpture is represented in this Museum, viz. as a "fine art," and also . . . as a decorative art or industry. . . . It is not more certain than unfortunate, that in our times an imaginary . . . line of distinction has been drawn betwixt these two aspects. The idea has gradually grown up, especially in this country, that it is scarcely the business of an artist-sculptor to concern himself with anything but the human figure, and as one result of this short-sighted view, when any architectural or ornamental accessories are required, an unfortunate want of power is too often manifested; whilst, on the other hand, no ornamentist sculptors, worthy of the name, are likely to arise from amongst the . . . skilled artizans, to whom ornamental sculpture has been virtually abandoned.[9]

Though he justified his acquisitions to Cole, Redgrave, and the Department of Science and Art by using their rhetoric, Robinson's eloquent descriptions suggest that he valued them primarily as masterpieces of art. Criticized (especially by Redgrave) for spending too much on originals when reproductions were available, Robinson successfully defended his decisions by citing "that natural feeling of the human mind, which attaches the highest value only to original works," and by describing reproductions as "imperfect" and useful only to "supply missing links in the series."[10] Robinson praised Adrian de Vries's 1609 bronze relief *Emperor Rudolf II* (cat. 69) as "a masterpiece of bronze casting and chasing," yet its ostensibly supplemental merit—"excellence in point of art"—reflects just as accurately his reason for acquiring it in 1860.[11]

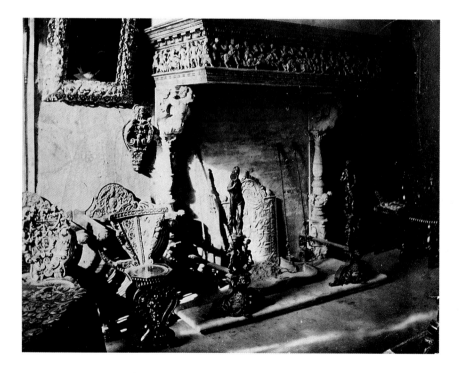

Fig. 83. Part of the collection of Jules Soulages, photographed at his house in Toulouse by V&A photographer Thurston Thompson in 1855

Entirely different in temperament and character, Robinson and Cole nonetheless collaborated by traveling regularly across Europe to take advantage of strategic opportunities offered by dealers, collectors, and estate sales. The redevelopment of historic city centers (such as Paris) and the Continental passion for church restoration helped create a ready supply of artworks. Robinson used his unparalleled knowledge—all the more remarkable given the paucity of literature available—to assemble a collection of Italian Renaissance sculpture, majolica, metalwork, textiles, and furniture that remains unmatched. He told *The Times* in 1883 that "the noble masterpieces of sculpture now at South Kensington . . . are now the envy of the most celebrated museums of Europe. . . . [A]s a collective series [they] have no parallel, even in Italy."[12]

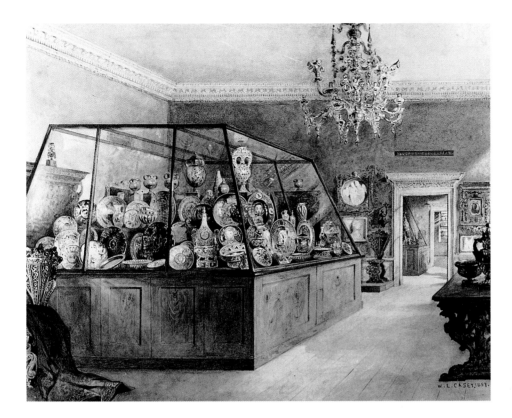

Fig. 84. A watercolor rendering (V&A 7280) of Marlborough House in 1857, by W. L. Casey. This room displayed items on loan from the collection of Jules Soulages, subsequently purchased by the V&A over a number of years.

Like the National Gallery's Director, Sir Charles Eastlake, Robinson capitalized upon Italy's political troubles through the 1850s and early 1860s to secure the best objects. His fortunate timing was enhanced by a virtual withdrawal from the market by Berlin's acquisitive curators, though the Louvre was still active during these decades. In view of its status as a government agency, the Museum's competitive collecting overseas can be seen as an expression of Britain's imperial ambitions, comparable to the Foreign Office's search for new colonies.

In 1855, the Museum's photographer visited Toulouse to record the Soulages collection of 749 objects—the first known use of this new medium to reinforce an acquisition proposal (fig. 83).[13] Robinson then catalogued the collection (rich in French Renaissance material) and showed it at Marlborough House (fig. 84) and in the 1857 Manchester Art Treasures exhibition.[14] These presentations familiarized the public—and the parliamentary leaders who could approve purchase funds—with this collection, which the Museum managed to buy with government support in the early 1860s.

The government was prepared to underwrite some, not all, purchases of historical art, as it was doing for the National Gallery. Although Cole's arguments for government assistance always emphasized how a nationwide training scheme in design would benefit Britain's economy by raising the standard of modern industrial products, the fact that a large proportion of these government funds were used to purchase historical objects suggests Cole had more sympathy with Robinson's aims than his official statements reveal. Robinson's acquisitions were treasures in their own right, and many fulfilled Cole's educative objectives, too. Starting in 1854 with the Gherardini collection, for example, Robinson developed superb holdings in sculptors' models that joined fine art criteria to Cole's concern for processes of making (fig. 85).

At home, the Museum organized a loan exhibition of almost ten thousand medieval, Renaissance, and "more recent" artworks to coincide with the International Exhibition of 1862 occurring nearby.[15] Although this massive display must have delighted him on aesthetic grounds, Robinson observed that these pieces also "show at all events what ample scope there is for the posthumous teaching of the great ceramic artists of the 15th and 16th centuries through their great work which still remains to us."[16] Visited by 1.2 million people, the Museum's exhibition featured objects borrowed primarily from English dealers and collectors being cultivated by Robinson and Cole. By displaying and promoting these and other loans, the pair rapidly secured first-rate material it had taken other connoisseurs decades to gather.

Like Cole, Robinson was determined that the Museum's canon should be rigorously taxonomic. Aware that the British Museum already held the field in ancient art, Robinson specified in his 1862 catalogue of Italian medieval and Renaissance sculpture where South Kensington's emphasis should be placed:

> It is the intimate connection of mediaeval and renaissance sculpture with the decorative arts in general, which clearly indicates this Museum as the proper repository for this class of the National acquisitions; consequently the present Collection should be regarded as part of a methodic series, following the antique sculptures of the British Museum, to be eventually continued down to our own time, so as to form a complete collection of what, in contradistinction to the similarly general term *antique,* may be fitly designated *modern* sculpture.[17]

If the Museum could not possess a great historical artwork or piece of architecture, it instead commissioned plaster casts, drawings, or photographs so that the entire canon could be represented in some form.[18] This is demonstrated by a photographic series of the twelfth-century cathedral at Santiago de Compostela in Spain. The views were taken by the Museum's photographer Charles Thurston Thompson in 1866 during a carefully planned campaign to cast the Portico de la Gloria, which still graces one of the V&A's Architectural (Cast) Courts (see fig. 52). The images were published in London by the Arundel Society (established to make major artworks better known) in 1868, when the cast was unveiled. Together, the photographs and cast gave the hitherto unknown portal a prominence that Robinson—acting without encouragement from outside parties such as the British public or Spanish government—believed it deserved.[19]

During the 1860s, the Museum moved to validate the canonical storehouse it was creating with the "Kensington Valhalla." This was a series of fictional life-size portraits (painted and then created as mosaic murals in the South Court) of the greatest European artists and craftsmen, each holding a

work already in the Museum's collections. In its choices of Raphael, Michelangelo, and Donatello (cat. 52, holding the Martelli Mirror, cat. 54, then attributed to him), the Museum reflected current views of the canon. When, however, it included a representation of the little-known potter Maestro Giorgio of Gubbio with his lusterware vase (cats. 51, 53), South Kensington was not merely reflecting an existing concept of excellence but shaping and modifying the canon. The theme of a major artist holding his creation also surfaces in the Cafaggiolo dish (cat. 50) acquired in 1855 and displayed prominently thereafter. This strategy continued until 1905, when the sculpted figures of thirty-two British artists were "admitted" to the canon through placement on the grand facade of Aston Webb's Main Building (see fig. 110).

During the nineteenth century, few qualities bestowed masterpiece status on an object more rapidly than its association with a historical, romantic, or notorious figure. Sometimes fictitious, such links often attracted other objects with similar provenances, effectively profiling not the people who created the artworks, but those who owned them. Among these pieces are the Holbein Cabinet (cat. 68) thought to have belonged to Henry VIII; the Boudoir of Marie Antoinette's Lady of Honor, the Marquise de Serilly; and a group of pieces made for the Medici family (cats. 75–77). The treasures of past rulers have proven to attract and fascinate visitors, and, equally significant, possession of such talismanic objects both enhances the institutional owner and underscores Britain's status as a leading world power.

Methods of display have been explored and exploited as a means for the Museum to bestow canonical status on its strongest acquisitions. After the Soulages collection was acquired in the 1860s, for example, its rare pieces by Bernard Palissy (see cat. 71) were showcased in the Ceramics Gallery, where Cole included this hitherto ignored figure among the leading potters depicted on the windows. (The collection's comprehensiveness was underscored by the fact that most factories named on the Gallery's frieze were represented by their products in the cases below.) Like the William Morris legacy nurtured by the Museum today, Europe's craze for Palissy in the late nineteenth century bloomed largely due to South Kensington's coordinated strategy of acquiring, displaying, and publishing his work (see fig. 28). The subsequent decline in Palissy's popularity was reflected in his decreased visibility in the Museum, yet he remained in its canon, awaiting "rediscovery" in the 1960s.[20]

Intended to evoke objects' original contexts, the device of period room displays emerged in the 1870s, confirming the Museum's gradual shift from technical toward stylistic concerns. The elegant Serilly Boudoir, for example (fig. 86), served as a key period room until 1882, when the Museum received John Jones's enormous collection of

Opposite: Fig. 85. A wax model (6⅝" [16.8 cm] high) for a marble figure of a slave by Michelangelo, acquired from the Gherardini collection (V&A 4117–1854)

Fig. 86. The Marquise de Serilly's Boudoir (V&A 1736–1869) as it was displayed by 1874, containing a harp said to have belonged to Marie Antoinette

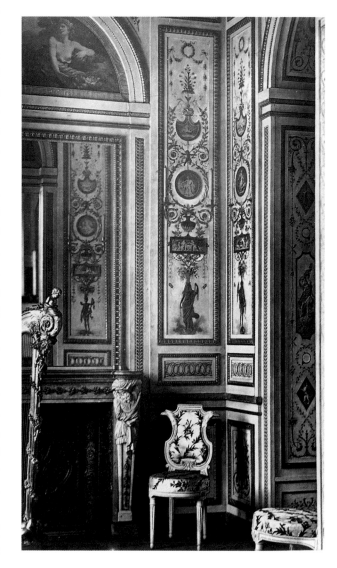

eighteenth-century French applied arts (see figs. 41–44).[21] At a single stroke, the bequest's excellence lowered the Boudoir's standing within the canon, though the room did not disappear from view immediately.

Despite its preeminence, the V&A has paid careful attention to its colleagues' display techniques, as well. Wilhelm von Bode's dramatic period installations at the Kaiser Friedrich Museum electrified Berlin from 1904, even as South Kensington had been moving in this same direction. However, the Committee on Re-arrangement's pivotal decision in 1908 to reorganize artworks by material, rather than by period, radically diminished the visual impact of the galleries, and it was only in 1948 that director Leigh Ashton's Primary Galleries returned key masterpieces to prominence in compelling historical contexts more appealing to the public. Since then, the excitement of collecting masterpieces has been conveyed through ever more striking displays and temporary exhibitions, a trend developed most clearly beginning in the 1970s under director Sir Roy Strong.

Publishing is fundamental to the validation of a subject's importance, so Robinson and Cole developed their catalogues strategically. With his landmark 1862 catalogue, Robinson firmly secured names such as Andrea and Luca della Robbia (see cat. 56) and Giovanni Pisano (see cat. 44) in the canon. The campaign continued with a series of *South Kensington Museum Art Handbooks* and has been sustained by distinguished specialists such as C. D. Fortnum, George Birdwood, John Hungerford Pollen, Bernard Rackham, and Charles Oman—a tradition of curatorial scholarship still alive today. Collectively these connoisseurs can be described as the canon's third builder. Generations of them have published the collections in their care to tell the story of a particular medium or style, implying that the subject can be traced adequately at South Kensington alone. For example, both the scale and encyclopedic range of the ceramics displays were noted in guidebooks from the 1880s onward. The collecting of contemporary ceramics—a tradition started by Cole—has been continuous, and he would probably be gratified by the collection's ongoing influence upon ceramic production in Britain.

The Museum has often positioned an artwork as the type specimen by which examples from a particular group can be identified, much as species of plants are identified in the Natural History Museum across Exhibition Road. This is demonstrated, for example, by a panel with a scene of the Resurrection (cat. 49), around which has been assembled a large group of majolica decorated by the "Master of the Resurrection Panel," or by *The Girl-in-a-Swing* figure (cat. 141) that has given its name to a distinctive group of English porcelains. By 1900 the size and quality of the V&A's majolica collection, among other types, meant that serious study was effectively constructed around the Museum's holdings.

Emphasizing acquisitions exclusively, however, gives a false picture of what visitors actually saw during the nineteenth century, when many loans enabled the Museum to highlight areas in which its collections were weak, and at the same time to encourage the eventual donation of these objects. This strategy had its own risks in that curators tended not to acquire in areas already represented by loans. As it turned out, the Museum gambled well by not acquiring Renaissance objects similar to those bequeathed by the Australian George Salting in 1910, yet lost when J. Pierpont Morgan sent most of his medieval treasures to New York in 1912. Like the

Continental buying strategies of Robinson and Cole at mid-century, South Kensington's bestowal of canonical status on the gifts of such donors as Jones and Salting must be considered not only in view of their quality, but also in light of the Museum's fierce competition for private collections with Berlin's museums and New York's Metropolitan Museum of Art, among others.

Throughout the twentieth century, important acquisitions have been made in many of the areas developed by Robinson and Cole. Curator (and ultimately director) John Pope-Hennessy built on Robinson's achievement through his own purchases of Italian sculpture (fig. 87). The continuity from Robinson to Pope-Hennessy emerges most clearly, however, in their publications. Robinson's 1862 catalogue set a new standard for scholarship in Italian sculpture. The Museum's holdings in this field were further burnished by V&A curators when Eric Maclagan and Margaret Longhurst published their catalogue in 1932, followed three decades later by magisterial volumes from Pope-Hennessy and Ronald Lightbown (1964) that redrew the field's map again.

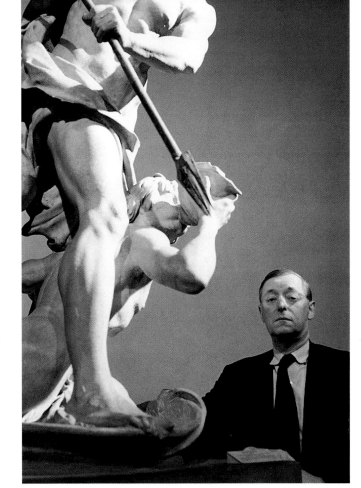

Fig. 87. John Pope-Hennessy, director of the V&A (1967–74), photographed alongside a statue of Neptune and Triton by Gianlorenzo Bernini (V&A A18–1950)

Other twentieth-century acquisitions, such as the seventeenth-century ivory by Balthasar Permoser (cat. 82) and Pietro Piffetti's eighteenth-century mother-of-pearl stand (cat. 83), illustrate how the Museum's curators have molded the canon to respond to new interest in previously neglected areas. These shifts are often stimulated by individuals, such as the ivory specialist H. Delves Molesworth (on staff 1931–66) or the collector Dr. W. L. Hildburgh, who gave important metalwork and sculpture between 1916 and 1955. Reshaping of the canon was encouraged by Robinson himself, as in 1860 when he declared that recently acquired pieces of "Medici porcelain" were "henceforward a new feature in the history of the art."[22] This expansive, quintessentially Victorian brand of confidence—critiqued as arrogance whenever certain styles are excluded—has ensured both the constant growth of the V&A's collections and their preeminence worldwide.

Robinson's collaboration with Cole and Redgrave weakened over time: in 1863 his title was changed from Superintendent of Art Collections to Permanent Art Referee, and his authority began to ebb as his philosophical views diverged further from those of his colleagues. Robinson noted ironically in 1863 that "there is an implicit belief in the minds of most people, that someone else— entire classes, in fact—are making profound and earnest use of [museums] in directly practical ways." He went on to observe that intuitive good taste comes only to "certain continental people . . . familiar from childhood with the most refined works of art. . . . But then London is not Venice."[23] After Cole forced him out in 1868, Robinson enjoyed an illustrious career as an author on art and

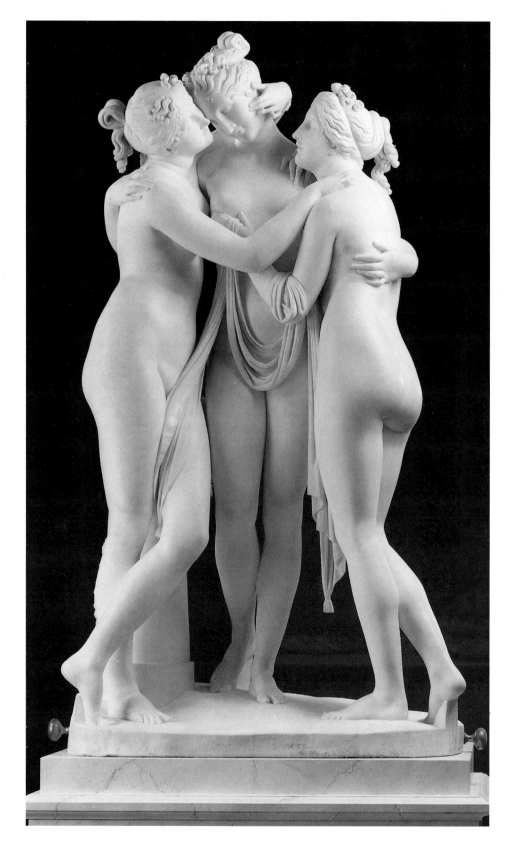

Fig. 88. Antonio Canova (Italian, 1757–1822). *The Three Graces.* 1814–17. Marble, 68⅛ x 38¼ x 22½" (173 x 97.2 x 57 cm). Victoria and Albert Museum: Purchased jointly with the National Galleries of Scotland. V&A A.4-1994

Surveyor of the Queen's Pictures (1882–1901). In 1883 he wrote, "I relinquished the direction of the acquisitions to the South Kensington Museum years ago, when it became no longer possible for me to keep out a vast influx of trivial and useless matter, which, in my opinion, tended only to vitiate and vulgarise the collection."[24]

Though Cole won his battle, it can be argued that he lost the war with Robinson's values. The Museum's gradual abandonment of contemporary acquisitions after Cole retired in 1873 (exemplified by the transfer of modern manufactures to Bethnal Green from 1880) suggests that Robinson's vision of a three-dimensional encyclopedia of connoisseurship proved more attractive to subsequent curators than did Cole's elusive objective of an accessible patternbook. In his annual report for 1854, Cole had argued:

> A museum may be a passive, dormant institution, an encyclopedia as it were, in which the learned student, knowing what to look for, may find authorities; or it may be an active teaching institution, useful and suggestive. The latter has emphatically been the status of this museum from its origin.[25]

In 1880, however, he described the Museum as having too many "Virgins and Childs."[26] By the turn of the century, potential acquisitions were no longer assessed on whether they exemplified good taste or were suitable models for students and consumers. Instead, it could be argued that they represented styles, periods, or other categories that—no matter how objectionable—belonged in a collection showing the entire history of a particular type.

Increasingly, the Museum has been forced to use its limited purchase funds to acquire works threatened with export from Britain, such as Antonio Canova's marble sculpture of *The Three Graces* (fig. 88) commissioned by the duke of Bedford. The widely publicized debate about acquisition of this object in the early 1990s not only raised issues about Britain's "heritage" but also illustrated how the canon evolves. Seen by his contemporaries in the early nineteenth century as Europe's leading artist, Canova was far less highly regarded a century later. Yet in acquiring *The Three Graces* in 1994, the Museum again marked Canova as a major figure in the history of art. The acquisition also built on the collecting tradition of Robinson and his successors by adding to the Museum's holdings of work by Donatello and Bernini an outstanding example by the last great Italian sculptor of the premodern era. Two years later the Museum reinforced an aspect of the canon firmly established in the nineteenth century by joining in partnership with the National Heritage Memorial Fund to acquire a twelfth-century Limoges enamel casket associated with Saint Thomas à Becket.

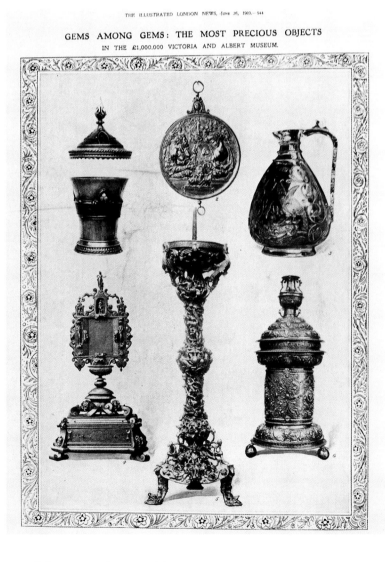

THE ILLUSTRATED LONDON NEWS, June 26, 1909.—944

GEMS AMONG GEMS: THE MOST PRECIOUS OBJECTS
IN THE £1,000,000 VICTORIA AND ALBERT MUSEUM.

Fig. 89. "Gems among Gems," from *The Illustrated London News,* 26 June 1909. This page illustrated some of the treasures acquired by the V&A up to that time. These included, at top center, the Martelli Mirror (cat. 54).

Though its original didactic mission prompted the births of similarly chartered museums worldwide, the V&A's encyclopedic aspirations and metamorphosis into a treasure house influenced an even greater number of institutions. By 1874—only a year after Cole retired—Murray's *Guide to London* was praising South Kensington's "very precious objects" and observing that "this truly national museum of Art, and of Manufactures allied to Art, has sprung up in short time to be one of the most considerable and important in Europe" (fig. 89; also see fig. 33).[27] Within the V&A, where installations of selected objects arranged according to period complement the denser displays of particular materials, the well-known treasures tend to remain prominently on view and have become "destination objects" for countless visitors. Indeed, most applied arts museums today seek to engage and awe visitors by demonstrating through striking displays how distinctively their objects illustrate the widely accepted canon nurtured by the Victoria and Albert Museum. Though the validity and sociocultural implications of such terms as "prototype" and "masterpiece" continue to be debated, the canon still resonates.

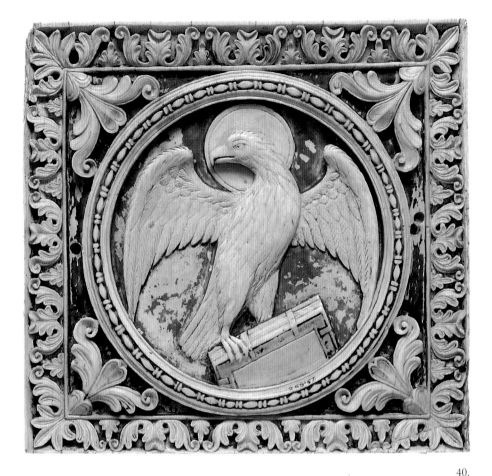

40.

40. Carolingian. *Eagle: Symbol of St. John the Evangelist.*
c. 800–10. Ivory, with remains of paint, 4⅝ x 5 x ⅜"
(11.7 x 12.7 x 1 cm). V&A 269–1867

This plaque was among the many medieval ivories acquired by
the Museum in the 1860s, their prominence reflecting the significance that medieval objects had for Henry Cole and John
Charles Robinson. This eagle plaque (purchased for £48) once
formed part of a diptych, subsequently cut into pieces, that
showed the other three evangelist symbols and busts of Christ
and (probably) the Virgin. In 1867 the plaque was considered to
be Byzantine; it was not until 1914, when Adolph Goldschmidt
published the first volume of his great corpus of early medieval
ivory carvings, that it was recognized as Carolingian and dated
to the early ninth century. Possibly carved in a northern Italian
center, it exemplifies the refined sophistication characteristic of
Carolingian ivories, most of which hark back to Early Christian
models.

Already by the late 1860s the South Kensington Museum
possessed one of the most comprehensive and high-quality collections of medieval ivory carvings in the world. This was due
largely to the London dealer John Webb, who placed large numbers of ivories on loan to the Museum until purchase funds
could be found; the ivories were bought in batches over time.
These ivories—the misleadingly titled "Webb collection"—

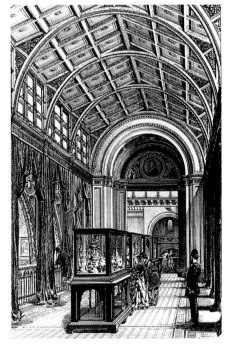

Fig. 90. The Prince Consort Gallery—named
for Prince Albert and reflecting his importance in the Museum's history—where the
V&A displayed many of its most precious
objects

came from a wide variety of sources. Some had been acquired at the Soltikoff sale in Paris in 1861, but many were bought by Webb on his travels in Europe, and their earlier provenances have never been established. At South Kensington the medieval ivories were shown with some later ivories and many plaster casts of ivories from other collections, first in the North Court, by 1881 in the Prince Consort Gallery (fig. 90) alongside the goldsmiths' work, and later in the South Court. Because of the strength of this part of the collection, the Museum has—since the formation of the materials-based departments in 1910—always kept on the staff an expert in this field. A striking manifestation of this expertise was provided in 1974 with the V&A's exhibition, "Ivory Carvings in Early Medieval England 700–1200," organized by John Beckwith, deputy keeper of architecture and sculpture: of the sixty-four works in the exhibition, twenty (including *Head of a Tau-Cross* [cat. 41]) were from the Museum's collection.

Lit. Goldschmidt, 1914, vol. I, cat. 34; Longhurst, 1927, vol. I, pp. 63–4; Williamson, 1996, pp. 68–9

PAUL WILLIAMSON

41. English. *Head of a Tau-Cross.* c. 1140–50. Walrus ivory, 2½ x 6¼ x 1⅜" (6.4 x 15.9 x 3.6 cm). V&A 371–1871

Certain acquisitions of medieval art subsequently came to be seen as significant also in the history of English art. Although described simply as from "northern Europe" when acquired in 1871, this ivory was, by 1927, accepted as English, and of twelfth-century date. The attribution seems firm insofar as the foliage and figure style of the tau-cross has been linked with Winchester manuscript illuminations of the second quarter of the twelfth century.

This tour de force of walrus ivory carving originally formed the upper terminal of an ecclesiastical staff. Known to have been in the collection of the Baron de Crassier of Liège by 1715, the piece is said to have come from Liège Cathedral. Such pieces are called tau-crosses because of their T shape, and in the Old Testament (Ezekiel 9:4) the mark of the tau is a symbol of righteousness. On one side is the Virgin and Child in a central medallion between two men struggling with serpents; on the other, Christ is flanked by Saint Michael subduing the dragon and another struggling figure.

Lit. Longhurst, 1927, vol. I; V&A, 1974b, no. 51; Williamson, 1996, pp. 124–5

PAUL WILLIAMSON

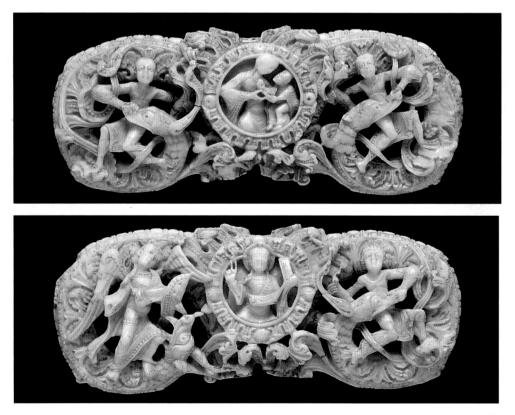

41.

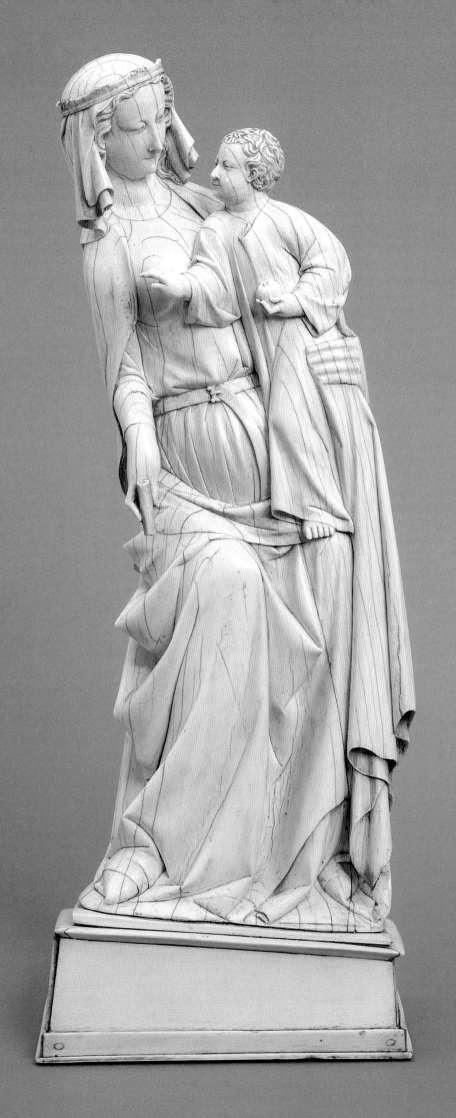

42. French (Paris). *The Virgin and Child.* c. 1320–30. Ivory, 16 x 3½ x 3⅝" (40.6 x 8.9 x 9 cm). V&A 4685–1858

This Virgin and Child was one of the Museum's earliest acquisitions of medieval ivory carving. Formerly in the Daugny collection, Paris, it was purchased from John Webb (see cat. 40) in 1858 for £100. Large numbers of ivory Virgin and Child statuettes were carved in Paris in the years between 1250 and 1350. This is one of the largest and most well known of these figures, which were predominantly intended for private devotion. The imposing figure is carved from a single piece of ivory, and the elegant sway of the Virgin's pose follows the slight curve of the elephant's tusk. In her right hand she once held a separately made lily, which the infant Christ reaches out to touch.

Lit. Longhurst, 1927–29, vol. II, p. 30; Williamson, 1996, pp. 196–7

PAUL WILLIAMSON

43. Hispano-Arabic (Madinat al-Zahra, Córdoba). *Casket of the Daughter of Abd al-Rahman III.* c. 961–65. Ivory with engraved silver mounts enriched with niello, 1¾ x 3¾ x 2½" (4.5 x 9.5 x 6.5 cm). V&A 301–1866

This ornate casket, richly carved with foliate decoration, was perhaps used for jewelry or perfumes since a related piece has an inscription referring to musk and camphor. The V&A casket has a Kufic inscription referring to the daughter of the powerful ruler Abd al-Rahman III. It belongs to a group of Hispano-Arabic ivory carvings that were produced in Córdoba when southern Spain was under Arabic rule and are therefore considered part of the history of Islamic art. Although catalogued as "Moorish," this piece was included among the European medieval ivories in William Maskell's 1872 *Description of the Ivories Ancient and Modern;* these "ancient Spanish ivories" were discussed in the same author's handbook on ivories—one of the series issued by the South Kensington Museum during the 1870s—in terms of their use as Christian reliquaries in the treasuries of medieval cathedrals.

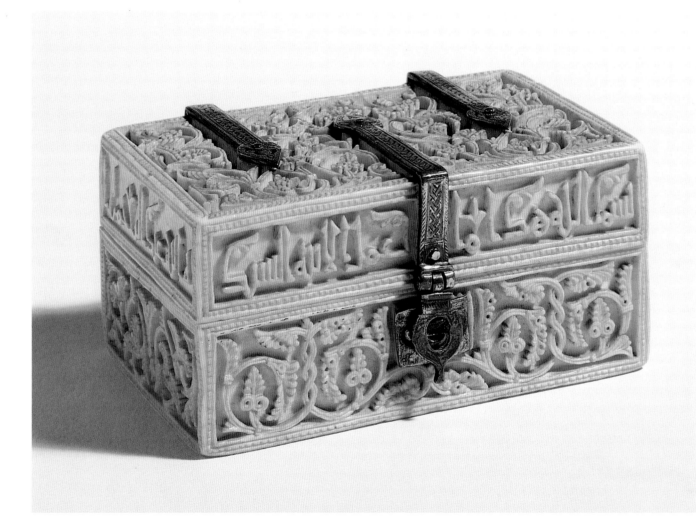

43.

The way in which this casket was described and classified by the Museum following its acquisition in Madrid in 1866 indicates the ambiguous position such a Moorish ivory occupied between the medieval ivories (cats. 40–42, 44) and the Alhambresque ornament of the thirteenth and fourteenth centuries admired by Owen Jones and well represented in the collections (cats. 14–15).

A plaster cast was made of this piece by the Museum, and partial copies probably based on the cast were made by D. Francisco Pallas y Puig working in Valencia. One of those copies, with a misunderstood version of the original's Arabic inscription, was acquired by George Salting and entered the Museum with his bequest in 1910.

Lit. Maskell, 1872; Longhurst, 1927, vol. I, p. 52; Beckwith, 1960, pp. 6–7, plates 2–4; Kühnel, 1971, cat. 20

PAUL WILLIAMSON

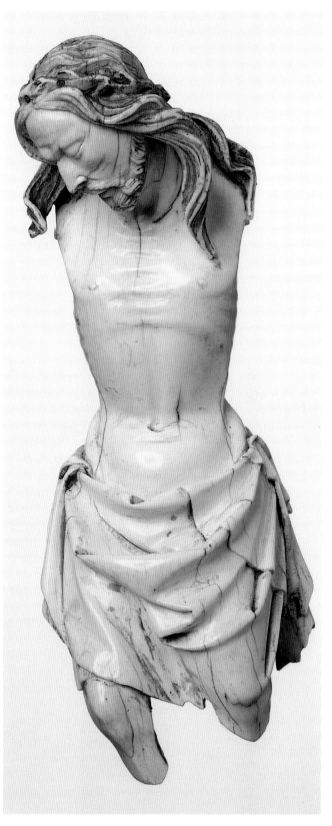

44.

44. GIOVANNI PISANO (Italian, born c. 1250, died after 1314). *The Crucified Christ.* c. 1300. Ivory, with traces of pigmentation, 6 x 2¼ x 2" (15.3 x 5.7 x 5 cm). V&A 212–1867

One of the most celebrated objects in the Museum's collections, this powerful crucifix figure in ivory has a monumentality and presence that belie its small size. Purchased as "French(?), 14th century," it was bought from John Webb in 1867 for the comparatively modest price of £15 (the Carolingian ivory eagle plaque [cat. 40], for example, was purchased in the same year for £48). This must have been partly due to the fact that it was in fragmentary condition, but also reflects its anonymous status at that time; moreover, Gothic ivories do not appear to have been in short supply in the mid-nineteenth century. The piece was reclassified as Italian in 1929. The later perceptive and convincing attribution to Giovanni Pisano was made by John Pope-Hennessy in 1965 on the basis of stylistic comparisons with other works by the artist in wood and marble, one of which—the head of a prophet from the facade of Siena Cathedral—he had recently acquired for the Museum, in 1963.

Lit. Longhurst, 1929, vol. II, p. 58; Pope-Hennessy, 1965; Williamson, 1995, pp. 260–1

PAUL WILLIAMSON

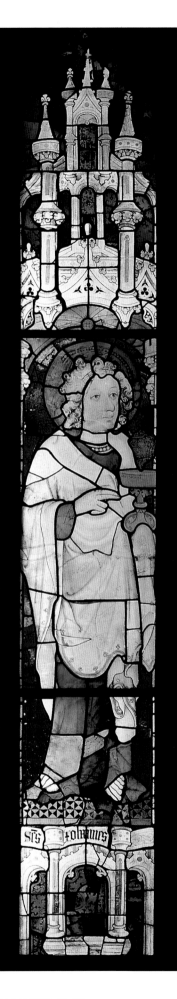

45.

45. WORKSHOP OF THOMAS OF OXFORD (English). *Saint John the Evangelist.* c. 1393. Stained and painted glass (potmetal glass and white glass with silver stain), 139½ x 23⅝" (354.3 x 60 cm). V&A 4237–1855

The Saint John was one of many figures produced for the chapel of Winchester College by the workshop of Thomas of Oxford, one of the most important glass painters in England around 1400 and among the first artists in England to adopt the Perpendicular (or International) Gothic style. By the early nineteenth century, the defective composition of the glass had resulted in its darkening to such a degree that the College decided wholesale cleaning was required. Between 1821 and 1828 all the glass except for the tracery lights was replaced with a copy.

Much of the original glass was jettisoned because of its poor condition; the Saint John and two other figures are the only survivors of the windows on the north and south sides of the church. The Reverend W. G. Rowland, vicar of St. Mary's, Shrewsbury, purchased the three figures for installation in his church. They were acquired by the Museum from Mr. P. Corbett of Shrewsbury, who had inherited them from Rowland.

Although two panels of contemporary glass were purchased in 1844, the Museum's first acquisition of earlier glass was in 1855 when ten Continental pieces were bought from the Bernal collection, along with Continental and English panels, including the saints from Winchester. Over the next fifty years, further additions made the Museum's collection one of the world's major holdings of stained glass; its importance was reinforced by the gift in 1919 of the glass collected by J. Pierpont Morgan, which was left in London at the outbreak of World War I, although his many other objects previously on loan to the V&A had been taken for safekeeping across the Atlantic to The Metropolitan Museum of Art in New York. The full extent and significance of the V&A's collection of stained glass became apparent with the publication of ceramics curator Bernard Rackham's guide in 1936.

In the 1930s, the three figures were displayed individually as specimens of English medieval glass. When installed in the Gothic Primary Gallery in 1950, they were not only juxtaposed with medieval textiles and metalwork, but also arranged in what appeared to be a single window, thus creating a darkened chapel-like interior considered appropriate to the style. These contrasting installations show the different ways in which a work from a specific context could be presented within the Museum.

Lit. Rackham, 1936, pp. 50–1

MICHAEL ARCHER

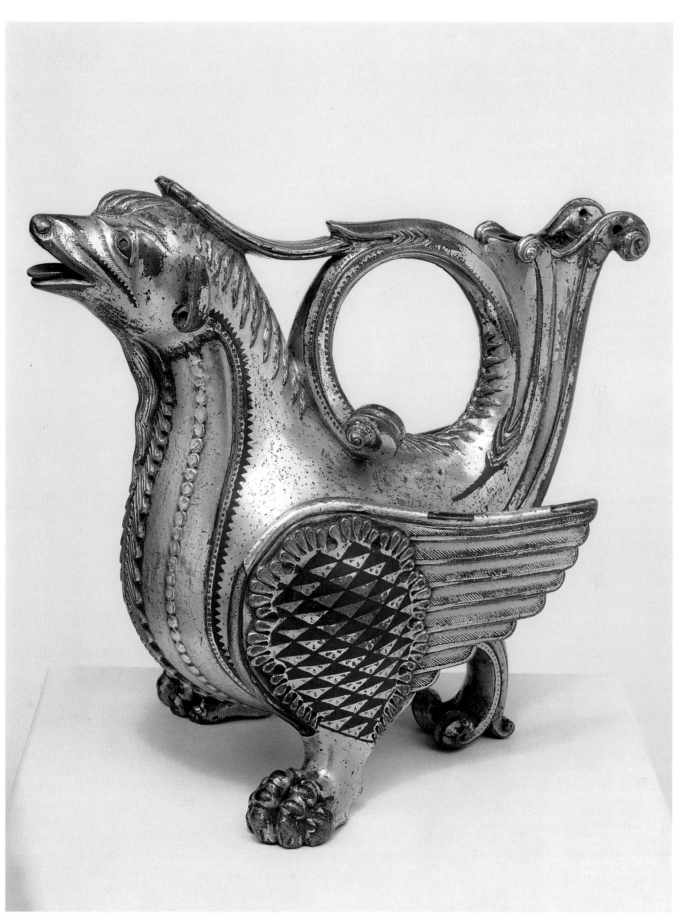

46.

46. Mosan region (modern Belgium). *Ewer: Griffin Aquamanile.* c. 1130. Cast-copper alloy, inlaid with sheet silver and niello, engraved and gilt, 7⅜ x 8¼ x 5" (18.7 x 20.9 x 12.8 cm). V&A 1471–1870

The Griffin ewer has been considered an important medieval piece since it was acquired in 1870 on the recommendation of Sir Matthew Digby Wyatt, art referee (consultant to the Museum on acquisitions), architect, journalist, and author of *Metalwork and Artistic Design* (1852). According to Digby Wyatt, "so fine and historical a piece of metalwork seldom occurs for sale. . . . designed and executed by a master of his craft [with] admirable 'hardiesse'."

Medieval ewers are often called aquamanilia (from the Latin *aqua:* water and *manus:* hand). They were used both in the home and especially in church, where washing rites (of hands, feet, and head) played an important part in the ceremonies of the Mass and baptism. From the twelfth century onward ewers often took the shape of real or fantastic animals and were made of either precious or base metal, or ceramic. Only a few dozen survive; this is one of the oldest and most technically sophisticated, the cast-copper alloy inlaid with sheet silver and niello—an ancient and skilled technique that goes back at least to ancient Egypt.

Originally the ewer would have been filled through the opening in the tail (the lid is missing), the mouth acting as the spout. Its shape resembles the fabulous beast known as a griffin, combining the head and wings of an eagle and the body of a lion. The form of griffins was influenced by Eastern *senmurvs,* images of which were woven into ancient Sassanid and Byzantine silks imported into Europe and preserved in cathedral treasuries. Since 1986 the ewer has been displayed at South Kensington in the Medieval Treasury, alongside a Sassanid textile with a depiction of this type of beast.

Lit. Fortnum, 1876, p. 112, plate xvi; Hungerford Pollen, 1878, p. 23; Williamson, 1986, p. 137, plate 9; Montevecchi and Rocca, 1988, p. 228; Mende, 1995, p. 228

MARIAN CAMPBELL

47. France (Limoges). *Reliquary Chasse.* c. 1200–50. Copper-alloy plaques enameled in champlevé on an oak core, with gilt copper alloy figures; the eyes of glass, 10¼ x 10⅝ x 4⅝" (26 x 26.9 x 11.7 cm). Bequeathed by George Salting. V&A M572–1910

In the Middle Ages, Limoges was the center of large-scale manufacturing of enameled objects, particularly reliquaries (to contain the relics of saints), crosses, candlesticks, and wares for ecclesiastical and domestic use. Found from the Outer Hebrides to southern Italy, these enamels were widely exported; more products from Limoges survive than from any other medieval center. Limoges enamels—made of ground glass laid into an engraved copper surface and fired at great heat—are characterized by a range of brilliant blues and stylized multicolored rosettes. Although their manufacture involved great skill, enamels had the advantage of being cheap to produce and enabled metalwork to be colored permanently in a range of vivid hues. This example uses a form popular for reliquaries—that of a miniature stylized church, with pointed gables at either end and a steep "roof." None of the applied and engraved figures of saints can be identified, and almost identical forms can be found on other Limoges objects to which this type of figure seems to have been applied rather indiscriminately.

Although certainly medieval, the two applied figures on the cresting make little iconographic sense and may have been placed there by a restorer; also, the central crystal nearby has been reset. Both changes evidently predate the Heckscher sale at Christie's in 1898, when John Webb—perhaps the son of the dealer of the same name (see cat. 40)—acquired the piece. Further work is recorded (in a notebook in the Museum archives) by Webb, who paid "André" (of Paris) £12 for unspecified restoration, which can be determined (from the Heckscher sale photograph) as having been the replacement of the left-hand cresting spike, a nicely "worn" detail.

When this piece was bequeathed to the Museum in 1910 by the Australian George Salting, along with his bronzes, Chinese porcelain, and English miniatures, enamels from Limoges were already prominent among the Museum's medieval collection. The enamels were on display with other metalwork, ivories, and jewelry in the Prince Consort Gallery by 1874 and, together with this Salting chasse, still have an important place today in the Medieval Treasury.

Lit. Rupin, 1890, pp. 331–2 and figs. 386, 394; Christie's, 1898, lot no. 182; Gomez-Moreno, 1968, no. 164; Campbell, 1983, p. 32, plate 23d; Taburet-Delahaye and Boehm, 1995

MARIAN CAMPBELL

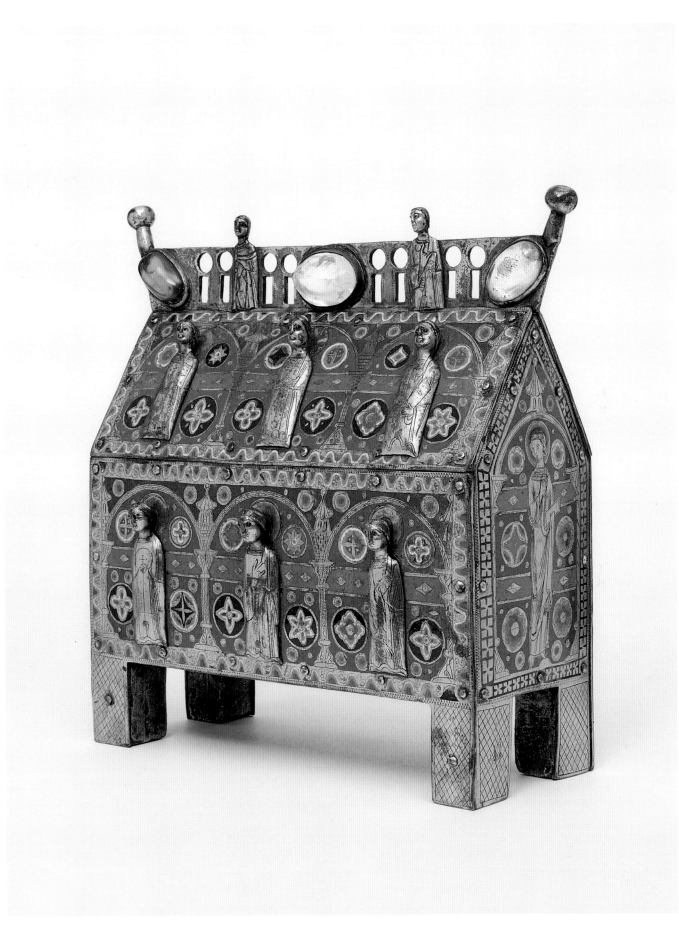

47.

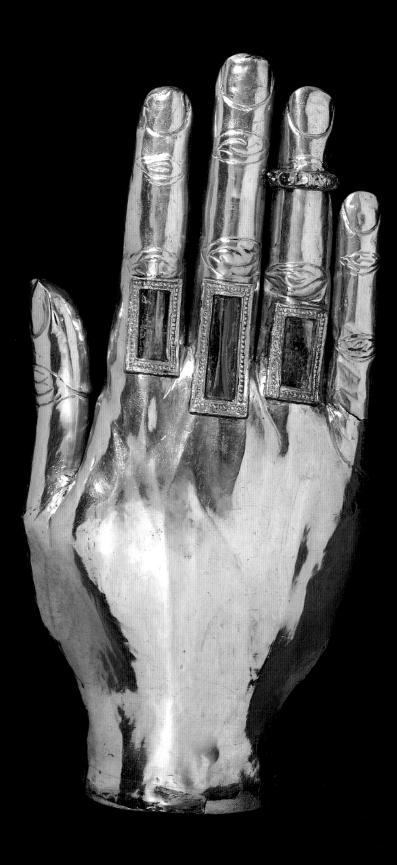

48. Flemish (modern Belgium). *Hand Reliquary.* c. 15th century. Sheet silver, parcel-gilt, set with mica and a stone (with modern wooden base), 9 x 4½ x 2¼" (22.8 x 11.5 x 5.7 cm). Bequeathed by Dr. W. L. Hildburgh. V&A M356–1956

The practice of acquiring medieval objects, well established by the 1860s, was sustained in the twentieth century in part through the scholarly enthusiasm and generosity of Dr. W. L. Hildburgh. An American settled in London, Hildburgh wrote extensively about English alabaster carvings and medieval enamels, and between 1916 and 1955 he gave numerous pieces of metalwork and sculpture to the Museum. This hand reliquary, lent to the Museum in 1930 and later bequeathed, appropriately overlaps these two categories.

Relics of saints were often housed in reliquaries that were shaped to represent the part of the body preserved, encased in gold or silver, and enameled or set with gems. In this case the hand may have originally formed part of an arm. The relics (now lost) would have been visible through the windows in the fingers. The sheet silver has been skillfully worked to produce a realistically modeled hand, complete with veins and lines. The style of the ring, worn almost at the fingertip, suggests a date of between 1400 and 1500.

Lit. Braun, 1940, pp. 338–411 and nos. 443–70; Williamson, 1986, p. 180; Montevecchi and Rocca, 1988, pp. 190–1, 194–5

MARIAN CAMPBELL

49. Italian. *The Resurrection of Christ.* 1510–20. Tin-glazed earthenware, painted in colors, 9⅞ x 8⅛ x ¾" (25 x 20.5 x 2 cm). Marked on the back with T and B in a monogram. V&A 69–1865

When this majolica (tin-glazed earthenware) panel appeared in the sale of the Pourtalès collection in 1865, it was described by Robinson in his recommendation for purchase as "most exquisite and rare [and] by one of the greatest of the early maiolica painters." Its importance was widely recognized with the publication in 1873 of C. D. Fortnum's catalogue of the majolica at South Kensington, in which it was described as "perhaps the most artistic production of the Italian painters on enamelled pottery which has descended to us." A study by ceramics curator Bernard Rackham in 1930 made it the central example in a group of ten pieces attributed to the "Master of the Resurrection Panel."

Although the TB monogram has not been identified convincingly with any named painter, the style in which the panel is painted suggests that it was executed by someone, probably working in Faenza or Urbino, who had as precedent examples the work of artists such as Andrea Mantegna, Melozzo da Forlì, or Girolamo Genga, as well as the distinctive Resurrection woodcuts of Albrecht Dürer. Taken together, these features suggest a date after 1510, which is confirmed by comparison with dated pieces of majolica.

Attitudes toward majolica, what was essentially a painting on a ceramic ground, were somewhat ambivalent. An extreme viewpoint, held by Richard Redgrave and quoted in the 1853 Marlborough House catalogue, was that "Landscapes and pictures are almost always out of place in pottery." Italian majolica was regarded technically, Redgrave continued, as "a ceramic art ... [but] important primarily for its painted decoration, often of a pictorial character." Rackham was likewise very much attuned to the qualities considered appropriate to ceramics, but in his writings about majolica he made constant reference to contemporary painters and concluded that because of the Resurrection Master's "skill of hand and his gifts of imagination alike he must be accorded an honourable place in the history of Italian art."

By claiming it to be "quite as excellent in its degree as great works of painting and sculpture of the same period," majolica pieces such as this were given canonical status, thus legitimizing applied arts through reference to the fine arts. It is perhaps an irony that, following the transfer of the ceramics collection to the top floor of the Aston Webb building in 1910, this canonical masterpiece has been almost lost among the many riches of the collection, with no visual indication of its importance.

Lit. Robinson, 1856, pp. 1–2; Robinson, 1865; Fortnum, 1873; Rackham, 1930; Falke, 1934; Wilson, 1985; Wilson, 1991, pp. 157–65

REINO LIEFKES

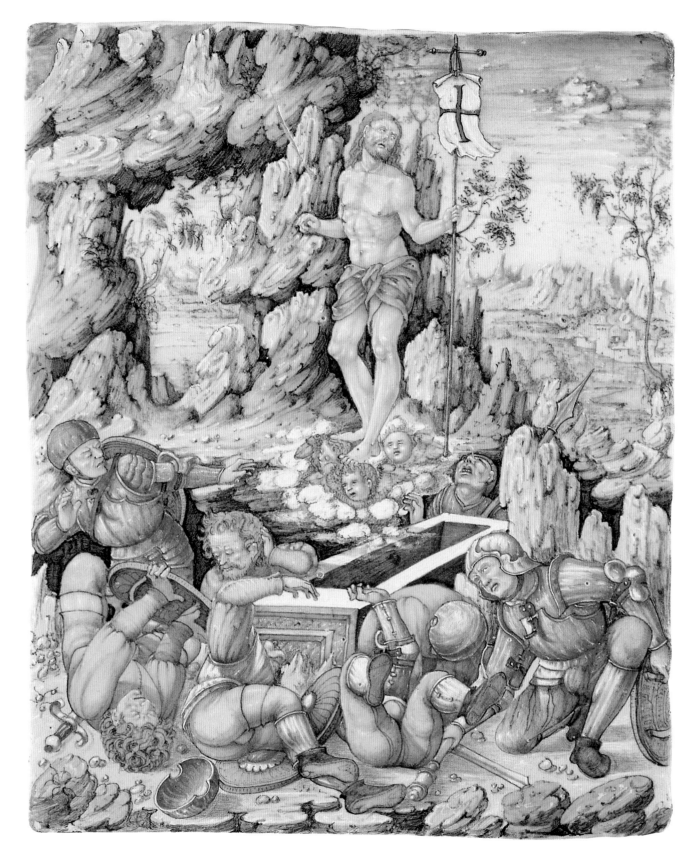

49.

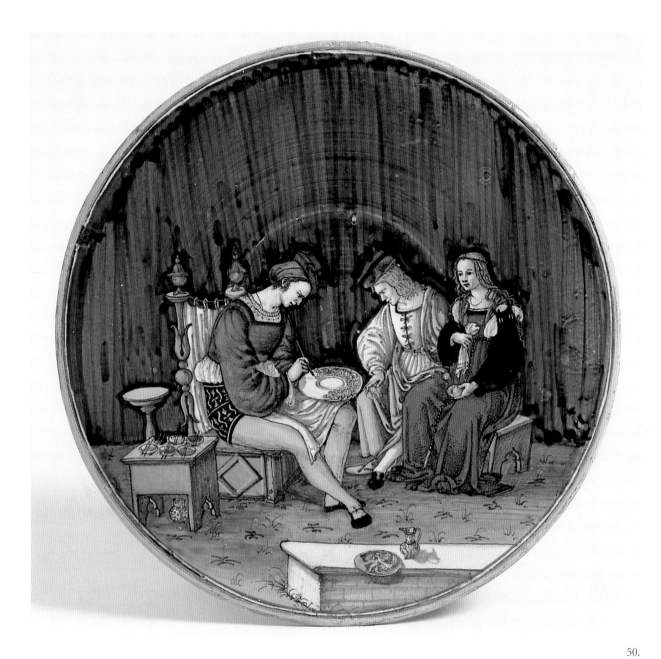

50.

50. Italian. *Plate: Majolica Painter at Work.* c. 1510. Tin-glazed earthenware, 9¼" (23.5 cm) diam., 1⅛" (3 cm) deep. V&A 1717–1855

As perhaps the most frequently illustrated piece of Italian majolica (tin-glazed earthenware), this plate has been given a central place in both the literature on the subject and the representation of ceramic techniques in the Museum. The monogram SP on the back probably stands for the names of Stefano and Piero di Filippo, who in 1458 took over the pottery that was housed at the Medici villa at Cafaggiolo. The style of the painting is closely related to pieces associated with a majolica painter at Cafaggiolo named Jacopo. Its Medici connections have recently been further strengthened by its identification in an inventory in 1784 of the Real Galleria in Florence, the core of which goes back to the collections of Lorenzo il Magnifico (1449–1492) and Cosimo I (1519–1574).

Shortly after leaving the Medici collection, the plate was seen by Carl Friedrich von Rumohr who in the 1820s was traveling around Italy to collect Italian art for the newly established Berlin museum. In October 1828 he reported his discovery of a collection of about 140 pieces of "terre d'Urbino." In the end, the piece was not purchased by the Berlin museum but acquired very shortly after its discovery "for an old song" by the duke of Buckingham, only to be sold with his vast collection at Stowe in 1848. From there, via the dealer Forrest, it entered the collection of Ralph Bernal. At the Bernal sale in 1855, the Museum acquired the plate along with other important examples of majolica, thus making the South Kensington Museum unrivaled for its ceramics collection.

Rumohr had reported an old story about Raphael's collaboration with a potter, suggesting that the young painter illustrated on the plate might be Raphael himself. By the time of the Bernal sale, the catalogue described the subject as "Raffaelle himself and the Fornarina seated in the studio of an artist." This refers to the myth of Raphael falling in love with a potter's daughter, called La Fornarina, and painting majolica in her father's workshop in order to gain her affections. Although entirely fictitious, this story could be linked with the description of majolica with figurative scenes as "Raffaelle ware," on the assumption that it was all produced in Raphael's home town of Urbino. This romantic story may account for the unusually high price of £120 paid by the Museum at the Bernal sale.

From the start, however, the story was not accepted by the Museum, where detailed knowledge of majolica was already being developed by J. C. Robinson and scholar-collector C. D. Fortnum, whose catalogue in 1873 provided the framework for later serious study of this material. Consequently, the Museum described the scene on the plate simply as "A maiolica painter in his studio, painting a plate in the presence of two persons of distinction." Since the frequent use of Raphael compositions on majolica linked the master's name to the applied arts, the temptation to exploit the more fanciful story must have been considerable.

The plate with an image of a majolica painter at work was complemented by the acquisition six years later of Cipriano Piccolpasso's mid-sixteenth-century illustrated manuscript, *Arte del Vasaio,* about the manufacture of majolica. The importance attached to both manuscript and plate was registered by their depiction in the stained-glass window representing majolica—one of the windows created in 1867–68 illustrating the history of ceramic production that formerly lined the Ceramics Gallery.

Lit. Fortnum, 1873; Rackham, 1930; Cora and Fanfani, 1982; Wilson, 1985

REINO LIEFKES

51. SOLOMON ALEXANDER HART (English, 1806–1881). *Maestro Giorgio of Gubbio.* c. 1870. Oil on canvas, 103⅞ x 34½" (264 x 87.6 cm). V&A 46–1874

The "Kensington Valhalla" is a series of life-size portraits of those artists understood in the 1860s to be the major figures in the history of European art; the portraits were created and then copied in mosaic to decorate the South Court of the Museum (see fig. 25). The "Valhalla" included not only painters and sculptors, such as Donatello (cat. 52), but also figures from the applied arts such as the potter Maestro Giorgio of Gubbio. By including craftsmen within the pantheon and describing them as "maestri," Henry Cole and the South Kensington Museum asserted a belief in the connection between the fine and applied arts. Through both these images and what the Museum collected and displayed, a canon of applied arts was formulated that paralleled one already established in the fine arts.

Giorgio di Pietro Andreoli, known as Maestro Giorgio, worked between 1492 and 1536 as a potter of majolica at Gubbio, one of the two main centers for the production of luster pottery in sixteenth-century Italy. Giorgio, whose modeling tools are shown in a pouch fixed to his belt, holds up the two-handled vase acquired for the Museum by J. C. Robinson in 1865 (cat. 53), as was a bowl corresponding to that on the table in the painting. Both the vase and the bowl have the characteristic luster glaze about which Robinson had written in his introduction to the 1856 catalogue of the Soulages collection.

When the Hart portrait was composed, the vase was not attributed to Giorgio himself and was used either as an example of a technique associated with his name or as a work by his master, to whom Giorgio was shown paying tribute. More recently, new evidence has led to an attribution to Giorgio himself.

Lit. Parkinson, 1990, 120–1

RONALD PARKINSON

52. RICHARD REDGRAVE (English, 1804–1888). *Donatello.* c. 1867. Oil on canvas, 103⅞ x 34½" (264 x 87.6 cm). V&A 1707–1869

Prominent among artists selected for the "Kensington Valhalla," a series of life-size portraits painted and then copied in mosaic for the Museum's South Court, were those—most notably Donatello—whose original works were then being collected by the Museum. Sculptures by Donatello, including the marble *Ascension* relief and the bronze *Winged Putto with a Fantastic Fish* (cat. 55) figured significantly among J. C. Robinson's acquisitions of Italian Renaissance sculpture and continue to be considered outstanding pieces in the most comprehensive collection of Italian sculpture in the world. The decision to represent the sculptor not with one of these works but instead with the Martelli Mirror (cat. 54), then attributed to him, was perhaps prompted by the statement in Vasari's biography that Donatello had been brought up by the Martelli family.

The artist Richard Redgrave occupied various positions in the School of Design at Somerset House and was one of Cole's

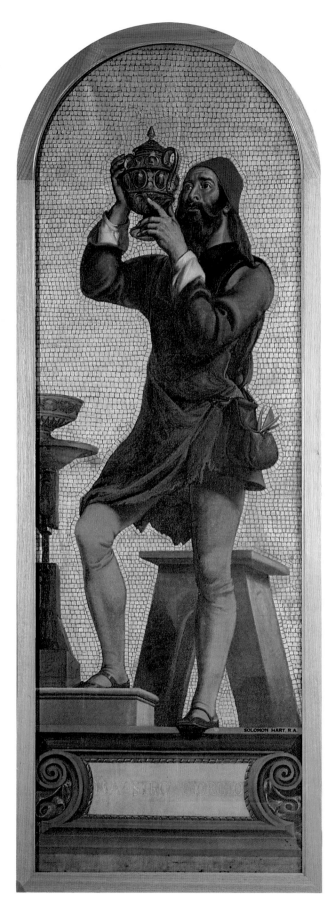

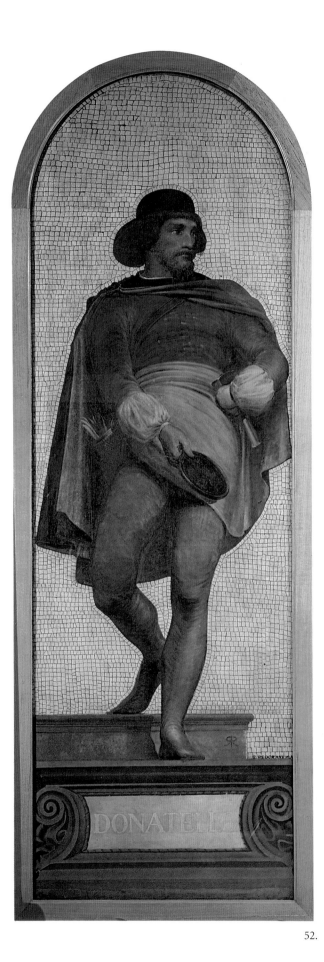

51.

52.

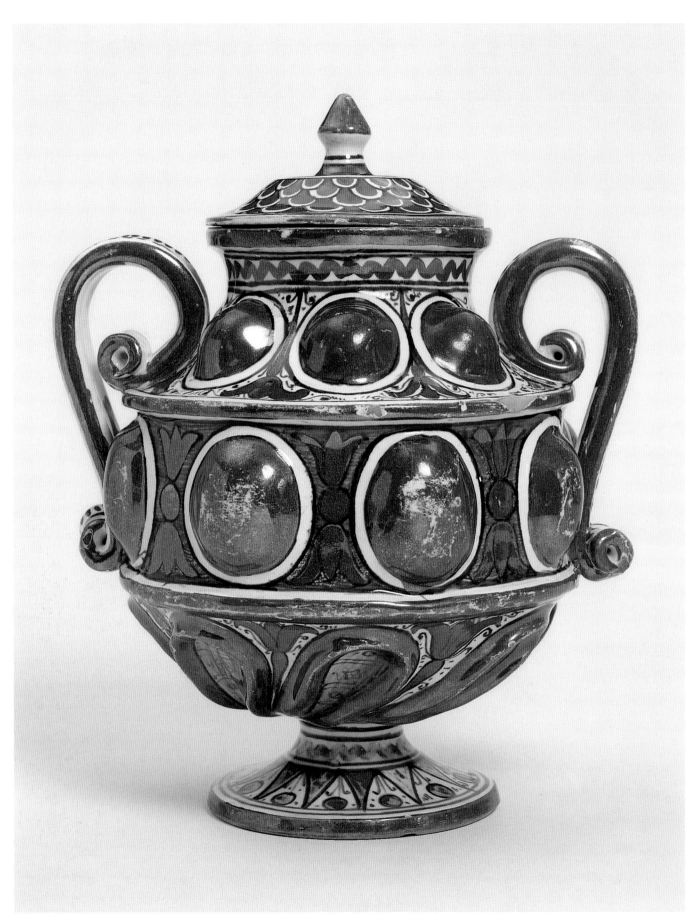

53.

most influential lieutenants at South Kensington. Like Charles Eastlake at the National Gallery, Redgrave was both a distinguished artist and a talented Museum official.

Lit. Casteras & Parkinson, 1988, pp. 140–1, 165; Parkinson, 1990, p. 245

Ronald Parkinson

53.
Attributed to GIORGIO DI PIETRO ANDREOLI (Italian, active c. 1490/92–1536). *Vase and Cover.* 1500–10. Tin-glazed earthenware with luster decoration, 10¼ x 9½ x 6⅞" (26 x 24 x 17.5 cm). V&A 500–1865

Purchased along with the outstanding ceramics in the Soulages collection, this vase is one of the earliest and most successful examples of Italian lusterware, a technique much admired and imitated in the late nineteenth century. Although depicted in Solomon Alexander Hart's painting of Giorgio di Pietro Andreoli, known as Maestro Giorgio of Gubbio (cat. 51), the vase was not attributed to him by J. C. Robinson, who described its unusually intense tint as "approximating rather to the Hispano-Arab copper lustre than to the genuine ruby of the Gubbio school." C. D. Fortnum's catalogue of 1873 attributed the vase not to Giorgio but to an anonymous potter earlier identified by Robinson as the "master or immediate predecessor of Giorgio." Maestro Giorgio's work was known primarily by his signed pieces, all dated within the range of 1518 to 1541. Recent archival research has shown, however, that as early as 1495 Maestro Giorgio entered a partnership with Maestro Giacomo di Paoluccio di Gubbio with the intention of producing "vasi di maiolici," which at that date referred to luster-decorated earthenware. In 1501 he signed another contract with Paoluccio for a duration of ten years, again to produce lusterwares. Now, for the first time in over a hundred years, it seems likely that Maestro Giorgio was depicted with his own vase after all.

Lit. Robinson, 1856, pp. 1–5, 15, 57, no. 99; Fortnum, 1873, pp. lii, 228; Rackham, 1940, p. 167, no. 510; Fiocco and Gherardi, 1988–89, pp. 401–9; Wilson, 1993a, pp. 163–72; Mattei and Cecchetti, 1995

REINO LIEFKES

54.
Possibly by CARADOSSO FOPPA, called CARADOSSO DEL MUNDO (Italian, 1452–1527). *The Martelli Mirror.* c. 1495–1500. Bronze with gold and silver, 7½" (19.1 cm) diam., 1⅝" (4 cm) deep. V&A 8717–1863

Set in the back of this mirror is a bronze relief with an unusually high finish, its refinement indicating it to be the work of a major Italian Renaissance sculptor. Originally attributed to the fifteenth-century Florentine sculptor Donatello and represented in Richard Redgrave's painting of him (cat. 52), the mirror is an outstanding example of the type of small-scale object acquired by the V&A in the 1860s; it remains characteristic of the Museum's collections in both its high quality and its merging of sculpture and the applied arts.

The relief on the reverse of the mirror shows the profile figures of a satyr and a bacchante beneath a term (a tapered pedestal that supports a bust or merges at the top into a figure) representing the ancient Greek fertility god, Priapus. These figures, together with a Latin inscription meaning "Nature encourages what necessity demands," suggest that the relief is an allegory of procreation. Robinson, evidently concerned that the subject would cause offense to polite society, suggested that a gold "leaf or spray of foliage should be added" to the genitals of Priapus before it went on public view.

The mirror was purchased in Florence in 1863 from the Martelli family for the colossal sum of £650, more than twice the amount paid two years earlier for Donatello's marble *Ascension.* Although J. C. Robinson's comment that this "celebrated work is supposed to be from the hand of Donatello" (18 August 1863) already suggests a certain doubt about the object's authorship, the mirror continued to be labeled as by Donatello. It was initially displayed among enamels, bronzes, clocks, and other precious objects in the Prince Consort Gallery. The *Art Journal* in 1865 criticized the validity of presenting such "curiosities" in the context of "a museum purporting to be *established solely for the working student.*" Enamels and bronzes were seen as "little else but reckless and useless expenditure," and the price paid for the Martelli Mirror was contrasted with the "£3 and £4" for which casts—the electrotype copies of the mirror made by Franchi and Son and sold by the Museum—could be bought, "particularly as the latter serve every useful purpose, and are more pleasant to the eye than the original." But such criticism was anticipated by Robinson, who had justified the policy of acquiring originals in addition to casts in his 1862 catalogue of Italian sculpture.

Although the attribution to Donatello was maintained by C. D. Fortnum in his 1876 catalogue of bronzes in the Museum, his keen eye led him to recognize that the detailed tooling was more "worthy of the practised goldsmith," such as Caradosso or Cellini. Long considered one of the Museum's masterpieces (see fig. 89), the mirror was one of the few bronzes included in John Pope-Hennessy's catalogue of Italian sculpture, in which it was described as Mantuan. Recently found inside the mirror was a

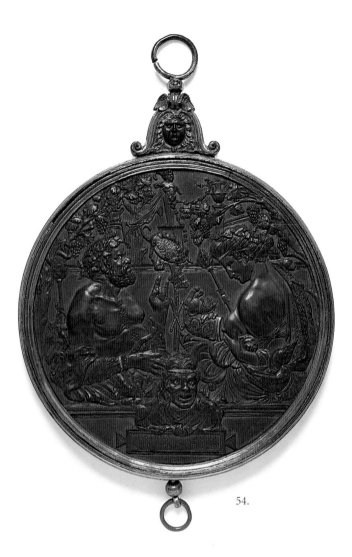

54.

fragment of a document about enemy French troop movements written in a secret code used by Milanese diplomats. Such a discarded scrap of paper would have been available only to someone working within the Milanese court. This has prompted reconsideration of the attribution to Caradosso (who was active in Milan between 1475 and 1505), first tentatively suggested by Fortnum a century before.

Lit. Fortnum, 1876, pp. 58–9; Pope-Hennessy, 1964, pp. 325–9; Ebert-Schifferer, Beck, and Blume, 1985, pp. 446–8

PETA MOTTURE

55. Attributed to DONATELLO (Italian, c. 1386–1466). *Winged Putto with a Fantastic Fish.* c. 1435–40. Bronze, parcel-gilt, 15¾ x 16 x 4⅛" (40 x 40.6 x 10.6 cm). V&A 475–1864

In 1864 J. C. Robinson was particularly keen to supplement the Museum's "comparatively poor" holdings of bronzes with examples from the Eugène Piot collection to be sold that April in Paris. He noted, however, that his own acquisitions of Italian sculpture for the Museum in past years were the main cause of the much higher prices that the finest pieces were likely to command. Much to Robinson's annoyance, his recommendations were largely rejected by the board, both before and immediately after the sale, when other bronzes from the Piot collection were offered by London dealer John Webb. *Winged Putto* was one piece that the Museum did acquire at the sale, primarily as an example of bronze casting. At this time it was associated by Robinson with Andrea del Verrocchio (Italian, 1435–1488), but soon afterward it was classified almost unanimously as a product of Donatello's workshop. Despite being described as merely from Donatello's workshop, the bronze was regarded as such a major work that it was included in the Museum's publication, *Fifty Masterpieces of Sculpture,* published in 1951 (with a second edition in 1964). In 1977 a layer of corrosion and hard, black wax was removed, revealing the exceptional quality of the modeling and chasing, prompting Anthony Radcliffe, then an assistant keeper in the V&A's Department of Architecture and Sculpture,

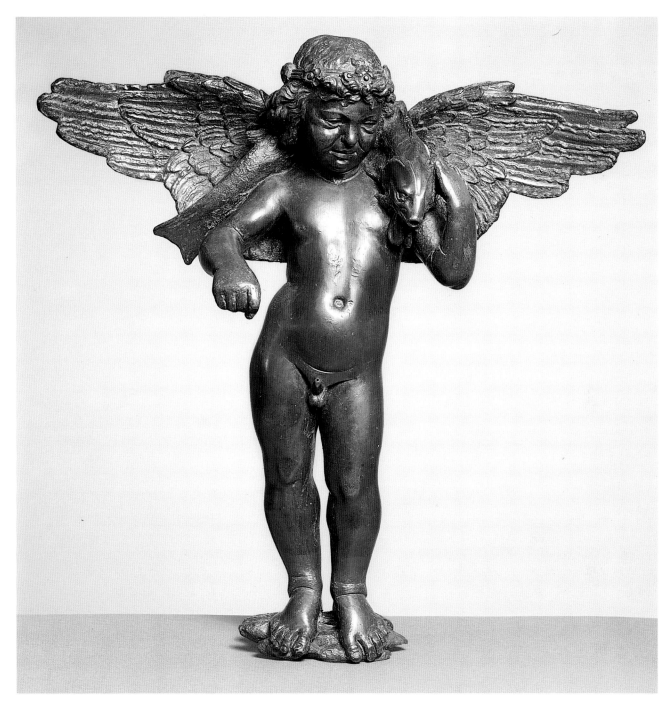

to attribute it to Donatello himself. The conservation treatment also revealed that the object on which the boy stands—described as a "rocky base" by John Pope-Hennessy—was in fact a tortoise, an emblematic device of the Medici family (though it is unknown if it was intended as such in this piece).

The same conservation examination also led to a rethinking of the bronze's setting, which in turn has been reflected in changes over time in how the Museum has displayed it. Described by Robinson as the crowning figure of a fountain, it was suggested by Eric Maclagan and Margaret Longhurst in their catalogue of 1932 that the boy originally stood on a dolphin, guiding it with reins. The putto was therefore displayed in

the round and was at one time mounted on a column. The figure was, in fact, designed to function as a wall fountain, the water entering through a round hole in the back and issuing out through two jets: one in the mouth of the fish and the other in the penis of the boy; the water played on an object once held in his right hand, probably a water wheel.

Lit. Maclagan and Longhurst, 1932; Pope-Hennessy, 1964, pp. 78–80; Radcliffe, 1985, pp. 124–5

Peta Motture

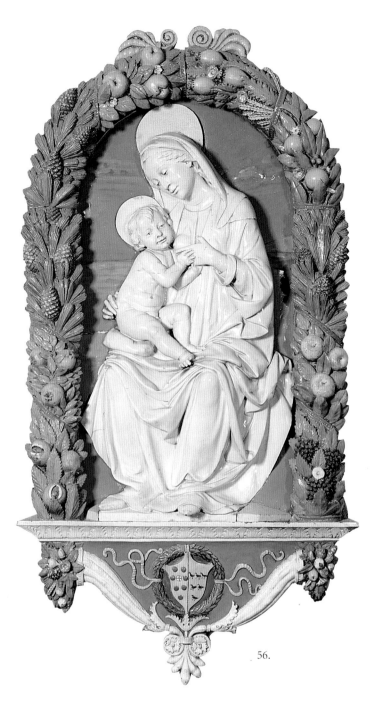

56.

cially relevant to the Museum's founding mission. This relief of the Virgin and Child—a characteristic devotional subject—is supported by a console bearing the arms of the Medici and Rondinelli families, suggesting that it was commissioned by Gabriele di Cambio de' Medici, whose marriage to Lucrezia di Alessandro Rondinelli took place in 1487–88.

While in the collection of Marchese Giovan Pietro Campana, *Virgin and Child* was attributed to Luca della Robbia, whose works were considered superior to Andrea's. The objects in the so-called Gigli-Campana collection were of mixed quality, and in 1861 J. C. Robinson purchased a selection, including this relief. He reattributed it to Andrea and suggested that there was "probably no finer specimen" surviving from the artist's early period.

The popularity of della Robbia ware was reflected in the rapid increase in its value during the 1860s (Robinson papers, 18 January 1864). At that time the Museum was actively pursuing the acquisition of casts of Italian sculpture, and lists were drawn up of those considered suitable for casting, including "all the works of . . . the Robbias." Copies were made in vast numbers in the late nineteenth and early twentieth centuries by specialist firms in Italy, and the ware's polychrome effects were imitated in England by the della Robbia pottery at Birkenhead, as well as by the Minton factory in its ceramic decoration of South Kensington's refreshment room, designed by James Gamble. In 1874 this example was displayed among "fifty specimens of enamelled terracotta or Luca della Robbia ware" in the North Court. Removed for safekeeping in World War II (see fig. 45), it was placed in the new Italian Renaissance galleries upon its return to the Museum.

Lit. Museo Campana, 1859, classe xi, p. 2, no. 9; Robinson, 1862b, p. 63; Pope-Hennessy, 1964, pp. 213–4

PETA MOTTURE

56. ANDREA DELLA ROBBIA (Italian, 1435–1525). *Virgin and Child.* 1487–88. Enameled terra cotta, 65⅜ x 34 x 6½" (166 x 86.5 x 16.5 cm). V&A 7630–1861

Sculpture in glazed terra cotta produced by the family workshop founded by Luca della Robbia was particularly highly esteemed in the second half of the nineteenth century and figured prominently among the Museum's early acquisitions of Italian sculpture. The reproductive method used by the workshop in its later years also provided a link with manufacturing, which was espe-

57. BARTOLOMMEO BELLANO (Italian, c. 1437–1496/97). *Lamentation over the Dead Christ.* c. 1470–75. Marble, 40 x 43⅞ x 5¾" (101.6 x 111.6 x 14.6 cm). V&A 314–1878

This strongly carved relief of the Lamentation, which formed part of an altarpiece or antependium, was made for the church of SS. Trinità in Padua. The tonsured figure to the left appears to represent the donor, who probably held the office of Prevosto della SS. Trinità.

Acquired in 1878 as a work of the school of Donatello, this attribution was subsequently erased from the Museum register at the suggestion of J. C. Robinson who, despite having resigned as an art referee (advisor on acquisitions) two years before, was one of three experts whose views were reported before the relief

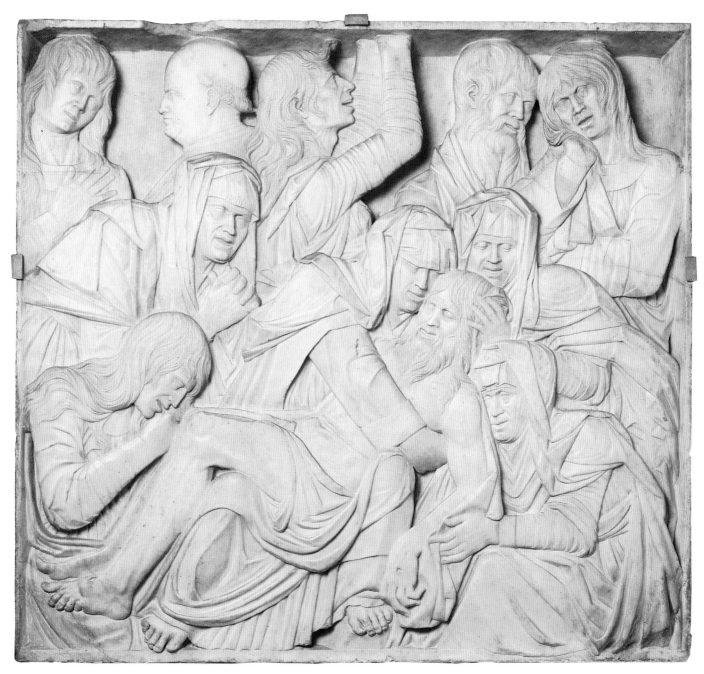

57.

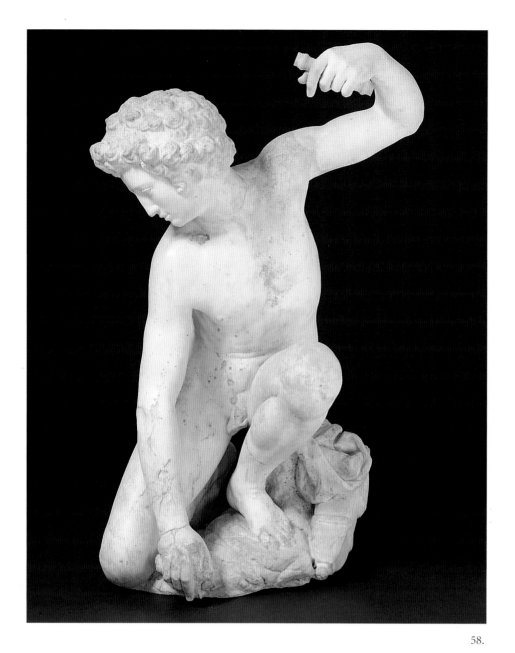

58.

was purchased. Another was Edward Poynter, who regarded the marble as "a remarkably fine specimen of religious art," which, though "somewhat archaic in treatment," was notable for "the intensity of tragic expression and devout feeling which it displays." This powerful image, with its figures agonized in grief, has a directness of expression seen in other works by both Donatello and Bellano (who worked with Donatello in Padua and Florence). The connection with Bellano was soon recognized and has been widely accepted ever since.

Lit. Pope-Hennessy, 1964, pp. 335–7; Krahn, 1988, pp. 89–97

PETA MOTTURE

58. Italian. *Narcissus.* Antique, probably recut c. 1564 by VALERIO CIOLI (Italian, c. 1529–1599). Marble, 39⅜ x 26¾ x 21¾" (99.9 x 67.8 x 55.3 cm). V&A 7560–1861

A dramatic example of how the status of objects may change, this figure was once thought to be a representation of Cupid by the young Michelangelo and was one of the most celebrated works in the Museum. It is now thought to be an antique fragment restored in the sixteenth century and, accordingly, a relatively minor piece. (The documented *Cupid* that this figure was once thought to be has recently been tentatively linked with a marble in New York.)

The statue was acquired from the so-called Gigli-Campana collection for £1,000 as the *Cupid* carved by Michelangelo for Jacopo Galli in 1497. The 1861 purchase of eighty-four works from the combined collections of Ottavio Gigli and Marchese Giovan Pietro Campana—although ultimately understood to be of uneven quality and unreliable attributions—was widely praised in the press at the time, and overnight made the V&A's sculpture collection "one of the most important features of the Museum" (*Athenaeum*, 27 April 1861). The *Cupid* was selected for particular praise, being considered in the same article as of "a far higher status as a work of Art" than Michelangelo's *Bacchus* in the Museo Nazionale, Florence, then believed to have been carved at the same time.

The sculpture was first displayed in the newly erected North Court where, according to Wilson's 1876 biography of Michelangelo, it became "the chief ornament of the South-Kensington-Museum." Although doubts as to its authenticity had been expressed since the end of the last century, it was not until 1945 that it was relabeled as "formerly attributed to Michelangelo." Despite this, the sculpture was the centerpiece of the influential 1946 exhibition, "Style in Sculpture" (see fig. 49); it was placed as the focal point of the Renaissance Galleries in 1949 (see fig. 48); and it continued to be highlighted in the guidebooks as the work of Michelangelo. John Pope-Hennessy's reappraisal of the figure showed that the body was an ancient copy of a Hellenistic model of a warrior; the figure was extensively recut in the sixteenth century, when a new head set in a downward gaze was added, prompting Pope-Hennessy to reinterpret the subject as Narcissus gazing into a pool.

In the course of Pope-Hennessy's intensive research for his monumental catalogue of Italian sculpture, published in 1964, he established that not only the "Cupid," but eighteen other pieces in the V&A collection—including terra cottas and wax models—all thought to be by Michelangelo, were not by the master. Only one of the wax models, a *Slave* (see fig. 85), survived Pope-Hennessy's careful scrutiny as an authentic work by Michelangelo, and today it enjoys a prominent position in the Renaissance galleries.

Lit. Wilson, 1876, p. 34; Pope-Hennessy, 1964, pp. 452–5; Pope-Hennessy, 1968; Summers, 1979, pp. 461–2

Peta Motture

59. Pier Jacopo Alari-Bonacolsi, called Antico.
(Italian, c. 1460–1528). *Meleager*. c. 1484–90. Bronze, parcel-gilt with silver inlay, 13⅝ x 6⅞" (34.6 x 17.5 cm). Purchased through the Horn Bequest and Bryan Fund and with the assistance of the National Art Collections Fund. V&A A.27–1960

With the purchase of this exquisite bronze statuette in 1960, curator John Pope-Hennessy continued the tradition of collecting Italian Renaissance bronzes established by J. C. Robinson one hundred years earlier (see cat. 55). Meleager, a famous warrior in Greek mythology, led a band of heroes to kill a boar that was sent to ravage his land. The statuette, which shows Meleager in the act of spearing the boar (see also cat. 8), is based on a lost antique marble popularly known as the "peasant"; this Antico is probably the "figure of metal called the little peasant" referred to in the 1496 inventory made after the death of Gianfrancesco, son of Marchese Ludovico Gonzaga of Mantua. Antico was court artist to the Gonzaga dynasty and developed his sophisticated technique for reproducing small bronzes within the cultivated humanism of the Gonzaga court for which Andrea Mantegna was also working. Although he often used molds to reproduce different versions of the same figure, this is the only known version of *Meleager*. The figure's hair, mustache, beard, teeth, tunic, and sandals are gilded, and the eyes are inlaid with silver. The gold and silver contrast with the darkly patinated bronze surface of the body, making this a refined, luxurious decorative object, almost as close to goldsmiths' work as to sculpture. Seen in this way—as a work, equally, of fine and applied art, thus teasing at the distinctions between the two—*Meleager* exemplifies many of the issues addressed in the Museum's collections.

London antiques dealer H. C. Baxter had brought the bronze into the Department of Architecture and Sculpture and, within a week, Pope-Hennessy wrote to the Museum's director Trenchard Cox to report his discovery, describing it as "one of the most beautiful Antico bronzes in the world" and urging its purchase. The importance of the find was underscored by his assertion that it was "the first occasion in . . . [his] experience in which it has been possible to buy an absolutely first-rate parcel-gilt bronze Antico statuette."

When discussing the potential price with the dealer, Pope-Hennessy pointedly mentioned that the Museum had paid £2,126 for two Antico bronze roundels the previous year. Despite the valuation of £6,000 attached to *Meleager*, it was offered to the Museum at the reduced price of £4,000. In making his case to the director, Pope-Hennessy noted that the price was a large sum but not "in any way excessive for a bronze of this rarity and quality." In a handwritten annotation, the director responded that the Museum was "greatly indebted to . . . [Pope-Hennessy] for this important discovery."

Confident of substantial support from the National Art Collections Fund, the director approached its chairman, Lord Crawford, a formidable scholar of Italian Renaissance art, but the initial response was unexpectedly disappointing. Rather ambiguously, Crawford replied that the bronze was "a most 'desirable acquisition': marvellous—& quite horrible," but begged the Museum to "let . . . [the Fund] off lightly" because of other commitments. In particular, he was concerned by the price, which he considered "a great deal: as bronzes really cant [sic], even if by Donatello, be expected to vie in price with a scribble by Dufy in this brave[?] world." Undeterred, the director sent photographs with the assurance that "I believe you will

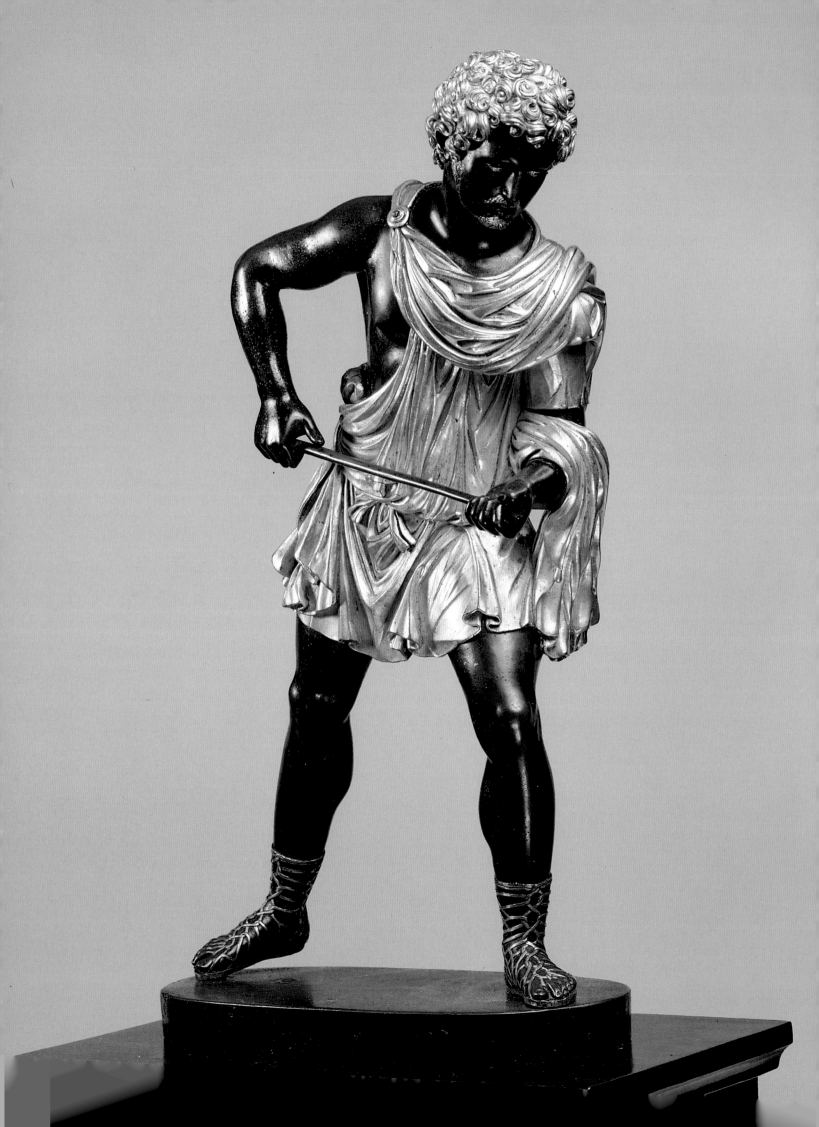

think it less horrible than you supposed." His gambit was successful, and Lord Crawford conceded that "it must be marvellous—& very beautiful. And of course it is not dear: perhaps I made[?] a naughty joke. . . ." The Fund finally donated £2,900 toward the purchase.

Pope-Hennessy believed the bronze base to be a later addition and removed it; subsequent comparison with bases on other Antico bronzes—as art-historical attention focused more on settings, frames, and bases—revealed that the base was original. Figure and base were reunited only in 1974.

Lit. Chambers and Martineau, 1981, pp. 134–5; Ebert-Schifferer, Beck, and Blume, 1985, pp. 410–1; Allison, 1993/1994, pp. 168–71

Peta Motture

Opposite: Cat. 59.

60. Carlo Crivelli (Italian, working 1457–94). *Virgin and Child.* c. 1480. Tempera on panel, 19⅛ x 13¼" (48.5 x 33.6 cm). Signed "OPUS. CAROLI. CRIVELLI. VENETI." Bequeathed by John Jones. V&A 492–1882

Although collector John Jones was attracted above all to eighteenth-century French art (cats. 84–86), he shared his contemporaries' enthusiasm for the rich imagery and ornate embellishments of paintings by Carlo Crivelli. In the 1860s the National Gallery purchased four paintings by Crivelli, including the spectacular Demidoff altarpiece in 1868. Jones probably bought this panel in Italy in the early 1860s. Crivelli's intricate details, rich fruits and foliage, and sinuous linear qualities greatly influenced Dante Gabriel Rossetti and the second generation of Pre-Raphaelite artists such as Edward Burne-Jones.

Lit. Kauffmann, 1973, pp. 78–9

Ronald Parkinson

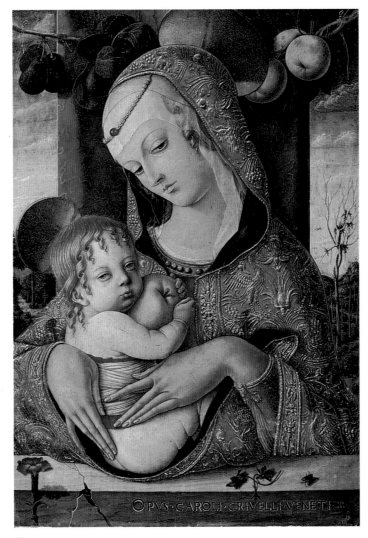

60.

61. BENVENUTO CELLINI (Italian [Florence], 1500–1571). *Head of Medusa.* c. 1545–50. Bronze, 5⅜ x 3¾ x 5¾" (13.8 x 9.5 x 14.5 cm). V&A A.14-1964

Like the gilt bronze figure of Meleager (cat. 59), this expressive head was acquired by John Pope-Hennessy, who recognized its significance as one of the few surviving models by Benvenuto Cellini, the most celebrated of Italian Renaissance sculptor-goldsmiths. In Greek myth, the Gorgons Stheno, Euryale, and Medusa (the only mortal of the three) were hideous sisters, winged and snake-haired, who turned all who looked at them to stone. Cellini's famed monumental statue of Perseus (fig. 91) shows the hero holding the head of Medusa, with hair of writhing snakes, after he had beheaded the Gorgon with the aid of a reflection in the polished bronze surface of his shield (the gift of the goddess Athena) so as to avoid her deadly gaze.

The *Perseus* was commissioned by Cosimo I de' Medici in 1541 when Cellini returned to Florence from France but was not finished until 1554 when it was placed in the Loggia dei Lanzi in the Piazza della Signoria in the center of the city. Because of its prominent site it is familiar to every visitor to Florence but its fame, and its position as the sculptor's masterpiece, were assured by the vivid account of its commissioning and casting given in Cellini's autobiography. Cellini reported in his *Life* that Duke Cosimo responded enthusiastically to the artist's suggestion of Perseus as a subject (the hero Perseus was a dynastic emblem of the Medici, first adopted by Cosimo's predecessor Alessandro de' Medici). When presented with a model in wax (now in the Museo Nazionale in Florence) Cosimo declared: "If you could translate this little model, Benvenuto, into a full-scale work, it would be the finest piece in the Piazza." This was a high compliment—as well as a purposeful challenge—to Cellini since the dominant works then on the Piazza della Signoria were two acclaimed masterpieces, Michelangelo's *David* and Donatello's *Judith* (with the head of Holofernes), the latter positioned as a pendant to the site Cosimo designated for Cellini's *Perseus.*

The finished statue rose an imposing seventeen feet from the bottom of its base to the top of Perseus's left hand gripping the head of Medusa, with gore hanging from its severed head and blood spewing from the headless body's neck. Pope-Hennessy writes convincingly that Cellini's "purpose was to depict not a dead but a newly decapitated body, with blood pouring from its neck and still coursing through its veins, an Amazon so powerful that the magnitude of Perseus' achievement stood in no doubt." Contemporaries were astonished at the fearsome realism of these details of the *Perseus,* one reporting that "Though metal, it seemed like human blood, and one stood aside for fear of being splashed by it." The new sculpture was an unqualified success with the populace (it was a tradition of the time, based on classical precedent, to "test" public work on its public audience and, depending on the response, modify the work accordingly before committing it to permanent installa-

tion); and Cellini was praised by fellow artists, scholars, and poets, one of whom declared that "the bronze Perseus turned the onlooker to marble," while another compared Cellini "to a star which in the star-strewn sky outshone the other stars."

Between the making of the first wax model shown to Cosimo and the casting of the full-scale bronze, Cellini made many other models—almost all now lost—some of which, rather unusually, were in bronze. One of them (now in the Museo Nazionale) was for the head of Medusa—for which the artist's mistress Dorotea was the model—and, sharing some features of the early wax and others of the finished statue, had long been accepted as a model by Cellini. When a second model of Medusa's head with the hand and wrist of Perseus appeared in the 1960s, Pope-Hennessy recognized its similarities to the bronze head in Florence, suggesting that this newly discovered piece might be the "head of Medusa, of bronze" recorded in the inventory of Cellini's studio at the sculptor's death. His rigorous analysis of the material and documentary evidence led him to conclude that this was "not only an autograph sculpture by Cellini but ... a sketch-model for the head of Medusa in his masterpiece, the *Perseus.*" It was acquired by the Museum and placed alongside the Italian Renaissance sculptors' models purchased by J. C. Robinson almost exactly a century earlier. Subsequent thermoluminescent testing of the clay "core" within the head established that the bronze must have been cast between 1415 and 1570, a period that spans the ten years when Cellini is known to have been working on the *Perseus.*

Lit. Pope-Hennessy, 1965; Pope-Hennessy, 1985

MALCOLM BAKER/BRENDA RICHARDSON

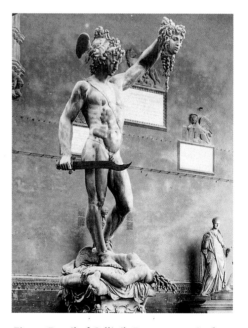

Fig. 91. Detail of Cellini's *Perseus,* 1554, in the Loggia dei Lanzi, Piazza della Signoria, Florence

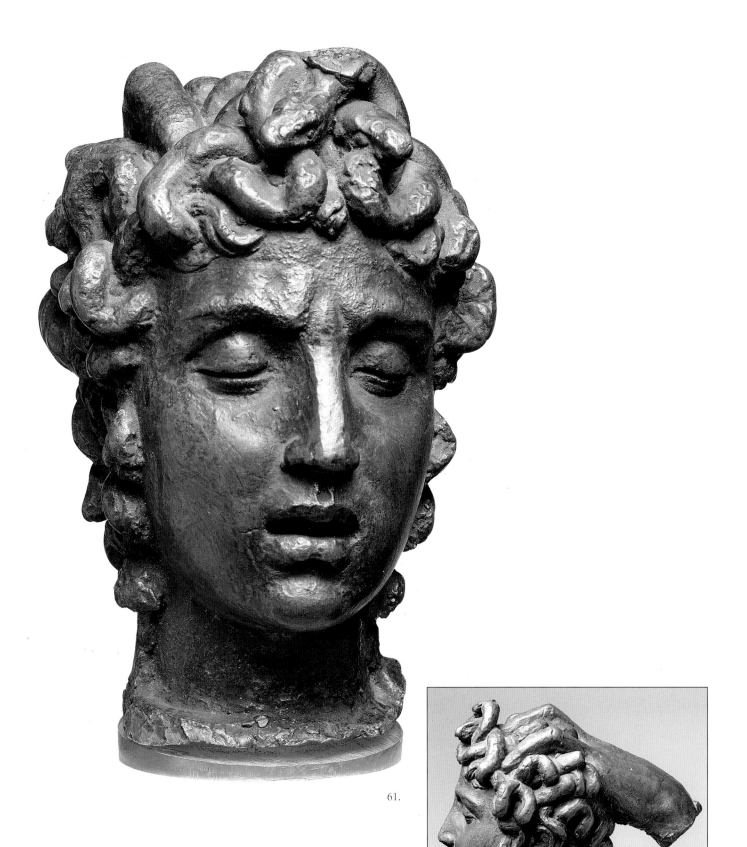

61.

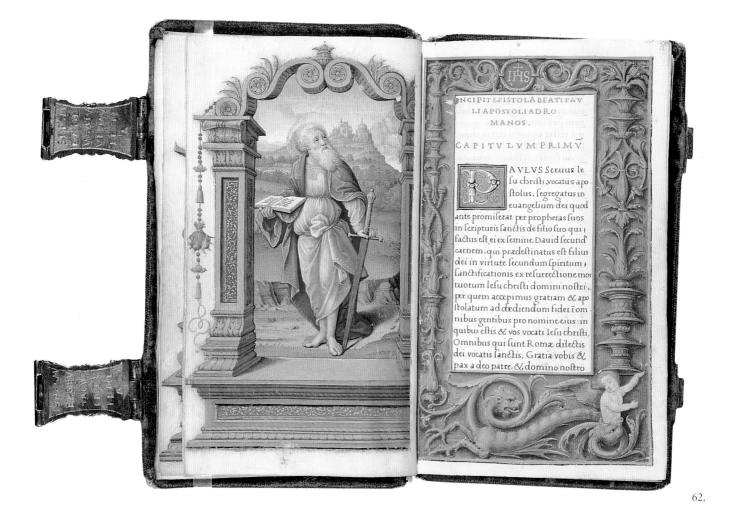

62. French (Loire Valley?). *Illuminated Manuscript: The "Leuville Epistles"*. Written and illuminated c. 1525–26. Tempera and brushed gold on vellum; binding, green velvet on pasteboard covers and gilt metal clasps with enamel, 195 ff., 4½ x 3⅜ x 1⅜" (11.5 x 8 x 3 cm). Bequeathed by David Currie. V&A MSL.1721–1921. [Illustrated: pages depicting Saint Paul and the beginning of Chapter 1 of The Epistle of Paul the Apostle to the Ephesians]

From the mid-nineteenth century, illuminated books, particularly in their original bindings, became essential to any collection that purported to give a comprehensive account of European artistic production. As well as buying books on art and collections of engraved ornament (see cat. 14) for use by students, the Museum's library purchased for the art collections both complete manuscripts and manuscript cuttings from 1855 onward.

Books used by laypeople in the decades around 1500 for their private devotions (Books of Hours, prayerbooks, books with selections from the scriptures) were often produced in luxury formats with rich illustrations and elaborate border decoration; they were especially popular among nineteenth-century collectors. Such books were mass-produced in considerable quantities throughout the fifteenth century, initially by traditional handmade techniques (manuscript books—from the Latin *manus*: hand and *scriptus*: written) and, from the 1480s, by the new technology of printing. Images were integral to such books and the devotional practices they served, though only the wealthy could afford to employ skilled craftsmen using expensive pigments and gold. Illuminators decorated both printed and manuscript books.

In the *Leuville Epistles,* images of Saint Jerome and five authors of the epistles (including Saint Paul) are placed in ornate settings alongside meticulously written texts imitating printed characters in Italian versions of roman and italic letter forms. The luxurious nature of the book is also apparent in the binding's exquisite clasps, which bear the heraldic arms of the original owner, a member of the Olivier de Leuville family.

By the late nineteenth century, the *Leuville Epistles* were in the collection of David Currie, a shipping magnate with a magnificent assemblage of historical arms, armor, and metalwork, as well as other objects, from an "antique Persian Rug" to a "piece of gothic tapestry." Many pieces from the Currie collection were placed on extended loan to the Museum from 1887 on, including the present manuscript, which was bequeathed in 1921.

Rowan Watson

63. LEONARDO DA VINCI (Italian, 1452–1519). *Notebook from the "Codex Forster"*. 1487–90 and 1505. Pen and ink, 55 ff., 5⅜ x 4⅛ x ¾" (13.5 x 10.5 x 2 cm). Bequeathed by John Forster, 1876. V&A Forster MS.141/1

The presence at South Kensington of works by Italian High Renaissance artists such as Michelangelo and Raphael would seem to make the Museum's acquisition in 1876 of a work by their contemporary, Leonardo da Vinci, very appropriate. However, while its significance within a collection already renowned for its Renaissance holdings was clearly recognized, this notebook was initially displayed with other manuscripts— alongside examples of autographs—rather than with other Renaissance works.

This volume of the *Codex Forster,* composed of three volumes, dates from a period when Leonardo's notebooks reveal an increasing preoccupation with mathematics; the contents of this notebook address the geometrical problem of transforming a solid or shape into another of equal volume or area. In treating a single subject at length, it differs from most of the artist's other surviving notebooks (including the other two that make up the *Codex Forster*), which are fragmentary, containing isolated thoughts, observations, and sketches on a variety of subjects. As in some other Leonardo manuscripts, the notebook is written in mirror script; this has been attributed to his left-handedness and even to a desire for secrecy.

Leonardo was a famous artist during his lifetime. He left his manuscripts and drawings to Francesco Melzi of Milan, where they were seen by art historian Giorgio Vasari before 1568. The dispersal of the manuscripts began before Melzi's death, and later Charles I of England and Napoleon were among those who attempted to acquire manuscripts and drawings by Leonardo's hand.

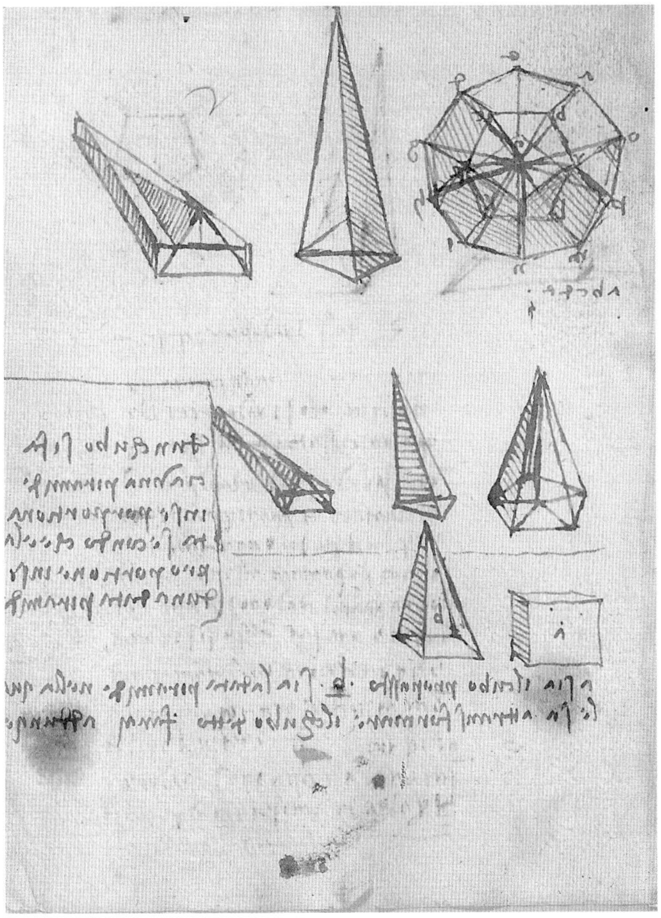

63. (folio 15)

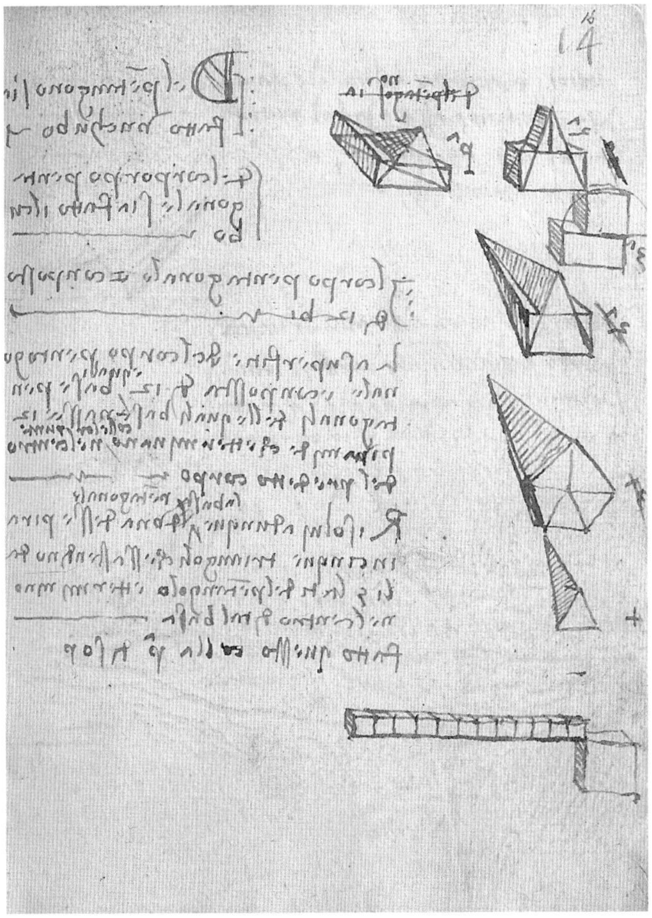

63. (folio 16)

Nothing is known about the early provenance of the *Codex Forster* notebooks. They were purchased in Vienna by Edward Robert Lytton, first earl of Lytton (1831–1891), who gave them to his close friend John Forster (whose name identifies the notebooks, as is traditional). Lytton appears to have been unsure of the authorship and value of the notebooks: plagued by financial problems, he wrote to his wife, probably in about 1868, "What do you think? Mr Robinson the Art Connoisseur [at South Kensington] tells me that the note books of Leonardo which I gave Forster (if genuine) [are] worth £500 or £600." J. C. Robinson later confirmed their authenticity and they were bequeathed to the Museum in 1876 along with Forster's collection of books, paintings, and manuscripts, including those by Charles Dickens (cat. 155). The bequest's fame owed much to its collection of "autographs," a major feature of a display set up in the Museum after 1876. Leonardo's notebooks were prominent in that display and are mentioned repeatedly in London guidebooks from 1881 onward, when Baedeker's guide described them as having been those carried by "the master . . . at his belt."

From the mid-1920s (though planned from as early as 1911), a series of ambitious facsimiles of Leonardo manuscripts (including the *Codex Forster*) was produced by the Italian government as part of the fascist promotion (and attempted appropriation) of an Italian Renaissance hero. After much discussion with the Foreign Office (and partly in return for Italian loans to a major exhibition of Italian art at the Royal Academy in 1930), all three notebooks of the *Codex Forster,* together with Leonardo drawings from Windsor Castle, were reluctantly lent in 1939 to a major exhibition in the Palazzo dell'Arte in Milan. This exhibition, promoted at the insistence of the "greatest Italian of today" (Benito Mussolini) to celebrate the "greatest Italian of the past" (Leonardo) sought to demonstrate the cultural, economic, and political self-sufficiency of Italy. The British government managed to retrieve its Leonardo notebooks and drawings in mid-July, before the end of the exhibition in October 1939.

Lit. Richter, 1879, pp. 344–5; Hayward Gallery, 1989

ROWAN WATSON

64. HANS DAUCHER (German, c. 1485–1538). *Saint John the Evangelist.* c. 1523. Limestone, 32 x 10½ x 7¼" (81.2 x 26.7 x 18.5 cm). V&A 49–1864

This figure of Saint John was almost certainly intended to form part of a Crucifixion group, along with a crucified Christ and the mourning Virgin Mary. It is a distinguished example of the religious sculpture being produced in stone or wood in Germany around 1500. It was probably commissioned by Hans Lamparter von Greiffenstein, a member of a prominent Nuremberg family, whose coat of arms is carved below the saint's feet. A commission for such a Crucifixion group from an Augsburg sculptor was mentioned by Lamparter in a letter of 1524; this evidence led to an attribution to Hans Daucher, the leading sculptor of Augsburg in the early sixteenth century. The letter also says that he intended the group to be erected in a church in Nuremberg as a monument to his father but, having heard that the people of the city were destroying images, he had decided not to proceed with the plan. Therefore, the other figures in the Crucifixion group were never completed. The figure is a telling case of an image produced at exactly the time when attitudes toward religious sculpture were changing dramatically as a result of criticism from Protestant Reformers.

The purchase in Munich in 1864 of this "youth with clasped hands, probably St John," reflected a growing admiration for German Late Gothic and Renaissance art that is also to be seen in the additions of German silver and plaster casts to the collections around the same time. But as an example of carving in limestone, the piece was also valued in accord with the Museum's concern with materials and processes of making. By 1946 its authorship had long been established and it was shown in the Museum's "Style in Sculpture," a display organized by the postwar director Leigh Ashton, which set out to encourage a fresh evaluation of sculpture by juxtaposing works of different nationalities and periods (see fig. 49), including the "Michelangelo *Cupid*" (cat. 58) and Michael Rysbrack's *Newton* (cat. 137). *Saint John* was described as "a typical synthesis of late medieval and Renaissance elements" and, placed on a marble column, was presented within a history of style without any reference to its function or context. More recently, attention has been given to the circumstances in which it was commissioned, Lamparter's change of mind over its setting, and shifts in attitude toward sculpture around 1520. In response to this reevaluation of the work, as well as current interest in the original setting and function of objects, the figure is now displayed as part of a group of images illustrating changing patterns of devotion in sixteenth-century Europe. Cultural significance has now taken precedence over questions of authorship.

Lit. Lieb, 1952, p. 218; Baxandall, 1974, pp. 62–4; Baxandall, 1980, p. 72

MALCOLM BAKER

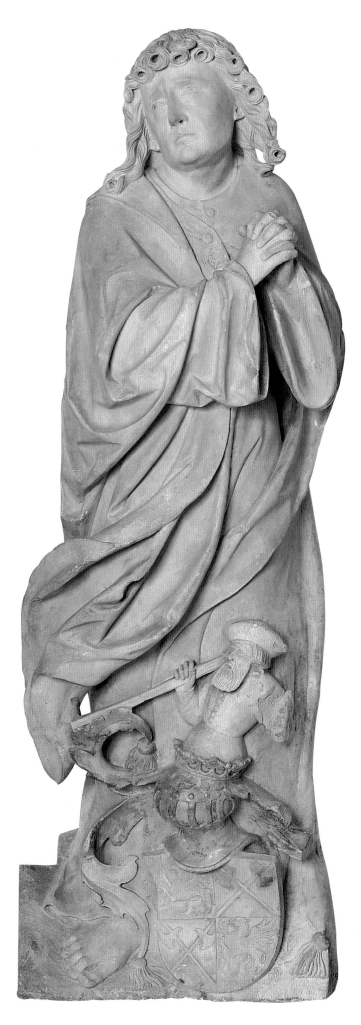

64.

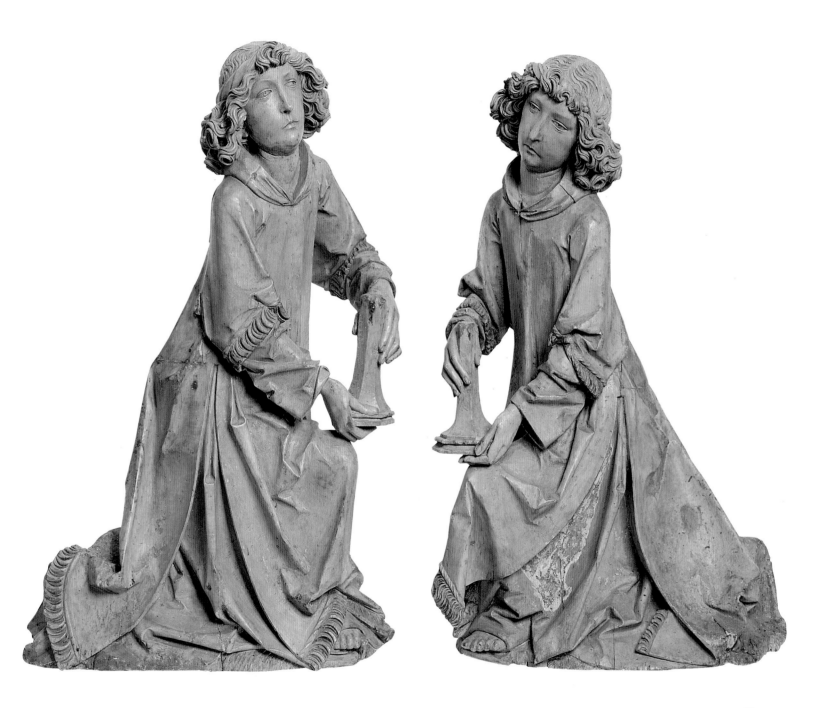

65.

65. Tilman Riemenschneider (South German [Würzburg], c. 1460–1531). *Two Angels*. c. 1505. Limewood, A.16 angel 25 x 16½ x 6½" (63.5 x 42 x 16.5 cm), A.17 angel 25⅝ x 14⅛ x 7⅛" (65 x 36 x 18 cm). V&A A.16–1912 & A.17–1912

The purchase of these two figures in 1912 shows the Museum's continuing interest in German art up to the outbreak of World War I and, in particular, the attention paid to Tilman Riemenschneider, the Late Gothic South German sculptor who was in the nineteenth century one of the most widely admired German artists. Riemenschneider's standing was such that many new acquisitions in the field of German Late Gothic sculpture were initially attributed to him, including *Saint John* by Hans Daucher (cat. 64) when it was acquired in 1864. (Ironically, however, when Riemenschneider's limewood group, *Mary, Salome, and Zebedee*, came into the Museum in 1878, it was at first ascribed to the Ulm sculptor Jörg Syrlin.) The admiration for Riemenschneider was evident at the Museum by virtue of the place given to plaster casts of his works; in 1906 the Museum bought five painted examples, including a cast of the monumental tomb of Rudolph von Scherenberg (1496–99) from the Würzburg Cathedral. The pair of angels was bought from the church of Wolferstetten near Külsheim in Baden. The two kneeling angels, "bearing every sign of the master's remarkably individual style" and "charming examples of his rather recondite type of beauty," may originally have stood on either side of a tabernacle (fig. 92).

Lit. V&A, 1913, pp. 4–5; Baxandall, 1974, pp. 46–7

Norbert Jopek

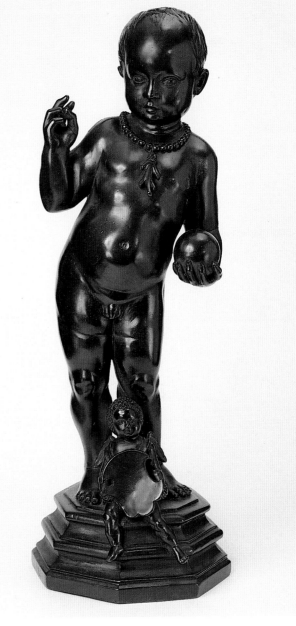

66.

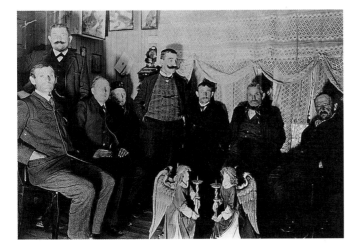

Fig. 92. The Riemenschneider angels photographed in 1912 with representatives of the seven farm families who together owned the chapel of Wolferstetten. The angels were sold by the families once the chapel was no longer in use. Originally polychromed, the angels were stripped of their paint and gesso, much of it certainly nineteenth-century, after their acquisition by the V&A.

66. Attributed to Pankraz Labenwolf (German, 1492–1563). *Christ Child*. c. 1550–60. Bronze, 18¾ x 6¾ x 7¼" (47.5 x 17 x 18.5 cm). V&A 411–1854

Although German sculpture figured prominently among the Museum's early acquisitions, this exceptional finely cast German bronze was first considered to be Italian, perhaps because of its technical qualities. When acquired in 1854, its curatorial assessment stated: "Admirable in pose and sentiment, the modelling of this figure denotes, as we believe, the Florentine school of the revival, and may even be by the hand of Verrocchio, the great pupil of Donatello." This view was reiterated in C. D. Fortnum's catalogue of 1876 and again in its 1910 edition. In 1926, however,

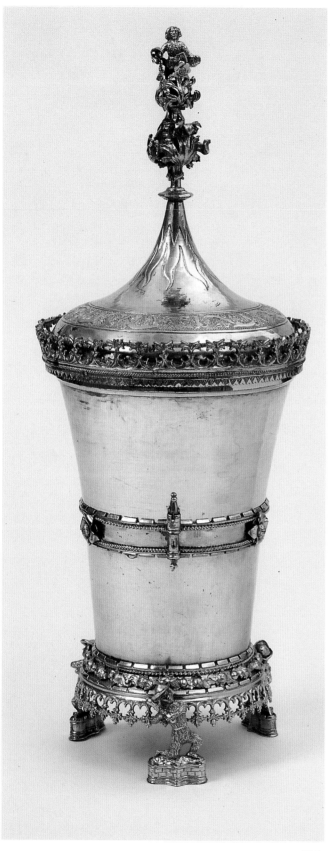

Christ Child was associated with the bronze foundry of Pankraz Labenwolf (1492–1563) in Nuremberg. This is still regarded as largely valid. The wood model for *Christ Child* may have been provided by an unknown contemporary Nuremberg wood sculptor; however, the cherub with the shield seems to be cast after an older model which may have been available in the Labenwolf foundry. Despite its Italianate style, this depiction of a nude Christ Child, with his right hand raised in blessing and with an orb in his left hand, is deeply rooted in the Gothic devotional tradition. Numerous wood figures of this type from the fourteenth century and later have survived, and these were often placed in the cells of nuns as an aid to their private prayer.

Lit. Fortnum, 1876, p. 14; Meller, 1926, plate 40; Radcliffe, 1966, p. 65

Norbert Jopek

67.1 South German or Swiss. *Beaker and Cover.* c. 1450. Silver, parcel-gilt, raised and chased; the mounts, feet, and finial cast; the finial partly enameled, 12 x 3½ x 4⅜" (30.5 x 9 x 11 cm). Unmarked. V&A 7941–1862

This example of German Late Gothic silver was acquired as a "rare and most beautiful specimen" with a number of other outstanding medieval objects, including the twelfth-century Gloucester Candlestick, from the Soltikoff sale in 1862.

As is unusual for a medieval silver object, much of its early history is known. Inventory records show that it was a gift to the Basel Cathedral treasury from a chaplain, Eucharius Vol, who died in 1502. The treasury survived the Reformation intact, but was broken up in 1827 following a dispute between the cathedral and the canton, and its contents were dispersed into antiquarian collections. The beaker thus reflects the vicissitudes of the nineteenth-century art market, as well as the Museum's interest in German material in the 1860s.

The beaker is plainer than much Late Gothic silver, lacking any elaborate mounts or richly embossed or chased surfaces. The wild men that appear as the feet and finial are a frequently used medieval motif and were a symbol of power and fertility. Such beakers were secular objects and were intended mainly for display.

Lit. Hungerford Pollen, 1878, pp. 115–6; Burckhardt, 1956, vol. I, pp. 49–50, no. 58, and vol. II, pp. 315–20, no. 60; Oman, 1960; Badisches Landesmuseum, 1970, p. 269, no. 234, plate 214; Fritz, 1982, p. 274, no. 625

67.1.　Pippa Shirley

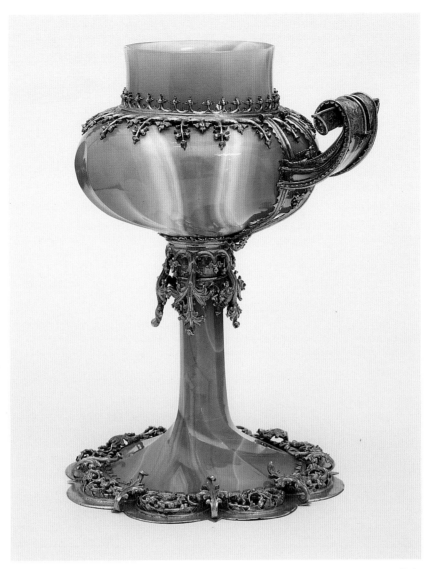

67.2.

67.2 German(?). *Cup.* 19th century, in the style of c. 1475. Agate with silver-gilt mounts, 8¼ x 6⅛ x 5⅝" (21 x 15.5 x 14.3 cm). V&A 389–1854

Another supposedly Gothic metalwork object acquired in the same era as cat. 67.1 has had a rather different later history. This exotic and sumptuously decorated cup was bought on the recommendation of J. C. Robinson in 1854 for the then considerable sum of £80, at a time when the Museum was actively seeking out German silver. When it was acquired, it was considered a splendid example of Late Gothic metalwork and was embraced as one of the stellar pieces in the collection. Exotic mounted pieces, such as hard stone, rock crystal, or mother-of-pearl, were greatly prized in late medieval and Renaissance times and were within the grasp of only the very wealthy. With their implications of status, sophistication, and taste, such jewel-like objects were given a prominent place in aristocratic "cabinets of curiosities."

These very qualities also made such pieces highly attractive to eighteenth- and nineteenth-century collectors. Since few genuine examples had survived, however, a thriving market developed for made-up and "improved" mounted hard stones. This cup, consistently published in the standard accounts of Gothic goldsmiths' work, has only recently been reconsidered in relation to comparable objects in European collections. On the basis of certain construction features—such as the jointed stem, separate handle, and round foot disguised with a lobed mount—along with the object's total lack of wear and the absence of information about its early provenance, the cup has been reclassified as an example of nineteenth-century rather than Gothic goldsmiths' work.

Lit. Somers Cocks, 1980, p. 18, pl. 21; Fritz, 1982, no. 639; Tait, 1991, p. 172, fig. 188

PIPPA SHIRLEY

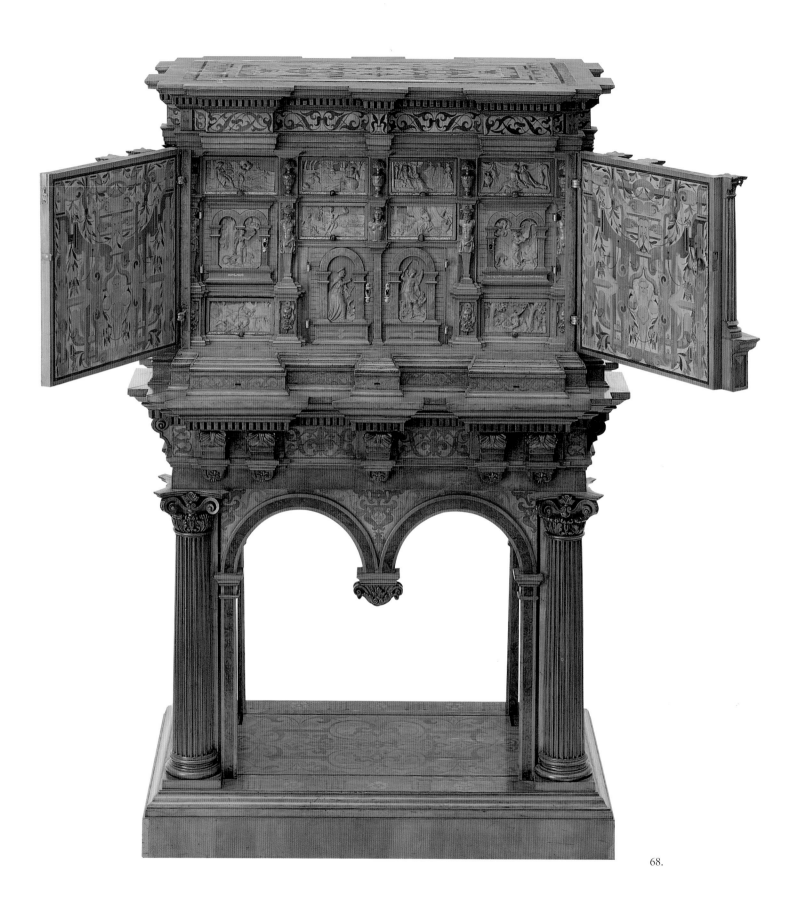

68.

68. South German, probably Augsburg. *The Holbein Cabinet.* 1550–80. (Stand: English? 1800–20?). Oak carcase, ash drawer linings, boxwood carvings, marquetry of various woods, 55⅛ x 35¼ x 23⅝" (140 x 89.5 x 60 cm). V&A 27-1869

The history of this cabinet, both before and after it entered the Museum's collection in 1869, illustrates the ways in which presumed associations with a major artist (Hans Holbein, the Younger) and a historical figure (Henry VIII) influence how an object is viewed and assessed. It also reflects the Museum's changing views about the relationship between English and European material and its attempts to balance stylistic qualities with historical significance. The cabinet—now considered to be sixteenth-century South German—was in the collection of author and antiquarian William Beckford (1760–1844) at Fonthill Abbey in the early nineteenth century. In the catalogue of the abortive 1822 sale of the Beckford collection, the piece was described as "A CABINET of the Greatest CURIOSITY . . . from the PALACE at WHITEHALL, and executed from designs of HOLBEIN for KING HENRY the VIIIth," thus attracting interest for its historical associations as well as its virtuosity. The cabinet's stand is later in date and may have been commissioned by Beckford, or possibly earlier in the eighteenth century.

When the cabinet was acquired by the Museum from the dealer Henry Durlacher in 1869 it still retained the Henry VIII provenance and its association with designs by Holbein, who had settled in England in 1532 and in 1537 became the king's court painter. Having experienced overwhelming success in England (he portrayed nearly a quarter of the nation's peerage), Holbein had been regarded by both Horace Walpole and Beckford as a talismanic figure in the history of English art. The cabinet's importance, according to Matthew Digby Wyatt's recommendation for its acquisition, thus resided in its national historical significance and its place in the development of specifically English design. Although Digby Wyatt strongly recommended the acquisition, he was, in comparison to later appraisers, noticeably cool about its artistic merit, probably because he regarded it as English work: "Of course the workmanship (which I believe to be English—as it is certainly neither French, Spanish, nor Italian, and I cannot think it to be German) does not fully realise . . . the admirable life and ease of Holbein's drawings. . . ." Thus thought to be of English workmanship, the piece was displayed among a varied and changing assortment of English furniture during the later nineteenth century.

However, as early as 1874 John Hungerford Pollen noted that the piece was "perhaps of mixed German and English workmanship" and focused upon the exceptional quality of the interior carvings, which he felt made the cabinet "the most remarkable in the Museum." The furniture specialist Percy Macquoid, discussing the piece in 1904, similarly praised the carvings: ". . . there is no possible ground for attributing the marvellous little carv-

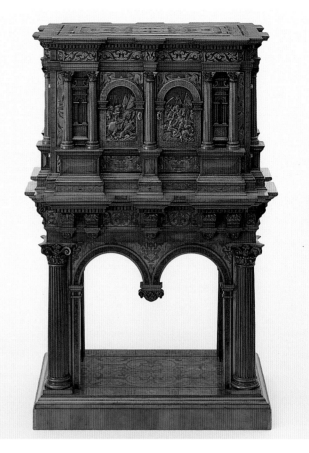

68.

ings in boxwood on the faces of the drawers, and the skill shown in the portrayal of the human form to this [English] source." By at least 1913 the cabinet was recognized as typically South German in its form, and displayed with other European Renaissance furniture. More recent discussions of the piece—coinciding with the rise of interest in antiquarianism—have focused on its presence in Beckford's collection. Given its name because of a misunderstood association, the cabinet nonetheless retains its name as the Holbein Cabinet to the present day.

The cabinet's numerous drawers and compartments were intended to house a collection of precious objects or "curiosities," and the clever intellectual aspects of the cabinet's decoration make it a very appropriate receptacle for such a collection. Whereas the exterior is decorated on the front and sides with intense and violent battle scenes, the interior carvings, sometimes accompanied by moral maxims in Latin, strike a more contemplative tone; for example, a ruler is urged to listen to the advice of Age, Mars (the god of war) is chastised by Saint Michael, and Time leads Youth from ignorance to understanding.

Lit. Christie's, 1822; Hungerford Pollen, 1874, pp. 42–6; Macquoid, 1904, pp. 102–4; Möller, 1956, pp. 101–5; Wainwright, 1971; Alfter, 1986, pp. 42–6; Wilk, 1996, p. 38

ELEANOR JOHN

69. ADRIAN DE VRIES (Dutch, c. 1545–1626 [working in Prague c. 1601–12]). *Emperor Rudolf II.* 1609. Bronze, 30 x 24 x 4½" (76.2 x 61 x 11.5 cm). V&A 6920–1860

The collection assembled by the Emperor Rudolf II in Prague, which included natural objects and raw materials along with works of art, was the most celebrated of those "cabinets of curiosities" often seen as forerunners of the modern museum. It therefore seems appropriate that the Museum's 1860 acquisition of Rudolf's bronze portrait relief—once in the emperor's personal collection—was justified as much for its technical merits as a bronze casting as for its artistic qualities: "This work is a masterpiece of bronze casting and chiselling, irrespective of its excellence in point of art," commented J. C. Robinson.

The most distinctive sculptor active in northern Europe in the early seventeenth century, the Dutch-born de Vries worked with Giovanni Bologna, called Giambologna, in Italy before joining the artists assembled by Rudolf II at his court in Prague.

The bronze portrait is signed under the left edge; the sitter is identified by another inscription in Latin on the edge of the arm, "Rudolph II, Roman Emperor, Caesar Augustus, aged 57, in the year 1609." The lion's mask on the shoulder guard, the imperial eagle, and the allegorical reliefs on the cuirass (depicting "Hercules holding up the world" and "Minerva with a trophy of arms and a statuette of Victory") allude to the Emperor's position and power. The portrait was recorded in the inventory of Rudolf's cabinet of curiosities in Prague by 1611; after 1652, it formed part of the collection of Queen Christina of Sweden.

Lit. Larsson, 1967, p. 48, plate 92; Robinson, 1862b, p. 167

NORBERT JOPEK

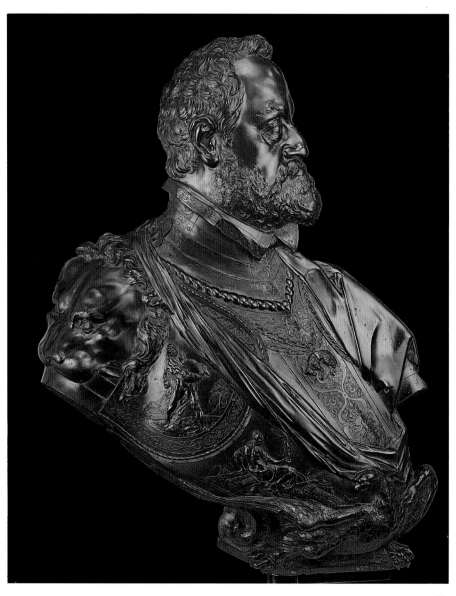

69.

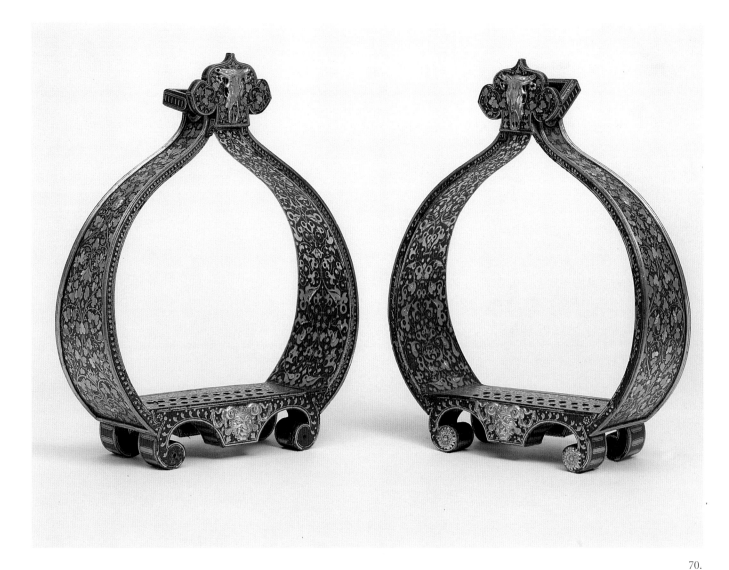

70. Italian (Pesaro). Probably made by BARTOLOMMEO CAMPI. *Pair of Stirrups.* 1546. Iron damascened and overlaid with gold and silver, each 6¾ x 5⅜ x 2¾" (17.3 x 13.7 x 7 cm). Marks: each stirrup inlaid with the initials "A. C. F." Bequeathed by George Salting. V&A M662–1910

The stirrups formed part of a suit of armor in the Royal Armory, Madrid, made in 1546, probably by the Italian armorer and goldsmith Bartolommeo Campi of Pesaro, for Duke Guidobaldo II of Urbino. By tradition, this ceremonial armor was presented by the duke to the emperor Charles V. The decoration of vine leaf tendrils damascened in gold and silver on the exterior differs markedly from the interior decoration, which is in an Islamic style with arabesques and half-palmettes. It is possible that the stirrups were decorated by two goldsmiths working in collaboration. This might explain the discrepancy between the initials B. C. F. (Bartolommeo Campi fecit) on the armor and the A. C. F. on the stirrups. The stirrups became separated from the armor in the 1830s when a quantity of items were stolen from Madrid's Royal Armory and sold in England. They were first in the Warwick Castle collection and later acquired by Salting, who bequeathed them to the Museum.

Arms and armor had from the sixteenth century formed part of antiquarian and aristocratic collections in which they were displayed to evoke associations of a medieval chivalric past. In precisely such a collection in the early nineteenth century, these elaborately decorated stirrups were esteemed by Salting as examples of goldsmiths' work and were accordingly placed alongside bronzes and porcelains in his collection. After Salting's bequest to the Museum, the stirrups became part of a collection of predominantly decorative arms and armor, interpreted in terms of design, decoration, and technique rather than in terms of either function or social significance.

Lit. Laking, 1907; Laking, 1920, vol. 3, p. 282; V&A, 1951, no. 35; Boccia and Coelho, 1967, nos. 275 & 276

ANTHONY R. E. NORTH

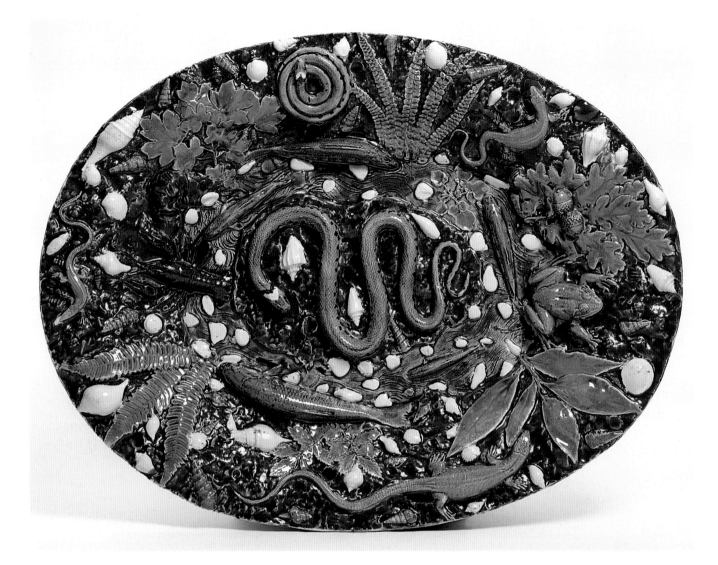

71. Possibly made by BERNARD PALISSY (French [Paris], c. 1509/10–c. 1585) or his sons, Nicolas and Mathurin
Dish. 1565–85, or possibly 17th century. Earthenware with colored glazes, 16 x 21 x 1⅝" (40.6 x 53.3 x 4 cm). Marks: paper label for "Dept.S&A Museum."
V&A 5476-1859

Trained as a glass painter, Bernard Palissy studied the chemistry of glazes and by 1565 had set up a kiln on the grounds of the Palais des Tuileries in Paris for which he was commissioned to make a *grotte rustique* by Catherine de' Medici, daughter of Lorenzo de' Medici, duke of Urbino. Catherine, who became queen consort to Henry II of France in 1533, gained real power in 1560 when she was named regent for her second son, Charles IX, who ascended the throne as a ten-year-old. During the 1850s and over the next three decades, excavations around the Louvre and Tuileries gardens revealed parts of the *grotte rustique* and also a tile-maker's kiln then thought to be Palissy's, along with

fragments of his wares. This contributed further to the rapidly increasing cult status of the artist and the value of the wares associated with him.

This dramatic dish, with its lush decoration of reptiles, plants, and shells characteristic of Palissy ware, was bought by the Museum as part of the Jules Soulages collection in 1859 for £60. Palissy wares in the Soulages collection were described as "a series of the highest aesthetic value. . . . [A]ccess to such examples must improve the taste of the people." By the late 1850s a new school of potters imitating Palissy was flourishing, the artist's complete writings had been reprinted, and the historian Lamartine considered Palissy of such heroic achievement as to link his name with those of Joan of Arc, Homer, and Gutenberg.

At South Kensington, Palissy was accorded his own window in the Ceramics Gallery, in company with Luca della Robbia and Josiah Wedgwood. By 1900 the Museum had acquired over fifty ceramics by "Palissy or school of . . . ," paying a record sum of £1,102 10s. for one piece in the 1880s. These were among the "choice collection of Palissy ware" that, together with the "specimens of rare 'Henri-Deux'" (or Saint-Porchaire) ware (cat. 72), were constantly mentioned in guidebook accounts of the day. It is therefore not surprising that this object is the most prominent piece shown in a *Punch* cartoon of visitors looking at a Museum display in 1869 (see fig. 28).

Although they retained their importance within the context of ceramics study and display, Palissy wares were out of fashion from the turn of the century until the 1960s, and only then were they introduced into the Primary Galleries. Around the same date, Palissy's work was placed within a wider cultural framework in John Shearman's *Mannerism* of 1967, where the artist's "wonderfully capricious dishes" were seen as combining "the imaginative fecundity of an artist with the resource of a practical technologist."

Lit. Conway, 1875, p. 500; Honey, 1952; Reitlinger, 1963, pp. 119, 253; Amico, 1987; Dufay, 1987; Lecocq, 1987; Britton, 1991, pp. 169–76

JENNIFER H. OPIE/MALCOLM BAKER

72.
French, probably Paris or Fontainebleau. *Candlestick.* c. 1550. Lead-glazed earthenware; techniques include throwing, hand modeling, molding, stamping, incising, and inlay work, 12⅝ x 6¾" (32 x 17 cm).
V&A 261–1864

Decorated with the cypher of King Henri II and the arms of France, this elaborate candlestick is one of about seventy surviving pieces in a mannerist style characteristic of French court fashion around 1550. Although known as Saint-Porchaire ware, these pieces were manufactured probably in or near Paris rather than at the village of Saint-Porchaire. The way in which they combine different components in several tiers is more typical of contemporaneous metalwork and architectural design than of pottery. By 1842 these pieces were described as "faïence de Henri II" because the emblems of the French king and his wife, Catherine de' Medici, together with those, as was then thought, of his mistress Diane de Poitiers, appear on more than one example. Because of its presumed royal connection, its style, its technical complexity, and its rarity, Saint-Porchaire ware became the type of ceramic most sought after by collectors, along with so-called Medici porcelain (see cat. 75). The prominence given to it at South Kensington enhanced its reputation still further.

From the late 1860s onward the Saint-Porchaire ware was displayed in a special case in the Ceramics Gallery. The name of François Charpentier of Orion, at that time thought to be the maker, was included among the ten most important potters whose names appeared on the ceramic columns made by

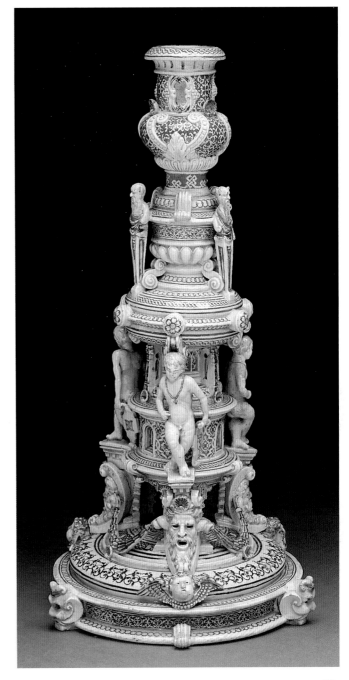

72.

Minton & Co. that lined the gallery. Several nineteenth-century manufacturers, notably Minton, produced copies of Saint-Porchaire ware. In 1871 Minton & Co. of Stoke-on-Trent showed a candlestick modeled on this piece at the international exhibition in London.

Lit. Delange and Bornemann, 1861; Robinson, 1862a; Fillon, 1864; Schnitzer, 1987; Barbour, Sturman, and Vandiver, 1993; Wilson, 1993b; Barbour and Sturman, 1996

REINO LIEFKES

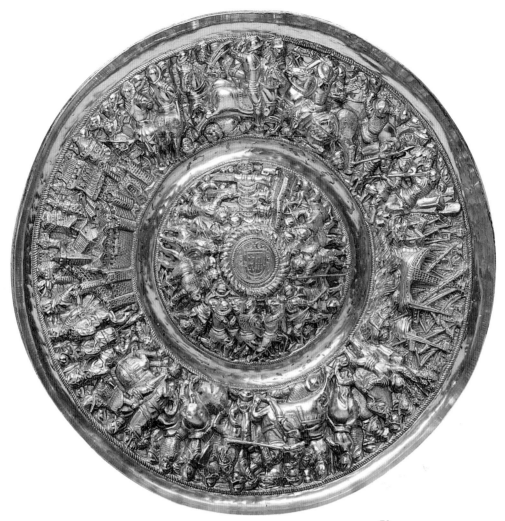

73.

73. Portuguese (Oporto?). *Dish.* Early 16th century. Silver, parcel-gilt, embossed, chased, and engraved, 11⅞" (30.1 cm) diam., 2⅛" (5.4 cm) deep. Unmarked. V&A M2–1938

From the 1860s when J. C. Robinson made several visits to Spain and Portugal, an interest in the fine and applied arts of the Hispanic peninsula was reflected in the Museum's acquisitions and publications. This interest was continued by later curators, most notably Charles Oman, who wrote an authoritative catalogue of the silver collection and was responsible for acquiring this dish for the Museum. Embossed with scenes from the siege of Troy, it shows the Trojan commander Hector and the Greek hero Achilles in combat, with the city to the left. Dateable to between 1500 and 1520, it is attributed to Oporto on the basis of the central medallion with the arms of the Pintos da Cunha family, added in the seventeenth century.

Although the Museum did not formally acquire it until 1938, the dish had long been recognized as a masterpiece of early Renaissance silver. It first appeared in the Museum's 1881 "Special Loan Exhibition of Spanish and Portuguese Ornamen-

tal Art," where it was catalogued as "Gothic work." In 1927 the dish appeared on the London art market. A note from C. M. Koop, then curator of metalwork, reveals the Museum's aspirations: "Dr Hildburgh succeeded in acquiring . . . two pieces of silversmithing work which I was anxious for him to get. . . . [T]he Portuguese dish is a particularly fine and outstanding specimen." The dish was duly deposited on loan, and the Museum clearly hoped that Hildburgh would, as usual, turn the loan into a gift. However, due to unspecified financial difficulties, he was forced to sell it in 1938. There was no question of letting the dish go. In a note of 18 January 1938 (in the Bryan papers) metalwork curator Oman described the embossing as approaching that of Christian van Vianen, calling it "superior to any piece of its sort in the Lisbon Museum . . . and naturally to anything we have here."

Lit. Robinson, 1881, no. 489; Oman, 1968, pp. xxv, 30–1, figs. 156–69; Levenson, 1991, p. 141

Pippa Shirley

74. Italian (Ferrara). *Lucrezia Borgia Mirror.* 1504–34. Walnut, parcel-gilt, 19" (48.2 cm) diam., 2¾" (7 cm) deep. V&A 7694–1861

Although the Museum has collected objects primarily for their stylistic or technical interest, rather than as historical documents, associations with romantic or notorious figures of the past have often been highlighted in guidebook accounts of the Museum's collections. When the Soulages collection, with its Renaissance furniture, was bought between 1859 and 1865, this richly carved frame, priced at £150, was regarded as perhaps the most glamorous item. It enclosed a bronze disk, one side smooth and the other depicting the Virgin and Child. It was assumed to have been a mirror belonging to Lucrezia Borgia (1480–1519), duchess of Ferrara, a character with a legendary reputation for wickedness and extravagant vices. In this case, the object's assumed association with a notorious personality is not without foundation, as the piece includes the flaming grenade, the personal emblem of Alfonso d'Este (1486–1534), who became Lucrezia Borgia's third husband in 1501 and was named duke of Ferrara in 1505.

The frame has always been prized for the quality of its carving and abundance of symbolism, ranging from allegorical beasts to the Pythagorean "Y," signifying the choice between good and evil. However, so attached have furniture historians been to the idea of the mirror belonging to Lucrezia Borgia that they have overlooked the significance of the Virgin and Child on the other side. Recent research by Peter Thornton and Kent Lydecker on fifteenth-century Italian interiors and inventories, coupled with the moralizing nature of the frame, suggest that the object served originally not as a mirror but rather as a religious icon or *ancona*, which would have hung in the chamber of Lucrezia's husband, Alfonso.

Lit. Hungerford Pollen, 1874, pp. 185–7; Thornton, 1991, pp. 261–8; Lydecker, 1993, pp. 175–83; Wilk, 1996, p. 32

JAMES YORKE

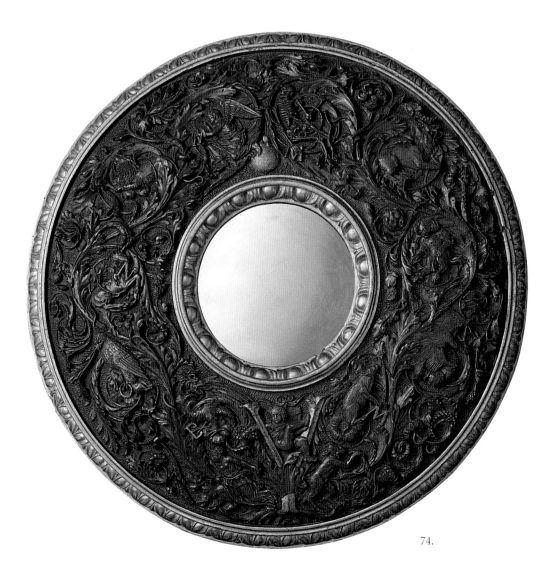

74.

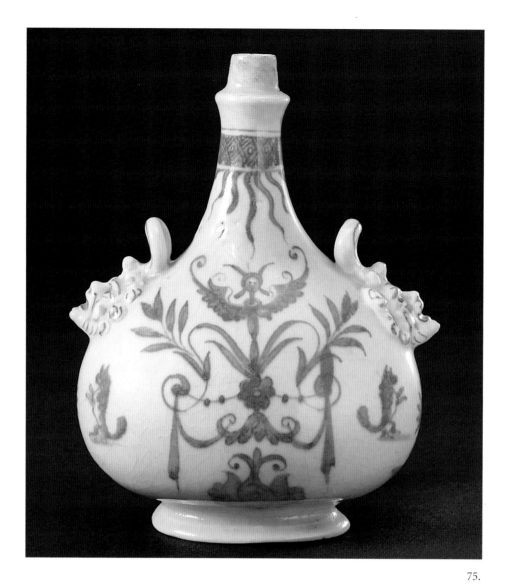

75.

75. Italian (Florence). *Pilgrim Bottle.* c. 1580. "Medici porcelain" painted in underglaze blue, 7⅞ x 6¼ x 3⅞" (20 x 16 x 10 cm). Bequeathed by George Salting. V&A C.2301–1910

This bottle, with its glassy body and hazy delicate painting, is an example of the first European hybrid porcelain, produced before 1587 for Francesco Maria de' Medici, second grand duke of Tuscany, in an attempt to imitate the Chinese blue-and-white porcelain then reaching Italy via Persia. It was among the porcelain bequeathed to the Museum by George Salting in 1910. By 1859 South Kensington had already acquired two Medici pieces; J. C. Robinson was among the first to recognize the importance of so-called Medici porcelain in the history of ceramics, following its neglect in the seventeenth and eighteenth centuries. After the first attempt to identify these wares appeared in 1859, Robinson acquired from its author a twin-bottle cruet and a large bowl, and in October 1860 signaled their significance in a note in the *Art Journal:* "Dr Foresi, by his inductive reasoning and close research, brought together history and specimens of ware. The 'Medici porcelain' is henceforward a new feature in the history of the art." At that time the total number of surviving pieces was estimated at fewer than fifteen, and strong interest from Paris ensured that many pieces subsequently found their way to the Louvre, the Musée National de Céramique at Sèvres, and the Musée Jacquemart André.

Over the next fifty years the Museum acquired nine out of over sixty surviving pieces of Medici porcelain, assembling the largest single collection anywhere. Initially considered a subdivision of majolica rather than early Italian porcelain, the earlier acquisitions were discussed in C. D. Fortnum's 1873 catalogue of majolica, but later they were seen as precursors of true porcelain. Already in 1908 the V&A's four examples of the "rare Florentine porcelain of the 16th cent." were singled out with a star in a Baedeker guidebook account of the "Keramic Gallery." By 1935, in the new Ceramics Galleries, the Medici porcelain was shown by itself in a "front pedestal case."

Lit. Foresi, 1859; Fortnum, 1873, pp. lxv–lxix; Lane, 1954, p. 3; Cora and Fanfani, 1986

ROBIN HILDYARD

76. Probably by GASPARO MOLA or MASTER GUGLIELMO THE FRENCHMAN (Italian [Florence]). *The Medici Casket.* 1609–21. Chiseled steel, 10 x 7¼ x 7¼" (25.4 x 18.4 x 18.4 cm). V&A M.95–1960

A tour de force in steel, this jewel casket was made for the Medici ruler Cosimo II, grand duke of Tuscany, who admired work in chiseled steel and employed two Florentine craftsmen noted for their skill in this difficult medium: Maestro Guglielmo the Frenchman and the armorer Gasparo Mola. Probably made by one of the two, the casket has applied decoration that owes much to Florentine architecture of the late sixteenth century. Indeed, despite its modest size, the object has a striking monumentality. At the front are Mars and Minerva in chiseled steel; the lid is surmounted with the Medici arms, with the grand ducal crown above. A separate steel plate within the lid is also pierced with the Medici arms. One key gives access to a shallow compartment immediately below the lid, probably for gems or cameos; another allows the entire lid to be lifted.

Although the casket was purchased by the Museum only in 1960, an attempt to acquire it was made nearly a hundred years

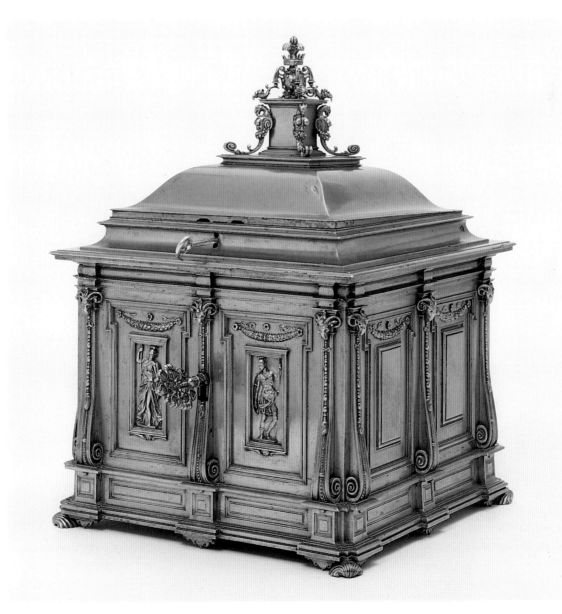

76.

before. The casket was already well known by 1847 when it was in the famous Debruge Dumesnil collection. It then passed into the collection of Lord Cadogan and was shown at the "Manchester Art Treasures" exhibition in 1857, before being sold with the Cadogan collection in 1865, when the Museum failed to buy it. At that time, the attraction of this object lay both in its Medici associations and its virtuoso use of this difficult material. When acquired in 1960, these features were still considered important; but the casket also allowed the Museum to represent on a small scale those stylistic features of High Renaissance Florentine architectural decoration that were then being reevaluated.

Lit. Labarte, 1849, p. 375; Burlington Fine Arts Club, 1900, pp. 74–5; Lightbown, 1967

Anthony R. E. North

77. French or Italian. *Cabinet on Stand.* 1840–55, possibly incorporating earlier gilt-bronze plaques and woodwork. Ebony and ebonized wood, veneered on a carcase of pine, poplar, and walnut, the interior with marquetry of padouk, purpleheart, and kingwood(?), with mounts of gilt-bronze, 67⅛ x 61¾ x 21⅝" (170.5 x 157 x 55 cm). Purchased by H. M. Government and allocated to the Museum. V&A W.64–1977

Although a Continental piece, this cabinet was acquired as the result of efforts to save a collection considered part of England's national heritage. In 1977 the Museum's curators were heavily involved in a campaign to avert the break-up of the Rothschild collection at Mentmore Towers, Buckinghamshire. Although the

effort failed, this cabinet and a handful of other items were purchased by the British government and allocated to the Museum to document this important nineteenth-century collection.

When the cabinet was acquired, it was celebrated as a supreme example of the ebony cabinets fashionable in French courtly circles between 1640 and 1660. Such cabinets usually showed carved decoration based on literary sources. This cabinet was more luxuriously decorated than usual, with gilt-bronze plaques illustrating episodes from the Italian poet Torquato Tasso's romantic epic, *Gerusalemme Liberata* (Jerusalem Delivered), first published in 1580.

In 1884, in a privately printed catalogue of Mentmore, the cabinet was said to have been presented to Marie de' Medici (1573–1642) by the city of Florence in 1600, for her marriage to Henri IV of France. This aristocratic provenance may well have been accepted when the piece was acquired by the Rothschilds in 1855 from the distinguished and knowledgable collector Alexander Barker. Although the date of 1600 seemed unrealistically early, it was later recognized that the piece related to a drawing for a cabinet bearing the monogram of Marie de' Medici, bound in an album (Ashmolean Museum, Oxford) with drawings by Jean Cotelle (1607–1676).

It was always clear that the cabinet and stand had been altered and enriched with new mounts in the nineteenth century. Rigorous conservation inspection has revealed that much of the structure and most of the mounts are also of nineteenth-century date. Some carcase work and marquetry may have been taken from an earlier cabinet. The carcase, which uses no oak, is more suggestive of an Italian than a French workshop. The main plaques have been heavily regilt, but may be from a German workshop of the late seventeenth or early eighteenth century; it is clear that the plaques have been cut down, suggesting re-use. The trade in altering and enriching furniture for collectors was well established by the middle of the nineteenth century, and in

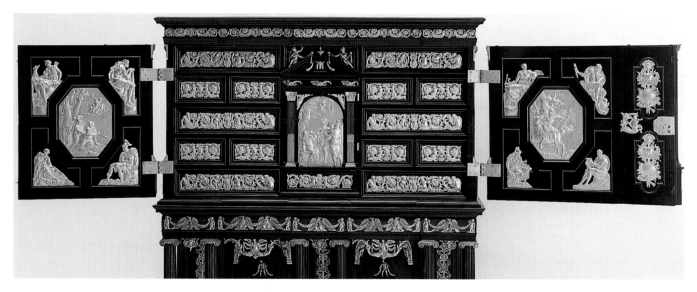

77. (detail)

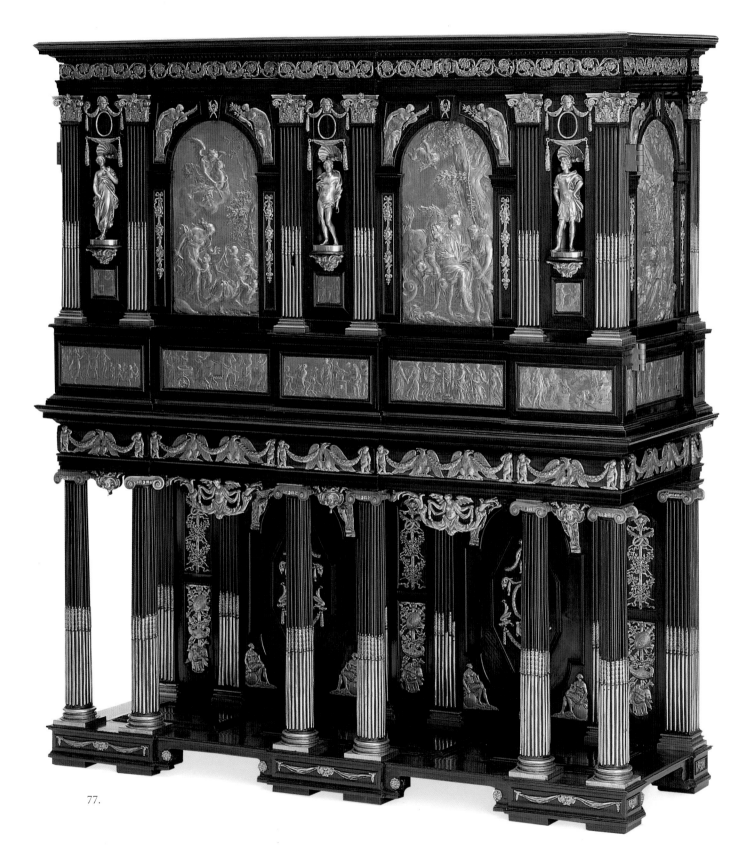

77.

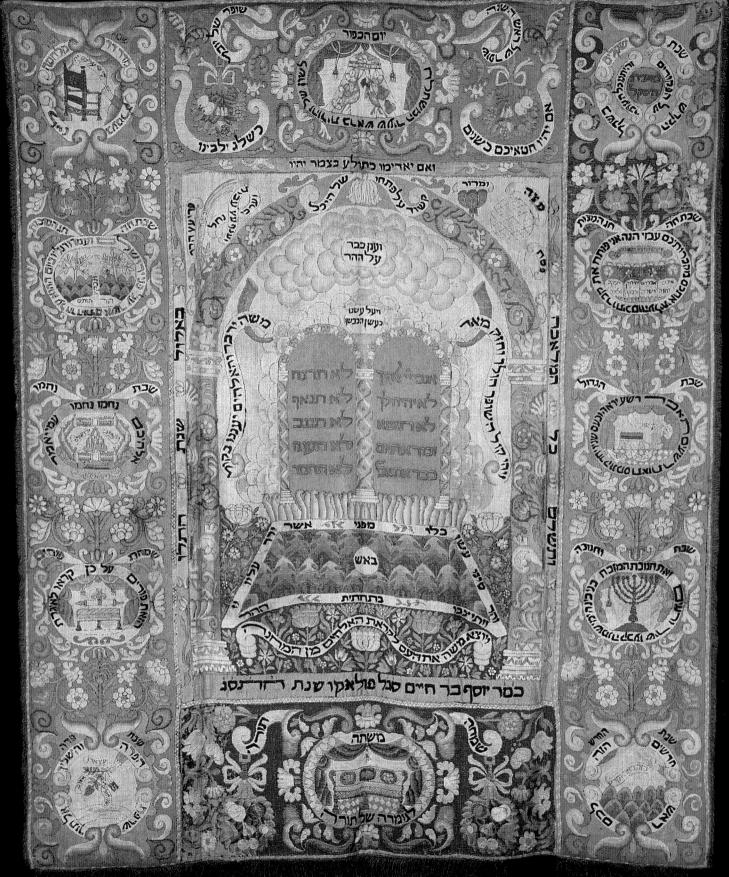

recent years—with the rise of interest in the history of collecting—has become a subject of enthusiastic study. This cabinet remains the subject of debate and investigation.

In the mid-nineteenth century, carved ebony cabinets, of which this is an exotic hybrid, were keenly sought by both private collectors and those forming the new Museum collections. The value placed on such cabinets as works of art at that time is also attested to by the contemporary re-creation of the form for one of the most ambitious exhibition pieces shown in Paris in 1867 (cat. 7).

The allure of such a richly mounted version must have been strong for the Rothschilds, of whom Lady Eastlake wrote after a visit, "I do not believe the Medici were ever so lodged at the height of their glory."

Lit. Thornton, 1978

SARAH MEDLAM

78. Italian. *Parochet (Ark Curtain).* Dated Ellul 5436 (August–September 1676). Linen embroidered with colored silks and silver-gilt thread in a variety of canvaswork stitches, 75 x 65" (190.5 x 165.1 cm). V&A 511–1877

Early acquisitions of Jewish ritual objects included a thirteenth-century spice box bought from the Bernal collection in 1855, a seventeenth-century Torah mantle purchased in 1870, and this *parochet,* bought in 1877 together with several other Jewish textiles from Caspar Purdon Clarke, who was later to be the Museum's director. Although South Kensington was among the first museums to collect Jewish material, the ritual and cultural significance of these acquisitions was probably considered far less important than their interest as metalwork or textiles (indeed, the spice box was misidentified as a reliquary). All these items were acquired before the "Anglo-Jewish Historical Exhibition" held at the Albert Hall in 1887. This exhibition, according to Judaica scholar Cecil Roth, "marked an epoch in the history of Jewish collecting and the development of the study of Jewish ritual art," and prompted the formation of Jewish museums in various Continental cities. No comparable interest was, however, shown at South Kensington, and little additional Jewish material came into the Museum collection until the Hildburgh bequest in 1956, with its twenty-three Jewish objects. In that same year the Museum mounted the exhibition of Anglo-Jewish art commemorating the tercentenary of the Resettlement of the Jews in England; two decades later, in 1978, the V&A held an exhibition of Anglo-Jewish silver.

Like most *parochets* (the cloth that covers the doors of the ark containing the Torah scrolls in a synagogue), this one is decorated with traditional symbols and inscriptions which focus attention on basic beliefs. Two dates are included: the narrow border around the central panel states that "All work was completed by Ellul 5436" (1676), and a later addition in the lower border gives the name of the donor and date of the donation, "The honoured Joseph bar Haim Segal Polacko 5463" (1703).

Lit. Cohen, 1953; Salomon, 1988, p. 73, fig. 52; Keen, 1991, pp. 26–7; Nachama and Sievernich, 1991, p. 88

JENNIFER WEARDEN

79. Flemish (Brussels). *Esther Hearing of Haman's Plot.* c. 1510–25. Tapestry woven in wool and silk, 138 x 156" (350.5 x 396.2 cm). V&A 5669–1859

The subject of this fine Gothic tapestry is taken from the Book of Esther in the Old Testament and shows Esther hearing that her husband, King Ahasuerus, had given his servant Haman permission to send out instructions to kill all the Jews in his lands. In the background, the messengers are dispatched, and the queen, covering her head with sackcloth, prays for the deliverance of her people. Such biblical stories were often used for tapestries.

This was one of four early-sixteenth-century Flemish tapestries among the few textiles purchased in 1859 from the collection assembled by the Toulouse lawyer Jules Soulages. The first examples of Flemish tapestry purchased by the Museum, they joined two earlier acquisitions of German work in forming the nucleus of an expanding collection of Gothic and Renaissance tapestries, numbering thirty-seven pieces by 1900 and now standing at around a hundred. Of the four Soulages hangings, the Esther tapestry was the most expensive, at £25.

Lit. Robinson, 1856, p. 164; Cole, 1888, pp. 96–7; Kendrick, 1924, p. 37; Rock, 1970, pp. 307–9; Wingfield Digby, 1980, p. 42

WENDY HEFFORD

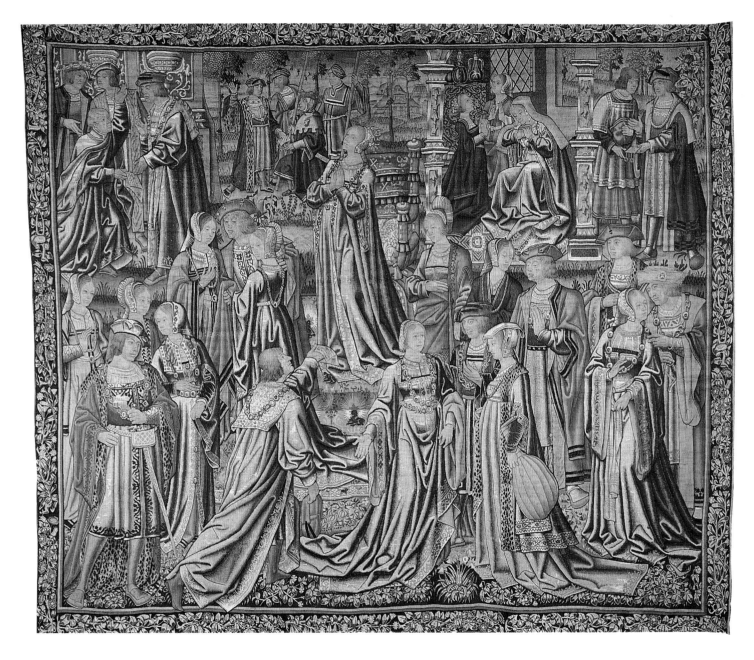

79.

80. DOMINIK STAINHART (South German, 1655–1712). *Saint George and the Dragon.* c. 1690–1700. Ivory, 4¾ x 3⅜ x 1⅛" (12.1 x 8.6 x 3 cm). Given by Dr. W. L. Hildburgh. V&A A.36–1949

The European ivory carvings acquired by the Museum in such large numbers during the 1850s and 1860s were almost all medieval in date; little attention was paid to the exquisite small-scale sculpture in this material produced for the courts of central Europe and Italy during the seventeenth and early eighteenth centuries. During the late 1940s and 1950s, however, this area of the collection was greatly increased as a result of the enthusiasm of the keeper of sculpture, Delves Molesworth, and the donations (often encouraged by Molesworth) of Dr. W. L. Hildburgh. Such acquisitions were usually small-scale pieces, unlike the larger examples of German Rococo wood sculpture purchased by some American museums during this period.

This finely carved Baroque piece by Dominik Stainhart, based on an Italian engraving by Antonio Tempesta (1555–1630), is characteristic of this category of artistic production, which makes up a significant part of the Museum's sculpture collection. These ivories form a link between large-scale monumental sculpture and the porcelain figures that imitated and eventually supplanted them. Neither small-scale works in ivory, nor the artists who made them, are usually given a significant place in histories of art, although both the works and the artists were highly regarded by their aristocratic patrons. Stainhart's career is typical: after six years in Italy (c. 1674–80), he returned to Germany where he worked in his native town of Weilheim in Bavaria and, from 1690, at the court of the elector Max Emmanuel in Munich.

The *Saint George* was bought in 1931 by Dr. Hildburgh from the Berlin dealer Ferdinand Knapp, possibly at the instigation of the V&A's Eric Maclagan, or Margaret Longhurst, who had recently published her catalogue of Gothic and later ivories. Knapp's invoice states that it came direct from the Hermitage in Leningrad, and it may have been one of the works of art sold from the Hermitage in the 1920s. Like most of the other fifty or so ivories bought by Hildburgh, it was immediately placed on loan to the Museum. When the ivories were offered as a gift, Molesworth recommended their acceptance to the director:

> There are 55 items in all, the greater number of which are examples of baroque carving in which our own collections are not very rich. A few items are particularly fine, some others are rather of study interest, though they are very useful to the Museum in view of the number of enquiries we get for this type of object . . . .

To this, director Leigh Ashton wryly replied: "Well—most of them are unlookable at—but I agree."

Lit. Theuerkauff, 1971; Theuerkauff, 1972

MARJORIE TRUSTED

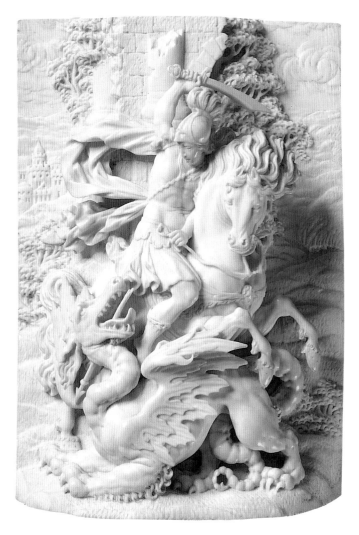

80.

81. PETER HENCKE (German [Mainz], died 1777). *Saint John Nepomuk.* c. 1750. Ivory, 9⅝ x 2¾ x 2¾" (24.5 x 7 x 7 cm). Purchased with funds from the Bequest of Captain H. B. Murray. V&A A.2–1958

When this dramatic figure was acquired in 1958, the Museum's director, Trenchard Cox, considered it a "very charming & precious object" (Museum Records RP 58/338)—a far more enthusiastic response than that of his predecessor to the gift of Dr. W. L. Hildburgh's ivories nine years earlier (see cat. 80). During the 1950s the interest in central European Baroque and Rococo art was fostered by curators such as Delves Molesworth, whose dramatically illustrated picture books about sculpture of this period complemented the attempts of the British man of letters Sacheverell Sitwell (1897–1988) to stimulate a wider popular interest in central European architecture and decoration.

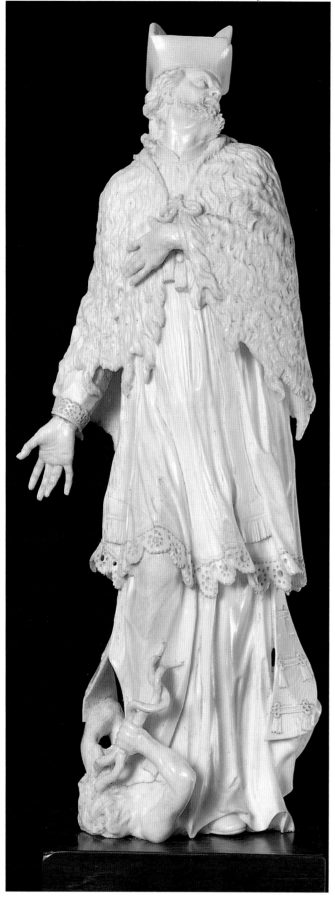

No subject was more typically central European than that of Saint John Nepomuk (c. 1350–1393), a Bohemian saint who was widely depicted in paintings and sculpture even before his canonization in 1729. This ivory version (initialed PH on the back) is based on the life-size bronze figure of 1683 on the Charles Bridge in Prague, near where Nepomuk had been martyred by drowning in the Vltava river. Here the Mainz ivory carver Peter Hencke has added the attribute of an allegorical figure of Treachery being trodden underfoot by the saint. No doubt reflecting Molesworth's interests, another larger wood figure of the saint by the Mainz sculptor F. M. Hiernle was prominently placed in the Museum's newly created Primary Gallery for seventeenth-century Continental art in the 1950s.

Lit. Philippovich, 1966; Baker, 1997

MARJORIE TRUSTED

82. BALTHASAR PERMOSER (German, 1651–1732 [active Italy 1675–89]). *The Entombment.* c. 1677–80. Ivory, 9½ x 5¾ x 1" (24.1 x 14.6 x 2.5 cm). Given by Dr. W. L. Hildburgh. V&A A.30–1949

This impressively monumental relief, like cat. 80, was among the Baroque ivories collected by Dr. W. L. Hildburgh for loan to the Museum from 1930 onward, and given in 1949. According to Museum records, *The Entombment* was purchased by Hildburgh from the Munich dealer Julius Böhler in 1930 on the recommendation of the Museum. Shortly after its purchase, it was published as being by Balthasar Permoser, best known for his monumental sandstone figures executed between 1712 and 1723 for the Dresden Zwinger, the richly decorated court building designed for Augustus the Strong (1670–1733), elector of Saxony. Like many German sculptors, he also produced small-scale sculpture, and this ivory is thought to have been produced early in his career, soon after the sculptor had gone to work in Florence in 1677. The attribution to Permoser was subsequently disregarded; it is only relatively recently that Permoser has once again been accepted as the carver of this piece.

Lit. Asche, 1978, pp. 36–7, 148

MARJORIE TRUSTED

81.

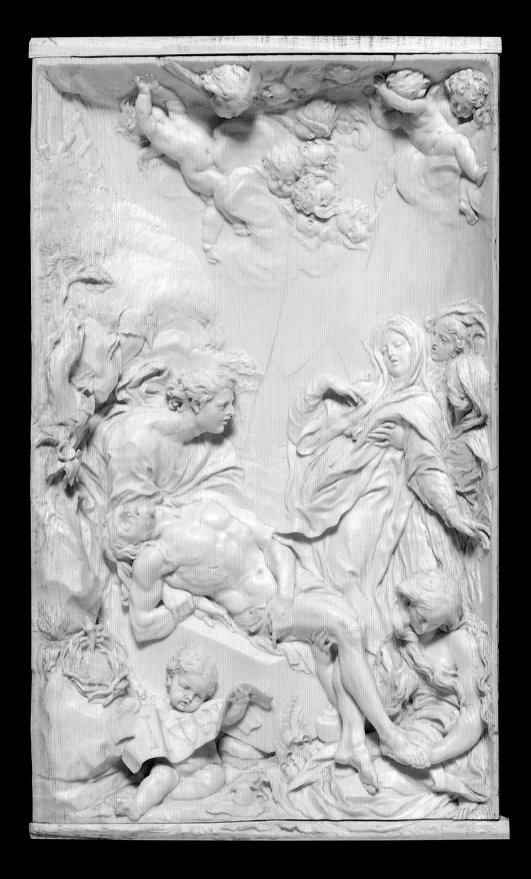

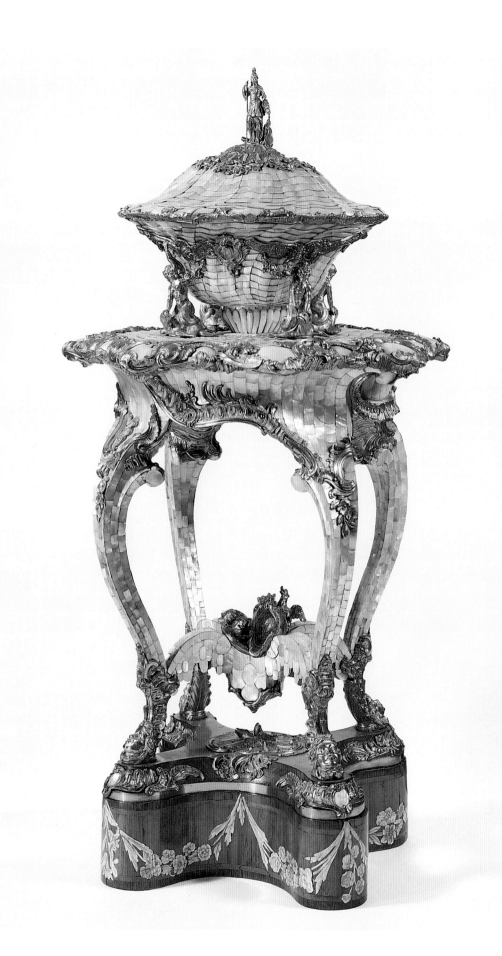

83.

83. PIETRO PIFFETTI (Italian [Turin], 1700–1775). *Ornamental Stand.* c. 1745. Poplar carcase, mother-of-pearl veneer, gilt-bronze (ormolu) and gilt-copper mounts, kingwood and spindle wood veneered base, with engraved and painted ivory, 56¾ x 27⅛ x 22¾" (144 x 69 x 57.7 cm). V&A W34–1946

When this amazing stand was acquired from Lionel de Rothschild's collection at Exbury House in 1946, it was assumed that it had come from "one of the great German Palaces." On that assumption, the stand was shown as an uncatalogued addition to the exhibition "Brunswick Art Treasures" at the V&A in 1952. The excessively decorative nature of the object—almost a parody of a piece of furniture—would have been understood at that time in relation to the fantastic ornament and polychromatic effects of South German Rococo.

In the early 1950s little was known of Italian Rococo and, indeed, the V&A had recently disposed of a set of gilt chairs made for Doge Paolo Renier (1710–1789), under the mistaken impression that they were English Rococo Revival work of about 1860. During the 1960s, however, research by Italian scholars on the Piedmontese Baroque suggested other possibilities, and this stand's relationship to work by Pietro Piffetti was first recognized. This attribution was confirmed by the recent discovery of a sale catalogue of Piffetti's estate, which included a mother-of-pearl stand that formed a pair with the V&A example. Piffetti is now recognized as perhaps the finest Italian cabinetmaker of the eighteenth century, and this stand as one of his most important pieces in any collection outside Italy.

The purchase of Continental furniture such as this was a departure from the focus on English walnut and mahogany pieces that was dominant during the interwar years. This shift, also evident in the acquisition of Baroque ivories (cats. 80–82), reflected the attention shown by authors such as Sacheverell Sitwell (see cat. 81) in German Baroque and Rococo art, as well as the knowledge of such material brought by the relatively few refugee Jewish scholars and dealers allowed residence in Britain in the 1930s. By the later 1950s, the Museum's expertise in this area was also strengthened through the experience of V&A curators such as John Hayward and Peter Thornton, who had earlier been employed in postwar Germany surveying the damage done to architecture and works of art during World War II.

Lit. Viale, 1963, pp. 12–27; González-Palacios, 1986, pp. 382–6; Ferraris, 1992, pp. 13–142; Wilk, 1996, p. 94

JAMES YORKE

84. French (Sèvres). *Pair of Vases "Choiseul".* 1763–69. Soft-paste porcelain in "bleu nouveau" with gilt-bronze (ormolu) mounts. Bequeathed by John Jones

84.1. 11 x 17⅜ x 10" (28 x 44 x 25.5 cm). Mark: incised "ae". V&A 743–1882

84.2. 11 x 17⅜ x 9⅞" (28 x 44 x 25 cm). V&A 743a–1882

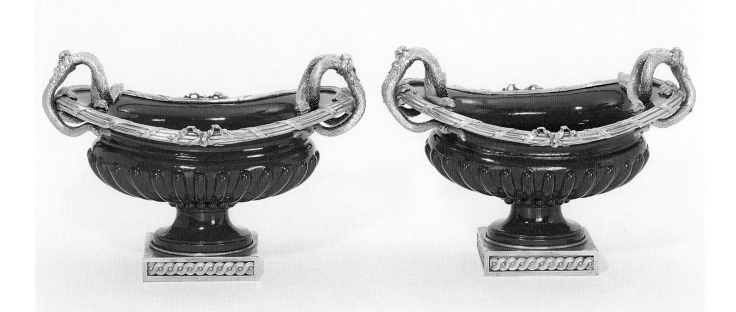

84.

These vases were among eighty-nine pieces of Sèvres porcelain bequeathed with a collection especially rich in eighteenth-century French decorative art by John Jones in 1882. As the handbook to the Jones collection stated in 1883: "Suddenly . . . a collection has been given . . . which contains the very objects so much to be desired, and, as it seemed a year ago, so hopeless of attainment." A military tailor who made his fortune during the Crimean War, Jones (1799–1882) started collecting seriously in the 1850s, sharing a taste for luxury objects of the *ancien régime* with aristocratic collectors such as the fourth marquess of Hertford and Sir Richard Wallace (founders of London's Wallace Collection), John Bowes, and Baron Ferdinand de Rothschild.

With their brilliant blue porcelain bodies and gilt snake handles, these vases, along with a gray "marbled" version also owned by Jones, were based on a real marble vase (now in the J. Paul Getty Museum) that may have been owned by the art collector the duc de Choiseul (whose name they carry). An early, pioneering example of a neoclassical form, in a color launched by Sèvres in 1763, they must still have been considered highly fashionable in 1769 when these versions (along with another, similar piece) were ordered directly from the Sèvres factory by the English writer and collector Horace Walpole for his friend John Chute. Prominently displayed at Walpole's "Gothick" style villa at Strawberry Hill (see cats. 134 and 135), they were bought at the Strawberry Hill sale in 1842 (erroneously described as "Oriental") by John P. Beavan, and later passed to Jones. In Jones's overcrowded house at 95 Piccadilly these vases were displayed with the single marbled version in his dining room in front of windows overlooking Green Park (see fig. 41).

Immediately upon its acquisition, the Jones collection was placed on display in galleries newly painted for the occasion. The objects were arranged by type, color, and shape, with the porcelain in serried ranks of heavy wooden cases (see fig. 42). According to the Museum's 1883 Jones collection handbook, ". . . it would have been impossible, as well as useless, to have retained . . . any memorial of their old arrangement," indicating that various styles of display must have been debated at the Museum. When the Jones collection was reinstalled in 1922, objects and furniture were intermixed to give the suggestion of eighteenth-century period settings; this approach has been refined in two subsequent reinstallations of the collection (see figs. 43 and 44).

Lit. South Kensington Museum, 1883a, no. 232; South Kensington Museum, 1883b; Thorpe, 1962; Charleston and Bolingbroke, 1972; Sutton, 1972; Eriksen and de Bellaigue, 1987

JUDITH CROUCH

85. Perhaps made by ROBERT ARNOULD DRAIS (French, active 1776–84). *The Five Orders of Architecture.* c. 1780. Lapis lazuli columns, mounted in gold, on a base of red porphyry and in ormolu resting on ball feet, 11 x 14⅛ x 6⅛" (27.8 x 36 x 15.5 cm). Bequeathed by John Jones. V&A 853–1882

This precious, elegant object of a courtly type—the last word in luxury—has been associated with Marie Antoinette (1755–1793), queen of France as the wife of Louis XVI from 1774 to 1793, as it was listed in the Jones collection inventory, 15 May 1882, alongside furniture also supposedly linked with Marie Antoinette. Although there is no firm documentary evidence, the connection made in the Jones document at least indicates the importance attached by the collector and the Museum to such putative royal connections when collecting French decorative art. This miniature representation of the orders of architecture as defined by Vitruvius—Tuscan, Doric, Ionic, and Corinthian, with the later addition of Composite—continued to be described in label and publication texts as linked to the French queen. William Maskell's 1883 Jones collection handbook, for example, stated that the piece was "designed and made for Marie Antoinette, in order to teach her (it is said) something of the science." This information may have originated with Jones's manservant Arthur Habgood, who inherited Jones's house and probably assisted curators in compiling the inventory. Versailles curator Christian Baulez has recently found a reference to a payment made by the goldsmith R.-A. Drais in 1790 for a set of seven lapis columns that may or may not be related to this object.

Under the terms of the 1882 Jones bequest, this object was displayed with other material from the Jones collection until, a century later, the stringent stipulations concerning display were lifted by the National Heritage Act of 1983. Having previously epitomized the art of pre-Revolutionary France in the Museum's displays, this exquisite object has since 1992 been used in the Ornament Gallery to demonstrate to a twentieth-century public the precepts of architecture known to educated viewers from the Renaissance until the nineteenth century.

Lit. South Kensington, 1883b; V&A, 1924, pp. 53, 69; Sutton, 1972, pp. 160–1

WENDY FISHER

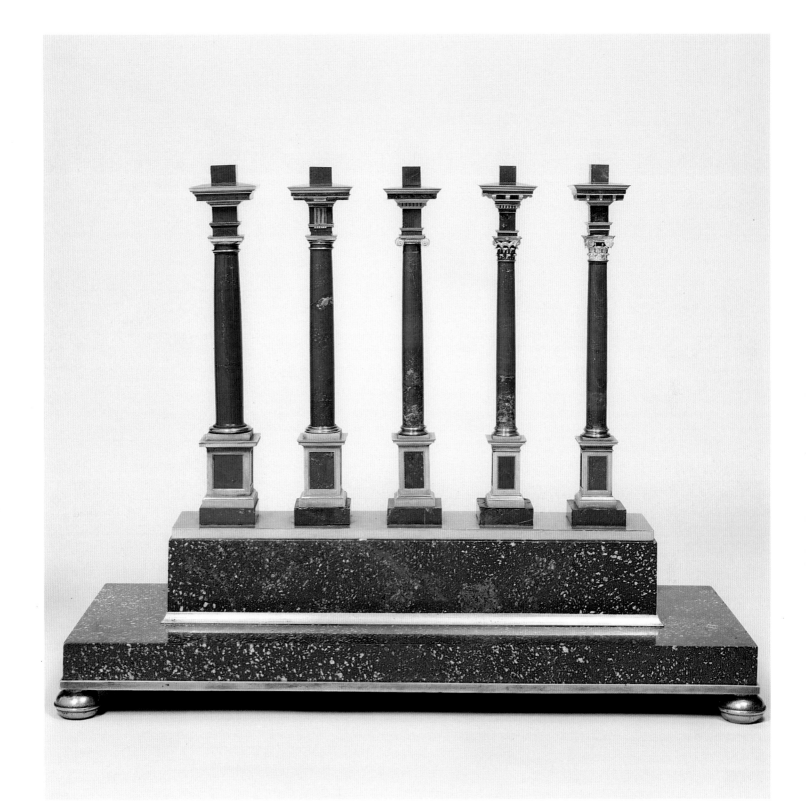

85.

86. Françoise Boucher (French, 1701–1770). *Portrait of Madame de Pompadour.* 1758. Oil on canvas, 22¾ x 20⅝" (57.8 x 52.4 cm). Signed and dated "f.Boucher 1758." Bequeathed by John Jones. V&A 487–1882

The collection bequeathed by John Jones to the Museum in 1882 contained a significant number of objects associated with historical, especially royal, figures, including Marie Antoinette's *The Five Orders of Architecture* (cat. 85). This portrait of Louis XV's mistress, a great patroness of the fine and applied arts, would presumably have appealed to Jones because of its subject as well as for its qualities as a work by the king's principal painter.

More than half of Boucher's portraits are of Madame de Pompadour (1721–1764), and most were painted when she was at the height of her influence in the later 1750s, including that in Munich of 1756 (on which this version is based) and a full-length standing figure of 1759 in London's Wallace Collection. Unlike the Crivelli from the Jones collection (cat. 60), Boucher's work accorded well with the eighteenth-century applied arts that Jones collected so assiduously. Its bequest to the Museum came two years after the National Gallery's acquisition of its first Boucher.

Lit. Kauffmann, 1973, pp. 78–9

Ronald Parkinson

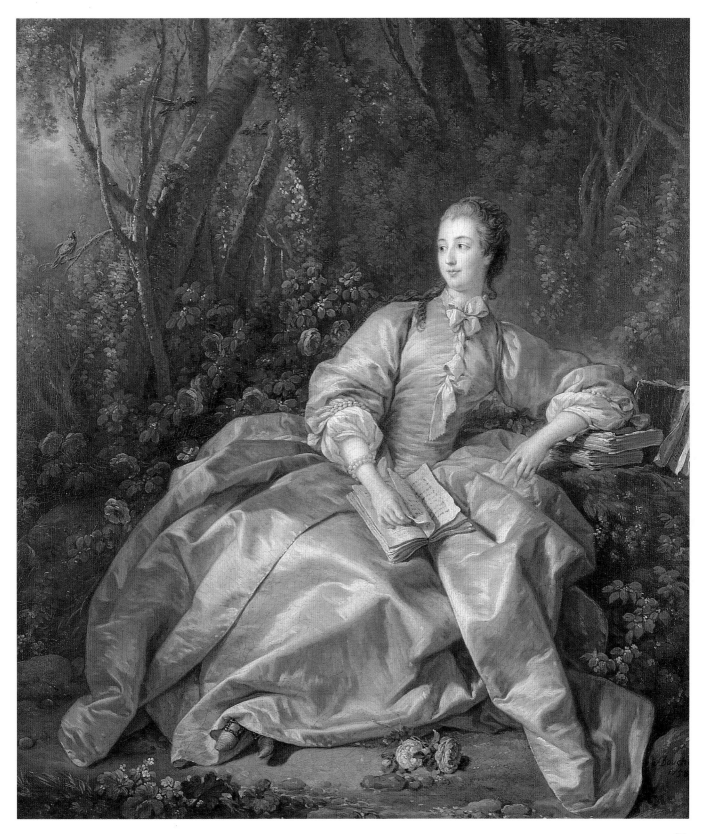

86.

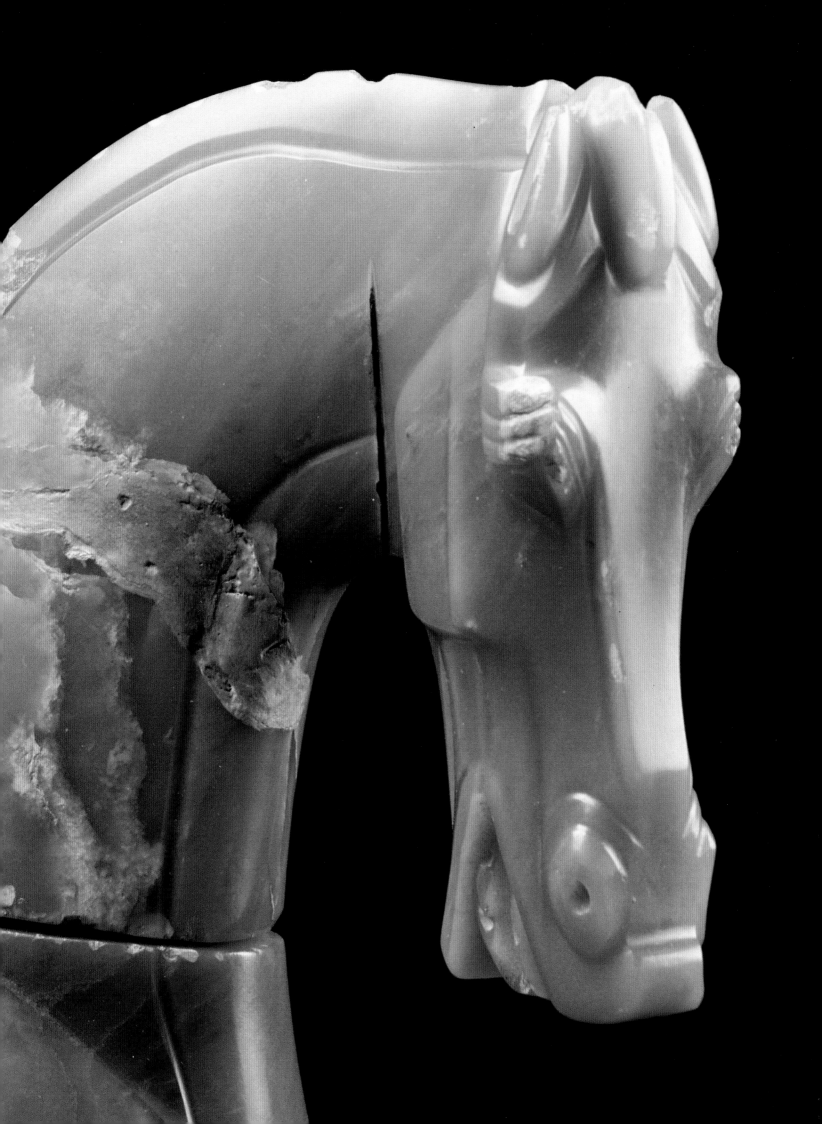

The Empire of Things: Engagement with the Orient

PARTHA MITTER AND CRAIG CLUNAS

RECENT STUDIES OF THE ROLE OF MUSEUMS in nineteenth- and twentieth-century British culture have addressed these institutions as complicit in sustaining British rule in Asia and elsewhere. Their activities of collecting and cataloguing have been viewed as analogous to the acquisition of territory and the classifying of populations necessary to maintain British supremacy in a political and economic sense. This might seem particularly apt in the case of museums with especially close ties to the imperial state, such as the British Museum and the Victoria and Albert Museum. These recent views must now be tested against the empirical facts of museum history covering a period of more than a century and a half. And if this exercise provides plenty of evidence to implicate the museum in the enforcement (or maintenance) of colonial rule itself, there is no single pattern, no master model that can articulate the distinction between politics and culture in museology.[1]

The history of the Eastern art collection of the V&A represents a complex network of interactions between official policies and the individual attitudes of different curators. But it also reflects the way in which imperial ideology assigned a marginal and subordinate, and yet essential, role to such material within the "universal" Western canon. A national institution such as the Victoria and Albert Museum was an important adjunct of the empire, classifying and displaying the art of non-European nations in an assertion of political control over them. The displays of Indian, Persian, Chinese, and Japanese art in the "East Cloister" were meant to highlight the "racial" character of the people who produced them. Imperial policy varied from country to country: thus, the display of Indian arts underscored the Raj trusteeship of the races, tribes, and castes of India. Since China and Japan were not British possessions, Britain had to compete for advantage with other European powers in those regions. Hence, the Far Eastern collection assumed great symbolic and diplomatic importance.

Fig. 93. Detail of cat. 109, Han Dynasty jade head and partial torso of a horse

The public perception of the Eastern art collection was linked with a categorization of non-Western art as ethnographic in earlier so-called cabinets of curiosities, in which the arts of other cultures had been collected in the same vein as specimens of natural history. With nineteenth-century public museums applying taxonomies of fine and applied arts to all artistic traditions, non-Western sculpture and painting were classified as decorative arts, which further confirmed their "ethnographic," rather than aesthetic, status. The situation was more complex at South Kensington. In an institution founded to foster the decorative arts, the distinction between fine and applied arts was more ambiguous, especially with regard to Eastern art.

The Imperial Collections: Indian Art

Partha Mitter

The Indian collection of the V&A served as a perfect tool for constructing cultural difference and reinforcing racial hierarchy. The evolution of the collection and its display reveal—to a degree that few Western collections can—the British ambivalence toward India, especially Hindu India, as evoked by E. M. Forster in *A Passage to India*. India's size and complexity, its extremes, and its seeming lack of understatement have both fascinated and repelled the West. Just when one felt confident that India was under control, it suddenly reverted to its true nature: eluding understanding, escaping into its own world of disgusting cults, weird customs, and lascivious fakirs. And no other aspect of India evoked more fascinated horror in the West than the sculptures of Hindu "monstrous" gods.[2]

The nucleus of the Indian collection, the rich array of Indian applied arts, goes back to the Great Exhibition of 1851, where Indian textiles (see cat. 4) and other applied arts were admired for preserving a traditional sense of design and used as exemplars for students. Owen Jones pointed out that in "the equal distribution of the surface ornament over the grounds, the Indians exhibit an instinct and perfection of drawing perfectly marvellous,"[3] while Richard Redgrave used Indian design to challenge the Victorian weakness for illusionist patterns, agreeing with Jones that decoration should not be constructed but construction should be decorated.[4]

Paradoxically, this new appreciation only helped reinforce the prevailing antipathy toward Hindu sculpture and architecture. Sir George Birdwood, a great champion of Indian decorative arts and an advisor to the Museum, spoke for the educated Victorian when he declared that the "monstrous shapes of the *Puranic* deities are unsuitable for the higher forms of artistic representation; and this is possibly why sculpture and painting are unknown, as fine arts, in India."[5] Hindu art could, however, be of antiquarian interest. The commissioning of the model of Tirumal Nayak's Pudu Mandapa (cat. 87) and related drawings—among the earliest examples of Hindu art to arrive in Britain—illustrates not only the curiosity shown by antiquarians but also the burgeoning interest in Hinduism prompted by the Enlightenment.[6] Another "mirror of Hindoo life held up to Englishmen," showing India's "venerable civilisation and native artistic genius," was a group of Mughal hard stones (cats. 94–97), among the finest objects from the imperial household. This impressive collection was assembled by Colonel Seton Guthrie, a wealthy officer in the Bengal Engineers, and included Shah Jahan's exquisite white nephrite wine cup, which was shown at the Paris exhibition in 1867. Part of the collection was

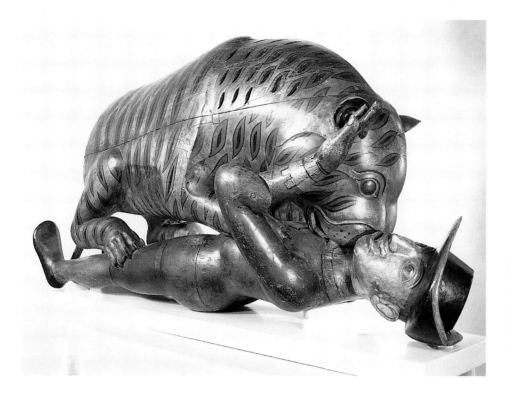

Fig. 94. *Tipoo's Tiger* (Mysore, c. 1790, painted wood, 70" [177.8 cm] long, V&A IS2545), an organ made for Tipu Sultan, ruler of Mysore, in the form of a tiger mauling a British officer. A favorite exhibit at the East India Company's India Museum, it continues to be popular at the V&A today.

acquired by the Museum the following year, although the Shah Jahan wine cup remained with Guthrie and, in fact, did not reach the Museum until 1962.[7]

Both the model and the Guthrie hard stones came to the V&A with the contents of the India Museum, formed by the East India Company.[8] From the early nineteenth century the India Museum, located in the nation's capital, had been a showcase for the manners and customs of India, "the jewel in the imperial crown." The busts of British conquerors and the spoils of the Indian wars were proudly displayed alongside art manufactures and natural products of India. *Tipoo's Tiger,* an organ in the form of a tiger mauling an Englishman (fig. 94), originally belonged to one of the great adversaries of the Raj, and its display vindicated Britain's "civilizing mission" by emphasizing the sadistic nature of an Oriental despot. In this museum of curiosities, religious sculptures, Richard Johnson's fine collection of miniatures, and other art objects jostled for attention with wood and metalwork, textiles, carpets, furniture, and assorted crafts. Even Hindu sculptures were included on the grounds that they were "the idols [that were] given up by their former worshippers from a full conviction of the folly and sin of idolatry."[9] Finally, the display of artificial and natural products of India was meant to underline the protective role of the British Raj in shielding traditional India from the threat of Western progress. The India Museum was essentially an ethnographic one, paralleled by the Royal Danish Cabinet of Curiosities with its fourteen Chola bronzes acquired in 1799, or the collection of Indian paintings in the Bibliothèque Nationale, Paris, used by Denis Diderot in his *Encyclopédie* (1751–72) to illustrate the manners and customs of mankind.[10]

The India Museum drew large crowds to the pageant of empire. Yet, despite its importance and popularity, it had a checkered history, shunted from the premises of the East India Company to Whitehall and then to the galleries opposite the V&A

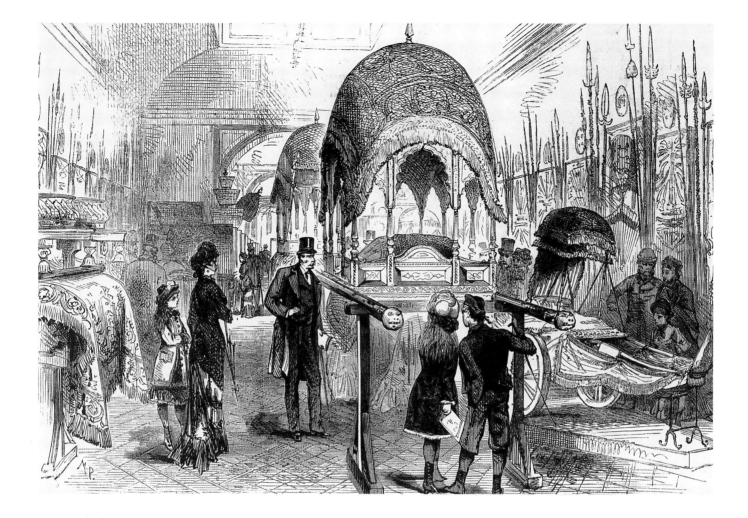

Fig. 95. "The New Indian Section, South Kensington Museum," from *The Illustrated London News,* May 1880

on the other side of Exhibition Road in South Kensington. From the 1860s, many of the objects in its collection were loaned to international exhibitions periodically held in South Kensington. In 1878–80 the collection was broken up, for it could no longer be maintained on the premises of the India Office. Following a power struggle within the British Raj, the objects were divided between the British Museum and the South Kensington Museum (fig. 95). Significantly, the magnificent early Buddhist reliefs from Amaravati were sent to grace the hallowed portals of the British Museum rather than transferred to South Kensington, even though the reliefs had already been displayed in the latter's Eastern Galleries in 1875. Mistakenly identified as "marble" sculptures, though in a "debased" Hellenistic style, the British Museum accorded the Amaravati reliefs a place adjacent to the Elgin Marbles.[11]

In 1880 the holdings of the India Museum were formally transferred to the Cross Gallery in South Kensington, although many objects from the collection had already been moved there. With the addition of Near and Far Eastern art, the Cross Gallery became a showcase for Oriental art. Indian textiles, metal and wood objects, and carpets exhibited at South Kensington had already been used for the teaching of design. It is ironic that while these same Indian industries had been fatally damaged by mass-produced goods from Britain, they were then extolled as the product of Indian "village republics," ideal communities untouched by modern technol-

ogy.[12] Two other key institutions on the South Kensington site propagated this same image of the Indian collection: the Imperial Institute and its close ally, the Society for the Encouragement and Preservation of Indian Art—together acting as Victorian guardians of the "authentic" Indian tradition.

If the India Museum was intimately bound up with colonial imperatives of power and control, we may learn much about that imperial ideology through the ways the collection was presented to the English public and described in contemporary guidebooks. Murray's 1874 guide, for example, recommended the India Museum, just before its move to South Kensington, "not only [for its] antiquities and historical relics, but also as an assemblage of the chief and natural productions of India, with specimens of the arts and manufactures, and illustrations of the industry, manners and customs of the various races."[13]

In the Eastern Galleries of the South Kensington Museum itself, the most striking exhibit was a massive plaster cast of the Eastern Gateway of the Great Buddhist Stupa at Sanchi (fig. 96). Henry Cole's son Henry Hardy Cole, the writer of the first "history of Indian art," arranged the Indian collection into three different periods—Buddhist, Hindu, and Islamic—to indicate the contributions to Indian art attributed to the different races, although such a racial classification is not supported by evidence.[14]

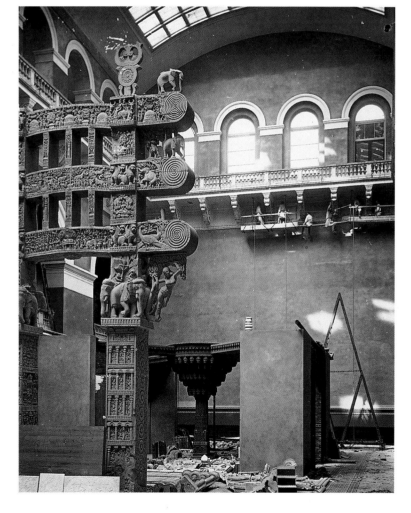

Fig. 96. A cast (V&A 1872–113–122) of the Eastern Gateway of the Great Buddhist Stupa at Sanchi, photographed in 1872 during the completion of the east Cast Court

Public response to the Eastern Galleries at South Kensington can be sensed from a report in the American journal *Harper's New Monthly Magazine* (1875). Seeing the displays as a triumph of Western rationality and order over Oriental superstition and chaos, the writer commented that it "is wonderful indeed that it should be left to this age and to England to appreciate the romance of the East, and to revise, correct and estimate the traditions of the Oriental world concerning its own monarchs."[15] In a further paean to Western science, the writer continued, "[T]he large casts of Oriental objects which occupy a grand building to themselves . . . will probably be of paramount interest to an American. It is here shown that the most notable and interesting objects in the world can be copied with the utmost exactness and in their actual size, [and] brought within the reach of the people of any country. . . . Here we have the grand topes of India . . . brought before us in full size."[16] Accompanying photographs showed how the casts were made and transported with the "aid of astonished Orientals."

In 1880 the newly opened India Museum in South Kensington attracted huge crowds, and the curator, Caspar Purdon Clarke, set about augmenting the collection

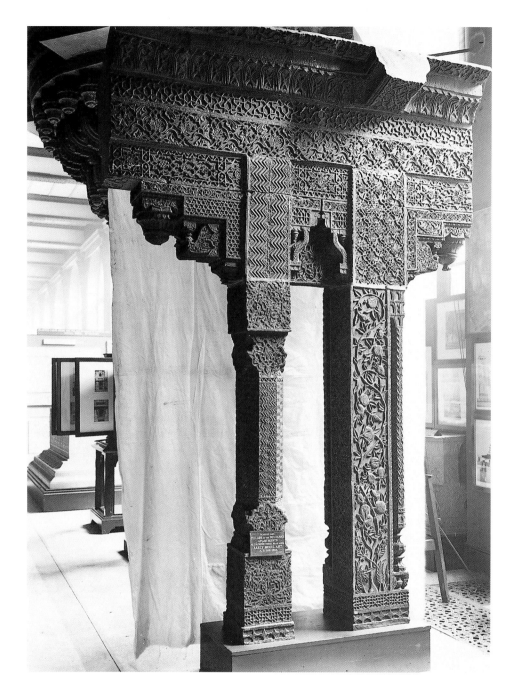

Figs. 97–98. Fragments of plaster casts of Indian architecture, including examples from the Sultana's apartments at Fâthpúr Sikri, near Agra (this page); the Mausoleum of Akbar at Secundra, near Agra; and the Pearl Mosque of Shah Jahan in the Fort of Agra. As early as 1909 such casts were displayed alongside drawings and photographs of the original buildings.

with thousands of additional items imported from India. As the 1885 Baedeker guide indicates, the display was once again based on an ethnographic taxonomy that explicated the cultures of alien races. Apart from eye-catching objects like the Sanchi Gateway and *Tipoo's Tiger,* fragments of architecture ranging from residential buildings to Mughal public monuments and palaces were featured (figs. 97 and 98), along with a wide variety of fabrics and objects of everyday use, as well as information on Indian mores provided by models of domestic scenes and festivals.[17] The arrangement in the nine rooms and the landing continued ethnographic convention by burying Gandharan sculptures among the applied arts.[18]

When the V&A's Committee on Re-arrangement reported in 1908, this whole display was threatened by the recommendation that the India Museum be abolished

and its collections transferred to the main building. Following a vigorous press campaign and the intervention of Lord Curzon, the former viceroy of India, the India Museum was left intact until the 1950s, although the Islamic and Far Eastern collections were incorporated into the V&A. But a grand Oriental Museum combining the resources of the British Museum and the Victoria and Albert Museum never ceased to be the dream of the old India hands—most of whom were former members of the imperial civil service, many of whom took up academic or cultural posts upon their return from India, and who became an informal lobby of paternalists deeply committed to preserving traditional Indian culture as they defined it.[19]

The same period also marked a watershed in Western perceptions of Indian art. A small group of influential writers, led by E. B. Havell and Ananda Coomaraswamy, aimed at undermining the sacrosanct character of the Western fine arts by arguing that all "true" artistic traditions (i.e., medieval European and Indian) were decorative, the function of other arts being to serve architecture. Havell turned to Indian art as the ideal product of a traditional society. He influenced nationalist artists of Bengal during his tenure as an art teacher in Calcutta (1896–1906). After a stormy meeting at the Royal Society of Arts in 1910 at which Sir George Birdwood made disparaging remarks about Indian art, William Rothenstein, a founder of the New English Art Club, joined with Havell and Coomaraswamy to found the India Society, which, with the support of cultural nationalists such as the poet Rabindranath Tagore, propagated the merits of Indian art.[20]

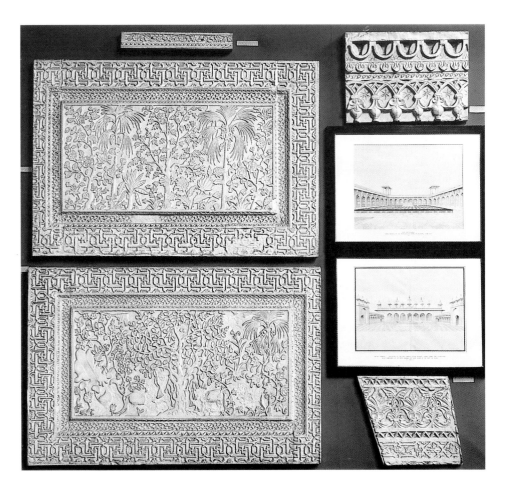

A shift of attitude was signaled by a 1918 guidebook's reference to the "important and varied collection of Indian antiquities and modern art in the India Museum," as well as by the clear separation of fine and applied arts in the display of the collection.[21] Sculpture, pictorial art, and calligraphy were assigned separate rooms in the museum, and the elegant Sanchi Torso (mistakenly identified as Gandharan) was given pride of place (fig. 99). However, despite the prominent display of Indian paintings from 1918 (fig. 100), Coomaraswamy's reevaluation of Rajput and Pahari miniature painting (cat. 93), the expansion of the sculpture section in 1923, and the eloquent pleading for Hindu art by Havell, pieces such as the Nepalese Bodhisattva, *Padmapani, the Lotus Bearer* (cat. 89), still hardly qualified as art. The archaeologists continued to carry the day.

In 1935, K. de B. Codrington, historian of ancient art, took charge of the collection, inaugurating an archaeological approach to Indian art that brought to an end the dominance of decorative art. The thirties were crucial in that under Codrington's influence, Buddhist art was thematically displayed, and, as photographs show, many of the aesthetically important objects were clearly on view. In the same decade, a Chola bronze (cat. 88), an important piece of Hindu sculpture, came to the Museum as part of the Ampthill bequest. Lord Ampthill was governor of Madras in the last century. Among the objects acquired in the 1930s, the large Fremlin carpet (cat. 98) is especially significant for its association with colonial history. Produced probably in Lahore for William Fremlin, an official of the East India Company between 1626 and 1644, the carpet was identified in 1882 by its owner as Spanish. Indeed, identifying Indian carpets has been fraught with difficulties.[22]

Indian independence in 1947 was marked by an ambitious exhibition of Indian art at the Royal Academy (1948–49), in which the V&A played a major part; with the Museum's appointments of W. G. Archer and the textile scholar John Irwin in 1949, the Indian art collection began a new life. As a district officer in Bihar in India in the 1940s, Archer had published on primitive Indian sculpture, collected Indian miniatures, and translated Indian poetry. He had also met modern Indian artists in Calcutta. He set about transforming the Indian Section into "a true art museum" by getting rid of ethnological material accumulated from industrial exhibitions over the years, which, he felt, obscured the art objects. To make the art objects intelligible, Archer initiated a regime of specialization, with John Irwin investigating Indian textile styles and their relationship to European designs, and he himself working on miniatures

Fig. 99. Central Indian (Sanchi), *The Bodhisattva Avalokiteśvara,* called the Sanchi Torso, c. 900, sandstone, 34" (86.4 cm) high (V&A IM184–1910)

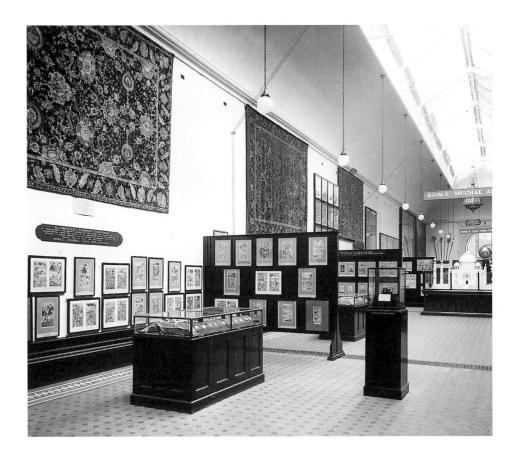

Fig. 100. The Mughal Room in 1936, including a display of Mughal paintings

Fig. 101. Mughal, c. 1565, "Hamsa's Son, Rustam, with His Mistress, in a Garden Pavilion," painting from the *Hamzanama* (V&A IS1506–1883)

(fig. 101). The latter could be studied particularly profitably at the V&A which, with the acquisition of William Rothenstein's collection in the 1950s, had exceptionally rich material.[23]

In 1955 the India Museum was transferred to the main Museum premises, and by 1965 the collection attained virtually its present status and shape, with the best-known objects prominently displayed. The latest twist in the dream of a separate Oriental art museum was the St. George's Hospital site proposed in the 1980s, but this too fell by the wayside.[24] During the heyday of the Raj, the preservation and display of Indian traditional arts was deemed to be an obligation owed to its Indian subjects as part of the imperial trusteeship. With the loss of empire and the ensuing economic decline, that motivation no longer existed.

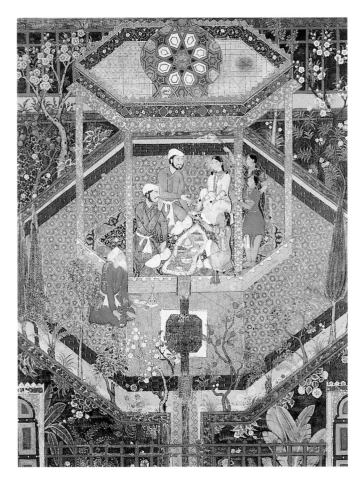

The Imperial Collections: East Asian Art

CRAIG CLUNAS

Though sharing certain assumptions, the practices of British rule in Africa, in South Asia, and in East Asia were experienced (and resisted) quite differently by the peoples who had to deal with them. The length of British rule, its direct and indirect nature in different parts of the globe, and the involvement of its agents with cultural work all varied greatly. Such variety is visible too within the Victoria and Albert Museum's East Asian collections (fig. 102), just as within the Indian collection. The very differential practices of racism in nineteenth-century Britain also need to be borne in mind, especially to explain the absence of African art from the collections at South Kensington. Although included in Owen Jones's *The Grammar of Ornament*, African art was implicitly categorized, even more consistently than the Indian works, as "ethnography" rather than as "art," and as such was collected far more extensively by the British Museum than by the V&A.

In East Asia, particularly in the states of China, Japan, and Korea, full British rule was never imposed, although territory such as Hong Kong was seized, and political and economic concessions were extracted by force. However, in contrast to

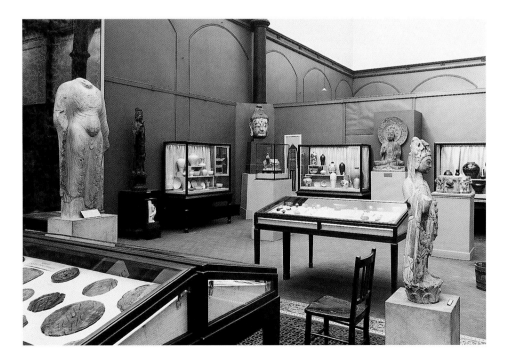

Fig. 102. Chinese objects displayed in the North Court in 1939

parts of Africa and South Asia, local rule was never extinguished or fully subordinated to British control. It is possible to argue that in this situation, in which Britain was in competition for economic and political advantage with other imperialist powers (including the United States), the *symbolic* importance of comprehensive art collections was even greater than it might otherwise have been. In this interpretation, objects from China, Japan, and Korea have played a central role within the Museum's larger mission of cultural self-definition. Precisely by acting as the "margins," these arts have been crucial in defining the center, the normal, the familiar—in allowing the V&A to function fully as a "national" institution. These arts are the marginal others that allow the centering of the self.[1]

British merchants exhibited both Chinese and Japanese material at the Great Exhibition of 1851, although neither China nor Japan assembled a display to represent itself in an arena of international competition. An East Asian presence was, however, of major symbolic importance in Hyde Park. Britain's imperial possessions in India certainly received great prominence,[2] while Henry Selous gave a highly visible role in his large canvas commemorating the Exhibition's opening (cat. 1) to a figure in Chinese official dress. This figure was not an accredited ambassador (which is how he is sometimes described) but, rather, seems to have been appropriated by Selous for his painting from an individual on display in another exhibition of Chinese people then on view in Hyde Park. (The public exhibition of humans to demonstrate "foreign" types and lifestyles was common in Britain and on the Continent, as well as in the United States, from the mid-nineteenth century well into the twentieth century.) Almost all of the Chinese and Japanese material shown at the Great Exhibition was of contemporary manufacture. However, very shortly after the 1850s a sharp divergence began to be noticeable in the way these two nations were treated, and in what their artifacts were made to signify in Museum displays.

The acquisition of Japanese material, which was very sporadic up to about 1865, continued to be characterized thereafter by currently manufactured goods, including major pieces made for the international exhibitions (cats. 10, 11, 112), in which Japan very quickly became an active participant.[3] This mirrored the position of Japanese art as a central focus of nineteenth-century debates about "art" and "craft" that swirled around the new Museum at South Kensington. In discussions of the period, admiration for the technical skill of Japanese makers is never without racist condescension about the supposed "semi-barbarous" nature of the decoration. As was standard in this period, the character of objects is taken in Museum publications as a direct reflection of the essential "character" of the people who made them. Thus, the 1872 *Catalogue of Chinese Objects in the South Kensington Museum* is thick with statements about "the Chinese character" where "art [for the Chinese] has to a large extent supplied the place God holds with us [the English]." Even more extreme judgments were made:

> It would hardly be supposed that an effeminate race like the Chinese should
> have a taste for working in metal; but it must be remembered that they have
> not always been a degenerate race, softened by luxury and by too great
> facility for enjoyment, but that on the contrary, they are still a hardy race,
> delighting in contending with resisting Nature.[4]

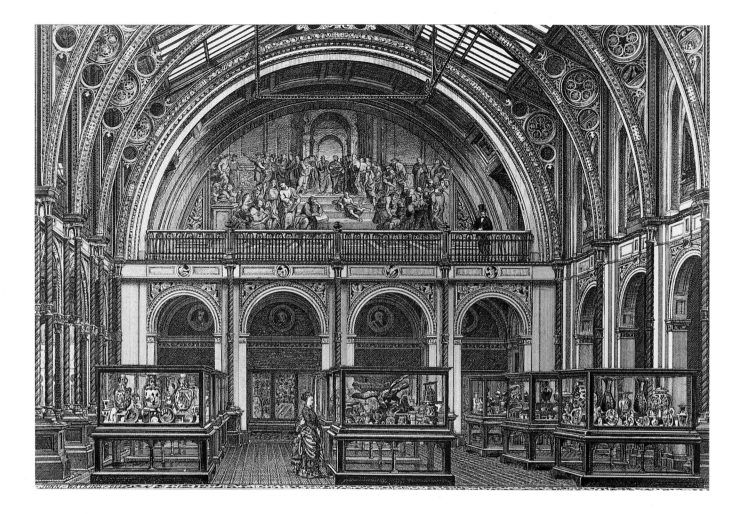

Fig. 103. The South Court, c. 1876, as depicted in an ink drawing (V&A 8089L) by John Watkins (English, died 1908). The central case contains the Japanese eagle incense burner acquired from the Mitford collection (cat. 113). Watkins's drawing was probably a proposal (never realized) to incorporate in the South Court an enlarged version of a recent copy by South Kensington artist F. W. Moody of Raphael's *School of Athens.* Watkins's vision was, ironically, realized in part four decades later when the V&A acquired the Anton Mengs copy of Raphael's *School of Athens* and installed it as a prominent feature of the west Cast Court.

Such racist attitudes were not created by the South Kensington Museum, but its role, along with that of other similar institutions, in putting before a middle-class public "physical evidence" of such theories in the form of actual artifacts makes these institutions of some importance to the Victorian imagination's grasp on "the East."

This "East" was a coherent physical presence at South Kensington in its earlier years. Between 1864 and 1865 a section of the building known as the East Cloister was decorated in elaborate "Oriental" designs by Owen Jones and used to house "objects of Indian, Persian, Chinese, Japanese and Oriental Art generally."[5] The contents of this area were initially made up primarily of loans from the private collections of Asian art, such as that of George Salting (cat. 107), which were increasing in number and size in late-nineteenth-century Britain. Through the 1870s in particular the space allocated to Japanese art increased (fig. 103), as the Museum acquired from these private collections elaborate display pieces such as the iron sea eagle from the Mitford collection (cat. 113). But perhaps the most significant expansion of the Japanese collection in this decade was the large quantity of ceramics, both historic and contemporary, acquired for the Museum in Japan by Sano Tsunetami and displayed at the Philadelphia Centennial Exposition of 1876.[6] This group was designed to be "an historical collection of porcelain and pottery from the earliest period until the present day, to be formed in such a way to give fully the history of the art."[7] Including both modern pieces and some very significant earlier ones (cats. 114–116), the collection served not only to make manifest the Museum's program of a series of "complete" taxonomies of the arts, but also to confront Britain's main commercial rival in Japan, the United States, making evident Britain's willingness to spend resources to "acquire" Japan on a symbolic level.

The acquisition of the collection was not matched by the development of professional scholarship on the subject of Asian art at South Kensington, and the catalogue of the ceramics from the 1876 Philadelphia exhibition was carried out instead by Augustus Franks (1826–1897). A major collector of Japanese and Chinese art, Franks was also director of the British Museum and, as art referee at the South Kensington Museum, a formal advisor on acquisitions for the Museum. As such, he represented one kind of expertise available in the formation and study of collections in this period. Another type of expertise was provided by those with direct experience of living in Asia in a colonial or commercial capacity. Perhaps the prime example of this type was Robert Murdoch Smith, director of the British-owned telegraph company in Iran. Murdoch Smith not only acted as the Museum's agent in Iran—buying both contemporary and historical items for the collection (cat. 99)—but he was also commissioned to write a guidebook to the material, published in 1876 as *Persian Art*.[8]

This same pattern was followed with the art of China, where from the early 1880s Stephen Wooton Bushell (died 1908) combined the post of medical officer at the British legation in Peking with the role of purchasing agent for the Museum. He too was commissioned to publish the collection; his *Chinese Art* of 1904 was the first work on the subject to be based on the holdings of a single Museum, equating the boundaries of the subject itself with the parameters of South Kensington's holdings.[9]

Through much of the nineteenth century, the relationship between British perceptions of Chinese and Japanese art was complex but clearly connected. Most frequently, praise for contemporary Japan was bound up with a critique, often voiced in contemptuous terms, for the products of contemporary China. Comparisons were frequently drawn to China's detriment. As a consequence, the collecting of contemporary Chinese objects by the V&A ceased very early in the twentieth century. Likewise, there was at the Museum a degree of Japanese language expertise, as in the case, for example, of the keeper of metalwork A. J. Koop, who worked at the Museum from 1900 to 1937, devoting himself to a complex taxonomy of the Museum's very large collection of Japanese sword fittings (fig. 104).[10] No one with the ability to read Chinese was employed by the Museum until the early 1970s, and until that time certain Chinese artists were catalogued in the Department of Prints and Drawings under the *Japanese* forms of their

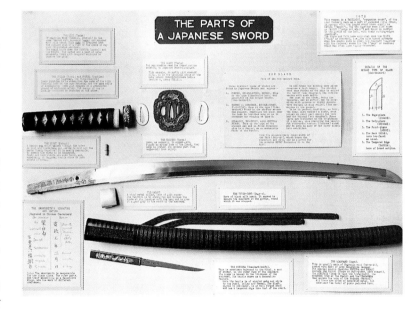

Fig. 104. Japanese sword fittings displayed along taxonomic lines

names; thus, the famous Chinese painter Wen Zhengming (1470–1559) appeared in the catalogue in Japanese, unrecognizably, as "Bun-cho-mei."

The division of the East Asian collection, supposedly by "material," took place in 1897 along with the European collections but unlike the Indian collection, which was kept together by political pressure from imperial interests within the establishment. This led to very different approaches to Asian materials within respective departments, approaches that were to influence the acquisition of and scholarship on objects of varying types. The early twentieth century saw a certain marginalization, a faltering of esteem for Japanese work generally, which went hand in hand with a growing awareness of earlier Chinese art, one of the areas that was to dominate collecting and display through the second half of this century. Koop's assiduous cataloguing activities were never at the center of aesthetic debate in the way Japanese objects had been in the 1870s. An increased supply of goods from China, together with new currents in aesthetics that valued the supposedly "spontaneous" over the highly finished,[11] led to new appreciation for types of ceramics that would have seemed unreasonably crude to earlier eyes.

Throughout the twentieth century until 1970, the Department of Ceramics was at the forefront in displaying East Asian objects at the V&A. It was in Ceramics that advanced aesthetic theories, associated in Britain with names like Roger Fry and Herbert Read (the latter a curator in the department, though never publishing on Asian art) were most explicitly applied to Chinese, Japanese, and (for the first time) Korean ceramics. When the keeper of ceramics, W. B. Honey (1891–1956), wrote in 1947 of Korean ceramics (cat. 111), praising the "hard but immensely vital linear fantasy in scroll work . . . vital and rhythmic brushwork, with an authentic life of its own,"[12] his stress on "vitality" led directly back to the enormously influential ideas of French philosopher Henri Bergson (1859–1941), as interpreted by Fry and Read, among others.

It was this philosophy of "vitality" that also drove the formation of major private collections of early Chinese art such as that of George Eumorfopoulos (1863–1939), subsequently sold to the state and divided between the V&A and the British Museum (cats. 108–109). The difference between the two Chinese ceramic pieces from the Salting and Eumorfopoulos collections (cats. 107–108) was interpreted in the advanced circles of British culture—for example, those around the British potter Bernard Leach (cat. 175)—as one between "sterile" decoration and "vital spirit." It would be wrong, however, to see the Museum as simply a reflection of cultural trends happening elsewhere, or as being totally in thrall to the universalist modernism seen in the writings of Herbert Read. While some of its staff certainly responded to a degree to such intellectual currents, the Museum continued to display and acquire the types of art that were fashionable in earlier times, a bias that grew even stronger in the twentieth century.

This retrograde tendency was particularly true of objects with an "imperial" provenance (cats. 105-107). Indeed, as British political hegemony in East Asia waned, the fascination with objects from the imperial court of the Qing dynasty (1644–1911) only intensified.[13] The looting of the imperial Summer Palace outside Beijing, carried out by British and French troops in 1862 in the course of the "Second Opium War" of 1858–62, an event that arguably marked the acme of British

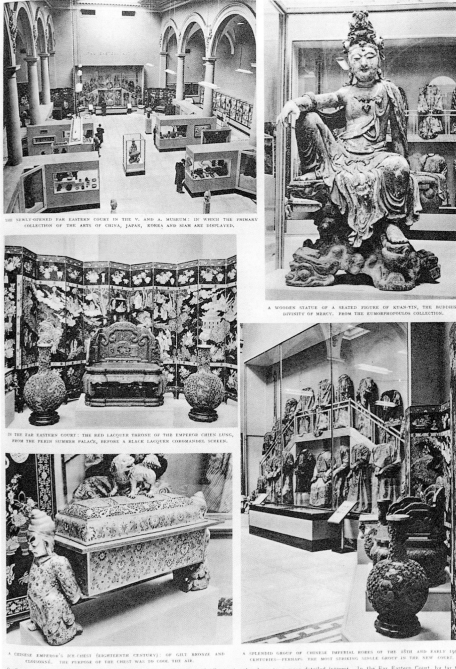

THE NEWLY-OPENED FAR EASTERN COURT IN THE V. AND A. MUSEUM: IN WHICH THE PRIMARY COLLECTION OF THE ARTS OF CHINA, JAPAN, KOREA AND SIAM ARE DISPLAYED.

A WOODEN STATUE OF A SEATED FIGURE OF KUAN-YIN, THE BUDDHIST DIVINITY OF MERCY. FROM THE EUMORPHOPOULOS COLLECTION.

IN THE FAR EASTERN COURT: THE RED LACQUER THRONE OF THE EMPEROR CHIEN LUNG, FROM THE PEKIN SUMMER PALACE, BEFORE A BLACK LACQUER COROMANDEL SCREEN.

A CHINESE EMPEROR'S ICE-CHEST (EIGHTEENTH CENTURY): OF GILT BRONZE AND CLOISONNÉ. THE PURPOSE OF THE CHEST WAS TO COOL THE AIR.

A SPLENDID GROUP OF CHINESE IMPERIAL ROBES OF THE 18TH AND EARLY 19TH CENTURIES—PERHAPS THE MOST STRIKING SINGLE GROUP IN THE NEW COURT.

On September 12 the Far Eastern Court was opened in the Victoria and Albert Museum. This follows the extremely successful post-war policy of the Museum in arranging what are called " primary collections "—that is to say, illustrating a single theme, such as the art of a particular civilisation, country or age, by grouping together the finest things available in a single gallery in such a way that they summarise the theme and at the same time serve, as it were, as a

shoe horn to a more detailed interest. In the Far Eastern Court, by far the greatest number of the objects are Chinese (from about 2500 B.C. to the early nineteenth century); next come objects from Japan (most of the sixteenth century or later); and there are as well selections from the arts of Korea and Siam. As can be seen from our general view of the gallery, the Court is dominated by a magnificent group of Chinese Imperial robes.

Fig. 105. The new Primary Gallery of Far Eastern Art from *The Illustrated London News,* 20 September 1952. The reconfigured installations emphasized the imperial provenance of many of the objects, including the throne of Emperor Qianlong (cat. 105).

imperial power in East Asia, actually brought fewer goods onto the art market than did the "Boxer uprising" of 1900–01 and the collapse of imperial rule in 1911. The acquisition of many of the most "imperial" objects in the V&A can in fact be dated to the years after 1920. The famous throne of the Emperor Qianlong (cat. 105) was purchased in 1922, a time when taste in ceramics was swinging decisively away from works of the eighteenth century to the less finished products of earlier dynasties.[14] (It was the year after the founding in London of the Oriental Ceramic Society, with Eumorfopoulos as its first president.) Only in 1952 did the throne, together with the robes from the Vuilleumier collection (cat. 106) and the Museum's much-published enameled ice chest (V&A 255–1876), which *is* part of the Summer Palace loot, finally form part of a new Primary Gallery of Far Eastern art (fig. 105). The throne retained that focal role until the 1980s, alongside the ceramics, bronzes, and sculptures of the Eumorfopoulos collection, and other objects more palatable to critical taste of the period (cat. 110). The main figure in the creation of this centralized focus for Chinese art was Sir Leigh Ashton (1897–1983), who rose (significantly) from the Ceramics Department to be director of the Museum from 1945 to 1955 (fig. 106).

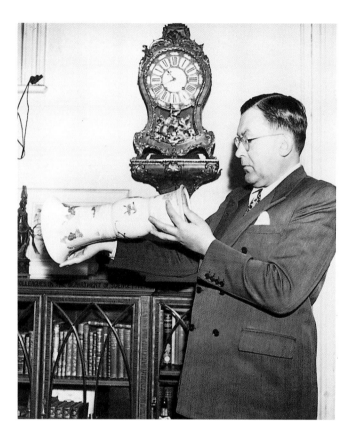

Fig. 106. Leigh Ashton, director 1945–55, with a Chinese vase. Ashton, a key figure in centralizing the V&A's focus on Chinese art, had previously worked in the Ceramics Department.

Japan and Korea had only a very marginal presence in the new gallery in its initial stages and, indeed, the story of Japanese art in the V&A is one of increasing marginalization from the prominence it once enjoyed, until the 1970s saw a revival of interest and commitment. Hostility to Japan after Britain's defeats in World War II played a part in this attitude, at least according to oral history within the Museum. The founding of a Far Eastern Department in 1970 began the rehabilitation of Japan within the Museum, as well as marked the beginning of scholarship on China, which was able to draw on the extensive historical record and research on the recent archaeological discoveries in China. Nevertheless, economic as well as cultural forces led to the large-scale expansion of the profile of Japanese art in the Museum in the 1980s, as the feasibility of commercial sponsorship from Japanese business made possible the creation of the Toshiba Gallery of Japanese Art in 1986, followed by the T. T. Tsui Gallery of Chinese Art in 1991 (fig. 107), and the Samsung Gallery of Korean Art in 1992.

The power of East Asian companies and individuals to assert the presence of their culture in British national museums has been one of the principal influences of the last decade. These commercial interests also motivated efforts to demonstrate that Japan, China, and Korea are still artistically productive, resulting in the acquisition of large quantities of contemporary objects—and generating debates around questions of "modernity," "tradition," and "national style" that have in no sense been resolved (and are perhaps incapable of resolution). Curators trained within the disciplines of Sinology or Japanology have once again come to deploy the collection as signifying the cultures that produced them, trying to put the objects "in context," as is now standard in museum practice worldwide. The Museum itself has even become the subject for exploration as "a context," one in which the presence of Asian artifacts in particular may not stand in need of apology, but still rightly demands constant and self-critical explanation.

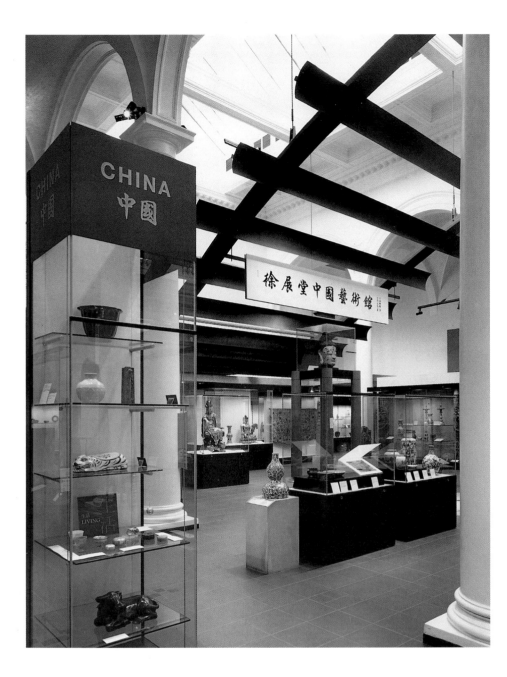

Fig. 107. The V&A's T. T. Tsui Gallery of Chinese Art, opened in 1991

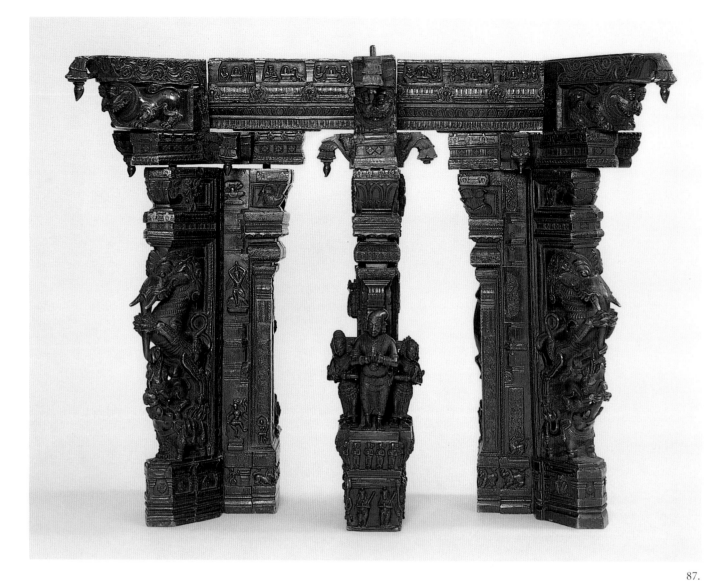

87.

87. Indian. *Model of Tirumala Nayak's Pudu Mandapa.* 1780–89. Commissioned by Adam Blackader. Copper alloy, 12⅝ x 16⅛ x 6¼" (32.5 x 41 x 16 cm). Given by the J. Heywood Hawkins Collection, 1870. V&A 98–98D–1870

The antiquarian enthusiasms of an eighteenth-century English-man motivated him to commission this intricate model. Such private interests played an important role in the growth of knowledge about India and the formation of Indian collections in Britain. The model represents a freestanding hall built to the east of the great Hindu temple of Minaksi-Sundaresvara at Madurai, which was a center for the revival of traditional Hindu architecture. The model was sent—along with the scale draw-ings made in its preparation (fig. 108)—by Adam Blackader, a British surgeon resident at Madurai, to Sir Joseph Banks, who read Blackader's letter to the Society of Antiquaries in London on 2 July 1789. This remarkable model represents one of the ear-liest attempts by a European to understand the aesthetics of

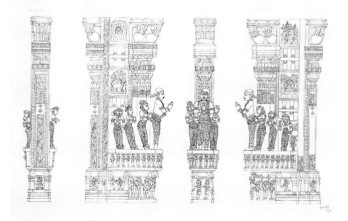

Fig. 108. Indian (Madurai). *Drawing of a Pillar from the Model of Pudu Mandapa, Depicting the Patron Tirumala Nayak and His Wives.* c. 1780s. Ink on paper, image 9½" (24.1 cm) high. V&A AL7766(87)

Hindu temple architecture. It was acquired by the South Kensington Museum in 1870. In 1879 the Museum absorbed the collection of the East India Company, formed largely as a result of the initiatives of enlightened employees of the company who sent back to England objects of antiquarian interest.

The model and preparatory drawings dropped from sight for a century until they emerged in the 1870s. The model came to the Museum in 1870 with the gift of the J. Heywood Hawkins collection; further sections were acquired with the purchase of the Charles Seton Guthrie collection in 1875. Subsequently, both the model and the drawings languished in obscurity until their rediscovery and display in the Museum's Nehru Gallery of Indian Art, opened in 1990.

Lit. Blackader, 1792; Guy, 1990; Guy and Swallow, 1990

JOHN GUY

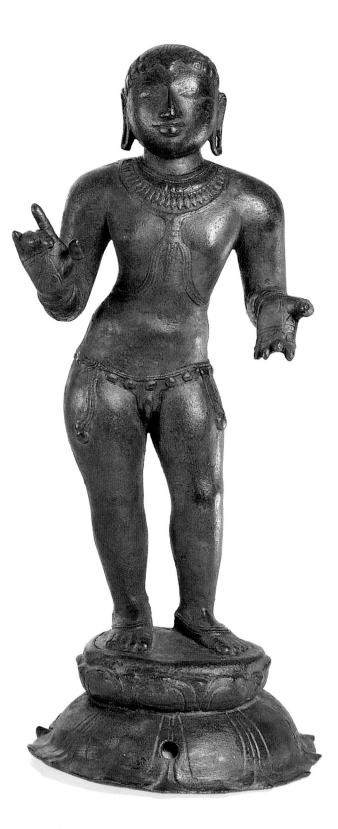

88. South Indian. *Sambandar, the Child Saint.* Chola dynasty (11th century). Copper alloy, 17" (43.2 cm) high, 7⅛" (18 cm) diam. Given in Memory of Lord Ampthill by his Widow, 1935. V&A IM 75–1935

This refined figure represents Sambandar, one of the sixty-three Saiva saints of Tamilnadu. He is represented as a child, naked but for a belt garland, bracelets, and other ornaments. Sambandar makes his characteristic gesture of the raised index finger with which, as an infant, he first pointed to Shiva and Parvati. The veneration of saints had become a feature of popular Hindu worship in South India by the Chola period (850–1279), when this image was cast. Sculptures of the saints were regularly installed for veneration alongside those of the divinities and retain this place of honor today.

Like many Indian artifacts in the Museum's collection, this child saint was acquired by a senior colonial official in the early decades of the twentieth century. The piece was reportedly excavated in Tinnevelly District, Tamilnadu, and entered the collection of Lord Ampthill, governor of Madras from 1900 to 1906. Lord Ampthill lent it for exhibition at the Festival of Empire, Crystal Palace, in 1911, and it was finally given to the Museum in 1935 by Lord Ampthill's widow in his memory.

JOHN GUY

88.

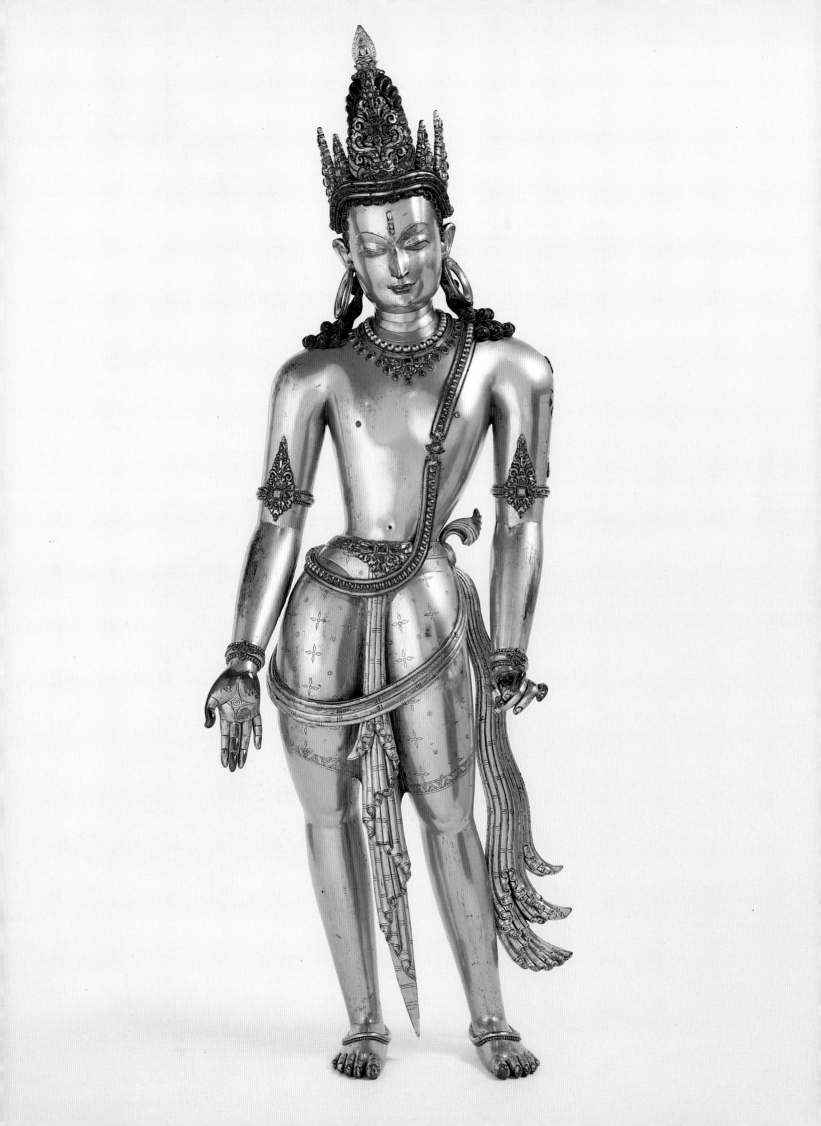

89. Nepalese. *Padmapani, the Lotus Bearer.* Late 14th–early 15th century. Gilt-copper with inset precious and semiprecious stones, 36⅝ x 13⅜ x 6½" (93 x 34 x 16.5 cm). V&A IM 239–1922

This exquisite sculpture was acquired by Brigadier-General C. G. Rawlings while in the Xigazê (Shigatse) District of central Tibet in 1904. He was a member of the Younghusband Expedition which that year fought its way from India to Lhasa in an attempt to force Tibet to engage in trade with British India. It is recorded that several members of the expedition acquired examples of "Lamaist" art en route.

The Buddhist lord of compassion, Avalokitesvara, is represented in his popular manifestation as Padmapani, the Lotus Bearer. Padmapani is one of the bodhisattvas, an enlightened being who voluntarily postpones passing into nirvana in order to help others gain salvation. The concept of the bodhisattva was developed in the Mahayanist school of Buddhist thought and gained enormous popularity in the Himalayas. The stillness and serenity of this figure speaks of the state of harmony to which the bodhisattva aspires, while the sensuous contrapposto of Padmapani's sleek, androgynous body ties him to the human world.

By 1922, when this piece was purchased for £210, Indian sculptures in general—not just Gandharan works in the Western taste (such as cat. 90)—were becoming valued for their aesthetic as well as their antiquarian worth.

JOHN GUY

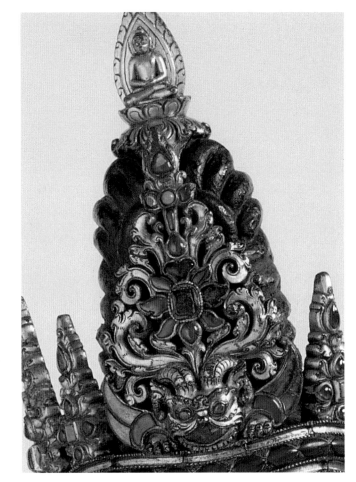

89. (detail)

90. Afghanistan. *Head of the Buddha.* Gandharan style, 4th–5th century. Lime plaster with traces of pigment, 11⅜ x 7⅛ x 7½" (29 x 18 x 19 cm). V&A IM 3–1931

No style of Indian art is more easily assimilated into the Western canon than Gandharan sculpture. The prominence given to this head in the Museum's collection vividly illustrates the ways in which Indian art has often been read in terms of Western art history. The Gandharan region of Afghanistan emerged in the early centuries A.D. as a stronghold of Buddhist practice. Numerous monasteries, shrines, and stupas, richly decorated with stone and stucco, were commissioned by the prosperous merchant communities. Like other Gandharan stucco, this head was originally richly colored. It displays several of the characteristic marks of the Buddha: the prominent hair-knot, here treated in a Greco-Roman manner unlike contemporary Indian styles; the forehead mark; and the elongated earlobes.

The Greco-Roman influence in Gandharan art explains the Western interest in this provincial style of Indian art at a time when Indian sculpture was viewed with puzzlement, even disdain. In the nineteenth century the Gandharan school fueled a theory of Mediterranean cultural diffusion that attributed India's sculptural tradition to Western inspiration and achieved a high status in nineteenth- and early-twentieth-century perceptions of Indian art. Yet the Gandharan style existed only on the margins of India and had no lasting influence on mainstream stylistic developments. Nonetheless, it is the best represented of Indian sculptural traditions in Western collections, and this piece is one of the V&A's most reproduced pieces of Indian sculpture. Indian sculpture was gradually reappraised early in the twentieth century to encompass not only Hellenistic-inspired Gandharan work but also mainstream Indian styles.

Lit. Ashton, 1950, no. 130, plate 21; Hallade, 1968, p. 143, plate 106; Bussagli, 1984, p. 229, fig. 1; Czuma, 1985, no. 120

JOHN GUY

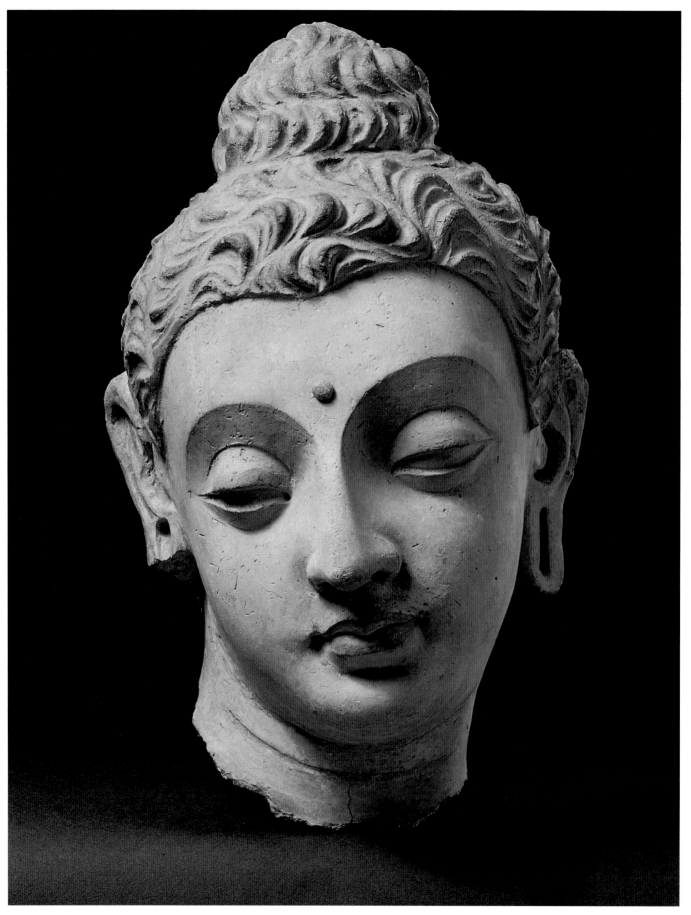

90.

91. Indian (Southern Deccan). *Nandi, Shiva's Sacred Bull.*
Late 16th–17th century. Serpentine, 24⅝ x 33⅛ x 15"
(62.5 x 84 x 38 cm). V&A IS 73–1990

Temples dedicated to the deity Shiva, the Hindu lord of creation
and destruction, are to be found throughout the Indian subcon-
tinent. An essential element in any Shiva temple is the image of
Nandi, the sacred calf-bull, whose name means "joyfulness" or
"blissfulness." In the ordering of temple space, Nandi occupies
an axial position, focusing the attention of the faithful from the
outer halls of the temple directly into its spiritual heart, the *garb-
hagrha,* or "womb chamber." Images of this scale and larger were
usually housed in a pillared hall or *mandapa,* which stood independent of the temple and was oriented toward the east, facing
directly into the temple, so that Nandi's intimate relationship
with Shiva was made explicit.

Lit. Guy, 1991

JOHN GUY

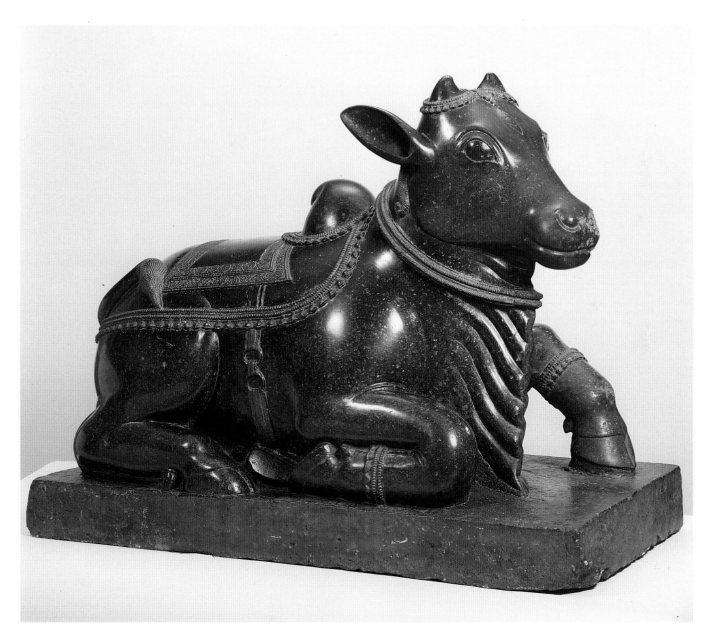

91.

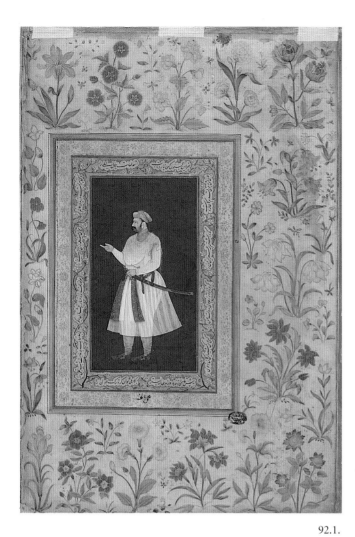

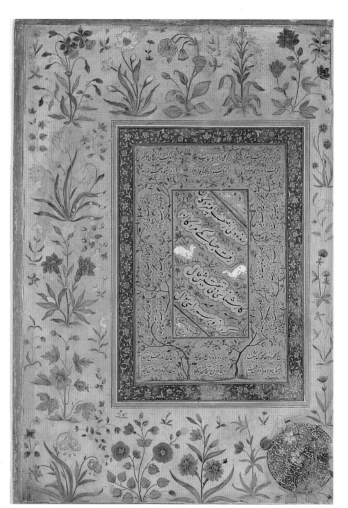

92.1.

92.2.

92. *Painting: Indian* (Mughal). Opaque watercolor and gold on paper, sheet 15⅜ x 10⅜" (38.9 x 26.4 cm). Bequeathed by Lady Wantage

92.1. Recto: Ascribed to Balchand. *Portrait of Mirza Abu'l Hasan 'Itiqad Khan (1579–1641)*. c. 1620–30. Image, 9⅝ x 6⅜" (24.6 x 16.3 cm). V&A IM 120–1921

92.2. Verso: Sultan Ali al-Mashhadi (Iranian, 16th century). *Panel of Calligraphy*. Decorated in Mughal India c. 1640. Image, 9½ x 6¼" (24.1 x 15.8 cm). V&A IM 120a–1921

This portrait depicts one of the most significant Mughal courtiers of the early seventeenth century, Mirza Abu'l Hasan, whose family belonged to the Iranian elite effectively ruling the empire. The painting was described on acquisition simply as "An amir of the court of Jahangir, by Balchand, about 1614"; it remained unidentified until 1976 when it was compared with authentically inscribed examples and redated.

The painting was originally mounted on a page for inclusion in an album, the front beautifully calligraphed with Persian verses, and both sides decorated with floral borders in the style of the 1640s. The album was probably broken up in about 1800 when some of the pages were copied and mixed with original seventeenth-century works such as this. Many of the authentic and copied pages in the Wantage bequest have been stamped on the borders with a genuine, though anachronistic, round seal of Jahangir. A smaller seal of one Pandit Nandaram is not entirely distinct but seems to be dated "1211 [of the Islamic era]/1796–97 A.D." The copying was presumably done in order to increase the number of pages for sale, authenticity "guaranteed" by the royal seal, which made the original buyer (and the Museum) overlook the many impostors in the Wantage collection.

The drawings in the Wantage bequest—once in the collection of the Mughal emperor Shah Jahan—had been purchased in a London salesroom and presented to Lady Wantage by her father in 1868 on her twenty-first birthday. The collection was exhibited as a loan to the Indian collection from 1916 to 1918 and bequeathed to the Museum on Lady Wantage's death in 1921. The Wantage paintings have been prominently displayed ever since. The perceived importance of the Museum's collection of Indian paintings has been such that they have become the focus for a great deal of scholarly activity.

Lit. V&A, n.d. [1918], no. 14; Clarke, 1922; Pinder-Wilson, 1976, no. 128; Smart, 1991, p. 147

SUSAN STRONGE

93. Indian (Kangra). *Shiva and His Family at the Burning Ground.* c. 1810. Opaque watercolor on paper, 9¾ x 5⅞" (24.8 x 14.9 cm). V&A IM 6–1912

The central figure in this painting is the Hindu god Shiva, "the destroyer," who sits with his consort Parvati and their sons at the burning ground where corpses are taken to be cremated. Despite its mournful subject, it is painted with the delicacy and control typical of the early-nineteenth-century Kangra style of Pahari (Punjab Hills) painting.

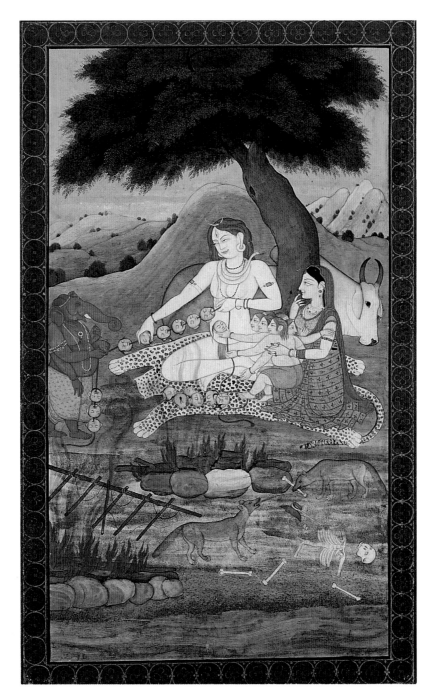

93.

In contrast to the Westernized works of the Mughal court artists (cat. 92), paintings of the Hindu courts of the Punjab Hills and Rajasthan began to be collected in the West for their artistic value only in the early twentieth century. One of the first champions of Rajput painting was the half–Sri Lankan critic and collector Ananda Coomaraswamy, from whom this painting was bought for £4 in 1912, together with four others. These were the first significant acquisitions of Pahari painting by the India Museum and laid the foundation for what was to become one of the finest collections of paintings from the Punjab Hills area. The collection was largely built up by W. G. Archer (keeper of the Indian section, 1949–60), who identified most of the Pahari schools that now form the basis of study of the area's painting styles. The collection benefited greatly not only from further purchases from Coomaraswamy, but also from the acquisition of paintings from the collection of the artist William Rothenstein who, like Coomaraswamy, had been one of the few enthusiasts for Indian painting in the early years of the twentieth century.

Lit. Archer, 1973, vol. 1, p. 304

Rosemary Crill

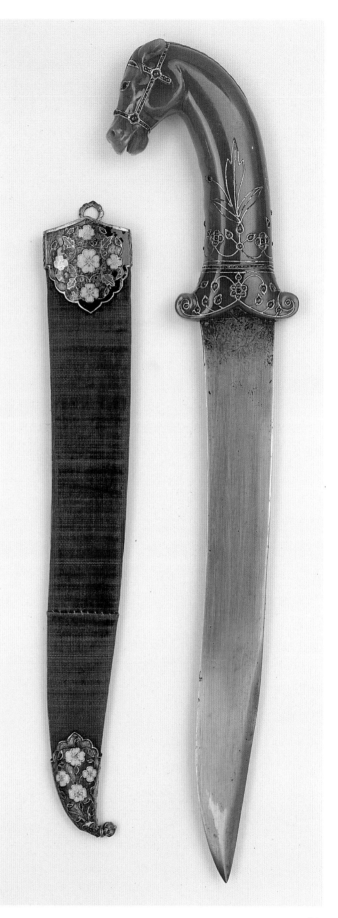

94.

94. Indian (Mughal). *Dagger and Scabbard.* Probably period of Aurangzeb (1658–1707). Hilt, nephrite jade with rubies; blade, steel; scabbard, with enameled silver mounts: Dagger 16½" (42 cm) long, 3½" (9 cm) wide; scabbard 11⅝" (29.5 cm) long, 1¾" (4.5 cm) wide. V&A (IS)02566

Daggers with animal head hilts first appeared during the reign of Mughal emperor Shah Jahan (1628–58) and were worn only by members of the royal house. Subsequently, their use proliferated, particularly by the eighteenth century, reflecting the decline in central Mughal power and concomitant inability to restrict the use of royal emblems.

This dagger formed part of the collection of Colonel Charles Seton Guthrie, who joined the Bengal Engineers in 1828 and remained in India until 1857. Possessed of "an ample fortune," he acquired hard stones as well as built the single largest private collection of Eastern coins. Guthrie's main preoccupation was with the virtuosity of lapidary work.

The Guthrie collection was shown at the Paris Exposition Universelle in 1867. The following year Guthrie offered the entire collection of 244 pieces to the India Museum. The case for acquiring the collection was strongly argued. Jade-working had virtually disappeared in India, and, as many of the pieces had come from royal collections dispersed through war or sold because of financial hardship, Guthrie's collection was unique. However, the Museum was funded from Indian revenues, and doubts over the propriety of expending these funds "for the mere purposes of exhibition" prevailed. Only eighty-one pieces from the collection were acquired.

In 1879, the Guthrie acquisitions were transferred with a large part of the India Museum collection to the South Kensington Museum. Guthrie had died in 1874, and the following year his possessions were dispersed in a sale at Christie's. Some of the hard stones were acquired by connoisseurs who then sold, gave, or bequeathed them to South Kensington, thus reuniting a significant part of the collection. The last Guthrie jade to be acquired was the famous wine cup of Shah Jahan in 1962.

Western connoisseurs in the nineteenth and early twentieth centuries were well aware of the quality of Mughal lapidary work, but a school of thought later developed that denied the existence of an independent Indian jade tradition, claiming it to be simply an offshoot of Chinese craftsmanship. The argument was largely based on the fact that jade was not found in India, thus ignoring the sixteenth- and seventeenth-century Mughal and European accounts of its importation. The ensuing debate led to an exhibition at the V&A in 1966, which examined the distinctly different styles and techniques of Mughal and Chinese jades, as well as introduced jades from elsewhere in the Islamic world, notably Iran and Turkey. Subsequent research focused on

the development of style in historic Mughal jades, with the Guthrie collection providing key reference material.

Lit. Skelton, 1972; Stronge, 1993

Susan Stronge

95. Indian (Mughal). *Pen Box and Utensils.* Early 18th century. White nephrite jade set with rubies, emeralds, and diamonds in gold, 8¼" (20.9 cm) long x 3½" (8.8 cm) wide x ¾" (2 cm) deep. V&A (IS)02549

The precious stones with which Mughal jades are set provide an instantly recognizable Indian character. The Mughal aspect is reinforced by the decoration, derived from the floral patterns inlaid into the white marble of Shah Jahan's buildings, such as the Taj Mahal, of the 1630s and 1640s.

Lit. Koezuka, 1993, no. 22

Susan Stronge

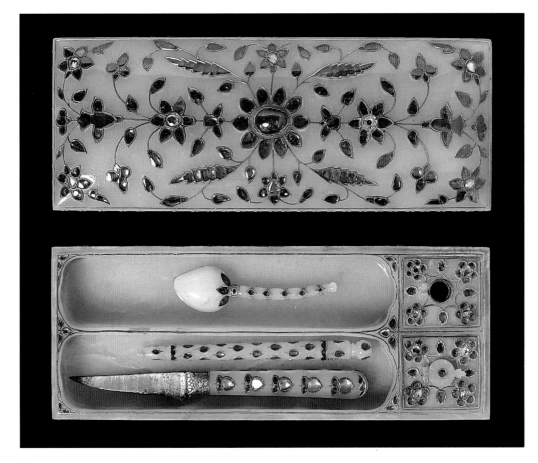

95.

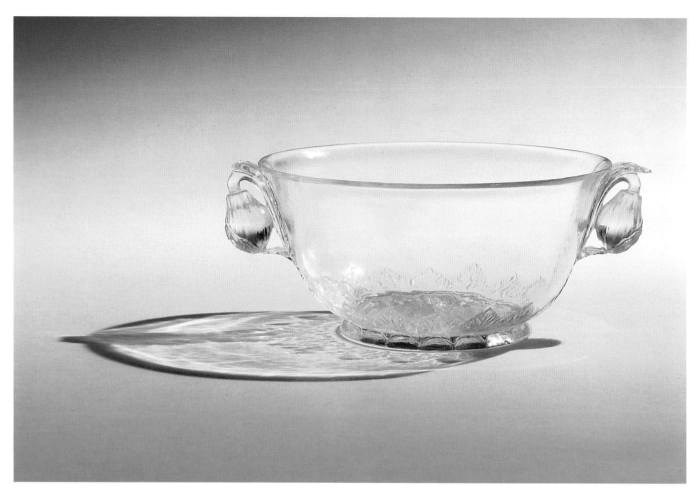

96.

96. Indian (Mughal). *Cup.* Mid-17th century. Rock crystal, 2⅛ x 5¾ x 4¾" (5.5 x 14.5 x 12 cm). V&A (IS)02608

Although Charles Guthrie had in his collection a small number of vessels of similar, almost flawless, rock crystal, Mughal cups of this quality are extremely rare and were presumably made only for the court. The decoration is deliberately restrained to reveal the unblemished nature of the hard stone.

Lit. Koezuka, 1993, no. 26

SUSAN STRONGE

97. Indian (Mughal). *Mirror.* 18th century. Dark green nephrite jade inlaid with white nephrite jade and rubies in gold, 5¼ x 4½ x ½" (13.4 x 11.4 x 1.3 cm). V&A (IS)02587

The inlays on the mirror-back are secured by highly refined gold. In this quintessential Mughal jewelry technique, the stone is pressed into the soft gold, which also provides a reflective foil for translucent stones. Trellis designs similar to this were used on tiles, textiles, and metalwork.

Lit. Koezuka, 1993, no. 31

SUSAN STRONGE

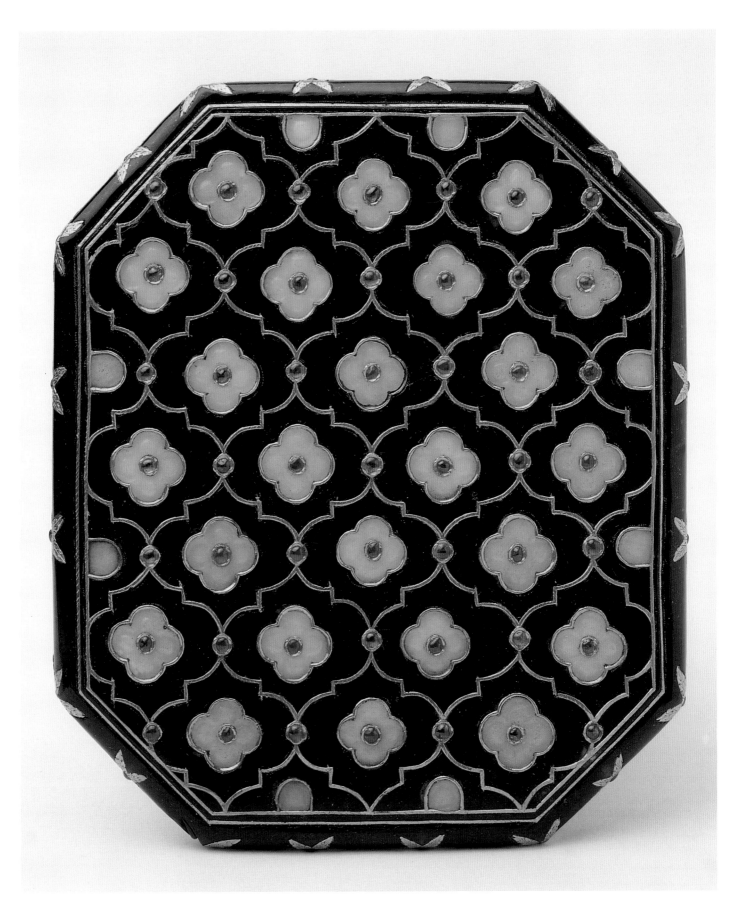

97.

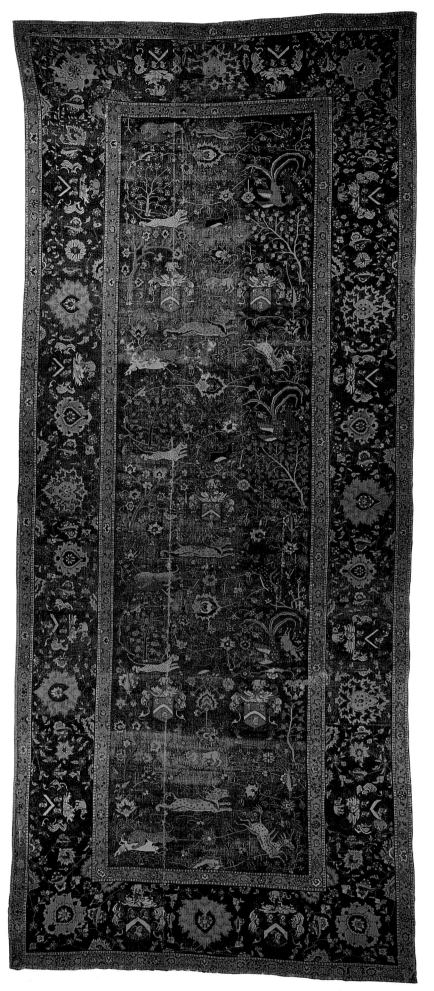

98.

98. Indian (probably Lahore). *The Fremlin Carpet.* c. 1640. Wool pile on cotton warp and weft, 226 x 100" (574 x 254 cm). Purchased with the assistance of the National Art Collections Fund and Frank Fremlin. V&A IM 1–1936

The Fremlin Carpet is among the most impressive of those many works in the Museum's collection made by Indian crafts-men for members of the British trading and administrative community, particularly those working for the East India Company. This stunning Mughal carpet is named after William Fremlin, an official of the East India Company who became president of the Council at Surat. He commissioned it during his service in India from 1626 to 1644. It is one of only three Mughal carpets with British coats of arms known to have survived: a second was commissioned in Lahore in 1631 for the Girdlers Company in London, and a third (known only by repute) was apparently commissioned by Sir Thomas Roe, James I's ambas-sador to the Mughal court fron 1615 to 1619.

The design of the Fremlin carpet is based on a standard type of animal or "hunting" carpet which derives from Persian prototypes, although it is unmistakably Indian in the drawing and coloring of its lifelike figures, flora, and scenes of fierce tigers attacking prey. The carpet would have been made to be spread over a table, which was the normal usage of carpets in England at that time, rather than on the floor as it would have been in India. Considered Spanish in 1882, this carpet was not alone in being misidentified at that time: Indian carpets were frequently called Persian, or at best labeled "Indo-Persian" and considered a provincial offshoot of Persian carpet weaving, until they were studied in their own right in the twentieth century. (The Fremlin Carpet was bought in Paris in 1936.)

Controversy over the provenance and dating of Mughal carpets has arisen mainly through the lack of documented examples, which is why pieces such as the Fremlin Carpet, trace-able to a certain owner at a fairly secure date, have become key objects in this field of study. Although it is known that fine car-pets were being made in Agra and Lahore (both at times capitals of the Mughal Empire) since the late sixteenth century, there is very little evidence to link specific carpets to either center. The link with Lahore for the Fremlin Carpet is based on the prove-nance of the related Girdlers Carpet and also on references to Lahore in the labels on contemporaneous Mughal carpets still in the palace at Jaipur. Although William Fremlin is known to have been stationed in Agra in 1630 and 1633, he is unlikely to have commissioned such a grand object for himself until after he attained the rank of president in 1637.

Lit. Robinson, 1882, plate 9; Irwin, 1976, pp. 65–6

Rosemary Crill

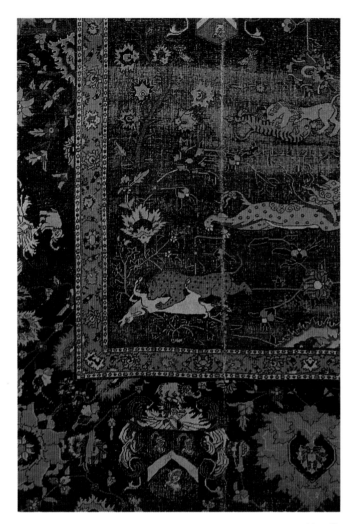

98. (detail)

99. Iranian (Kāshān). *Frieze Tiles.* c. 1200–15. Fritware (artificial porcelain) with luster-painted decoration on an opaque white glaze, each 18½ x 18½" (47 x 47 cm), overall 52⅜" (133 cm) long x 18½" (47 cm) high x 2⅜" (6 cm) deep. V&A 1481–, 1481a–, 1481b–1876

From the 1870s on, interest in Islamic pottery focused on luster-ware, an Islamic invention that involved the deposition of a thin layer of metallic silver and copper on the surface of the glaze during firing. These lusterware tiles came from a major shrine which had undergone continual renovation since the medieval period. The tiles originally formed part of a cornice above a tiled dado on an interior wall. The religious inscriptions are now only fragmentary.

Travelers acquired such tiles through the antiques trade or from archaeological sites and ruins. Less scrupulous methods—"persuading" caretakers to sell, or simple theft—are also record-

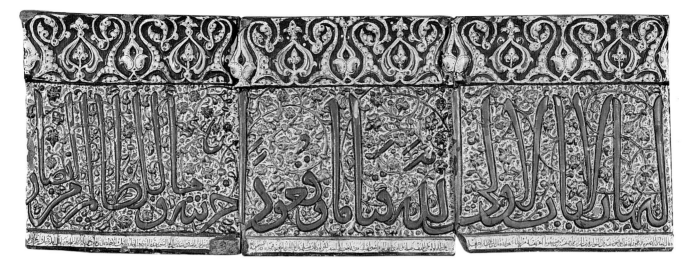

99.

ed. This group was acquired by Robert Murdoch Smith, director of the Persian Telegraph Department and one of the most significant of the expatriates used by South Kensington to develop its collections. At his own instigation, Murdoch Smith was commissioned to purchase examples of Persian art for the South Kensington Museum, a task he carried out from 1873 to 1885. The material acquired was both contemporary and historical, and by 1876 no fewer than 1,889 of those acquisitions (including these tiles) were on display. In the same year the Museum published a book by Murdoch Smith that effectively defined the notion of Persian art around the collection he had amassed for South Kensington.

Lit. Murdoch Smith, 1876; Scarce, 1973

OLIVER WATSON

100. Anatolian (Iznik). *Bowl.* c. 1550–55. Fritware (artificial porcelain) with polychrome underglaze painting, 11" (28 cm) high, 17" (43.2 cm) diam. V&A 242–1876

This elegant piece is representative of the range of material from the court of the Ottoman Empire collected throughout the Museum's history. Like the decorative architectural model of the Alhambra (cat. 16), this kind of material became a focus of interest for manufacturers in the nineteenth century.

The establishment of a high-quality ceramics industry in Iznik, western Anatolia, stemmed from the desire of the Turkish Ottoman court for luxury ware. Although imported Chinese porcelains were more luxurious, Iznik ware offered some advantages. Since the Ottoman court designers supplied patterns, they were in the most refined Turkish taste; they were decorated in a bright polychrome, not just in blue-and-white; and they could be made in any shape desired.

In the late nineteenth century, Iznik wares began to be enthusiastically collected and were an inspiration for William Morris and others in the Arts and Crafts movement, who saw in them an ideal of non-naturalistic pattern-making. Their origin, however, was uncertain, and variously attributed to Persia, Rhodes, or Damascus. Persia was seen as a natural home, as the Persians were generally considered to be the most artistic race in the Islamic world; a fantastic tale even developed that these wares were the product of Persian artisans marooned on the island of Rhodes. But since the mosques of Damascus were still decorated with tiles (ironically made by an inferior offshoot of the Iznik industry), the term "Damas" was already used in sixteenth-century English archives. Indeed, this bowl entered the Museum in 1876 as "Damascus," although C. D. Fortnum commented that these wares "were also made, in all probability, in Egypt, Turkey, Syria, Asia Minor, &c., and . . . pieces of Persian manufacture may be included." The real origin of the bowl was not established until the 1930s. The price—£21.75—was modest in its day given the bowl's size, rarity, and splendor.

Lit. Fortnum, 1873

OLIVER WATSON

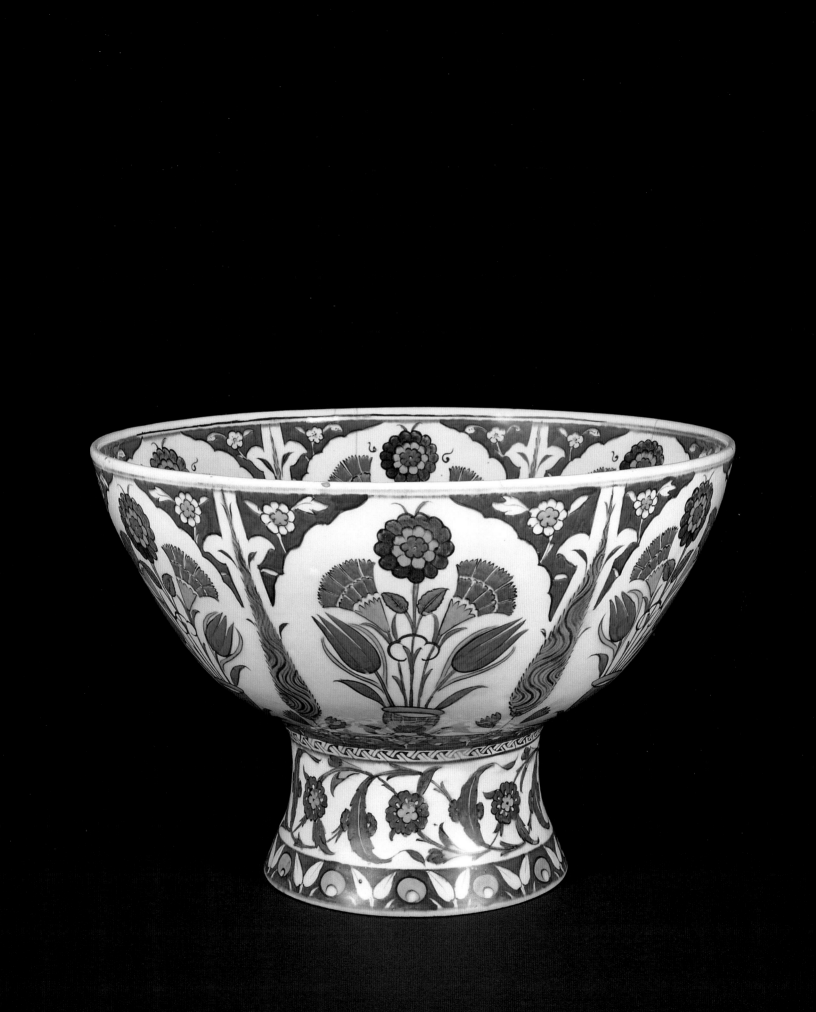

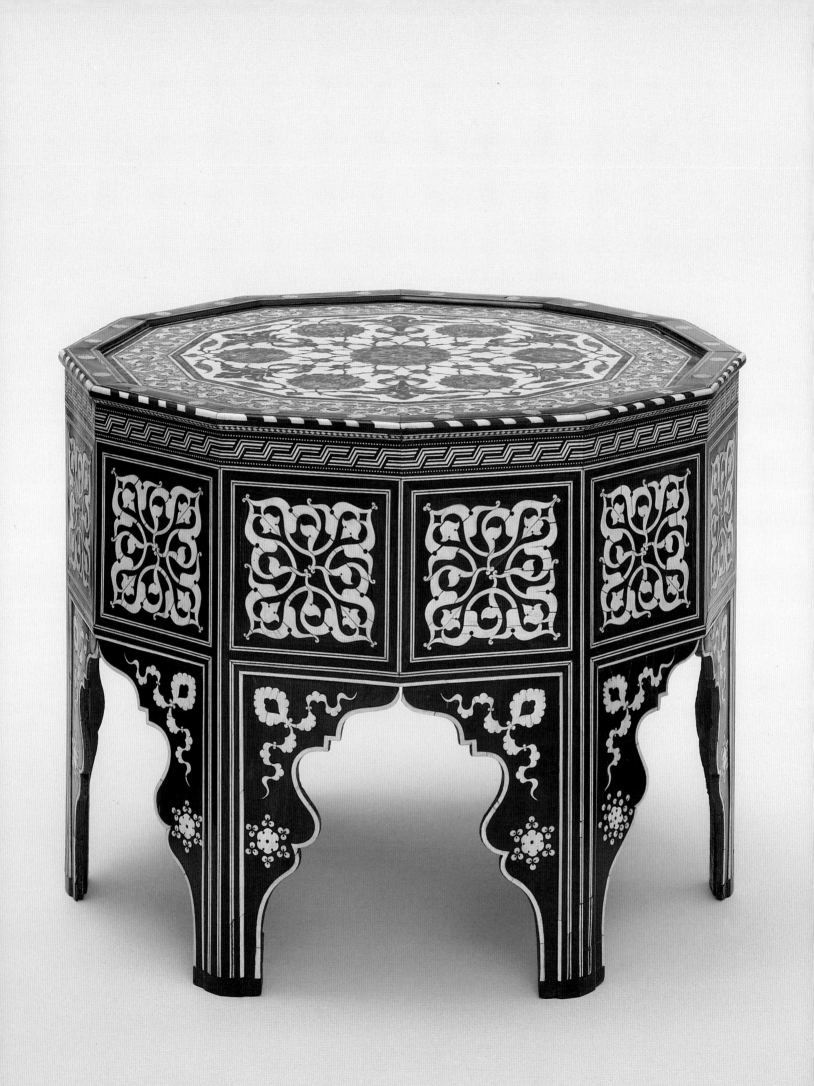

101. Turkish (the tile from Iznik, the woodwork probably from Istanbul). *Table.* 16th century. Tile, fritware (artificial porcelain) with polychrome underglaze painting; table, wood with ivory, ebony, and mother-of-pearl marquetry, 18⅞" (48 cm) high, 24¾" (63 cm) diam. Purchased with the assistance of the J. R. Vallentin Fund, Horn Bequest, Bequest of Captain H. B. Murray, Bryan Fund, and Barbar Fund. V&A C.19–1987

It has been commonly assumed that "there is no furniture" in the Islamic world and that carpets and built-in cupboards alone served as seating and storage. Thus there was great unease when this "coffee table" appeared in a London auction house in 1986. It was catalogued as mid-sixteenth-century and compared to the throne of Sultan Suleyman the Magnificent, in Istanbul's Topkapi Palace Museum. Most experts doubted it, believing it to be either a nineteenth-century object made to satisfy the European fashion for "Oriental" rooms, or an assemblage of disparate fragments—bits of an old Qu'ran-box married to a wall tile. A different view was taken by the V&A, and the table was acquired the following year on the recommendation of the Museum's Islamic specialist.

Subsequent investigation revealed that the woodwork was complete and integral, with no later alterations. The technique, materials, and style also closely matched the imperial Turkish throne to which it had been compared. While the tile matches those installed in Suleyman's mosque in 1557, it does not compare in size or shape to any wall tiles and thus can only have been a tabletop. Further research revealed that tables of this type were used in the Topkapi Palace in the sixteenth century, for example, to serve food in the council chamber to officials seated on built-in benches around the walls. Because of both its rarity and simplistic notions of what an Islamic object should be, doubts were needlessly raised. At the V&A the table is prominently displayed as a key example of Islamic imperial-quality sixteenth-century Turkish furniture.

OLIVER WATSON

102. Egyptian (Cairo). *Mosque Lamp.* Late 15th century. Bronze overlaid with silver and gold, 64⅛" (163 cm) high (exclusive of chain), 29⅛" (74 cm) diam. at base. V&A 109–1888

This imposing hanging lamp was originally made for a mosque in Cairo built by the Mamluk sultan Qaytbay. The central medallions carry the engraved blazon of Abu'l-Nasr Qaytbay, which reads "Glory to our master the Sultan al-Malik al-Ashraf Abu'l-Nasr Qaytbay. May his victories be glorious." This same

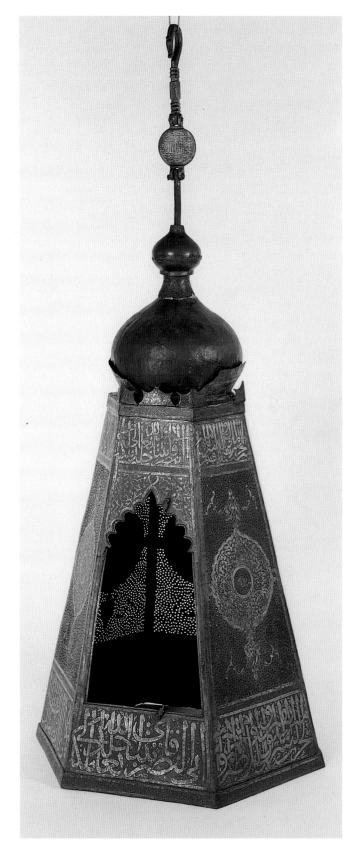

102.

inscription appears on the lamp's dragon-shaped suspension hook. The lamp also bears two bands, overlaid with silver and inscribed with an invocation to the Sultan in which each letter is decorated with fine punch-work. This exquisite decoration would have been invisible when the lamp was suspended, but gives some indication of the quality of the craftsmanship.

The lamp was acquired in 1888 for £80 from a dealer who recorded that it was said to have been dug up near Cairo in the 1860s. From an early date the importance of the lamp was appreciated. It has maintained a prominent place among the Museum's displays of Islamic material and is frequently cited in London guidebooks. The Islamic collection has had a varied display history at the Museum. Shown together by the end of the nineteenth century, it was split up according to material—as were other Museum collections—after the 1908 rearrangement (the lamp was displayed with Saracenic and Persian metalwork [see fig. 36]). After World War II, however, the Islamic collection was reassembled in one gallery, where the lamp has also been displayed in recent years.

Lit. Jones and Michell, 1976, no. 227

ANTHONY R. E. NORTH

103. Ottoman, possibly Egyptian. *Table Carpet.* Mid-16th century. Woolen pile on woolen warp and weft, asymmetrical knot, 91 x 99" (231 x 251.5 cm) max.; 24 x 25" (61 x 63.5 cm) min. V&A 151–1883

This carpet was woven to fit over a small square table and was almost certainly made for export to Europe, since tables were not normally part of the furnishings of an Ottoman house (see cat. 101). It was woven in a single cruciform piece, beginning with a narrow panel and extending the knotted pile when required to form the complete width.

The carpet was purchased as a fine specimen of Persian seventeenth-century weaving in 1883 at a sale at the firm of Bon Marché in Paris. It was thought at that time to be a canopy "for carrying above a person of rank going in procession." Carpets with this combination of design and technique are now believed to date from the mid-sixteenth century and to come from the East Mediterranean, although their precise attribution is still uncertain.

Lit. Erdmann, 1966, p. 22; Pinner and Franses, 1981, pp. 36, 45, 47, 49; Yetkin, 1981, p. 105

JENNIFER WEARDEN

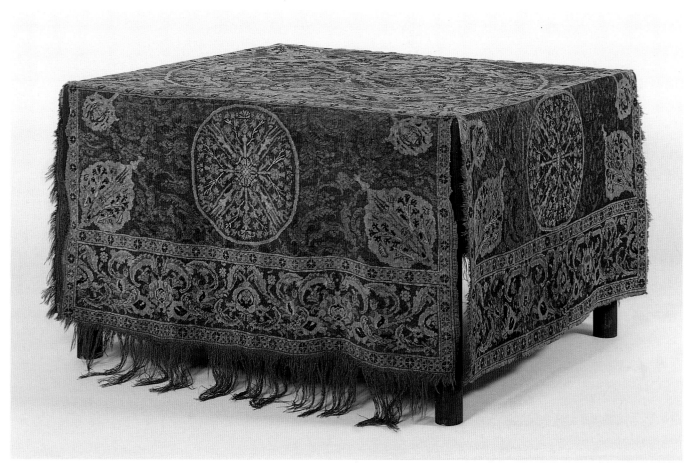

103.

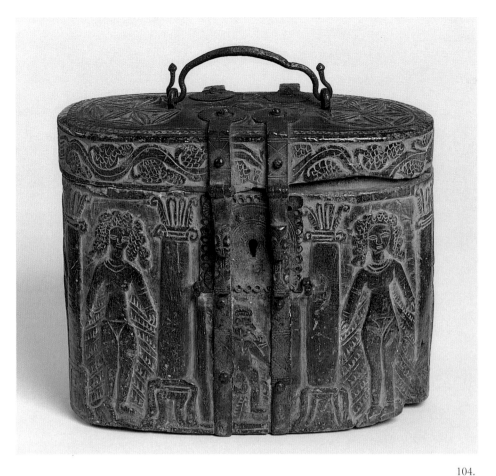

104.

104. Nubian. *Box.* 7th or 8th century. Steatite (soapstone), mounts of copper alloy, 5½ x 6¾ x 3¼" (14 x 17.1 x 8.3 cm). V&A 873–1876

Found in Nubia in 1832 and acquired by the Museum in 1876 for £4 10s. from Edinburgh dealers in antiques and curiosities, among other things, this carved stone box was thought to be Roman at the time of its purchase. The Museum's register on the piece was revised in 1894 when the director, Dr. John Middleton, described the box as a "curious half savage work of doubtful date; probably executed in Upper Egypt or Abyssinia in the 6th or 7th centy A.D." Dr. Middleton identified the central figure under the lock as the youthful Horus (called Harpocrates by the Greeks and Romans)—the ancient Egyptian god of light and goodness—with his finger on his lip (a symbol of childhood). A very similar figure, also with his finger to his lips, appears on the opposite side of the box. Middleton's identification of this figure as Horus is problematic, however—as, indeed, is the nature of the object in many other respects. The figure does not have the head of a hawk, as Horus is usually represented. Perhaps more significantly, Nubia was Christianized by the sixth century, and the Egyptian god Horus thus would be an unlikely subject for a seventh- or eighth-century object.

In 1904 the Cairo Museum included this piece in its catalogue of Coptic art, citing it as a remarkable example of Coptic work. The attribution was taken up by the V&A, not least for its appeal in relation to the Coptic textiles in the Museum's collection. The Coptic attribution was repeated in 1932 by the scholar W. F. Volbach, who added, however, that the figures recalled Nubian work. The piece is now believed to be Nubian.

As a result of the Nubian attribution, this box is one of the very few objects in the V&A's collections that can be described as African—thus creating a conundrum. The V&A does not collect African art, and most of the African material once held by the Museum has long since been transferred, largely to the British Museum. In respect to the art historical, sociocultural, and even political questions this raises, the box can be compared with many objects in the collections which have Egyptian provenances but have been classified as Islamic (for example, cats. 102–103). In certain cultural and academic quarters in the late twentieth century, especially in France and the United States, premodern Egyptian materials have become the subject of lively dialogue (sometimes disputatious) about the origins of African art, the exclusion of Egypt from African studies, and the geopolitics that distinguish ancient Egypt from Africa.

Lit. Strzygowski, 1904, p. 109; Volbach, 1932, p. 100

RICHARD DUNN/BRENDA RICHARDSON

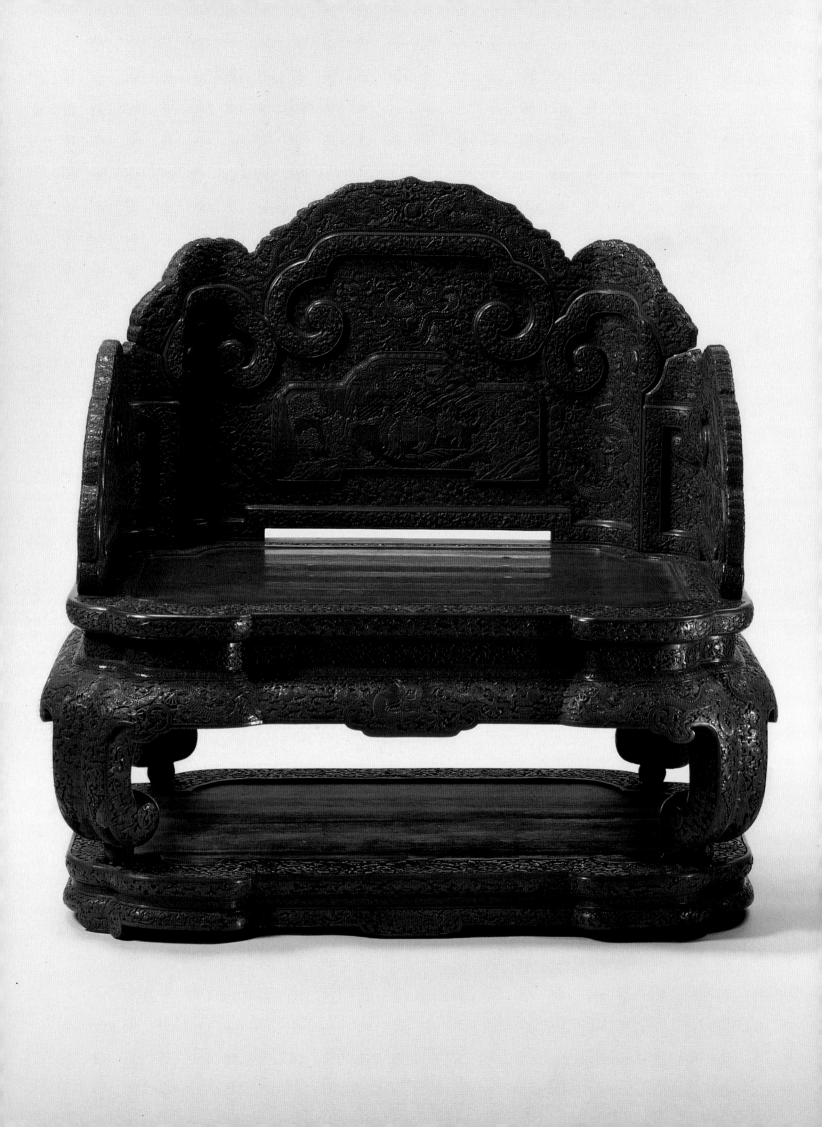

105. Chinese. *Imperial Throne.* Qing dynasty, Qianlong reign, 1736–95. Carved polychrome lacquer on wood core, 47 x 49½ x 36" (119.3 x 125.7 x 91.4 cm). V&A W399–1922

Artifacts from the Chinese imperial court, including this grand and ornate throne (and cats. 106–107), enthralled many nineteenth-century collectors and consequently figure prominently in the Museum's collection. The throne was almost certainly commissioned in the late 1780s for the Tuanhe Traveling Palace, one of several temporary abodes of the emperors of the Qing dynasty in the Nan Haizi ("southern ponds") hunting park immediately south of Beijing. This park formed the setting for a number of military reviews celebrating the apogee of Manchu power in Asia, but was neglected in the nineteenth century and gradually fell into decay. The Nan Haizi park was looted by Russian troops in 1900–01, in the aftermath of the occupation of Beijing by troops of the eight allied powers (including the United States and Great Britain) that invaded China, ostensibly to suppress the so-called Boxer Uprising. The czarist Russian ambassador Mikhail N. Girs acquired the throne in China and brought it to Britain following the Soviet revolution of 1917.

The throne was displayed by the dealer Spink & Son at its St. James's premises and bought from the firm on behalf of the Museum by George Swift, a major figure in the wholesale pota-

to industry in Britain and, during World War I, a colleague of Edward Fairbrother Strange, the V&A's furniture curator.

Neither Spink nor the Museum has ever attempted to conceal the origins of the throne, which is valued as much for its imperial associations as for its craftsmanship. It has been on continuous display since its acquisition, labeled until the 1980s as "Throne of Emperor Ch'ien-lung" (Qianlong). Until 1952 the throne had pride of place in the displays of Oriental furniture and woodwork (see fig. 105), and since then has been prominent in the Far Eastern Primary Gallery and the T. T. Tsui Gallery of Chinese Art.

In his 1925 *Catalogue of Chinese Lacquer,* Strange made the first serious attempt in a European language to provide an overview of lacquer, concentrating on itemizing the medium's most common decorative motifs and their symbolic significance, a style of scholarship derived from the study of Chinese ceramics. More recently, attention has shifted away from the throne's glamorous lacquer medium and toward the object's provenance, with an attempt to provide a more precise date and place of manufacture and to understand its role as symbolic of British hegemony in Asia in the popular and institutional imagination.

Lit. Strange, 1925; Clunas, 1991; Clunas, 1994

CRAIG CLUNAS

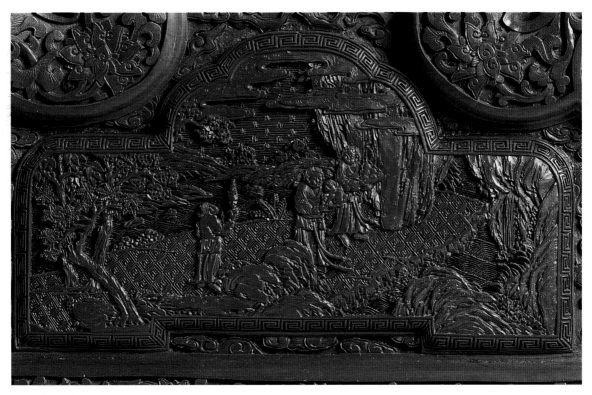

105. (detail)

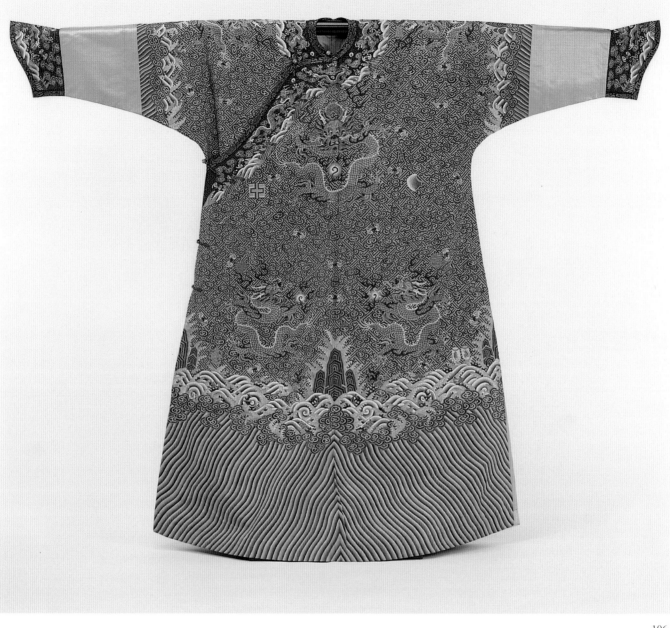

106. Chinese. *Imperial Dragon Robe.* Qing dynasty, 18th–19th century. Silk tapestry weave, 61 x 77" (154 x 194 cm). Purchased with a grant from the National Art Collections Fund. V&A T.199–1948

Dragon robes of such magnificence were worn by Chinese emperors on formal occasions. These imperial clothes are distinguished from those worn by Chinese bureaucrats by the frequent use of yellow and the patterning of twelve small motifs within the standard dragon-and-cloud layout.

Although it is not known whether any Chinese ruler wore this particular garment, the supposed imperial connection and the emphasis placed by Westerners on the perceived symbolic nature of all Chinese patterns legitimized the collecting of such dress. Bernard Vuilleumier, a Swiss banker, accentuated both aspects in a handbook that accompanied a display of his collection of Chinese robes in London in 1939. Today, the book is regarded as a blueprint of Orientalist fantasy, although it retains some credence among collectors. This splendid robe was purchased along with the rest of Vuilleumier's extensive collection upon his death.

VERITY WILSON

107. Chinese. *Vase.* Qing dynasty, mark and reign period of Qianlong (1736–95). Porcelain with celadon green glaze and overglaze enamel decoration, 14⅜ x 10⅞ x 7⅞" (36.5 x 27.5 x 20 cm). Bequeathed by George Salting. V&A C.1466–1910

Unlike other, more recently formed museum collections of Chinese pottery, the V&A's Chinese ceramics contain an unusually high proportion of eighteenth-century imperial porcelain. This vase, made at the imperial porcelain factory at Jingdezhen in Jiangxi province, central southern China, is characteristic of the highest quality of Chinese porcelain produced in the eighteenth century. Its finely painted scenes depict landscapes of the four seasons with appropriate short poems, a common and auspicious theme.

The vase was among 1,405 pieces of Chinese and Japanese porcelain bequeathed by George Salting in 1910. The bulk of the Salting collection comprised items made in China for export to the West during the seventeenth and eighteenth centuries. This piece, however, was made for the highest echelons of the Chinese home market, a fact indicated by its form and decorative style, which closely resemble the form and style of pieces from the former Chinese court now held in the Palace Museum, Beijing, and the National Palace Museum, Taipei.

Lit. Honey, 1927, p. 101; Ayers, 1980, p. 68; Kerr, 1986, pp. 94–118

ROSE KERR

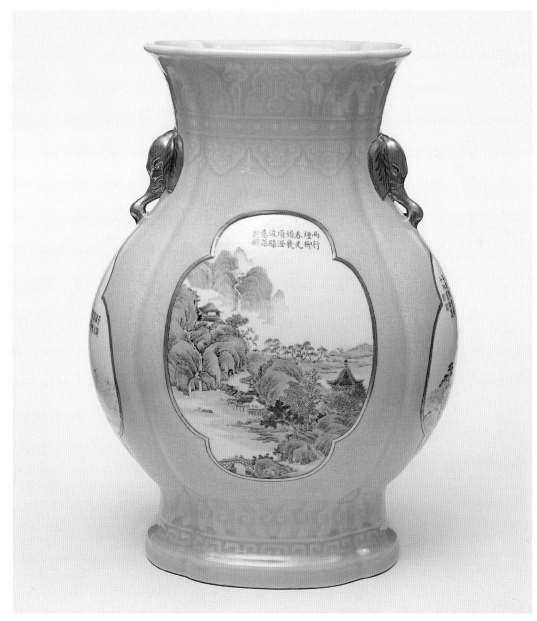

107.

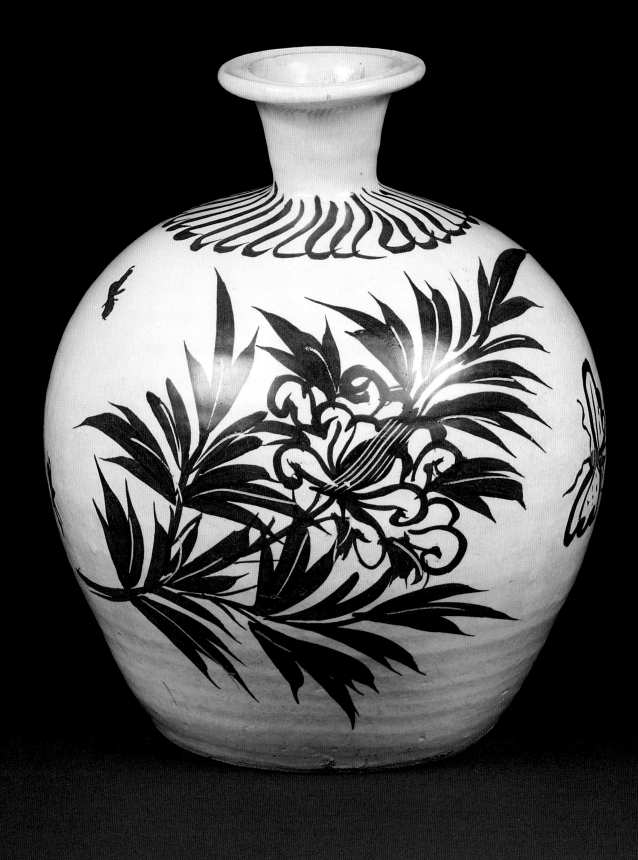

108. Northern Chinese. *Vase.* Jin dynasty, 1115–1200. Stoneware, 9⅝" (24.5 cm) high, 8¼" (21 cm) diam. V&A C.32–1935

An example of vernacular rather than imperial applied art, this vase was purchased in 1935 as part of the collection of George Eumorfopoulos. Formed in accordance with a modernist aesthetic, Eumorfopoulos's collection contained earlier Chinese ceramics, thus complementing the later pieces bequeathed twenty-five years earlier by George Salting (cat. 107).

The vase was made in Cizhou, formerly a county in present-day Hebei province, north of the Yellow River. Using iron oxide as a colorant, the potter painted two large peony sprays on each side, adding fluttering butterflies and smaller insects between the sprays and a row of stylized petals on the shoulders. Cizhou ware, though popular into the sixteenth century, never enjoyed imperial patronage, apart from a few court orders for wine jars. When the Qing dynasty collapsed in 1912 and the imperial collection of ceramics in the Forbidden City was examined, no Cizhou ware was found. Private collectors were, however, interested in it, although primarily for its antiquity. *The Ge Gu Yao Lun* (*A Discussion of the Essential Criteria of Antiquities*) of 1388 commends "old Cizhou ware" but warns that "contemporary pieces are not worth discussing."

Collectors in the West became interested in Cizhou ware only during the early years of this century, when excavations unearthed many pieces. This vase was lent by Eumorfopoulos to an exhibition, "Chinese Applied Art," at the City of Manchester Art Gallery in 1913, two years before a chapter on Cizhou was included in R. L. Hobson's *Chinese Pottery and Porcelain* (1915).

Eumorfopoulos was one of the first collectors to show an interest in vernacular art, at a time when colorful overglaze enameled porcelain and blue-and-white pieces were the fashion. As first president of London's Oriental Ceramic Society, he played a major role in introducing early ceramics into the canon of Chinese art. Such was his influence that a generation later the renowned English potter Bernard Leach (1887–1979) expressed great admiration for the free and vigorous brushwork evident in pots such as this one and produced work in much the same style.

Following the collapse of Eumorfopoulos's fortunes in the slump of the 1930s, his immense collection, particularly strong in Chinese ceramics, bronzes, and sculpture of the pre-Song (960–1279) period, was purchased at an advantageous price by the British government and divided between the British Museum and the V&A. These acquisitions profoundly influenced the study and acquisition of Chinese material in both institutions.

Lit. Manchester City Art Gallery, 1913, no. 750; Hobson, 1926, no. C273; Royal Academy, 1935, no. 1264; Ayers, 1980, no. 25; Ayers, 1983, p. 22; Kerr, 1991, p. 242

Ming Wilson

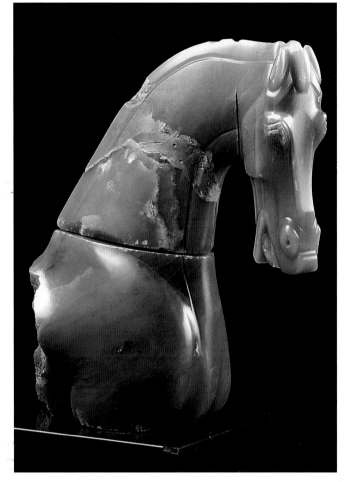

109.

109. Chinese. *Head and Partial Torso of a Horse.* Han dynasty, 206 B.C.–A.D. 220. Jade, 7⅝ x 6¾ x 2½" (19.3 x 17.2 x 6.5 cm). V&A A16–1935

This horse's head from the Eumorfopoulos collection—one of the most popular and reproduced of all the Chinese objects in the Museum's collection—comes from a tomb of the Han dynasty (206 B.C.–A.D. 220). By this period it was common in China for tombs to be highly decorated and for beautiful objects to be buried alongside the body, since it was thought that the burial place became the home for the immortal soul. Jade was especially important in this process, due to its supposed magical powers to preserve the dead body.

The unique nature of this head—no other animal carving in jade of its size is known—has caused uncertainty over its dating. However, recent archaeological discoveries in China, and the growing body of comparable objects in metal and ceramic, have made its assignment to the Han period more secure.

Lit. Kerr, 1991, p. 44

Craig Clunas

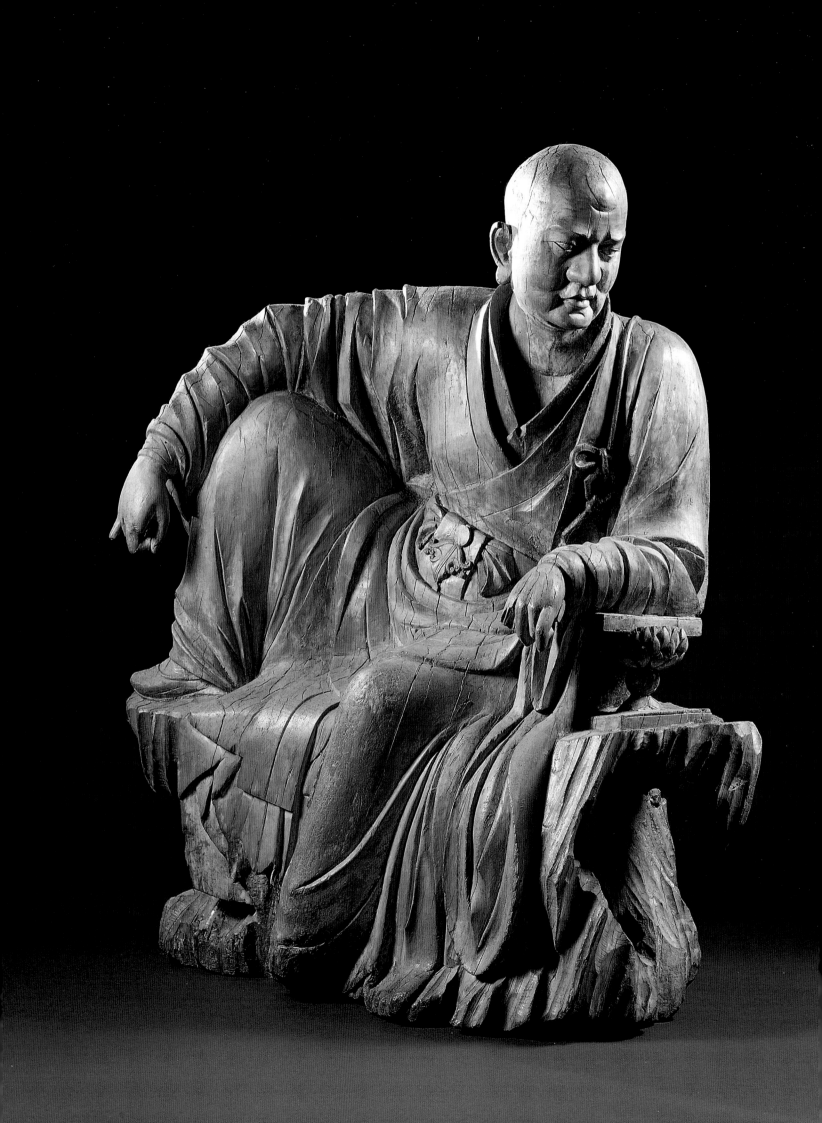

110. Chinese. *Figure of a Luohan, an Enlightened Holy Man.* Yuan dynasty (1271–1368). Wood with traces of polychromy, 38⅝ x 32¼ x 16⅞" (98 x 82 x 43 cm). V&A A.29–1931

An appreciation for Chinese sculpture developed with the enthusiasm for earlier Chinese ceramics, and during the 1920s and 1930s the Museum acquired some impressive examples, including this *luohan*. Sets of *luohan* were placed in attendance of the Buddha in temples. Their number varied, but a common set comprised eighteen figures. This type of sculpture was encouraged by Buddhist Ch'an (Zen) sects, which stressed the importance of the religious teacher and of the interaction between master and pupil. This sculpture portrays a vigorous, middle-aged Chinese monk in the act of turning to his neigh-

bor. From the style it is thought that the piece comes from one of the northern Chinese provinces that excelled in carved and painted wooden sculpture.

Lit. Nara National Museum, 1981, no. 198; Ayers, 1983, p. 24

Rose Kerr

111. Korean (Choson dynasty, 1392–1910). *Jar.* 18th century. Porcelain, with underglaze red painted decoration, 11⅜" (28.9 cm) high, 9¼" (23.5 cm) diam. V&A C.131–1913

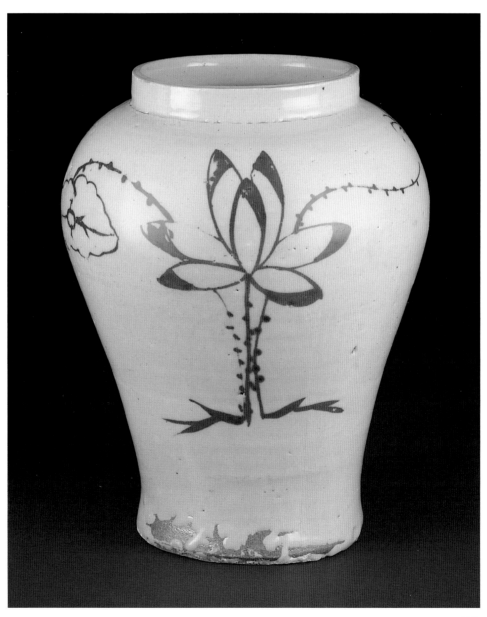

111.

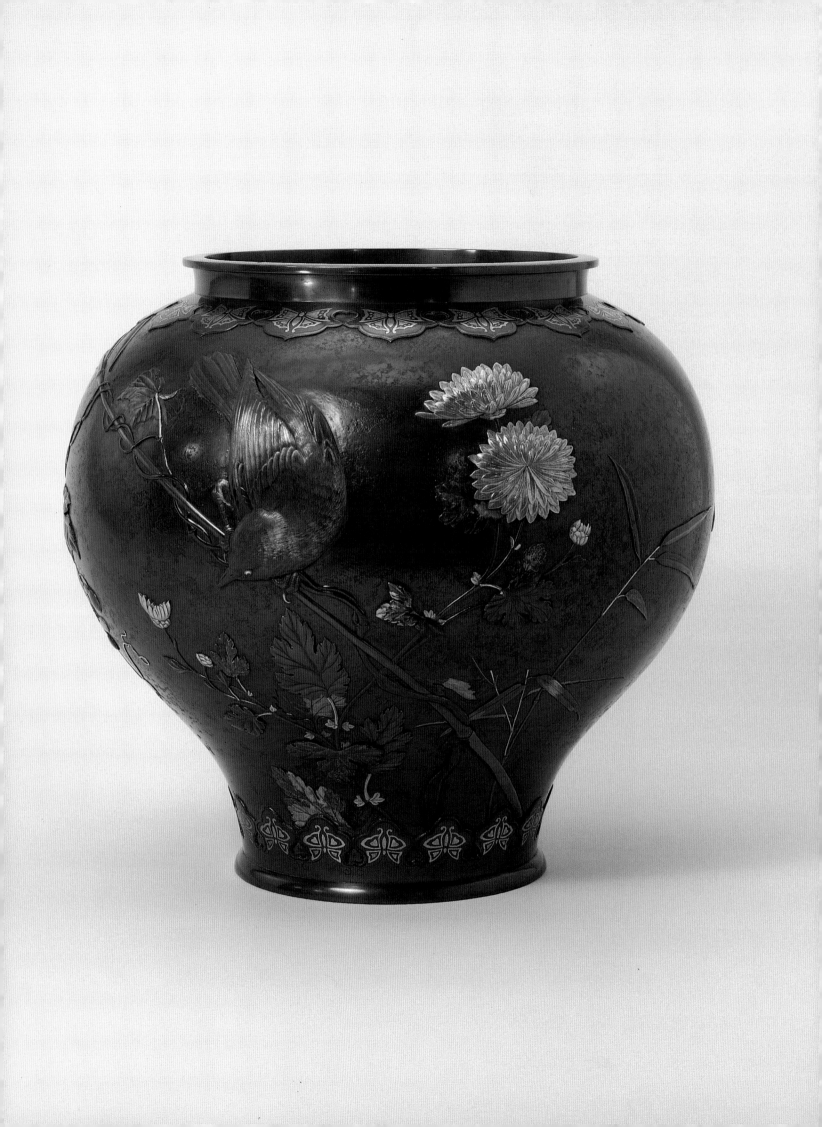

Although acquired by the Museum in 1913, this stunning jar first became the focus of attention in the 1940s, when its "rugged" qualities were seen as exemplifying the potter's art. It is one of several examples of decorated white porcelain showing a boldly painted lotus flower. Porcelain decorated solely in underglaze red was produced at small private kilns rather than at the official kiln established at Punwon after 1752. When acquired, this jar was thought to be seventeenth-century, but it has now been redated, on stylistic grounds, to the eighteenth century.

The jar was among a group of twenty-one pieces of Chinese and Korean pottery acquired in 1913 from S. M. Franck & Co., an importer of goods from the Near and Far East, a firm from which the Museum had made regular purchases since 1883. The jar cost £10 and was recommended for acquisition by ceramics curator Bernard Rackham, who described it as "a remarkable specimen." It was similarly regarded as a masterpiece by his successor, William Honey, who published extensively on Korean ceramics during the 1940s and wrote of this piece:

> There is a great jar at South Kensington, an old possession of the Museum, which was the first example to reveal to me the peculiar beauty of the Yi dynasty wares. . . . I like to regard this rugged pot as a test of ceramic education.

Lit. Honey, 1946, pp. 64–7; Honey, 1947, pp. 15–6; McKillop, 1992a, pp. 70–4

Liz Wilkinson

112.
Cast by Suzuki Chōkichi (Japanese, 1848–1919), designed by Kasson. *Vase.* c. 1880. Cast and patinated bronze with gold, *shakudo*, *shibuichi*, and copper inlay, 11" (28 cm) high, 13" (33 cm) diam. V&A 30–1886

Although acquisitions of Chinese material in the nineteenth century consisted predominantly of imperial objects from the seventeenth and eighteenth centuries, purchases of Japanese material during the same period centered on contemporary manufactures, often from international exhibitions (cats. 10–11). This extraordinary vase displays the virtuoso craftsmanship that the Museum sought to represent in its collections at that time, and, indeed, it was purchased at the Universal Exhibition in Amsterdam in 1883, directly from the Kiritsu Kosho Kaisha of Tokyo, a company set up to promote traditional Japanese craft industries.

Following the downfall of the ruling military government of Japan in 1868, and the eventual banning in 1876 of the wearing of swords in public, the market for decorative metalwork on weapons and armor effectively disappeared. Consequently, craftsmen had to find new outlets for their talents. This superbly executed bronze vase, produced by the notable bronze-caster Suzuki Chōkichi, is one such example. It combines the decorative inlay techniques derived from the manufacture of sword fittings, the naturalistic depiction of nature from the Shijō school of painting, and the overall composition of the *rimpa* (Sotatsu-Korin) school.

Lit. Earle, 1986a, pp. 200–1; Harris, 1994, pp. 23–4

Greg Irvine

113.
Attributed to Myōchin Muneharu (Japanese, late Edo period, 1615–1868). *Incense Burner in the Form of an Eagle.* c. 1860. Hammered iron, 28¾" (73 cm) high, 40¾" (103.5 cm) wide [wingspan], 22⅝" (57.5 cm) deep. V&A 603–1875

This unusually dramatic piece of relatively modern manufacture was admired for its virtuoso craftsmanship, characteristic of the very best of nineteenth-century Japanese metalwork, at the same time that it was invested with historical associations that provided a spurious link with earlier traditions. Described on its acquisition as a "model of a Sea-eagle, or osprey," it was originally made as an incense burner. A container for the incense is set in the eagle's back, covered by a pierced plate, continuing the design of feathers, which would have allowed the smoke to escape. As a decorative yet functional object, it shows the changing application of metalwork skills in nineteenth-century Japan as the power of the ruling military class declined and traditional arms and armor were less in demand.

The eagle was purchased from A. B. Mitford, secretary of the British legation in Japan from 1866 to 1870; it is likely that Mitford acquired the eagle there during this period. When bought by the Museum, the eagle was not seen as modern but was believed to be "the work of Myōchin Muneharu, a celebrated native worker in metal, Japanese, sixteenth century." In fact, the first name referred to the Myōchin family of armor manufacturers (who had a long if somewhat questionable genealogy), and the second name to one of five makers using this name in the latter part of the Edo period (1615–1868). The high price of £1,000—a sum equivalent to thirteen percent of the total cost of all the Museum's purchases in 1875—reflected the high values commanded by nineteenth-century Japanese works at that time, in contrast to the cheaper prices then being paid for earlier works.

At the time of acquisition, the Western mania for Japan was at its height, and this eye-catching eagle became a centerpiece of

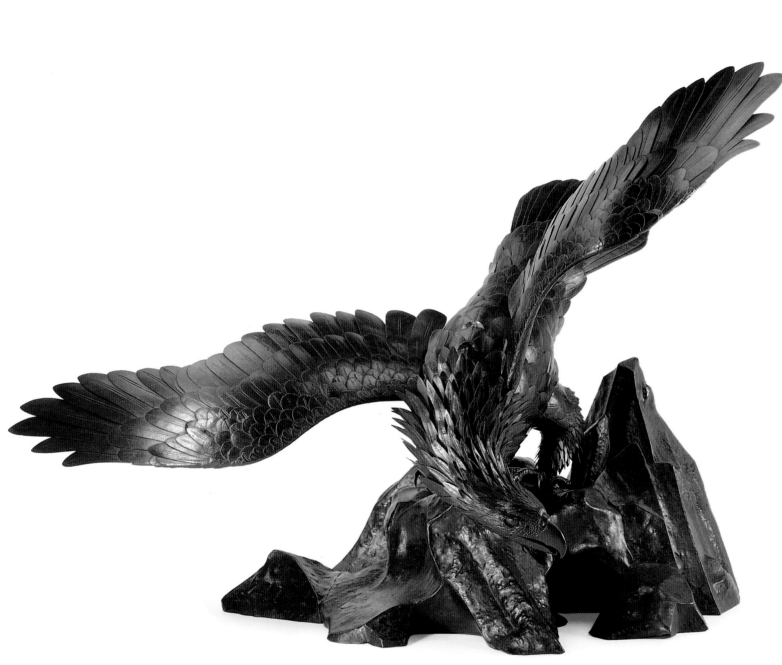

113.

the Museum's display of Japanese art. Only a week after the Museum acquired it, *The Building News and Architectural Review* of 21 May 1875 described the eagle in glowing terms that perpetuated the myth of the sixteenth-century maker: "a Japanese artist . . . whose name is so revered by his countrymen that, in a native biographical dictionary, he is mentioned in the following terms: —Under Heaven there never was a smith the equal of Myōchin Muneharu." This is seemingly a reference to the Japanese title of *Tenka Ichi* (First under Heaven) given to outstanding craftsmen. The importance attached to the piece is indicated by its appearance in the center of a display scheme intended for the newly erected South Court (see fig. 103).

In 1881 Professor J. J. Rein of the University of Bonn visited the Museum

> with a learned Japanese . . . and with the permission of the directors undertook an examination of the origin and age of the Japanese metal articles. . . . [W]e found no inscription, name or sign which would indicate its [the eagle's] origin. We have also not been able to trace the history of this remarkable piece of art-industry.

Despite these doubts, successive descriptions of the Museum in London guidebooks continued to mention the eagle until about 1910. After that date, when interest in the Japanese collections focused increasingly on earlier artifacts, the eagle was placed in storage. Its history and significance have been reappraised only recently as attention has been given to the history of Western perceptions of Japan and its culture.

Lit. Gonse, 1886, pp. 200–2; Rein, 1889, pp. 433–4

GREG IRVINE

114.   Japanese. *Fresh-Water Jar with Lug Handles.* Late 16th–early 17th century. Stoneware with natural ash glaze, 8 x 10¼ x 8" (20.3 x 26 x 20.3 cm). V&A 191–1877

During the 1870s the Museum expanded its holdings of Japanese ceramics, both historical and contemporary. While this acquisition policy reflected contemporary consumer demand for Japanese objects, it was also an attempt to establish a complete taxonomy and thus understanding of Japanese arts.

This heavily sculpted jar, along with a teabowl and incense burner (cats. 115–116), were displayed with a large group of Japanese ceramics at the Philadelphia Centennial Exposition of 1876. The jar was made at Bizen, one of the first Japanese kiln

groups to produce purpose-made tea ceramics during the late sixteenth century. The deposits of melted ash that enhance the powerfully organic form result from firing in a wood-fired kiln. The jar was used as a container from which cold water was ladled into a cast-iron kettle.

The Philadelphia Centennial Exposition was the first major exhibition of its kind to be mounted in America. Japan was the largest overseas contributor after Britain. Even before the exhibition opened, however, the Museum had already purchased one section of the display of Japanese ceramics. In 1875—in anticipation of the Philadelphia show—Philip Cunliffe Owen paid £1,000 to the Exposition's Japanese commissioners to "make an historical collection of porcelain and pottery from the earliest period until the present time, to be formed in such a way as to give fully the history of the art." At Philadelphia this group was labeled "The Property of the South Kensington Museum." This acquisition strategy enabled Britain to assert cultural hegemony over Japan, ahead of America, its rival for power in the East.

Despite Cunliffe Owen's intention, the collection was uneven in its coverage. Many objects, including the most costly, were contemporary products of the type that the Japanese were promoting for export to the West. The collection did, however, include some important sixteenth- and seventeenth-century tea ceramics.

The Philadelphia group was in London by the following year, where it was displayed prominently in the Museum's South Court and was featured in subsequent Museum guides, although the tea ceremony ceramics were not specifically singled out. It was not until after World War II that the Museum realized that, for the mere nine shillings paid for this fresh-water jar, it had acquired what is now considered one of the most important objects in the Japanese collection.

Lit. Cunliffe Owen, 1875; Varley and Isao, 1989; Wilson, 1991; Jackson, 1992

ANNA JACKSON/RUPERT FAULKNER

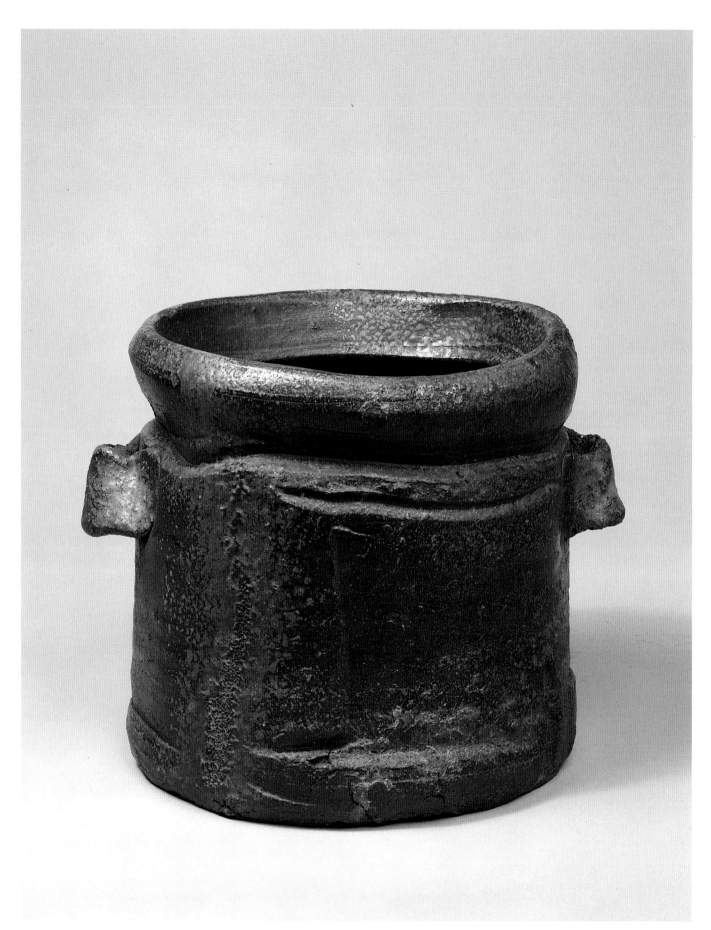

114.

115. Attributed to HON'AMI KÔETSU (Japanese, 1558–1637). *Teabowl.* Early 17th century. Black Raku ware, 3⅜ x 5 x 4½" (8.5 x 12.7 x 11.5 cm). V&A 247–1877

This bowl is one of a small number of surviving ceramics by Hon'ami Kôetsu, a noted designer-connoisseur who played a prominent role in Kyoto artistic circles during the late six-

teenth and early seventeenth centuries. He used techniques pioneered in Kyoto by the Raku family during the 1580s. The process of making black Raku ware involves pinch-formed shapes and the removal of the ware from the kiln at peak temperature. This rare piece was among the Japanese ceramics shown at the Philadelphia Centennial Exposition of 1876 (see cat. 114).

ANNA JACKSON/RUPERT FAULKNER

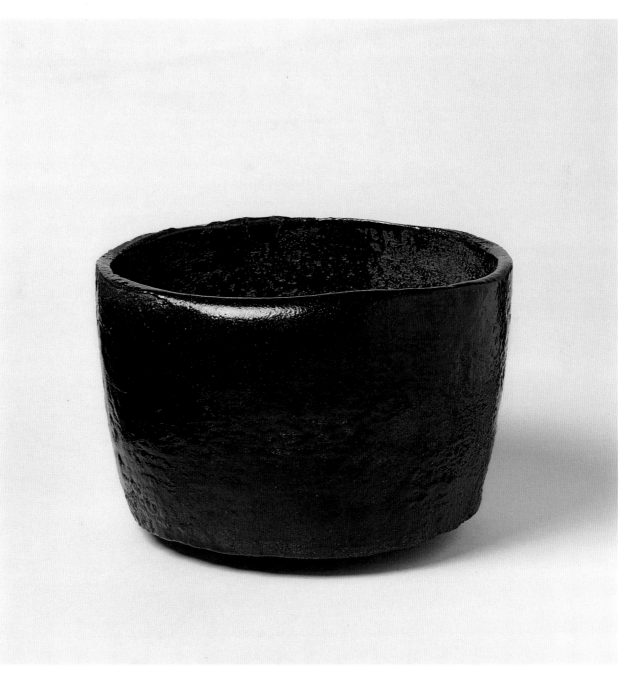

115.

116. NONOMURA NINSEI (Japanese, active 1645–75). *Incense Burner in the Form of a Conch Shell.* Mid-17th century. Stoneware with clear glaze and stippled underglaze iron decoration, 4⅝ x 10¾ x 6⅛" (11.6 x 27.3 x 15.5 cm). V&A 260–1877

Nonomura Ninsei was a prominent figure in Kyoto's rise as a major ceramic-producing center during the seventeenth century. He is renowned for his use of overglaze enamels in the production of elegantly decorated stonewares. This trompe l'oeil work in the form of a seashell, with its underglaze iron oxide painting, is subdued and naturalistic. Adoption of an underwater mollusk as a container to burn incense associates it with the use of conch shells by both the military and itinerant priests in Japan. This piece too was among the Japanese ceramics proudly presented by the South Kensington Museum as its property at the Philadelphia Centennial Exposition in 1876 (see cat. 114).

ANNA JACKSON/RUPERT FAULKNER

117. Japanese. *Writing Table.* c. 1620. Wood, covered with gold and silver *takamaki-e* and *nashiji* lacquer with gold and silver details; silvered metal fittings, 3½ x 23½ x 13¾" (9 x 59.7 x 35 cm). Given by the Misses Alexander. V&A W.339–1916

This writing table is a fine example of the extensive and varied collection of Japanese art formed by William Cleverly Alexander, an English collector active in the 1850s, after Japan was opened up to the West. Gifts and bequests from collectors like Alexander helped form the basis of the V&A's Japanese holdings.

The table's lacquer decoration illustrates themes from classical Japanese literature, especially poetry. The building on the island has been identified as the Sumiyoshi Shrine near Suma, a place famous for salt making. Other motifs, such as the Nagara Bridge with broken planks, an island topped by a pine tree, a dilapidated palace, and chrysanthemums by a fence are all subjects found in poetry, frequently alluding to loneliness and separation.

Lit. Earle, 1984; Earle, 1986a, p. 57

JULIA HUTT

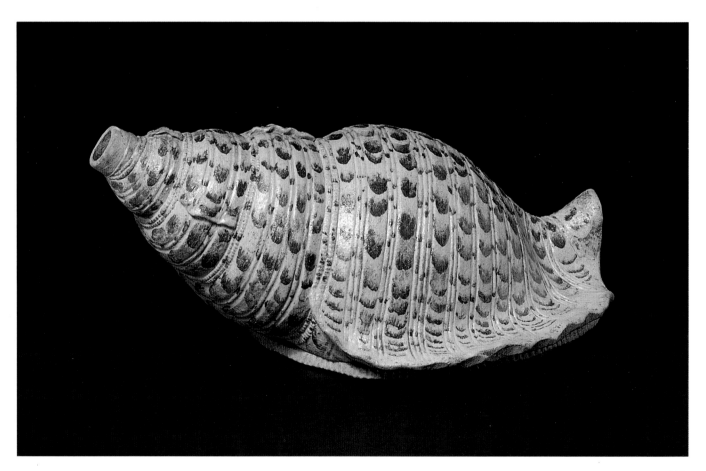

116.

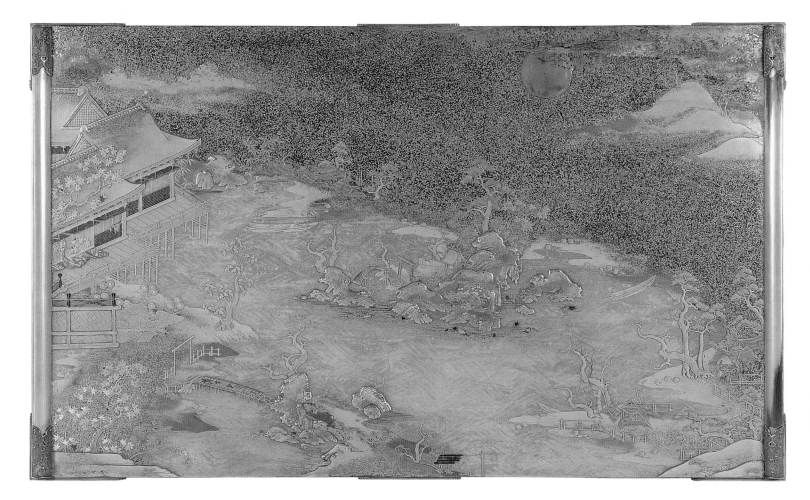

117.

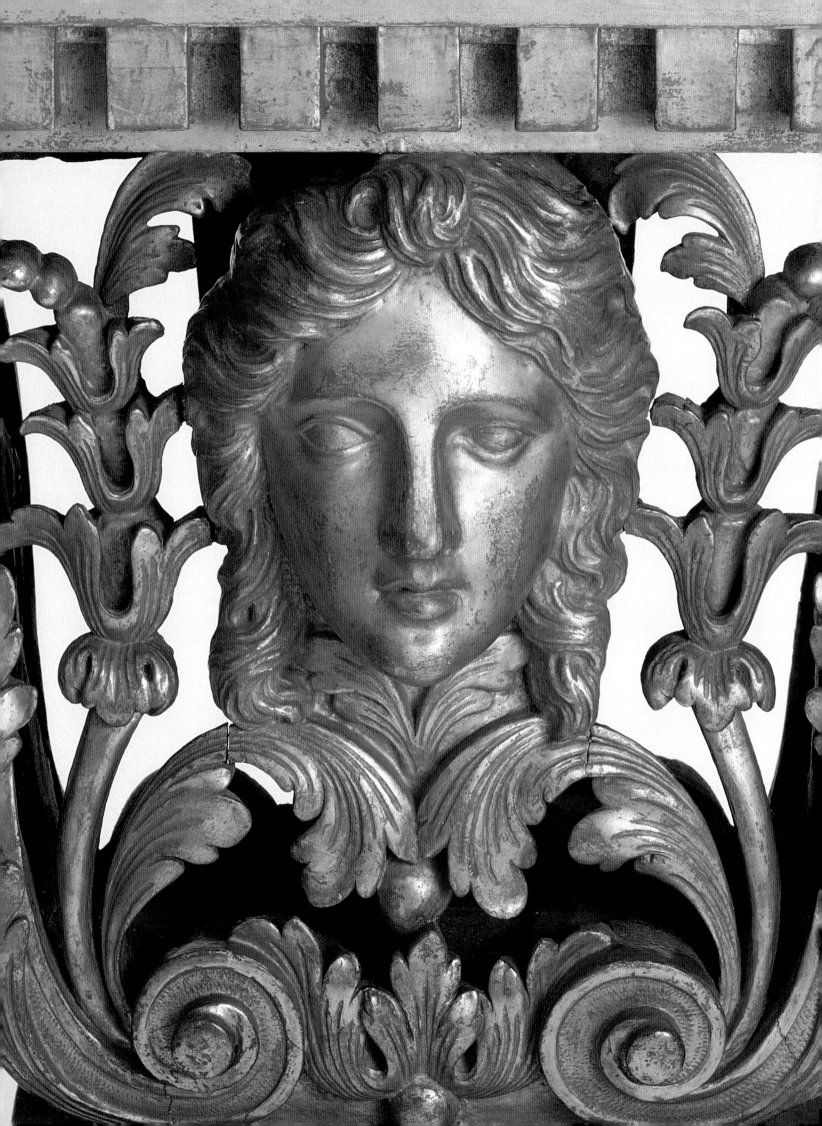

National Consciousness, National Heritage, and the Idea of "Englishness"

Charles Saumarez Smith

THE ORIGINAL IMPULSE BEHIND THE ESTABLISHMENT of the South Kensington collections was essentially imperial. Nationally, economically, and industrially self-confident, Britain fervently desired to encompass within its reach the full spectrum of world cultures. In the spirit of the Great Exhibition, British manufactures were intended to form only one, relatively small, part of collections that would encompass the whole of what were regarded as the significant cultures of the world. The pattern of early collecting thus demonstrates a willingness to go on predatory expeditions, buying up medieval and Renaissance works of art in Italy, France, and especially Spain, while ignoring equivalent British ecclesiastical treasures in the churches of Herefordshire and East Anglia.

On the other hand, from the start, there was also a countervailing tendency—a wish to document and describe the specific characteristics of the British contribution to the cultures of the world and a desire to establish the legitimacy of British art and design, alongside British preeminence in industry and imperial conquest. Part of the spirit of South Kensington lay in an oppositional view of what are normally regarded as the constituent elements of mid-Victorian culture. The Museum was intended to be not academic, but popular; it was not dominated by the scholarly ideals of Oxford and Cambridge, but by a belief that the state should be actively engaged in public education. Its staff were civil servants, many of them linked by professional friendships and residence in Kensington. They wanted to foster interest, not in classical antiquity as represented by the British Museum, nor in masterpieces of Western European art as at the National Gallery, but in the products of contemporary British industry, in genre painting, and in new technologies, such as photography. They came from a milieu which regarded the past with the utilitarian view that the South Kensington Museum needed to contribute to an improvement in ornamental art and industrial production.

The principal figure behind the view that the South Kensington Museum should have a role in the interpretation of British culture was Richard Redgrave, a narrative painter and the least well known of the triumvirate of Henry Cole, Redgrave, and John Charles Robinson that was responsible for the early development of the Museum and its collections.[1] Redgrave believed that the South Kensington Museum should encompass a National Gallery of British Art, and he

Fig. 109. Detail of cat. 152, William Kent's Console Table, c. 1730, for Chiswick House

persuaded John Sheepshanks, who had inherited a fortune from his father's textile mills, to bequeath his collection of British paintings, drawings, and watercolors (cats. 118–119) to South Kensington rather than keeping them in situ in his private house in Rutland Gate.[2] It was Redgrave, too, who was responsible for a number of initiatives during the 1860s to document aspects of British painting, including the Ellison gift of watercolors in 1861, a loan exhibition of portrait miniatures in 1865, and a series of exhibitions on British portraits.

If the collection of paintings during the 1860s suggests a purposeful view of establishing a National Gallery of British Art, the collection of British objects was more haphazard and consisted generally of works that exhibited a high degree of surface ornament. They included, for example, representative examples of sixteenth- and seventeenth-century metalwork such as the Torre Abbey Jewel (cat. 124), key examples of *opus anglicanum* (English work), including the Syon Cope and the Clare Chasuble, and even works of vernacular pottery by Thomas Toft (cat. 128), presumably bought as interesting examples of workmanship. During the Museum's early pioneer days, however, British objects did not live up to the high Victorian appetite for rich surface imagery, so that when, in 1865, the Museum was offered a silver cup presented by Charles II to the Lord Almoner, Archbishop Sterne, it was turned down by Robinson on the grounds that "from its boldness of style and paucity of ornamentation, I do not think that it can be considered as coming within the category of works of art."[3]

A change of attitude came about under the influence of the Arts and Crafts movement. During the 1880s and 1890s, there was a shift in interest on the part of scholars and antiquarians toward an appreciation of English domestic architecture of the sixteenth and seventeenth centuries and of the artifacts produced between the age of Queen Elizabeth and the age of Queen Anne.[4] This was motivated by a sentimental appreciation of the relics of old English life, which were being swept away by urbanization. It was the period of the establishment of many of the public and private institutions which have ever since been responsible for the preservation of English cultural life, including the founding of the National Trust in 1895; the opening of a proper building for the National Portrait Gallery in 1896; the opening of the Tate Gallery on Millbank in 1897; and the publication of *Country Life*, which, more than other institutions of this period, promoted nostalgia for a preindustrial past (see cat. 128). It was also the period in which the idea of England as an entity, with distinctive characteristics of language, landscape, and tradition, was more sharply differentiated from a broader belief in the imperial destiny of Great Britain.[5]

As a result of this nostalgia for English folk life, there was increasing public interest in old English crafts, including pewter, ironwork, and oak furniture. For example, Lady Dorothy Nevill presented a collection of Sussex ironwork to the Museum, with a telling description:

> It was owing to Sir Purdon Clarke that I placed my collection of Sussex iron-work at the Victoria and Albert Museum, where it still remains. I formed this collection years ago when I used to live in Sussex, purchasing the different pieces for the most part in old cottages and farmhouses. Some

of the old firebacks were extremely ornamental, but the fire-dogs, of which I collected a great number, were my especial favourites. . . . Most of the iron-work in my collection, such as rush-holders, fire-tongs, and the like neces-sities of old-world cottage life, has now become completely obsolete in the farmhouses and cottages, to which they formed a useful and artistic adorn-ment. At the time I was collecting, many people did not fail to express their scepticism as to the value of all "the old rubbish", as they called it, which I was getting together; but I am glad to say that my judgement has been com-pletely vindicated, and today, instead of "old rubbish", I am told it is a "valu-able collection".[6]

This passage suggests the attitudes current at the end of the nineteenth century that prompted an idealization of the products of rural industry. Such attitudes inevitably influenced the Museum and its collecting—Queen Elizabeth's Virginal in 1887 (cat. 123), the Sizergh Castle Room in 1891, an early-seventeenth-century room from Bromley-by-Bow in 1894, the Waltham Abbey Room in 1899, and the Clifford's Inn Room in 1903. Their acquisition, which was associated with the establishment of the *Survey of London*—and in the case of the Bromley-by-Bow Room directly inspired by English Arts and Crafts architect and designer C. R. Ashbee (influential founder in 1888 of the Guild of Handicraft)—suggests the extent to which the Museum was prepared to consider a role in what would now in England be called "rescue archae-ology" (one aspect of historic preservation).

During the 1890s there was also an increasing interest in producing a more accurate and scholarly history of English furniture and the decorative arts, a prod-uct of growing professionalism in the writing and documentation of all aspects of English history.[7] Following Caspar Purdon Clarke's establishment of specialist departments at the Museum in 1896, a number of young scholars were appointed who were subsequently to revolutionize their fields in the decorative arts. Among these pivotal figures were A. F. Kendrick, who was appointed curator-in-charge of textiles in 1898 and was to transform the academic study of English tapestries, car-pets, and embroidery; Bernard Rackham, who was appointed a Museum assistant in 1898 and retired in 1938, having made immense contributions to the study of English ceramics; Martin Hardie, who was likewise appointed an assistant in 1898, and who became the leading scholar of English watercolors; and H. Clifford Smith, who became curator of furniture in the 1920s. These Young Turks of the late 1890s were inspired not so much by a sentimental attachment to relics of English life as by a bureaucratic zeal to classify the full range of artifacts in the Museum's collections and to do so with properly scholarly apparatus.

By 1909, when the new building opened, the Victoria and Albert Museum had been transformed from an eclectic institution that collected a range of products of human industry from all corners of the world into an institution that was able to project a much more uniform image of itself. On the Cromwell Road facade were statues of famous and less famous British artists, including six sculptors, ten painters, and six architects (fig. 110), and on the Exhibition Road facade were stat-ues of ten craftsmen. An official document of 1911 specified the Museum's responsi-bilities toward the acquisition and display of specifically English works of art:

The Victoria and Albert Museum, so far from being intended as a collection illustrating the decorative arts of England, may be said in fact to have originated with the desire of bringing from abroad such models and examples as might influence and improve English design and workmanship. Nevertheless, not only does the increased interest in English art make it incumbent to show prominently on English soil a representative and full illustration of the best work of English craft for the instruction of Colonial students and of the large number of foreigners who come to London for the purpose, but also on purely aesthetic grounds it may be held that the national element in the collections must be fully recognised as of great importance.[8]

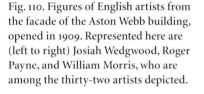

Fig. 110. Figures of English artists from the facade of the Aston Webb building, opened in 1909. Represented here are (left to right) Josiah Wedgwood, Roger Payne, and William Morris, who are among the thirty-two artists depicted.

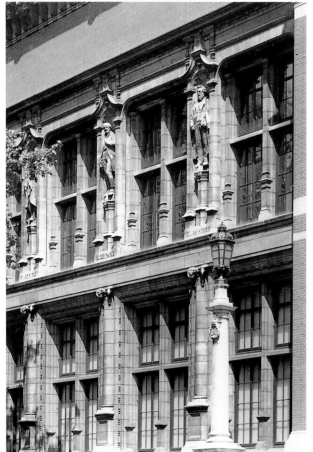

Within the galleries of the new Aston Webb building, an increasing amount of space was given over to displays of English objects (fig. 111). V&A ceramics curator Oliver Watson's study of the English glass collection demonstrates that it was during this period that interest switched from European, especially Venetian, glass to English. In 1903 Charles Wylde described how "the Museum Collection of English glass is very poor and quite unworthy of a National Museum of Industrial Art." Between 1900 and 1909, the Museum acquired 157 pieces of English glass; between 1909 and 1919, it acquired 371; in the 1920s it acquired 685.[9] English glass thus moved from being marginal to the V&A's glass collection to being its most important part. Similarly, guidebooks to the Museum demonstrate that when the Aston Webb building first opened, English sculpture was displayed alongside Spanish sculpture in Room 9; yet, by 1933, part of Room 9 and the whole of Room 10 were devoted exclusively to English sculpture, including alabaster carvings, busts by eighteenth-century artists Thomas Banks, John Bacon, and Michael Rysbrack, and even "modern alphabets and works on loan by Eric Gill."[10]

Changes in the patterns of acquisition and display reflected the changing interests of the curatorial staff. By the 1920s, the system of organization adopted by the Museum had resulted in a series of discrete departments, each with its own ethos, but each promoting scholarship in English decorative arts. In the Department of Architecture and Sculpture, Margaret Longhurst worked on medieval English ivories. In the Department of Ceramics, Bernard Rackham worked on the classification of English porcelain. In 1922 Rackham was joined by Herbert Read, who applied for a transfer from the Treasury on the grounds that, although less well paid, the Museum position offered him more freedom to write. As Richard Aldington wrote to him, "The South Kensington . . . is a better job than bum-sucking a duke."[11] Together Rackham and Read wrote a pioneering book, *English Pottery,* and Read also wrote the important books *English Stained Glass* (1926) and *Staffordshire Pottery Figures* (1929). In 1926, William Thorpe moved from the Library to the Department of Ceramics, bringing a formidable knowledge of antiquarian source material that was evident in his definitive two-volume study, *English Glass* (1929). In the Department of Engraving, Illustration and Design, Basil Long undertook original research on English miniatures, and James Laver embarked on his studies of English fashion and theater.

Because of the fragmentation of scholarship into different subjects according to material, each department cultivated its own view of the British past. The Department of Furniture had close contacts with landowners and viewed the country house as the cradle of fine design; the Department of Ceramics was interested in the more popular aspects of pottery figures; the Department of Textiles—because of the necessity of storing, classifying, and looking after different types of fabric and costume—had a strong interest in techniques of production. While there were connections across the Museum, members of the staff frequently worked in isolation from one another, not sharing approaches to their subjects, and were inclined toward historical research that was documentary and taxonomic. It is hard to detect a nostalgic approach to England and its past in the Museum's publications, which were frequently dry-as-dust lists of the collections. Indeed, the life of the

Fig. 111. A display of English decorative art, arranged by period, in the Central Court of the Aston Webb building, c. 1910

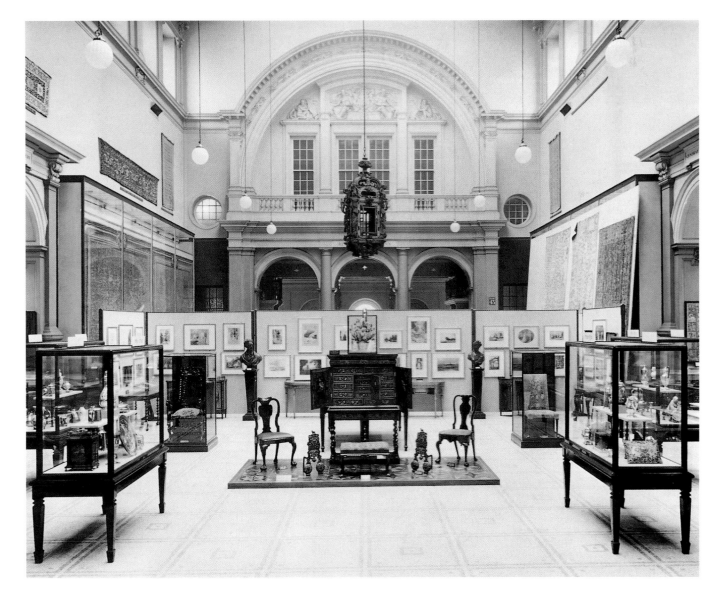

assistant keeper owed as much to the traditions of the British civil service—diligent and narrow-minded—as to the broader currents of Oxbridge and the academy.[12]

Throughout the 1920s the majority of departments, following the intellectual interests of the staff, concentrated on acquisitions of English objects. Many of these have now lost their original interest, since they were bought on the basis of their visual quality without regard for proper documentation. At the same time, these acquisitions included key works, such as the Chinese Bed from Badminton House, bought in 1921; the cabinet designed by Horace Walpole to house his miniatures and enamels at Strawberry Hill, bought in 1925 (cat. 134); and the virtuoso limewood cravat carved by Grinling Gibbons (cat. 135).

The only point at which the Museum may have had an intellectually coherent approach to the English past was in the establishment of the so-called English Primary Galleries after World War II. Since the reorganization of the Museum in 1909, there had been pressure to display objects chronologically and stylistically rather than by material. As the Royal Commission on National Museums and Galleries stated in its final report in January 1930:

> Nowhere in London is it at present possible to see any ordered sequence or illustration of the English arts and crafts. In accordance with the "classification by material" arrangement of the Victoria and Albert Museum, English work will be found scattered among a large number of different departments. If there were also an English Museum, this would be a matter of little moment. But until it is possible to develop a separate Museum illustrating the artistic civilization of this country, we think that the nucleus of an English collection might be developed within the Victoria and Albert Museum.[13]

In 1936 the first steps toward an integrated display of English objects were taken in the Octagon Court (see fig. 39). Then, after World War II, Leigh Ashton, who succeeded Eric Maclagan as director in 1945, seized the opportunity, provided by the fact that the Museum's collections had been stored in a Welsh slate quarry during the war, to reinstall the finest examples of English decorative arts together in a long sequence of galleries on two floors on the west side of the Aston Webb building. Preparation of these galleries coincided with the 1946 "Britain Can Make It" exhibition (fig. 112). The desire to display the greatest works of English decorative art to impress schoolchildren and tourists no doubt reflected a similar patriotic urge. But accounts of the English Primary Galleries at the time that they opened suggest that their atmosphere was not so much chauvinist as aesthetic, consisting of what were regarded as the best objects in the collections, spaced tastefully far apart from one another in a

Fig. 112. The V&A's 1946 exhibition "Britain Can Make It" was presented as an impetus to "buy British" and thus support postwar economic recovery.

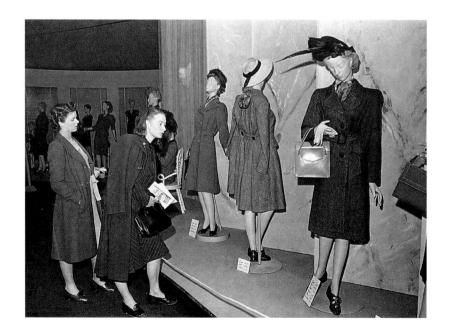

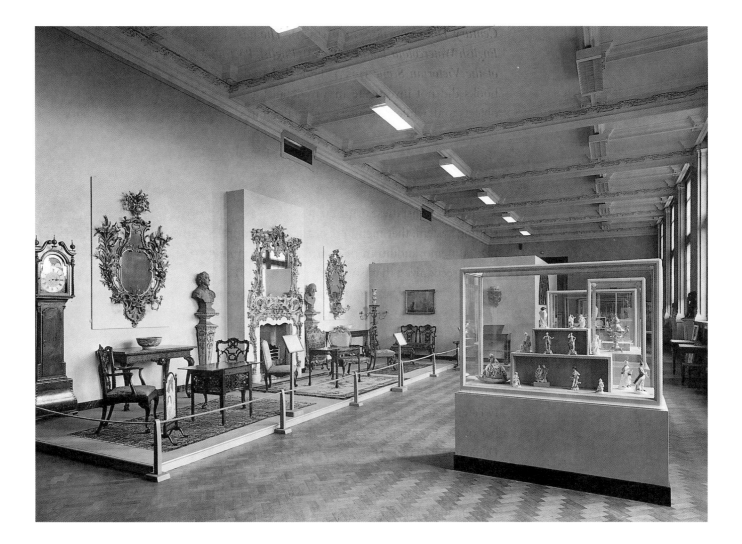

three-dimensional equivalent to the *Connoisseur Period Guides,* which concentrated on style in line with what was then art-historical orthodoxy (fig. 113). In these galleries—more than at any other time in the history of the Museum—there was a demonstration of the belief that English art, particularly the art of the eighteenth century, could and should stand comparison with Italian art, and that it was a legitimate part of a national cultural history. Objects from Scotland, Wales, and northern Ireland were not included unless they had been designed by Robert Adam.

During the 1950s, the characteristics of scholarly research and publication continued more or less as before the war. This was the most prolific period in the Museum's history for independent publications by the Museum staff, which helped to establish the V&A's status as a research institution. Arthur Lane, a classical scholar who committed suicide in 1963, published *Style in Pottery* (1948) and *Early Porcelain Figures of the Eighteenth Century* (1961). Ralph Edwards, a Welshman who was keeper of furniture from 1937 to 1954, published *Early Conversation Pictures from the Middle Ages to about 1730* and the revised edition of his magisterial *Dictionary of English Furniture* in 1954. John Hayward published *English Cutlery* (1956), *English Watches* (1956), and *Huguenot Silver in England 1688–1727* (1959). Graham Reynolds, a great authority on the art of Constable, wrote *Nineteenth-*

Fig. 113. The V&A's Gallery of English Decorative Art, 1750–1820, in 1951. This was one of the new period displays created after World War II. The case on the right contains the Chelsea porcelain tureen and cover in the form of a chicken (cat. 145).

Century Drawings, 1850–1900 (1949), *Thomas Bewick* (1949), *An Introduction to English Watercolour Painting* (1950), *English Portrait Miniatures* (1952), and *Painters of the Victorian Scene* (1953). Though based on the Museum's collections, these books did not investigate in any detail the visual or aesthetic characteristics of objects and, while incorporating meticulous documentary research, they showed no interest in methodology. They also tended to assume a common belief that the eighteenth century was the high point of English design, that Tudor objects were interesting in an antiquarian but not necessarily an aesthetic way, and that the taste of the nineteenth century was mostly execrable.

It was against these orthodoxies, established by the high priests of the Museum's staffing system, that members of the Circulation Department rebelled. As early as 1921, a memorandum in the Furniture Department (probably written by Clifford Smith) recognized that "sooner or later we shall be obliged (if the collection is to be historically complete) to include characteristic pieces of Victorian furniture, provided, of course, that such pieces are reasonably good models of design and craftsmanship, and if we delay too long we may find it difficult to acquire them at all." Oliver Brackett replied, "As a matter of princ[iple] I agree that we must, very cautiously, take opportunities of acquiring really good examples of Early Victorian Furniture."[14] This cautious approach to the study of Victorian design did not satisfy Peter Floud, a graduate of the London School of Economics and an active member of the Communist party in the 1930s, who became keeper of the Circulation Department in 1947. He was the leading force behind the 1952 exhibition, "Victorian and Edwardian Decorative Arts," which played an important role in the rediscovery of Victorian design, and he gathered around him a group of especially capable women, including Shirley Bury, Natalie Rothstein, and Barbara Morris, who made strenuous efforts to break the essentially male monopoly of scholarship in the Museum by studying previously unfashionable subjects, such as Victorian jewelry. They were responsible for the layout of the Victorian Primary Gallery in the early 1960s along the lines established by Nikolaus Pevsner's *Pioneers of the Modern Movement,* with the greatest amount of space given to the leading figures of the Arts and Crafts movement, especially William Morris; and they inspired the acquisition of high Victorian objects such as the Yatman Cabinet designed by William Burges (cat. 157).

In the recent history of the Museum it is more difficult, and much more invidious, to identify characteristic traits in both the ways that objects were acquired and how the Museum staff studied them. There were a number of versions of the English past in competition, if not at war, with one another. There was the romantic version of the English past promoted by Sir Roy Strong, who was fascinated by the crafts, a vigorous exponent of modern design, and, at least during the 1970s, an enthusiastic propagandist for the national heritage, as evident in exhibitions such as "The Destruction of the Country House" held at the V&A in 1974 (see fig. 50). Then there was the self-consciously grand view of England as a network of country houses, to which the Furniture Department staff would pay regular visits. This was the England of Peter Thornton's monograph, *Seventeenth-Century Interior Decoration in England, France and Holland* (1978), a monumental work of documentary scholarship concentrating on the work of foreign craftsmen in England. Then there were the Victorianophiles: Clive Wainwright, dressed in tweed and with a beard modeled on William Morris; Michael Darby, who was always said to be a great expert on beetles as well as on Owen Jones; and Stephen Calloway, a fin-de-siècle dandy. Somewhere at the top of the Henry Cole Wing was the "People's Republic of Prints and Drawings." As an institution, the V&A was a disorderly place, a model of England in decline, full of people with recondite specialist interests. It did not appeal to the reformist zeal of Mrs. Thatcher's Britain.

Nonetheless, at the Museum the question of England and what to do about it remains. In 1985, an internal report, "The V&A: Towards 2000," stated:

> The present division of the primary galleries involves . . . the separation of both England and Italy (1400–1500) from the rest of the European sequence. Despite some considerable arguments for the integration of English and continental, this division remains fundamentally sound reflecting the nature of the collections and the way in which the public use them. The collections are particularly strong in English . . . material and to integrate these into a single sequence would result in awkward imbalances of display. . . . As well as presenting a survey of the applied arts internationally, the V&A has a role as the foremost display of the English applied arts and many visitors, both British and foreign, come here for this reason.[15]

Not long after release of this document, the committee in charge of the redisplay of the twentieth-century collections decided to amalgamate the British and Continental holdings on the grounds that to display British objects on their own was a historical anachronism.

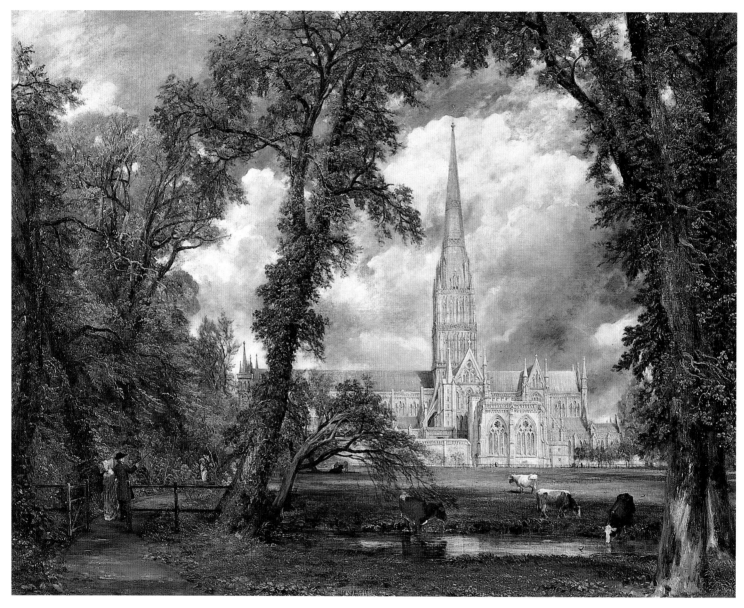

118.

118. JOHN CONSTABLE (English, 1776–1837). *Salisbury Cathedral from the Bishop's Grounds.* 1823. Oil on canvas, 34½ x 44" (87.6 x 111.8 cm). Given by John Sheepshanks, 1857. V&A FA 33

This great Constable painting was acquired by the Museum in 1857 as part of the large collection of British paintings given by John Sheepshanks, a collection displayed together for the first thirty years of the Museum's history, first as the "National Gallery of British Art" and then as the "British Fine Art Collection." Although Constable was only one artist represented in that context, his central place within the Museum's collection was reinforced in 1888 by the gift and bequest of 390 works from the painter's daughter. As the two collections were thereafter shown together, *Salisbury Cathedral* was no longer seen simply as an example of nineteenth-century British art, but as one of the most important works in a large oeuvre of a painter who had come to exemplify a notion of Englishness expressed through a view of landscape.

This painting was commissioned in 1820 by John Fisher, the bishop of Salisbury, and later purchased back from Fisher's family by the artist. The Fishers were among Constable's closest friends; the painting was begun in 1822 and finished in time for the Royal Academy's annual summer exhibition in May 1823. The bishop was dismayed by the stormy sky with dark clouds against which Constable had set the cathedral, and two further versions painted for the Fisher family (one now in the Huntington Art Collections in San Marino, California, and the other in The Frick Collection, New York) have, in the bishop's words, "a more serene sky."

Salisbury and its cathedral have a special place in the English imagination: the southern English county of Wiltshire—with historic Salisbury Plain and the ancient sites of Old Sarum and Stonehenge—is one of the most rural areas in England and among the least changed by the revolutions of industry and commerce over the past three hundred years. As a splendid example of early English architecture—and with the highest spire of all the churches in Britain—Salisbury Cathedral (1220–60), set in a gently undulating plain, dominates the landscape and has long appealed to painters.

Lit. Reynolds, 1984, vol. I, pp. 117–8, vol. II, plate 393; Parris and Fleming-Williams, 1991, pp. 258–60

RONALD PARKINSON

119. THOMAS WEBSTER (English, 1800–1886). *A Village Choir.* 1847. Oil on panel, 23¾ x 36" (60.3 x 91.4 cm). Given by John Sheepshanks, 1857. V&A FA 222

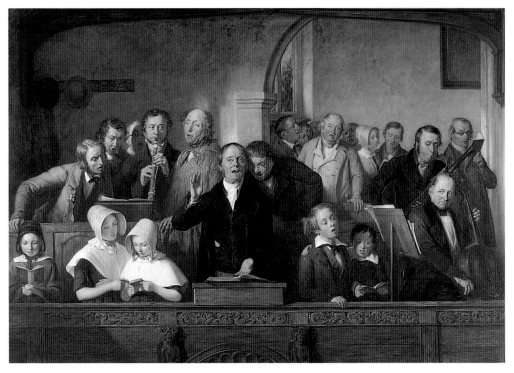

119.

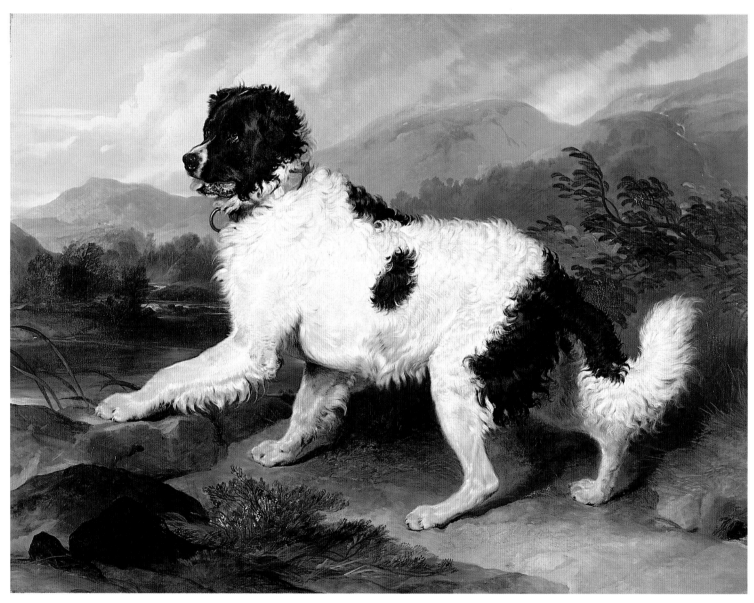

120.

A characteristic example of the type of English genre painting that John Sheepshanks collected and gave to the Museum, this nostalgic representation of a mythical English rural past has since its acquisition remained a popular work. Webster painted *A Village Choir* on commission from Sheepshanks, who already owned five works by the artist, and who exhibited it at the Royal Academy in 1847.

Sheepshanks inherited the family cloth manufacturing business, retiring in the late 1820s at the age of forty. He had already begun collecting old master prints and copies after Italian Renaissance pictures, but from about 1830 he concentrated on buying contemporary British paintings, either from the Royal Academy's summer exhibitions or direct from the artist. Sheepshanks owned a house in Rutland Gate, just around the corner from the South Kensington Museum, and a "country" home in Blackheath in South London. It seems likely that, in common with some of his contemporaries, he favored paintings of rural life for nostalgic reasons, given the increasing urbanization of London and its environs.

The subject of *A Village Choir* was inspired by Washington Irving's *The Sketch Book* of 1820, which described the various "characters" in a rural church choir and band. Perhaps the success in the later 1830s and 1840s of Dickens's earlier novels also prompted Webster to tap this similar vein of humor and sentiment. To quote two contemporary critics in 1847, the diversity of "true expression" in this painting ranges from "the region of more laughter into that of gentle character and homely English romance." It is without a doubt Webster's most famous picture and has been reproduced many times in magazines and newspapers, especially at Christmas. V&A files record the survival of the musical instruments depicted and two of the kerchiefs worn, as well as identifications of several members of the choir.

Lit. Parkinson, 1990, pp. 298–300

RONALD PARKINSON

120. SIR EDWIN HENRY LANDSEER (English, 1803–1873). *Lion: A Newfoundland Dog.* 1824. Oil on canvas, 59⅞ x 78⅛" (152 x 198.5 cm). Bequeathed by Mrs. Ann de Merle. V&A 852-1894

When this large painting was bequeathed to the South Kensington Museum in 1894, it joined nineteen other oil paintings by Landseer, including sixteen alone from the 1857 John Sheepshanks gift. But *Lion* was the most impressive acquisition, not least because of its sheer size. The painting was commissioned in 1824 by the dog's owner, W. H. de Merle, for fifty pounds. As a teenager Landseer had established himself as a precocious and prodigious talent, specializing in Scottish domestic

subjects and animals, especially dogs. This is Landseer's earliest treatment of the Newfoundland breed, famous for its lifesaving abilities; a variety of the breed was even named after the painter. Landseer is even better known through his engravings of certain others of his Newfoundland paintings, including *A Distinguished Member of the Humane Society* of 1838 and *Saved!* of 1856. The subject appealed greatly to nineteenth-century taste, with its combination of animal magnificence and canine heroism. There is a story—unsupported by evidence—that this painting was dispatched in a large case to Paris during the Revolution (either of 1830 or 1848) and narrowly escaped being used as a barricade.

Lit. Parkinson, 1990, p. 152

RONALD PARKINSON

121. ISAAC OLIVER (English, died 1617). *Pair of Miniatures.* 1590. Each, watercolor on vellum in an ivory frame, 2½" (6.4 cm) diam. Bequeathed by George Salting

121.1. *Girl Aged Four, Holding an Apple.* V&A P.145–1910

121.2. *Girl Aged Five, Holding a Carnation.* V&A P.146–1910

These two charming portraits of young sisters were among eighty miniatures acquired with the George Salting bequest in 1910. This bequest effectively established the V&A as the national collection of miniatures. At the time, however, debate in English newspapers could not identify a logical home for these important miniatures. The National Gallery received Salting's "pictures" and the British Museum his "drawings," but public opinion was divided about whether miniatures should be categorized as pictures or drawings. The V&A's own 1908 Committee on Re-arrangement argued that miniatures had "no relation to applied art" and thus no place at the V&A. (Significantly and perhaps defiantly, it was in 1908 that the V&A published the first catalogue of miniatures.)

In fact, the V&A had long played an active role in promoting the importance of miniature painting in the history of English art. An 1859 Museum catalogue devoted to "pictures" (but ironically including no miniatures) stated that "from the earliest time there was one branch of art in which English artists had a reputation even on the continent . . . [and] excelled other nations, namely miniature painting in watercolours." By the 1850s the invention of photography had all but destroyed the contemporary miniature, but the history of miniature painting began to be nostalgically reappraised, led by the V&A. Without precedent, "antiquarian" miniatures figured prominently in a

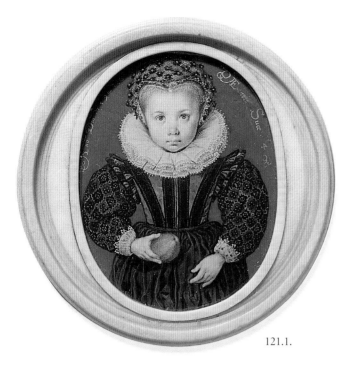

121.1.

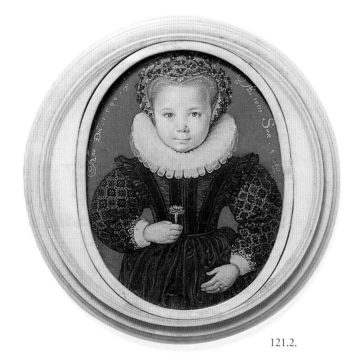

121.2.

huge 1862 loan exhibition at the Museum. Their popularity led in 1865 to an extraordinary loan exhibition of nearly four thousand miniatures (including *Queen Elizabeth I,* cat. 122).

The acquisition of the Salting bequest was seen as the moment to settle Museum policy regarding miniatures. Salting's collection unofficially established the V&A as the primary institution for the collecting of miniatures and for research on this subject. The Museum also houses the National Collection of Watercolours, which has subtly influenced the collecting and interpretation of miniatures. Within the V&A miniatures took their place as early forms of watercolor painting, as an integral part of what was seen as an essentially English tradition.

A specific outcome of this research was the rejection of the earlier attribution of this pair of miniatures to Levina Teerlinc, and the pair's acceptance as two of the earliest surviving works of Isaac Oliver, one of the foremost English miniature painters. Later discussion has drawn attention to the symbolic, if enigmatic, significance of the apple and carnation, the figures' frowning and smiling expressions, and the possible dynastic meanings of these portraits of children, so rare before the eighteenth century.

Lit. Williamson, 1904, addendum, p. xx; V&A, 1926, p. 46; Strong, 1983, p. 102; V&A, 1985a, pp. 44–5

KATHERINE COOMBS

122. NICHOLAS HILLIARD (English, 1547–1619). *Queen Elizabeth I.* c. 1595–1600. Watercolor on vellum, 3⅜ x 2½" (8.5 x 6.5 cm). Bequeathed by John Jones. V&A 622–1882

Painted when Elizabeth I was sixty, this portrait by Nicholas Hilliard, the best known of English miniature painters, conferred on the queen a "mask of youth," reducing her features to a few schematic lines and concentrating on her magnificent dress. This is not the portrait of an individual but an icon for a nation apprehensive about an aging, childless queen, a symbol of power not withered by time.

Although miniatures now have a place in national culture, Horace Walpole, an eighteenth-century owner of this miniature, set such early works against Continental standards and found them more alien than English. He wrote that painting Elizabeth I was as limiting to "genius" as painting an "Indian Idol." The first miniature purchased by the Museum, in 1857, also of Elizabeth I by Hilliard, was in fact catalogued and displayed for its decorative case. At that time no English national museum had a brief to collect miniatures.

This Hilliard miniature was included in the Museum's groundbreaking 1865 exhibition of miniatures and entered the V&A permanently in 1882. It was acquired as part of the John

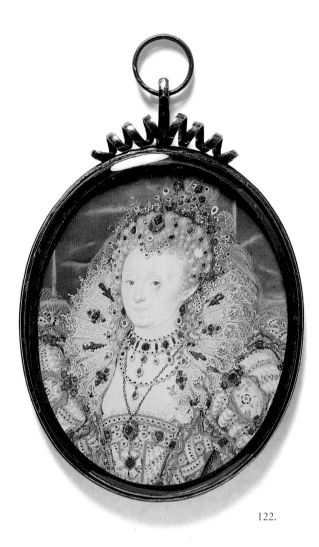

122.

Jones bequest, primarily devoted to French decorative art (cats. 84–86). Although Jones's numerous examples of foreign miniatures painted in enamels could be accommodated in the Museum's already substantial collection of enamels, the few English watercolor miniatures as yet had a less certain role.

Lit. Long, 1923, part III, pp. 80–1; Winter, 1943, plate VI(a); Strong, 1987, p. 146

KATHERINE COOMBS

123. Italian (Venice). *The Queen Elizabeth Virginal.* c. 1570. Painted cypress wood case and soundboard, parchment rosette, ebony and bone *certosina* keys, 63" (160 cm) long, 15⅞" (40.4 cm) wide, 7½" (19 cm) deep. V&A 19–1887

The connection of objects to historical figures has often been based purely on legend and wishful thinking, but the Queen Elizabeth Virginal is an exception. Very similar to a Venetian example of 1571, it is decorated with both the royal coat of arms of the Tudors and the raven with the scepter, the personal emblem of Queen Anne Boleyn, the mother of Queen Elizabeth I (reigned 1558–1603). Since Elizabeth was noted for her ability to play keyboard instruments "excellently well," it is quite possible that she used this very instrument. It was acquired in 1887 partly on account of these associations but

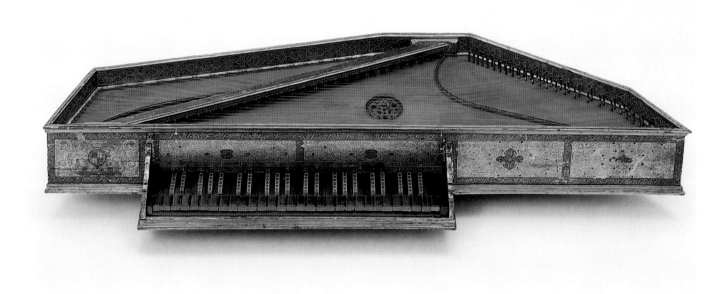

123.

also because of its musicological interest. Its similarity to Italian spinets had been noted some thirteen years earlier by Carl Engel, the Museum's consultant musical specialist, in a period when musical instruments were acquired in their own right. The 1960s ushered in a revival of early music and with it an interest in early instruments; during this period, the V&A catalogued its musical collections and put them on display. Playable replicas of this virginal are much sought after by early keyboard specialists.

Lit. Engel, 1874, pp. 349–50; Russell, 1968, pp. 36–7; Schott, 1985, pp. 29–31; Starkey, 1991, p. 105; Wilk, 1996, p. 42

JAMES YORKE

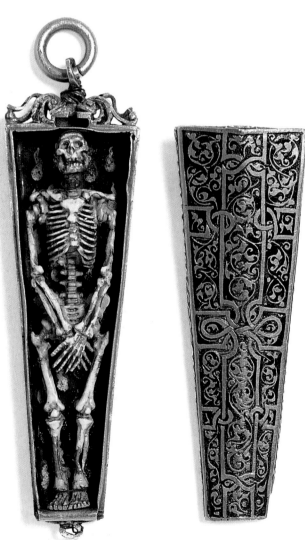

124.

124. English. *The Torre Abbey Jewel.* c. 1540–50. Gold, enameled in white and black, with the remains of opaque pale blue, white, yellow, translucent green, and dark blue enamel on the upper scrollwork, 3⅛ x ⅞ x ½" (8 x 2.3 x 1.3 cm). Inscribed THRONGH.[*sic*] THE. RESVRRECTION. OF. CHRISTE. WE. BE. ALL. SANCTIFIED. V&A 3581–1856

This jewel, reputedly found on the grounds of Torre Abbey, is one of the Museum's early acquisitions of Tudor goldsmiths' work. In the mid-sixteenth century—around the time the pendant was made—the Torre Abbey property passed from the ownership of the church to that of a private family named Pollard following the dissolution of the monasteries during the Reformation. Memento mori jewelry such as this, with its unflinching use of the symbols of death and its purposeful message—"remember you must die"—was widely worn in Western Europe during the sixteenth and early seventeenth centuries. Its intention was to encourage virtuous living, thereby distinguishing it from mourning jewelry of later periods, which most often commemorated the deaths of particular individuals. Moresque decoration such as that on the coffin was in wide use throughout Europe from the 1530s, but the inscription confirms the pendant's English origin.

Lit. Clifford Smith, 1908, p. 365; Evans, 1970, p. 143; Somers Cocks, 1980, p. 51; Llewellyn, 1991, p. 96; Scarisbrick, 1995, p. 51

CLARE PHILLIPS

125. English (Fulham), made at JOHN DWIGHT's FULHAM POTTERY, by an unidentified modeler. *Figure of Lydia Dwight, Half-Length Recumbent.* 1674. Gray salt-glazed stoneware, 10 x 8⅛ x 4⅜" (25.5 x 20.5 x 11 cm). Inscribed "Lydia Dwight dyed March 3 1673" [1674 in the modern calendar]. V&A 1055–1871

A touching image of the potter John Dwight's dead child, this is one of the most striking of a group of pieces that played a key role in the writing, in the 1860s, of a history of English ceramics. Lydia Dwight was less than seven years old when she died, and this highly personal memorial vividly evokes the feelings of bereaved parents. The very material—indestructible stoneware—chosen to represent the fragility of the lace, the impermanence of the flowers, and the vulnerability of the dead child herself, adds considerably to the pathos.

Little was known about the Dwight family until the death of the last descendant released a cache of heirlooms that were

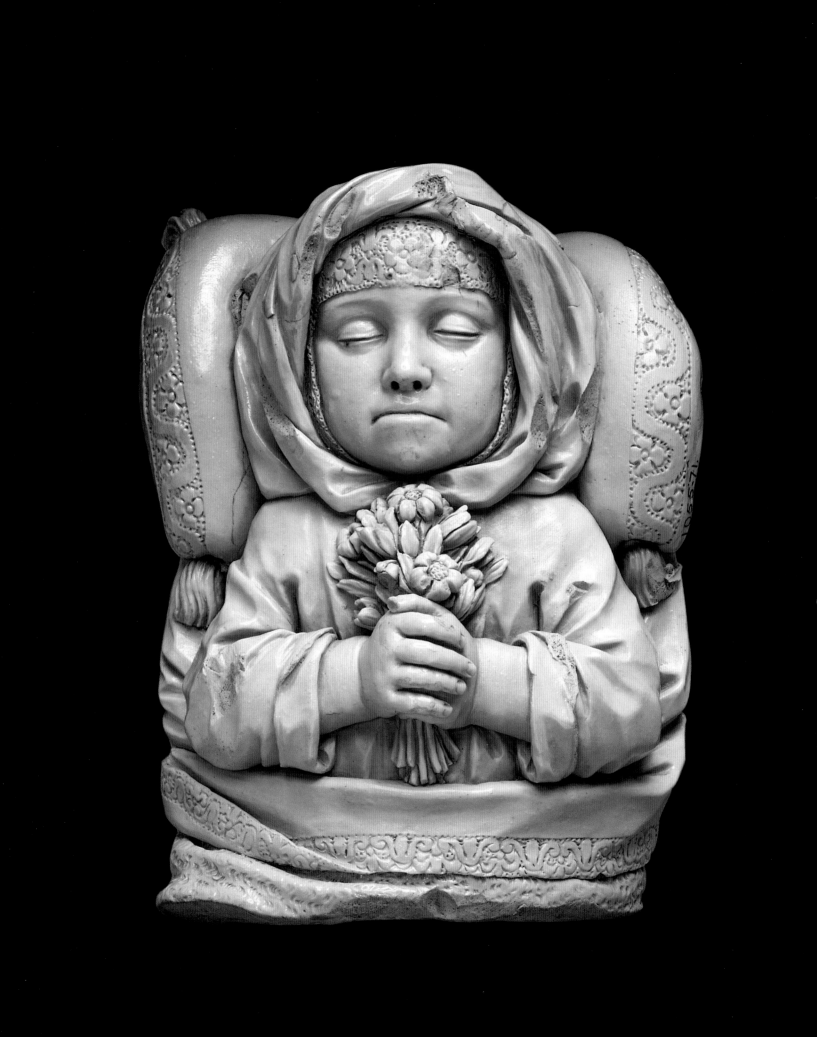

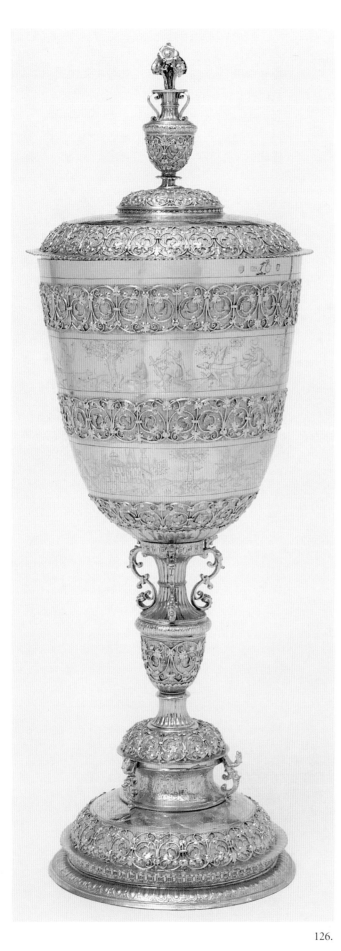

bought by a Fulham antiquary, Thomas Baylis, who published them along with a fanciful account of Dwight in the *Art Journal* (October 1862). The objects were then acquired by C. W. Reynolds, who exhibited them in the 1862 Special Loan Exhibition at South Kensington, with an introduction giving details of Dwight's "Statues and Figures" covered by his second patent of 1684. A fuller account, including the first patent of 1672, given by William Chaffers in the *Art Journal* (June 1865), finally established Dwight's reputation as the father of English fine ceramics, which in turn provided the basis for the huge expansion of the Staffordshire potteries in the second quarter of the eighteenth century.

Dwight's activities as a chemist (including his association at Oxford with Robert Boyle, the "Father of Chemistry") and his nearly successful attempts to make porcelain preceded the experiments of Bottger at Meissen by some fifty years. Furthermore, Dwight's intention of raising the status of his refined stonewares by employing artist-modelers, and his eventual reliance upon the mass production of functional brown stoneware, offer interesting parallels with the life of Josiah Wedgwood a hundred years later. When the Dwight heirlooms were sold at Christie's in 1871, the British Museum and the South Kensington Museum agreed to divide them; *Lydia Dwight* was purchased for £158.

It has long been known that John Dwight was neither a modeler nor a practical potter. Recent writers have concluded that Dwight employed four professional modelers—possibly from the Low Countries or Italy—to create pieces. But in the complete absence of documentary evidence, it has proved impossible on stylistic grounds alone to identify any of the four. Recent excavations at the Fulham Pottery and the publishing of copious surviving documentation have confirmed Dwight's pivotal role in converting English ceramics from a position of struggling imitation to one of successful stylistic innovation.

Lit. Bimson, 1961; Haselgrove and Murray, 1979

ROBIN HILDYARD

126. Probably Flemish maker, working in England (London). *Standing Cup and Cover.* 1611–12. Silver gilt, 19½ x 6¼ x 6¼" (49.6 x 16 x 16 cm). Mark of an unidentified goldsmith TvL in monogram, perhaps Thierry [Dierick] Luckemans. V&A 5964–1859

This handsome cup, recognized as English at the time of its acquisition in 1859 (for £260), has long been greatly admired as an example of goldsmiths' work. The cup's decoration, with its intricate bands of vine scrolls alternating with engraved hunting scenes, was clearly appreciated from the outset. The cup was copied in electrotype as early as 1863, and by 1881 it was on view with other especially precious examples of goldsmiths' work and enamels in the Prince Consort gallery, indeed being one of the pieces singled out in Baedeker's guide.

The TvL cup was made by an unidentified goldsmith, most likely one of many Flemish makers active in London during a period when foreigners, more rigorously trained in drawing and technical skills, could offer rich effects that were appreciated by English patrons. This artisan's technique of creating and laying down fine wires and cast leaves for the vine scrolls is unusual and closer to the workmanship of a jeweler than of a silversmith.

The covered standing cup was the principal type of display plate in early modern Europe; because so many were preserved by museums, a disproportionate number of such cups have survived. The cup had special significance as a gift, with its use governed by rules of ceremony.

Lit. Jackson, 1911, pp. 669–700; Hayward, 1976, plate 663; Glanville, 1990, pp. 405–6

PHILIPPA GLANVILLE

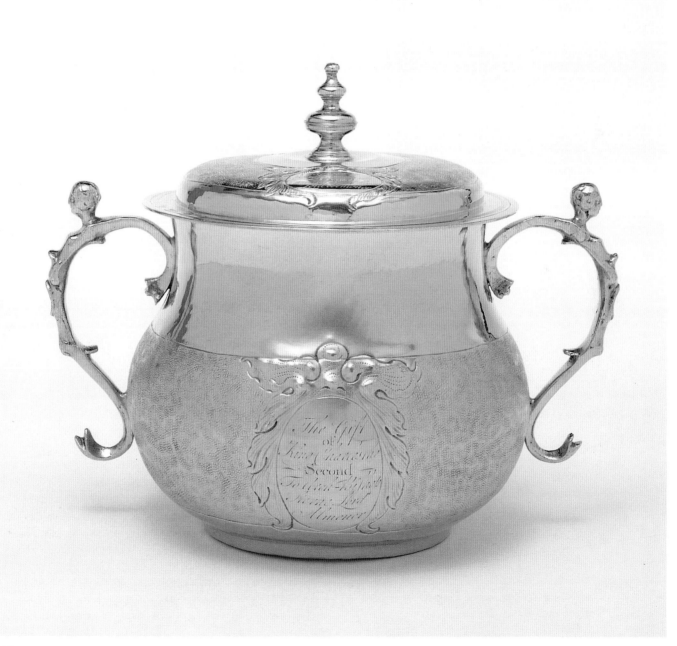

127.

127. English (London). *The Sterne Cup.* 1673–74. Silver, 7⅞ x 10 x 6½" (20 x 25.4 x 16.5 cm). Mark of unidentified goldsmith "AC." V&A M.103–1925

This two-handled cup is a presentation piece, given by King Charles II to Richard Sterne, the archbishop of York (as the later inscription records), and then handed down in his family. From the form's introduction in the early seventeenth century, the large two-handled cup had a high status in England; used as a ceremonial drinking vessel, it was presented as a mark of honor and reward. Until Charles II abolished the practice as an economy measure in about 1680, it had been the tradition since the Middle Ages to exchange presents at court on New Year's Day. For an archbishop, the customary gift from the king was an object weighing forty-six ounces, close to the weight of the Sterne Cup.

Acquired in 1925, the cup had been offered to the Museum as early as 1864. But the Museum's curator at that time, J. C. Robinson, took the view that English silver of this period was merely "useful plate" and rejected the piece, saying, "I do not think it can be considered as coming within the category of works of art." By the time the cup was offered to the Museum in 1925, its acquisition was suppported, as it was described by a curator in the metalwork department as "a piece of English silver of remarkably fine character, very much more important than anything of the kind we have. It is precisely such examples of outstanding quality which are needed to give weight and solidity in building up the national collection." The Museum was in competition with the leading London silver dealer Lionel Crichton, and the cost, £1,000, swallowed up the entire annual acquisition budget of the Metalwork Department. Although it was stressed then that "this is just the kind of really fine work of art which we must increasingly aim at supporting," the antiquarian emphasis on the cup's royal association and the link, however tenuous, with the archbishop's great-grandson, the novelist Lawrence Sterne, author of *Tristram Shandy,* have together given the cup a special standing. This seems to have outweighed what is now perceived as its rather poor quality as a piece of goldsmith's work.

Lit. Oman, 1970, plate 11B

Philippa Glanville

128. Thomas Toft (English [Staffordshire], died 1689). *Mermaid Dish.* c. 1670–80. Slip-trailed earthenware, 17⅜" (44 cm) diam., 2¾" (7 cm) deep. V&A 299–1869

By the 1920s the remarkable signed dishes of Thomas Toft, the earliest and most accomplished member of several families of slipware makers working in Staffordshire, were admired as a distinctive English vernacular style of pottery. But this ware had already attracted interest as early as 1869 when the Museum acquired this piece, at a time when those involved in ceramic production showed an interest in collecting examples from the preindustrial past.

The freehand pictorial use of slip which appeared on Toft's dishes in the 1660s was old-fashioned in style. Much of the patriotic imagery on these dishes (though not, in fact, the mermaid) may well have been stimulated, like that on the urban delftware portrait chargers, by the Restoration of Charles II. The dishes' high survival rate and lack of wear show that they were made solely for decoration. None have worthwhile provenances, either as family heirlooms or to taverns with names that match the heraldic motifs. If the huge makers' signatures were intended as advertisement, it is ironic that their names as well as their products were completely lost until the wealthy manufacturer Enoch Wood collected for his private museum the two examples mentioned by Simeon Shaw in his 1829 *History of the Staffordshire Potteries.* Wood's "very scarce" dishes were acquired by Henry Cole and his advisor Herbert Minton for the new Museum of Practical Geology in 1846, six years before the Museum of Ornamental Art was established at Marlborough House. (The collections from the Museum of Practical Geology in 1901 formed an important addition to the already vast holdings of ceramics of the V&A.) This Mermaid Dish, the first example of Toft's work to be acquired, was purchased by the Museum at auction for £15.

Wealthy collectors in the Midlands, such as Thomas Greg and Charles J. Lomax, glutted on the mechanically perfect products of the Industrial Revolution and disinclined to collect foreign Renaissance pottery, soon began to search for the "pre-Wedgwood English pottery" remaining in farms and cottages in the counties around Staffordshire. Although in 1883 even Louis Marc Emmanuel Solon, the French art director of Minton & Co., felt compelled to apologize at length for the "modest artists" of "so primitive a community," he chose to display the dishes in his own collection in broad ebonized frames. Thus, these peasant pots with their bold linear style went from quaint antiquarian curio to artistic icon, acquiring status as examples of pure Englishness—in part through the collecting zeal of Dr. James Whitbread Lee Glaisher (whose collection is now at the Fitzwilliam Museum) and the writings of Bernard Rackham and Herbert Read. According to Rackham and Read in their 1924 *English Pottery,* this ware "owes nothing to servile imita-

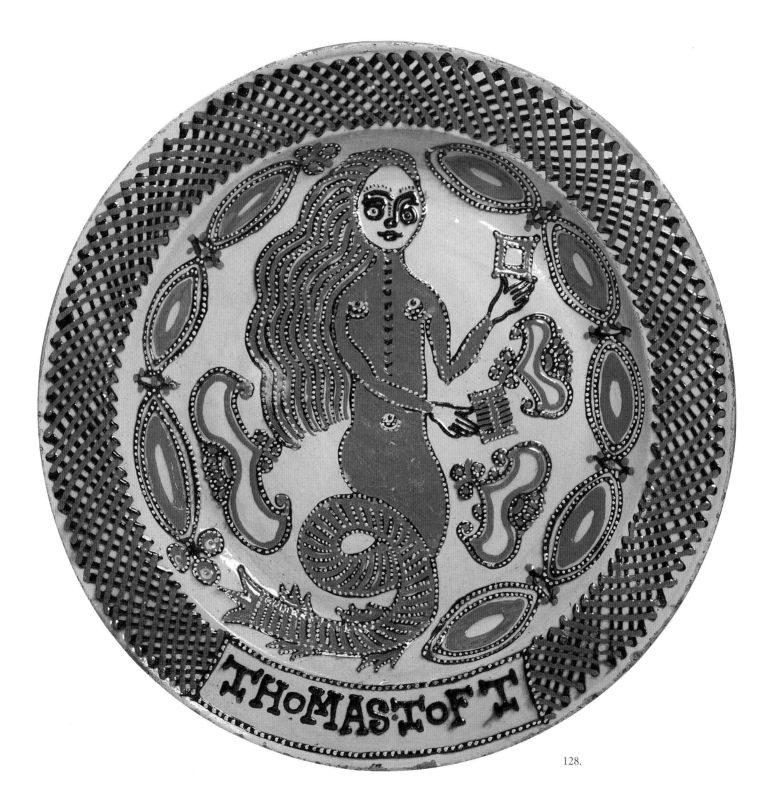

128.

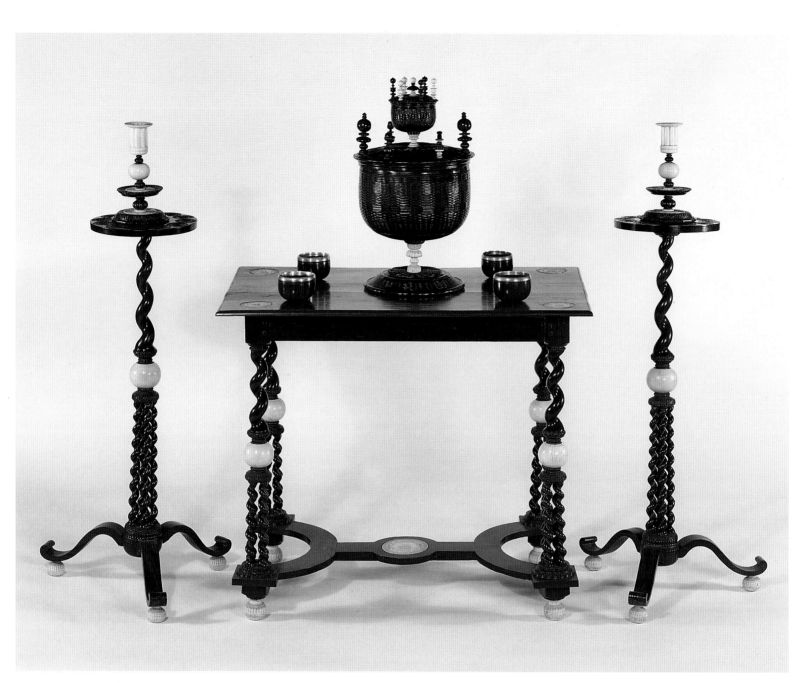

tion," proof indeed that "art tends to reach its highest levels when narrowly restricted in its means."

Considered a formative influence in the 1920s upon the cross-cultural pioneering studio potter Bernard Leach, English trailed slipware is now highly regarded in Japan. In America, popularized by collections formed in Kansas by Frank P. and Harriet C. Burnap in the 1930s–40s and by Colonial Williamsburg in Virginia in the 1950s–60s, such ware has come to represent part of the shared cultural roots of the New and Old Worlds.

Lit. Solon, 1883; Rackham and Read, 1924; Goodby, 1992

ROBIN HILDYARD

129. English. *Wassail Table and Furnishings.* c. 1640–80. Lignum vitae with ivory decoration, table 30 x 35 x 23" (76 x 89 x 58.4 cm); candlestands 36⅝" (93 cm) high; candlesticks 9½" (24 cm) high; bowl 19⅝" (50 cm) high; cups 3" (7.7 cm) diam. V&A W.8-K-1976

Preserved in part through its supposed family connections and its associations with English folk life traditions, this exceptional suite of furniture was acquired by the Museum in 1976 as a virtuoso example of woodturning and for its significance for English antiquarianism. It was used to serve wassail, or spiced ale (the word derives from the Middle English *waeshaeil,* or "be healthy"), a drink traditionally offered at Christmas. Other wassail bowls survive with dipper cups, but this set is uniquely elaborate in having a matching table, candlestands, and candlesticks. The entire set is lavishly enriched with "rose engine turning" (in which decoration is incised into the surface of the material while it is spun on a lathe), making this the most important known seventeenth-century example of turning.

The set was passed down as a treasured possession through generations of the Cokayne family, who knew it as "King Charles' Wassail Table"; family tradition maintained that it was given to Sir Charles Cokayne, the first Viscount Cullen (1602–1661), by Charles I after the battle of Naseby in 1645, during the English Civil War. Cokayne's seat, Rushton Hall, Northamptonshire, was close to the site of the battle. Stylistic assessment, however, casts doubt on the family legend, as the table and candlestands probably date not from the 1640s but from the 1670s, when their spiral-twisted supports and delicate silhouettes would have been newly fashionable. The wassail bowl itself could date from the 1640s, and it is possible that the rest of the set was added later. The high quality of this luxury furniture is certainly worthy of royal connections; and it may indeed have been acquired by the second viscount's wife Elizabeth, who was a noted beauty at the court of Charles II and was lady of the bedchamber to Queen Catherine of Braganza.

During the nineteenth century, antiquarian interest in early English furniture and interiors resulted in the publication of this set both in the background of a view of the great hall at Rushton (in J. P. Neale's *Views of Seats of Noblemen and Gentlemen* [1826]) and in Henry Shaw's *Specimens of Ancient Furniture* (1836), ranking it among the most important sets of early furniture in the country. This interest in early furniture continued later in the century, when the Museum's acquisitions of English furniture were chiefly of sixteenth- and seventeenth-century pieces. While interest later moved on to the eighteenth century, furniture historians kept in mind the items illustrated by Shaw, and in 1927 H. Clifford Smith, later the Museum's keeper of furniture and woodwork, published an article in *Connoisseur* establishing the current whereabouts of the Rushton Hall suite. About the same time wassail bowls began to attract the attention of collectors of treen (small wooden objects), ultimately resulting in a detailed description of the Rushton Hall furniture in Edward Pinto's 1969 *Treen and Other Wooden Bygones.*

By 1976, when the set was purchased, its acquisition was a dramatic restatement of the Furniture and Woodwork Department's interest in British art and traditions, at a time when emphasis was placed on acquiring important pieces of Continental furniture.

Lit. Neale, 1826, vol. III; Shaw, 1836, plate XXII; Clifford Smith, 1927; Pinto, 1969, p. 52; Wainwright, 1973; Thornton and Jervis, 1976; Wilk, 1996, p. 56

Catherine S. Hay

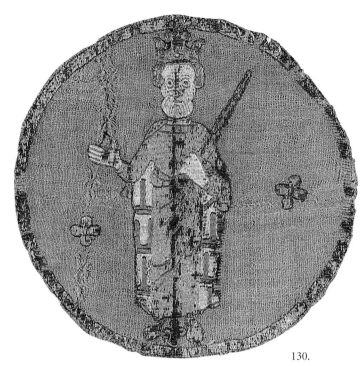

130.

130. English. *Roundel with a Saint.* c. 1220-50. Linen, originally covered with silk twill, embroidered with silk and silver-gilt threads in underside couching and stem stitch, 6¾ x 7" (17.2 x 17.8 cm). V&A 1249–1864

Originally applied to an ecclesiastical vestment, this roundel with the figure of an unidentified saint is an example of a type of embroidery that was already identified as distinctively English in the Middle Ages through its description in inventories such as *opus anglicanum* (English work). Although its English origins were never in doubt, the roundel was among a large number of medieval textile fragments acquired in the 1860s, not as examples of English material, but as part of the wider context of European medieval art. The tiny fragment was acquired from Dr. Franz Bock who, though a canon of Aachen cathedral, was very active as a dealer. Bock's scholarly investigation of medieval cathedral treasuries in Germany and Austria resulted in substantial publication, including a history of textiles, but it also seems to have involved the removal of numerous sample specimens (such as this) snipped from complete vestments. The collection of textiles assembled in this way was sold by Bock (who was on very good terms with J. C. Robinson) to South Kensington; in addition, the applied arts museums in Vienna and Berlin, as well as South Kensington, continued to buy other works from him. By the 1920s, however, such textiles were being seen in terms of their national significance, a position reinforced by the publication in 1938 of A. G. I. Christie's monumental study, *English Medieval Embroidery.* This shift was

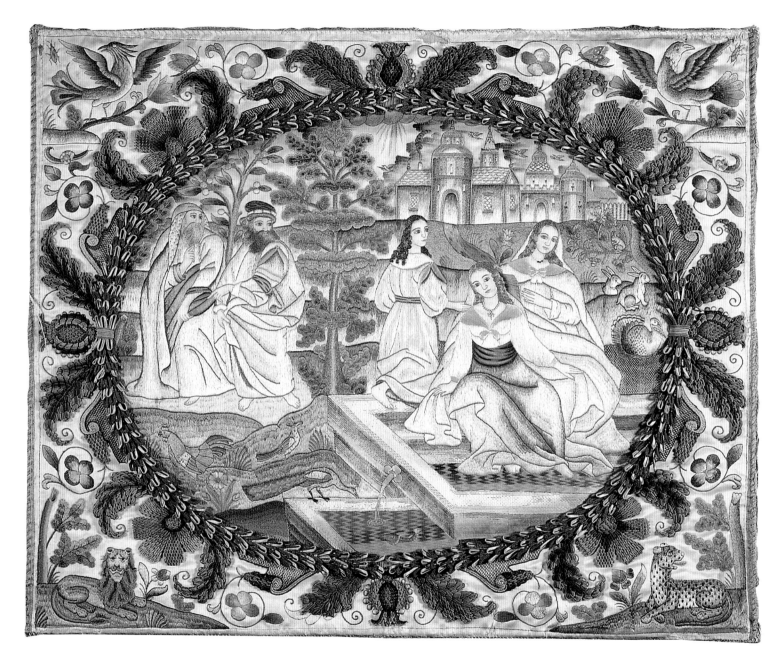

131.

also reflected in publications on other aspects of medieval art by scholars associated with the Museum, including Mary Chamot's *English Medieval Enamels* (1930) and Margaret Longhurst's *English Ivories* (1926), with its most notable manifestation the major exhibition, "English Medieval Art," mounted by the Museum in 1930.

Lit. King, 1963, p. 18; Jopek, forthcoming

LINDA WOOLLEY

131. English. *Embroidered Picture: "Susanna and the Elders".* c. 1660. Satin embroidered with colored silks and metal purl in long and short, split and back stitches, detached darning, French knots, and couched work; silk-covered parchment; additional details in watercolor, 18⅛ x 22 x ⅜" (46 x 56 x 1 cm). Bequeathed by Sir Frederick Richmond. V&A T.50-1954

This exceptionally well-preserved picture, which retains its fresh original colors, is a fine example of professional English embroidery of about 1660. The panel depicts an early moment in the biblical story of Susanna and the Elders, from the Apocrypha. Susanna, a beautiful and righteous wife, walked each afternoon with her handmaidens in the garden adjoining her wealthy husband's house. Two Elders, newly appointed as judges, watched her in the garden every day and began to lust after her. The Elders waited for an opportune moment to take advantage of her, finding it one hot day when Susanna decided to bathe and sent her maids to the house for bath oils. The Elders shut the garden gates and ordered Susanna to lie with them or they would falsely accuse her of adultery. Despite their power as judges, Susanna chose the virtuous course, rejecting the Elders, and was condemned to death upon their testimony to the people's assembly. She was saved by Daniel, in whom the Lord—hearing Susanna's cries of innocence—instilled the spirit of truth.

The details of this picture are unusual. The story of Susanna is one of the few biblically justifiable opportunities to depict female nudity, and it is rare to find a composition of the story in which Susanna is fully clothed. Nor is she commonly posed with her maids; on the contrary, Susanna is almost always portrayed in a suggestive manner, flanked by the Elders. (It has been suggested by art historian Mary Garrard that depictions of Susanna in which she does not invite the Elders' advances were sometimes the work of women artists, who would have been more sympathetic to her plight and perhaps given greater emphasis to her chastity.)

Biblical stories recounting the deeds of virtuous women were a popular choice for English needlework pictures in this period. They were mostly made by young needlewomen (girls from age eight could already be accomplished in such work), for whom biblical heroines like Susanna represented the virtues of chastity, faith, and sacrifice.

The amateur needleworker did not ordinarily create her own designs. The figures, birds, animals, insects, architectural elements, and trees and flowers were usually copied from woodcuts and engravings (mostly Flemish) by professional pattern drawers and print sellers, who would transfer line drawings on fabric for the needleworker to embroider. It is thought that this elaborate and refined piece is by a professional embroiderer; indeed, it has decorative elements—notably its ornate wreath "frame"—similar to those found in a surviving signed work by the London "broderer" John Nelham. An oval wreath of silk-wrapped parchment, very like the one in this "Susanna and the Elders," also occurs on a signed and dated (1673) beaded jewel case—in the Victoria and Albert Museum's collection—worked by the very skilled amateur Martha Edlin (English, born 1660).

This embroidered picture was bequeathed to the Museum in 1954 by Sir Frederick Richmond, together with other outstanding examples of seventeenth-century English embroidery. The Richmond collection was one of the finest in private hands, exemplifying the growing appreciation for English needlework among collectors. Such gifts or bequests from private collectors—complementing purchases made with public funds—have played a major role, especially in the twentieth century, in the Museum's collection development in the field of English material.

Lit. Sumner, 1987, no. 38

CLARE BROWNE/SUSAN DACKERMAN/ANITA JONES

132. English or French. *Valance with a Garden Scene.* Late 16th century. Linen canvas embroidered with wool and silk in tent stitch, details in stem stitch and couched work, 22⅛ x 71¼" (56.3 x 181 cm). Bequeathed by Miss M. Ochs. V&A T137-1991

Although French in style, most valances of this type with secure provenances have English associations, suggesting they are, in fact, either English or were made for an English market. The ambiguity as to whether or not a work is indeed English has been an issue of constant and lively debate as the Museum attempted to present "Englishness" through its collection.

Valances (or borders) such as this formed friezes which ran around the Elizabethan bed and were particularly suitable for embroidery with figure subjects. The style and workmanship of this example suggest a professional workshop strongly influenced by French fashion, if not the product of a French work-

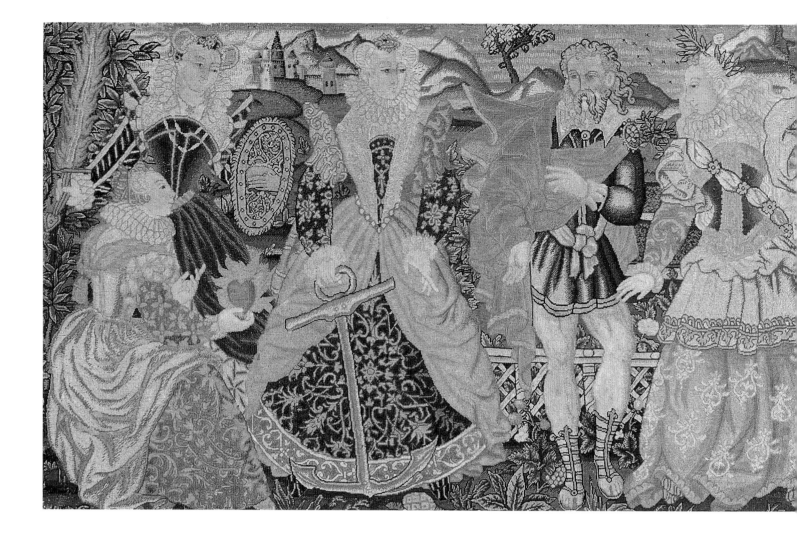

shop itself. The setting is an ornamental garden scene with a mountainous skyline, an extremely popular type of background for such scenes. The subject is unidentified, but the four female figures on the left may represent four of the seven Virtues.

Linda Woolley

133. English (probably made by the Bickford family, royal locksmiths). *Queen Mary's Jewel Casket.* c. 1688–94. Steel, covered with velvet, overlaid with gilt-brass studs and openwork quatrefoils of blued steel, 9⅝ x 18¾ x 12⅝" (24.5 x 47.5 x 32 cm). Purchased with funds from Bequest of Captain H. B. Murray. V&A M19–1937

The acquisition in 1937 of this elaborate jewel casket, with its complicated locking system of four bolts, openwork ornament in blued steel, and finely engraved gilt-brass, was a significant addition to the Museum's collection of objects made of iron and steel. But no doubt one of the main reasons for its purchase was its royal connection and the traditional view that it was made for the dowry paid on the marriage of Queen Mary to William III; this view was supported not only by the crowned cipher of William and Mary around the keyholes but also by an eighteenth-century provenance linking it with Sophia Dorothea, sister of George II, and wife of Frederick William I of Prussia, who took it to Berlin. By 1918 the jewel casket was in the Schlossmuseum in Berlin. It was sold to the V&A for £500 to raise funds for the acquisition of part of the collection of medieval goldsmiths' work known as the Guelph Treasure, regarded as a notable part of the German heritage. The V&A's opportunity to acquire what was considered an English national treasure thus came about through Berlin's attempts to retain a national treasure of its own.

Lit. V&A, 1951, no. 39; Haedeke, 1970, plate viii

Anthony R. E. North

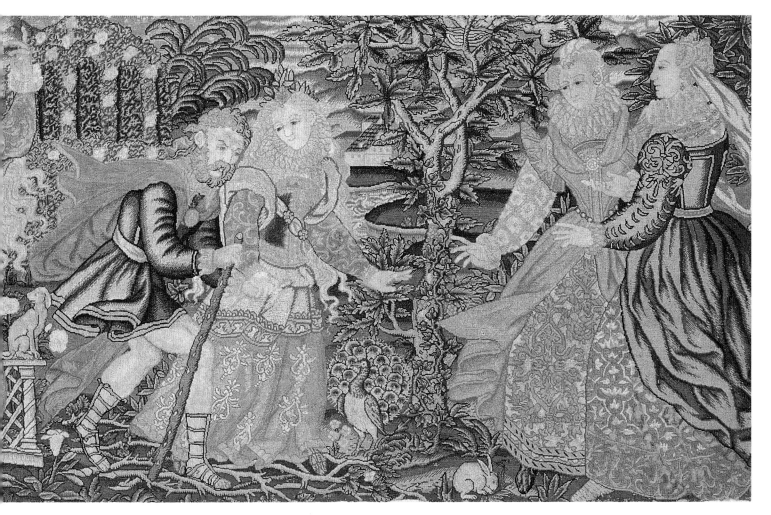

132.

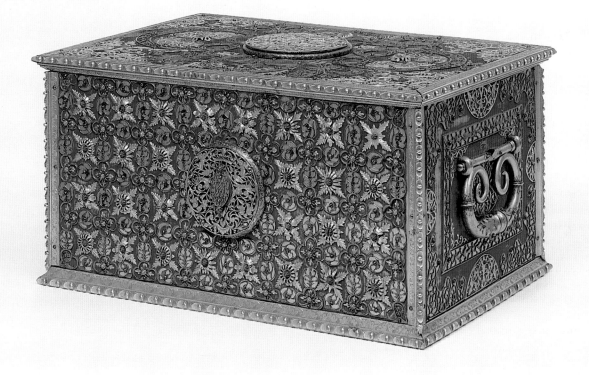

133.

134. Designed by HORACE WALPOLE (English, 1717–1797), perhaps in collaboration with WILLIAM KENT (English, 1685–1748). *The Walpole Cabinet.* 1743. Kingwood with ivory, 60 x 36 x 8½" (152.4 x 91.5 x 21.6 cm). V&A W.52–1925

This richly decorated cabinet was made to house the portrait miniatures collected by the connoisseur Horace Walpole and, through both its original contents and the images of artists represented on its exterior, was from the start conceived as a statement about the history of art in England. Its own later history, including its acquisition and use by the Museum, reveals not only how English art has been revalued in the twentieth century but also the symbolic role accorded to Walpole in this process. As well as gathering together some of the most informative sources about eighteenth-century and earlier English art, Walpole was an important patron and collector, his most notable achievement being his Gothic Revival house at Strawberry Hill and the works displayed there.

The cabinet was described by Walpole in 1743 as a "new cabinet for my enamels and miniatures," designed by himself, possibly with the assistance of the architect William Kent. It is decorated with the owner's arms and surmounted by ivory figures of three earlier artists whom Walpole held in especially high esteem: the Flemish sculptor François Duquesnoy (1594–1644), flanked by two architects—Andrea Palladio (1508–1580) and Inigo Jones (1573–1652)—whose designs formed the basis for the neo-Palladian style in mid-eighteenth-century England. The ivory figures were carved by the otherwise unknown Verskovis after models by Michael Rysbrack (cat. 137). Most of the ivory reliefs of classical subjects were by Andrea Pozzo, who worked in eighteenth-century Rome mainly for British patrons on the grand tour, and these were probably acquired by Walpole himself in Italy in 1740. The Judith relief was erroneously, if significantly, thought by Walpole to be by the seventeenth-century English sculptor Grinling Gibbons, who carved the cravat also in his collection (cat. 135).

The cabinet was first placed in Walpole's London house in Arlington Street around 1743 but was moved to Strawberry Hill in the early 1760s (fig. 114). As E. Edwards's drawing of 1781 shows, it there formed the centerpiece of a room in which some of the most precious small objects in the collection were displayed; these included miniatures by Hans Holbein and Isaac Oliver. Through both its contents and its external imagery, the cabinet was used in this context as a statement about English art and aesthetic ideals. The English miniatures inside were presented as the equal of the works of ancient art reproduced in ivory on the outside.

The piece, sold with Walpole's collection in 1842, was purchased by the V&A in 1925 at a period when new interest was being shown in Walpole and his collection. This parallels the enthusiasm for eighteenth-century English culture at this date in Britain and the United States, one notable outcome being the

beginning of the forty-eight-volume Yale edition of Walpole's correspondence. Employed by Walpole to frame his collection of earlier English works, the cabinet has been used in evolving Museum settings to exemplify eighteenth-century English taste.

Lit. King and Longhurst, 1926; Wainwright, 1989, pp. 74–5, 101

MALCOLM BAKER

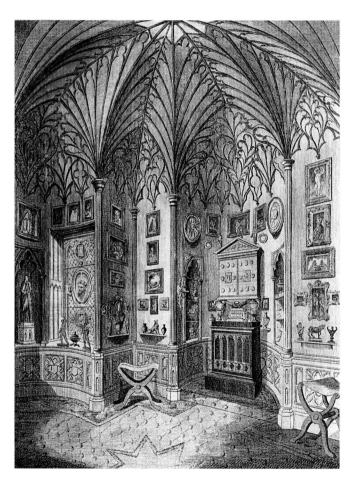

Fig. 114. The Walpole Cabinet in Walpole's famous Gothic Revival house, called Strawberry Hill

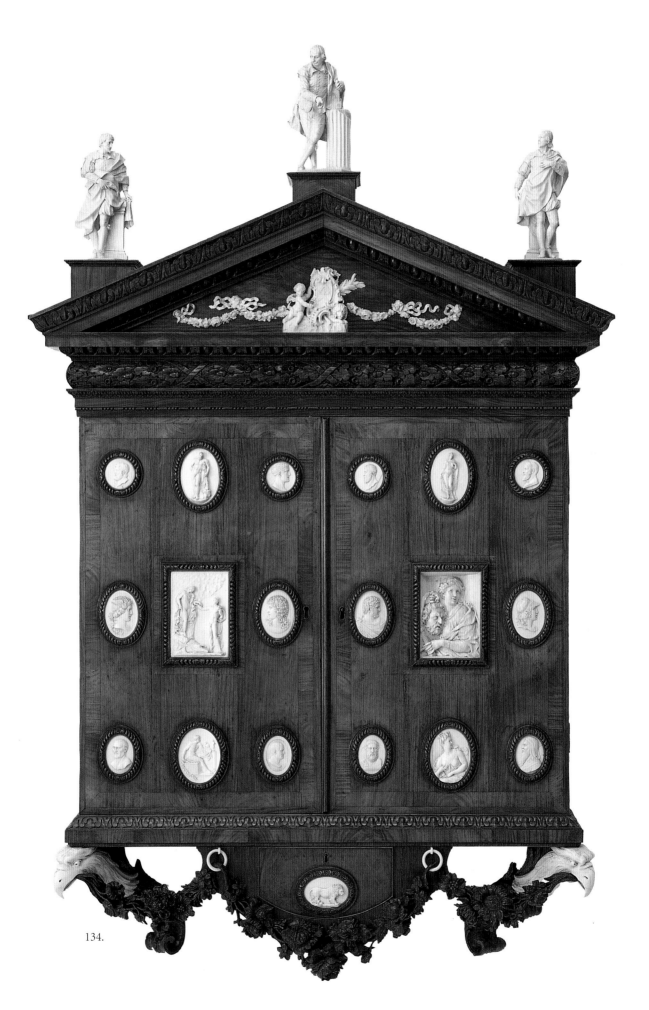

134.

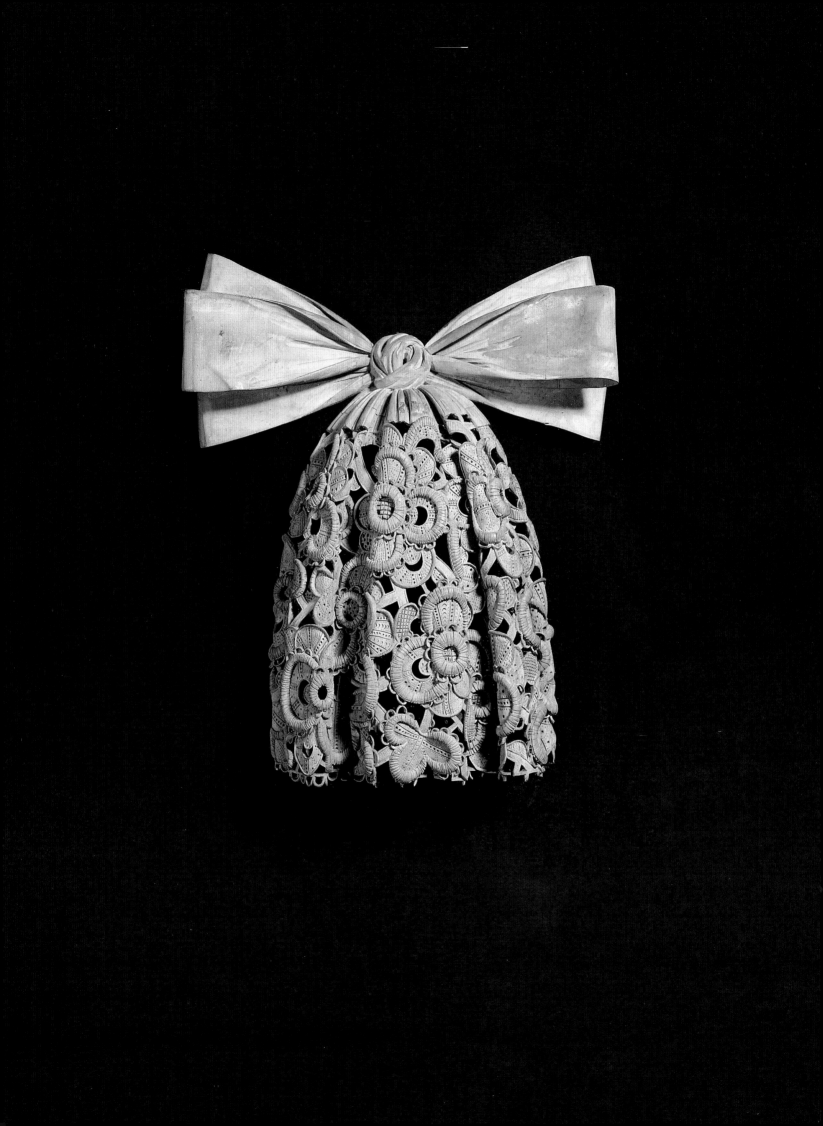

135. GRINLING GIBBONS (English, born Rotterdam [of English parents], 1648–1721 [in England by 1670–71]). *Cravat.* c. 1690. Limewood, 9½ x 8¼ x 2" (24.1 x 20.9 x 5.1 cm). Given by Mrs. Basil Ionides. V&A W.181–1928

When this astonishing carving was given to the Museum in 1928 by Mrs. Basil Ionides, Grinling Gibbons was already established as the archetypal English craftsman genius. He is perhaps best known for his work for Sir Christopher Wren at St. Paul's Cathedral and for his royal commissions. Another example of his work—a relief of the stoning of Saint Stephen—had for some time been prominently displayed in the Museum. Not surprisingly, this trompe l'oeil "cravat," carved in imitation of Venetian needlepoint lace fashionable in the late seventeenth century and similar to those used in other schemes of carved decoration associated with Gibbons, was described then as a virtuoso example by a craftsman "so highly gifted that he transformed existing practice and originated a style." Making Gibbons a canonical figure was largely due to connoisseur and collector Horace Walpole, who included an account of Gibbons in his *Anecdotes of Painting.* As well as attributing one of the ivories on his cabinet (cat. 134) to Gibbons, Walpole also owned this cravat, "the art of which arrives even to deception," and displayed it near the cabinet at Strawberry Hill, Twickenham. In a letter of 11 May 1769, Walpole described receiving a number of distinguished foreign visitors, for which occasion he dressed in the Gibbons cravat and wore a pair of embroidered gloves that had belonged to King James I, reporting that "the French servants stared and firmly believed that this was the dress of English Country Gentlemen."

In 1874 Gibbons's life was celebrated in Austin Clare's popular historical novel, *The Carved Cartoon,* and his work was promoted by those interested in English art and design. Although not among the artists represented in the Museum's so-called Kensington Valhalla created from 1862 to 1871, his statue appeared on the facade of the Aston Webb building in 1909, five years before a monograph about him was published by H. Avray

Tipping, editor of *Country Life* (and the donor of Thomas Carter's *Chaloner Chute* [cat. 136], with its Walpole associations). However, as a woodcarver his work occupied an ambiguous position between woodwork and sculpture, allowing the Saint Stephen relief to be displayed with English furniture in 1923 and then alongside English sculpture in 1930. With the formation of the English Primary Galleries in 1950, both the relief and this cravat were shown together as part of a narrative about English art.

Lit. Avray Tipping, 1914, pp. 82–3; Edwards, 1929; V&A, 1955, no. 30; Green, 1964, p. 52; Oughton, 1979, pp. 136–7; Beard, 1989, p. 44

TESSA MURDOCH

136. THOMAS CARTER (English, died 1795). *Chaloner Chute.* c. 1775. Terra cotta, 2½ x 7⅞ x 3⅞" (6.4 x 19.9 x 9.9 cm). Given by H. Avray Tipping. V&A A.8–1911

This model for a figure on a monument in the chapel of the Chute family's country house, The Vyne in Hampshire, was given to the Museum by H. Avray Tipping, the editor of *Country Life,* whose writings played a role in encouraging interest in eighteenth-century English art and architecture. The work itself is the result of an eighteenth-century interest in an earlier English past.

136.

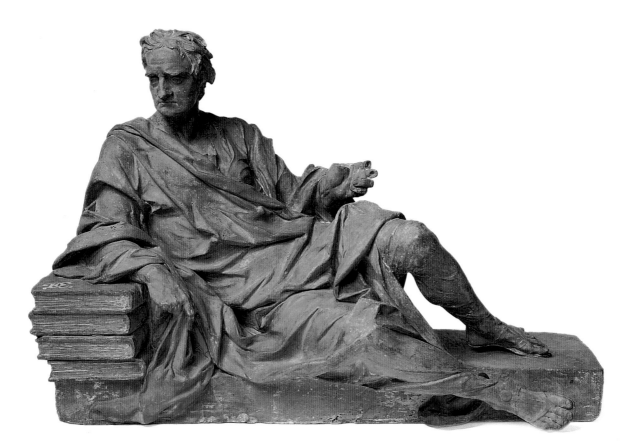

137.

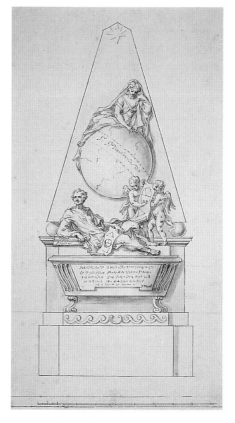

The full-scale monument, which is based on this small pre-liminary model, was commissioned by Chaloner Chute to com-memorate his seventeenth-century ancestor. It was placed in a family chapel attached to the house at the same time as the windows were set with fragments of medieval glass under the guidance of Chute's friend, Horace Walpole. From the start, the monument was conceived as a conscious revival of earlier English styles.

Early in the twentieth century Avray Tipping wrote about Chute and his house in *Country Life* and presumably acquired the model around this time. In giving it to the Museum in 1911, he was not only adding to an already substantial collection of sculptors' models but making an early contribution to the Museum's eighteenth-century English sculpture. The model was identified as being by Thomas Carter through the archival work of Rupert Gunnis, whose *Dictionary of British Sculptors* (1953) remains a standard work. The *Chaloner Chute* thus represents two distinct phases in the historiography of "Englishness" and English art, involving several key figures from both periods.

Lit. Whinney, 1971

Malcolm Baker

Fig. 115. William Kent (English, 1685/1686–1748). *Design for the Memorial to Sir Isaac Newton Erected in 1731 in Westminster Abbey.* V&A E.424–1946

137. Michael Rysbrack (English, born Belgium, 1695–1760). *Sir Isaac Newton.* c. 1730. Terra cotta, 14⅛ x 20⅞ x 9" (36 x 53 x 23 cm). Given by Dr. W. L. Hildburgh. V&A A.1–1938

Sculptors' models were acquired by the Museum from the 1860s as examples of processes of design and making. Although drawings for English sculpture, including William Kent's design for the monument to Lord Stanhope, were purchased for this reason, most of the three-dimensional models acquired at this date were French or Italian. Models for eighteenth-century English sculpture were acquired only in the 1930s when the Museum was prompted by scholars such as Katherine Esdaile and the donor Dr. W. L. Hildburgh to take serious account of postmedieval English sculpture. As a result, the Newton model was acquired in 1938 and Kent's design for it (fig. 115) in 1946, complementing the companion design for the Stanhope monument bought seventy years earlier. This reassessment of the artistic qualities of English sculpture led to the inclusion of several English models, including the Newton piece, in the V&A's 1946 exhibition, "Style in Sculpture."

   This terra cotta was made as a preliminary model for the central marble figure on the monument to the scientist Sir Isaac Newton erected in Westminster Abbey in 1730. By his death in 1727 Newton was already included among English "worthies" (or celebrated men), and his monument immediately attracted wide attention. Commissioned by John Conduitt (the husband of Newton's niece), the monument was designed by the architect William Kent, and drawings by both Kent and Rysbrack preceded the making of this model. Models such as this were already being collected in the eighteenth century, and in the 1770s some of Rysbrack's models for monuments in Westminster Abbey were advertised as "ideal for any library or grotto."

Lit. Whinney, 1971, pp. 38–9; Baker, 1986

Malcolm Baker

138. English (Spitalfields). *Dress Fabric.* c. 1708. Silk damask brocaded with colored silks, 65 x 20½" (165 x 52 cm). V&A 711–1864

Acquired by the Museum in 1864 as Italian, this silk was recognized as English workmanship largely through the study of the English silk industry by Peter Thornton and Natalie Rothstein, whose research on the subject culminated in *Silk Designs of the Eighteenth Century in the Collection of the Victoria and Albert Museum* (1990). Thornton and Rothstein's work established that throughout the first half of the eighteenth century dress silks designed and woven in Spitalfields were of a quality to rival

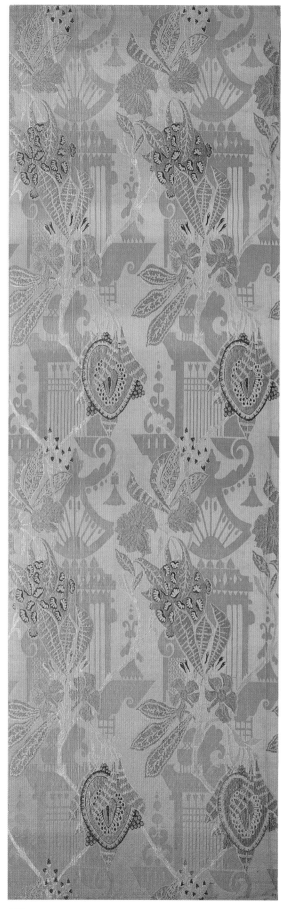

138.

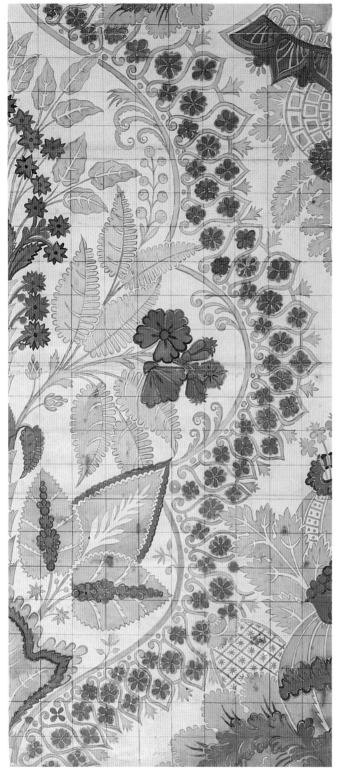

139.

imported fabrics from France, but with a uniquely English character to their design. The exotic pattern of this example is typical of the taste for the bizarre in textile design in Europe at the beginning of the eighteenth century, though the English interpretation of the bizarre style was less extreme than the French or Italian.

Lit. King, 1980, vol. I, plate 121; V&A, 1995, no. 76

CLARE BROWNE

139. CHRISTOPHER BAUDOUIN (Anglo-French, c. 1665–c. 1735). *Design for Woven Silk.* 1724. Pencil and watercolor, 24 x 9⅞" (61 x 25 cm). V&A 5973.17

This is one example from several volumes of designs for silks compiled by Anna Maria Garthwaite (English, 1690–1763), the most prominent successor to Christopher Baudouin, the founder of silk design in Britain. The design volumes were purchased by the Museum in 1868 with the express intention of encouraging and instructing students, particularly future textile designers in the Government Schools of Design. To make them exhibitable and available, the volumes were broken up and the items individually mounted, framed, and traveled in exhibitions around Britain. Although still used as a source for designers, the volumes are now regarded as key evidence in the history of silk design and production in eighteenth-century Britain.

Although at first regarded to be by Garthwaite, some of these designs are now thought to be by Baudouin and collected by her. In the never-ceasing trade rivalry between Britain and Lyon, the French had undermined their own dominance in figured silk weaving. Persecuted Huguenot designers and weavers (like the Baudouin family) escaped religious intolerance in France by fleeing to England in the 1680s, where they set up a manufactory that rivaled Lyon's. Elaborate figured silks for dress and furnishings remained fashionable in Europe and America until the 1770s, but thereafter the silk weavers had to produce much simpler and smaller Neoclassical motifs and stripes to appeal to changing tastes. As late as the middle of the nineteenth century, the British government was still concerned to maintain silk weaving at Spitalfields in London—and elsewhere in Britain—although the industry was in severe decline in comparison with the massive production of printed cotton for world markets.

CHARLES NEWTON

140. JOSIAH WEDGWOOD (English [Etruria, Staffordshire], 1730–1795). *Copy of the "Portland Vase".* c. 1790. Blue-black jasper ware, with jasper dip and white relief, 9⅞ x 7⅞" (25 x 20 cm), 5⅛" (13 cm) diam. at base. Unmarked. Transferred from the Museum of Practical Geology, Jermyn Street. V&A 2418–1901

The Portland Vase, a Roman cased-glass vase of about 30–20 B.C., was in the eighteenth century the most celebrated artifact to have survived from ancient Rome. Of Greek amphora form, it is of the darkest cobalt blue translucent glass, with decoration of white opaque glass carved in cameo relief. Once called the "Barberini Vase" (because it was in the Barberini family collection in Rome from 1626 for nearly 150 years), it passed through a number of owners before coming into the possession sometime before 1785 of the dowager duchess of Portland, from whom it derived its present name. The Portland Vase is known to have been cracked in 1786, and then in 1845 it was smashed into more than 200 fragments by a drunken visitor. Restored at that time, it was purchased by the British Museum in 1945 and was more expertly restored by the museum in 1948, and again in 1988–89. The vase remains an iconic image, prominently dis-

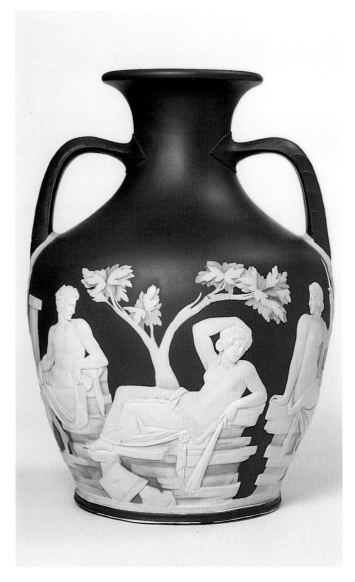

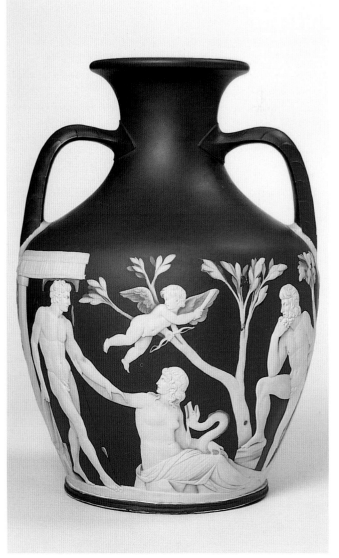

140.

played at the British Museum and known worldwide through mass-produced reproductions of generally poor quality.

In 1786 the Portland Vase was loaned by the third duke of Portland, the duchess's son, who purchased it at auction after the duchess's death, to Josiah Wedgwood for the purpose of making a limited-edition copy in jasper ware (a hard, fine-grained stoneware of Wedgwood's invention).

Wedgwood's pottery exemplified the "industrial arts," and work from his factory was prominent among the ceramics collected for the Museum of Practical Geology, with which Henry Cole was closely involved. Included in the Wedgwood material represented there was Josiah Wedgwood's famous copy of the Portland Vase, which he had perfected in 1790 after four years of painstaking trials; the copy was introduced at his London showrooms in an exhibition open to those members of the nobility and gentry who had applied for admission tickets.

Although copied by other manufacturers of ceramics and glass, the Wedgwood version came to serve as a symbolic icon for the whole of Josiah Wedgwood's life and achievements and, increasingly, as a masterpiece of English applied art. As such, it appears on the spines of Eliza Meteyard's monumental 1865–66 two-volume biography of the potter; and Wedgwood is shown holding his Portland Vase copy in both Edward Davis's monu-

ment to him at Stoke-on-Trent (unveiled in 1863), and in the sculpture of him included in the pantheon of ten English craftsmen on the 1909 facade of the Museum. There is a paradox here, for although the copy can be taken as the crowning technical achievement of Josiah Wedgwood's work as a potter, those made in his lifetime were extremely costly, limited-edition productions—full-blown works of art made as exhibition and presentation pieces. Thus, they scarcely represent what nineteenth- and early-twentieth-century admirers saw as his greatest accomplishment—the harnessing of art and design to the needs of commerce and industry.

Lit. Painter and Whitehouse, 1990, pp. 24–84

Hilary Young/Brenda Richardson

141. English (London). *The Girl-in-a-Swing.* c. 1749–59. Soft-paste porcelain, 6¼ x 7¼ x 3⅞" (16 x 18.5 x 10 cm). Unmarked. Given by Lt. Col. Dingwall. V&A C.587–1922

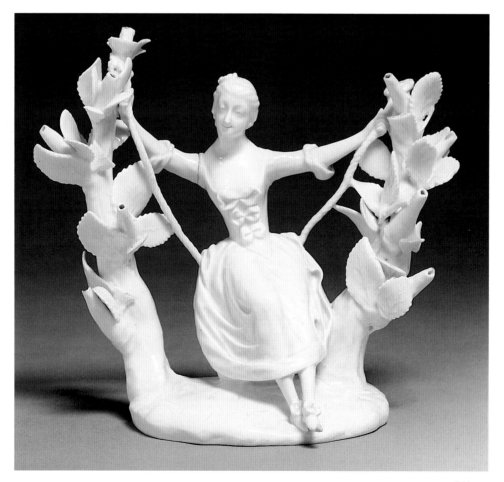

141.

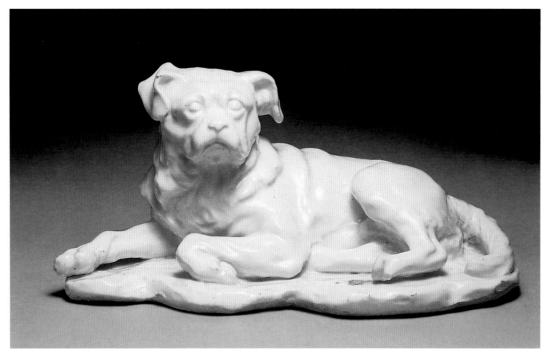

142.

This seemingly unassuming figure is the prototype (or "type specimen") that has named a highly problematic group of English porcelain figures—all unmarked—that have attracted collectors of ceramics because of the distinctive glassy, reflective qualities of their material and their charmingly naive modeling. The difficulty in identifying their place of production has also intrigued specialists exploring the smaller, more problematic English porcelain factories.

The *Girl-in-a-Swing* figure was given to the Museum in 1922, when it was taken to be an early product of Nicholas Sprimont's Chelsea factory. It was later suggested that the *Girl-in-a-Swing* group could have been made at a rival factory at Chelsea set up by Staffordshire workmen who had seceded from Sprimont's works. In 1962 V&A curators Arthur Lane and Robert Charleston greatly enlarged the group to include a large number of "toys" (etuis, scent bottles, and similar small objects), proposing an attribution to a factory of unknown location run by Charles Gouyn, a jeweler with premises in St. James's, London, who had been a partner in Sprimont's Chelsea factory until sometime before March 1749. Support for this conjecture has been provided by a recently discovered document stating that "Mr. Gouin left [the Chelsea factory] . . . and makes at his house in St. James's Street, very beautiful small porcelain figures." Despite many remaining questions, the identity of the *Girl-in-a-Swing* manufacturer—and the general nature of the maker's relationship with Chelsea—are now far clearer.

Lit. Lane and Charleston, 1962; Dragesco, 1993, pp. 14–21; Valpy, 1994, pp. 317–26

HILARY YOUNG

142. English (Chelsea), after LOUIS FRANÇOIS ROUBILIAC (English, born France, 1702–1762). *Hogarth's Dog, Trump.* c. 1747–50. Soft-paste porcelain, 4⅞ x 10½ x 5⅞" (12.4 x 26.5 x 15 cm). Unmarked. V&A C.101–1966

Acquired in 1966 at a time when the Museum was showing a new interest in the mid-eighteenth-century Rococo style, this appealing piece links Nicholas Sprimont's Chelsea porcelain factory to the painter William Hogarth and the sculptor L. F. Roubiliac. An icon of Englishness, the figure combines a popular English animal subject with the names of two major figures in the history of English art.

The figure of Hogarth's much-loved pet dog Trump is based on a lost terra cotta by Roubiliac that was originally associated with the sculptor's bust of Hogarth (now in the National Portrait Gallery). Casts and molds of pugs and dogs are recorded at the sale that followed Roubiliac's death in 1762; some of these must have passed into the hands of Richard Parker, a dealer in plaster casts, who subsequently sold a "Pug Dog" to Josiah Wedgwood.

By linking Hogarth, Roubiliac, and Sprimont, a silversmith who transferred his skills to porcelain at his Chelsea factory, *Trump* provides a vivid illustration of the interconnections among a group of artists who congregated at Slaughter's Coffee House and at the St. Martin's Lane Academy in London's Soho district, and who were seen as pioneering the Rococo style in England.

The figure of *Trump* intersects a number of points of scholarship significant to the Museum's collections: archival research on English sculpture (for example, establishing that Sprimont

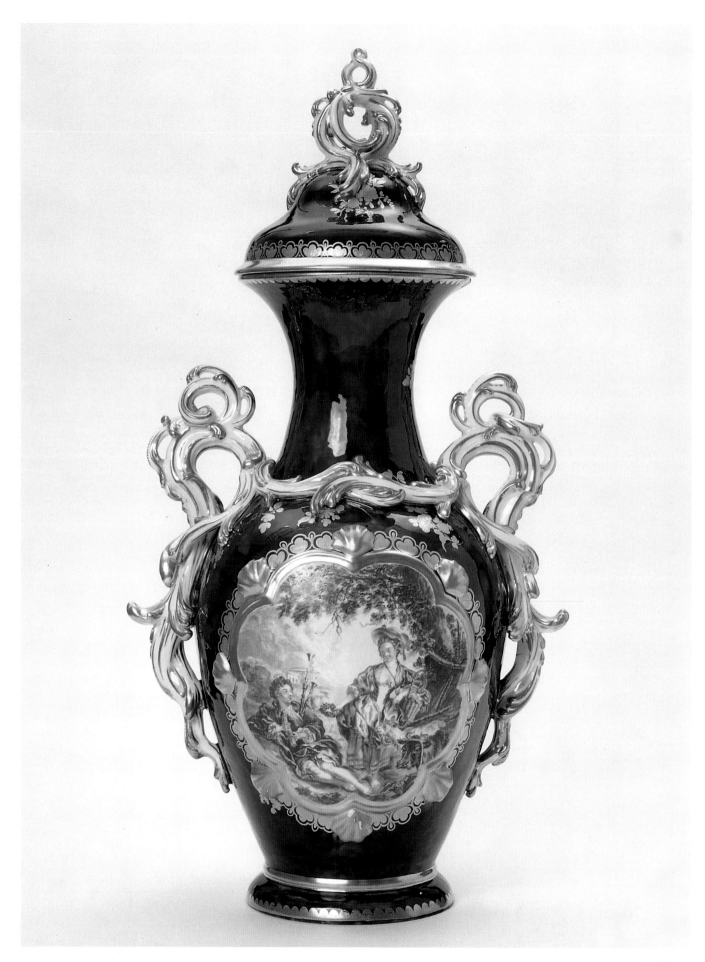

143. (front)

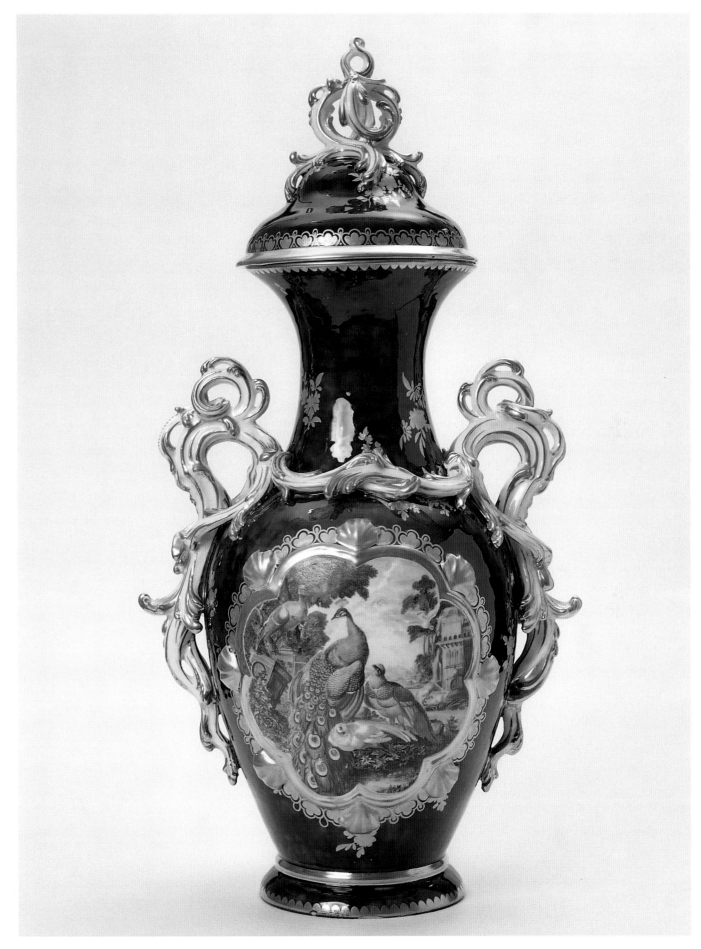

144. (back)

was the godfather of Roubiliac's daughter); interpretation of the decorative arts in terms of a sequence of period styles; a more recent focus on the consumption of luxury objects and its relationship to social history; and a renewed interest in such a piece as evidence of the relationship between the porcelain factories and the London plaster shops. In addition, the discovery of documentation indicating Roubiliac's interest in using Chelsea porcelain in one of his monuments in 1745 has prompted a reappraisal of the relationship between this important sculptor and the equally important Chelsea porcelain factory.

Lit. Mallet, 1967; Snodin, 1984, cat. E4; Baker, forthcoming

HILARY YOUNG

143. English (Chelsea). *The Foundling Vase.* c. 1762–63. Soft-paste porcelain, painted in enamel colors in reserves on a Mazarine blue ground, and gilt, 23⅝ x 11⅜ x 9½" (60 x 29 x 24 cm). Unmarked. V&A C.52&A–1964

By adding this ornate vase and its companion (cat. 144) to the Museum's collection of Chelsea porcelain, the curators of the 1960s were revising the accepted canon of English porcelain by giving prominence to a style and type that had been held in low esteem by twentieth-century collectors. The vase, one of six similarly decorated and extremely ambitious pieces to survive, was presented in 1763 to the Foundling Hospital, which housed Britain's first public art gallery. It remained there until it was bought in 1869 by the earl of Dudley, who had acquired its pair, the Chesterfield Vase (cat. 144), in the previous year. The two vases were widely exhibited in the 1850s and 1860s, when the opulence of their Rococo scrollwork embellishments, rich enameled decoration inspired by engravings by French painter François Boucher, and lavish use of burnished gilding—all heavily influenced by Sèvres porcelain of the years around 1760—were much admired. At the sale of the earl of Dudley's collection in 1886, they failed to reach the very high reserves placed on them, and on being returned to Dudley House their whereabouts became unknown to scholars.

By the time the pair of vases reappeared on the London art market in 1963, taste had evolved and the simplicity of the earlier "triangle," "raised-anchor," and "red-anchor"—referring to the marks used by the factory between 1745 and 1758—Chelsea wares was preferred. Many in the 1960s would have embraced connoisseur Horace Walpole's much-quoted judgment on the well-known Mecklenburg-Strelitz dinner service (now at Buckingham Palace) of 1762–63—"the forms are neither new, beautiful, nor various"—to describe a great deal of "gold-anchor" period (1758–84) production. The vases clearly owe their whole inspiration to French art and design, and they were probably made as showpieces intended to demonstrate that the leading English factory could compete with those of France. Writing in 1963, one commentator condemned the "English Sèvres" of Chelsea as a "shabby provincial product."

Lit. Reitlinger, 1963, vol. II, pp. 168–9; Mallet, 1965

HILARY YOUNG

144. English (Chelsea). *The Chesterfield Vase.* c. 1762–63. Soft-paste porcelain, painted in enamel colors in reserves on a Mazarine blue ground, and gilt, 23⅞ x 12¾ x 9½" (60.5 x 32.5 x 24 cm). Mark: an anchor in brown enamel. V&A C.53&A–1964

The vase was made as the companion piece to the Foundling Vase (cat. 143), but remained unsold until the final sale of Nicholas Sprimont's remaining stock of the Chelsea factory in 1770. In 1862 it was in the collection of the earl of Chesterfield, who sold it to the earl of Dudley "for upwards of £2,000" in 1868. Like its pair, the Chesterfield Vase is decorated with pastoral subjects taken from engravings by the French painter François Boucher.

Lit. Mallet, 1965

HILARY YOUNG

145. English (Chelsea). *Tureen, Cover, and Stand in the Form of a Chicken.* c. 1755. Soft-paste porcelain painted in enamels, chicken 9⅞ x 13¾ x 8⅝" (25 x 35 x 22 cm), plate 18½ x 15¾ x 1" (47 x 40 x 2.5 cm). Marks: an anchor in red (twice). Given by Stephen, 6th Baron Lilford, in accordance with the wishes of his brother John, 5th Baron Lilford. V&A C.75 to B–1946

Strengthened by the acquisition in 1901 of the ceramics collection assembled in the 1850s for the Museum of Practical Geology, the Ceramics Department continued to benefit from individual bequests made with an awareness of the Museum's work on English porcelain factories. This charming tureen was

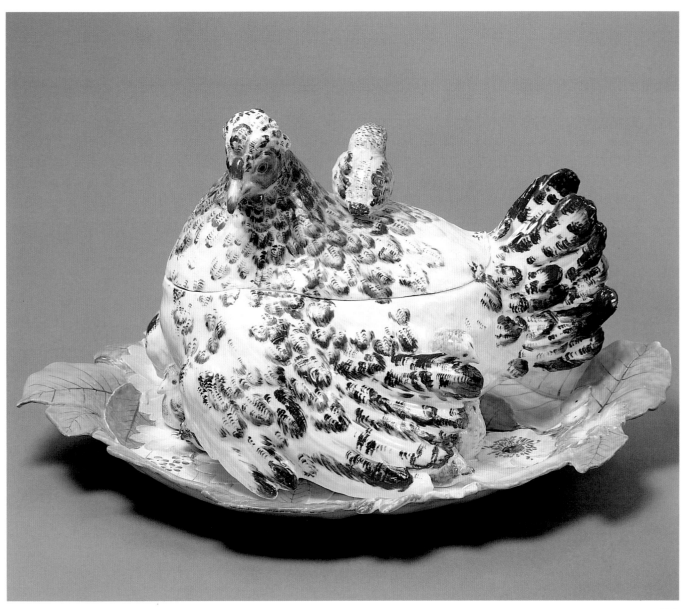

145.

probably the piece offered at the 1755 sale of Chelsea porcelain, where it was described as "A most beautiful tureen in the shape of a HEN AND CHICKENS, BIG AS THE LIFE in a curious dish adorn'd with sunflowers." Although apparently based on a print by the English artist Francis Barlow, the basic idea derives from the naturalistically modeled tablewares made during the 1740s at the great Meissen porcelain factory (founded 1710) near Dresden. The Meissen type is here translated into the English soft-paste material in which the sharpness of detailing characteristic of Meissen is muted, an effect much appreciated by connoisseurs of early English porcelain.

Lit. Honey, 1948a, p. 58 and plate 14B

HILARY YOUNG

146. English (Bow). *Chocolate or Coffee Pot.* c. 1760–65. Soft-paste porcelain painted in enamels, 12 x 8½ x 5½" (30.5 x 21.5 x 14 cm) high. Mark "To" impressed. V&A C.231–1993

This fanciful design is especially intriguing for the puzzle of its sources. The spout and handle recall coffeepots made at the Italian porcelain factory of Doccia in the middle of the eighteenth century; a Doccia service is in fact recorded at the sale of the Bow warehouse in May 1764, when it was described as "a rich and elegant Tea and Chocolate Equipage, of the curious and rare Tuscan Manufactory. . . ." Although Rococo shellwork is common in Doccia porcelain, all known Doccia pots lack both the scrolled upturned cover (a shape rarely found on ceramic coffeepots), and the Rococo scrollwork and cartouches that

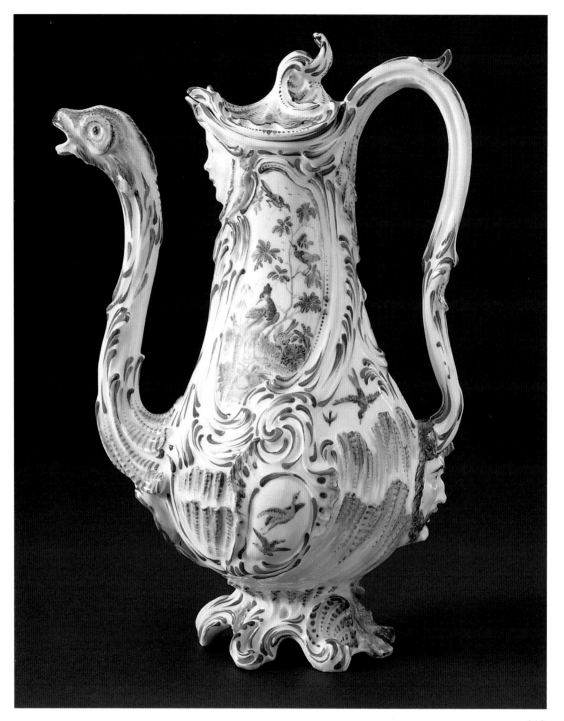

146.

enliven the body. Similar Rococo scrollwork occurs in mid-eighteenth-century silversmiths' work, in which zoomorphic spouts and high-looped handles are found. (The latter two features are particularly common on Italian silver coffeepots of the 1750s and 1760s.) As Italian silver was clearly an important influence on the design of the lobed Doccia coffeepots of the 1750s, it may be that the Bow design derives from a silver prototype by way of a Doccia adaptation. The scrolled base, however, occurs on other Bow productions of the early 1760s, on occasions in

combination with the same mark—"To"—impressed on the foot of this piece. The significance of this mark has been the subject of a great deal of speculation, but is thought to be that of a craftsman who worked as a modeler and a "repairer" (the workman who assembled the objects from piece-molds prior to firing), and who worked at a number of porcelain factories.

This relatively recent acquisition was made in part so that the English porcelain collection would include an unusually exuberant form of Rococo, of a type that the Museum had only begun to collect in other materials with the purchase of the Ashburnham Centerpiece (cat. 147). The Bow coffeepot was also seen as a way of linking the British and Continental collections. With its looped handle and body overrun by wildly asymmetrical scrollwork, the pot takes a Rococo theme to an extreme rare in English porcelain.

Lit. Tait, 1963, p. 209

HILARY YOUNG

147. NICHOLAS SPRIMONT (English, probably born Liège [modern Belgium], 1716–1771 [in London by late 1730s]), perhaps working in collaboration with PAUL CRESPIN (English [London], 1694–1770). *The Ashburnham Centerpiece.* 1747. Silver, 18¼ x 23⅞ x 22" (46.5 x 60.8 x 56 cm). Mark of Nicholas Sprimont. Purchased with the assistance of the National Art Collections Fund. V&A M.46–1971

When the Ashburnham Centerpiece, commissioned in 1747 by an English earl from a foreign-born designer and silversmith, was acquired in 1974, it was only the second major example of

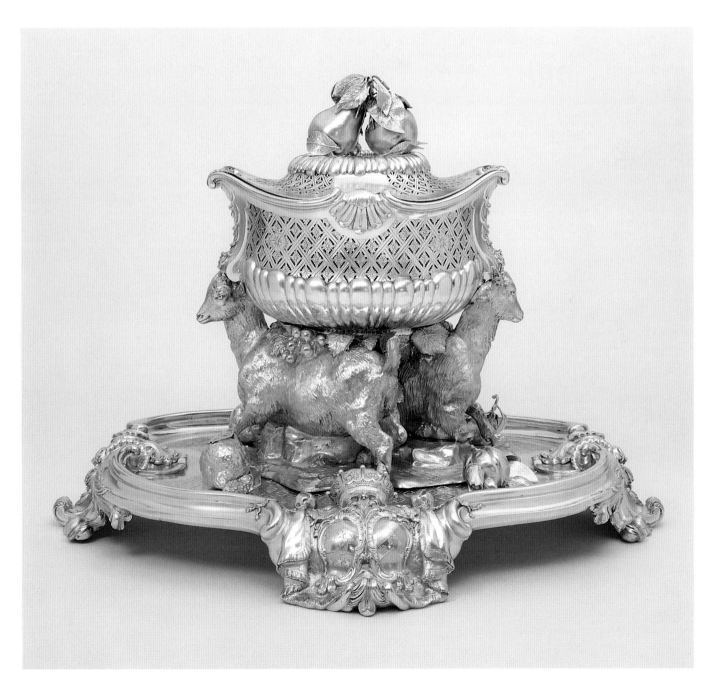

147.

English Rococo silver to enter the Museum's collection. Named after John, second earl of Ashburnham, whose arms are engraved on it, the centerpiece was made by Nicholas Sprimont, best known as the manager from 1748 of the newly founded Chelsea porcelain factory. His personal vocabulary in both silver and porcelain included decorative motifs of carefully modeled, naturalistic fruit and animals like those on this centerpiece.

The silver centerpiece or epergne was the most costly and elaborate item on fashionable dinner tables in Europe from about 1700. Originally devised at the court of Louis XIV as a composite object and a container for soup or a hot dish, the form became increasingly ornamental and fanciful by 1740. In the Ashburnham example, a pierced covered bowl rests on two kids, echoing a design of two hundred years earlier for a saltcellar by the much-admired Italian Renaissance artist Giulio Romano. A similar theme was used on a centerpiece made for the duke of Somerset by Sprimont's Soho neighbor, Paul Crespin, in 1746 (indeed, the relationship between the Ashburnham and the Somerset centerpieces has been much debated by scholars). This plundering of the past for design motifs is characteristic of the best English Rococo silver, which was inventive and eclectic at the same time.

When the Ashburnham family silver was sold in 1914, the centerpiece was purchased by an American collector. Until after World War II, important Rococo silver was rarely featured in exhibitions. There was a residual English collectors' distaste for what were seen by Charles Eastlake (internationally influential English architect, critic, and designer) and other High Victorian aesthetes as the wilder fantasies of the Rococo—a view that was partly due to the heavy-handed late Georgian and Victorian reinterpretations of the style in all mediums. The tone of Charles Oman's comment on Rococo silver in the first edition of his *English Domestic Silver* (1934) is characteristic of the prevailing attitude toward "imported" ornament: "The monumental centrepiece naturally found favour in the 19th century which gloried in massive effects. . . . We may allow a tempered admiration for some of those produced within our period." Oman later became a great admirer of Sprimont's silver and recognized the close links with Crespin as early as the 1950s, but until the 1970s the V&A had only one outstanding example of Rococo silver, Charles Kandler's Kettle on Stand, which was on loan from 1925 and purchased in 1939.

Lit. Oman, 1934; Grimwade, 1974

PHILIPPA GLANVILLE

148. After a design by GEORGE MICHAEL MOSER. English [London], born Switzerland, 1706–1783). *Apollo and Daphne Candlesticks.* c. 1743. Silver, each 14⅝ x 7⅛ x 6⅞" (37 x 18.1 x 17.5 cm). Unmarked. V&A M.329–1977

The conceit of a candlestick designed as a figure holding a candlestick is an ancient one, although the earliest such forms to survive in silver date only from the late seventeenth century. This pair, unusually refined in design and modeling, takes its subject from Greek mythology: the nymph Daphne, amorously pursued by the Olympian god Apollo, prays for rescue and is transformed into a laurel tree by Gaea, the primal goddess, the mother of all things.

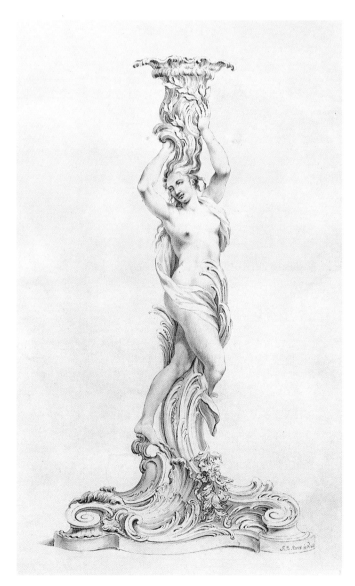

Fig. 116. G. M. Moser. *Design for a Candlestick in the Rococo Style, Incorporating the Figure of Daphne Turning into a Laurel Tree.* Pen and ink and brown wash, 13¾ x 7¾" (34.9 x 19.7 cm). V&A E.4885–1968

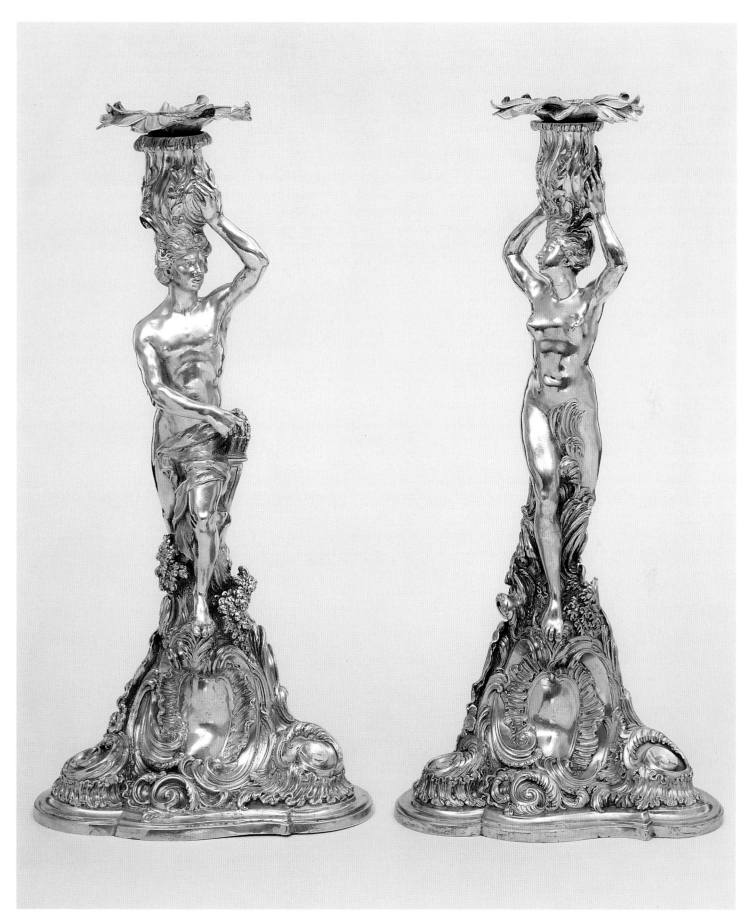

148.

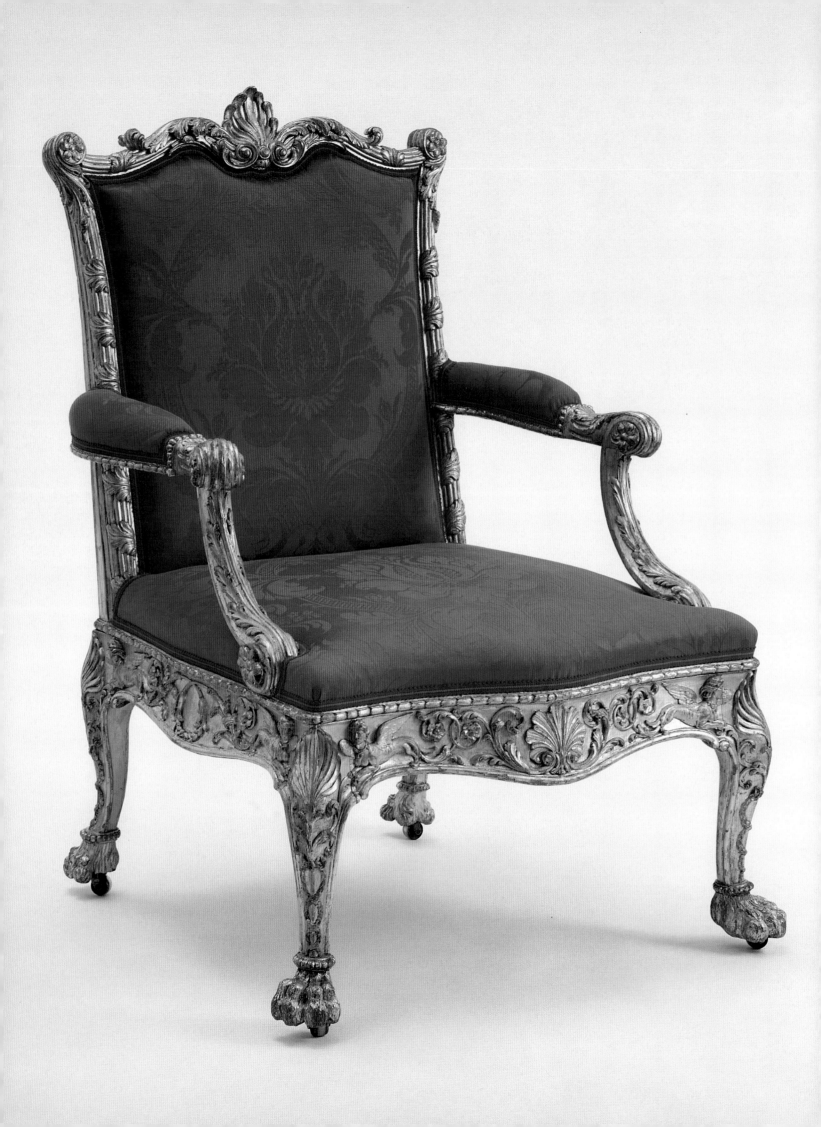

Felicitously, the Apollo and Daphne Candlesticks related to a drawing by George Michael Moser already in the V&A collection, thus making the pair an especially desirable acquisition. There are many works in the Museum collection that are represented by original design drawings, offering rich opportunity for firsthand comparisons between an object's design and its final form. Acquisition of the Moser candlesticks, however, also marked a shift of aesthetic attitude. Until at least the 1960s, this type of English Rococo work had been dismissed by V&A curators as no more than an interesting aberration.

Although Moser's drawing for the Daphne candlestick (fig. 116) has been described "more as a pleasant *jeu d'esprit* of the artist than as a sober design for execution by a working goldsmith," the drawing nonetheless attributes the design to this Swiss modeler and enameler who taught life drawing in London at St. Martin's Lane Academy. Founded as a drawing school for artists and craftsmen in 1735, the Academy was one of the key centers for exploring and disseminating new design ideas in England. As scholarly work on the English Rococo developed, the Academy's members—including Moser—were increasingly seen as important for an understanding of this style.

Lit. Grimwade, 1974; Snodin, 1984, p. 70

PHILIPPA GLANVILLE

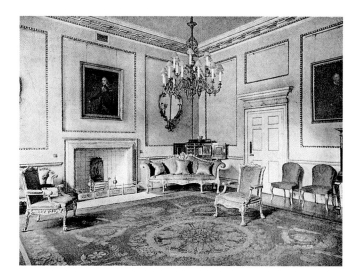

Fig. 117. Interior of the house of Sir Lawrence Dundas, showing two of the seven chairs and two of the four sofas from the original Adam/Chippendale suite (*Country Life*, September 1921, p. 350)

149. Designed by ROBERT ADAM (Scottish, 1728–1792 [active London 1758–92]); made by THOMAS CHIPPENDALE (English, 1718–1779). *Armchair.* 1764–65. Walnut and beech, carved and gilded, 42⅜ x 30⅜ x 31⅛" (107.5 x 77 x 79 cm). V&A W.1–1937

This imposing chair was part of a set with seven other chairs and four sofas (fig. 117) from the house of Sir Lawrence Dundas at 19 Arlington Street, London, all of which were sold during the 1930s when the dispersal of country house collections and the demolition of many aristocratic London townhouses led to the sale of much important English furniture. Designed by Robert Adam for an interior that he also designed, the chair was proudly presented by the Museum as an iconic work of the late-eighteenth-century architect.

The association of the suite with an Adam design (a watercolor design, dated 1764, for one sofa, is among the Adam drawings in Sir John Soane's museum) was made in 1922 by Arthur Bolton in *The Architecture of Robert & James Adam,* where it was suggested that the suite was the work of the cabinetmaker Samuel Norman. Bolton's book crystallized the admiration for Adam that had developed in the late nineteenth century, using the large body of surviving drawings to make firm attributions to Adam with unusual documentary precision. It was Bolton's

discovery of the design that allowed the chair to be claimed for England, though "hitherto regarded as French."

In 1936 the Museum had received architectural woodwork and plasterwork from the Adam brothers' speculative development at London's Adelphi. Its demolition was to provoke outrage among those concerned with architectural preservation. The purchase of this chair a year later, however, generated little comment: it was assumed to be an important document of English design, and its acquisition brooked no dissent.

A further significant connection was established in 1967 when Anthony Coleridge's archival research linked the chair to a suite that had been described in a bill of 9 July 1765 from Thomas Chippendale to Sir Lawrence Dundas. According to this document, the chairs were "exceedingly Richly Carv'd in the Antick manner" and cost the very large sum of £20 each. This was not only the single recorded instance of Chippendale working to Adam's designs but, equally significant, it was the cabinetmaker's first use of the term "Antick" to describe his furniture. Evidently, Chippendale was proud of his interpretation of Adam's design in the emergent Neoclassical taste.

Already associated with Adam, and then with Chippendale, the iconic significance of the suite soared as it was recognized as the only fully documented evidence of a collaboration between these two preeminent figures in the history of decorative arts in Britain.

Lit. Bolton, 1922, vol. II, pp. 291, 293; Coleridge, 1967; Tomlin, 1972, pp. 2–3; Gilbert, 1978, pp. 154–60; Wilk, 1996, p. 118

SARAH MEDLAM

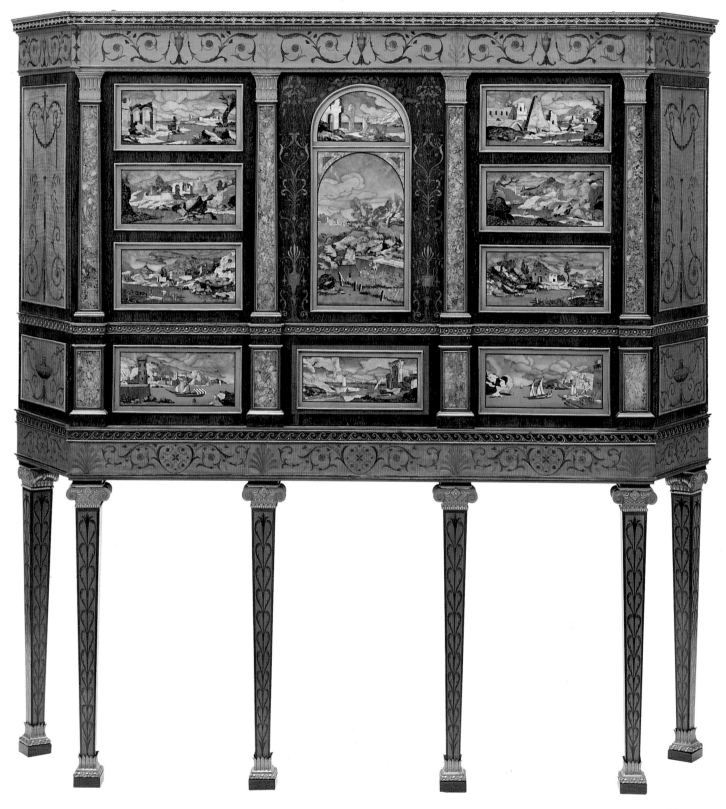

150.

150. Designed by ROBERT ADAM (Scottish, 1728–1792 [active London 1758–92]); made by INCE AND MAYHEW with mounts by BOULTON AND FOTHERGILL. *The Kimbolton Cabinet.* 1771–75. Mahogany and oak, with marquetry in satinwood, rosewood, and other woods, inset panels of *pietre dure* and ormolu (gilt-brass) mounts, 74⅜ x 71⅝ x 14⅜" (189 x 182 x 36.5 cm). Inscribed "Baccio Cappelli Fecit anno 1709 Fiorenza." V&A W.43–1949

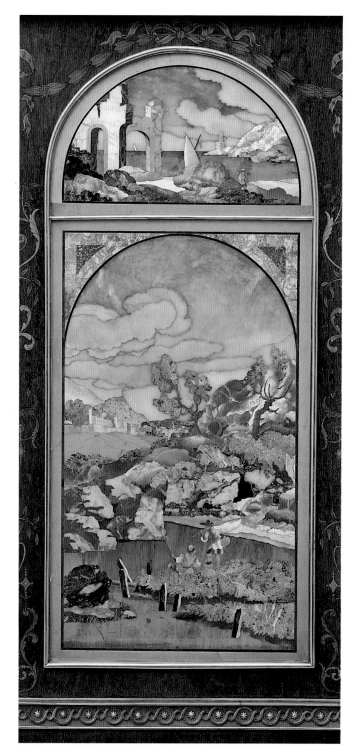

150. (detail)

The Kimbolton Cabinet was given a key place in the history of English furniture in the 1920s, status that has been reinforced by its prominent position in the Museum since its acquisition in 1949. It was made for the duchess of Manchester for Kimbolton Castle, Northamptonshire, to display eleven Florentine *pietre dure* (hard stone inlay) panels made by Baccio Cappelli in 1709. It is not known how these marble panels, depicting romantic seascape and mountainous pastoral scenes, came into the possession of the duchess, but they were the type of souvenir frequently bought by young Englishmen while on the grand tour of Europe. The duchess commissioned the architect Robert Adam to design the cabinet; a related Adam design in the Soane Museum is dated 1771 and inscribed "Design of a Cabinet for Her Grace The Duchess of Manchester." The cabinet was made by one of the largest cabinetmaking firms of the eighteenth century, Ince and Mayhew, with fine ormolu (gilt-brass) mounts by the Birmingham metal manufacturers Boulton and Fothergill. The panels are arranged to suggest drawer and cupboard fronts, although the only real doors are the two in the angled ends.

The panels were the main focus of interest when the cabinet appeared in the 1857 Manchester "Art Treasures" exhibition, alongside other furniture inlaid with marble and semiprecious stones. Described then as a "monument of labour and materials misapplied," it was seen very differently in 1924 when Adam's eminence as a designer had been recognized and the cabinet was featured as one of the few color plates in Macquoid and Edwards's *Dictionary of English Furniture.* Illustration in the *Dictionary* became for many pieces of furniture a form of certification, and the V&A was not alone among museums in accepting this as a primary criterion for purchase. In 1949 Edwards, by then keeper of the furniture and woodwork collection, purchased the cabinet, and it was placed with other furniture by Adam (including cat. 149) in the newly created English Primary Galleries.

Lit. Macquoid and Edwards, 1924, p. 171; Boynton, 1966; Goodison, 1974, pp. 133–5, plates 52–62

CATHERINE S. HAY

151. English. *Commode.* c. 1750–55. Mahogany with padouk cross-banding, ormolu (gilt-brass) moldings, mounts, and inlay, 35⅜ x 63¼ x 28¾" (90 x 160.5 x 73 cm). Acquired with assistance from the National Art Collections Fund. V&A W.4-1956

This bombastic piece is linked, though without firm documentary evidence, with the famous Fonthill Splendens, Wiltshire, the sumptuous Palladian mansion built by Alderman William Beckford (1709–1770) between 1757 and 1770. Beckford's son William (1760–1844), one of the most significant of early-nineteenth-century collectors, demolished his father's house in 1805, and in 1796–1807 built on the family property the Gothic Revival extravaganza he called Fonthill Abbey, designed by James Wyatt. Family tradition, a description in *Gentleman's Magazine* (1801) of "Two library tables . . . of the most elegant construction and exquisite workmanship" sold in the 1801 Fonthill sale, and furniture mentioned in John Britton's account of an unnamed Wiltshire house identifiable as Fonthill Splendens all lead to an association between Beckford and these extravagant pieces of furniture.

The V&A's commode was probably sold with its mate at the first Fonthill sale in 1801, though the pair, it was reported, "hardly brought one half of what was expected of them." By the 1950s, such richly decorated objects were even more unfashionable than they had been in 1801. The commode was first associated with the cabinetmaker John Channon in 1966 when his signed brass-inlaid bookcases from Powderham Castle, Devon, 1740, became the key to the attribution of a group of mid-eighteenth-century English brass-inlaid furniture. Like the Powderham bookcases, the V&A commode is embellished with dolphin mounts; as a dolphin forms part of the crest of the Courtenay family, this led to speculation that the commode was made for the same patron as the bookcases, Sir William Courtenay

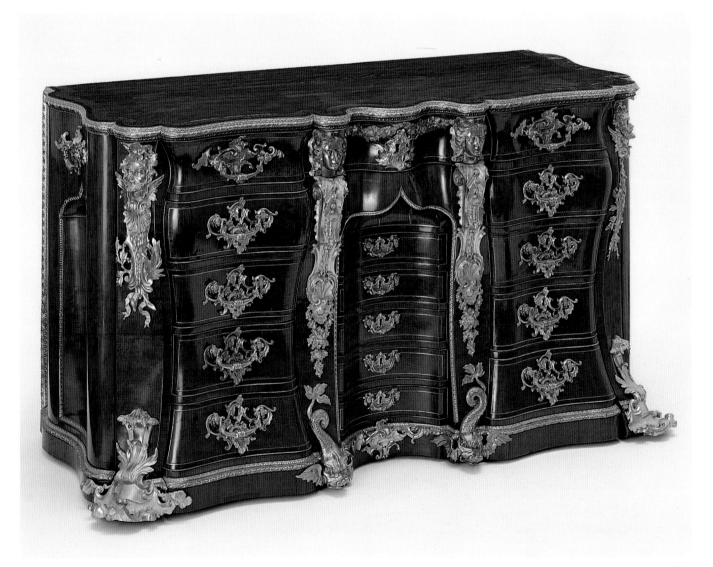

151.

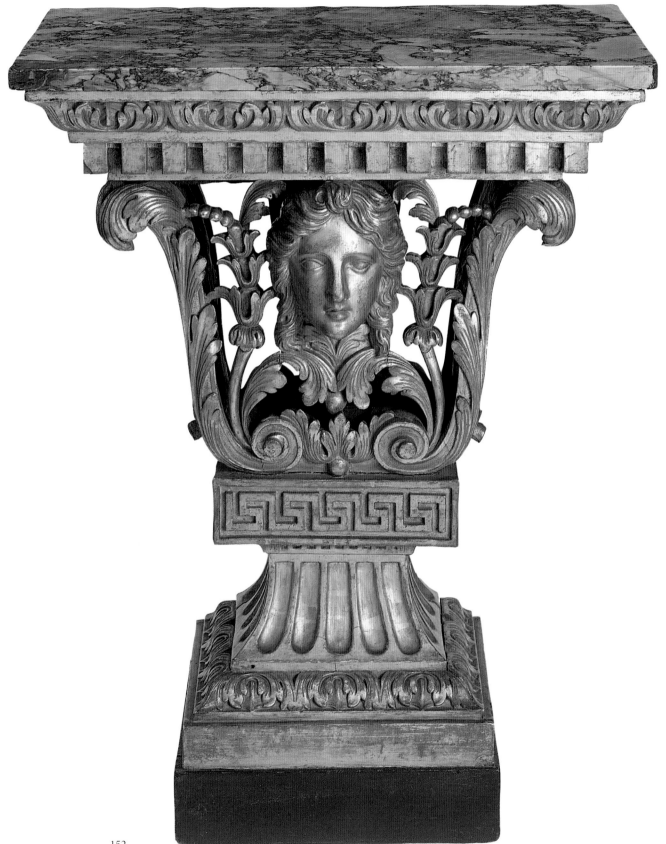

152.

(1709–1762). The dolphin link became tenuous, however, when the carved dolphin mounts on the Powderham bookcase plinths were recently found to be nineteenth-century additions.

The design of the commode is more sophisticated than the Powderham bookcases. Research undertaken for the recent exhibition "John Channon and Brass-Inlaid Furniture" uncovered seven other cabinetmakers whose workshops were producing brass-inlaid furniture in the mid-eighteenth century. Still, in the absence of more complete documentation, the authorship of this commode and related pieces remains uncertain.

Lit. Symonds, 1956; Hayward, 1965; Hayward, 1966; Gilbert and Murdoch, 1993, pp. 91–6; Gilbert and Murdoch, 1994

TESSA MURDOCH

152.
Designed by WILLIAM KENT (English, 1685–1748); probably made by JOHN BOSON (English, active 1720–43) for Richard Boyle, third earl of Burlington (1694–1753), for Chiswick House. *Console Table.* c. 1730. Gilt pinewood supporting a Siena marble slab, 35 x 27 x 17½" (88.9 x 68.6 x 44.5 cm). V&A W.14–1971

The Museum's acquisition in 1971 of this piece of furniture designed by William Kent for the earl of Burlington's Chiswick House acknowledged the importance of both a designer and a patron who are recognized as central figures in the development of English Neo-Palladianism. The acquisition of such a securely documented piece also reflected the growing concern of furniture historians from the 1960s onward about issues related to provenance and original setting.

The table was made for Lord Burlington's villa at Chiswick, west of London, built in the mid-1720s as an English response to Andrea Palladio's famous Villa Rotonda in Vicenza. Chiswick's interior was decorated and furnished under Lord Burlington's supervision to the designs of William Kent, whom he met on the grand tour in Italy. Chiswick became the touchstone of Neo-Palladian architecture, and Lord Burlington was known as the "Modern Vitruvius." The table is one of a pair, and passed through Burlington's daughter to the duke of Devonshire's family; its counterpart, like much original furniture from Chiswick, now forms part of the Devonshire collections at Chatsworth, Derbyshire. While still part of this collection, then at Devonshire House in London, the table was catalogued by V&A curator Oliver Bracket, and thus was well known to the Museum. During the next few decades the roles of Kent and Burlington received more attention, notably through the work of H. Avray Tipping, the editor of *Country Life;* Margaret Jourdain; and the architectural historian Rudolf Wittkower.

The reassessment of Kent and Burlington has been carried further by recent attempts to reconstitute the interiors of Chiswick House by placing some examples of the home's original contents (including this table) in their original settings. In making a long-term loan of this fine table to Chiswick House, the Museum is acknowledging the importance of understanding applied arts objects in context, that is, pointing up how the furniture was designed for and used in a particular interior. The display of furniture in period houses and its display in museums offer different but complementary perspectives on objects as form and function.

Lit. Vardy, 1740, plate 40; Brackett, 1919, nos. 6, 7; Wilk, 1996, p. 88

TESSA MURDOCH

153.
Designed by JOHN THURSTON (English, 1774–1822), modeled by EDMUND COFFIN (English, born 1761). *The Islington Cup.* 1802–03. Silver, parcel-gilt, 19¼ x 12¼ x 8½" (49 x 31 x 21.5 cm). London date hallmarks; presentation inscription engraved by John Roper; mark of the silversmith Joseph Preedy. Purchased with the assistance of the National Art Collections Fund, the Associates of the V&A, the Worshipful Company of Goldsmiths, the Islington Cup Appeal, and the citizens of the London Borough of Islington. V&A M.12–1987

This cup, every part of which is decorated with a trophy, symbol, or inscription, was purchased in 1986 following a public campaign led jointly by the V&A and a group of supporters that included the customers of the Canonbury Tavern in Islington, North London—an unusual consortium of local interests and a national museum. According to *The Times* on 23 January 1803, "A magnificent Silver Cup, of the value of 250 guineas" was presented at the Canonbury Tavern to Alexander Aubert, the commanding officer of the Loyal Islington Volunteers, a regiment of local part-time volunteers formed in 1797 in response to the threat from post-Revolutionary France. Alexander Aubert (1730–1805), whose arms the cup bears, lived at Highbury House, Islington, where he owned one of the finest observatories in Britain. The head of Mercury with a star above its forehead and the instruments on the base allude to Aubert's interest in astronomy, including the transit of Venus, which he observed on 3 June 1769. In addition to its local historical significance, the particular importance of the cup for the V&A was that the inscriptions provided a rare opportunity to identify the designer, modeler, and engraver, individuals who often remain anonymous even in the case of major commissions in silver.

Lit. Nelson, 1811, pp. 141–9; Culme, 1977, pp. 100, 130–1; Fox, 1992, no. 462

RICHARD EDGCUMBE

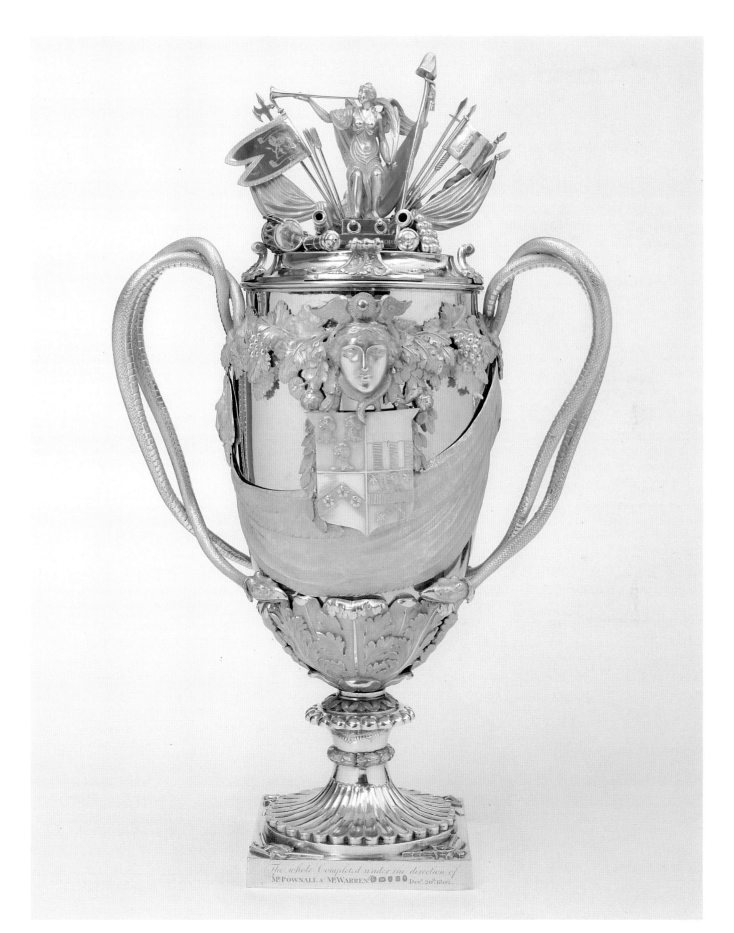

153.

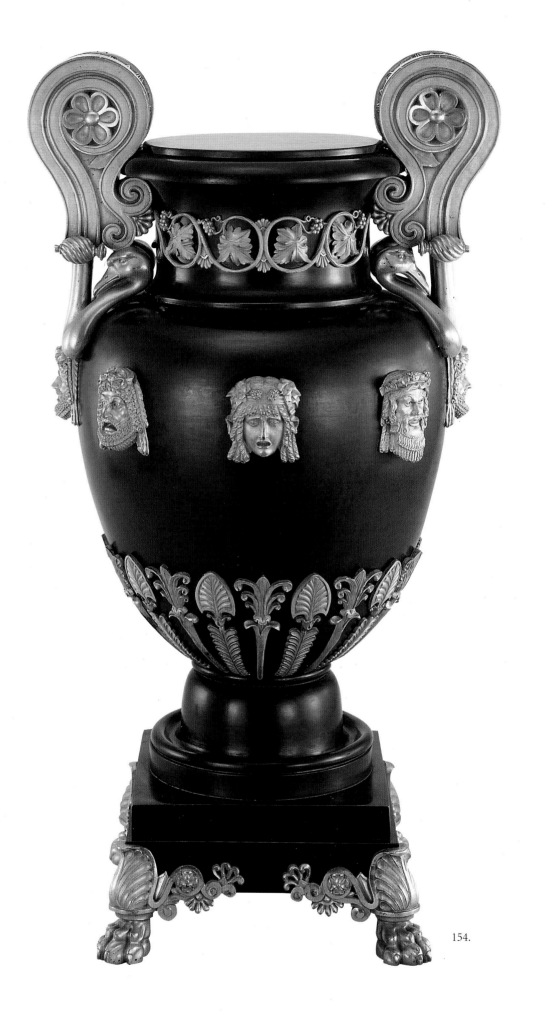

154.

154. THOMAS HOPE (English, born The Netherlands, 1769–1831 [London resident from 1795]); made by ALEXIS DECAIX, French (active in London 1794–1812). *Vase.* c. 1802–03. Patinated copper with ormolu (gilt-brass) mounts, 23¼" (59 cm) high, 13¼" (33.5 cm) diam. V&A M.33–1983

The revival of influential designer-collector-propagandist Thomas Hope's name and the Museum's acquisition of works designed by him form a significant part of the reevaluation of the Regency style that began among avant-garde collectors in the 1920s. When the contents of The Deepdene, Hope's country house in Surrey, were sold in 1917, their significance went unrecognized except by Edward Knoblock, the author of the musical *Kismet.* Knoblock's interest was shared by V&A curator H. Clifford Smith, who acquired some important Regency furniture for the Museum, including several pieces by Hope. Although interest waned in the postwar period, the collecting activities and publications of connoisseur Mario Praz led to Hope's work being featured prominently in the Council of Europe's "Age of Neo-Classicism" exhibition in 1972, part of which was presented at the Museum.

Based on the Greek krater form, this impressive vase is illustrated in Thomas Hope's *Household Furniture and Interior Decoration Executed from Designs by Thomas Hope,* published in 1807. In his introduction to the book, Hope describes how he employed Alexis Decaix—a *bronzier* and native of France—for "the more enriched portion" of his designs. This vase was made for Hope's London house, designed by Robert Adam, in Duchess Street (demolished in 1851), and was probably displayed in the dining room. The house was an outstanding example of Neoclassical design, and Hope's account of the house and its furnishings published in 1807 was a work of very considerable influence. The ormolu mounts are of extremely high quality and represent the work of a French *bronzier* at his best.

Lit. Chapman, 1985, p. 217; Wainwright, 1978

ANTHONY R. E. NORTH

155. CHARLES DICKENS (English, 1812–1870). All except cat. 155.3 bequeathed with the library of John Forster, 1876

155.1. *Manuscript: Bleak House* (Beginning of Chapter 46). 1853. 12⅜ x 11⅜ x 1⅞" (31.3 x 29 x 4.7 cm). V&A Forster MS 162

155.2. *Corrected Proof: Bleak House* (Beginning of Chapter 46). 1853. 10¼ x 7½ x 1⅞" (26 x 19 x 4.7 cm). V&A Forster 2412

155.3. *Monthly Serialization: Bleak House* (Beginning of Chapter 46). Published in serial form by Bradbury & Evans, London, beginning in 1852; Chapter 46, April 1853, Issue no. XIV. 8¾ x 5½ x ¼" (22.3 x 14 x .5 cm). V&A L.1041–1988

155.4. *First Complete Edition: Bleak House* (illustration for Chapter 46, "Tom all alone's," by Hablot Knight Browne [English, 1815–1882], called Phiz). Published by Bradbury & Evans, London, 1853. 8¾ x 5⅞ x ¼" (22.3 x 15 x .5 cm). V&A Forster 2411

Charles Dickens, one of the great fiction writers in English and the most popular writer of his time, is admired for the insightful character studies and sharp social awareness he evoked in novels like *Oliver Twist, David Copperfield, A Tale of Two Cities,* and

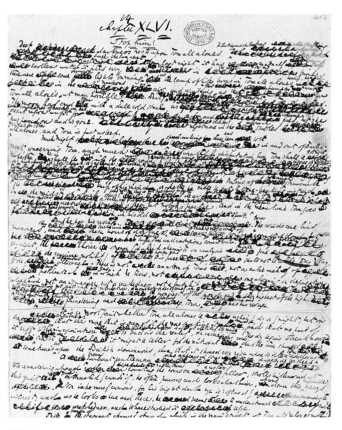

155.1.

"You do not think he is ill?" said I.

No. He looked robust in body.

"That he cannot be at peace in mind, we have too much reason to know," I proceeded. "Mr. Woodcourt, you are going to London?"

"To-morrow or the next day."

"There is nothing Richard wants so much as a friend. He always liked you. Pray see him when you get there. Pray help him sometimes with your companionship, if you can. You don't know of what service it might be. You cannot think how Ada, and Mr. Jarndyce, and even I—how we should all thank you, Mr. Woodcourt!"

"Miss Summerson," he said, and seemed more moved than he had been from the first, "before Heaven, I will be a true friend to him! I will accept him as a trust, and it shall be a sacred one!"

"God bless you!" said I, with my eyes filling fast; but I thought they might, when it was not for myself. "Ada loves him—we all love him, but Ada loves him as we cannot. I will tell her what you say. Thank you, and God bless you, in her name!"

Richard came back as we finished changing these hurried words, and gave me his arm to take me to the coach.

"Woodcourt," he said, unconscious with what application, "let us meet in London!"

"Meet?" returned the other. "I have scarcely a friend there, but now, where shall I find you?"

"Why, I must get a lodging of some sort," said Richard, pondering. "Say at Vholes's, Symond's Inn."

"Good! Without loss of time."

They shook hands heartily. When I was seated in the coach, and Richard was yet standing in the street, Mr. Woodcourt laid his hand upon his shoulder, and looked at me. I understood him, and waved mine in thanks.

And in his last look as we drove away, I saw that he was sorry for me. I was glad to see it. I felt for my old self as the dead may feel if they ever revisit these scenes. I was glad to be tenderly remembered, to be gently pitied, not to be quite forgotten.

CHAPTER XLVI.

Deep darkness rests upon Tom-all-alone's. Dilating and dilating since the sun went down last night, it has gradually swollen until it fills every void in the place. For a time there were some dungeon lights burning, as the lamp of Life burns in Tom-all-alone's—heavily, heavily, in the nauseous air, and winking—as that lamp, too, winks in Tom-all-alone's—at many horrible things. But they are blotted out. The moon has eyed Tom with a dull cold stare, as admitting some puny emulation of herself in his desert region unfit for life and blasted by volcanic fires; but she has passed on, and is gone. The blackest nightmare in the infernal stables grazes on Tom-all-alone's, and Tom is fast asleep.

155.2.

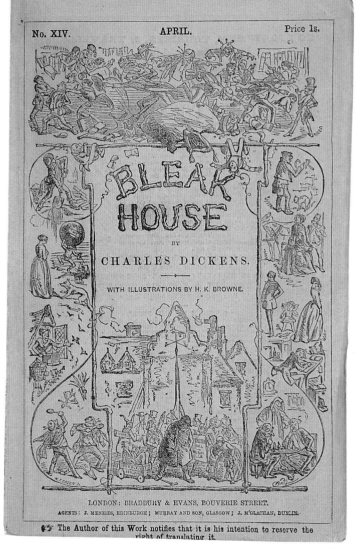

155.3.

"You do not think he is ill?" said I.

No. He looked robust in body.

"That he cannot be at peace in mind, we have too much reason to know," I proceeded. "Mr. Woodcourt, you are going to London?"

"To-morrow or the next day."

"There is nothing Richard wants so much, as a friend. He always liked you. Pray see him when you get there. Pray help him sometimes with your companionship, if you can. You do not know of what service it might be. You cannot think how Ada, and Mr. Jarndyce, and even I —how we should all thank you, Mr. Woodcourt!"

"Miss Summerson," he said, more moved than he had been from the first, "before Heaven, I will be a true friend to him! I will accept him as a trust, and it shall be a sacred one!"

"God bless you!" said I, with my eyes filling fast; but I thought they might, when it was not for myself. "Ada loves him—we all love him, but Ada loves him as we cannot. I will tell her what you say. Thank you, and God bless you, in her name!"

Richard came back as we finished exchanging these hurried words, and gave me his arm to take me to the coach.

"Woodcourt," he said, unconscious with what application, "pray let us meet in London!"

"Meet?" returned the other. "I have scarcely a friend there, now, but you. Where shall I find you?"

"Why, I must get a lodging of some sort," said Richard, pondering. "Say at Vholes's, Symond's Inn."

"Good! Without loss of time."

They shook hands heartily. When I was seated in the coach, and Richard was yet standing in the street, Mr. Woodcourt laid his friendly hand on Richard's shoulder, and looked at me. I understood him, and waved mine in thanks.

And in his last look as we drove away, I saw that he was very sorry for me. I was glad to see it. I felt for my old self as the dead may feel if they ever revisit these scenes. I was glad to be tenderly remembered, to be gently pitied, not to be quite forgotten.

CHAPTER XLVI.

STOP HIM!

DARKNESS rests upon Tom-all-Alone's. Dilating and dilating since the sun went down last night, it has gradually swollen until it fills every void in the place. For a time there were some dungeon lights burning, as the lamp of Life burns in Tom-all-Alone's, heavily, heavily, in the nauseous air, and winking—as that lamp, too, winks in Tom-all-Alone's—at many horrible things. But they are blotted out. The moon has eyed Tom with a dull cold stare, as admitting some puny emulation of herself in his desert region unfit for life and blasted by volcanic fires; but she has passed on, and is gone. The blackest nightmare in the infernal stables grazes on Tom-all-Alone's, and Tom is fast asleep.

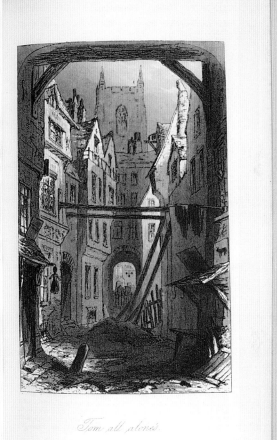

Tom-all-alone's

155.4.

Great Expectations, as well as a story beloved by generations of readers, *A Christmas Story.*

John Forster (1812–1876), a man of letters and scholar of seventeenth-century history, was a good friend of Dickens and acted as the writer's literary agent from the 1830s. Forster's library and collection of paintings were famous, the former especially for its "autograph collection." Collecting autographs was a cult activity in Victorian England, reflecting an interest in documenting outstanding individuals, also evident in the period's outpouring of *Life and Letters* biographies of notable Victorians (Forster published his own *Life and Letters of Charles Dickens* in 1872–74).

Forster bequeathed his library to the South Kensingon Museum in support of the educational movement represented by the institution, and the Dickens manuscripts became a major attraction in the Museum's display of the Forster collection. The Baedeker guide of 1881 refers to the Dickens material in a central case devoted to autographs in the room housing the Forster collection; the manuscripts were still on display in 1935.

Dickens's *Bleak House,* an indictment of the British legal system, was begun late in 1851. Its publication in monthly parts was a major public event: 30,000 copies of the first part were sold in March 1852, with later parts up to September 1853 reaching 40,000 and more. The progressive stages of *Bleak House* from manuscript to proof to first edition were all included in the Forster bequest.

Dickens wrote methodically between 9:00 a.m. and 2:00 p.m. every day; the manuscripts show him correcting and reworking the text as he wrote. Publication of novels in monthly parts became common in the 1840s; serialization allowed individuals to buy twenty issues at a shilling each over time rather than make a single payment of ten shillings for the conventional "triple-decker" three-volume novel. Like magazines, serial publications carried a variety of advertisements.

Phiz (Hablot Knight Browne) provided etchings for ten of Dickens's novels between 1837 and 1859. Dickens supervised Phiz's work closely, choosing the scenes to be illustrated and providing the captions. "Tom all alone's" was one of ten "dark plates" in the novel; fog, darkness, and shadow were meant to evoke the interminable mysteries of the courts and the tribulations of those involved in litigation there.

Lit. Cohen, 1980; Davies, 1983

Rowan Watson

156. Designed by William Burges (English, 1827–1881); made by Josiah Mendelson with gems and coins supplied by Richard A. Green for James Nicholson. *Decanter.* 1865–66. Glass bottle, mounted in silver, parcel-gilt set with rock crystal, malachite, mother-of-pearl, semiprecious stones, intaglios, and coins, 11 x 7½ x 5⅜" (27.9 x 19 x 13.5 cm). London date hallmarks; inscribed "JAMES NICHOLSON ANNO DOMINI MDCCCLXV." V&A Circ.857–1956

There can be no more handsome example of the work of William Burges, perhaps the most inventive and exuberant designer of the mid-Victorian period, than this richly ornamented and stylistically eclectic decanter. Burges looked to the arts of China, Assyria, ancient Greece and Rome, and medieval Europe as inspiration for the design. The most antiquarian of the exponents of the High Victorian Gothic, Burges used an exotic array of materials, from genuine antique coins and intaglios to colored glass and gemstones to create his opulent and dramatic effect.

The piece was ordered by James Nicholson through Richard A. Green, whose firm appears to have been largely concerned with the manufacture of jewelry. As a retailer, Green would not have made the decanter, though he probably supplied the expensive and unusual decorative embellishments, such as the semiprecious stones, Greek and Roman coins, and the large, rare piece of mother-of-pearl which forms the lion's head on the handle. The maker was the silversmith Josiah Mendelson.

Lit. V&A, 1952, no. J6; Wardle, 1963, plate 158; Mordaunt Crook, 1982, no. C47

Ann Eatwell

157. Designed by William Burges (English, 1827–1881); made by Harland and Fisher, London; painted by E. J. Poynter (English, 1836–1919). *The Yatman Cabinet.* 1858. Pine and mahogany, painted, stenciled and gilded, with metal leaf, lock and hinges of iron, 92⅞ x 55⅛ x 16" (236 x 140 x 40.5 cm). Given by Lt. Col. P. H. W. Russell. V&A Circ.217–1961

This splendid cabinet was commissioned from William Burges, along with two smaller side cabinets (V&A Circ.216–1961 and V&A Circ.218–1961), by H. G. Yatman, one of Burges's earliest and most important patrons. A serious medievalist, Burges based his design on the famous painted armoires he had seen in the cathedrals of Noyon and Bayeux in northern France. He adapted several medieval features for the Yatman cabinet, including a sloping roof and double folding doors, and revived an eleventh-century technique by covering the roof with layers of metal leaf and transparent paint. Burges's furniture is also dis-

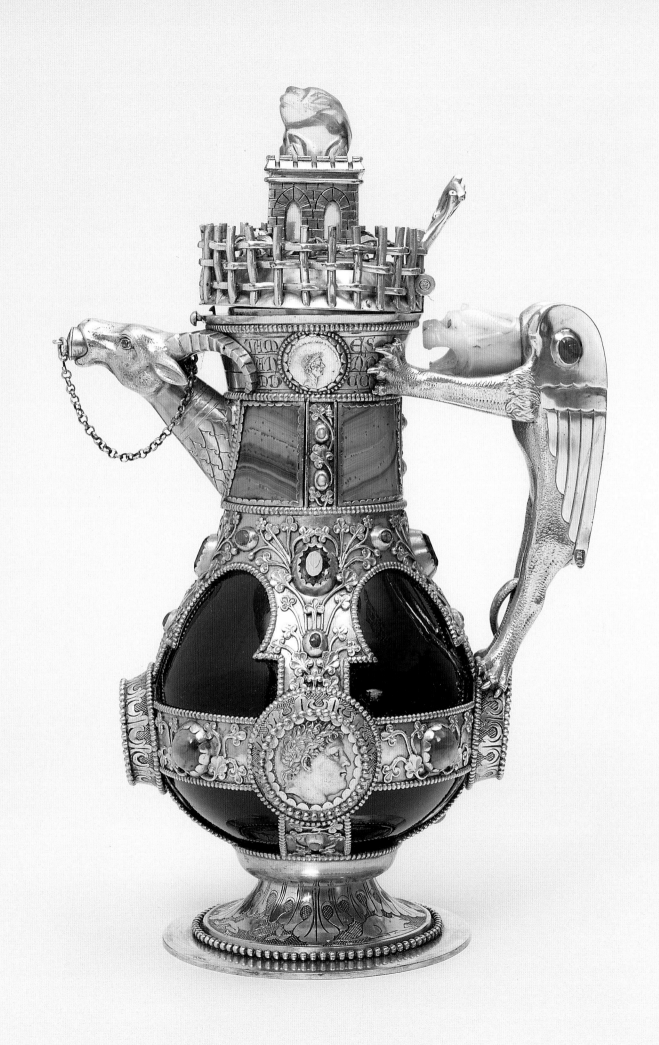

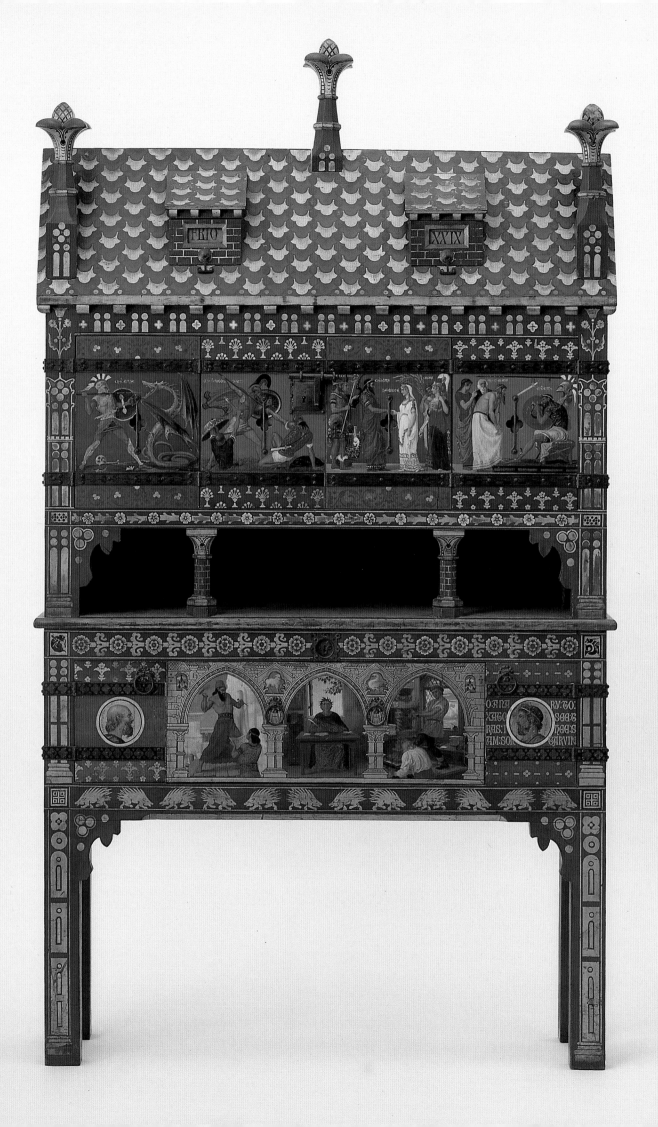

Opposite: Cat. 157.

tinguished by its iconographic painted decoration. This cabinet, fitted with a writing flap and pigeonholes, is painted with appropriately thematic scenes taken from classical and medieval history representing literature, the alphabet, and printing.

Lit. Mordaunt Crook, 1981, pp. 296–7; Wilk, 1996, p. 154

Frances Collard

shown together by 1908. By 1935, though still on display, *The Day Dream* was described in Muirhead's London guide simply as a "portrait" by Rossetti, evidently overshadowed in this later era by the French works in the Ionides collection.

Lit. Surtees, 1971, vol. I, pp. 153–4, vol. II, plate 388

Ronald Parkinson/Brenda Richardson

158. Dante Gabriel Rossetti (English [London], 1828–1882). *The Day Dream.* 1880. Oil on canvas, 62½ x 36½" (158.7 x 92.7 cm). Signed and dated "D. G. Rossetti 1880." Bequeathed by Constantine Ionides. V&A CAI 3

Dante Gabriel Rossetti was born in London, the son of a refugee Italian scholar. Poet (as was his sister Christina Rossetti), painter, and designer, Rossetti had a profound influence on English cultural life of the period. One of the founding members, in 1848, of the Pre-Raphaelite Brotherhood, Rossetti is credited with bringing to the movement its interest in the symbolism and mystical spiritualism of the art and literature of the Middle Ages.

A friend of the American-born artist James Abbott McNeill Whistler, who lived and worked in London from 1859, Rossetti in his later years came to share Whistler's idealization of women; Rossetti took as his feminine ideal the image of his wife, Elizabeth Siddal, who died in 1862. (His impressive portrait of her, painted in 1864 and now in London's Tate Gallery, *Beata Beatrix,* was titled after the romantic memorial character of Beatrice in Dante's *The Divine Comedy*). The art patron Constantine Ionides visited Rossetti's studio in the late 1870s and saw over the chimneypiece the artist's large chalk drawing of Jane Burden Morris (fig. 118), the wife of William Morris, which inspired him to commission *The Day Dream* (the title taken from the poem of the same name by Alfred, Lord Tennyson [see also cat. 9]), another highly romanticized female portrait and Rossetti's last masterpiece.

Ionides, whose grandfather had moved the family business of banking, shipping, and stockbrokering from Greece to London in 1815, was one of the principal collectors in England of contemporary art from the mid-1860s to his death in 1900. He bought an Edgar Degas at auction in Paris in 1881 some five years after it was painted, a late Gustave Courbet, and flower pieces by Henri J.-T. Fantin-Latour—the kind of modern art then unrepresented in any British public museum. Ionides was also interested in the work of contemporary British painters associated with the Pre-Raphaelite brethren, including Edward Burne-Jones as well as Rossetti. *The Day Dream* was included in the 1900 Ionides bequest to the Museum, all of which was being

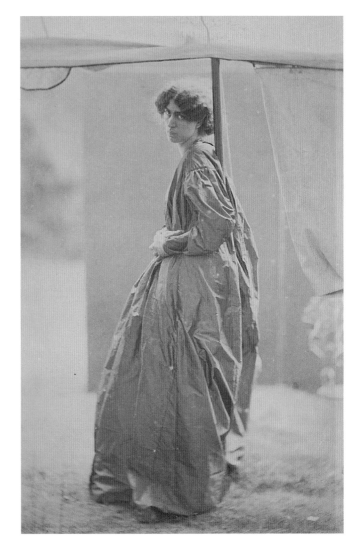

Fig. 118. Jane Burden Morris, the inspiration for Rossetti's *The Day Dream.* This image is from an album of photographs posed by Rossetti in his garden in Chelsea in July 1865 and taken by London studio professional John Parsons. Original albumen prints, 7¾ x 5⅛" (19.6 x 13 cm). Given by Dr. Robert Steele. V&A Ph.1735 to 1752–1939

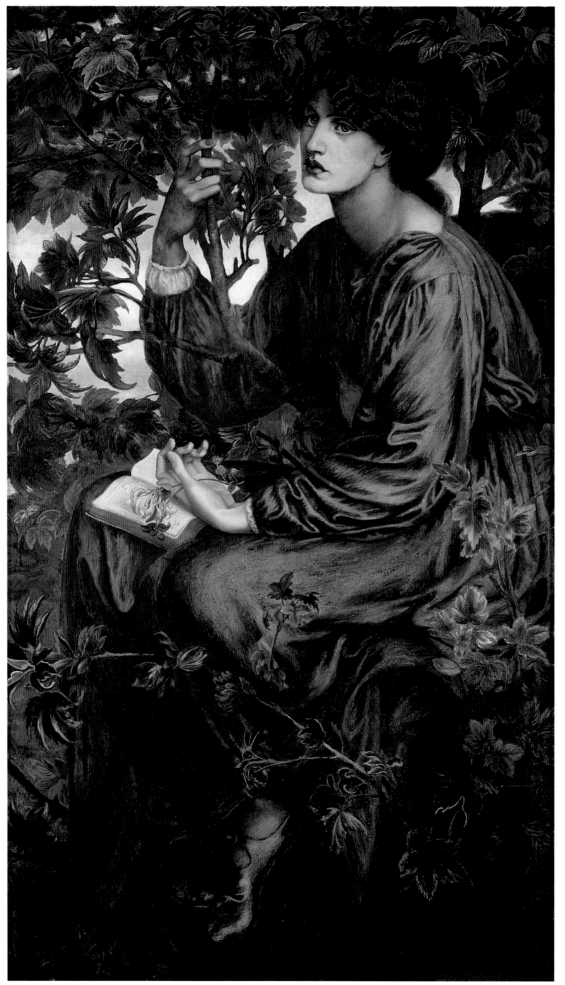

158.

159. Designed by Sir Edward Burne-Jones (English, 1833–1898) and John Henry Dearle (English, 1860–1932); made by Morris & Company (Merton Abbey Tapestry Works). *Pomona.* c. 1900. Tapestry-woven wool and silk on a cotton warp, 66½ x 43" (168.9 x 109.2 cm). V&A T.33–1981

William Morris (English, 1834–1896) is undoubtedly among the most beloved and internationally influential of all English designers. Ironically, Morris's influence derives more from his power and energy as a teacher, leader, and propagandist than as an artist. Morris first entered a partnership business in 1861 with designer Ford Madox Brown, painter Edward Burne-Jones, artist Dante Gabriel Rossetti, and architect and designer Philip Webb; he took sole control of the firm in 1875, when it became Morris & Co. Morris continued to collaborate with other artists and designers, executing many ambitious decorative schemes throughout England (including the exquisite Green Dining Room at the South Kensington Museum in 1866). Morris personally designed only a few figure pieces, for the most part confining his design work to layouts and backgrounds.

In 1881 Morris founded a print works at Merton Abbey, and from that date he worked seriously on the design and technique of textiles, including chintzes, carpets, tapestries, embroidery kits, and silk and wool fabrics. Burne-Jones was active at Merton Abbey, designing most of the figures used in tapestries woven by Morris & Co., including *Pomona.* Dearle, Morris's chief assistant for many years, increasingly took over his mentor's role at Morris & Co., and it was Dearle who designed the luxuriant background foliage and fruits of this and other major pieces. In his later years, Morris himself turned increasingly to fine book design and production (cat. 161), setting up his own press, the Kelmscott Press, in 1891, in which Burne-Jones was also an active design partner. Burne-Jones had first met Morris in 1855 when they were at Oxford; together they started a magazine, and at the same time Burne-Jones took up painting studies with Rossetti. From this youthful beginning, Burne-Jones and Morris forged a working partnership that endured for the remainder of their lives.

Few objects associated with Morris were acquired by the V&A during the nineteenth century, even from the 1870s until the artist's death, when he was actively using the collections of the Museum for his own inspiration and edification, and at the same time advising curators on the acquisition of objects, a role he took on informally, and at times officially. His advice was confined exclusively to what the officers of the Museum classed as "early" artifacts—medieval tapestries, sixteenth- and seventeenth-century Oriental carpets, and woven silks from both the East and the chief Mediterranean centers of production. He was never asked to comment on the acquisition of contemporary work nor, as far as records can be traced, did Morris ever volunteer such information. His association with the Museum was one of mutual respect and benefit, and he was one

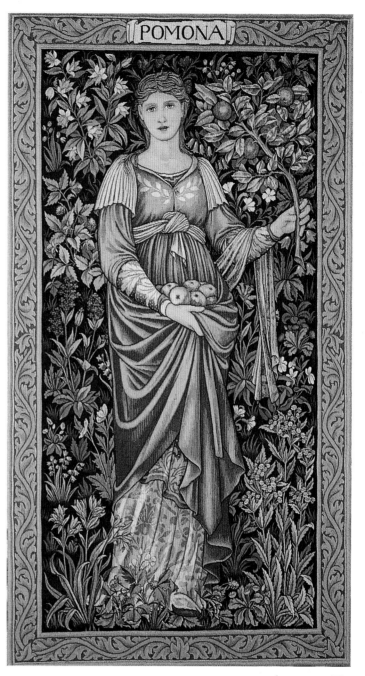

159.

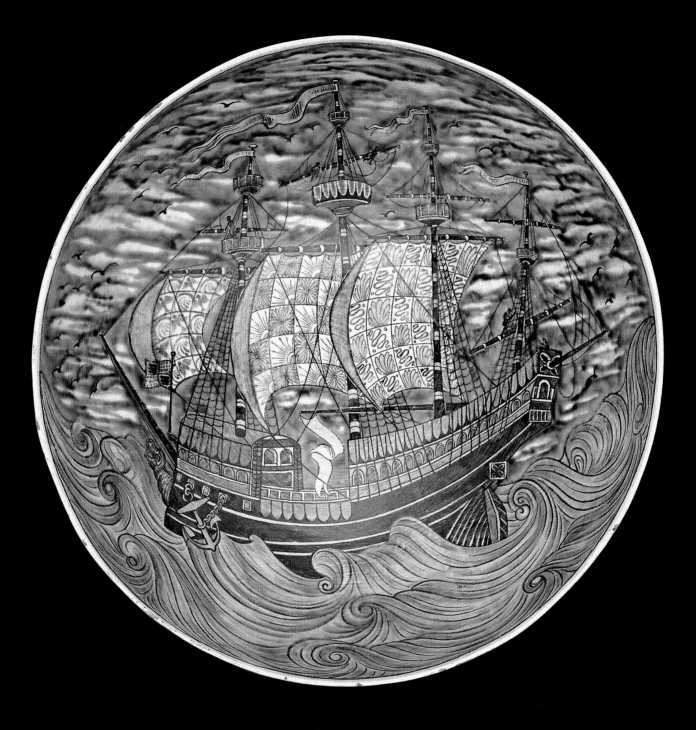

of its greatest supporters as well as most informed critics. One of his last public acts was a series of letters to the press vehemently opposing the removal of medieval tapestries (many of which he had helped the Museum to acquire) from their important central display area near the main entrance on the ground floor of the Museum to make way for a permanent exhibition of plaster casts.

Morris believed tapestry to be the most refined and worthwhile of crafts, "so deep, rich and varied, as to be unattainable by anything else other than the hand of a good painter in a finished picture." In 1893 Morris gave the Museum a personal gift of a miniature tapestry loom on which apprentices were taught the craft at Merton Abbey, clear indication of his view of the importance of the Museum's teaching role at this time.

Lit. Parry, 1983, p. 108; Parry, 1996, p. 29, cat. M126

LINDA PARRY/BRENDA RICHARDSON

160. Designed by WILLIAM FREND DE MORGAN (English [London], 1839–1917); made at the DE MORGAN POTTERY, Merton Abbey; painted by FRED PASSENGER (English, 1864–1935). *Bowl.* c. 1885. Earthenware, painted in colors, 18⅛" (46 cm) diam., 6⅛" (15.5 cm) deep. Marks: "F.P." painted in black. Presented to the Museum by Miss Evelyn Brooke in memory of her father, the Revd. Stopford Brooke. V&A C.78–1923

A designer of tiles and glass for the William Morris firm in the early 1860s, William De Morgan began to decorate pottery and was running his own successful firm in London by 1873. He was a close friend of Morris and is thus associated with the English Arts and Crafts movement. In 1882 De Morgan moved to Merton Abbey and established a pottery site near Morris's textile works. Characterized by flat, stylized plant and animal motifs drawn with great liveliness, De Morgan's designs were generally applied to the pottery forms by assistants.

De Morgan's most formative influences were not English or European but rather more exotic. This substantial bowl, painted in deep turquoise blues and purples, is an example of De Morgan's "Persian" wares. Described as a punch bowl, in both its generous proportions and the subject of the decoration—fantastic ships were one of his favorite subjects—it refers most closely to the celebrated Hispano-Moresque "ship bowls" of Malaga. De Morgan, with Morris, was part of a circle including Edward Burne-Jones and Dante Gabriel Rossetti that collected the ceramics and textiles of "Arabia" or "Persia," Spain, Turkey, and China. His richly colored and lustered pottery was inspired in particular by the lustered and ornamented wares of Persia,

the Iznik wares of sixteenth-century Turkey, and by Italian Renaissance majolica, although his depiction of quirky birds and animals belongs unmistakably to the Victorian world.

De Morgan ceased production in 1907, and by his death in 1917 he was better known as a novelist. When in 1923 De Morgan's daughter, Miss Brooke, wrote to the Museum saying that his work was "but poorly represented" in the Museum's collection and offering "many of the most beautiful pieces" by her father, ceramics curator Bernard Rackham chose four examples, including this striking bowl with its ship design evocative of travel to exotic foreign lands.

Lit. Stirling, 1922; John, 1951; V&A, 1952, no. I92; Pinkham, 1973, no. 24; Catleugh, 1983; Greenwood, 1989, plate 127

JENNIFER H. OPIE

161. Edited by F. S. ELLIS; illustrated by SIR EDWARD BURNE-JONES (English, 1833–1898); published by the KELMSCOTT PRESS, Hammersmith. *The Works of Geoffrey Chaucer.* 1896. Printed on paper, sheet 16⅞ x 11¾ x 2¾" (43 x 30 x 7 cm). V&A 757–1896

The Museum's library (the National Art Library) regularly acquired books from William Morris's Kelmscott Press at the time of publication, all of them in their simple quarter-linen binding with blue paper over boards, redolent of pre-Victorian English publishing. When the library was allocated an exhibition gallery in 1909 to display "the best examples of lettering, writing, illumination, types, type-ornaments . . . and bookbindings," the Kelmscott *Chaucer* appeared in a case devoted to "Modern British Presses."

William Morris had studied books all his life, and in 1888 an illustrated lecture at the Arts and Crafts Exhibition Society on fifteenth- and sixteenth-century Italian printing led him to embark on the designing and making of fine books. Morris's Kelmscott Press represents the artist's investigation of the whole process of making books: typefaces, paper, inks, page design, and printing methods were all examined anew. Controlling every aspect of the design process, Morris recruited and directed a number of highly skilled craftsmen experienced in every aspect of printing to make books by hand.

The Kelmscott *Chaucer*, published in an edition of 425 copies on paper and thirteen on vellum, was the Press's most ambitious production. Work on the book was mentioned in *The Athenaeum* as early as 1892; when the *Chaucer* was published— four months before Morris's death—the print run had been sold out in advance. The total investment in the work amounted to more than £7,218 over four years. Despite the high price of the *Chaucer* (£20 for paper copies, £126 for those on vellum), Morris

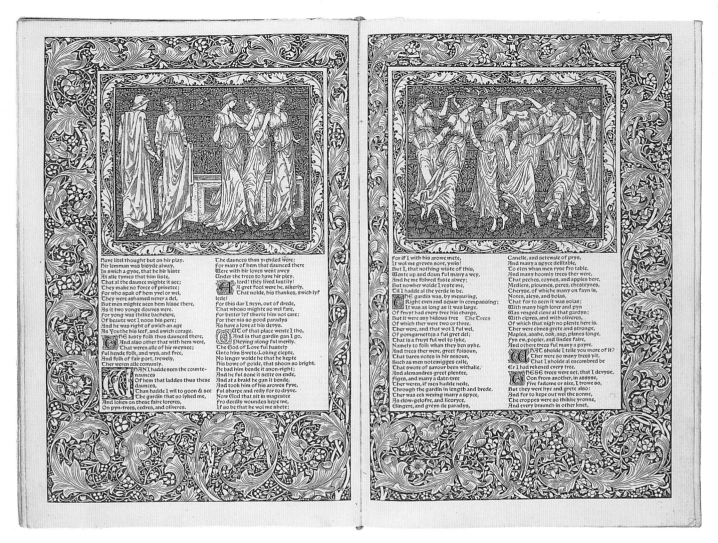

had to extend the print run by 100 copies as a means of meeting production costs. In the end, costs were met only from profits realized on other Kelmscott titles. A reviewer in *Library* (1896) described the work as "the finest book ever produced," one of many such panegyrics.

Lit. Isherwood, 1986; Peterson, 1991

Rowan Watson

162. C. F. A. Voysey (English, 1857–1941); made by Alexander Morton & Co., Darvel, Scotland. *The Owl.* 1898. Jacquard-woven woolen furnishing fabric, 57½ x 49½" (146.1 x 125.7 cm). Given by C. Cowles Voysey FRIBA. V&A T.11–1953

Although the designer C. F. A. Voysey epitomizes the Arts and Crafts movement at its most British, and he was enormously influential abroad, the Museum began to collect objects designed by Voysey only in the second half of the twentieth century. Exhibited at the Museum in 1952, this fabric composition of stylized owls was acquired with a number of other items from the designer's family shortly afterward. Trained as an architect, Voysey was one of the most original, versatile, and commercial of freelance designers. He produced an enormous number of designs for wallpapers, textiles, metalwork, and woodwork, and his repeating patterns were frequently duplicated in a number of different forms. This pattern was used for both wallpaper and woven fabric. Voysey was a shrewd businessman, adapting his work to fashion, and was under contract to the notable Scottish manufacturer Alexander Morton to produce a certain number of patterns each year.

Lit. Brandon-Jones, 1978, no. D13; Naylor, 1971, p. 66; Parry, 1988, p. 38

Linda Parry

162.

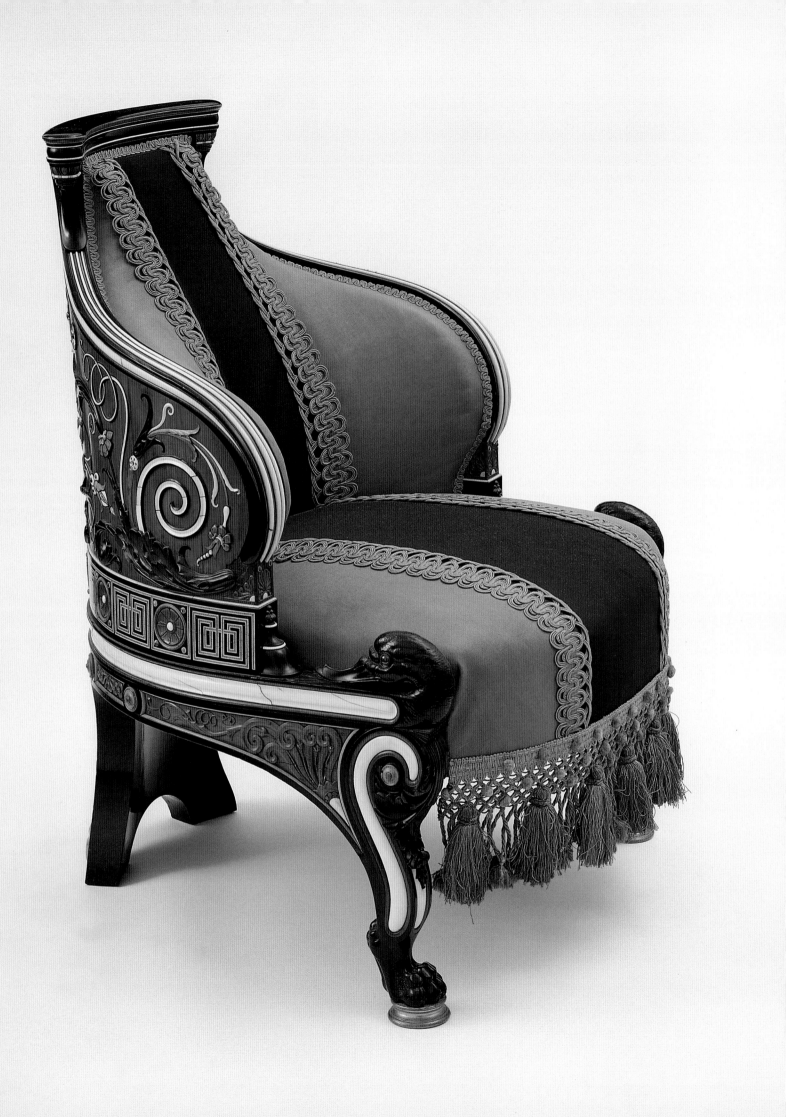

163. Sir Lawrence Alma-Tadema (English, born Friesland, 1836–1912); made by Johnstone, Norman and Company, London. *Armchair.* c. 1884. Mahogany with cedar and ebony veneer and inlay of ebony, sandalwood, ivory, boxwood, and abalone (replacement upholstery based on original evidence), 35⅜ x 27⅛ x 26" (90 x 69 x 66 cm). V&A W.25–1980

Although the Museum was collecting examples of furniture by influential Victorian designers such as William Burges (cat. 157) and Bruce J. Talbert (cat. 9) during the 1950s, 1960s, and 1970s, Alma-Tadema's work remained unrepresented. By 1980 the Museum's knowledge of the development of Victorian furniture design was sufficiently advanced to recognize this dramatic chair's importance as an example of late-nineteenth-century taste for elaborate Greco-Roman classicism.

The armchair is part of a large suite of Greek Revival furniture commissioned by the American collector Henry G. Marquand (1819–1912) for the music room in the Marquand residence at Madison Avenue and East 68th Street, New York. Alma-Tadema, a fashionable artist famous for his genre paintings set in ancient Greece and Rome, also designed the classical furnishings for the music room. The distinctive appearance of the furniture, their exotic materials, and the high quality of workmanship attracted favorable publicity on both sides of the Atlantic. Unusually, the furniture was displayed in Johnstone and Norman's Bond Street showroom and shown to the Prince and Princess of Wales before shipment to New York.

Lit. Kisluk-Grosheide, 1994; Wilk, 1996, p. 176

Frances Collard

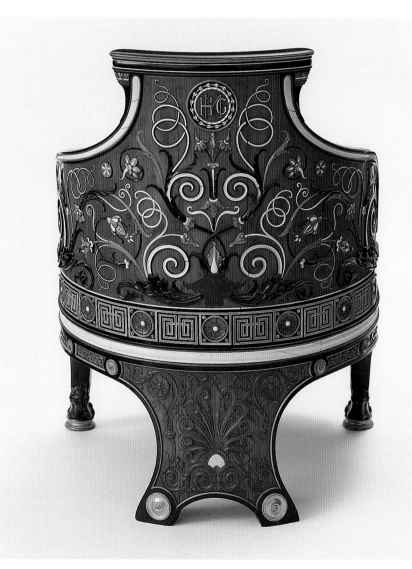

163.

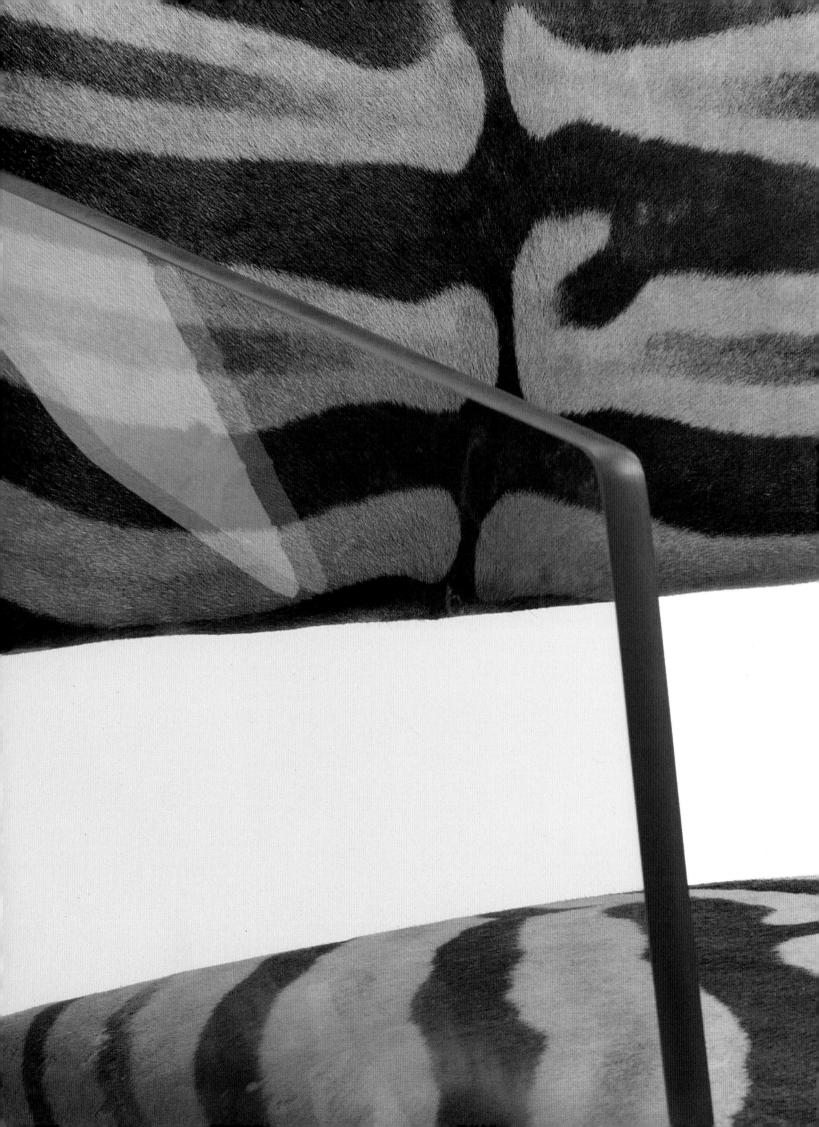

Collecting the
Twentieth Century

CHRISTOPHER WILK

THE STORY OF THE V&A'S COLLECTING OF TWENTIETH-CENTURY material and contemporary objects is largely an episodic one, undirected by museum-wide policies until quite recently.[1] It begins with the important gift of objects made for the Paris exhibition of 1900 but, with rare exceptions in a few departments, the Museum largely kept objects made during the twentieth century at arm's length until the late 1960s. The Circulation Department, established to generate exhibitions that could travel throughout Britain, then began collecting a much wider range of contemporary objects, in some cases with the encouragement of director John Pope-Hennessy (1967–74). During the directorship of Roy Strong (1974–87), the curatorial departments of the Museum actively began to collect twentieth-century objects, although the main impetus for this on a Museum-wide basis was, ironically, the 1977 closing of the Circulation Department, at which point its objects were dispersed throughout the V&A's respective materials-based departments. While the refusal to engage with design of the present might seem to conflict with the Museum's founding principles, it was hardly exceptional, since few institutions then actively collected recent design.[2]

Ironically, it was a traditional Bond Street antique dealer, George Donaldson, who was responsible for the Museum's first and, in many ways, most exciting purchase of contemporary decorative arts in this century (cats. 164–165). His gift of thirty-eight pieces of Art Nouveau furniture (and one ceramic object) personally selected from exhibits at the Paris Exposition Universelle of 1900 was welcomed by the Museum. By the time the collection was shown at the V&A in 1901, however, it was the subject of venomous attack. Despite support and interest from some in the art press, British architects in particular fulminated in the pages of *The Times,* the *British Architect,* and the *Architectural Review.* Significantly, the purchase was vehemently attacked by the Council of the Royal College of Art, and it was this criticism—from an influential body closely allied to the Museum by history and by virtue of the structure of government administration—that was particularly damaging. Despite great demand that the Donaldson collection travel to art schools, the Council's criticism resulted, initially, in a warning that students viewing the collection should consult their instructors before forming an opinion of it, and, in 1909,

Fig. 119. Detail of cat. 179, Denham Maclaren's glass and zebra skin chair of about 1930

in the transfer of the collection from South Kensington to the Bethnal Green branch of the Museum in East London.

The furor over the Donaldson collection had a profound impact on future Museum policy. Not only was the controversy public in nature but also, and even more significantly, it coincided with the deliberations about the nature of the Museum's collection and its redisplay. This culminated in the 1908 Report of the Committee on Re-arrangement, in which the case against collecting design of the previous half-century was set out under the heading of "Acquisition of Modern Specimens":

> It may occasionally happen that manufactured objects of say less than 50 years old may convey valuable artistic lessons . . . and it would be impolitic to exclude altogether such objects from the scope of the Museum. On the other hand, it is obvious that the principle of admitting modern specimens presents grave difficulties; taste is apt to change with time; and the admission of the work of any one living manufacturer or craftsman would not improbably expose the administration to attack from others, and even to the charge of advertising for ulterior ends.[3]

However, the Committee stopped short of an outright ban and reached the conclusion that "after full consideration, [the Committee members] are not disposed to make any definite recommendation on this point; but consider it would be better to leave such questions to be dealt with as they arise."[4]

The Museum distanced itself further from collecting and displaying new work when, in 1914, director Cecil Harcourt Smith (1909–24) proposed that the V&A refrain from collecting "modern industrial art." He proposed instead "a central Museum and Institute of modern industrial art," which was established following World War I, in 1920, as the British Institute of Industrial Art.[5] This act may accurately be described as the single largest factor in discouraging the collecting of modern design within the V&A during the post-Donaldson period; the Museum did not merely sidestep the issue—which would have allowed for serendipitous collecting or even a change in policy—but, instead, helped to establish an alternative organization to exhibit and collect contemporary design.

Although a classical scholar from the British Museum, Harcourt Smith wrote with conviction of the need of the State to promote "Art as applied to Manufacture" and devoted considerable time during his directorship and in his retirement to the new institute, even suggesting that it be located adjacent to the V&A.[6] He acknowledged that it was the Museum's policy to show "very little which is not at least 50 years old" and that "this break in continuity in a Museum which has for its principal object to illustrate and stimulate the craft of design and workmanship by means of the finest examples obtainable is, to say the least, unfortunate."[7]

Yet Harcourt Smith could not bring himself to consider this task as relevant to the Museum of his own time, agreeing with the 1908 report that perspective and distance are required in matters of taste (fifty years was the duration almost always mentioned), and that in showing contemporary work the Museum authorities "lay themselves open to the charge of using public funds to encourage selected tradesmen and give them advertisement at the expense of their rivals."[8] While Henry Cole and his colleagues enthusiastically embraced the Museum's connection with trade,

Harcourt Smith and some of his successors felt what might be described as the educated class's dread of commerce.[9]

Although the attribution of the Museum's retreat from contemporary collecting solely to the Donaldson affair is too simplistic, it was an important factor, especially within a civil service environment where maintaining equilibrium was prized. Larger cultural forces also played their part, though it is hardly surprising that they do not surface explicitly in Museum files. The Museum's new emphasis on historic British, specifically English, design, which began around 1900 and gained force in the decades after World War I (see pp. 277–83), both reflected a new form of romantic nationalism and mitigated against attention being paid to contemporary design.[10] This nationalism surely contributed to the antimodernism of British culture (still prevalent today), which, in general, was hostile to the influence of modernist, specifically foreign, architecture and design.[11] By contrast, the acceptance of modernist influence in Germany, France, and America was responsible for the spate of design exhibitions and museum collecting in those countries during the same period.[12]

The British Institute of Industrial Art (BIIA) eventually established a presence for modern design within the Museum, although the extent to which the BIIA was identified in the mind of the public with the V&A is difficult to gauge.[13] From 1922 (at the latest) to 1929, exhibitions of contemporary "industrial art" were mounted in the Museum's North Court, and accompanying catalogues were published. The Museum also organized traveling exhibitions for the BIIA. Starved of government funds, the BIIA closed in 1934; some of its collection was returned to lenders, and other pieces were transferred to the V&A.[14]

Mrs. Margaret Armitage, author (under her maiden name of Bulley) of numerous books on art appreciation, was foremost among the lenders of BIIA material that came to the Museum the year before the BIIA's closing. The Armitage collection, consisting mainly of textiles (cat. 178), glass, and ceramics, was the single largest gift of twentieth-century material to come to the Museum up to that time. It was a particularly unusual gift, since Mrs. Armitage had agreed with the BIIA and the V&A that, with consultation, she would be allowed to add to it, which she did from 1934 to 1956.[15] In general, however, the Museum's attitude to contemporary collecting remained distant. When the silver craftsman R. E. Stone, for example, sought an appointment to show a celebrated piece of his work to the keeper of metalwork, director Eric Maclagan wrote that the V&A "hardly ever acquires the work of living artists . . . [and] I fear that it is very unlikely that we should be able to contemplate its purchase."[16] Nonetheless, some new or recently made objects found their way into the collections.

During the 1920s and 1930s the Department of Engravings, Illustration and Design enthusiastically collected contemporary work in numerous fields. Its attention to contemporary printmaking, etching especially, was due to the interests of Martin Hardie (keeper 1921–35), a professional etcher who collected the work of distinguished practitioners and friends. Posters were also well represented (fig. 120), largely through the acceptance of numerous gifts from firms that commissioned innovative work (including, from 1911, the London Underground and, slightly later, Shell-Mex), as well as through the 1921 gift of Mrs. Joseph T. Clarke.[17]

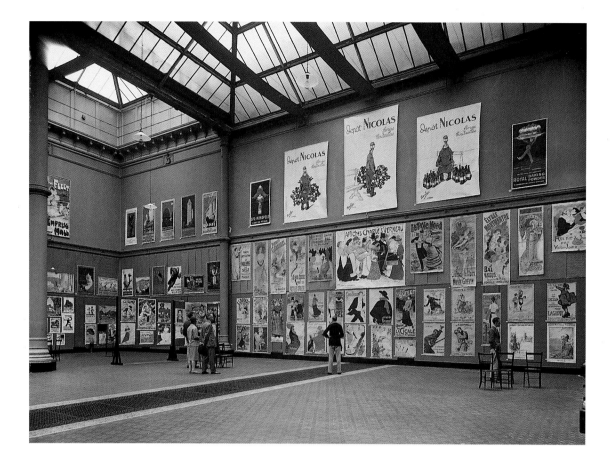

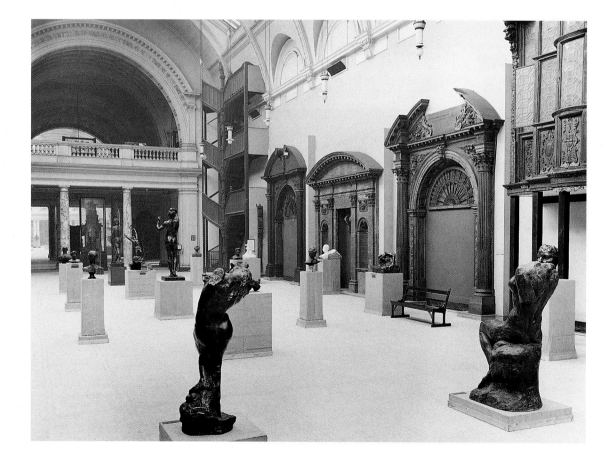

Acquisition by gift was the norm for twentieth-century objects, including not only mass-produced objects such as posters but also the sculptures donated by Auguste Rodin (1840–1917) (fig. 121).[18] Of the fifty-one studio pots acquired by 1930, only six were purchased.[19] The predominance of gifts is explained both by the lack of funds available for acquisitions by the Circulation Department and by the initiative and generosity of donors who included makers, designers, and manufacturers, especially in the interwar period.

Most of the Museum's twentieth-century collections until 1977 were acquired by the Circulation Department. Its role in collecting twentieth-century objects throughout the twentieth century cannot be overstated, although it is important to distinguish between the department's approach before and after World War II. During the first half of the century, Circulation concentrated on traveling exhibitions—mainly small collections of objects displayed in a single case (fig. 122)—and on loans to art schools, intended to supplement the school collections. Both were generally restricted to relatively inexpensive objects deemed suitable to be placed in the care of other institutions. Circulation had few large objects, such as furniture or sculpture; its collecting favored small pieces, such as ceramics or glass, or flat objects, including textiles. Costume was deemed too wide a field to collect and too difficult to display.

With the appointment of Peter Floud as keeper of the Circulation Department (1947–60), the department's ambitions expanded. He embarked on a program of organizing larger traveling exhibitions, as well as internal V&A exhibitions (including those with objects borrowed from other departments and museums). Most importantly, he decided that Circulation would specialize in the fields of nineteenth- and (mainly early-) twentieth-century decorative arts. For the first time, subject expertise was actively developed in the department, notably through the groundbreaking 1952 exhibition, "Victorian and Edwardian Decorative Arts." Staff members, including Floud, Elizabeth Aslin, Shirley Bury, and Barbara Morris, became the leading authorities on the subject, and they were largely responsible for amassing the collections that led to the V&A's preeminent reputation, especially regarding work from the Victorian period.

Circulation had its own culture that set it apart from the rest of the Museum. Most of its staff were trained at art schools rather than at private schools and universities. Floud was an active member of the Communist party, and most of his staff were decidedly left-wing. Their attention to the later nineteenth and early twentieth century was determined by several factors: a desire to stake out territory in which they would not compete with the materials departments; an ambition to engage the audience, especially students, designers, and enthusiasts; and a generally more skeptical attitude toward prevailing taste and hierarchies. Even within the most important decorative arts museum in the world, traditional notions of the relative merits of fine and decorative art held sway. Throughout the century, it was general-

Opposite, top: Fig. 120. "Exhibition of British and Foreign Posters," held in the North Court in 1931

Opposite, bottom: Fig. 121. Sculptures by Rodin on display alongside architectural woodwork in the East Hall, 1914

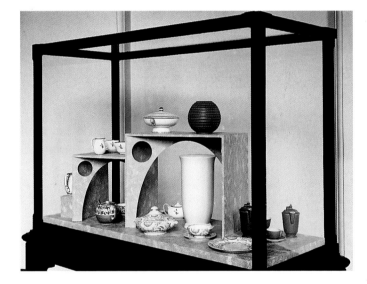

Fig. 122. A display of contemporary ceramics about 1940, typical of the small traveling exhibitions of twentieth-century material mounted by the Circulation Department. This case includes work by Keith Murray, Harold Stable, Pountney & Co., Spode, and Gray's.

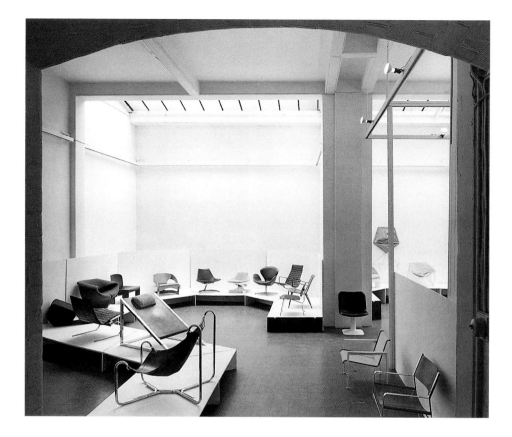

Fig. 123. A view of the "Modern Chairs, 1918–1970" exhibition, mounted by the Circulation Department at the Whitechapel Art Gallery in 1970

ly works by artists or those associated with artists' groups—for example, Roger Fry, Vanessa Bell, or William Staite Murray (see cats. 171 and 185)—that would occasionally find their way into the collections of the materials departments, while manufactured goods or those by craftsmen generally ended up in Circulation.

The Circulation exhibition program expanded during the 1950s and 1960s. Floud's successor, Hugh Wakefield (keeper, 1960–75), had a particular interest in Scandinavian design, which led to several exhibitions, culminating in "Finlandia" in 1961. Acquisitions resulted from virtually all of these exhibitions, as they did on a large scale from the "Modern Chairs" exhibition organized by curator Carol Hogben for the Circulation Department but held at the Whitechapel Art Gallery in 1970 (fig. 123). Circulation also organized the Museum's first photography exhibition in some years, the Henri Cartier-Bresson retrospective of 1966 (also curated by Hogben), which contributed to the reevaluation of the place of photography within the V&A.[20] The department mounted "40 Years of Modern Design" at Bethnal Green, which became, in effect, the Museum's first twentieth-century gallery, since this exhibition remained on view for many years.

The last two decades have been an uncommonly active period during which the status of twentieth-century objects and their study have risen immeasurably. Within the arena of collecting, the Museum seriously addressed the revival of interest in "classic" designs of the high period of modernism (see cats. 170, 173, and 177), as well as historically important traditional design and technically significant work. A notable and unusually large acquisition in 1974 was a complete interior by American architect Frank Lloyd Wright (fig. 124), which in 1993 was installed as the Museum's first twentieth-century period room.

A new factor in collecting modern objects has been the application of traditional notions of connoisseurship. Whereas the Museum had often been satisfied in the 1960s and 1970s with collecting newly made reproductions of 1920s or 1930s furniture, by the mid-1980s original modern objects were sought and valued for the same reasons as were original eighteenth-century objects. Despite the fact that a museum with rich historical collections is, of course, the natural place for such a development, it has been only in the final years of the century that modern objects have become accepted at the V&A in their own right. The changed view of the twentieth century as a historical period—and the acceptance of such objects into the canon of historical objects worthy of attention—created a new atmosphere in the Museum, encouraging serious study and reappraisal.

The promotion of contemporary design within the Museum also coincided with a period of research into the Museum's own history. Following on the heels of the Victorian revival that began in the 1950s and gained momentum in the 1960s, the Museum's part in the history of design became a topic for investigation.[21] This, in turn, led to a renewed desire among some Museum staff to return to the original mission and ideals of Henry Cole. The vast majority of twentieth-century objects in the Museum were acquired after 1974, following the appointment of Roy Strong as director.

Strong made contemporary collecting a priority, firstly by allocating to each department a fund specifically for buying objects made after 1920 and, secondly, by making these traditional materials departments responsible for the care of all of the twentieth-century material through the controversial decision to abolish the Circulation Department.[22] Responsibility, funds, and expertise for twentieth-

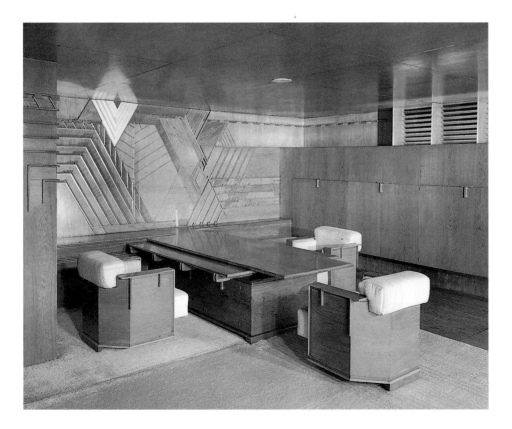

Fig. 124. The Edgar J. Kaufmann Office, designed by Frank Lloyd Wright, 1937. Acquired by the V&A in 1974, the Kaufmann Office is a permanent period-room installation (V&A W.9–1974).

century objects were now firmly and exclusively vested with the V&A's curatorial departments. The 1980s saw the Museum dramatically raise the profile of twentieth-century design within its walls.

In 1980, the Museum announced the establishment of the Boilerhouse exhibition space, intended to exhibit industrial design, to be operated independently by the Conran Foundation.[23] Beginning in the following year, the Boilerhouse exhibitions took advantage of a wider public interest in contemporary design and edged the V&A further toward an institutional commitment to it. Then in 1983 the Museum opened its first gallery devoted to its own twentieth-century collections, "British Art & Design 1900–1960," and in 1987 the Boilerhouse was transformed into the Museum's own twentieth-century exhibition gallery, in which regular exhibitions are mounted. In 1986, and again in 1988, internal Museum committees considered the issues surrounding the acquisition and display of twentieth-century objects.[24]

Both Strong and his successor, Elizabeth Esteve-Coll, devoted greater attention and resources to the twentieth century, and in 1989 the Board of Trustees decided to allocate at least half of the Museum's annual purchase grant of £1.4 million (less £500,000 for the library) to twentieth-century objects. Although competition with "heritage" objects continued to make it difficult to obtain major sums of money for expensive pieces from the first quarter of the century, a sea change had undoubtedly occurred. A Museum-wide acquisitions policy published in 1989 reaffirmed the Museum's commitment to the aims of its founders—a special responsibility to collect contemporary design was acknowledged. In many ways these efforts were successful, for by the 1990s most of what the Museum collected—in numerical terms—was produced in the twentieth century, and most of those objects were contemporary. This fact was acknowledged in the first Museum-wide exhibition devoted exclusively to contemporary collecting, "Collecting for the Future: A Decade of Contemporary Acquisitions" (1990).

Once the profile of twentieth-century objects was raised, subtler issues about the nature of the Museum's twentieth-century collecting arose. The new Twentieth Century Art and Design Gallery that opened in 1992 (figs. 125 and 126) included not only a mixture of British and non-British objects, but also many types of industrial design hitherto not collected in a conscious way, including stereo equipment, flashlights, and household appliances.[25] There is still active debate within the Museum about the extent to which the V&A can incorporate into its various departments the wide variety of design objects currently made. Some argue against collecting objects which fall beyond the traditional materials-based categories covered by the V&A's departments. The language of 1908 periodically reappears. Although now considered eccentric, occasional protests against collecting things newer than fifty years old continue, as does an unease with exhibiting the products of companies currently in business. Conversely, there are those who argue persuasively that during its first decades the Museum could claim to cover the work of professional designers, whereas today that is no longer the case. While the Museum may acquire contemporary design that corresponds to the collecting interests of particular departments (say, ceramic or furniture), it neither collects nor consistently addresses in exhibitions the majority of work undertaken by professional designers, especially the utilitarian mass-produced objects of industrial design. The Museum's ability to refer to itself with conviction as a Museum of design, to embrace its Victorian roots as well as to re-create itself for a new century, will depend largely upon its grappling with this issue in the years to come.

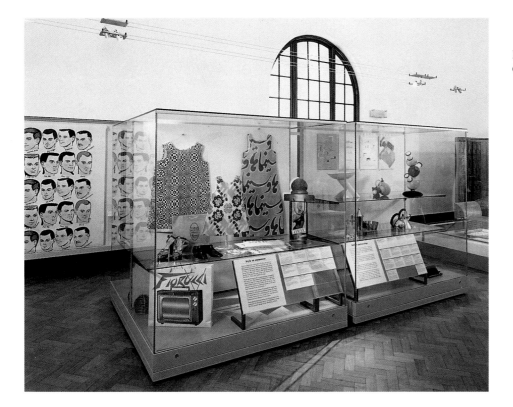

Fig. 125. The new Twentieth-Century Gallery, opened in 1992

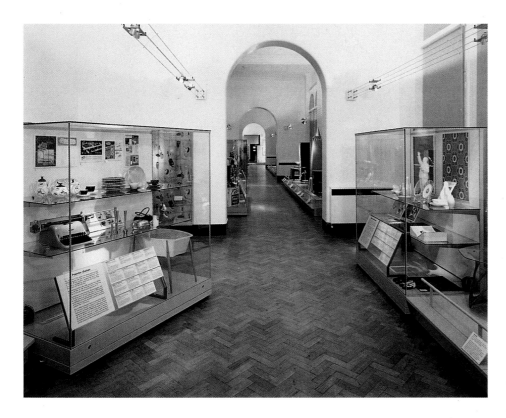

Fig. 126. Another view of the Twentieth-Century Gallery

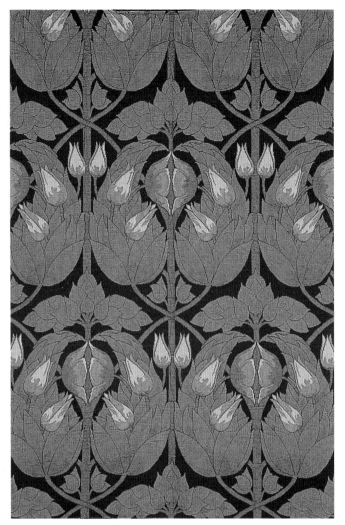

164.

164. CHARLES HARRISON TOWNSEND (English, 1851–1928); manufactured by ALEXANDER MORTON & Co., Darvel, Scotland. *Tapestry: "Omar".* 1896. Jacquard-woven wool and cotton furnishing textile (double-cloth called "Darvel tapestry"), 94½ x 63⅜" (240 x 161 cm). Given by Jocelyn Morton and Courtaulds Ltd. V&A T.154–1977

The buildings of architect Charles Harrison Townsend are recognized as among the most spectacular of the British Arts and Crafts movement. His two best-known London examples, the Horniman Museum and the Whitechapel Art Gallery, are now considered extremely significant expressions of the style. The manufacturer Alexander Morton was an avid follower of William Morris, and he set up his firm with Morris's principles in mind. With important technological developments in dyeing and weaving techniques, and patronage of the most influential

contemporary designers, the products of Morton & Co. reflect an ideal union of traditional patterns advanced by modern interpretation.

The name of the *Omar* textile—an elegant pattern of stylized lotus blossoms, on a deep red ground, aligned in ogival repeats derived from sixteenth- and seventeenth-century Turkish sources—may have been suggested by the popularity of *The Rubáiyát of Omar Khayyám,* translated by British poet Edward FitzGerald and first published in 1859. *Omar,* along with its original design drawing, was part of a large collection of Morton & Co. products given in the 1960s and 1970s by Jocelyn Morton and Courtaulds Ltd., a gift that filled a major gap in the V&A's holdings of English Arts and Crafts, one of the most original and popular British movements of modern times.

Lit. *Art Journal,* 1900, p. 12; Parry, 1993, no. 134, pp. 28, 111

LINDA PARRY

165. LOUIS MAJORELLE (French, 1859–1926). *Cabinet.* 1900. Walnut and oak veneered with coromandel and burl walnut and enriched with marquetry of various woods; wrought-iron mounts, 70⅞ x 33⅞ x 19⅝" (180 x 86 x 50 cm). Signed: "Majorelle Nancy." Given by George Donaldson. V&A 1997–1900

This cabinet was given to the Museum as part of a large and controversial gift from George Donaldson of objects purchased from the 1900 Exposition Universelle in Paris. Donaldson (1845–1925), a Bond Street dealer whose clients included George Salting, was well known among connoisseurs of the decorative arts at the turn of the century and was a prolific collector in his own right, in particular of musical instruments. As vice-president of the Jury of Awards for furniture at both the 1889 and 1900 Paris Expositions, he was one of a group asked to purchase works of decorative art for the Museum. Donaldson was so impressed by the "superior ingenuity and taste" evident in the Art Nouveau objects at the 1900 show, which he considered far better than British products on display, that he felt that the Museum's £500 purchase allocation was insufficient. Consequently, he offered to donate whatever funds were necessary "to secure an adequate representation of the objects illustrating the 'New Movement.'" The objects he acquired included furniture by Gallé, Majorelle, Spindler, and other lesser-known Hungarian, Norwegian, and German designers, as well as metalwork, pottery, glass, and textiles.

Earlier a cabinetmaker in the Rococo Revival style, by the 1890s Louis Majorelle—increasingly under the influence of his friend and fellow artist Emile Gallé (cats. 166–167)—had

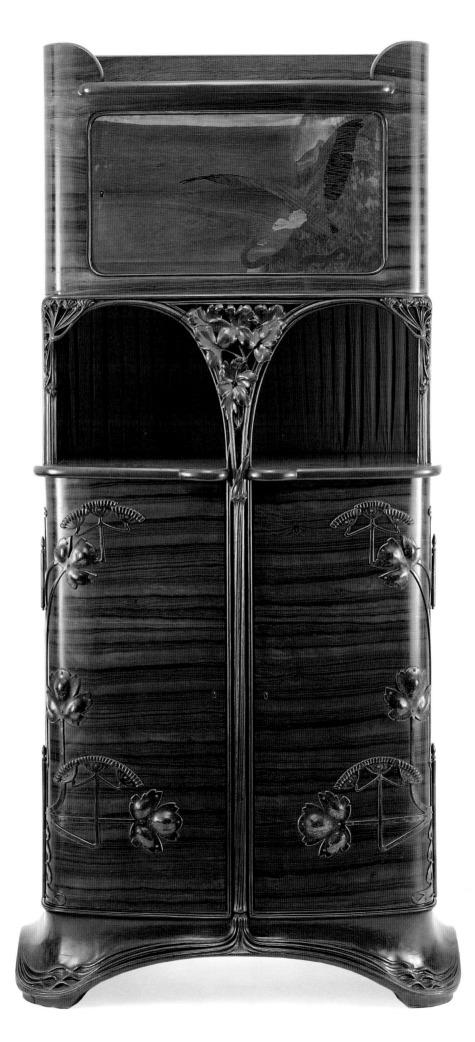

165.

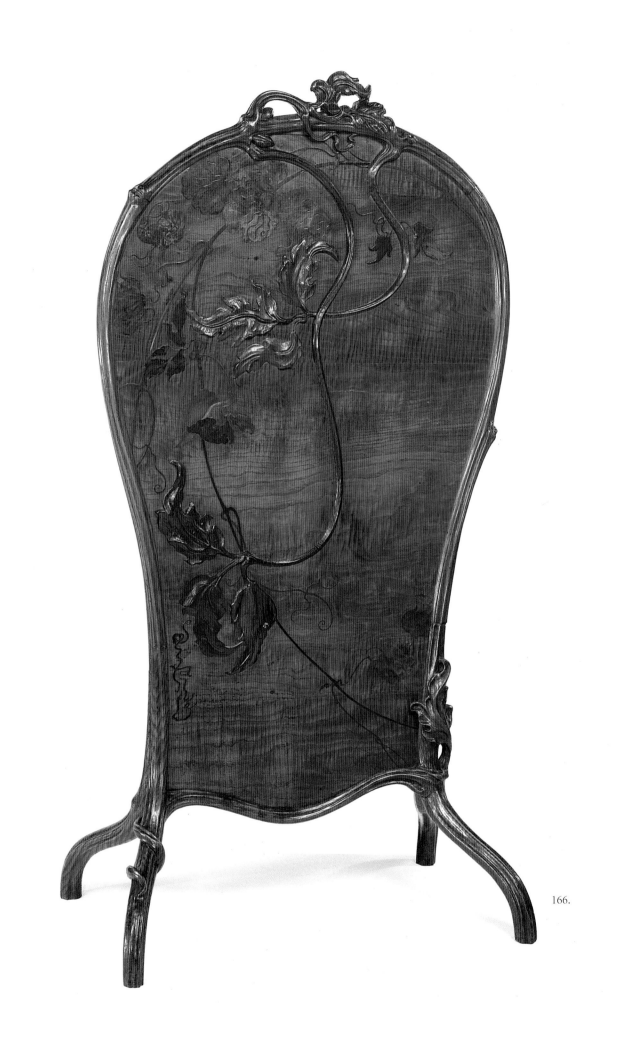

166.

become one of the foremost exponents of the naturalistic Art Nouveau style. He adopted the theme of the water lily (or lotus) for the room he designed for the 1900 Paris exhibition. The wrought-iron mounts of this cabinet—whose elegant lines and abstract forms are typical of Majorelle's best work—delineate lotus blossoms in the stylized geometry of Egyptian forms. The cabinet's upper panel constructs in delicate marquetry a horrific scene of a great winged eagle fiercely defending her nest and its three eaglets (just visible to the right of her upraised left wing) against a large predatory snake.

Donaldson was convinced of the importance of the Art Nouveau objects he generously acquired for the Museum, but he suspected that others might not agree. In fact, the reaction in Britain and, significantly, at the V&A was astonishingly hostile.

Lit. Wilk, 1996, p. 186

RICHARD DUNN/CHRISTOPHER WILK/BRENDA RICHARDSON

166. EMILE GALLÉ (French, 1846–1904). *Firescreen.* 1900. Ash, with applied floral decoration and marquetry in various woods; back veneered with maple, 42⅜ x 22 x 13¾" (107.5 x 56 x 35 cm). Given by George Donaldson. V&A 1985–1900

This firescreen, like the Majorelle cabinet (cat. 165), was one of the Art Nouveau objects purchased for the V&A by George Donaldson from the 1900 Paris Exposition Universelle. Emile Gallé was a leading designer and manufacturer of glass (by 1900 he employed more than 300 workers at his Nancy factory) and, from 1884, furniture as well; he won prizes for both at the 1900 exhibition. Gallé studied botany and mineralogy at university, and he passionately advocated natural ornament in furniture.

The firescreen's decoration of dancing leaves and swooping vines—whose tendrils snake along the screen's framework and even wrap around its legs, thus integrating structure and decoration—is archetypal Art Nouveau and quintessential Gallé.

RICHARD DUNN/BRENDA RICHARDSON

167. EMILE GALLÉ (French, 1846–1904). *Vase.* 1900. Glass, colored, acid-etched inside, enameled and gilded, 18½" (47 cm) high, 11" (28 cm) diam. Marks: "Gallé Exposition 1900" enameled within the decoration. V&A 1622–1900

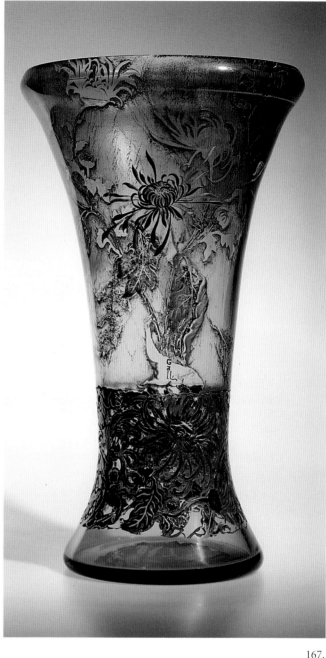

167.

Shown at the Paris Exposition Universelle in 1900, this elegant vase was purchased from Gallé by the Museum itself, rather than as part of the controversial Donaldson gift (see cats. 165–166). The vase's decoration of stylized chrysanthemums is characteristic of Gallé's introspective and slightly morbid symbolism; he would have been well aware of the chrysanthemum's Japanese significance as an imperial flower as well as the flower's French association with funerals and death. A serious student of both science and art, Gallé was familiar with Chinese glass and hard stones, which he studied at the South Kensington Museum when he was in London for the international exhibition of 1871; thirteen years later in Berlin he saw the Brandt collection of Chinese glass, as well as Islamic glass. From the 1880s, he developed a passion for Japanese lacquer and prints; like many other late-nineteenth-century French artists, he adopted a style that came to be called Japonisme, perhaps the single most significant precursor of Art Nouveau.

Spending only £258 19s. from its own funds, the Museum's choice of objects from the 1900 exhibition was more conservative than those chosen by Donaldson. From that perspective, this vase (purchased for £7 19s. 6d.) fit within the established "Japanese" style. Part of the "New Art" collection exhibited in Birmingham, Edinburgh, and Dublin following its first, contentious showing in the Museum, the vase apparently remained in storage until 1971.

Lit. Gallé, 1908; Garner, 1976; Charpentier, 1985–86; Morris, 1986

JENNIFER H. OPIE

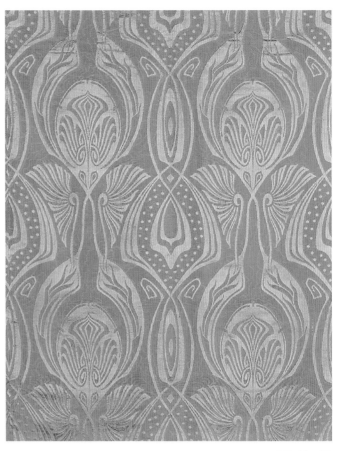

168. (detail)

168. Probably designed by EDWARD COLONNA (American, born Edouard Klönne in Germany, 1862–1948 [to U.S. 1882, active Paris 1898–1903]); possibly woven by CORNILLE FRÈRES, Lyon. *Curtain.* (c. 1900). Woven silk, 129⅞ x 56⅜" (330 x 143.3 cm). V&A T.357–1990

An influential figure in the Art Nouveau movement in both Europe and America, Colonna was born near Cologne and trained as an architect in Brussels. Immigrating to the United States in 1882, he designed for Tiffany's in New York and later moved to the Midwest where he designed railroad cars. From 1898 to 1903 Colonna lived in Paris and designed jewelry, furniture, porcelain, and textiles for Samuel Bing, the influential dealer whose shop, L'Art Nouveau, gave its name to the art style just then assuming prominence. Colonna produced Bing's L'Art Nouveau pavilion at the 1900 Exposition Universelle in Paris. The pattern of this silk is very similar to Colonna's *Les Orchidées* which was part of that display, and it is assumed from the high quality of their manufacture that both examples were woven by one of the leading French silk weavers, Cornille Frères of Lyon. The V&A's example reflects the stylized organicity of Art Nouveau, and its watered-style ground has parallels in the subpatterning seen in Colonna's designs in other mediums, for example, the opalescence in his glass and the wood inlays of his furniture.

Although the Museum concentrated at the end of the nineteenth century on building up its early textiles collection, it did not acquire examples of the two most fashionable contemporary styles—Arts and Crafts and Art Nouveau. Examples such as this curtain by Colonna have been purchased only retrospectively.

LINDA PARRY/BRENDA RICHARDSON

169. CHARLES RENNIE MACKINTOSH (Scottish, 1868–1928). *Chair.* 1897–1900. Oak, upholstered seat, 53¾ x 19⅞ x 18⅛" (136.5 x 50.6 x 46 cm). V&A Circ.130–1958

The Scottish architect and designer Charles Rennie Mackintosh was celebrated in Europe in the early 1900s, largely because of his contribution to the 1900 Vienna Secession exhibition, but his significance was forgotten in Britain until the 1950s. The V&A's 1952 exhibition "Victorian and Edwardian Decorative Arts" included ten pieces by Mackintosh; the Museum's first acquisition of his work, a small smokers' cabinet, followed in 1956. This chair was given by the Glasgow School of Art in 1958, with an additional group of furniture from the Ingram Street tearooms. Mackintosh had designed chairs of this rectilinear, elongated form for Miss Cranston's tearooms, 114 Argyle Street, Glasgow. When he married fellow artist and designer Margaret Macdonald in 1900, the couple reused the design for their own dining chairs, of which this is probably an example. Like much of Mackintosh's furniture, the design originated on the drawing board rather than at the work bench—construction and comfort were secondary to radical and elegant appearance.

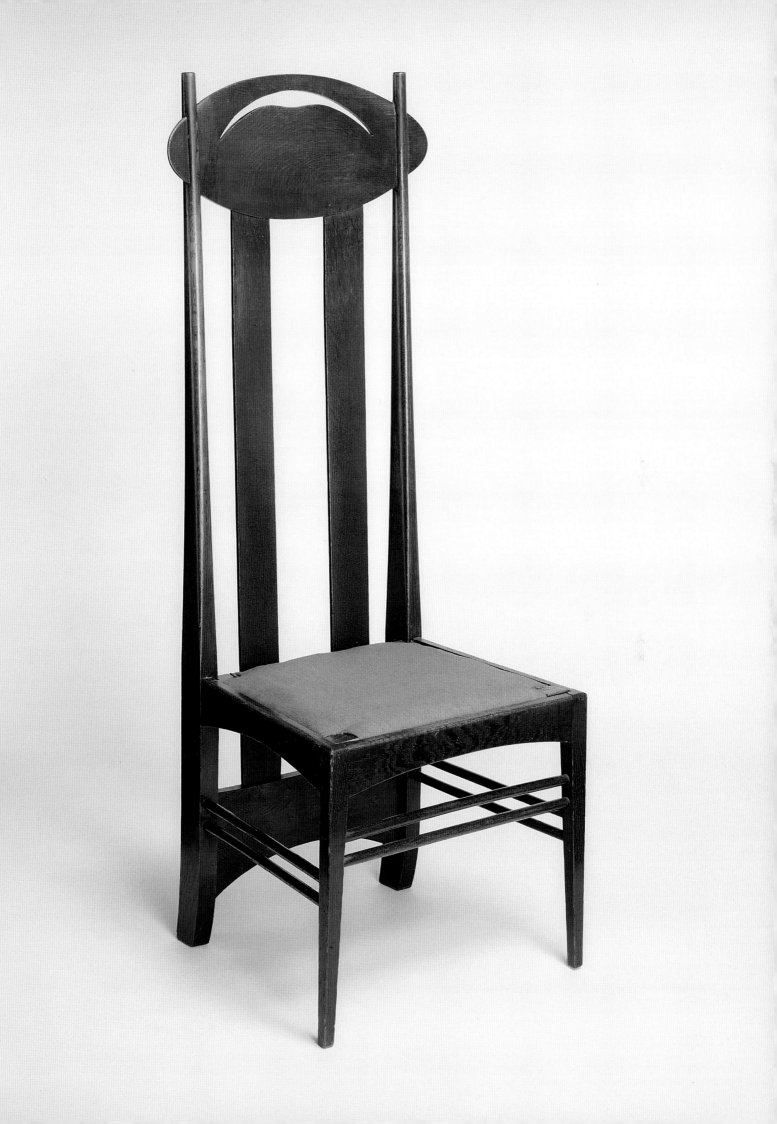

Although Mackintosh was first recognized as a pioneer of modernism in the 1930s, his reputation was more firmly established by major international exhibitions in the 1960s, including the V&A's Mackintosh centenary exhibition of 1968.

Lit. Billcliffe, 1986, pp. 47–8; Wilk, 1996, p. 182

GARETH WILLIAMS

170. KOLOMAN MOSER (Austrian, 1868–1918); made by CASPAR HRAZDIL (Austrian, active 1890–c. 1945). *Lady's Writing Desk and Armchair* (designed for the Hölzl apartment, Vienna). 1903. Thuya wood, inlaid with satinwood and brass, engraved and inked; gilt-metal feet; mahogany interior, oak drawers, deal carcase, later upholstery: desk, 57¼ x 47 x 23⅝" (145.5 x 119.4 x 60 cm); chair, 27½ x 23⅝ x 23⅝" (70 x 60 x 60 cm). Paper label of maker under lower right drawer. V&A W.8&A–1982

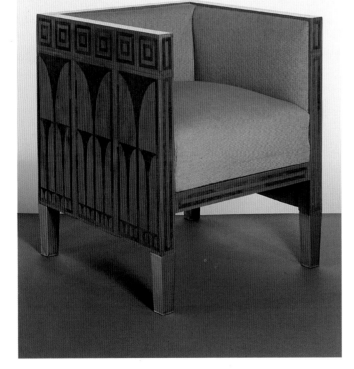

170.

During the last twenty years, the V&A has attempted to redress earlier neglect by retrospective acquisition of objects, such as this desk and armchair considered central to a history of twentieth-century design. In this extraordinary piece, Koloman Moser, one of the Viennese Secession group that also included Gustav Klimt, combined the elegance of early-nineteenth-century Biedermeier furniture with a simplicity and geometry that was entirely new to the style, perhaps inspired by Mackintosh (see cat. 169). While recognizably "protomodern," this Moser piece is also in the grand cabinetmaking tradition of earlier centuries. Made for Dr. Hölzl's apartment, the set's design was coordinated with the unified decoration of the furniture and the interior.

Exhibitions in New York in 1978 and in Vienna in 1981 reawakened interest in this period of Viennese design. Subsequently, the V&A acquired many of the objects shown in Vienna, as the Museum concentrated on the formation of a representative collection of twentieth-century material. The desk now forms the centerpiece of a group of Viennese objects collected by the Museum in the early 1980s, including luxury furniture and bentwood for mass production.

Lit. Adlmann, 1978; Asenbaum, Asenbaum, and Witt-Dörring, 1981; Jervis, 1986, pp. 48–9; Wilk, 1996, p. 194

GARETH WILLIAMS

171. VANESSA BELL (English, 1879–1961); printed by MAROMME, Rouen, France, for the OMEGA WORKSHOPS. *Maud.* 1913. Printed linen, 32 x 30½" (81.3 x 77.5 cm). V&A Circ.425–1966

The Omega Workshops were founded in 1913 by the English critic, painter, and designer Roger Fry (1866–1934), with Vanessa Bell, also a painter and designer, as coordinator. A central figure of the legendary Bloomsbury Group, Vanessa Bell was married to critic Clive Bell, was Virginia Woolf's sister, and often collaborated on artworks with painter Duncan Grant. The Omega style was heavily influenced by developments in contemporary painting, especially French Fauvism and Cubism, and Omega designs often feature the brilliant color of the former and the faceted abstraction of the latter. Omega produced six printed linens, each of which—in keeping with the painterly traditions the workshop emulated—self-consciously showed evidence of the artist's hand. These designs were used as dress fabrics by the most daring customers of the time. The unstructured, abstract patterns of the fabrics struck an unusually modernist note during the pre–World War I period when retrospection in design—especially the use of reproduction patterns—was favored.

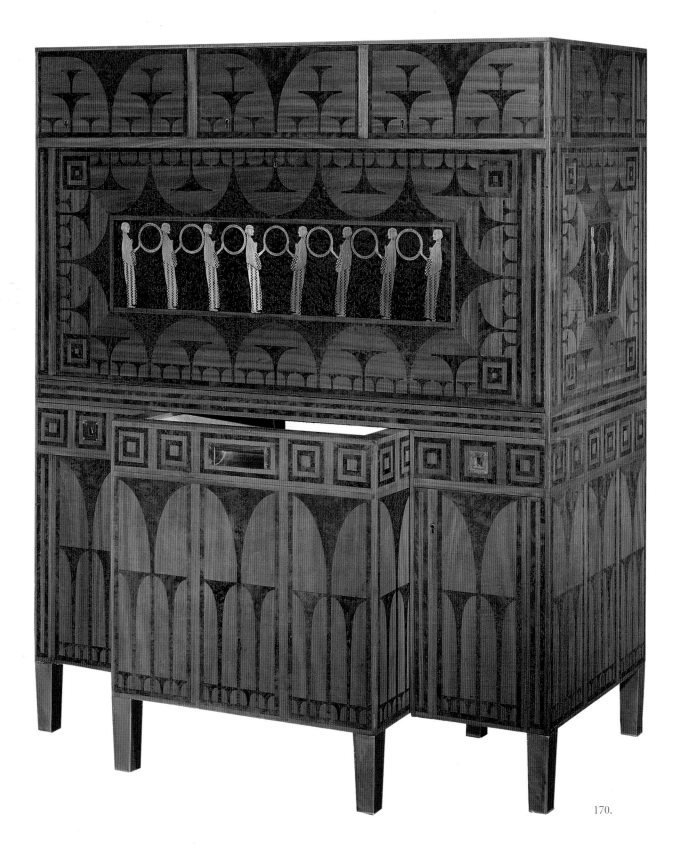

170.

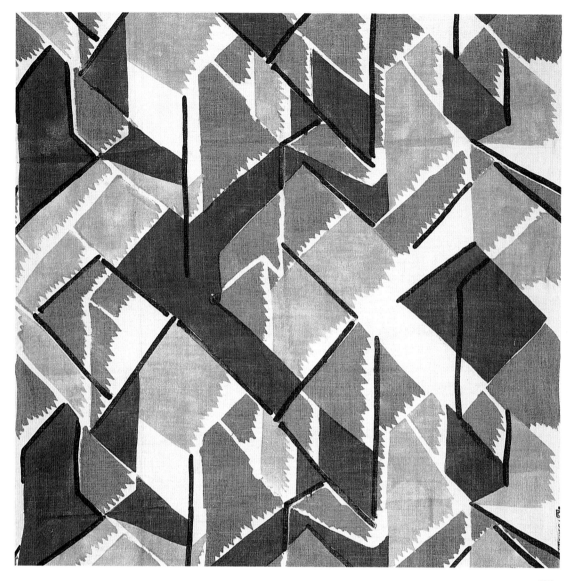

171.

Maud, presumably named after Lady Maud Cunard, a patron of Omega, was available in four different colorways.

Omega textile production was limited, and surviving fabric examples are rare. When the workshops closed in 1920, the V&A acquired several Omega pieces, noting that "they might become great curiosities in the future." This panel of *Maud* was acquired in 1966 by the Circulation Department as part of a large collection of copyright registrations transferred to the Museum from the Design Registry in Manchester. However, it was only in the 1980s, with a strong revival of interest in the Omega Workshops, that the "great curiosities" first acquired in 1920 assumed wider interest.

Lit. V&A, 1995, p. 155

LINDA PARRY/VALERIE MENDES/BRENDA RICHARDSON

172. EDWARD MCKNIGHT KAUFFER (American, 1890–1954 [resident London, 1914–1940]). *Soaring to Success! Daily Herald—The Early Bird.* 1918–19. Color lithograph, 118 x 59⅞" (299.7 x 152.2 cm). Given by Ogilvy Benson and Mather Ltd. V&A E.35–1973

Born Edward McKnight in Great Falls, Montana, the artist adopted the name Kauffer in gratitude to an American mentor who paid for the young man to travel to Paris to study painting. By 1914 he was in London and by 1915 he already had a commission for a poster from the London Underground. The origin of the designer's signature poster image, *Soaring to Success!,* was a 1916 print called *Flight,* a geometric flock of birds (derived from a Japanese print) whose rendering reflected the strong influence of the English Vorticist style of the period. First published in the English periodical *Colour* in 1917, the image was used in 1919 as

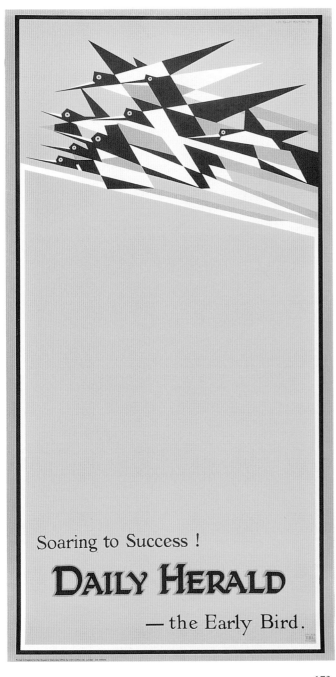

172.

Meynell (proprietor of Nonesuch Press, for which Kauffer illustrated books), who designed and wrote the caption. Meynell considered the design "a symbol, in those days of hope, of the unity of useful invention and natural things." Already a leader of the new profession of graphic design, Kauffer quickly gained international recognition. Subsequently, the design became emblematic of Kauffer and influenced many young designers. He presented the upper third of the poster (the "Flight" image) to The Museum of Modern Art, New York, which honored him with a retrospective exhibition in 1937. This same motif was used as the catalogue cover of the V&A's 1955 Kauffer memorial exhibition, opened by his intimate friend and fellow Anglo-American, the poet T. S. Eliot.

Although Kauffer (like Francis Meynell) was a member of the V&A's Advisory Council, this poster, which represents an unusually ambitious use of modernist design in British advertising, is one of many important twentieth-century objects acquired only retrospectively, in the 1970s. The V&A had collected Kauffer's work from 1916 onward through regular gifts from the Underground Electric Railways Co. of London (predecessor of London Transport), and Museum curators had every opportunity to acquire the poster from Kauffer in his lifetime. But it was only when V&A staff were invited to examine a cache of old posters in a basement in London's Kingsway—from campaigns undertaken by S. H. Benson Ltd., which had handled the *Daily Herald* campaign of 1919—that *Soaring to Success!* finally entered the Museum collections. The company's successors gave the entire poster archive to the V&A, including the very rare complete version of this poster.

Lit. Haworth-Booth, 1979

MARK HAWORTH-BOOTH

173. GERRIT RIETVELD (Dutch, 1888–1964); made by Rietveld with the assistance of G. VAN DER GROENEKAN, for Piet Elling. *Armchair.* 1918. Purpleheart, stained brown, 35 x 26 x 26" (88.9 x 66 x 66 cm). V&A W.9–1989

This example of a design classic by a leading figure of the Dutch de Stijl group has a provenance that can be traced back to the original patron. It was not, however, the first version of this famous chair to be acquired by the Museum, and its purchase reflects a significant shift in thinking about twentieth-century acquisitions. Popularly known as the Red Blue Chair, this Rietveld form has become synonymous with the geometry and primary colors of the influential modernist de Stijl movement. This version, however, predates the use of color on the chair by about five years. With this design, Rietveld attempted to con-

an advertising poster to promote the Labour Party newspaper, the *Daily Herald*. According to family tradition the poster aroused Winston Churchill's attention, who sent for Kauffer with a view to commissioning a new flag for the Royal Air Force. Churchill's enthusiasm waned, however, when he learned that Kauffer was an American.

Although the original design seems an inspired symbol of modernity, aspiration, and the union of industrial power with natural grace—thus typifying the ideals of a new, radical newspaper—it was conceived independently of client or product. The poster was bought for the *Daily Herald* campaign by Francis

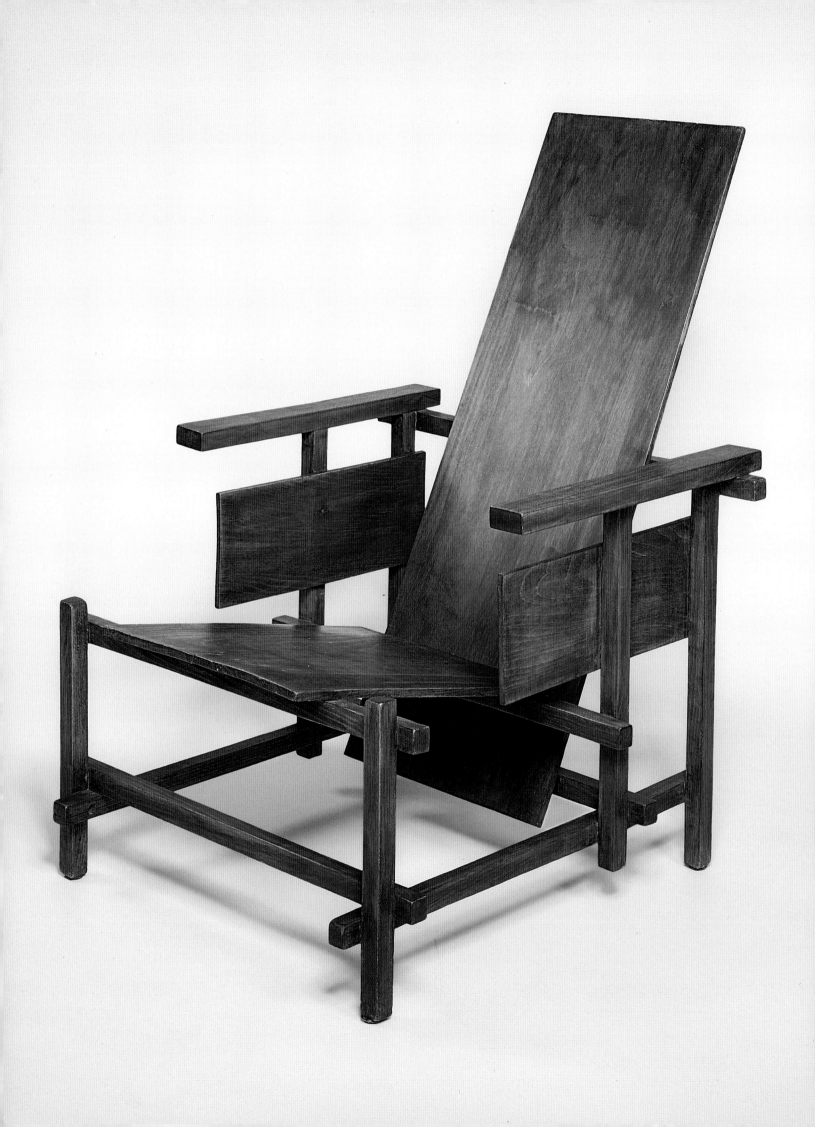

struct a chair from its most basic components, assembled in their simplest form, while also experimenting with modular design adaptable to cheap, mechanized production. The result is an abstract, architectural construction that has, since the 1950s, become an icon of modernism. Later painted versions of the chair dispensed with the side panels, which are the only non-functional elements of the earlier design.

Rietveld organized the first major retrospective exhibition of de Stijl for the Stedelijk Museum in Amsterdam in 1951; the show was also presented at New York's Museum of Modern Art, in 1952. Reproductions of the Red Blue Chair and the Zig-Zag Chair (1934) were acquired by the V&A's Circulation Department for its 1971 exhibition, "Modern Chairs." However, it was not until 1987 that the Museum acquired an original Rietveld piece, the Crate Chair of 1934.

Lit. Küper & van Zijl, 1992, pp. 74–6; Wilk, 1996, p. 196

GARETH WILLIAMS

174. Decoration designed and painted by ALFRED HOARE POWELL (English, 1865–1960); made at JOSIAH WEDGWOOD & SONS, Etruria, Stoke-on-Trent. *Vase.* 1920. Earthenware painted in colors, 28¾" (73 cm) high, 11¾" (30 cm) diam. Marks: "Wedgwood" impressed; the artist's monogram painted. Purchased with the assistance of a group of subscribers and the National Art Collections Fund. V&A C.134–1938

After training as an architect, Alfred Powell moved to Gloucestershire at the turn of the century, where he learned local crafts such as chair-making. In 1906 he and his wife Louise were engaged to work for Wedgwood, and their ceramics were particularly sought after by country house owners enamored of the designs of the Arts and Crafts movement. When V&A ceramics curator Bernard Rackham was offered this vase in 1938, by the artist, he described it as

> a large vase . . . with painted landscape decoration . . . a spare piece from a set of vases made to decorate the house of Sir Hugh Bell [at Rounton] and certainly an important piece of pottery decoration in the manner fashionable two or three decades ago. It was thrown at Wedgwood's and is a remarkable example of pottery, quite apart from the very individual decoration.

The director, Sir Eric Maclagan, responded less enthusiastically: "It seems very difficult to refuse this offer. But I am not very anx-

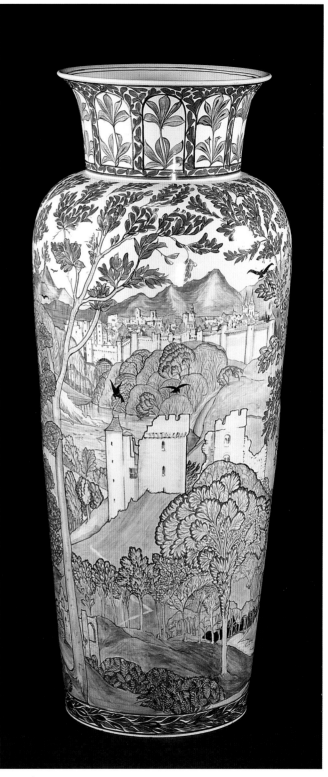

174.

ious to make additions to our collections of Modern Pottery at Bethnal Green at the present. . . . Still this particular vase had better in the circumstances be accepted." The vase cost £50, which was raised by Powell's friends, including George Eumorfopoulos (see cat. 108), as a gift to the Museum.

At the time of its acquisition, the Museum was more interested in the vase's technical superiority than in its aesthetic merit; Rackham, for instance, stressed the tour de force of potting in this enormous size. Its artistic significance was first recognized in the Museum's influential 1952 exhibition, "Victorian and Edwardian Decorative Arts."

Lit. Honey, 1948b, pl. 86; V&A, 1952, no. Q29; Batkin, 1983

Jennifer H. Opie

175.
Designed by C. F. A. Voysey (English, 1857–1941); manufactured by Morton Sundour Fabrics, Carlisle. *Alice in Wonderland.* c. 1920. Roller-printed cotton, 53⅜ x 36¾" (135.5 x 93.5 cm). Given by Jocelyn Morton. V&A Circ.856.1967

C. F. A. Voysey, an architect by training, became one of the most popular and prolific of freelancers, providing designs for all aspects of the domestic interior, including furniture, metalwork, wallpapers, and textile furnishings. As a designer, he came to specialize in flat pattern design, although he also continued to design many houses. Voysey's "Alice" design was taken directly from the original illustrations by Sir John Tenniel (English, 1820–1914) for *Alice's Adventures in Wonderland* (1865) by Lewis Carroll (Charles Lutwidge Dodgson, English, 1832–1898). A well-known caricaturist, Tenniel was already admired for his

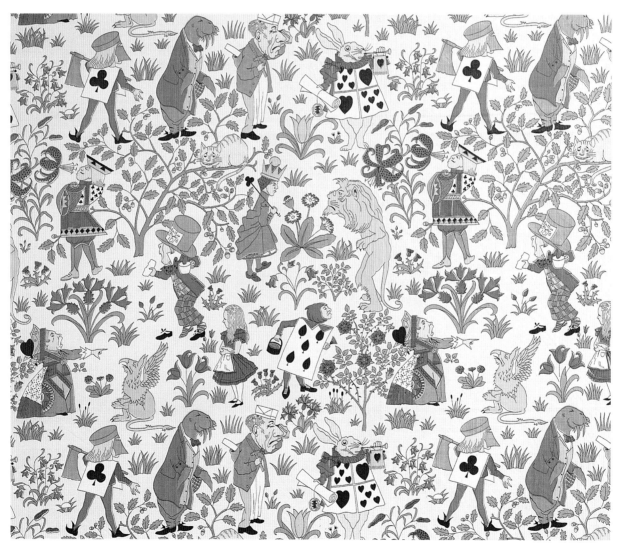

175. (detail)

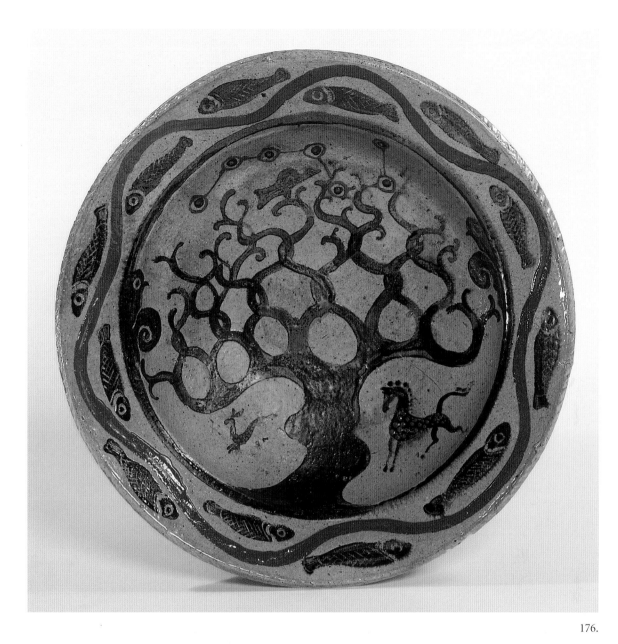

political cartoons in *Punch* when he took on the *Alice* illustrations and, later, those as well for Carroll's "Alice" sequel, *Through the Looking Glass* (1872).

Beginning in the 1880s, a strong interest in children's book illustration developed in England, and this Voysey pattern, typical of his original and witty style, continued to be popular for a very long time after its introduction. The *Alice in Wonderland* fabric came to the Museum as part of a large group of textiles and original design drawings donated by Jocelyn Morton, a descendant of the founder of Alexander Morton & Co. of Darvel, Scotland, which manufactured some of the best of English Arts and Crafts textiles.

Lit. Brandon-Jones, 1978, no. D.28

LINDA PARRY/BRENDA RICHARDSON

176. BERNARD LEACH (English [St. Ives], 1897–1979).
Dish: "The Tree of Life". 1923. Earthenware with slip decoration, 16½" (42 cm) diam., 4¾" (12 cm) deep.
V&A Circ.1278–1923

This dish by Bernard Leach, purchased for £5 (reduced from £7.50) from an exhibition at the British Institute of Industrial Art, is now ranked as a masterpiece by one of the twentieth century's greatest artist-potters. It combines old English earthenware techniques, particularly those of Thomas Toft and other seventeenth-century Staffordshire potters (cat. 128), with a "tree of life" motif from a Chinese Han Dynasty tomb decoration that Leach may have seen during a visit in 1916. Leach commented that the design "may be seen as symbolic," and, though not explicit about his interpretation of the motif, he reused it many times.

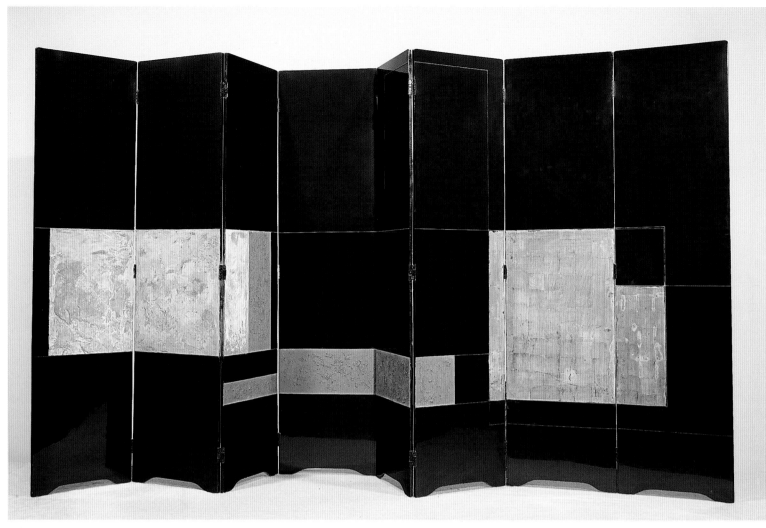

177.

The Museum's Circulation Department acquired this dish in 1923 not as a work of art in its own right, but as "a very interesting revival of an old technique" at a time when slipware was arousing great interest among collectors and museums. The technique was considered the true English style, uncontaminated by the foreign influences perceived in porcelain and delftware, and was thought to demonstrate a "racy vitality" that the sterile perfection of industrialized products could not match.

Leach set up his workshop in St. Ives in 1920 after working for ten years in Japan, where he studied pottery under the master Ogata Kenzan. Leach's aim was to "re-create" the English pottery tradition that he believed had been swept away by industrialization. He also wished to introduce the techniques and styles of Chinese ceramics of the Tang and Song periods, which he regarded as the highest achievements in the potter's art (see cat. 108).

OLIVER WATSON

177. EILEEN GRAY (Irish, 1878–1976 [resident Paris, 1902–1976]). *Screen.* c. 1928. Wood with red and black lacquer, silver leaf, and composite decoration, brass hinges; eight-fold screen, each leaf, 81½ x 21¼ x ⅝" (207 x 54 x 1.7 cm); overall, 81½ x 171¼ x ⅝" (207 x 435 x 1.7 cm). Gift of Prunella Clough. V&A W.40–1977

An important figure in design of the 1920s and 1930s, Eileen Gray was largely forgotten from the 1940s until 1970. Born in Ireland and trained as an artist in London, Gray moved to Paris in 1902, where she lived until her death. She studied the art of lacquer there with the Japanese master Sugawara, and even before World War I her lacquer furniture had already found an influential patron in the couturier Jacques Doucet. After the war years (which she spent with Sugawara in London), Gray expanded into interior decoration and developed a more refined, minimal, and innovative modern style in her work, which, from 1922 to 1930, she sold through her own shop, called

Jean Désert. From 1922, too, Gray had active contact with the Dutch de Stijl group, whose influence moved her toward architecture with integrated interiors featuring highly refined furniture in advanced materials.

A reappraisal of Gray's work began around 1968; the sale in 1972 of Doucet's collection further enhanced her standing. In 1971 she gave the V&A two chairs, and in 1972 the Museum acquired one of the famous lacquer "Brick" screens from the Handley-Read collection. The Royal Institute of British Architects held an exhibition of Gray's work in 1973, and in 1976 her chrome, steel, and glass furniture was licensed for reproduction.

This elegant screen, which remained in Gray's Paris apartment until her death, shows her moving away from the decorative symbolism of her early lacquerware toward a more architectural, abstract, modernist style, dependent on texture, reflection, and light. The screen came to the Museum in 1977 as a gift from her niece, who had reworked areas of it under Gray's supervision around 1970. It was included in an exhibition of her work organized jointly by New York's Museum of Modern Art and the V&A in 1978–79.

Lit. Rykwert, 1972; Johnson, 1979, p. 28; Adam, 1987

GARETH WILLIAMS

178. EDWARD McKNIGHT KAUFFER (American, 1890–1954 [resident London, 1914–1940]); manufactured by THE WILTON ROYAL CARPET FACTORY, near Salisbury. *Rug.* 1929. Hand-knotted woolen pile on a jute warp, 45 x 82⅝" (114.3 x 210 cm). Transferred from the British Institute of Industrial Art, 1934. V&A T.440-1971

Designed by the American Edward McKnight Kauffer (see cat. 171), this rug was acquired by the Museum in 1934 as part of the collection assembled by Margaret Bulley for the British Institute of Industrial Art, an organization in which the V&A's former director Cecil Harcourt Smith played a key role.

In the late 1920s and 1930s the Wilton Royal Carpet Factory, in addition to its mechanized production, made hand-knotted carpets to order. These exclusive, signed carpets provided decorative focal points and injected color into the modish interiors of the period, whose walls and upholsteries were generally in neutral shades. In financially depressed times, the business thus boosted income by attracting clients who could afford custom-designed works.

A signed gouache by Kauffer in the Wilton archives relates closely to this carpet; the design is stamped with the statement that it "can be suitably adapted for any size carpet and any desired alterations in colouring or ornament effected."

Lit. Arts Council, 1979, p. 146; Mendes, 1992, p. 82

VALERIE MENDES

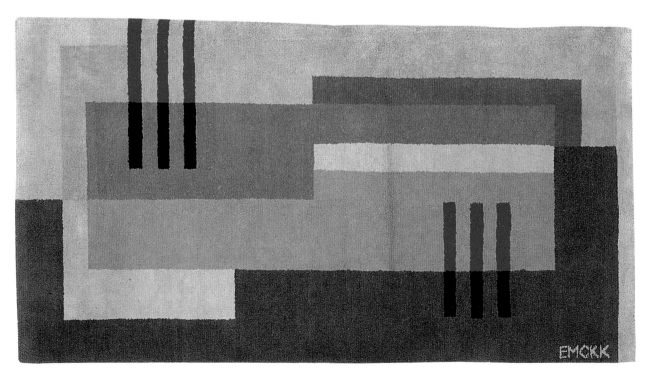

178.

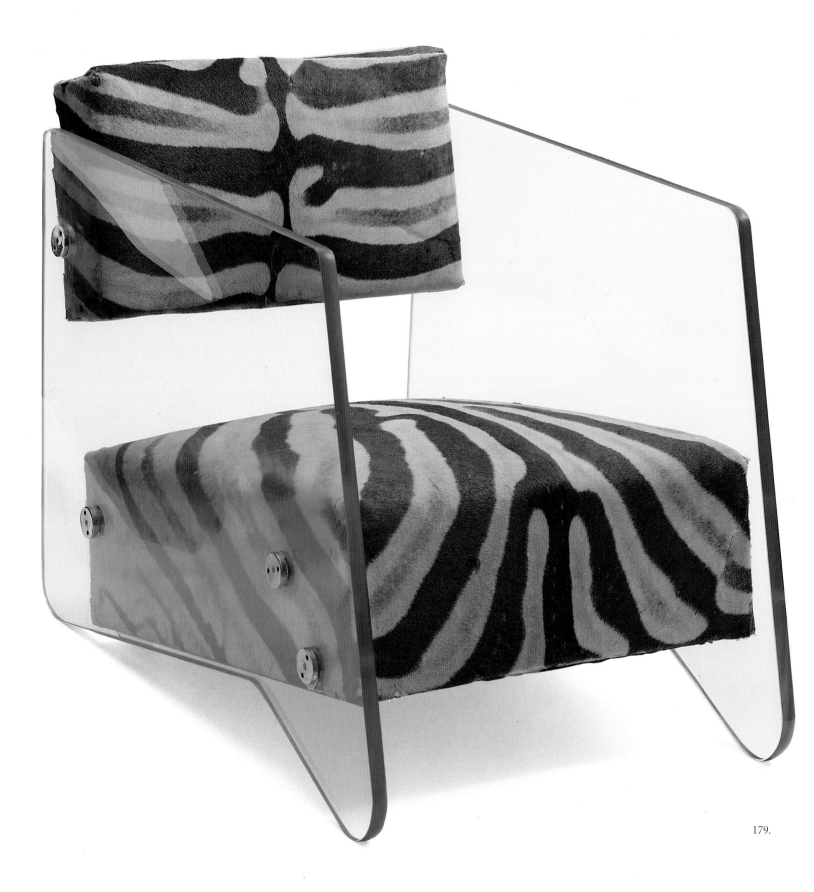

179.

179. Denham Maclaren (English [London], 1903–1989). *Chair.* c. 1930. Glass, metal fittings, zebra skin upholstery, 26¾ x 22½ x 33½" (68 x 57 x 85 cm). V&A W.26–1979

Although contemporary British textiles and ceramics were purchased by the Museum during the 1930s, many of the most significant examples of British modernism, including this inventive, exotic chair of glass and zebra skin, were acquired only in the late 1970s in connection with the "Thirties" exhibition, a joint venture of the V&A and the Arts Council of Great Britain.

While Denham Maclaren designed only a relatively small quantity of furniture from the late 1920s to the end of the 1930s, he of all British designers best captured the spirit of contemporary European modernism. He followed the functionalist precepts of Le Corbusier and Walter Gropius, and most of his furniture was constructed of steel and glass. Reflecting the glamor of Hollywood of the period, this chair, like many of Eileen Gray's contemporaneous designs, tempers the austerity of modernism with sophisticated wit. Maclaren maintained his own London showroom from 1930 to 1936, and retailed his designs through Duncan Miller's West End showroom from 1936; he designed radios prior to the outbreak of war in 1939, although none were put into production. After 1945 his interests moved away from furniture design. This classic chair was purchased by the Museum directly from Maclaren in 1979.

Lit. Arts Council, 1979, p. 150; Greenhalgh, 1989; Wilk, 1996, p. 208

Gareth Williams

180. Susan Vera Cooper, called Susie Cooper (English, 1902–1995): shape and decoration designed by Susie Cooper; decorated by the Susie Cooper Pottery, Burslem, using blanks made by Wood & Sons Ltd. *"Kestrel" Coffee Set.* 1932. Earthenware with banded, painted, and sgraffito decoration: coffee pot with lid 7⅝" (19.5 cm) high; jug 3⅛" (7.8 cm) high; bowl 4⅛" (10.5 cm) diam., 3½" (9 cm) high; cups 2⅜" (6 cm) high; saucers 4⅜" (11 cm) diam. V&A C.127–, C.127A– through C.127K–1985

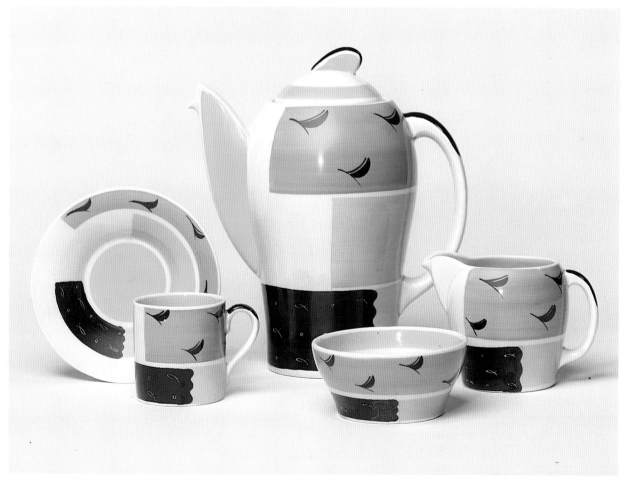

180.

Susie Cooper's original contribution to the design, production, and marketing of tableware has assured her a prominent place in the history of twentieth-century ceramics. Founding (in 1929) and managing her own factory, and designing pottery shapes as well as their decorations, Cooper broke away from the traditional roles ascribed to women in the pottery industry worldwide, moving into the design of shapes (which was, and remains, predominantly a male preserve) and, even more notably, into the management of the factory.

Praised by design critics of the 1930s for her understanding of the "fitness to purpose" philosophy of design, Cooper earned commercial success with a wide range of designs, including distinctly "feminine" petite floral and geometric patterns, boldly colored stripes and abstract forms, and exuberant animal decorations. This coffee set, an early product of the Susie Cooper Pottery in the classic "Kestrel" shape, was purchased by the Museum in 1985, prior to its exhibition of her work in 1987, although Cooper's work had been represented in the V&A's collection since 1934.

ALUN GRAVES

181. CHRISTIAN BARMAN (English, born 1898); made by HMV. *Electric Fan Heater.* Designed c. 1934, manufactured 1938. Chrome-plated metal, 12 x 16⅜ x 12¼" (30.5 x 41.5 x 31 cm). V&A W.71–1978

This fan heater—a classic image of 1930s streamlined industrial design—derives its effect from its reflective curvilinear form. Its designer, Christian Barman, the editor of *Architectural Review* and later publicity officer for the London Passenger Transport Board, was an influential propagandist for the modern movement.

Lit. V&A, 1994, p. 121

RICHARD DUNN/GARETH WILLIAMS

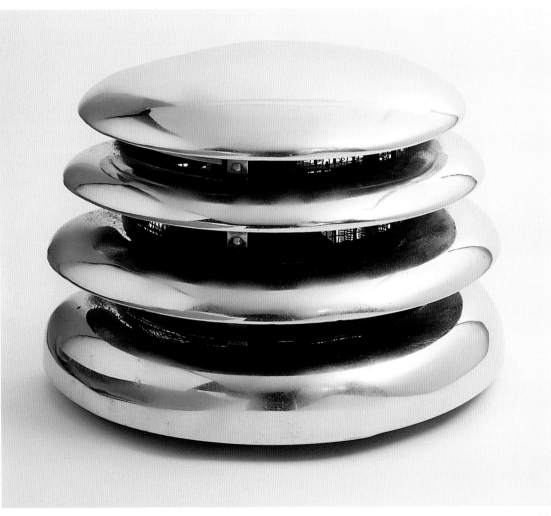

181.

182. *Radios*

182.1. WELLS COATES (Canadian, born Japan of Canadian parents, 1895–1958); made by E. K. COLE LTD., Southend-on-Sea, Essex. *Radio: "Ekco Model AD–65"*. Designed 1932, manufactured 1934. Molded phenol formaldehyde (Bakelite) case, 16 x 15½ x 8¼" (40.5 x 39.5 x 21 cm). Bequeathed by David Rush. V&A W.23–1981

182.2. NORMAN BEL GEDDES (American, 1893–1958); made by EMERSON. *Radio: "Patriot" Midget.* c. 1940. Blue catalin case, 7¼ x 10⅜ x 5⅜" (18.3 x 26.5 x 13.6 cm). V&A W.31–1992

182.3. WELLS COATES (Canadian, born Japan of Canadian parents, 1895–1958); made by E. K. COLE LTD., Southend-on-Sea, Essex. *Radio: "Ekco Princess Portable Model P63"*. Designed 1947, manufactured 1948–49. Case of acrylic and other plastics, 7½ x 8¼ x 2⅛" (19 x 21 x 5.4 cm). V&A W.29–1984

182.4. ROBERTS RADIO CO. LTD. (English). *Radio: "Roberts Model R500"*. 1964. Leopard-skin-covered wooden case, 7½ x 12⅜ x 4⅛" (19 x 31.5 x 10.5 cm). Given by Mr. Bob Burt of Roberts Radio Co. Ltd. V&A W.33–1992. (Roberts Radio does not today practice or support the killing of animals for their fur.)

182.5. DANIEL WEIL (English, born Argentina 1953); made by APEX, Tokyo. *Radio in a Bag.* Designed 1981, manufactured 1983. Transistor radio components in a printed plastic (PVC) bag, 11⅜ x 8⅛ x 1⅛" (29 x 20.7 x 3 cm). V&A W.9–1992

Product design involves different collecting criteria than are applied to more traditional objects. While a consistent, identifiable, and often aristocratic provenance is regarded as one determinant of significance for the historic objects in the Museum, examples of modern product design often come from everyday, anonymous consumers or international manufacturers. By virtue of its nature as a market- or consumer-led industrial activity within a capitalist economy, product design enables the Museum to chart the relationship of design, industry, and society in the twentieth century.

The advent of public radio broadcasts in Britain in 1922 inspired the development of domestic radio receivers. As a radically new form of appliance for the home, radio receiver styling had no precedent; many early valve sets were made in imitation of traditional cabinet furniture. With the introduction of molded plastic cases in the 1930s, however, the distinctive forms of radio sets were decisively defined. The E. K. Cole firm employed leading modernists, including Wells Coates, to design receivers suited to the technology of its Bakelite molding plant, established in 1931. Coates's "AD–65" model was pure geometry, completely unrelated to traditional domestic furniture. The radio's

streamlined curves were overtly modern, and at the same time disguised the technological mechanism of the object. In 1931 Wells Coates designed the interiors for the British Broadcasting Corporation studios, which, along with the BBC radio broadcasts, became synonymous with modernism. The "Patriot," designed in the United States by Norman Bel Geddes only a few years later, also used a molded plastic casing, although Geddes chose a rectilinear form with a red, white, and blue design, created as part of the celebration of the Emerson company's twenty-fifth anniversary.

Wells Coates was born in Japan, the son of a Canadian missionary; he studied engineering in Vancouver and, after World War I, continued advanced studies in London. He began work as an industrial designer in 1928 and became known for his innovative use of plywood. In 1931 he cofounded the Isokon Company, which set out to manufacture functional modernist design; in this period Coates was recognized as leading the vanguard of the modernist movement in England. The versatile American designer Norman Bel Geddes (born in Adrian, Michigan) exercised his talents in advertising, industry (including the design of cars, trains, and planes), window display, interiors, theater, and book design. His futuristic ideas only rarely found their way into production.

Miniaturization of radio components and the near saturation of the market for a single quality receiver in each of Britain's estimated eleven million homes encouraged postwar manufacturers to produce cheaper, portable radios. Comparison of the AD–65 with Wells Coates's 1947 Princess Portable shows the transformation of the radio from authoritative parlor piece to youthful fashion accessory. The brightly colored rectangular case and innovative clear plastic carrying handle of the "Princess" conformed to the functionalism of modernism, but the aesthetic was less austere and more playful than that of prewar sets, and shows the increased importance of styling in the marketing of radios. Roberts Radio promoted its products by encasing receivers in exotic materials such as mink, jewel-encrusted suede, and even gold leaf. These promotional models, made for trade fairs and as advertising stunts, presented the conservative Roberts radio as a glamorous fashion accessory. This leopard-skin model was shown at the Earl's Court Radio Show in 1964. Miniaturization moved forward again in 1956 with the introduction of transistor radios, from which point the center of innovation ceased to be Britain, Europe, or even America, but rather Japan and East Asia.

Daniel Weil's Radio in a Bag subverts our preconceptions of the appearance of audio equipment, which, by the 1970s, was dominated by hard-edged black and chrome boxes, visual indicators of high technology. The flexible and transparent bag features the radio's scattered components as the object's decoration, while also demystifying the mechanism and allowing for easy maintenance. About ten thousand were made, most of which were sold in Japan. Weil studied architecture in his native

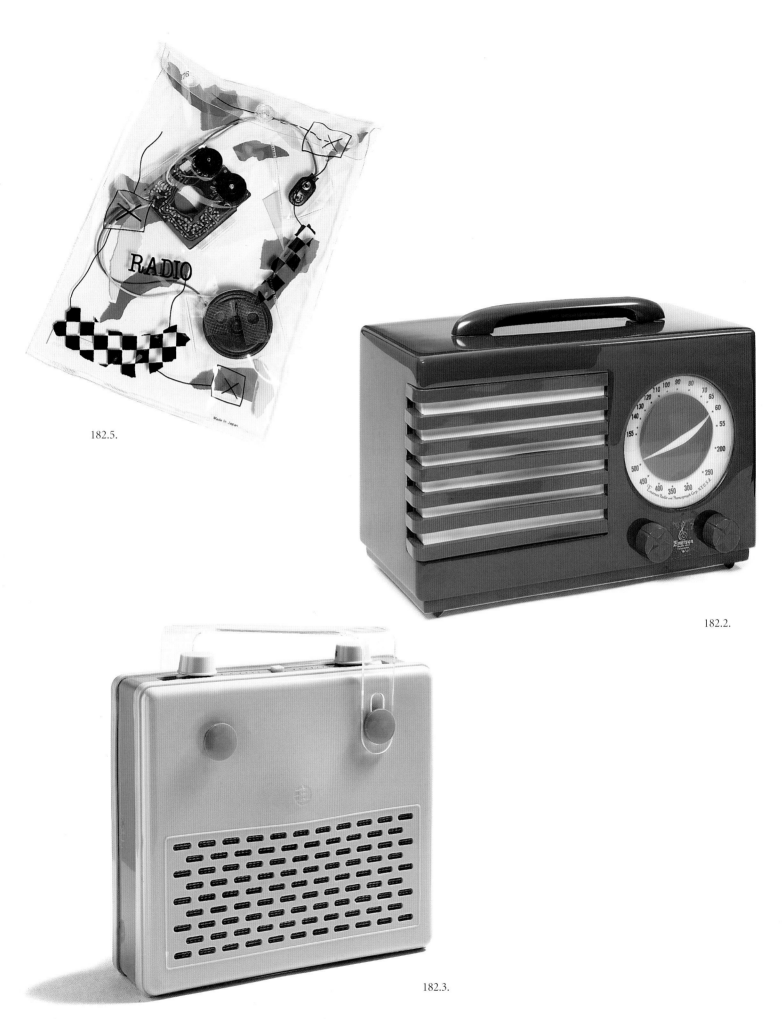

182.5.

182.2.

182.3.

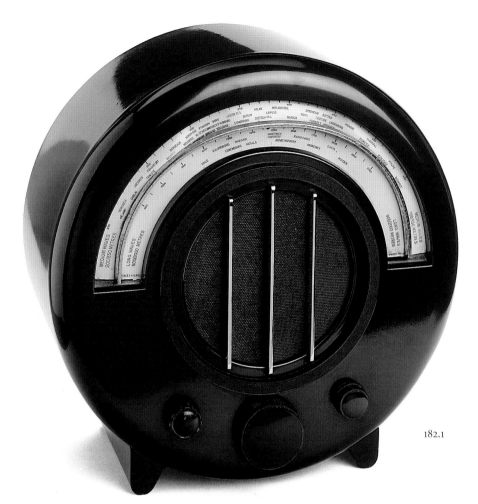

182.1

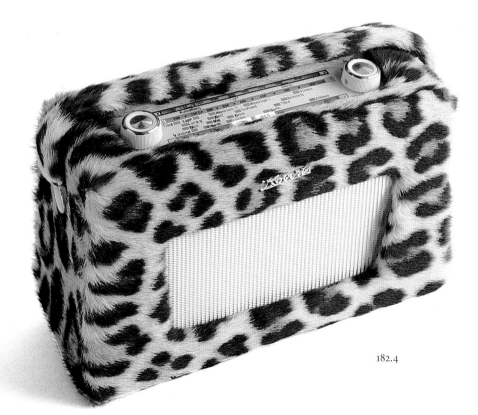

182.4

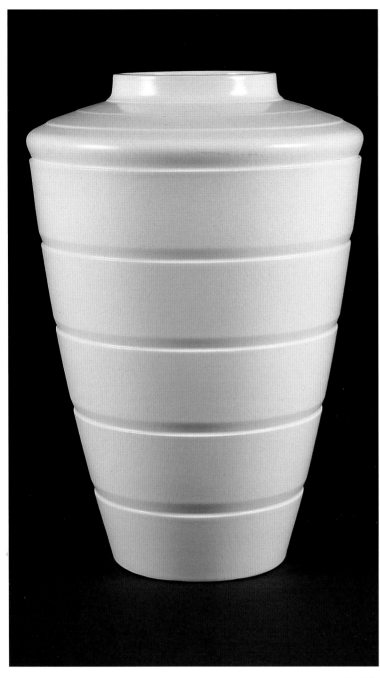

183.

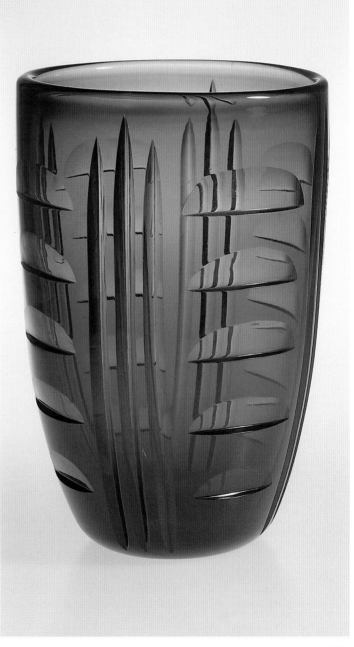

184.

city of Buenos Aires and then moved to London to study industrial design. His "plastic bag" clocks, radios, and lights earned him international recognition, and he has designed for several major manufacturers of quality products.

The V&A has collected approximately one hundred radios since 1963, selected for their aesthetic rather than technological advances.

Lit. *Studio Yearbook of Decorative Art,* 1949, p. 124; Council of Industrial Design, 1950, p. 3 and plate 10; Hogben, 1977, pp. 1, 5, 11; Arts Council, 1979, p. 148; Hiesinger, 1983, pp. 87, 95; Forty, 1986, p. 205; Hawes, 1991, pp. 46–7, 82, 108

Gareth Williams

183. Keith Murray (English, born New Zealand, 1892–1981); made at Josiah Wedgwood & Sons, Etruria, Stoke-on-Trent. *Vase.* 1933. Earthenware with "Moonstone" glaze, hand-thrown and turned, 11" (28 cm) high, 8¼" (21 cm) diam. Marks: "Keith Murray Wedgwood Made in England" printed in blue/green, "E H" impressed. V&A Circ.262–1975

184. Keith Murray (English, born New Zealand, 1892–1981); made at Stevens & Williams, Brierley Hill. *Vase.* 1937. Glass, mold-blown and cut, 11¼" (28.5 cm) high, 7½" (19 cm) diam. Given by Stevens & Williams. V&A Circ.16–1938

Trained as an architect, Keith Murray began designing glass in the 1920s when the depressed economic climate provided few opportunities for him to work within his chosen profession. Murray had immigrated to England in 1906, served in the air force in World War I, and then studied architecture in London. Interested in old glass and impressed with Scandinavian and Viennese glass he saw at the 1925 Exposition Internationale des Arts Décoratifs et Industriels Modernes held in Paris, he determined to improve English glass design. Murray was to play a major role in establishing a new, modern style in glass and ceramics and was hailed as Britain's best, indeed only truly International Modern designer. In *Design for Today* (1935), for example, the influential modernist designer Serge Chermayeff included Murray with Walter Gropius, László Moholy-Nagy, Wells Coates (see cat. 182), and Mies van der Rohe as those "who have in the last decade been directly or indirectly responsible for industrial design and exhibitions of the highest class."

Murray's modernism did, however, contain a strong element of traditional, particularly eighteenth-century, classicism. This strong glass vase, for instance, is a modernist reworking of Georgian-style flat-cutting. It also closely resembles the glass made at Orrefors in Sweden from the turn of the century (an influence Murray acknowledged). Similarly, this earthenware vase has overtones of eighteenth-century Wedgwood basalt ware, even as Murray's vase demonstrates a clean, architectural quality which his admirers identified with the 1930s modernist aesthetic.

As a leading exponent of modernism, Murray was an obvious choice in the selection of British designers for the 1937 international exhibition in Paris, where Murray showed this glass vase in the industrial design section. (The V&A's Circulation Department negotiated a gift of the vase from that show, adding to a group of Murray's works acquired beginning in 1934.)

In 1939 Murray returned to architecture, though production of his glass and ceramic designs continued into the 1950s; by the 1970s, however, the architect's 1930s design work was largely forgotten. In the mid-1970s Murray's work was featured in a traveling exhibition organized by the V&A as well as in the Museum's show of 1930s British design. Interviewed at the time, Keith Murray expressed astonishment that anyone would be interested in what he considered to have been "bread and butter" work undertaken only until he was able to practice as an architect.

Lit. Chermayeff, 1935; V&A, 1976

Jennifer H. Opie

185. William Staite Murray (English [Bray, Berkshire], 1881–1962; resident Rhodesia [now Zimbabwe] 1939–62]). *Vase: "Wheel of Life".* c. 1939. Stoneware with painted decoration, 24¾" (63 cm) high, 11¾" (30 cm) diam. V&A Circ.352–1958

Like English artists' books, British studio pottery was actively collected by the Museum throughout the twentieth century, particularly through the efforts of the Circulation Department. William Murray, a deeply spiritual man, believed that pottery was the bridge between sculpture and painting. Like other potters and collectors of the 1920s and 1930s, Murray was enthralled by the revelations of the newly excavated Chinese ceramics, with their strong forms, plain but rich glazes, and subdued decoration (see cat. 108). The title of this piece, *Wheel of Life,* demonstrates Murray's belief in the cosmic dimension of pottery:

> . . . the clay is formed on the wheel by opposing forces, it opens as an expanding spiral and so follows closely the evolving nature. . . . [T]he earth itself might almost be a vast potter's wheel and the potter's thumb on which is the spiral imprint, has then a deeper meaning, this spiral formation can be seen everywhere.

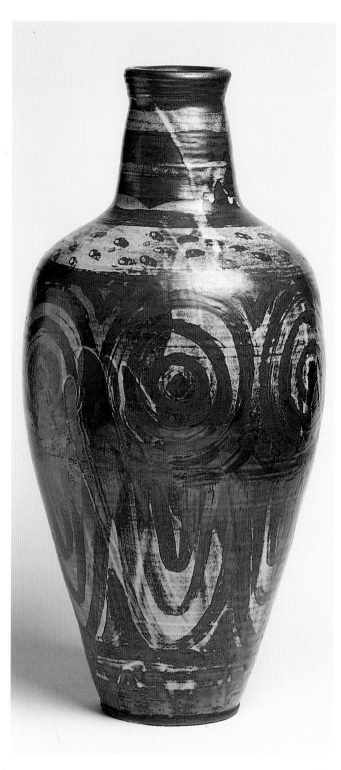

Murray chose to exhibit in fine art galleries. As a result of their status as art objects, Murray's pots tended to be expensive. Although the Museum acquired twenty-one pieces during Murray's working life (c. 1920–39), only five of these were purchases by the Museum. The others were acquired as gifts from patrons. One piece that was purchased by the V&A cost just over £20—the highest price paid for a piece of studio pottery before World War II. The *Wheel of Life* vase, made in 1937, was purchased from a farewell exhibition in 1958, when Murray returned from Rhodesia (now Zimbabwe) to clear out his studio. He had moved abroad and ceased potting in 1939. The piece was bought for £94.50, a price not paid again for studio pots until the 1970s. Murray's recognized status as an "artist" rather than a craftsperson justified the expense.

Oliver Watson

186. Lucienne Day (English, born 1917). *Calyx.* 1951

186.1. Design for a printed linen. Watercolor, gouache, and collage, 34⅝ x 29⅞" (88 x 76 cm). V&A Circ.285–1955

186.2. Produced by Heal's Wholesale and Export Ltd. Screenprinted linen, 67⅜ x 49" (171 x 124.5 cm). V&A Circ.190–1954

185.

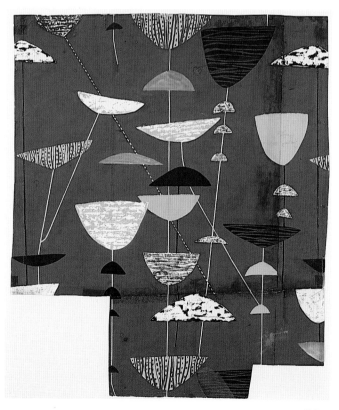

186.1.

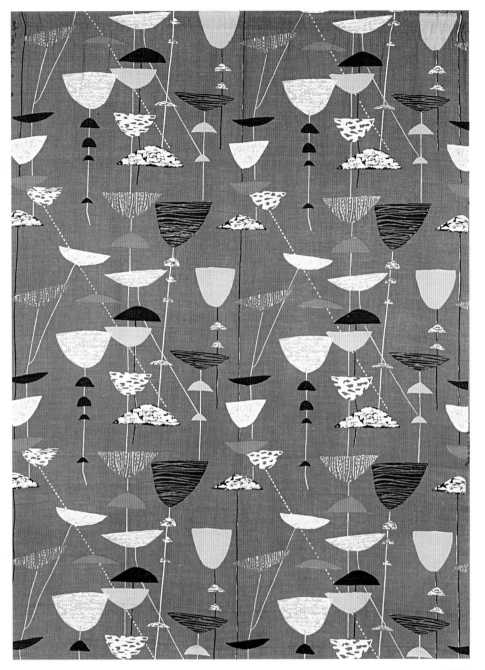

186.2.

The Museum's collecting of contemporary textiles was carried out with a knowledge of earlier traditions. For Circulation Department curators in the early 1950s who had researched the origins of English printed textiles, or "chintz," this Lucienne Day *Calyx* design was an obvious candidate for acquisition. Unlike most modern chintz, which revived nineteenth-century floral patterns, the Day design was a bold and forward-looking pattern that had already influenced other designers.

Calyx was created specially for a room designed by Lucienne's husband, Robin Day (English, born 1915), in the Homes & Gardens Pavilion in the 1951 Festival of Britain. The Festival of Britain showcased examples of both abstract designs and traditional floral chintzes. This design, in which the stylized floral forms (the calyx or fruiting body of a flower) appear almost completely abstract, typified the prevailing trend for nonrepresentational patterns. Its painterly style reflects the influence, acknowledged by Lucienne Day, of Paul Klee and Joan Miró. *Calyx* won a gold medal at the Milan Triennale later in 1951, as well as the International Design Award of the American Institute of Decorators in 1952, the first time a British designer had won this award. In the United States, the fabric was sold to over two hundred leading designers through Greeff Fabrics Inc.

Lit. Harris, 1993

CHARLES NEWTON

187. English (Staffordshire). Decoration designed by
ENID SEENEY; shape designed by TOM ARNOLD;
made by RIDGWAY POTTERIES LTD. *"Homemaker"
Tableware.* 1957–68. White earthenware, glazed and
printed: C.205:1&2 tureen and cover 9½" (24 cm)
diam., 4⅜" (11 cm) high; C.52 platter 13 x 10¼ x ¾"
(33 x 26 x 2 cm); C.231:1&2 soup bowl 6⅛" (15.5 cm)
diam., 2⅛" (5.5 cm) high; saucer 6¼" (16 cm) diam.;
C.179:1&2 coffee pot and lid 9¼ x 8⅝" (23.5 x 22 cm);
C.18:1&2 coffee cup 2 x 3½" (5.1 x 8.8 cm); saucer
4⅝" (11.7 cm) diam. V&A C.205:1&2–1991, C.52–1991;
C.231:1&2–1991; C.179:1&2–1991; C.18:1&2–1996

Although the Circulation Department acquired contemporary
British tableware during the 1950s, what was collected tended to
be quite conservative, following types popular in the interwar
period. It was not until the mid-1980s that highly styled and
thoroughly contemporary 1950s tableware—like Ridgway's
"Homemaker" series—was actively collected by the Museum.
This pattern, designed in 1957 by Enid Seeney and retailed
exclusively through Woolworth's, is an amusingly self-referential
1950s design. Depicting a range of contemporaneous furniture
and domestic objects, "Homemaker" provided an instant style
guide for the period. Ironically, the "Metro" shapes used for

"Homemaker" do not have nearly the vitality and fifties flam-
boyance of the items depicted on them. The success of the pattern had a great deal to do with the fact that it appeared stylish
and contemporary but was very cheap to produce by virtue of
its transfer-printed decoration. For the more complex shapes
such as the coffee pot, the large transfer print that would be used
whole for the plates was simply cut into pieces and applied
around the pot.

ALUN GRAVES

188. ALEXANDER CALDER (American, 1898–1976);
made by PINTON FRÈRES (French [Aubusson]).
Tapestry: "Autumn Leaves". 1971. Wool on cotton
warp, 65 x 93¼" (165 x 237 cm). V&A T.503–1974

Throughout the twentieth century, the Museum has actively collected contemporary textiles, ranging from unique tapestries
created independently by artist-weavers to those like this

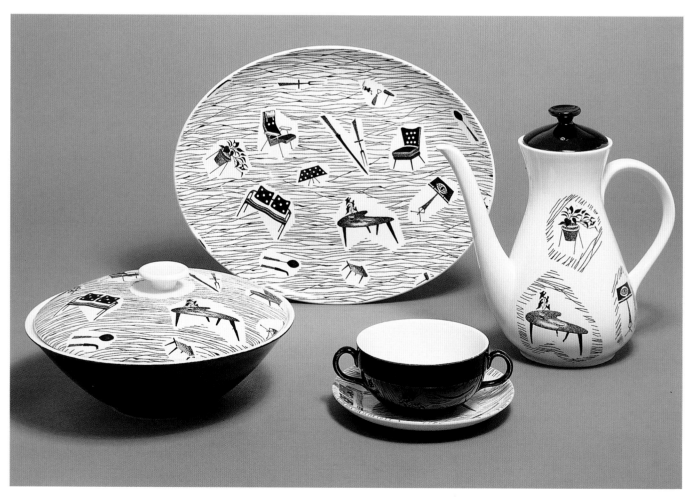

187.

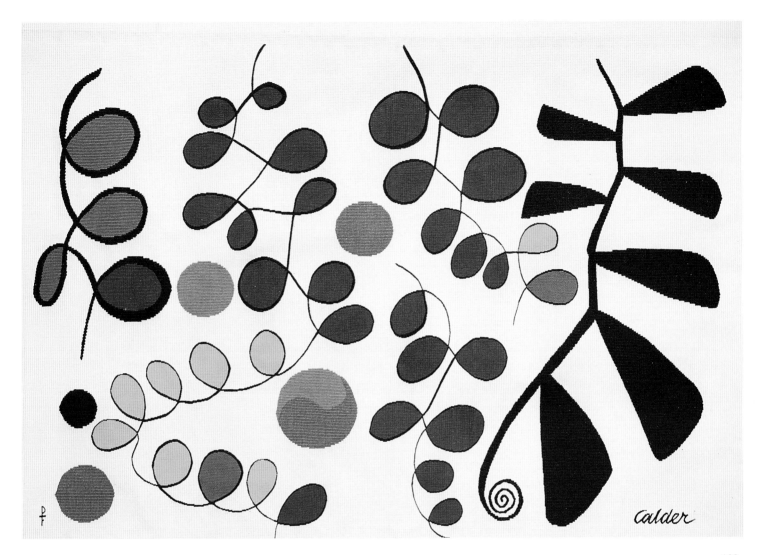

Calder, works made in large ateliers by professional weavers following designs by well-known painters and sculptors. At the time of this acquisition, a choice had to be made between the Calder and a tapestry by Sonia Delaunay; the director, John Pope-Hennessy, was adamant that it should be the Calder.

In 1971 Calder worked closely with Jean Pinton to produce a series of twenty-six tapestries that included *Autumn Leaves*. In its scale, its motifs, and its bright, clear colors set off by black and white, the tapestry is reminiscent of Calder's famous mobiles. The artist first designed textiles in 1929, although his energies from 1930 to 1962 were largely devoted to sculpture. He returned to the design of textiles in 1962, when he began a collaboration with French tapestry workshops that continued until his death.

Lit. V&A, 1991, front cover and p. 82

VALERIE MENDES

189. RONALD TRAEGER (American, 1937–1968). *Twiggy.* 1967; printed 1995. Photograph (gelatin-silver print), 19⅞ x 16⅛" (50.5 x 40.8 cm). Given by Tessa Traeger. V&A E.72–1996

Ronald Traeger trained at the San Francisco Art Institute and arrived in London—by way of Rome and Paris—in 1963. As a result of photographs Traeger had produced in Rome, the art director of British *Vogue* immediately published Traeger's work, and regular commissions followed to photograph fashion for *Vogue,* as well as for *Elle* in Paris. This dynamic image of the model Twiggy riding a motorized bicycle (or moped) was shot for "Young Idea's Shorts Supply," published in *Vogue* in July 1967. This particular image, however, is an outtake from the series and was not published. Contrasting Traeger's work with that of David Bailey from the same period, critic Martin Harrison wrote that this image is "much closer to most perceptions of mid-sixties London. Its throwaway exuberance captures exactly the spirit of the time."

Ronald Traeger died of cancer while young. His work received renewed attention in 1991 when it was shown at the V&A in the exhibition, "Appearances: Fashion Photography since 1945." As is common with the work of fashion photographers, many of Traeger's greatest negatives were lost or discarded by his clients. This print was copied by his widow, Tessa Traeger, from an apparently unique original. She made the print in 1995 using Ronald Traeger's darkroom procedures.

Lit. Harrison, 1991, pp. 216–21

MARK HAWORTH-BOOTH

190. STEPHEN WILLATS (English, born 1943)

190.1. *Variable Sheets (Design for a Dress).* 1965. Pencil and bodycolor, 43¾ x 29⅞" (111 x 76 cm). V&A E.1615–1984 & E.1615A–1984

190.2. *Variable Sheets/Optical Shift (Dress with Zipped Panels).* 1965. Plastic (PVC), 32⅛ x 19⅝" (81.5 x 50 cm). V&A T.19–1991

This boldly geometric dress was designed by the performance artist Stephen Willats so that the panels could be rearranged by the wearer in a variety of combinations, according to mood and environment. Willats chose PVC instead of more conventional materials because he felt that the new synthetic materials of the

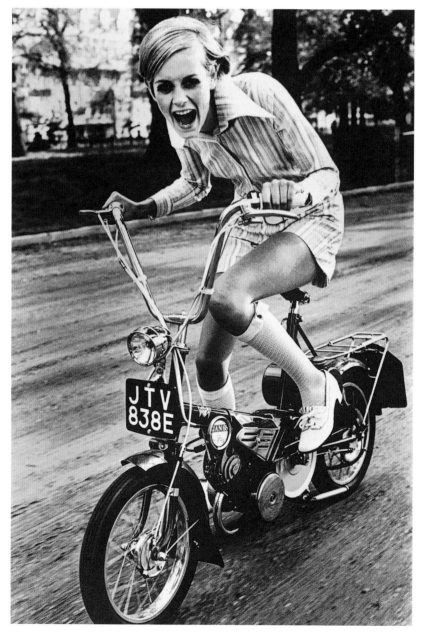

189.

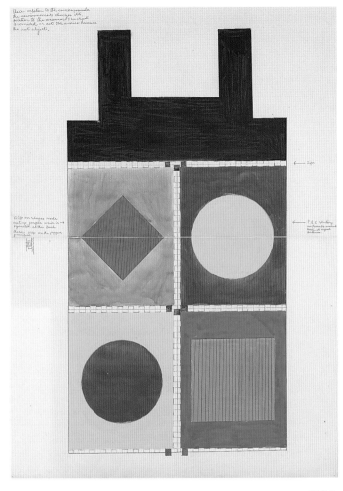

190.1.

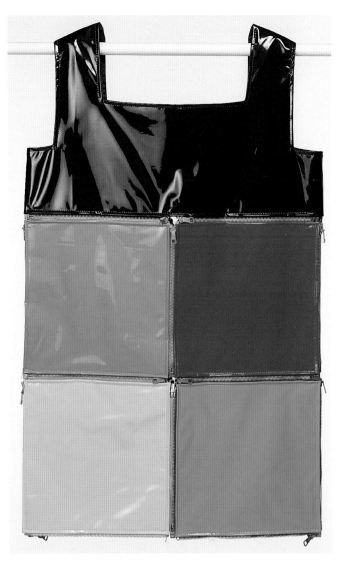

190.2.

1960s embodied the forward-looking spirit of the period. He designed similar dresses for sale in boutiques and other small outlets.

Willats has staged his performance pieces in a variety of venues—from housing developments to museums—with the aim of making art a dynamic public event. Such activities blur distinctions between painting/sculpture, theater, and design, making the art form difficult for museums to collect, record, illustrate, and explain. The acquisition of associated documentation and materials is one way of "collecting" this art. The Museum acquired the dress, the designs for it, and an accompanying helmet only in the 1980s; by then it had become clear that Willats's experimental design concepts were at the forefront of the artistic sensibilities of the 1960s.

CHARLES NEWTON

191. MARC FOSTER GRANT (American, born 1947). *Furnishing fabric: "Haircut? Yes Please!".* 1973. Cotton sateen, screenprinted, 144 x 48" (366 x 122 cm). Given by Marc Foster Grant. V&A Circ.189–1974

Marc Foster Grant is the chairman of Jeanne-Marc (named for Grant and his wife and design partner Jeanne Allen), an extremely successful San Francisco–based company, founded in 1974, specializing in fabric and clothing design. A quarter-century ago, however, Grant was a student in printmaking at Brighton Polytechnic School of Art and Design in England. After graduating from San Francisco State College in 1970, he and Allen (who met as coworkers at the San Francisco branch of the retailer Design Research) left for Europe, finding their way to Finland where Grant hand-screened fabrics for the Marimekko factory. Moving to England to pursue a master's

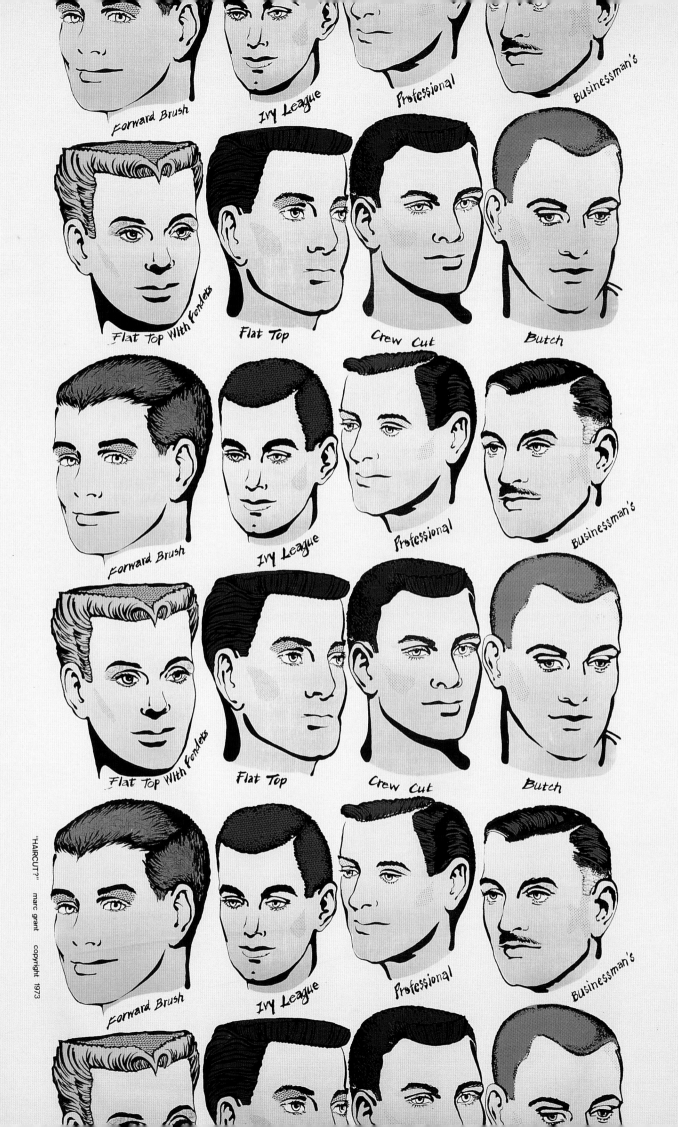

Forward Brush   Ivy League   Professional   Businessman's

Flat Top With Fenders   Flat Top   Crew Cut   Butch

Forward Brush   Ivy League   Professional   Businessman's

Flat Top With Fenders   Flat Top   Crew Cut   Butch

Forward Brush   Ivy League   Professional   Businessman's

"HAIRCUT?"   marc grant   copyright 1973

191.

degree in printmaking, Grant enrolled at Brighton and joined a class taught by Harvey Daniels, a charismatic teacher and Art Deco collector who assembled around him what Grant describes as an international group of students uncharacteristic of English schools.

One day in 1973 there were visitors to Daniels's class. Staff from the V&A's Circulation Department were looking for work suitable for "The Fabric of Pop," a traveling exhibition of Pop imagery in textiles and fashion of the late 1960s and 1970s. In those years, Circulation staff essentially scavenged door to door—often in art schools—to acquire contemporary design works. They selected from among Grant's work several screen-printed pieces, including his "Haircut" fabric, and a big quilted, tasseled pillow screenprinted with images of water-skiers that the artist recalls vividly. Grant reports that there was never a question of being paid for these works; the student designers were so excited by the Museum's interest and the prospect of exhibition that they gave to the V&A whatever the curators liked.

"Haircut? Yes Please!" is unique. Grant made the screen and printed a single twelve-foot run of cotton sateen (he printed enough of the "Haircut" pattern on muslin to make a pair of pajamas, specifically so that he could see how the print would drape in clothing.) The artist reports that in designing the print, he was remembering the commercial graphics common in barber shops in the United States in the 1950s and 1960s that depicted styles from which the customer could choose. *"Haircut? Yes Please!"* is entertaining and nostalgic by virtue of its subject—period haircut styles and their amusing period names—and it is visually compelling in the boldness of its pattern repeat. But there is also a subversive seriousness to the design, reflected in its spectrum of human skin colors and the sensitivity and variety of facial expressions among the rows of heads. Having come of age in an era of racial divide in America, Grant must have been conscious that his "Haircut" pattern was not simply a handsome abstraction but carried a specific sociopolitical subtext. In designing that duality into his fabric, Grant's "Haircut" pays homage to the form-and-content dualities of the best of classic sixties American Pop Art.

Lit. V&A, 1974a

Brenda Richardson

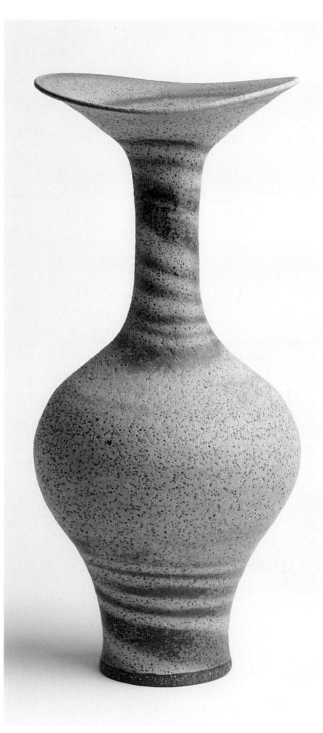

192.

192. Lucie Rie (Austrian, 1902–1995 [resident London from 1939]). *Bottle.* c. 1979. Stoneware, 15 x 6¾ x 6¾" (38 x 17 x 17 cm). V&A C.42–1982

The Museum bought this pot by Lucie Rie following a major Rie retrospective exhibition at the Museum in 1982. At the same time, the artist donated a group of her pots made in the 1920s and 1930s in her native Vienna. Toward the end of her career, Rie had come to be regarded as the greatest potter working in England. She was particularly championed by those who considered the Oriental styles of Bernard Leach (see cat. 176) and his followers to be overly restrictive. Working in a central

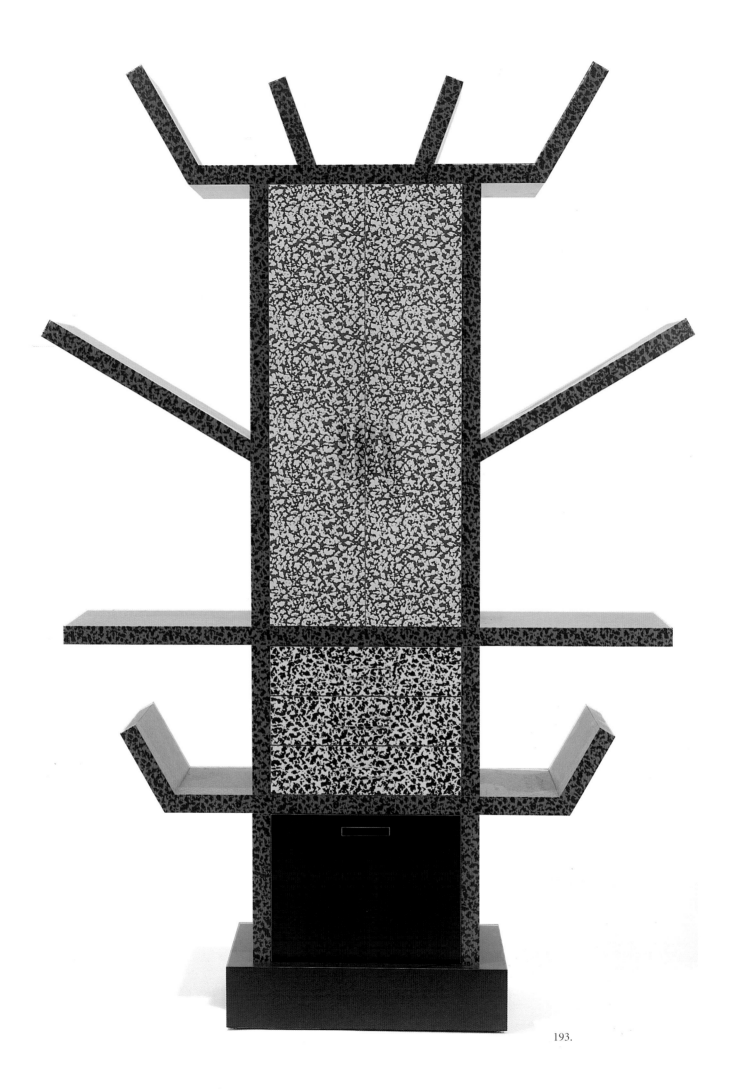

193.

London studio and buying her materials ready-made from industrial suppliers—she remarked of this vase that "the pink comes from the chemist"—Rie diverged from Leach in her approach to her work. She was a pragmatist, decidedly not of the "lifestyle" school of potters—epitomized by Leach—who believed the spiritual ways in which they lived their lives infused and shaped their work. As a consequence, she has been characterized as a "modernist" in contrast to the "traditionalist" Leach and has been criticized by purists for eroding traditional values. Yet she took inspiration from the same Chinese Song wares that inspired Leach and, like him, spent her entire life making useful tablewares or decorative vessels, all of them wheel-thrown. This vase, although entirely original, nonetheless echoes twelfth-century Chinese porcelains in its shape, medieval Persian ceramics in its coloring, and contemporary European art in its textures and softly distorted form.

OLIVER WATSON

193. ETTORE SOTTSASS (Italian, born Austria 1917); made by MEMPHIS, Milan, Italy. *Casablanca Sideboard.* 1981. Plastic laminate over fiberboard, 90½ x 63⅝ x 13¾" (230 x 161.5 x 35 cm). Acquired, in part, with the assistance of Memphis. V&A W.14–1990

In 1981 the design group and manufacturer Memphis, led by Ettore Sottsass, launched its first collection, in which the designers explicitly challenged preconceptions of good taste. Sottsass believed that contemporary design had become sterile under the influence of modernism and wished to reintroduce wit, color, and iconography. The improbable form of the Casablanca Sideboard (part of Memphis's first collection) and its bold laminated decoration, inspired by popular taste of the 1950s, identified the design as postmodern. The wit and iconoclasm of Memphis influenced many 1980s designers, particularly in the field of product design, and its contribution has been recognized as a defining moment in the history of late-twentieth-century industrial design.

Lit. Radice, 1985, p. 37; Radice, 1993; Wilk, 1996, p. 220

GARETH WILLIAMS

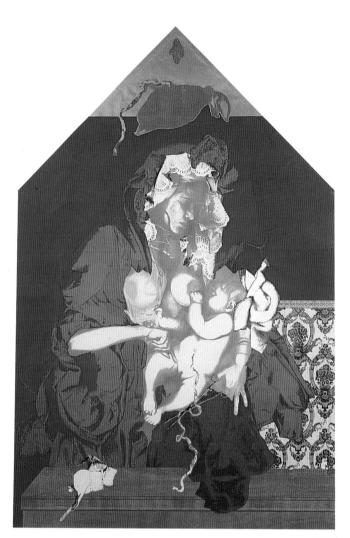

194.

194. HELEN CHADWICK (English, 1953–1996). *One Flesh.* 1985. Collage of photocopies, 66⅛ x 44½ x 2½" (168 x 113 x 6.5 cm). V&A Ph.146–1986

This is a Madonna and Child for modern, or rather, postmodern times. The title refers to the trinity of mother, child, and, above them (toned in gold), the placenta. Like Julia Margaret Cameron before her (cat. 33), Helen Chadwick used "low" technology to create high art. The artist photocopied imagery from various sources, then cut and collaged the copies to form a design inspired by Madonna compositions of the Early Renaissance. The result is both overwhelmingly frank and as elusive as an echo.

One Flesh has been described by Marina Warner, one of its principal feminist admirers, as "a Surrealist outrage," while Chadwick herself related the image to the idea of "jouissance" ("enjoyment") in the writings of Julia Kristeva. Shortly after its acquisition, *One Flesh* was shown at the V&A in "Towards a Bigger Picture: Contemporary British Photography" (1987), an

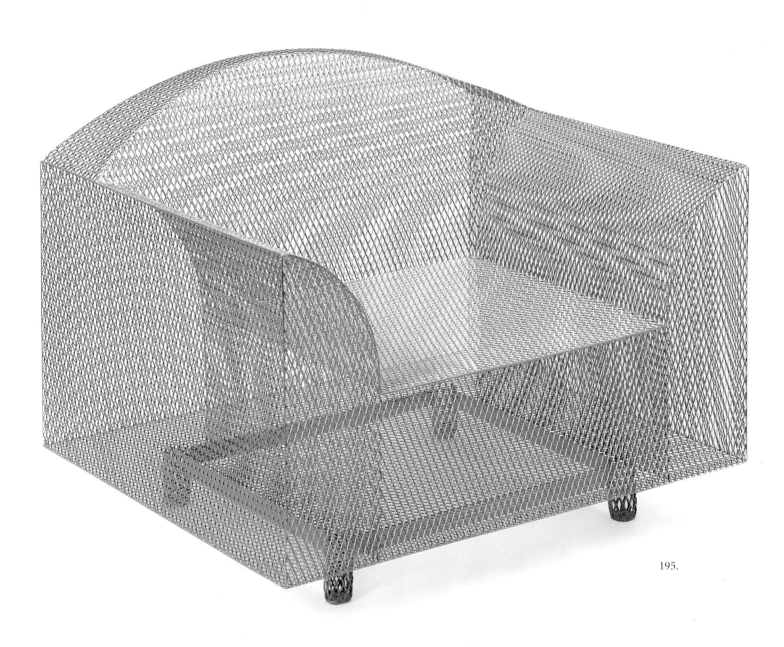

195.

exhibition that demonstrated the lively condition of the medium in the hands of a new generation of photographic artists and artist-photographers. In 1989 Chadwick produced a celebrated series of large-scale Polaroid photographs at the V&A. Her career was cut tragically short, however, when she died very suddenly, of unknown causes, on 15 March 1996.

Lit. Chadwick, 1989; Haworth-Booth, 1994b

MARK HAWORTH-BOOTH

195. SHIRO KURAMATA (Japanese, 1934–1991); made by VITRA, Basel, Switzerland. *Armchair: "How High The Moon".* 1986–87. Perforated zinc and steel mesh, 29⅝ x 37½ x 32⅛" (75.2 x 95.4 x 81.5 cm). Given by Vitra Ltd., London. V&A W.6–1990

While the form and proportions of this self-consciously artistic armchair are based on the traditional club chair—an upholstered and overstuffed easy chair with deep arms and a low back—the bulkiness and solidity of the club chair are transformed into weightlessness and transparency through the use of an unexpected material. Comfort is obviously not a priority in the design. Rather, its apparent contradiction between form and function invites reflection, and its distinctively aesthetic presence asserts its intention to be viewed as a work of art as much as a piece of furniture.

SORREL HERSHBERG

196. NORBERT BERGHOF (German, born 1949), MICHAEL LANDES (German, born 1948), and WOLFGANG RANG (German, born 1949); made by DRAENERT COLLECTION, Immenstaad, Germany. *Frankfurt Cabinet.* 1985–89. Number 50 of edition of 100. Bird's-eye maple, maple, burl walnut, walnut, masur birch, unidentified woods, brass, gold leaf, lasa and acosta marble, Bahia blue granite, 89¾ x 29½ x 15¾" (228 x 75 x 40 cm). V&A W.14–1989

The Frankfurt Cabinet is a modern example in the long tradition of furniture intended as display object, made of exotic materials and concealing its function beneath its decoration. Its design contrasts with the prevailing functionalism of much twentieth-century furniture collected by the Museum and

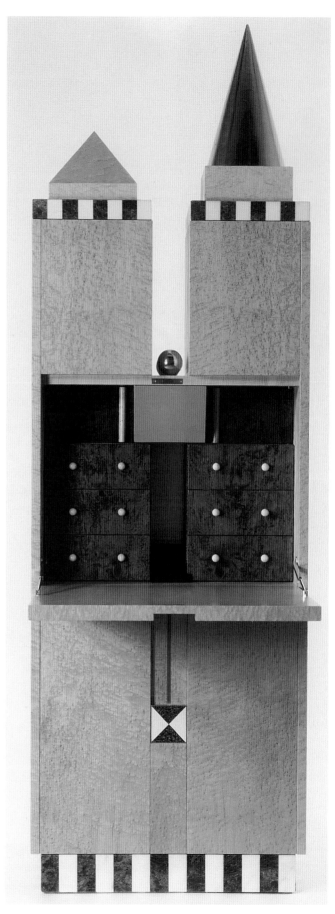

196.

demonstrates the eclectic use of historical sources typical of postmodernism, the most fashionable design style of the 1980s. The light wood and flat veneered surfaces recall central European Biedermeier furniture of the early nineteenth century, the checkerboard device and simplified geometry echo early-twentieth-century Viennese patterning, and the asymmetrical design and combination of rich materials are reminiscent of Art Deco.

Lit. Himmelheber, 1988, p. 287; Fischer, 1989, pp. 92–5

Gareth Williams

197. Designed by SWATCH, Switzerland; made in Taiwan. *Telephone: Pink Jelly XK200 Twinphone.* 1990. Plastic, 9⅝ x 2¾ x 2" (24.5 x 7 x 5 cm). Given by Swatch. V&A W.3–1996

This telephone, like a series of internationally popular wristwatches also produced by Swatch, uses internal functional components as a primary decorative feature (like Daniel Weil's Radio in a Bag, cat. 182.5). In its cheerful, candy colors and its visually accessible technology, the telephone signals youth and playfulness as well as contemporary style.

Richard Dunn

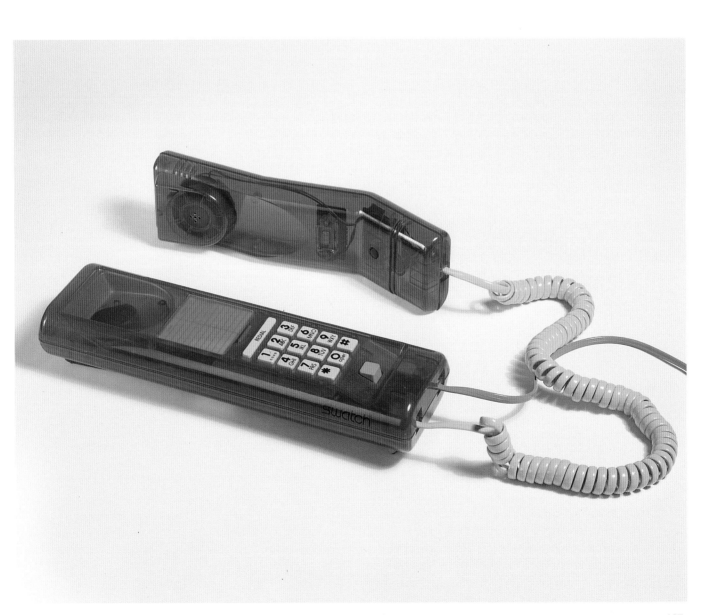

197.

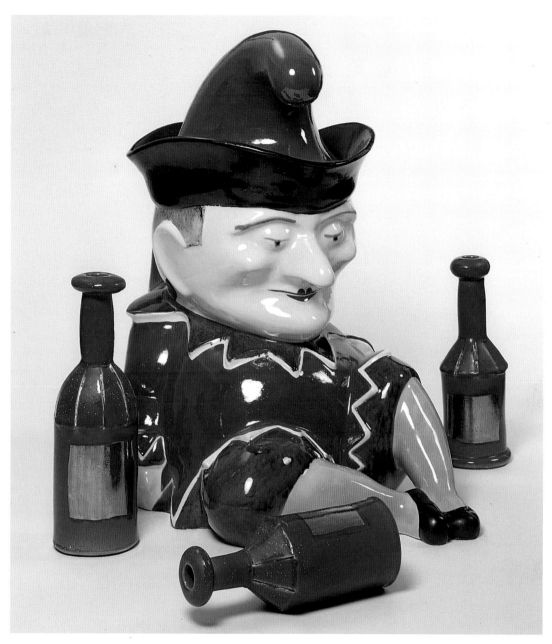

198. RICHARD SLEE (English [Brighton], born 1946). *Drunk Punch.* 1991. Earthenware, coiled, with colored glazes: Punch with hat 22 x 13¾ x 19⅝" (56 x 35 x 50 cm); small bottle 8¼ x 3⅛" (21 x 8 cm); medium bottle 9⅝ x 3¾" (24.5 x 9.5 cm); large bottle 11 x 3½" (28 x 9 cm). V&A C.15:1to5–1992

The grand wizard of contemporary British studio pottery, Richard Slee and his ceramics have not always found immediate favor with collectors. But the Museum has long regarded his work as important, acquiring several of his reworkings of traditional vase forms. In the early 1990s Slee began making large Tobies, playing with notions of "Englishness" and the ways in which appeals to the traditional past are often used to legitimize current attitudes and actions. The Toby jug (a large drinking mug, usually in the form of a stout man) was an eighteenth-century invention depicting characters that embodied typically English bluff and stalwart qualities. Slee combines Toby with another traditional character—the more sinister Punch, an alcoholic wife-beater from the seaside *Punch and Judy* show. With a title that inverts the phrase "punch drunk," Slee's *Drunk Punch* articulates the artist's view of England after a decade in which "Victorian" and "Traditional Family" values have been much vaunted by politicians, yet systematically eroded by government policy. The historic references thus acquire a biting contemporary meaning. The piece is normally exhibited at the end of a gallery that contains the eighteenth-century jugs to which it refers.

OLIVER WATSON

199. English
Pairs of Shoes

199.1.   Made by SHAFTESBURY SHOES LTD. 1940s. Sling-back sandals; plaited leather straps in red, yellow, and gray; leather-covered platform sole with circular inset layers; leather-covered heel. 7⅞" (20 cm) long, 7⅛" (18 cm) high. Given by Mrs. M. Bagel. V&A T.33–1988

199.2.   MARY QUANT (English [London], born 1934). 1960s. Yellow plastic injection-molded ankle boots with cotton jersey lining. 10⅞" (27.5 cm) long, 4⅜" (11 cm) high. Quant trademark daisy on bottom of heel. Given by Susannah Lob. V&A T.59:1&2–1992

199.3.   M. K. EGELI (Turkish-Cypriot?, 20th century [active England 1970s]). 1970s. Cream knee-high calfskin boots; round toe, platform sole. 10⅝" (27 cm) long, 24⅜" (62 cm) high. Given by M. K. Egeli. V&A T.129–1987

199.4.   VIVIENNE WESTWOOD (English, born 1941). Autumn/winter 1993–94. Bright blue punched leather "mock-croc" platform shoes, blue silk ribbon laces, platform soles, 9" (23 cm) long, 12" (30.5 cm) high. Given by Vivienne Westwood. V&A T.225:1&2–1993

199.5.   *Vegetarian Shoes.* 1994. Green polyester and polyurethane boots; Dr. Martens original "Air Wair" air cushion soles, resistant to oil, fat, acid, petrol, and alkali, 12¼" (31 cm) long, 8⅛" (20.5 cm) high. Given by Vegetarian Shoes, Brighton. V&A T.90:1&2–1994

The Museum's collection of shoes—like its larger twentieth-century dress collection—has been primarily of haute couture examples. It has been only in the past few years that the Museum has sought to expand its shoe collection—recent acquisitions have ranged from 1940s cowboy boots to 1990s Converse Allstars designs, each chosen for its significance in the changing history of fashion in the shoe industry.

Revivalism has been a major theme in the design of twentieth-century shoes. All five of these pairs of shoes demonstrate a nostalgia that is manifest in creating new styles from old. Platforms, although seen as a new style in the 1930s—and subsequently revived in the 1940s, 1970s, and 1990s—had their origins in the chopines of the sixteenth century. The use of synthetics has also become more common in the last century, motivated both by technological innovation and by the scarcity of leather during World War II. Today, synthetics are often seen as an ethical alternative to leather, and companies like Vegetarian Shoes have begun to manufacture design classics—like the "Doc Martens" boot—in brightly colored polyester.

CATHIE DINGWALL

199.3.

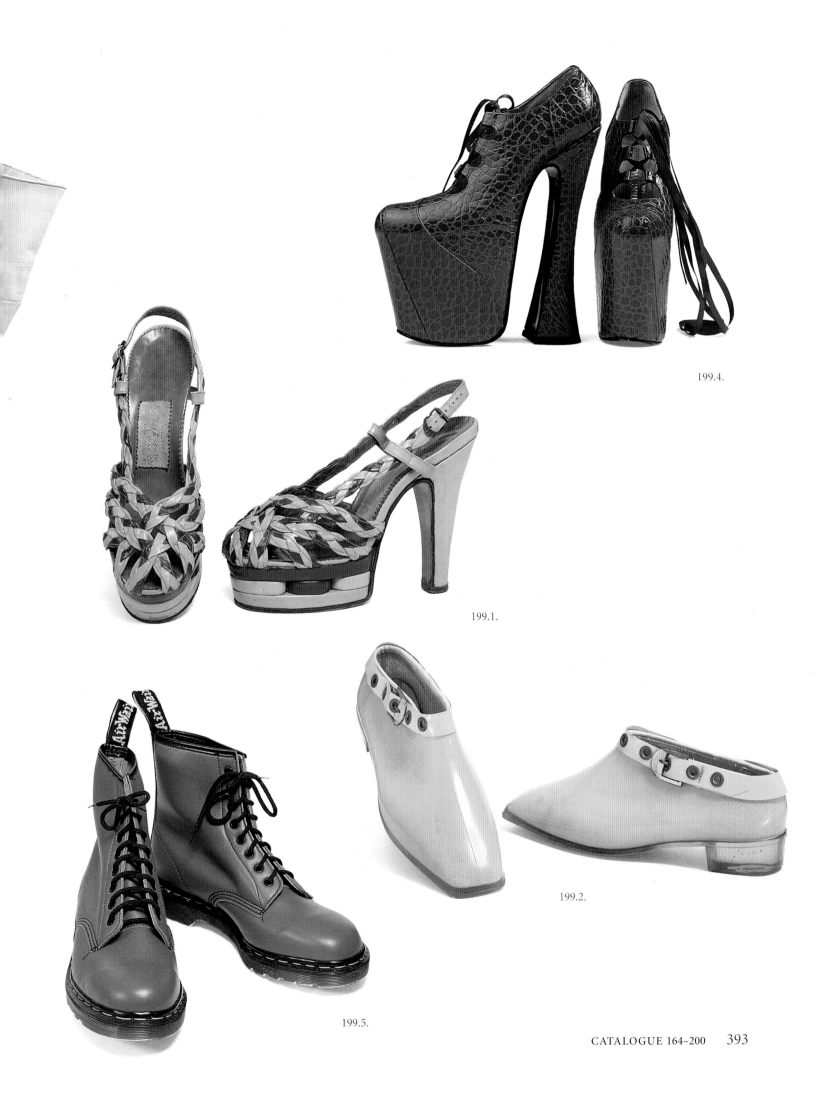

199.4.

199.1.

199.2.

199.5.

200. CHRISTIAN LACROIX (French, born 1951). *Evening Dress.* 1996. Chiné-printed silk taffeta and lace, embroidered with sequins, pastes, and beads, 59" (150 cm) long, 27½" (70 cm) bust, 24⅜" (62 cm) waist, 66⅞" (170 cm) hoop max. diam. Given by Christian Lacroix. V&A T.435–1996

This spectacular dress—the most recent V&A acquisition represented in *A Grand Design*—was given to the Museum very shortly after its first appearance on Lacroix's catwalk in the autumn 1996 Paris fashion shows.

Christian Lacroix opened his haute couture house in 1986. His luxurious fashions, typified by this hooped evening dress, reflect an abiding passion for historical styles, ornate textiles, and elaborate decoration, all of which he translates in a contemporary idiom.

In a striking palette of acidic yellow and pastels, the dress forms part of Lacroix's "18th-Century Haute Couture Collection," which draws on a wide range of pre-1968 fashion references. Lacroix describes this collection as elegant and slightly disheveled: "Nothing seems to be held in place. The fabric is wrapped. It pirouettes around obstinately asymmetrical necklines."

AMY DE LA HAYE

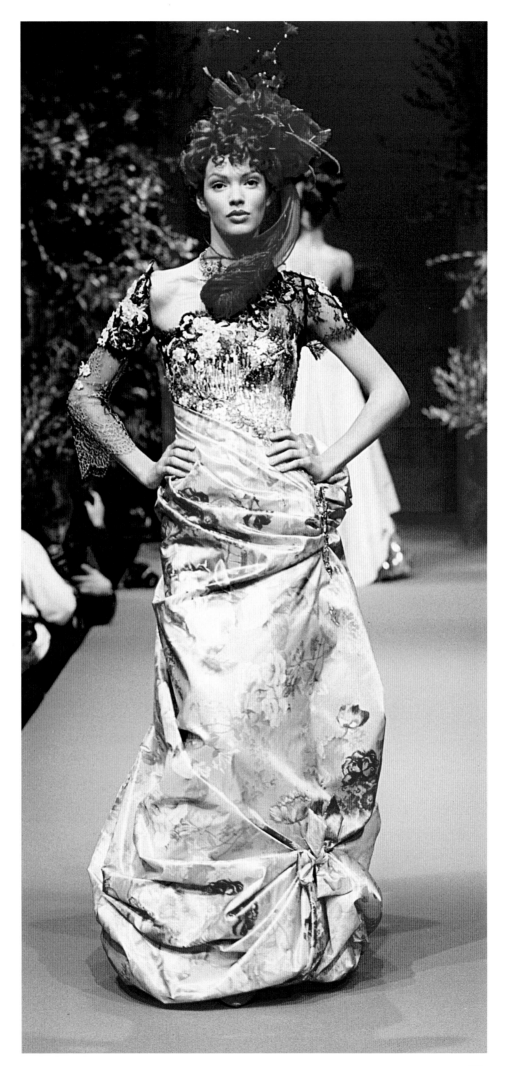

Notes

Preface: A Point of View

1. V&A, 1991, p. 6.

2. Ibid.

3. Lyle Rexer, "Art for Science's Sake Is a Whole Other Story," *The New York Times*, 21 July 1996, p. 28.

4. David Lowenthal, letter published in "The Mail," *The New Yorker*, 17 February 1997, p. 10.

Museums, Collections, and Their Histories

1. For one view of the relationship between the V&A and other national museums in London, see the discussion in the V&A's 1908 Report of the Committee on Re-arrangement.

2. Baker, 1996a.

3. The V&A has itself contributed to this study, notably through Physick, 1982; and the research of Charles Gibbs-Smith, one outcome of which was a display about the Museum's history mounted in the 1950s.

4. For discussions of some of this literature, see Pomian, 1993; Herklotz, 1994; Gordon, 1995; and Gaskell, 1995.

5. MacGregor, 1983; and Stafski, 1978. Other important studies have included McClellan, 1994; and a number of discussions of the Berlin museums, including Gaehtgens, 1992, and Joachimides, 1995.

6. Georgel, 1994; and Griffiths, 1996.

7. Significant contributions, among others, include Pearce, 1992; and Pointon, 1994. The current interest in these issues is registered by the space given last year to an extensive series of articles on "the problematics of collecting and display" in the *Art Bulletin 77* (1995). Especially telling articles were written by Vishakha Desai and Donald Preziosi, among others. A further significant response to recent critiques of the museum is Conforti, 1992.

The Idealist Enterprise and the Applied Arts

I want to thank Malcolm Baker, Anthony Burton, David Caccioli, and Ashley West for the considerable help they provided in research for this essay.

1. Taft, 1878, p. 10. John Adams's attitude is expressed in the letter to his wife that concludes his often quoted perspective on generational progress: "I must study politics and war, that my sons may have the liberty to study mathematics and philosophy . . . in order to give their children a right to study painting, poetry, music, architecture, statuary, tapestry, and porcelain" (John Adams to Abigail Adams, 1780, in Adams, 1876, p. 381).

2. These words from the "Influence of the South Kensington Museum" were underlined by William T. Walters in his personal copy of the catalogue for the 1889 Paris Exposition Universelle ("First Group"), 1889, p. 15. (I am grateful to William R. Johnston of Baltimore's Walters Art Gallery for this information.)

3. Menzhausen, 1985, pp. 69–75.

4. Neverov, 1985, pp. 54–61.

5. McClellan, 1994, pp. 124–54.

6. In 1865, Henry Cole made a study of the Conservatoire and his notes are in the National Art Library, V&A (55.AA.56.f.97). See also Tise, 1991, pp. 1–5; Froissart, 1994, pp. 83–90; and Conforti, in press [1997].

7. For Vienna's response to the French Ecole and Conservatoire, see Lackner and Mikoletsky, 1995, pp. 29–42.

8. Select Committee. *Report from the Select Committee Appointed . . .*, 1835–36.

9. The Museum opened in May 1852. It appears that Cole and Prince Albert initially looked to the British Museum as a source of collections: Cole's diary chronicles a meeting in which the prince discussed his plan "to buy plenty of ground at Kensington to provide Collection of History of Manufactures, Lectures and c. to reform school of design to Call it College of Applied Art. . . . I agreed that to bring there the overflowings of the Brit Mus: wd aid all other proceedings in that neighborhood." Cole Diaries, entry for 5 January 1852.

10. Privy Council, 1853, p. 27.

11. For Cole's early background and administrative attributes, see Cooper, 1992. For Benthamism, see Nesbit, 1966, pp. 20–37.

12. Cole's belief in the power of his institution to advance the level of public taste grew with each year. His aims were already evident in a lecture, "On Public Taste in Kensington," 5 April 1853 (Cole Miscellanies, vol. XI, f.8), in which he connects the future establishment of the school and Museum to a broad educational objective that he understood to have commercial benefit. In 1857 Cole was even successful in arranging for his Department of Science and Art to report to the Education Minister rather than the Board of Trade.

Cole realized the education of the consumer was fundamental to the Museum's role and he referred to it both in his early years at the Museum and after his retirement. For one of the first of the now common studies focusing on the indoctrination of the Museum's consumer audience (and its parallels to the development of the department store in the late nineteenth century), see N. Harris, 1990. For an interpretation of South Kensington's role in advancing consumer demand, see Purbrick, 1994.

13. Cole's hope that South Kensington might be self-supporting is suggested by an 1853 lecture in which he asks that Kensington residents tax themselves "as a parish" to make such an institution possible (Cole Miscellanies, vol. XI, f.8). As time went on, however, and significant public support appeared out of reach, Cole changed his perspective by suggesting that government support was the only way to ensure public purpose (Cole Miscellanies, vol. XV, f.48).

14. The circulation of objects from the collections, a fundamental requirement in the government mandate, began in 1854 (Department of Science and Art, 1881 [Ed. 84.29]). Cole's acquisition of photographic, electrotype, and plaster reproductions began early in the institution's history (Cole Miscellanies, vol. IX, f.282) and continued through his directorship, when his foreign travel was often consumed with adding to the Museum's collection of copies.

15. Cole lecture, *The Functions of the Science and Art Department*. While one cannot generalize on admission policies in eighteenth- and early-nineteenth-century European museums, most considered their "public" to be aristocrats, learned individuals, or artists. Often they were allowed to visit a collection only upon application or on certain days of the week. Admission fees were also fairly commonplace. Cole, therefore, took special pride in his introduction of evening hours, and in the number of days South Kensington was available free of charge, making it more accessible to the working classes than any museum at the time.

16. Cole spent much of his first official report in 1853 discussing teaching by example (Cole Miscellanies, vol. IX, f.80). In 1860 when John Charles Robinson testified to the Select Committee, he summarized institutional attitudes on the use of objects for educational purposes: "I do not consider that the mere reproduction of the things we have got is the right use, nor do I think it a principal one, but I think that manufacturers and workmen, and students, get a general education at the museum for having fine examples before them" (Select Committee, 1860, p. 109).

17. Cole Miscellanies, vol. VII, f.223. The effort Cole went through to secure great collections is first evidenced in his work acquiring the Gherardini sculpture models (Cole Diaries, 1854, entries for March 13, 20, 27, and April 10, 13).

18. Already in 1853, Marlborough House displays included a "specimen of Mexican pottery . . . [a] Ceylon sword . . . 2 Chinese filigree bracelets" (Cole Miscellanies, vol. IX, f.80). After citing the purchases of Indian objects from the Great Exhibition of 1851, Cole in 1866 justified broadening the Indian collections to casts of architectural elements, "[as] India and the United Kingdom are under the same sovereign, it appears most desirable to obtain a complete representation of Indian architecture for South Kensington" (Cole Miscellanies, vol. XIV, f.49).

19. Cole was an avid critic of all aspects of a museum's public face, including its installations. As early as 1842 in a pamphlet on the British Museum, he complained of works of art "hung so high, that the label attached to them cannot be deciphered" (Cole Miscellanies, vol. VII, f.51). The journals of his trips abroad are filled with the observations of a serious museum professional and critic. On an 1863 trip he worried in the Salle d'Apollon at the Louvre that the "real magnificence and finesse of the objects are overpowered by the splendor of the room." In Berlin, he complains of no W.C. before revealing his own aesthetic inclinations about the works on view: ". . . the collections here have been made from a learned point of view rather than of art. . . . but no cost has been spared to set off the collection" (Cole, "Notes on a Journey to Vienna . . . ," pp. 3, 29).

20. Robinson spoke of installation practice in educational terms as early as 1854: ". . . the judicious arrangement and juxtaposition of specimens for comparison . . . facilitate[s] the deduction of those abstract laws and principles, a proper acquaintance with which is the foundation of all true knowledge" (Robinson, *An Introductory Lecture on the Museum of Ornamental Art of the Department*, 1854). That South Kensington took particular notice of Cluny as a museum paradigm is evidenced not only by Cole's occasional references to the French museum (e.g., Cole Diaries, 27 March 1856 entry), but also by Robinson's comment of 1863 that the

"Musée de Cluny possessed a most valuable and practically useful collection of works of medieval and Renaissance art." Later, Robinson unwittingly suggested that it represented a standard for him. After buying art for South Kensington for ten years, he claimed in writing that his Museum's collection was "almost superior" to that exhibited at Cluny (Robinson, 1863).

21. Robinson felt that intuitive good taste came to "certain continental peoples . . . familiar from childhood with the most refined works of art." He went on to lament, "But then London is not Venice" (Robinson, 1854, p. 21).

22. Charles Yriarte's words are recorded in Select Committee, *Second Report from the Select Committee . . .*, 1897, (note 103), p. 493. While this comment introduced Yriarte's criticism of South Kensington's display philosophy after Cole's retirement, he clearly appreciated the high level of medieval and Renaissance objects acquired under Cole's directorship.

23. For the applied arts museum movement in France, see Michael Conforti, "Les musées des arts appliqués et l'histoire de l'art," in press [1997].

24. Cole Diaries, 20 May 1853 entry.

25. Semper's views on the "reuniting" of science and art are stated succinctly in his treatise on metalwork presented to Cole in August 1852, a few months before the department's name was changed: "National education will be perfect, when science shall be pervaded by art and art by science and all human relations by both. . . . [Public collections] must bear the double character of scientific and artistic institutions" (Semper, "Practical Art in Metals," 1854, nos. 2, 6).

26. For a summary of Semper's London years, see Mallgrave, 1996. For Semper's plans for South Kensington, see Physick, 1994, pp. 28–36.

27. Mallgrave, 1996, p. 206.

28. Semper, *Der Stil . . .* , 1860/63. This fundamental theoretical text in art history is about to be published in its first English translation, although, appreciating the importance of Semper to their project, such a translation was discussed at South Kensington in the mid-1880s. (I thank Harry Mallgrave for this information.)

29. I thank Harry Mallgrave and Christian Witt-Dörring for much of this information. For the early history of the Museum für angewandte Kunst, see Fliedl, 1986, and Noever, 1988. For Austria's early efforts at design education, see Lackner and Mikoletsky, 1995, pp. 29–42.
Cole was in Vienna in 1864 a few months before the opening of Eitelberger's museum, but he seems not to have been aware of this new enterprise (Cole, "Notes on a Journey to Vienna . . . ," 1870).

30. For comments on Italy's achievement in establishing museums and the country's concern over the loss of its cultural patrimony to the collections of other nations, see Odaschalchi, pp. 295–6.

31. For the history of applied arts museums in Germany, see Mundt, 1974.

32. Schwabe, 1866a. The Institut Minutoli, which opened in 1845 in Liegnitz, Silesia (now Poland), was organized by a Prussian civil servant, Alexander von Minutoli, who had been sent to Silesia to improve the region's textile, glass, and cast-iron industries. It appears that Henry Cole was not aware of Minutoli's institute when he planned his museum and school, although it anticipates the training program and purposeful arrangement of objects in Cole's enterprise. In 1853, however, Minutoli informed officials in London of his work, and an account of the Institut's achievements was published that year in the *Journal of the Society of Arts,* pp. 320–4.

33. Brinckmann, 1894, pp. V–VII. For Lessing's contribution to culturally focused installation, see Mundt, 1982.

34. For Bode's innovative and historically evocative installation, see Conforti, 1992, pp. 3–14. In 1896, Bode argued with Julius Lessing in print over whether applied arts museums were as advanced as his fine arts museum in embracing the new, more cultural-history approach to museum installation and collection growth. For differing responses to Bode's innovations, see Baker on "Bode and Museum Display," 1996a.

35. Brinckmann, 1894, as translated by Mallgrave and Hermann in Semper, *Four Elements of Architecture . . .* , 1989, p. 160.

36. Perkins, 1870, pp. 7–8.

37. Woodward, 1985, pp. 12–60. For further discussion of South Kensington and schools of design in the United States, see Morris, 1986, pp. 75–82.

38. Cincinnati Art Museum, 1981, pp. 8–12.

39. Tvrdik, 1977, p. 10; Saint Louis Art Museum, 1984–88, p. 3.

40. Corcoran Gallery, 1985, p. 2; Babbitt, Philadelphia, 1995, pp. 10–21; Morikawa, 1983, pp. 281–5.

41. For the early history of The Metropolitan Museum of Art, see Howe, 1913; and Tomkins, 1970, pp. 15–120. Choate's words seem to echo those of the Cincinnati promoter Charles A. Taft, delivered and published two years before (Tomkins, p. 23).

42. For Charles C. Perkins, see Whitehill, 1970, pp. 10–2. For a summary of Perkins's report on museums, see Perkins, op. cit., where his most complete perspective on the value of South Kensington is expressed.

43. Eliot, 1887, pp. 17–8. Walter Smith subsequently became an outspoken and respected advocate for the establishment of South Kensington–style art programs in the United States (see Morris, 1986, pp. 75–6).

44. Perkins's inaugural speech is referred to in N. Harris, 1962, p 554–66.

45. *The American Architect and Building News,* 1880, p. 207.

46. For a discussion of these Metropolitan Museum exhibitions, see Miller, 1990.

47. For the Boston building and plan, see Whitehill, pp. 172–88, 204–45; also, "Communications to the Trustees regarding the New Building" (privately printed, 1904); and "The Museum Commission in Europe" (privately printed, 1905), both in the Archives of the Museum of Fine Arts, Boston.
The new Boston building that opened in 1909 reflected the intelligent, indeed sophisticated, philosophies of its senior staff at the turn of the century. Gilman regularly published the programs and perspectives that shaped Boston's direction. His ideas significantly influenced American early-twentieth-century museums, especially his organization of the country's first lecture programs by "docents," a term Gilman coined.

Industrial Arts and the Exhibition Ideal

I am grateful for the assistance of Paul Greenhalgh, Head of Research at the V&A, and of Geoff Opie.

1. Durbin, 1994, p. 16.

2. Fay, 1951, p. 47.

3. Ibid., p. 56.

4. Bennett, 1996, p. 83.

5. Findling, 1990.

6. Luckhurst, 1951, p. 23.

7. Greenhalgh, 1988, pp. 3–6.

8. *Official, Descriptive and Illustrated Catalogue of the Great Exhibition of the Works of Industry of All Nations,* London, 1851 [hereafter, *Official . . .*].

9. Bennett, op. cit., p. 92.

10. Ibid., p. 93.

11. Alexander, 1983, p. 163.

12. South Kensington Museum, *Guide to the South Kensington Museum,* 1857b.

13. Art Journal, facsimile version of the Great Exhibition catalogue, 1995, p. viii.

14. Ibid.

15. Herbert is occasionally omitted from accounts of this committee's membership (see Frayling, 1987, p. 38; MacCarthy, 1972, p. 20).

16. "First Report of the Department of Practical Art," in British Parliamentary Papers [hereafter BPP], *Reports and Papers Relating to the State of the Head and Branch Schools of Design,* 1850–53, Irish University Press, Industrial Revolution, Design, IV, p. 229, cited in Purbrick, 1994, p. 79.

17. MacCarthy, op. cit., p. 20.

18. Hinsley, in Karp and Lavine, 1991, p. 345.

19. "Catalogue of the Museum of Manufactures," in BPP, op. cit., p. 481.

20. Richard Redgrave, *Reports by the Juries on the Subjects in the Thirty Classes into Which the Exhibition Was Divided,* London, 1852, pp. 708–49, as cited in Boe, 1957, p. 59.

21. "Catalogue of the Museum of Manufactures," in BPP, op. cit., p. 481.

22. Department of Science and Art, *List of Objects in the Art Division, South Kensington Museum, Acquired During the Year 1871,* 1872.

23. *List of Objects . . .* [for years 1878, 1889, and 1900] (see note 22).

24. Jackson, A., 1992, pp. 245–56.

25. *List of Objects . . .* [for the year 1867] (see note 22).

26. *Report from the Select Committee on the South Kensington Museum,* 1860, pp. 10–11, cited in Purbrick, 1994, p. 84.

27. *Official . . .* , op. cit., p. 1.

Teaching by Example: Education and the Formation of South Kensington's Museums

I wish to acknowledge the support of the Brazilian Ministry of Education (CAPES) in funding the research upon which this article is based.

1. For standard accounts of this process, see Pevsner, 1940, pp. 191–242; and Macdonald, 1970, pp. 20–31.

2. The history of the period 1837–52 is covered in Macdonald, 1970, chs. 3–5; as well

as being rather colorfully described in Bell, 1963.

3. On the formation of the collections, see Physick, 1982, esp. pp. 13–8; and Purbrick, 1994.

4. As a Royal Academician and former teacher at the metropolitan School of Design, Redgrave occupied an ambiguous position in the debate between those who believed in the virtues of fine art training for prospective designers and those who advocated an entirely different type of "technical" instruction geared to the particular demands of trade and industry; see Redgrave, 1891, pp. 358–9. For more on Redgrave's career, see Burton, 1988.

5. See, for example, Argles, 1964, p. 21; Macdonald, 1970, p. 157; or Allthorpe-Guyton, 1982, pp. 21, 83–5.

6. Redgrave, 1853, p. 59.

7. Department of Science and Art, 1856, pp. 26–7.

8. For an overview of the development of the London school, see Frayling and Catterall, 1996, pp. 20–8.

9. Department of Science and Art, 1856, pp. 26–7.

10. Amateur day classes, for instance—which were officially encouraged from 1853—usually cost not less than 10s. 6d. [ten shillings and sixpence] per quarter and often as much as 21s. Evening classes for artisans, on the other hand, usually cost around 2s. 6d. per quarter, sometimes less. For basic data on types of classes held in local Schools of Art and their operation, see Select Committee on Schools of Art, 1864, pp. 368–453.

11. See Department of Science and Art, 1854, pp. xi–xlvi; Cole, 1831–82, vol. 9, pp. 13–4; Department of Science and Art, 1865a, p. 14; A. S. Cole and H. Cole, 1884, vol. 1, p. 305; and Macdonald, 1970, p. 176.

12. Select Committee on Schools of Art, 1864, pp. 47–8; Royal Commission on Technical Instruction, 1881, Second Report (1884), pp. 98–103; and Bishop, 1971, pp. 177.

13. Herkomer, 1890, p. 20.

14. Select Committee on Schools of Art, 1864, pp. 65–9, 72, 92. For descriptions of the teaching regime at South Kensington, see Poynter, 1879, p. 106; Clausen, 1912, pp. 155–61; and Fildes, 1968, pp. 3–4.

15. See Department of Science and Art, 1857, p. 6; and A. S. Cole and H. Cole, 1884, vol. 2, p. 289; see also Burchett, 1858, p. 28.

16. For an insightful analysis of the inception and development of the Museum, see Purbrick, 1994.

17. Cole, 1831–82, vol. 9; Select Committee on Scientific Instruction, 1864a, vol. 15, pp. 47–8, 450–1.

18. Hansard's Parliamentary Debates, 3rd series, vol. 160, p. 1308. For examples of press criticism, see Building News, 1864, p. 320; and Smith, 1864, p. 219.

19. Select Committee on Schools of Art, 1864, pp. 74, 81; and Journal of the Society of Arts, vol. 16 (1868), p. 179.

20. Cole, 1831–82, vol. 16, pp. 51–2. The sum expended on purchases and acquisitions in 1869 was £30,147, equivalent to thirteen percent of the total parliamentary vote for that year.

21. V&A, 1908, pp. 4–5, 12.

22. Cole, 1878, p. 13.

23. Jones, 1856, pp. 1–3.

24. Unfortunately, the taxonomical dimension of this type of Museum project lent itself admirably to the worst excesses of cultural imperialism as well; for more on this, see "The Empire of Things" articles in the present publication.

25. For a fuller discussion of the social and ethical dimensions of collecting, see Elsner and Cardinal, 1994, esp. pp. 2–5.

An Encyclopedia of Treasures: The Idea of the Great Collection

We are grateful to Malcolm Baker, Anthony Burton, Paul Greenhalgh, and Clive Wainwright for their suggestions.

1. For notions of the changing canon, see Haskell, 1976; Gaskell and Kemal, 1991; and the essays by Michael Camille and others in Art Bulletin, 1996.

2. "Report from the Select Committee on Arts and Their Connexion with Manufactures," 1836, p. v, cited in Rhodes, 1983.

3. Frayling, 1987, p. 17.

4. Ibid., p. 23.

5. Hobhouse, 1950, p. 7; Altick, 1978, p. 456.

6. "First Report of the Department of Practical Art," in British Parliamentary Papers, Reports and Papers Relating to the State of the Head and Branch Schools of Design, 1850–53, Irish University Press, Industrial Revolution, Design, IV, p. 2, as cited in

Purbrick, 1994, p. 77.

7. Wainwright, 1994, p. 96.

8. Ibid.; Caygill, 1985, p. 199.

9. Robinson, 1862b, pp. viii–ix.

10. Ibid., p. xi.

11. Ibid., p. 167.

12. J. C. Robinson, letter to The Times, 1 October 1883.

13. Wainwright, 1989, p. 292.

14. Wainwright, 1988; Robinson, 1856.

15. Robinson, 1862a.

16. Ibid.

17. Robinson, 1862b, p. xi.

18. For these various forms of reproduction and their impact, see Baker, 1988; Fawcett, 1987; Galbally, 1988.

19. For Robinson's Spanish campaigns, see Oman, 1968; Baker, 1986; Trusted, 1996.

20. Jervis, 1983, p. 82. Beginning in 1852, when Henry Morley (1822–1894) published a two-volume biography of Palissy, the French potter's fame in England grew not only on account of his art, but also by virtue of his status as a persecuted Protestant.

21. Wainwright, 1989.

22. Art Journal, October 1860.

23. Robinson, "On the Art Collections at South Kensington, Considered in Reference to Architecture," Building News 12, 5 June 1863. We are grateful to Michael Conforti, whose research in conjunction with A Grand Design has brought a great deal of significant material to our attention, including this commentary by Robinson.

24. Robinson, letter to The Times, op. cit.

25. Alexander, 1983, pp. 159–60.

26. Ibid., p. 161.

27. Murray, 1874, p. 172.

The Empire of Things: Engagement with the Orient

1. For example, Mitchell, 1992; Richards, 1993.

The Imperial Collections: Indian Art

2. Mitter, 1992.

3. Jones, 1856, p. 2.

4. Cole, 1874, pp. 219, 241, passim.

5. Birdwood, 1879, p. 125.

6. Guy, 1990; Mitter, 1992, p. 233.

7. Stronge, 1993, p. 11.

8. It is variously called the India Museum, the East India Museum, and the East Indian Museum.

9. Desmond, 1982, p. 35.

10. Mitter, 1992, appendix I; National Museum, 1950; Wulff, 1966, p. 327.

11. See especially Desmond, 1982, chs. 11, 12, 13, and 14; Skelton, 1978, pp. 301–4.

12. Birdwood, 1879, pp. 134–43; Dumont, 1970.

13. Murray, 1874.

14. Cole, 1874, p. 88.

15. Conway, 1875, p. 658.

16. Ibid., p. 657.

17. Baedeker, 1885, pp. 278–80.

18. V&A, 1901, pp. 2–3.

19. V&A, 1908; Museums Journal 8 (1908–9), p. 435; Desmond, 1982, p. 201.

20. Mitter, 1992, ch. 6; Mitter, 1994, chs. 8 and 9, for discussion of Birdwood's remarks. See also "The Purposes and Functions of the Museum," proof of confidential memorandum dated 5 November 1912, National Art Library, V&A.

21. Muirhead, 1918, p. 278

22. See cat. 98.

23. Archer and Archer, 1994; Rothenstein, 1932, pp. 229–31. My forthcoming work documents Rothenstein's role in the India House mural project.

24. Skelton, 1978, pp. 301–4.

The Imperial Collections: East Asian Art

1. This interpretation follows Bhabha, 1994, especially p. 5, where he writes, "... the boundary becomes the place from which something begins its presencing. . . ." See also Coombes, 1988.

2. Breckenridge, 1989.

3. Faulkner and Jackson, 1995. This article is the major piece of scholarship on early collecting of Japanese art at South Kensington, and I am indebted to it for both facts and interpretations.

4. South Kensington Museum, 1872, pp. 2, 57.

5. Faulkner and Jackson, 1995, p. 158.

6. Ibid., p. 168.

7. Philip Cunliffe Owen, Minutes to the Lords of the Committee of Council on Education, 23 July 1875: Public Records Office, Education 84/30.

8. On Murdoch Smith and South Kensington see Helfgott, 1994, pp. 125–43.

9. This work has been astonishingly successful, remaining in print some ninety years after its original appearance, though no longer published by the V&A. Clunas, 1994, p. 334.

10. On Koop, see Earle, 1986b, pp. 867–8.

11. Gotlieb, 1986.

12. Quoted in McKillop, 1992a, p. 74.

13. Hevia, 1994.

14. Clunas, 1991; and Clunas, 1994, pp. 336–8.

National Consciousness, National Heritage, and the Idea of "Englishness"

In preparing this essay, I am indebted for information and advice to Malcolm Baker, Tim Barringer, Anthony Burton, Clive Wainwright, and Christopher Wilk.

1. For the life of Richard Redgrave and his contribution to South Kensington, see, in particular, Redgrave, 1891; and Casteras and Parkinson, 1988.

2. There are accounts of the Sheepshanks collection in Davis, 1963, pp. 74–9; and Parkinson, 1990, p. xviii.

3. This episode is recounted in Pope-Hennessy, 1991, p. 170.

4. The best introductions to attitudes toward domestic architecture of this period are Girouard, 1984; and Mandler, in press.

5. Attitudes toward English history at the end of the nineteenth century have been the subject of a considerable amount of recent study. See, for example, the essays in Colls and Dodd, 1986; Samuel, 1989; and Grant and Stringer, 1995.

6. Nevill, 1906, pp. 256–7.

7. For the professionalization of historical scholarship, see Levine, 1986.

8. "The Purposes and Functions of the Museum," proof of confidential memorandum dated 5 November 1912, National Art Library, V&A.

9. This evidence is drawn from Watson, 1995. I am indebted to him for allowing me to refer to it.

10. Muirhead, 1935, p. 413.

11. Richard Aldington to Herbert Read, 16 June 1925, The Read Archive, McPherson Library, University of Victoria, cited in King, 1990, p. 84.

12. There is a useful account of Museum life in the 1920s in Laver, 1963, pp. 86–111.

13. Royal Commission on National Museums and Galleries, 1930, p. 43.

14. Wilk, 1996, p. 19.

15. V&A, 1985b, p. 6.

Collecting the Twentieth Century

1. Contemporary here refers to the new or nearly new, things still available in the marketplace at the time, or manufactured objects made within the past fifteen years or so that remain in continuous production.

2. Prominent exceptions in the era after 1900 included the short-lived Deutsches Museum für Kunst im Handel und Gewerbe in Hagen (1909–c. 1921), the Würtemburgisches Landesmuseum in Stuttgart, and, from 1932, The Museum of Modern Art in New York.

3. V&A, 1908, pp. 19–20.

4. Ibid.

5. Harcourt Smith, 1914, p. 5. For the BIIA's history, see Pevsner, 1937, pp. 154–5; for its closing, see *Museums Journal* 33 (1933–34), pp. 369–70. An archive of BIIA papers is held at the British Architectural Library, RIBA, while the V&A holds Nominal Files on both the Institute of Modern Industrial Art (Proposed) and the BIIA.

6. Harcourt Smith, 1914, p. 1. The report also makes clear that Harcourt Smith was well aware of Continental developments such as the Deutscher Werkbund, an awareness that would continue during the 1920s.

7. Ibid., p. 4.

8. Ibid., p. 3.

9. Wiener, 1981.

10. Watkin, 1980, pp. 94–5.

11. Architect Sir Reginald Blomfield wrote, for example, that modernist architecture was "alien to the English tradition and temperament" (Blomfield, 1934, pp. 12–3).

12. Ironically, the V&A later hosted the 1989 exhibition, "A Vision of Britain," which was generally perceived as a direct attack on the influence of modernist design.

13. It is important to consider the BIIA within the context of the activities of other organizations, such as the Design and Industries Association (founded 1915) and the Council for Art and Industry (Frank Pick, chairman, begun 1934), the reports of various Board of Trade committees (including the Gorell Committee, 1931–32, on which Sir Eric Maclagan served), and various design exhibitions held in London (Dorland Hall, 1933, and Royal Academy, 1935). See Pevsner, 1937, pp. 154–75.

14. Numerous other attempts to found a Museum of Modern Industrial Art based on German models involved discussions between Harcourt Smith's successor, Sir Eric Maclagan (director, 1924–45), and modernist advocates such as Frank Pick and Sir Nikolaus Pevsner; any such prospects were presumably cut short by World War II. See "Institute of Modern Industrial Art (Proposed)," V&A Nominal File.

15. "Armitage, Mrs G. W., also Mrs Margaret H., 1915–1933," V&A Nominal File. Mrs. Armitage dealt directly with director Eric Maclagan.

16. Copy of letter from Maclagan to R. E. Stone, 8 March 1929, provided to Metalwork Department by Mrs. Dorothy Stone (brought to my attention by Eric Turner). For that department's modern collecting, see Turner, 1988.

17. See London Underground Electric Railways Nominal File; Joseph T. Clarke Nominal File; Hardie, 1931; V&A, 1979.

18. Although the Rodins remain at the V&A, almost all other twentieth-century sculptures, including those from Circulation, were transferred to the Tate Gallery in 1983.

19. Watson, 1990. The Ceramics Department was unusually involved in advising Circulation on the acquisition of modern objects due to the wide-ranging interests of the department's keeper, W. B. Honey.

20. In 1954 the director Leigh Ashton wrote to the photographer Roger Mayne that "photographs are entirely outside the terms of reference of this museum . . . ," adding later that "photography is a purely mechanical process into which the artist does not enter." See V&A, 1986, p. 6.

21. This work eventually resulted in Physick, 1982; and Morris, 1986.

22. Strong, 1978, p. 276, and his Milner Gray lecture to the Society of Industrial Artists and Designers, 1978.

23. "Art in the Boilerhouse," V&A Press Notice, 17 October 1980, V&A Nominal File 1980/1130, VA 375, "Premises, Policy & Precedent." The arrangement was that the Conran Foundation would pay for the renovation of the space, use it for about five years, and then move to Milton Keynes where it would establish "an industrial design centre with a permanent collection, constantly changing" ("Art at Work in the Boilerhouse," V&A Press Notice, 22 October 1980). Eventually, in 1989, the Conran Foundation plan was realized as the Design Museum in London. The V&A's view was that it would "complement and supplement those areas which are outside the scope of the V&A's collections." It seems clear that the Museum saw the Boilerhouse as a means to attract a wider audience, especially during a boom time for public interest in design. Within the context of the Thatcher years, it represented a collaboration between a publicly funded institution and the private sector, which was to result in the Museum gaining a fully renovated exhibition space at no capital expense.

24. "20th Century Acquisitions Policy Committee," V&A RP 86/369; and "20th Century Art & Design Gallery Team," V&A RP 88/2328.

25. There were exceptions, such as Circulation's formation of a radio collection, though few additions were made to this between 1977 and 1992.

Stop him!

Darkness rests upon Tom-all-Alone's. ... since the sun went ... last night ... it has ... gradually ... swollen until it fills every ... in the place. ... some ... light is burning ... as the lamp of life burns in Tom-all-Alone's ... in the ... nauseous ... air, and winking ... as that ... lamp ... Alone's, at many horrible things. But ... Tom has eyed ... with a dull cold stare ... as ... and ... and is gone. ... nightmare in the ... stables ... and Tom's fast asleep.

Much might ... speech-making ... there has been ... concerning ... in and out of Parliament, concerning Tom, and much ... wrathful disputation how Tom shall be ...

But he has his revenge ... The winds are his ... serving him ... and ... these hours of darkness ... infection and contagion somewhere ... choice of stream in which chemists on analysis ... the genuine nobility ... it shall ... There is not an atom of Tom's ... not a cubic inch ... pestilential ... in which he lives, not ... one ... in a ... not an ignorance, not a wickedness, not a brutality ... the ... highest of the high. ... plundering and ... Tom ... has his revenge.

It is a moot point whether Tom-all-Alone's be ... uglier by day or night; but on ... that the more that is seen of it the more ... and that no part of ... to bad as the ... decaying ... it might be better for the national ... that the sun should ... sometimes upon the British dominions, than that it should even rise upon so ... Tom ... A ... gentleman ... who appears in some ... in ... for sleep, ... rather ... counting the hours on ... fellow, strolls ... attracted ... if, he often pauses and looks about him, up and down ... Nor is he merely curious, for his bright dark eye is often ... and as he looks ... here and there, he ... seems ... to understand ... wickedness, and to have studied it ... often.

... the ... channel of mud which is the main street of Tom-all-Alone's ...

Bibliography

COMPILED BY SEANNA TSUNG

Adam, Peter. *Eileen Gray: Architect/Designer.* London and New York: Abrams, 1987.

Adams, C. F. E., ed. *Familiar letters of John Adams and His Wife Abigail Adams during the Revolution.* New York: Hurd and Houghton, 1876.

Adams, Nicholas, and Jennifer Krasinski. "La rocca roveresca di Mondolfo." In *Francesco di Giorgio architetto,* edited by Francesco Paolo Fiore and Manfredo Tafuri, 280–6. Milan: Electa, 1993.

Adlmann, Jan Ernst. *Vienna Moderne, 1898–1918: An Early Encounter between Taste and Utility.* Houston: Gallery of the University of Houston, 1978.

Alexander, Edward P. *Museum Masters: Their Museums and Their Influence.* Walnut Creek, Calif.: Altamira Press, 1983.

Alfter, Dieter. *Die Geschichte des Augsburger Kabinettschranks.* Augsburg: Historisches Verein für Schwaben, 1986.

Allen, Bernard Meredith. *Sir Robert Morant: A Great Public Servant.* London: Macmillan, 1934.

Allison, Ann Hersey. "The Bronzes of Pier Jacopo Alari-Bonnacolsi called Antico." *Jahrbuch der Kunsthistorischen Sammlungen in Wien* 89/90, n.F. 53/54 (1993–94): 37–310.

Allthorpe-Guyton, Marjorie, with John Stevens. *A Happy Eye: A School of Art in Norwich, 1845–1982.* Norwich: Jarrold, 1982.

Altick, Richard D. *The Shows of London.* Cambridge, Mass.: The Belknap Press of Harvard University Press, 1978.

American Architect. "The Museum of Fine Arts, Boston." *The American Architect and Building News* 7, no. 253 (1880): 207.

Ames, Winslow. *Prince Albert and Victorian Taste.* New York: Viking, 1967.

Amico, Leonard N. "Les céramiques rustiques authentiques de Bernard Palissy." *Revue de l'art* 78 (1987): 61–79.

Archer, William G. *Indian Paintings from the Punjab Hills.* London: Sotheby Parke Bernet, 1973.

Archer, William G., and Mildred Archer. *India Served and Observed.* London: BACSA, 1994.

Argles, Michael. *South Kensington to Robbins: An Account of English Technical and Scientific Education since 1851.* London: Longmans, 1964.

Armytage, W. H. G. "J. F. D. Donnelly: Pioneer in Vocational Education." *Vocational Aspect of Secondary and Further Education* 2 (1950): 6–21.

Art Bulletin. "The Problematics of Collecting and Display, Part 1." *The Art Bulletin* 77 (March 1995): 6–24. Articles by Janet Catherine Berlo and Ruth B. Phillips, Carol Duncan, Donald Preziosi, Danielle Rice, Anne Rorimer.

———. "The Problematics of Collecting and Display, Part 2." *The Art Bulletin* 77 (June 1995): 166–85. Articles by Richard R. Brettell, Vishakha N. Desai, Françoise Forster-Hahn, Rosamund W. Purcell.

———. "Rethinking the Canon." *The Art Bulletin* 78 (June 1996): 198–217. Articles by Michael Camille, Zeynep Çelik, John Onians, Adrian Rifkin, Christopher B. Steiner.

Art Journal. "Minor Topics of the Month." *Art Journal* (1852): 262.

———. "Early Italian Porcelain." *Art Journal* (October 1860): 300.

———. *The Illustrated Catalogue of the Universal Exhibition.* London: Virtue and Co., 1868.

———. *The Great Exhibition: London's Crystal Palace Exposition of 1851.* Reprint of the *Art Journal Illustrated Catalogue of the Industry of All Nations,* 1851. New York: Gramercy Books, 1995.

Arts Council. *Thirties: British Art and Design before the War.* London: Arts Council, 1979.

Arundel Society. *The cathedral of Santiago de Compostella in Spain. Showing especially the sculpture of the Portico de la Gloria, by Mestro Mateo. A series of twenty photographs recently taken by the late Mr Thurston Thompson.* London: Arundel Society, 1868.

Asche, Sigfried. *Balthasar Permoser: Leben und Werk.* Berlin: Deutscher Verlag für Wissenschaften, 1978.

Asenbaum, Paul, Stefan Asenbaum, and Christian Witt-Dörring, eds. *Moderne Vergangenheit Wien 1800–1900.* Vienna: Gesellschaft Bildener Künstler Österreichs, 1981.

Ashton, Leigh. "100 Years of the Victoria & Albert Museum." *Museums Journal* 53 (1953–54): 47.

———, ed. *The Art of India and Pakistan: A Commemorative Catalogue of the Exhibition Held at the Royal Academy of Arts, London, 1947–48.* New York: Coward-McCann, 1950.

Aslin, Elizabeth. *Nineteenth Century English Furniture.* New York: T. Yoseloff, 1962.

Athenaeum. "Fine Art Gossip." *Athenaeum* (1852): 633.

Atterbury, Paul, and Maureen Batkin. *The Dictionary of Minton.* Woodbridge: Antique Collector's Club, 1990.

Avray Tipping, Henry. *Grinling Gibbons and the Woodwork of His Age.* London: Country Life, 1914.

Ayers, John. *Far Eastern Ceramics in the Victoria and Albert Museum.* London: Sotheby Parke Bernet in association with the V&A, 1980.

Ayers, John, with contributions by Andrew Topsfield and John Lowry. *Oriental Art in the Victoria and Albert Museum.* London: Philip Wilson, 1983.

Babbitt, Sherry, ed. *Handbook of the Collections.* Philadelphia: Philadelphia Museum of Art, 1995.

Badisches Landesmuseum. *Spätgotik am Oberrhein: Meisterwerke der Plastik und des Kunsthandwerks 1450–1530.* Karlsruhe: Badisches Landesmuseum, 1970.

Baedeker. *London and Its Environs.* Leipzig: Baedeker, 1885, 1892, 1908, 1923, and 1930 editions cited.

Bagenal, Philip Henry. *The Life of Ralph Bernal Osborne M.P.* London: Richard Bentley and Son, 1884.

Baker, Malcolm. "The Cast Courts," pamphlet, 1982. National Art Library, V&A.

———. "Roubiliac's Models and 18th Century English Sculptors' Working Practices." In *Entwürf und Ausführung in der europäischen Barockplastik,* edited by Peter Volk, 59–84. Munich: Bayerisches Nationalmuseum, 1986.

———. "The Establishment of a Masterpiece: The Cast of the Portico de la Gloria in the South Kensington Museum, London in the 1870s." In *Actas simposio internacional sobre o Pórtico da Gloria é a arte do seu tempo.* Colección de difusión cultural, vol. 6. Santiago de Compostela: Xunta de Galicia, 1988.

———. "Bode and Museum Display: The Arrangement of the Kaiser-Friedrich Museum and the South Kensington Response." *Jahrbuch der Berliner Museen* 58 (1996a).

———. "De l'église au musée: les monuments du XVIIIe siècle (fonctions, significations et histoire)." In *Sculptures hors contexte: Actes du colloque international organisé au musée du Louvre par le Service culturel le 29 avril 1994,* edited by Jean-René Gaborit, 71–92. Louvre conférences et colloques. Paris: La documentation française, 1996b.

———. "Roubiliac and Chelsea in 1745." *Transactions of the English Ceramic Circle* 17 (1997), in press(a).

———. "Francis van Bossuit, Böttger Stoneware and the *Judith* Reliefs." In *Festschrift Alfred Schädler,* edited by R. Kahsnitz and P. Volk. Munich, in press(b).

Barbour, Daphne, Shelley Sturman, and P. B. Vandiver. "Technical Appendix II: The Saint-Porchaire Ceramics." In *Western Decorative Arts,* edited by Rudolf Distelberger et al. Vol. 1, *Medieval, Renaissance and Historicizing Styles, Including Metalwork, Enamels and Ceramics,* 242–80. Washington, D.C.: National Gallery of Art, 1993.

Barbour, Daphne, and Shelley Sturman, eds. *Saint-Porchaire Ceramics.* Washington, D.C.: National Gallery of Art, 1996.

Barocchi, Paola. "La scoperta del ritratto di Dante nel Palazzo del Podestà: Dantisom letterario e figurativo." In *Studi e ricerche di collezionismo e museografia Firenze 1820–1920,* 151–78. Quaderni del Seminario di storia della critica d'arte, vol. 2. Pisa: Scuola normale superiore di Pisa, 1985.

Fig. 127. Detail of cat. 155.1, Dickens's hand-corrected manuscript page from *Bleak House*

Barocchi, Paola, and G. Gaeta Bertela. "Ipotesi per un museo nel Palazzo del Podestà tra il 1858 e il 1865." In *Studi e richerche di collezionismo e museografia Firenze 1820–1920,* 211–378. Quaderni del Seminario di storia della critica d'arte, vol. 2. Pisa: Scuola normale superiore di Pisa, 1985.

Batkin, Maureen. *Wedgwood Ceramics, 1846–1959: A New Appraisal.* London: Richard Dennis, 1983.

Baur-Heinhold, Margarete. *Schmiedeeisen: Gitter, Tore und Geländer.* Munich: Gallwey, 1977.

Baxandall, Michael. *South German Sculpture, 1480–1530.* London: HMSO, 1974.

———. *The Limewood Sculptors of Renaissance Germany.* New Haven: Yale Univ. Press, 1980.

Beard, Geoffrey. *The Work of Grinling Gibbons.* London: Murray, 1989.

Beckwith, John. *Caskets from Cordoba.* London: HMSO, 1960.

Bell, Quentin. *The Schools of Design.* London: Routledge and Kegan Paul, 1963.

Benjamin, Walter. "The Work of Art in the Age of Mechanical Reproduction." In *Illuminations,* edited and with an introduction by Hannah Arendt and translated by Harry Zohn, 219–53. London: Cape, 1970.

Bennett, Tony. *The Birth of the Museum: History, Theory, Politics.* London: Routledge, 1995.

———. "The Exhibitionary Complex." In *Thinking about Exhibitions,* edited by Reesa Greenberg, Bruce W. Ferguson, and Sandy Nairne, pp. 81–112. London/New York: Routledge, 1996.

Bethnal Green Museum, 1872. *Catalogue of the Collection of Paintings, Porcelain, Bronzes, Decorative Furniture, and Other Works of Art Lent for Exhibition in the Bethnal Green Branch of the South Kensington Museum by Sir Richard Wallace, Bart.* London: G. E. Eyre and W. Spottiswoode, 1872.

Bhabha, Homi K. *The Location of Culture.* London: Routledge, 1994.

Billcliffe, Roger. *Charles Rennie Mackintosh: The Complete Furniture Drawings & Interior Designs.* London: J. Murray, 1986.

Bimson, M. "John Dwight." *Transactions of the English Ceramic Circle* 5, no. 2 (1961): 95–109.

Birdwood, George Christopher Molesworth. *The Industrial Arts of India.* 2 vols. London: Chapman and Hall, 1879.

Bishop, A. S. *The Rise of a Central Authority for English Education.* Cambridge: Cambridge Univ. Press, 1971.

Black, Jeremy. *The British and the Grand Tour.* London: Croom Helm, 1985.

Blackader, Adam. "Description of the Great Pagoda of Madura, and the Choultry of Trimul Naik, in a Letter from Mr. Adam Blackader, Surgeon, to Sir Joseph Banks, Bart. P.R.S.F.A.S." *Archaeologia* 10 (1792): 449–59.

Blomfield, Reginald. *Modernismus.* London: Macmillan and Co., 1934.

Boccia, Lionello Giorgio, and E. T. Coelho. *L'arte dell'armatura in Italia.* Milan: Bramante, 1967.

Bode, Wilhelm. "Aufgang der Kunstgewerbemuseen." *Pan* 2 (1896): 121–7.

Boe, Alf. *From Gothic Revival to Functional Form: A Study in Victorian Theories of Design.* Oxford: Basil Blackwell, 1957.

Bolton, Arthur. *The Architecture of Robert & James Adam.* London: Country Life, 1922.

Bonython, Elizabeth. *King Cole: A Picture Portrait of Sir Henry Cole, KCB, 1808–1882.* London: V&A, 1982.

Borowitz, Helen, and Albert Borowitz. *Pawnshops and Palaces: The Fall and Rise of the Campana Art Museum.* Washington, D.C.: Smithsonian Institution Press, 1991.

Boynton, L. "Italian Craft in an English Cabinet." *Country Life* 140, no. 3630 (1966): 768–9.

Brackett, Oliver. *Catalogue of Furniture from Montagu House, Devonshire House and Grosvenor House lent by the Duke of Buccleuch, the Duke of Devonshire, and the Duke of Westminster.* London: HMSO, 1919.

Brandon-Jones, J., et al. *C. F. A. Voysey: Architect and Designer, 1857–1941.* London: Lund Humphries, 1978.

Braun, Joseph. *Die Reliquiare des christlichen Kultes und ihre Entwicklung.* Freiburg am Breisgau: Herder, 1940.

Breckenridge, Carol A. "The Aesthetics and Politics of Colonial Collecting: India at World Fairs." *Comparative Studies in Society and History* 31, no. 2 (1989): 195–216.

Brinckmann, Justus. *Das Hamburgische Museum für Kunst und Gewerbe.* Hamburg: Hamburgische Museum für Kunst und Gewerbe, 1894.

British Parliamentary Papers. *Irish University Press Series of British Parliamentary Papers: Industrial Revolution: Design.* IUP Library of Fundamental Source Books. Shannon: Irish University Press, 1968–.

Britton, F. "Bernard Palissy and London Delftware." *English Ceramics Circle Transactions* 14 (1991): 169–76.

Bronowski, J., and Brian Peake. "Exhibition of Science." In *A Tonic to the Nation: The Festival of Britain 1951,* edited by Mary Banham and Bevis Hillier, 144–7. London: Thames and Hudson, 1976.

Brunhammer, Yvonne. *Le beau dans l'utile: Un musée pour les arts décoratifs.* Paris: Gallimard, 1992.

Building News. "The Schools of Art Grievance." *Building News* 11 (1864): 320.

Burchett, Richard. *On the Central Training School for Art: An Address Delivered December 7, 1857.* London: n.p., 1858.

Burckhardt, Rudolf F. *Der Basler Münsterschatz.* Die Kunstdenkmaler des Kantons Basel-Stadt, vol. 2. 1933. Reprint, Basel: Birkhauser, 1956.

Burke, Doreen Bolger, et al. *In Pursuit of Beauty: Americans and the Aesthetic Movement.* New York: Metropolitan Museum of Art and Rizzoli, 1986.

Burlington Fine Arts Club. *Exhibition of Chased and Embossed Steel and Iron Work of European Origin.* London: Burlington Fine Arts Club, 1900.

Burlington Magazine. "Reorganisation at South Kensington." *Burlington Magazine* 14 (1908–9): 129–33, 198–200.

Burton, Anthony. "The Image of the Curator." *V&A Album* 4 (1985): 372–87.

———. "Redgrave as Art Educator, Museum Official and Design Theorist." In *Richard Redgrave, 1804–1888,* edited by Susan P. Casteras and Ronald Parkinson, 48–70. New Haven: Yale Univ. Press in association with the V&A and the Yale Center for British Art, 1988.

———. *People and Politics in South Kensington: A History of the Victoria and Albert Museum.* Forthcoming (1999).

Burton, Anthony, with captions by Susan Haskins. *European Art in the Victoria and Albert Museum.* London: Philip Wilson, 1983.

Burty, Philippe. *Chefs d'Oeuvre of the Industrial Arts.* London: Chapman and Hall, 1869.

Bury, S. "The Lengthening Shadow of Rundell's." *Connoisseur* 108 (1966): 218–22.

Bury, Shirley. *Jewellery 1789–1910: The International Era.* Woodbridge: Antique Collector's Club, 1991.

Bussagli, Mario. *L'Arte del Gandhara.* Turin: UTET, 1984.

Cabinet Maker. "The Octagon Court." *The Cabinet Maker* 8 (1936): 238.

Campbell, Marian. *An Introduction to Medieval Enamels.* London: HMSO, 1983.

———. *An Introduction to Ironwork.* London: HMSO, 1985.

———. "L'oreficeria italiana nell'Inghilterra medievale, con una nota sugli smalti medievali italiani del Victoria and Albert Museum." *Oreficere e smalti traslucidi nei secoli XIV e XV,* 1–16. Rome: Istituto poligrafico e Zecca dello Stato Libreria, 1987.

Cannadine, David. *The Pleasure of the Past.* London: Collins, 1989.

Casteras, Susan P., and Ronald Parkinson, eds. *Richard Redgrave, 1804–1888.* New Haven: Yale Univ. Press in association with the V&A and the Yale Center for British Art, 1988.

Catleugh, Jon. *William De Morgan Tiles.* London: Trefoil, 1983.

Caygill, Marjorie. *Treasures of the British Museum.* New York: Harry N. Abrams, Inc., 1985.

Central Office of Information. *The Festival of Britain 1951: The Official Book of the Festival of Britain 1951.* London: HMSO, 1951.

Ceruti, Benedetto, and Andrea Chiocco. *Musaeum Francisci Calceolari.* Verona: A. Tamum, 1622.

Chadwick, Helen. *Enfleshings.* Text by Marina Warner. New York: Aperture, 1989.

Chambers, David, and Jane Martineau, eds. *Splendours of the Gonzaga.* London: V&A, 1981.

Chapman, Martin. "Thomas Hope's Vase and Alexis Decaix." *V&A Album* 4 (1985): 216–28.

Charleston, R. J., and J. Bolingbroke. "The Sèvres Collection in a New Light." *Apollo* 95 (1972): 186–95.

Charpentier, Françoise-Thérèse, and Philippe Thiébaut, eds. *Gallé.* Paris: Ministère de la Culture, Editions de la Réunion des musées nationaux, 1985.

Chermayeff, S. "Design for Selling." *Design for Today* 14 (1935).

Christie and Manson. *Catalogue of the Celebrated Collection of Works of Art from the Byzantine Period to That of Louis Seize of That Distinguished Collector Ralph Bernal . . . Messrs Christie & Manson at the Mansion No 93 Eaton Square Commencing on Monday March the 5th 1855.* London: Christie and Manson, 1855.

Christie's. *Magnificent Effects at Fonthill Abbey Wilts. to be Sold by Auction by Mr. Christie on October 1, 1822 and Nine Following Days.* London: Christie's, 1822.

———. *Catalogue of Works of Art of Martin Heckscher.* London: Christie's, 1898.

Cincinnati Art Museum. *Art Palace of the West: A Centennial Tribute, 1881–1981.* Cincinnati: Cincinnati Art Museum, 1981.

Clark, Kenneth. *The Gothic Revival: An Essay in the History of Taste.* New York: Harper and Row, 1962.

Clarke, C. Stanley. *Indian Drawings: Thirty Mogul Paintings of the School of Jahangir (17th century) and Four Panels of Calligraphy in the Wantage Bequest.* London: HMSO, 1922.

Clausen, G. "Recollections of the Old School." *Royal College of Arts Students' Magazine* 1 (1912): 155–61.

Clayton, Tim. "The Engraving and Publication of Prints of Joseph Wright's Paintings." In *Wright of Derby*, by Judy Egerton, 25–9. London: Tate Gallery, 1990.

Clifford Smith, Harold. *Jewellery.* London: Methuen, 1908.

———. "A Royal Wassail Table." *Connoisseur* 77, no. 307 (1927): 158–62.

Clunas, Craig. "Whose Throne Is It Anyway? The Qianlong Throne in the Tsui Gallery." *Orientations* 22, no. 7 (1991): 44–50.

———. "Oriental Antiquities/Far Eastern Art." *Positions: East Asia Cultures Critique* 2, no. 2 (1994): 318–55.

Cohen, Jane R. *Charles Dickens and His Original Illustrators.* Columbus, Ohio: Ohio State Univ. Press, 1980.

Cohen, S. "A 17th Century Parochet." *Jewish Chronicle* 10 (1953).

Cole, Alan Summerly. *A Descriptive Catalogue of the Collections of Tapestry and Embroidery in the South Kensington Museum.* London: HMSO, 1888.

Cole, Alan Summerly, and Henrietta Cole, eds. *Fifty Years of Public Work of Sir Henry Cole, K.C.B..* 2 vols. London: G. Bell and Sons, 1884.

Cole, Henry. Miscellanies, 1831–82. 17 vols. National Art Library, V&A.

———. Diaries, 1844–54. National Art Library, V&A.

———. "On the Facilities Afforded to All Classes of the Community for Obtaining Education in Art." In *Addresses of the Superintendents of the Department of Practical Art Delivered in the Theatre at Marlborough House.* London: Chapman and Hall, 1853.

———. *The Functions of the Science and Art Department.* Introductory Addresses on the Science and Art Department and the South Kensington Museum, no. 1. London: Chapman and Hall, 1857.

———. Study of the Conservatoire, 1865, 55.AA.56.f.97. National Art Library, V&A.

———. "Notes on a Journey to Vienna and back in October and November MDCCCLXIII." National Art Library, V&A. London, 1870.

———. *Catalogue of the Objects of Indian Art Exhibited in the South Kensington Museum.* London: G. E. Eyre and W. Spottiswoode, 1874.

———. *What is Art Culture? An Address Delivered to the Manchester School of Art, 21st December 1877.* Manchester: Reprinted for private distribution from the report on the Manchester School of Art, 1878.

Coleridge, Anthony. "Sir Lawrence Dundas and Chippendale." *Apollo* 87, no. 67, n.s. (1967): 190–203.

Colls, Robert, and Philip Dodd, eds. *Englishness: Politics and Culture, 1880–1920.* London: Croom Helm, 1986.

Commissioners. *Second Report of the Commissioners for the Exhibition of 1851 to the Right Hon. Spencer Horatio Walpole, one of Her Majesty's Principal Secretaries of State.* London: W. Clowes, 1852.

Conforti, Michael. "History, Value and the 1990s Art Museum." *Papers of the XXVII Internationaler Kongress für Kunstgeschichte,* Berlin, 15–20 July 1992. Also published in *Journal of Museum Management and Curatorship* 12, no. 3 (1993): 245–55.

———. "Les Musées des arts appliqués et l'histoire de l'art". In *L'Histoire de l'histoire de l'art IV.* Paris: Musée du Louvre, in press [1997].

Conway, M. D. "The South Kensington Museum." *Harper's New Monthly Magazine* 51 (1875): 486–503, 649–66.

Conway, William Martin. *The Domain of Art.* London: J. Murray, 1901.

Coomaraswamy, Ananda K. *Rajput Painting.* 2 vols. London: Oxford Univ. Press, 1916.

Coombes, Annie E. "Museums and the Formation of National and Cultural Identities." *Oxford Art Journal* 11, no. 2 (1988): 57–68.

Cooper, A. "For the Public Good: Henry Cole, His Circle and the Development of the South Kensington Estate." Ph.D. diss., The Open University, Milton Keynes, 1992.

Cora, Galeazzo, and Angiolo Fanfani. *La maiolica di Cafaggiolo.* Florence: Centro Di, 1982.

———. *La porcellana dei Medici.* Milan: Fabbri, 1986.

Corcoran Gallery. *A Guide to the Corcoran Archives.* Washington: Corcoran Gallery of Art, 1985.

Cork, Richard. *Vorticism and Abstract Art in the First Machine Age.* 2 vols. London: G. Fraser, 1976.

Council of Industrial Design. *Design Portfolio D.* London, 1950.

Country Life. "Changes at the Victoria and Albert Museum." *Country Life* 79 (1936): 124.

Coysh, A. W., and R. K. Henrywood. *The Dictionary of Blue and White Printed Pottery 1780–1880.* Vol. 1. Woodbridge: Antique Collector's Club, 1981.

Cullingham, Gordon Graham. *The Royal Windsor Tapestry Manufactory: 1876–1890.* Maidenhead: Royal Borough of Windsor and Maidenhead, 1979.

Culme, John. *Nineteenth-Century Silver.* London: Hamlyn for Country Life Books, 1977.

Cunliffe Owen, P. Minutes to the Lords of the Committee of Council on Education, 23 July 1875. Ed. 84/30. National Art Library, V&A.

Czuma, Stanislaw J., with the assistance of Rekha Morris. *Kushan Sculpture: Images from Early India.* Cleveland: Cleveland Museum of Art in cooperation with Indiana Univ. Press, 1985.

Daily Telegraph. "Art Notes: Victoria and Albert Museum." *Daily Telegraph,* 7 November 1908.

Darby, M. "Owen Jones and the Eastern Ideal." Ph.D. diss., University of Reading, 1974.

Davies, James A. *John Forster: A Literary Life.* Leicester: Leicester Univ. Press, 1983.

Davillier, Jean-Charles. *Histoire des faïences hispano-moresques à reflets métalliques.* Paris: Librairie Archéologique de Victor Didron, 1861.

Davis, Frank. *Victorian Patrons of the Arts: Twelve Famous Collections and Their Owners.* London: Country Life, 1963.

Davis, H. "The Life and Works of Sir John Charles Robinson, 1824–1913." Ph.D. diss., University of Oxford, 1992.

Day, L. F. "How to Make the Most of a Museum." *Journal of the Society of Arts* 56 (1908): 146–60.

Delange, Carle, and C. Bornemann. *Recueil des fayences françaises dites de Henri II et Diane de Poitiers.* Paris, 1861.

Deneke, Bernward, and Rainer Kahsnitz, eds. *Das Germanische Nationalmuseum Nürnberg, 1852–1977: Beiträge zu seiner Geschichte.* Munich: Deutscher Kunstverlag, 1978.

Department of Practical Art. *A Catalogue of the Articles of Ornamental Art Selected from the Exhibition of the Works of Industry of All Nations in 1851 and Purchased by the Government.* 3rd ed. London: Department of Practical Art, 1852.

———. *First Report of the Department of Practical Art.* London: G. W. Eyre and W. Spottiswoode, 1853.

Department of Science and Art. Minutes Relative to the Acquisition of Art Objects for the Benefit of Schools of Art, 1852–70. Ed. 84/34. National Art Library, V&A.

———. *A Catalogue of the Museum of Ornamental Art at Marlborough House, Pall Mall.* London: HMSO, 1853.

———. *Report of the Science and Art Department of the Committee of Council on Education* 1 (1854).

———. *Catalogue of a Collection of Works of Decorative Art . . . Circulated for Exhibition in Provincial Schools of Art.* London, 1855a.

———. *Report of the Science and Art Department of the Committee of Council on Education* 2 (1855b).

———. *Directory.* London, 1856.

———. *Addresses. The Advantages of Teaching Elementary Drawing Concurrently with Writing as a Part of National Education.* London, 1857.

———. *Report of the Science and Art Department of the Committee of Council on Education* 5 (1858).

———. *Art Directory.* London, 1865a.

———. *Report of the Science and Art Department of the Committee of Council on Education* 12 (1865b).

———. *List of Objects in the Art Division, South Kensington Museum, Acquired During the Year 1871.* London: George E. Eyre and William Spottiswoode, 1872.

———. *Report of the Science and Art Department of the Committee of Council on Education* 21 (1873).

———. *Report of the Science and Art Department of the Committee of Council on Education* 23 (1876).

———. Report on the Systems of Circulation of the Art Objects on Loan for Exhibition, 1881. Miscellaneous Correspondence, Ed. 84/29. National Art Library, V&A.

———. *Report of the Science and Art Department of the Committee of Council on Education* 38 (1890).

———. *Report of the Science and Art Department of the Committee of Council on Education* 39 (1891).

———. *List of Reproductions in Electrotype and Plaster Acquired by the South Kensington Museum in the Years 1889–1890.* London: Eyre and Spottiswoode, 1891.

Desmond, Ray. *The India Museum, 1801–1879.* London: HMSO, 1982.

Distelberger, Rudolf, et al., eds. *Western Decorative Arts. Vol. 1, Medieval, Renaissance and Historicizing Styles, Including Metalwork, Enamels and Ceramics.* Washington, D.C.: National Gallery of Art, 1993.

Dragesco, Bernard. *English Ceramics in French Archives: The Writings of Jean Hellot, the Adventures of Jacques Louis Brolliet and the Identification of the "Girl-in-a-Swing" Factory.* London: B. Dragesco, 1993.

Dreyfus, John. *Italic Quartet: A Record of the Collaboration between Harry Kessler, Edward Johnston, Emery Walker and Edward Prince in Making the Cranach Press.* Cambridge: Univ. Printing House, 1966.

———. "The Cranach Press." In *Into Print: Selected Writings on Printing History, Typography and Book Production,* 71–81. London: The British Library, 1994.

Dufay, Bruno, et al. "L'Atelier parisien de Bernard Palissy." *Revue de L'Art* 78 (1987): 33–57.

Dumont, Louis. "The Village Community from Munro to Maine." In *Religion, Politics and History in India: Collected Papers in Indian Sociology,* 112–32. Le monde d'outre-mer, passé et présent, première série, études, vol 34. The Hague: Mouton, 1970.

Duncan, Carol. *Civilising Rituals: Inside Public Art Museums.* London: Routledge, 1995.

Durbin, Gail, ed. *Studying the Victorians at the V&A: A Handbook for Teachers.* London: V&A, 1994.

Earle, Joe. "Three Japanese Lacquers." *V&A Album* 3 (1984): 220–9.

———, ed. *The Toshiba Gallery: Japanese Art and Design.* London: V&A, 1986a.

———. "The Taxonomic Obsession: British Collectors and Japanese Objects, 1852–1986." *Burlington Magazine* 128 (1986b): 864–73.

Eatwell, Ann. "The Collector's or Fine Arts Club, 1857–1874: The First Society for Collectors of the Decorative Arts." *Omnium Gatherum* 18 (1994): 25–30.

Eatwell, Ann, and A. R. E. North. "Metalwork." In *Pugin: A Gothic Passion,* edited by Paul Atterbury and Clive Wainwright. New Haven: Yale Univ. Press in association with the V&A, 1994.

Ebert-Schifferer, S., ed. *Natur und Antike in der Renaissance.* Frankfurt am Main: Liebieghaus Museum Alter Plastik, 1985.

Edwards, R. "On a Carved Cravat by Grinling Gibbons." *Connoisseur* (1929).

Egerton, Judy. *Wright of Derby.* London: Tate Gallery, 1990.

Eliot, Samuel. *Memoir of Charles Callahan Perkins.* Cambridge: J. Wilson and Son, 1887.

Elsner, John, and Roger Cardinal, eds. *The Cultures of Collecting.* Cambridge, Mass.: Harvard Univ. Press, 1994.

Engel, Carl. *A Descriptive Catalogue of the Musical Instruments in the South Kensington Museum.* London: Chapman and Hall, 1874.

Erdmann, Kurt. *Siebenhundert Jahre Orientteppich,* Herford: Busse, 1966.

Eriksen, Svend, and Geoffrey de Bellaigue. *Sèvres Porcelain: Vincennes and Sèvres, 1740–1800.* London: Faber and Faber, 1987.

Eudel, Paul. *Le Baron Charles Davillier.* Paris: Imprimeries réunies Matteroz, 1883.

Evans, Joan. *A History of Jewellery, 1100–1870.* 2nd ed. London: Faber, 1987.

Evening News. "The Dying Trades of London: The Cameo Cutter." *The Evening News,* 7 December 1908.

Exposition Universelle, Paris 1889. Catalogue, 1st group. Walters Art Gallery, Baltimore.

Fairbanks, A. "The Museum of Fine Arts in Boston in Its New Quarters." *Museums Journal* 9 (1909–10): 365–70.

Falke, Otto von. "Der Majolicamaler TB von Faenza." *Pantheon* 13 (1934): 18–22.

Falke, Otto von, and Erich Meyer. *Romanische Leuchter und Gefässe: Giessgefässe der Gotik.* Berlin: Deutscher Verein für Kunstwissenschaft, 1935.

Faulkner, R., and A. Jackson. "The Meiji Period in South Kensington: The Representation of Japan in the Victoria and Albert Museum, 1852–1912." In *Meiji No Takara: Treasures of Imperial Japan,* edited by Oliver R. Impey and Malcolm Fairley, 152–95. London: Kibo Foundation, 1995.

Fawcett, T. "Plane Surfaces and Solid Bodies: Reproducing Three-Dimensional Art in the Nineteenth Century." *Visual Resources* 4 (1987): 1–23.

Fay, C. R. *Palace of Industry, 1851: A Study of the Great Exhibition and its Fruits.* Cambridge: Cambridge Univ. Press, 1951.

Fergusson, James. *A History of Architecture in All Countries from the Earliest Times to the Present Day.* Vol. 2, *The History of Indian and Eastern Architecture.* London: J. Murray, 1876.

Ferraris, Giancarlo. *Pietro Piffetti e gli ebanisti a Torino, 1670–1838.* Turin: U. Allemandi, 1992.

Ferstel, Heinrich F. von. *Rede des Neues Antretenden Rectors.* Vienna, 1881.

Fildes, L. V. *Luke Fildes, R.A.: A Victorian Painter.* London: Joseph, 1968.

Fillon, Benjamin. *L'art de terre chez les Poitevins.* Niort: L. Clouzot, 1864.

Findlen, Paula. *Possessing Nature: Museums, Collecting and Scientific Culture in Early Modern Italy.* Berkeley: Univ. of California Press, 1994.

Findling, John E., ed., and Kimberly D. Pelle, assistant ed. *Historical Dictionary of World's Fairs and Expositions, 1851–1988.* New York: Greenwood Press, 1990.

Fiocco, Carola, and Gabriella Gherardi. *Ceramiche umbre dal medioevo allo storicismo.* 2 vols. Faenza: Litografie artistiche faentine, 1988–89.

Fischer, Volker, ed. *Design Now: Industry or Art?* Munich: Prestel, 1989.

Fleming, J. "Art Dealing and the Risorgimento." *Burlington Magazine* 115 (1973): 4–16; 121 (1979): 492–508, 568–80.

Fliedl, Gottfried, with contributions by Oswald Oberhuber. *Kunst und Lehre am Beginn der Moderne: Die Wiener Kunstgewerbeschule, 1867–1918.* Salzburg: Residenz, 1986.

Floyd, M. H. "A Terra-cotta Cornerstone for Copley Square." Ph.D. diss., Boston University, 1974.

Fontanella, Lee, and Gerdardo F. Kurtz. *Charles Clifford fotografo de la España de Isabel II.* Madrid: Ediciones el Viso, 1996.

Foresi, A. "Sulle porcellane medicee: Lettera al Barone di Monville." *Il piovano arlotto,* July 1859.

Fortnum, C. Drury E. *A Descriptive Catalogue of the Maiolica, Hispano-Moresco, Persian, Damascus and Rhodian Wares in the South Kensington Museum: with Historical Notes, Marks and Monograms.* London: Chapman and Hall, 1873.

———. *A Descriptive Catalogue of the Bronzes of European Origin in the South Kensington Museum.* London: Chapman and Hall, 1876.

Forty, Adrian. *Objects of Desire: Design and Society, 1750–1980.* London: Thames and Hudson, 1986.

Fox, Celina, ed. *London: World City 1800–1840.* New Haven: Yale Univ. Press in association with the Museum of London, 1992.

Frayling, Christopher, with research by John Physick, Hilary Watson, and Bernard Myers. *The Royal College of Art: One Hundred and Fifty Years of Art and Design.* London: Barrie and Jenkins, 1987.

Frayling, Christopher, and Claire Catterall, eds. *Design of the Times: One Hundred Years of the Royal College of Art.* Shepton Beauchamp: Richard Dennis, 1996.

Fritz, Johann Michael. *Goldschmiedekunst der Gotik in Mitteleuropa.* Munich: Beck, 1982.

Froissart, R. "Les collections du Musée des arts décoratifs de Paris: modèles de savoir technique ou objets d'art?" In *La jeunesse des musées: Les musées de France au XIXᵉ siècle,* under the direction of Chantal Georgel, 83–90. Paris: Editions de la réunion des musées nationaux, 1994.

Furniture Gazette. *Furniture Gazette* (1887–88).

Gaehtgens, Thomas W. *Die Berliner Museumsinsel im Deutschen Kaiserreich: Zur Kulturpolitik der Museen in der Wilhelmischen Epoche.* Munich: Deutscher Kunstverlag, 1992.

Galbally, A. "The Lost Museum: Redmond Barry and Melbourne's Musée des Copies." *Australian Journal of Art* 7 (1988): 28–49.

Gallé, Emile. *Ecrits pour l'art: Floriculture, art décoratif, notices d'exposition, 1884–1889.* Paris: H. Laurens, 1908.

Gardner, James. *James Gardner: The Artful Designer: Ideas off the Drawing Board by James Gardner.* N.p.: Lavis Marketing, 1993.

Garner, Philippe. *Emile Gallé.* London: Academy Editions, 1976.

Garrard, Mary. "Artemisia and Susanna." In *Feminism and Art History: Questioning the Litany,* edited by Norma Broude and Mary D. Garrard, 147–71. New York: Harper and Row, 1982.

Gaskell, Ivan. Review of *On the Museum's Ruins* by D. Crimp, and other titles. *Art Bulletin* 77 (1995): 673–5.

Gaskell, Ivan, and Salim Kemal, eds. *The Language of Art History.* Cambridge Studies in Philosophy and the Arts. Cambridge: Cambridge Univ. Press, 1991.

Gasnault, Paul, and Edouard Garnier. *French Pottery.* London: Chapman and Hall, 1884.

Georgel, Chantal. *La Jeunesse des musées: Les musées de France au XIXᵉ siècle.* Paris: Musée d'Orsay, 1994.

Gilbert, Christopher. *The Life and Work of Thomas Chippendale.* 2 vols. London: Studio Vista, 1978.

Gilbert, Christopher, and Tessa Murdoch. *John Channon and Brass-Inlaid Furniture, 1700–1760.* New Haven: Yale Univ. Press in association with Leeds City Art Galleries and the V&A, 1993.

———. "Channon Revisited." *Furniture History* 30 (1994): 66–85.

Gilman, Benjamin Ives. "Aims and Principles of the Construction and Management of the Museum of Fine Arts." *Museum Journal* 9 (1909–10): 28–44.

———. *Museum Ideals of Purpose and Method.* Boston: Museum of Fine Arts, 1918.

Girouard, Mark. *Sweetness and Light: The Queen Anne Movement, 1860–1900.* New Haven: Yale Univ. Press, 1984.

Glanville, Philippa G. *Silver in Tudor and Early Stuart England: A Social History and Catalogue of the National Collection, 1480–1660.* London: V&A, 1990.

Goldschmidt, Adolph. *Die Elfenbeinskulpturen aus der Zeit der karolingischen und sächsischen Kaiser und der romanischen Zeit.* Vol. 1. Berlin: B. Cassirer, 1914.

Gomez-Moreno, Carmen. *Medieval Art from Private Collections.* New York: The Cloisters, 1968.

Gonse, Louis. *L'art japonais.* Paris: Quantin, 1886.

González-Palacios, Alvar. *Tempio del gusto: Il Granducato di Toscana e gli stati settentrionali: le arti decorative in Italia fra classicismi e barocco.* 2 vols. Milan: Longanesi, 1986.

Goodby, M. F. "The Lost Collection of Enoch Wood." *Journal of the Northern Ceramic Society* 9 (1986): 123–51.

Goodison, Nicholas. *Ormolu: The Work of Matthew Boulton.* London: Phaidon, 1974.

Gordon, Jennifer. "Museum Fiction." *Art History* 19 (1995): 150–5.

Gotlieb, Rachel. "Vitality in British Art Pottery and Studio Pottery." *Apollo* 127 (1986): 163–7.

Government School of Design. *Fourth Report of the School of Design.* London, 1845.

Grant, Alexander, and Keith J. Stringer, eds. *Uniting the Kingdom? The Making of British History.* London: Routledge, 1995.

Gray, M. "Robin Day ARCA FSIA." *Art & Industry* 52 (1952): 154–9.

Great Exhibition. *Official, Descriptive and Illustrated Catalogue of the Great Exhibition of the Works of Industry of All Nations.* 4 vols. London: Spicer Brothers, 1851.

Green, David Brontë. *Grinling Gibbons: His Work as a Carver and Statuary, 1648–1721.* London: Country Life, 1964.

Greenhalgh, Paul. *Ephemeral Vistas: The Expositions Universelles, Great Exhibitions and World's Fairs, 1851–1939.* Manchester: Manchester Univ. Press, 1988.

———. "Denham Maclaren" (Obituary). *The Independent,* 22 November 1989.

Greenwood, M., 1989, *The Designs of William De Morgan: A Catalogue.* Ilminster: Richard Dennis and W. E. Wiltshire III, 1989.

Griffiths, Anthony, ed. *Landmarks in Print Collecting: Connoisseurs and Donors at the British Museum since 1753.* London: The British Museum Press and the Parnassus Foundation in association with the Museum of Fine Arts, Houston, 1996.

Grimwade, Arthur G. *Rococo Silver.* London: Faber, 1974.

Guy, J. "Tirumala Nayak's Choultry and an Eighteenth Century Model." In *Makaranda: Essays in Honour of Dr. James C. Harle,* edited by Claudine Bautze-Picron, 207–13. Delhi: Sri Satguru Publications, 1990.

———. "Nandi, the Joyful Bull." *The Art Quarterly of the National Art Collections Fund* 8 (1991): 28–31.

Haedeke, Hanns-Ulrich. *Metalwork.* Translated by Vivienne Menkes. London: Weidenfeld and Nicolson, 1970.

Hahnloser, Margrit. *Matisse: The Graphic Work.* Translated by Simon Nye. New York: Rizzoli, 1988.

Hallade, Madeleine. *The Gandharan Style and the Evolution of Buddhist Art.* London: Thames & Hudson, 1968.

Hansard's Parliamentary Debates. 3rd series, vol. 160, p. 1308.

Harcourt Smith, Cecil. Proposals for a Museum and Institute of Modern Industrial Art, 30 April 1914. National Art Library, V&A.

———. "The Modern Note in Industrial Art." *Journal of the Society of Arts* 74 (1925–26): 32–42.

Hardie, M. *Exhibition of British and Foreign Posters.* London: V&A, 1931.

Harris, Jennifer. *Lucienne Day: A Career in Design.* Manchester: Whitworth Art Gallery, 1993.

Harris, Neil. "The Gilded Age Revisited: Boston and the Museum Movement." *American Quarterly* 14, no. 3 (1962): 544–66.

———. "Museums, Merchandizing and Popular Taste: The Struggle for Influence." In *Cultural Excursions: Marketing Appetites and Cultural Tastes in Modern America,* 56–81. Chicago: Univ. of Chicago Press, 1990.

Harris, Victor. *Japanese Imperial Craftsmen: Meiji Art from the Khalili Collection.* London: British Museum Press, 1994.

Harrison, Charles. *English Art and Modernism, 1900–1939.* London: Allen Lane, 1981.

Harrison, Martin. *Appearances: Fashion Photography since 1945.* New York: Rizzoli, 1991.

Haselgrove, Dennis, and J. Murray, eds. "John Dwight's Fulham Pottery, 1672–1978: A Collection of Documentary Sources." *Journal of Ceramic History* 11 (1979).

Haskell, Francis. *Rediscoveries in Art: Some Aspects of Taste, Fashion and Collecting in England and France.* Ithaca, N.Y.: Cornell Univ. Press, 1976.

Hawes, Robert. *Radio Art.* London: Green Wood, 1991.

Haworth-Booth, Mark. *E. McKnight Kauffer: A Designer and His Public.* London: G. Fraser, 1979.

———. *Camille Silvy: River Scene, France.* Malibu, California: J. Paul Getty Museum, 1992.

———. "Julia Margaret Cameron." *British Journal of Photography* 6974 (1994a): 15.

———. "Interview with Helen Chadwick." *The Oral History of British Photography.* National Sound Archive, British Library, 1994b.

Hayward, J. "English Brass Inlaid Furniture." *Victoria and Albert Museum Bulletin* 1, no. 1 (1965): 11–23.

———. "The Channon Family of Exeter and London." *Victoria and Albert Museum Bulletin* 2, no. 2 (1966): 64–70.

Hayward, J. F. *Virtuoso Goldsmiths and the Triumph of Mannerism, 1540–1620.* London: Sotheby Parke Bernet, 1976.

Hayward Gallery. *Leonardo da Vinci.* New Haven: Yale Univ. Press in association with the South Bank Centre, 1989.

Hefford, Wendy. "A Windsor Tapestry Portrait." *The Victoria and Albert Museum Yearbook* (1969): 30–2.

Helfgott, Leonard Michael. *Ties That Bind: A Social History of the Iranian Carpet.* Washington, D.C.: Smithsonian Institution Press, 1994.

Herklotz, I. "Neue Literatur zur Sammlungsgeschichte." *Kunstchronik* 47 (1994): 117–35.

Herkomer, Hubert von. *Autobiography of Hubert Herkomer.* Printed for private circulation, 1890.

Herrmann, Frank. *The English as Collectors: An Exhibition of Books Selected by Frank Herrmann.* London: National Book League, 1972.

Herrmann, Wolfgang. *Gottfried Semper: In Search of Architecture.* Cambridge, Mass.: MIT Press, 1984.

Hevia, J. L. "Loot's Fate: The Economy of Plunder and the Moral Life of Objects from the Summer Palace of the Emperor of China." *History and Anthropology* 6 (1994): 319–45.

Hewison, Robert. *Culture and Consensus: England, Art and Politics since 1940.* London: Methuen, 1995.

Hibbert, Christopher. *The Grand Tour.* London: Thames Methuen, 1987.

Hiesinger, Kathryn B., and George H. Marcus, eds. *Design since 1945.* Philadelphia: Philadelphia Museum of Art, 1983.

Himmelheber, Georg, ed., with the assistance of Brigitte Thanner. *Kunst des Biedermeier 1815–1835: Architektur, Malerei, Plastik, Kunsthandwerk, Musik, Dichtung und Mode.* Munich: Prestel, 1988.

Hinsley, Curtis M. "The World as Market Place: Commodification of the Exotic at the World's Columbian Exposition, Chicago, 1893." In *Exhibiting Cultures: The Poetics and Politics of Museum Display,* edited by Ivan Karp and Steven D. Lavine, 344–65. Washington, D.C.: Smithsonian Institution Press, 1991.

Hobhouse, Christopher. *1851 and the Crystal Palace.* Rev. ed. London: J. Murray, 1950.

Hobson, R. L. *The George Eumorfopoulos Collection: Catalogue of the Chinese, Corean and Persian Pottery and Porcelain.* Vol. 3. London: E. Benn, 1926.

Hogben, Carol. *The Wireless Show! 130 Classic Radio Receivers, 1920s to 1950s.* London: V&A, 1977.

Hogben, Carol, and Rowan Watson, eds. *From Manet to Hockney: Modern Artists' Illustrated Books.* London: V&A, 1985.

Hollingshead, John. *Concise History of the International Exhibition of 1862: Its Rise and Progress, Its Building and Features, and a Summary of All Former Exhibitions.* London: Her Majesty's Commissioners, 1862.

Honey, William Boyer. *Guide to the Later Chinese Porcelain: Periods of K'ang Hsi, Yung Chêng, and Ch'ien Lung.* London: Board of Education, 1927.

———. *The Art of the Potter: A Book for the Collector and Connoisseur.* London: Faber and Faber, 1946.

———. *Corean Pottery.* London: Faber and Faber, 1947.

———. *Old English Porcelain: A Handbook for Collectors.* London: Faber and Faber, 1948a.

———. *Wedgwood Ware.* London: Faber and Faber, 1948b.

———. *European Ceramic Art.* 2 vols. London: Faber and Faber, 1952.

Horve, Winifred Eva. *A History of the Metropolitan Museum of Art.* 2 vols. New York: Gilliss Press, 1913.

Höver, Otto. *Das Eisenwerk: Die Kunstformendes Schmiedeeisens vom Mittelalter bis zum Ausgang des 18. Jahrhunderts.* 6th ed. Tübingen: E. Wasmuth, 1961.

Howe, Winifred E. *A History of the Metropolitan Museum of Art.* Vol. 1. New York: Printed at the Gilliss Press, 1913.

Hungerford Pollen, John. *Ancient and Modern Furniture and Woodwork in the South Kensington Museum.* London: Chapman and Hall, 1874.

———. *Ancient and Modern Gold and Silversmith's Work in the South Kensington Museum.* London: G. E. Eyre and W. Spottiswoode, 1878.

Impey, Oliver, and Arthur MacGregor, eds. *The Origins of Museums: The Cabinet of Curiousities in Sixteenth and Seventeenth Century Europe.* Oxford: Clarendon Press, 1985.

Impey, Oliver, and Malcolm Fairley, eds. *Meiji No Takara: Treasures of Imperial Japan.* London: Kibo Foundation, 1995.

Irwin, J., ed. *Indian Art in the V&A.* Bombay, 1976.

Isherwood, Andrew. *An introduction to the Kelmscott Press.* London: V&A, 1986.

Jackson, A. "Imagining Japan: The Victorian Perception and Acquisition of Japanese Culture." *Journal of Design History* 5, no. 4 (1992): 245–56.

Jackson, Charles James. *An Illustrated History of English Plate.* 2 vols. London: Country Life, 1911.

James, E. "Exhibitions and Displays at the V&A, 1852–1993," 1995. National Art Library, V&A.

Jervis, Simon. *High Victorian Design.* Woodbridge, Suffolk: The Boydell Press, 1983.

———. *The Penguin Dictionary of Design and Designers.* London: A. Lane, 1984.

———. *Furniture of about 1900 from Austria and Hungary in the Victoria and Albert Museum.* London: V&A, 1986.

———. *Art and Design in Europe and America, 1800–1900.* London: Herbert Press, 1987.

———. "Charles, Bevan and Talbert." In *The Decorative Arts in the Victorian Period,* edited by Susan Wright, 15–29. London: Society of Antiquaries of London, 1989.

Joachimides, Alexis, et al., eds. *Museumsinszenierungen: Zur Geschichte der Institution des Kunstmuseums: Die Berliner Museumslandschaft, 1830–1990.* Dresden: Verlag der Kunst, 1995.

John, William David. *Old English Lustre Pottery.* Newport, England: R. H. Johns, 1951.

Johnson, Stewart. *Eileen Gray: Designer, 1879–1976.* London: Debrett in association with the Victoria and Albert Museum and the Museum of Modern Art, 1979.

Jones, Dalu, and George Michell, eds. *The Arts of Islam.* London: Arts Council of Great Britain, 1976.

Jones, Joan. *Minton: The First Two Hundred Years of Design and Production.* Shrewsbury: Swan Hill Press, 1993.

Jones, Owen. *The Grammar of Ornament.* London: Day & Son, 1856.

———. *The Grammar of Ornament.* London: B. Quaritch, 1868.

Jopek, N. "Franz Bock und das South Kensington Museum." In *Festschrift für Franz Ronig,* edited by A. Schommers. Forthcoming.

Journal of the Society of Arts. "The Factory System in Prussia." *Journal of the Society of Arts* 2, no. 70 (1853): 320–4.

———. "Discussion." *Journal of the Society of Arts* 16, no. 792 (1868): 179.

Karp, Ivan, and Steven D. Lavine, eds. *Exhibiting Cultures: The Poetics and Politics of Museum Display.* Washington, D.C.: Smithsonian Institution Press, 1991.

Kauffmann, C. M., compiler. *Catalogue of Foreign Paintings.* Vol. 1, *Before 1800.* London: V&A, 1973.

Keen, Michael E. *Jewish Ritual Art in the Victoria & Albert Museum.* London: HMSO, 1991.

Kelvin, Norman. *The Collected Letters of William Morris.* 5 vols. Princeton: Princeton Univ. Press, 1984–87.

Kemp, Martin. "The Crisis at the V and A: A Loss of Balance, the Trustee Boards of National Museums and Galleries." *Burlington Magazine* 131, no. 1034 (1989): 355–7.

Kendrick, Albert Frank. *Catalogue of Tapestries.* 2nd ed. London: HMSO, 1924.

Kerr, Rose. *Chinese Ceramics: Porcelain of the Qing Dynasty, 1644–1911.* London: V&A, 1986.

Kerr, Rose, ed., with texts by Rose Kerr, Verity Wilson, and Craig Clunas. *Chinese Art and Design: Art Objects in Ritual and Daily Life.* Woodstock, N.Y.: Overlook Press, 1991.

King, Donald. *Opus Anglicanum: English Medieval Embroidery.* London: Arts Council, 1963.

King, Donald, director, with the collaboration of Santina Levey . . . [et al]. *British Textile Design in the Victoria and Albert Museum.* 3 vols. Tokyo: Gakken, 1980.

King, James. *The Last Modern: A Life of Herbert Read.* New York: St. Martin's Press, 1990.

King, W., and M. H. Longhurst. "A Relic of Horace Walpole." *Burlington Magazine* 48 (1926): 98–9.

Kisluk-Grosheide, Daniele O. "The Marquand Mansion." *Metropolitan Museum Journal* 29 (1994): 151–81.

Koezuka, Takashi, ed. *The Art of the Indian Courts: Miniature Paintings and Decorative Arts.* Osaka: NHK Kinki Media Puran, 1993.

Krahn, Volker. *Bartolommeo Bellano: Studien zur Paduaner Plastik des Quattrocento.* Munich: Scaneg, 1988.

Kühnel, Ernst. *Die islamischen Elfenbeinskulpturen.* Berlin: Deutscher Verlag für Kunstwissenschaft, 1971.

Kunstgewerbe-museum. *Das Kunstgewerbe-museum zu Berlin: Festschrift zur Eröffnung des Museumsgebäudes.* 1881. Reprint, Berlin: Frölich und Kaufmann, 1981.

Küper, Marijke, and Ida van Zijl. *Gerrit Th. Rietveld, 1883–1964: The Complete Works.* Utrecht: Centraal Museum, 1992.

Labarte, M. J. "Des collections d'objets d'art et d'industrie anciens." *Revue générale de l'architecture* 8 (1849): 302–12, 368–76.

Lackner, H., and J. Mikoletsky. "Zur Aufmienierung der Künste und der Gewerbe." In *Das K. K. National Fabriksprodukten-Kabinett: Technik und Design des Biedermeier,* edited by Thomas Werner, 29–42. Munich: Prestel, 1995.

Laking, G. F. "An Historical Pair of Stirrups." *Connoisseur* 29 (1907): 25–7.

Laking, Guy Francis. *Record of European Armour and Arms through Seven Centuries.* 5 vols. London: G. Bell, 1920–22.

Lane, Arthur. *Italian Porcelain.* London: Faber and Faber, 1954.

Lane, Arthur, and R. J. Charleston. "Girl in a Swing Porcelain and Chelsea." *Transactions of the English Ceramic Circle* 5, no. 3 (1962): 111–44.

La Niece, Susan. "Niello: An Historical and Technical Survey." *Antiquaries Journal* 63 (1983): 279–91.

Larsson, Lar Olaf. *Adrian de Vries.* Vienna: Schroll, 1967.

Laver, James. *Museum Piece, or the Education of an Iconographer.* London: A. Deutsch, 1963.

Lecocq, Anne-Marie. "Morts et résurrections de Bernard Palissy." *Revue de l'art* 78 (1987): 26–32.

Lessmann, Johanna. *Italienische Majolika: Katalog der Sammlung Herzog-Anton-Ulrich-Museum Braunschweig.* Braunschweig: Herzog-Anton-Ulrich-Museum, 1979.

Levenson, Jay A., ed. *Circa 1492: Art in the Age of Exploration.* Washington, D.C.: National Gallery of Art, 1991.

Levine, Philippa. *The Amateur and the Professional: Antiquarians, Historians and Archaeologists in Victorian England, 1838–1886.* Cambridge, England: Cambridge Univ. Press, 1986.

Lieb, Norbert. *Die Fugger und die Kunst.* Vol. 1. *Im Zeitalter der Spätgotik und frühen Renaissance.* Munich: Schnell and Steiner, 1952.

Lightbown, R. W. "A Medici Casket." *Victoria and Albert Museum Bulletin* 3 (1967): 81–9.

Little, Wilfred L. *Staffordshire Blue: Underglaze Blue Transfer-Printed Earthenware.* London: Batsford, 1969.

Llewellyn, Nigel. *The Art of Death: Visual Culture in the English Death Ritual, c. 1500–c. 1800.* London: Reaktion Books in association with the V&A, 1991.

Long, Basil Somerset. *Catalogue of the Jones Collection.* Vol. 3. London: HMSO, 1923.

Longhurst, Margaret Helen. *Catalogue of Carvings in Ivory: Victoria and Albert Museum.* 2 vols. London: Board of Education, 1927–29.

Lowenthal, David. *The Past Is a Foreign Country.* Cambridge, England: Cambridge Univ. Press, 1985.

Luckhurst, Kenneth William. *The Story of Exhibitions.* London: Studio Publications, 1951.

Lydecker, John Kent. *The Domestic Setting of the Arts in Renaissance Florence.* Ann Arbor, Mich.: University Microfilms, 1993.

Lynes, Russell. *More Than Meets the Eye: The History and Collections of the Cooper-Hewitt Museum, the Smithsonian Institution's National Museum of Design.* Washington, D.C.: Smithsonian Institution, 1981.

MacCarthy, Fiona. *All Things Bright & Beautiful: Design in Britain 1830 to Today.* London: George Allen & Unwin Ltd, 1972.

McClellan, Andrew. *Inventing the Louvre: Art, Politics, and the Origins of the Modern Museum in Eighteenth-Century Paris.* Cambridge, England: Cambridge Univ. Press, 1994.

Macdonald, Stewart. *The History and Philosophy of Art Education.* London: Univ. of London, 1970.

MacGregor, Arthur, ed. *Tradescant's Rarities: Essays on the Foundation of the Ashmolean Museum, 1683, with a Catalogue of the Surviving Early Collections.* Oxford: Clarendon Press, 1983.

———. *Sir Hans Sloane: Collector, Scientist, Antiquary, Founding Father of the British Museum.* London: British Museum, 1994.

McKillop, Beth. *Korean Art and Design.* London: V&A, 1992a.

———. "The Samsung Gallery of Korean Art at the Victoria and Albert Museum." *Orientations* 23, no. 12 (1992b): 34–8.

Maclagan, E. "Museum Planning." *RIBA Journal* 38 (1931): 527–48.

Maclagan, Eric, and Margaret H. Longhurst. *Catalogue of Italian Sculpture.* 2 vols. Oxford: Oxford Univ. Press, 1932.

Macquoid, Percy. *A History of English Furniture.* Vol. 1. London: Lawrence and Bullen, 1904.

Macquoid, Percy, and Ralph Edwards. *The Dictionary of English Furniture from the Middle Ages to the Late Georgian Period.* Vol. 1. London: Country Life, 1924.

Mallet, J. V. G. "Two Documented Gold Chelsea Gold-Anchor Vases." *Victoria and Albert Museum Bulletin* 1, no. 1 (1965): 29–37.

———. "Hogarth's Pug in Porcelain." *Victoria and Albert Museum Bulletin* 3, no. 2 (1967): 45–54.

Mallgrave, Harry Francis. *Gottfried Semper: Architect of the Nineteenth Century: A Personal and Intellectual Biography.* New Haven: Yale Univ. Press, 1996.

Manchester City Art Gallery. *Catalogue of an Exhibition of Chinese Applied Art.* Manchester: G. Falkner, 1913.

Mandler, Peter. *The Stately Homes of England: The English Country House and the National Heritage since the Eighteenth Century.* New Haven: Yale Univ. Press, in press.

Marryat, Joseph. *Histoire des poteries, faiences et porcelaines.* 2 vols. Paris: J. Renouard, 1866.

Martin, Theodore. *The Life of His Royal Highness the Prince Consort.* 5 vols. London: Smith, Elder and Co., 1875–80.

Maskell, William. *A Description of the Ivories Ancient & Medieval.* London: Chapman and Hall, 1872.

Mather, F. J. "Art in America." *Burlington Magazine* 9 (1906): 62–3.

———. "Museums." *Burlington Magazine* 13 (1908): 322.

Mattei, Pietro, and Tonica Cecchetti, eds. *Maestro Giorgio: l'uomo, l'artista, l'imprenditore.* Perugia: Camera di commercio, industria, artigianato e agricultura, 1995.

Meller, Simon. *Die deutschen Bronzestatuetten der Renaissance.* Florence: Pantheon, 1926.

Mende, U. *Heinrich der Löwe.* Braunschweig, 1995.

Mendes, Valerie. *The Victoria & Albert Museum's Textile Collection: British Textiles from 1900 to 1937.* New York: Canopy Books, 1992.

Menzhausen, Joachim. "Elector Augustus's Kunstkammer: An Analysis of the Inventory of 1587." In *The Origins of Museums: The Cabinet of Curiousities in Sixteenth and Seventeenth Century Europe,* edited by Oliver Impey and Arthur MacGregor, 69–75. Oxford: Clarendon Press, 1985.

Miller, R. Craig. *Modern Design in the Metropolitan Museum of Art, 1890–1990.* New York: Metropolitan Museum of Art and Harry N. Abrams, Inc., 1990.

Minihan, Janet. *The Nationalization of Culture: The Development of State Subsidies to the Arts in Great Britain.* London: Hamilton, 1977.

Mitchell, H. P. "W. H. J. Weale." *Burlington Magazine* 30 (1917): 241–3.

Mitchell, Timothy. "Orientalism and the Exhibitionary Order." In *Colonialism and Culture,* edited by Nicholas B. Dirks, 289–317. Ann Arbor: Univ. of Michigan Press, 1992.

Mitter, Partha. *Much Maligned Monsters: A History of European Reactions to Indian Art.* Chicago: Univ. of Chicago Press, 1992. First published Oxford: Clarendon Press, 1977.

———. *Art and Nationalism in Colonial India, 1850–1922: Occidental Orientations.* Cambridge, England: Cambridge Univ. Press, 1994.

Möller, Lieselotte. *Der Wrangelschrank und die Verwandten Süddeutschen Intarsienmöbel des 16. Jahrhunderts.* Berlin: Deutscher Verlag für Kunstwissenschaft, 1956.

Montevecchi, Benedetta, and Sandra Vasco Rocca, eds. *Suppellettile ecclesiastica.* Florence: Centro Di, 1988.

Moore, Andrew W. *Norfolk and the Grand Tour: Eighteenth-Century Travellers Abroad and Their Souvenirs.* Norwich: Norfolk Museums Service, 1985.

Moorman, David, ed. *Matisse Prints from The Museum of Modern Art.* Fort Worth, Texas: The Fort Worth Art Museum and The Museum of Modern Art, New York, 1986.

Mordaunt Crook, Joseph. *William Burges and the High Victorian Dream.* London: J. Murray, 1981.

Mordaunt Crook, Joseph, ed., with catalogue entries by Mary Axon and Virginia Glenn. *The Strange Genius of William Burges, Art-Architect, 1827–1881: A Catalogue to a Centenary Exhibition, Organised Jointly by the National Museum of Wales, Cardiff and the Victoria and Albert Museum, London, in 1981.* Cardiff: National Museum of Wales, 1982.

Morikawa, S. "The Rise and Development of the Art Museum as a Cultural Institution: The Philadelphia Story." Ph.D. diss., Syracuse University, 1983.

Morris, Barbara. *Inspiration for Design: The Influence of the Victoria and Albert Museum.* London: V&A, 1986.

Muirhead, Findlay. *London and Its Environs.* London: E. Benn, 1918.

Muirhead, Findlay, and L. Russell Muirhead, eds. *London and Its Environs.* 4th ed. London: E. Benn, 1935.

Muirhead, L. Russell, ed. *Short Guide to London.* 5th ed. London: E. Benn, 1947.

Mundt, Barbara. *Die deutschen Kunstgewerbemuseen im 19. Jahrhundert.* Munich: Prestel, 1974.

———. "Über einige Gemeinsamkeiten und Unterschiede von kunstgewerblichen und kulturgeschichtlichen Museen." In *Das kunst- und kulturgeschichtliche Museum im 19. Jahrhundert: Vorträge des Symposions im Germanischen Nationalmuseum Nürnberg,* edited by Bernward Deneke and Rainer Kahsnitz, 143–51. Munich: Prestel, 1977.

———. "125 Jahre Kunstgewerbemuseum: Konzepte, Bauten und Menschen für eine Sammlung, 1867–1939." *Jahrbuch der Berliner Museen* 34 (1982): 173–84.

Murdoch Smith, Robert. *Persian Art.* London: Chapman and Hall, 1876.

Murray, John. *Handbook to London As It Is.* London: J. Murray, 1874.

Museo Campana. *Cataloghi del Museo Campana.* Rome: n.p., 1859.

Museum of Fine Arts. "Communications to the Trustees Regarding the New Building," 1904. Archives Department, Museum of Fine Arts, Boston.

———. "The Museum Commission in Europe," 1905. Archives Department, Museum of Fine Arts, Boston.

Museums Journal. "The New Building for the Museum of Fine Arts in Boston." *Museums Journal* 8 (1908–09): 163–70.

———. "Indian collection at South Kensington." *Museums Journal* 8 (1908–09): 435.

———. "Art and Industry in Sweden." *Museums Journal* 20 (1920–21): 199–200.

———. "Art and Commerce." *Museums Journal* 24 (1924–25): 272.

———. *Museums Journal* 33 (1933–34): 369–70.

Nachama, A., and Gereon Sievernich, eds. *Jüdische Lebenswelten: jüdisches Denken und Glauben, Leben und Arbeiten in den Kulturen der Welt.* Berlin: Berliner Festspiele, 1992.

Naef, Weston J. *Early Photographs in Egypt and the Holy Land, 1849–1870.* New York: Metropolitan Museum of Art, 1973.

Nara National Museum. *Builders of Japanese Buddhism: Their Portraits and Calligraphy.* Nara, 1981.

National Museum. *Guides to the National Museum: The Ethnographical Department: High Civilizations of Asia.* Copenhagen: Nationalmuseet, 1950.

Naylor, Gillian. *The Arts and Crafts Movement.* London: Studio Vista, 1971.

Neale, John Preston. *Views of the Seats of Noblemen and Gentlemen in England, Wales, Scotland and Ireland.* 6 vols. London: Sherwood, Neely and Jones, 1818–23.

Nelson, John. *The History, Topography and Antiquities of the Parish of St Mary Islington in the County of Middlesex.* London: J. Nichols, 1811.

Nesbit, George L. *Benthamite Reviewing: The First Twelve Years of the Westminster Review, 1824–36.* New York: AMS Press, 1966.

Neverov, Oleg. "'His Majesty's Cabinet' and Peter I's Kunstkammer." In *The Origins of Museums: The Cabinet of Curiousities in Sixteenth and Seventeenth Century Europe,* edited by Oliver Impey and Arthur MacGregor, 54–61. Oxford: Clarendon Press, 1985.

Nevill, Dorothy Fanny. *The Reminiscences of Lady Dorothy Nevill.* Edited by Ralph Henry Nevill. London: E. Arnold, 1906.

Noever, Peter, ed. *Tradition und Experiment: Das Österreichische Museum für Angewandte Kunst, Wien.* Salzburg: Residenz-Verlag, 1988.

Odaschalchi, Baldassare. "The Industrial Arts in Italy." *The Builder* 40, no. 1988 (1881): 295–301.

Official, Descriptive and Illustrated Catalogue of the Great Exhibition of the Works of Industry of All Nations. 4 vols. London: Spicer Bros., 1851–52.

Oman, Charles. *English Domestic Silver.* London: A. and C. Black, 1934.

———. *German and Swiss Domestic Silver of the Gothic Period.* Small Picture Book, no. 55. London: HMSO, 1960.

———. *Caroline Silver, 1625–1688.* London: Faber, 1970.

———, compiler. *The Golden Age of Hispanic Silver, 1400–1665.* London: HMSO, 1968.

Oughton, Frederick. *Grinling Gibbons & the English Woodcarving Tradition.* London: Stobart, 1979.

Painter, K., and D. Whitehouse. "The History of the Portland Vase." *Journal of Glass Studies* 32 (1990): 24–84.

Parkinson, Ronald. *Catalogue of British Oil Paintings, 1820–1860: The Victoria and Albert Museum.* London: HMSO, 1990.

Parris, Leslie, and Ian Fleming-Williams. *Constable.* London: Tate Gallery, 1991.

Parry, Linda. *William Morris Textiles.* London: Weidenfeld and Nicolson, 1983.

———. *Textiles of the Arts and Crafts Movement.* New York: Thames and Hudson, 1988.

———, ed. *William Morris.* New York: Harry N. Abrams, Inc., 1996.

Paulson, Ronald. *Hogarth's Graphic Works.* 2 vols. New Haven: Yale Univ. Press, 1965.

———. *Hogarth: His Life, Art, and Times.* Vol. 2. New Haven: Yale Univ. Press, published for the Paul Mellon Centre for Studies in British Art, 1977.

Pearce, Susan M. *Museums, Objects and Collections: A Cultural Study.* Leicester: Leicester Univ. Press, 1992.

Penny, Nicholas. *Catalogue of European Sculpture in the Ashmolean Museum: 1540 to the Present Day.* 3 vols. Oxford: Clarendon Press, 1992.

Perez, Nissan N. *Focus East: Early Photography in the Near East, 1839–1885.* New York: Harry N. Abrams, Inc., 1988.

Perkins, C. "American Art Museums." *North American Review* 228 (1870).

Peterson, William S. *The Kelmscott Press: A History of William Morris's Typographical Adventure.* Oxford: Clarendon Press, 1991.

Pevsner, Nikolaus. *An Enquiry into Industrial Art in England.* Cambridge, England: Cambridge Univ. Press, 1937.

———. *Academies of Art.* Cambridge, England: Cambridge Univ. Press, 1940.

Pezone, R. "L'Union de l'art et de l'industrie: Les origines de I.U.C.A.D. et du Musée des arts décoratifs." Master's thesis, Université de Paris, IV Sorbonne, 1989.

Philippovich, E. von. "Peter Hencke, der Monogrammist JPH und PH." In

Mainz und der Mittelrhein in der europäischen Kunstgeschichte: Studien für Wolfgang Fritz Volbach zur seinem 70 Geburtstag, 679–86. Forschungen zur Kunstgeschichte und christlichen Archäologie, vol. 6. Gesellschaft für Bildende Kunst, 1966.

Physick, John. *Photography and the South Kensington Museum.* London: V&A, 1975.

———. *The Victoria and Albert Museum: The History of Its Building.* Oxford: Phaidon, 1982.

———. "Early Albertopolis: The Contribution of Gottfried Semper." *The Victorian Society Annual* (1994): 28–36.

Pinder-Wilson, Ralph H., compiler, with the assistance of Ellen Smart and Douglas Barrett. *Paintings from the Muslim Courts of India.* London: World of Islam Festival Pub. Co., 1976.

Pinkham, Roger. *Catalogue of Pottery by William De Morgan.* London: V&A, 1973.

Pinner, R., and M. Franses. "East Mediterranean Carpets in the V&A." *HALI* 4, no. 1 (1981): 36–52.

Pinto, Edward H. *Treen and Other Wooden Bygones: An Encyclopedia and Social History.* London: Bell, 1969.

Plinval de Guillebon, Régine de. *Paris Porcelain, 1770–1850.* London: Barrie and Jenkins, 1972.

Plunkett, G. T. "How an Art Museum Should Be Organised." *Magazine of Art* n.s. 1 (1902–03): 448–50.

Pointon, Marcia, ed. *Art Apart: Art Institutions and Ideology across England and North America.* Manchester: Manchester Univ. Press, 1994.

Pollen, Anne. *John Hungerford Pollen, 1820–1902.* London: J. Murray, 1912.

Pomian, K. "Collections et musées, note critique." *Annales* 6 (1993): 1381–1401.

Pope-Hennessy, John. "Obituary: Dr. W. L. Hildburgh." *Burlington Magazine* 98 (1956): 56.

———. "The Victoria and Albert Museum." Lecture given at the V&A, c. 1960. National Art Library, V&A.

———. "An Ivory by Giovanni Pisano." *Victoria and Albert Museum Bulletin* 1, no. 3 (1965): 9–16.

———. "A Sketch-Model by Benvenuto Cellini." *Bulletin of the Victoria and Albert Museum* I (1965): 5–9. Reprinted in *Essays on Italian Sculpture,* 141–44. London, 1968.

———. "Michelangelo's Cupid: The End of a Chapter." In *Essays on Italian Sculpture,* 111–20. London: Phaidon, 1968.

———. "The Gherardini Collection of Italian Sculpture." *Victoria and Albert Museum Yearbook* 2 (1970): 7–26.

———. "Perseus," *Cellini,* ch. VII, 163–86, plates 85–108. New York: Abbeville Press, 1985.

———. *Learning to Look.* New York: Doubleday, 1991.

Pope-Hennessy, John, assisted by Ronald Lightbown. *Catalogue of Italian Sculpture in the Victoria and Albert Museum.* 3 vols. London: HMSO, 1964.

Powell, J. C. "Hitcham: Notes on the 14th Century Glass in the Chancel of St Mary's Church." *Bucks Architectural and Archaeological Society: Records* 10 (1915): 370–3.

Poynter, Edward J. *Ten Lectures on Art.* London: Chapman and Hall, 1879.

Prince Consort. "Memorandum by the Prince Consort as to the Disposal of the Surplus from the Great Exhibition of 1851." In *The Life of His Royal Highness, The Prince Consort* by Theodore Martin, vol. 2, 569–73. London: Smith, Elder and Co., 1877.

Privy Council. Correspondence between the Lords of the Committee of the Privy Council for Trade and the Lords Commissioners of H. M. Treasury on the Constitution of the Department of Science and Art, March 16, 1853. National Art Library, V&A.

Pugin, Augustus Welby Northmore. *True Principles of Christian Architecture.* London: J. Weale, 1841.

Purbrick, Louise. "The South Kensington Museum: The Building of the House of Henry Cole." In *Art Apart: Art Institutions and Ideology across England and North America,* edited by Marcia Pointon, 69–88. Manchester: Manchester Univ. Press, 1994.

Rackham, Bernard. "The Master of the Resurrection Panel." In *Festschrift zum sechzigsten Geburtstage von E. W. Braum,* 70–84. Anzeiger des Landesmuseums in Troppau, vol. 2., 1930.

———. *A Guide to the Collection of Stained Glass.* London: Printed under the authority of the Board of Education, 1936.

———. *Catalogue of Italian Maiolica.* London: Board of Education, 1940.

Rackham, Bernard, and Herbert Read. *English Pottery: Its Development from Early Times to the End of the Eighteenth Century.* London: E. Benn, 1924.

Radcliffe, Anthony. *European Bronze Statuettes.* London: Connoisseur, 1966.

———. *Italian Renaissance Sculpture in the Time of Donatello.* Detroit: Founders Society, The Detroit Institute of Arts, 1985.

Radice, Barbara. *Memphis: Research, Experiences, Results, Failures and Successes of a New Design.* Translated from the Italian by Paul Blanchard. London: Thames and Hudson, 1985.

———. *Ettore Sottsass: A Critical Biography.* Translated by Rodney Stringer. New York: Rizzoli, 1993.

Redgrave, Richard. "Supplementary Report on Design." In *Reports by the Juries on the Subjects in the Thirty Classes into Which the Exhibition Was Divided.* London: Spicer Brothers, 1852.

———. "On the Methods Employed for Imparting Education in Art to All Classes." In *Addresses of the Superintendents of the Department of Practical Art, Delivered at the Theatre at Marlborough House.* London: Chapman and Hall, 1853.

———. *Richard Redgrave, C.B., R.A.A.: A Memoir, Compiled from His Diary.* Edited by Frances Margaret Redgrave. London: Cassell and Co., 1891.

Rein, J. J. *The Industries of Japan.* London: Hodder and Stoughton, 1889.

Reising, Gert. *Das Museum als Öffentlichkeitsform und Bildungsträger bürgerlicher Kultur: Unter besonderer Berücksichtigung der Entwicklungsgeschichte des South Kensington Museum in London.* Darmstadt: Roether, 1980.

Reitlinger, Gerald. *The Economics of Taste.* Vol. 2. London: Barrie and Rockliff, 1963.

Reynolds, Graham. *The Later Paintings and Drawings of John Constable.* 2 vols. New Haven: Published for the Paul Mellon Centre for Studies in British Art by Yale Univ. Press, 1984.

Rhodes, John Grant. *Ornament and Ideology: A Study in Mid-Nineteenth-Century British Design Theory* (Ph.D. diss., Harvard University, 1983). Ann Arbor: University Microfilms International, 1985.

Richards, Charles R. *Industrial Art and the Museum.* New York: Macmillan, 1927.

Richards, Thomas. *The Imperial Archive: Knowledge and the Fantasy of Empire.* London: Verso, 1993.

Richter, J. P. "The MSS of Leonardo da Vinci in the South Kensington Museum." *The Academy* 16 (1879): 344–5.

Riegl, Alois. *Stilfragen: Grundlegungen zu einer Geschichte der Ornamentik.* Berlin: G. Siemens, 1893.

Robinson, John Charles. *An Introductory Lecture on the Museum of Ornamental Art of the Department.* London: Chapman and Hall, 1854.

———. *Catalogue of the Soulages Collection.* London: Chapman and Hall, 1856.

———. *The Treasury of Ornamental Art.* London: Day and Son, 1857.

———. *On the Museum of Art.* Introductory Addresses on the Science and Art Department and the South Kensington Museum, no. 5. London, 1858.

———. Report for the Art Museum for 1859. Ed. 84/164, National Art Library, V&A.

———. *Italian Sculpture of the Middle Ages and Period of the Revival in Art: A Descriptive Catalogue of the Works Forming the above Section of the Museum, with Additional Illustrative Notices.* London: Chapman and Hall, 1862b.

———. "On the Art Collections at South Kensington, Considered in Reference to Architecture." *Building News* 10 (1863): 425–7, 445–6.

———. Report, 28th March 1865. Vol. 3, part 1, no. 6433. National Art Library, V&A.

———. "Our Public Art Museums: A Retrospect." *Nineteenth Century* (1897): 940–64.

———, ed. *Catalogue of the Special Loans Exhibition at the South Kensington Museum,* 1862a. National Art Library, V&A.

———, ed. *Catalogue of the Special Loan Exhibition of Spanish and Portuguese Ornamental Art.* London: Chapman and Hall, 1881.

Robinson, Vincent J. *Eastern Carpets: Twelve Early Examples.* London: H. Sotheran & Co., 1882.

Rock, Daniel. *Textile Fabrics: A Descriptive Catalogue of the Collection of Church Vestments, Dresses, Silk Stuffs, Needlework and Tapestries.* London: Chapman and Hall, 1870.

Rothenstein, William. *Men and Memories.* London: Faber and Faber, 1932.

Rothstein, Nathalie. *Silk Designs of the Eighteenth Century in the Collection of the Victoria and Albert Museum, with a Complete Catalogue.* London: Thames and Hudson, 1990.

Royal Academy of Arts. *Catalogue of the International Exhibition of Chinese Art, 1935–36.* London: Royal Academy of Arts, 1935.

Royal Commission on National Museums and Galleries. *Oral Evidence, Memoranda and Appendices to the Interim Report.* London: HMSO, 1928. National Art Library, V&A.

———. *Final Report.* London, 1930. National Art Library, V&A.

Royal Commission on Technical Instruction. *Second Report.* London, 1884. National Art Library, V&A.

Rupin, Ernest. *L'oeuvre de Limoges.* Paris: A. Piard, 1890.

Russell, Raymond. *Victoria and Albert Museum: Catalogue of Musical Instruments.* Vol. 1, *Keyboard Instruments.* London: HMSO, 1968.

Rykwert, Joseph. "Eileen Gray: Pioneer of Design." *The Architectural Review* 152 (1972): 357–61.

Saint Louis Art Museum. *Saint Louis Art Museum Bulletin* 17–18 (1984–88).

Salomon, Kathryn. *Jewish Ceremonial Embroidery.* London: Batsford, 1988.

Samuel, Raphael, ed. *Patriotism: The Making and Unmaking of British National Identity.* 3 vols. London: Routledge, 1989.

Saumarez Smith, Charles. "The Philosophy of Museum Display: The Continuing Debate." *V&A Album* 5 (1986): 30–8.

Scarce, J. "Travels with Telegraph and Tiles in Persia: From the Private Papers of Major-General Sir Robert Murdoch Smith." *Art and Archaeology Research Papers* 3 (1973): 70–81.

Scarisbrick, Diana. *Tudor and Jacobean Jewellery, 1508–1625.* London: Tate Gallery Publications, 1995.

Schaap, Robert, ed., catalogue compiled by Frits Scholten, Jan Dees, Robert Schaap. *Meiji: Japanese Art in Transition.* Leiden: Society for Japanese Arts and Crafts, 1987.

Schnitzer, B. K. "The 16th-Century French Ceramic Ware Called Saint-Porchaire." Ph.D. diss., University of Michigan, 1987.

Schott, Howard. *Victoria and Albert Museum: Catalogue of Musical Instruments.* 2nd ed. Vol. 1, *Keyboard Instruments.* London: HMSO, 1985.

Schwabe, Hermann. *Die Forderung der Kunst-Industrie in England und der Stand dieser Frage in Deutschland.* Berlin, 1866a.

———. Report on South Kensington and Its Programs, Berlin, 1866b. National Art Library, V&A.

Select Committee. *Report from the Select Committee Appointed to Inquire into the Best Means of Extending a Knowledge of the Arts, and of the Principles of Design, among the People of the Country.* London, 1835–36.

———. *Report from the Select Committee on Arts and Their Connexion with Manufactures.* London, 1836.

———. *Report from the Select Committee on the South Kensington Museum.* London, 1860.

———. *Second Report from the Select Committee on Museums of the Science and Art Department.* London: Printed for HMSO by Eyre & Spottiswoode, 1897.

Select Committee on Schools of Art. "Appendices." In *Parliamentary Papers* 12 (1864): 368–453.

Select Committee on Scientific Instruction. "Minutes of Evidence." *Parliamentary Papers.* London 15 (1864a): 47–8.

———. "Appendices." *Parliamentary Papers.* London 15 (1864b): 450–1.

Semper, Gottfried. "Practical Art in Metals," 1854. National Art Library, V&A.

———. *Der Stil in den technischen und tektonischen Künsten, oder praktische Aesthetik: Ein Handbuch für Techniker, Künstler, und Kunstfreunde.* 2 vols. Frankfurt: Verlag für Kunst und Wissenschaft, 1860/1863.

———. *Four Elements of Architecture and Other Writings.* Translated by Harry Francis Mallgrave and Wolfgang Herrmann. Cambridge, England: Cambridge Univ. Press, 1989.

Shaw, Henry. *Specimens of Ancient Furniture Drawn from Existing Authorities with Descriptions by Sir Samuel Rush Meyrick.* London: W. Pickering, 1836.

———. *The Encyclopedia of Ornament.* London: n.p., 1842.

Shearman, Daniel J., and Iirit Rogoff, eds. *Museum Culture: Histories, Discourses, Spectacles.* Minneapolis: Univ. of Minnesota Press, 1994.

Shearman, John K. G. *Mannerism.* Harmondsworth: Penguin, 1967.

Simmonds, Peter Lund. *Catalogue of the Collection of Commercial Products of the Animal Kingdom.* London, 1857.

———. *The Commercial Products of the Animal Kingdom Employed in the Arts and Manufactures: Shown in the Collection of the Bethnal Green Branch of the South Kensington Museum.* London: G. E. Eyre and W. Spottiswoode for HMSO, 1880.

Skelton, R. "The Relations between the Chinese and Indian Jade Carving Traditions." In *The Westward Influence of the Chinese Arts from the 14th to the 18th Century,* edited by William Watson, 98–108. Colloquies on Art and Archaeology in Asia, no. 3. London: Univ. of London, School of Oriental and African Studies, Percival David Foundation of Chinese Art, 1972.

———. "The Indian Collections: 1798–1978." *Burlington Magazine* 120, no. 902 (1978): 297–304.

Smart, Ellen S. "Balchand." In *Master Artists of the Imperial Mughal Court,* edited by Pratapaditya Pal, 135–48. Bombay: Marg Publications, 1991.

Smith, W. "The Department of Science and Art, and Its Reports." *Art Journal* 219 (1864).

Snodin, M., catalogue ed., assisted by Elspeth Moncrieff. *Rococo: Art and Design in Hogarth's England.* London: Trefoil, 1984.

Solkin, D. "Re-Wrighting Shaftesbury: The Air Pump and the Limits of Commercial Humanism." In *Painting and the Politics of Culture,* edited by J. Barrell, 73–99. Oxford: Oxford Univ. Press, 1992.

———. *Painting for Money: The Visual Arts and the Public Sphere in Eighteenth-Century England.* Chapter 6, 214–46. New Haven: Yale Univ. Press, 1993.

Solon, Louis Marc Emmanuel. *The Art of the Old English Potter.* London: Bemrose and Sons, 1883.

Somers Cocks, Anna. *The Victoria and Albert Museum: The Making of the Collection.* Leicester: Windward, 1980a.

———. *Princely Magnificence: Court Jewels of the Renaissance, 1500–1630.* London: Debrett's Peerage in association with the V&A, 1980b.

South Kensington Museum. *A Brief Guide to the Collection of Animal Products.* London: W. Clowes and Sons, 1857a.

———. *Guide to the South Kensington Museum.* London, 1857b.

———. *Catalogue of the First Special Exhibition of National Portraits Ending with the Reign of King James the Second on Loan to the South Kensington Museum.* London: Strangeways and Walden, 1866.

———. "Inventory of the Objects in the Art Division of the Museum at South Kensington Arranged According to the Dates of Their Acquisition." Vol. 1, For the Years 1852 to the End of 1867, 1868. National Art Library, V&A.

———, Bethnal Green Branch. Animal Products Registers, 1860s–1870s. 2 vols. National Art Library, V&A.

———. *Catalogue of Chinese Objects in the South Kensington Museum.* London, 1872a.

———. *Brief Guide to the Animal Products Collection.* London: Printed by Eyre and Spottiswoode for HMSO, 1872b.

———. *Handbook of the Jones Collection in the South Kensington Museum.* London: Published for the Committee of the Council on Education by Chapman and Hall, 1883.

———. *Forster Collection: A Catalogue of the Paintings, Manuscripts, Autograph Letters, Pamphlets, etc. Bequeathed by John Forster, Esq. LL.D..* London: HMSO, 1893.

Special Committee. *Report of a Special Committee of the Council of the School of Design . . . on the State and Management of the School.* London, 1847.

Spielmann, P. E. "Art, Books, and Friendships of Marion H. Spielmann." National Art Library, V&A.

Stafski, H. "Die Skulpturensammlung." In *Das Germanische Nationalmuseum Nürnberg, 1852–1977: Beiträge zu seiner Geschichte,* edited by Bernward Deneke and Rainer Kahsnitz, 607–33. Munich: Deutscher Kunstverlag, 1978.

Stangos, Nikos, ed. *David Hockney by David Hockney.* New York: Harry N. Abrams, Inc., 1977.

Starkey, David, ed. *Henry VIII: A European Court in England.* London: Collins and Brown in association with the National Maritime Museum, 1991.

Stewart, Susan. *On Longing: Narratives of the Miniature, the Gigantic, the Souvenir, the Collection.* Durham, N.C.: Duke University Press, 1993.

Stirling, Anna Marie Wilhelmina. *William De Morgan and His Wife.* London: T. Butterworth, 1922.

Strange, Edward Fairbrother. "Report on the Section of Prints and Drawings, Victoria and Albert Museum," 1908. Minutes and Memoranda of the Committee on Re-arrangement. National Art Library, V&A.

———. *Catalogue of Chinese Lacquer.* London: HMSO for the V&A, 1925.

Strong, Roy. "Forty Years On: The Victoria and Albert Museum and the Regions." *Museums Journal* 75 (1975): vi–viii.

———. "The Victoria and Albert Museum, 1978." *Burlington Magazine* 120 (1978): 272–6.

———. "Director's Report." *Victoria and Albert Museum: Report of the Board of Trustees* (1986) 8–9.

———. *Gloriana: The Portraits of Queen Elizabeth I.* London: Thames and Hudson, 1987.

Strong, Roy, with contributions from V. J. Murrell. *Artists of the Tudor Court: The Portrait Miniature Rediscovered.* London: V&A, 1983.

Stronge, Susan. "Colonel Guthrie's Collection." *Oriental Art* 39, no. 4 (1993): 4–13.

Strzygowski, Josef. *Koptische Kunst.* Catalogue général des antiquités égyptiennes du Musée du Caire, vol. 13. Vienna: A. Holzhausen, 1904.

Studio. *Studio Yearbook of Decorative Art* (1949).

Summers, John David. *The Sculpture of Vincenzo Danti: A Study on the Influence of Michelangelo and the Ideals of the Maniera.* New York: Garland, 1979.

Sumner, A. *Men, Birds, Beasts & Flowers: An Exhibition of Seventeenth Century Pictorial Needlework.* Bath, 1987.

———. "Sir John Charles Robinson: Victorian Collector and Connoisseur." *Apollo* 130 (1989): 226–30.

Surtees, Virginia. *The Paintings and Drawings of Dante Gabriel Rossetti, 1828–1882: A Catalogue Raisonné.* 2 vols. Oxford: Clarendon Press, 1971.

Survey of London. *Survey of London.* Vol. 38, *The Museums Area of South Kensington and Westminster.* London: Athlone Press for the Greater London Council, 1975.

Sutton, Denys. "A Born Virtuoso." *Apollo* 95, no. 121 (1972): 156–61.
———. "The Age of Robert Browning." *Apollo* 122 (1985): 96–110.
Swarzenski, Hanns. *Monuments of Romanesque Art.* London: Faber and Faber, 1955.
Symonds, R. W. "A Magnificent Dressing Table." *Country Life,* 16 February 1956, 286–8.
Taburet-Delahaye, Elisabeth, and B. D. Boehm. *L'oeuvre de Limoges: Emaux limousins du Moyen Age.* Paris: Réunion des musées nationaux, 1995.
Taft, Charles P. *The South Kensington Museum: What It Is, How It Originated, What It Has Done and Is Now Doing for England and the World, and the Adaptation of Such an Institution to the Needs and Possibilities of this City.* Cincinnati: Robert Clarke and Co., 1878.
Tait, Hugh. "The Bow Factory under Alderman Arnold and Thomas Frye (1747–1759)." *Transactions of the English Ceramic Circle* 5, no. 4 (1963): 195–216.
———. *Catalogue of the Waddesdon Bequest in the British Museum.* Vol. 3, *The Curiosities.* London: British Museum, 1991.
Theuerkauff, Christian. "Scultura Barocca in Avorio: Nuove attribuzioni ad Adam Lenckhardt e a Dominicus Stainhart." *Antichità Viva* 2 (1971): 33–51.
———. "Kunststücke von Helfenbein: Zum Werk der Gebrüder Stainhart." *Alte und Moderne Kunst* 17, no. 124/5 (1972): 22–33.
Thiekötter, Angelika, and Eckhard Siepmann, eds. *Packeis und Pressglas von der Kunstgewerbebewegung zum Deutschen Werkbund: Eine wissenschaftliche Illustrierte.* Giessen: Anabas-Verlag, 1987.
Thompson, L. B. "On the Working of Shell Cameos." *The Art Journal,* n.s. 14 (1898): 277–80.
Thornton, Peter. "A Very Special Year." *Connoisseur* 198, no. 191 (1978): 138–45.
———. *The Italian Renaissance Interior, 1400–1600.* New York: Harry N. Abrams, Inc., 1991.
Thornton, Peter, and S. Jervis. "King Charles' Wassail Table." *Connoisseur* 192, no. 772 (1976): 137–40.
Thorpe, W. A. "The French Taste of Mr. John Jones." *Antique Collector* 33, no. 5 (1962): 208–14.
Tise, Suzanne. "Between Art and Industry: Design Reform in France 1851–1939." Ph.D. diss., University of Pittsburgh, 1991.
Tomkins, Calvin. *Merchants and Masterpieces: The Story of the Metropolitan Museum of Art.* New York: E. P. Dutton, 1970.
Tomlin, Maurice. *Catalogue of Adam Period Furniture.* London: V&A, 1972.
Trusted, Marjorie. *Spanish Sculpture: Catalogue of the Post-medieval Spanish Sculpture in Wood, Terracotta, Alabaster, Marble, Stone, Lead and Jet in the Victoria and Albert Museum.* London: V&A, 1996.
Turner, Eric. "Toward a Modern Collecting Policy: The Metalwork Collections of the Victoria and Albert Museum." *Journal of Decorative and Propaganda Arts,* Summer 1988: 94–107.
Tvrdik, Valerie, ed. *The Antiquarian Society of the Art Institute of Chicago: The First One Hundred Years.* Chicago: Art Institute of Chicago, 1977.
Valpy, N. "Charles Gouyn and the Girl-in-a-Swing Factory." *Transactions of the English Ceramic Circle* 15, no. 2 (1994): 317–26.
Van Haften, Julia, introduction and bibliography. *Egypt and the Holy Land in Historic Photographs: 77 Views by Francis Frith.* New York: Dover Publications, 1980.
Vardy, John. *Some Designs of Mr. Inigo Jones and Mr. Wm. Kent.* London, 1740.
Varley, Paul, and Kumakura Isao, eds. *Tea in Japan: Essays on the History of Chanoyu.* Honolulu: University of Hawaii Press, 1989.
Viale, Vittorio, ed. *Mostra del Barocco Piedmontese: Palazzo Madama, Palazzo Reale, Palazzo di Torino Stupinigi.* 2nd ed., 3 vols. Turin: Città di Torino, 1963.
V&A. *Mogul Paintings Period of the Emperors Jahangir & Shah Jahan 1605–1658 and Persian Calligraphy formerly in the Imperial Collection at Delhi Lent by Lady Wantage to the Victoria and Albert Museum 1917.* London, 1918.
———. "Victoria and Albert Museum Oriental Collections." National Art Library, V&A. London, 1901.
———. "Report of the Committee on the Administration of the Victoria and Albert Museum." National Art Library, V&A. London, 1902.
———. *Catalogue of the Loan Exhibition of British Engraving and Etching Held at the Victoria and Albert Museum, South Kensington.* London: Printed for HMSO by Wyman and Sons, 1903.
———. "The Victoria and Albert Museum, Art Division: Report of the Committee on Re-arrangement, 1908." National Art Library, V&A.
———. *The Salting Collection.* Victoria & Albert Museum Guides. London: HMSO, 1911.
———. "The Purposes and Functions of the Museum." Confidential Memorandum dated 5 November 1912. National Art Library, V&A.
———. *Review of the Principal Acquisitions, 1912.* London: HMSO, 1913.
———. *Catalogue of the Jones Collection.* Vol. 2. London: HMSO, 1924.

———. *A Guide to the Salting Collection.* London: Board of Education, 1926.
———. "The History and Function of the Museum," 1929. National Art Library, V&A.
———. *Fifty Masterpieces of Metalwork.* London: HMSO, 1951a.
———. *Fifty Masterpieces of Sculpture.* London: HMSO for the V&A, 1951b.
———. *Victorian and Edwardian Decorative Arts.* London: HMSO, 1952.
———. *Fifty Masterpieces of Woodwork.* London: HMSO, 1955.
———. *V&A Circulation Department: Its History and Scope,* 1960. National Art Library, V&A.
———. *Fifty Masterpieces of Sculpture.* 2nd ed. London: HMSO for the V&A, 1964.
———. *The Fabric of Pop: A Travelling Exhibition Organised by the Circulation Department.* London: V&A, 1974a.
———. *Ivory Carvings in Early Medieval England, 700–1200.* London: Arts Council of Great Britain, 1974b.
———. *Keith Murray: A Travelling Exhibition Organised by the Circulation Department.* London: V&A, 1976.
———. "Teaspoons to Trains: The Work of Frank Pick, 1878–1941," 1979. Exhibition leaflet. National Art Library, V&A.
———. *100 Great Paintings in The Victoria & Albert Museum.* London: V&A, 1985a.
———. "The V&A: Towards 2000," 1985b. National Art Library, V&A.
———. *The Street Photographs of Roger Mayne.* London: V&A, 1986.
———. *The Victoria and Albert Museum.* London: Scala Books in association with the V&A, 1991.
———. Hisao Miyajima, ed. *British Design at Home: The Victoria & Albert Museum.* Osaka: NHK Kinki Media Plan, 1994.
———. Takahika Sano, ed. *The European Art of Textiles.* Osaka: NHK Kinki Media Plan, 1995.
Voak, J. "Directorship of Sir Roy Strong: A Chronology of Major Events, Acquisitions, Exhibitions, 1974–1987." *V&A Album Golden Edition* (1987): 27–48.
Vogelsang, Bernd. "Das Museum im Kästchen, oder, Die Erfindung des Kunstgewerbemuseums als Photosammlung durch den Freiherrn von Minutoli." In *Silber und Salz: Zur Frühzeit der Photographie im deutschen Sprachraum, 1839–1860,* edited by Bodo von Dewitz and Reinhard Matz, 524–47. Cologne: Edition Braus, 1989.
Volbach, W. F. "Das Christliche Kunstgewerbe der Spätantike und des frühen Mittelalters im Mittelmeergebiet." *Geschichte des Kunstgewerbes aller Zeiten und Völker,* edited by Helmuth T. Bossert, vol. 5, 46–125. Berlin: E. Wasmuth, 1932.
Vuilleumier, Bernard. *The Art of Silk Weaving in China: Symbolism of Chinese Imperial Ritual Robes.* London: China Institute, 1939.
Wainwright, Clive. "Some Objects from William Beckford's Collection Now in the Victoria & Albert Museum." *Burlington Magazine* 113 (1971): 257–8.
———. "Specimens of Ancient Furniture." *Connoisseur* 184, no. 740 (1973): 105–13.
———. "The Dark Ages of Art Revived." *Connoisseur* 198 (1978): 94–105.
———. "Models of Inspiration." *Country Life* 182 (1988): 266–7.
———. *The Romantic Interior: The British Collector at Home, 1750–1850.* New Haven: Published for the Paul Mellon Centre for Studies in British Art by Yale Univ. Press, 1989.
———. "Principles True and False: Pugin and the Foundation of the Museum of Manufactures." *Burlington* 137 (1994): 357–64.
Wardle, Patricia. *Victorian Silver and Silver-Plate.* London: H. Jenkins, 1963.
Waring, John Burley. *Masterpieces of Industrial Art and Sculpture at the International Exhibition, 1862.* 3 vols. London: Day and Son, 1863.
Watkin, David. *The Rise of Architectural History.* London: Architectural Press, 1980.
Watson, Oliver. "Justification and Means: The Early Acquisition of Studio Pots in the Victoria and Albert Museum." *Burlington Magazine* 132, no. 1046 (1990): 358–60.
———. "The Formation of the V&A Glass Collection." Paper presented at the annual conference of the Association of Art Historians, 8 April 1995.
Watson, P., and L. Marks. "Massacre of the Scholars." *Observer,* 12 February 1989, 19.
Whinney, Margaret. *English Sculpture 1720–1830.* London: HMSO, 1971.
White, Eva. *From the School of Design to the Department of Practical Art: The First Years of the National Art Library, 1837–1853.* London: V&A, 1994.
Whitehill, Walter M. *Museum of Fine Arts, Boston: A Centennial History.* 2 vols. Cambridge, Mass.: Belknap Press, 1970.
Wiener, Martin J. *English Culture and the Decline of the Industrial Spirit, 1850–1980.* Cambridge: Cambridge Univ. Press, 1981.
Wilk, Christopher, ed. *Western Furniture: 1350 to the Present Day in the Victoria and Albert Museum.* New York: Cross River Press, 1996.
Williamson, G. C. *History of Portrait Miniatures.* 2 vols. G. Bell and Sons, 1904.

Williamson, Paul. *Gothic Sculpture 1140–1300.* New Haven: Yale Univ. Press, 1995.

———, ed. *The Medieval Treasury: The Art of the Middle Ages in the Victoria and Albert Museum.* London: V&A, 1986.

———, ed. *The Medieval Treasury: The Art of the Middle Ages in the Victoria and Albert Museum.* 2nd ed. Wappingers Falls: Antique Collector's Club, 1996.

Wilson, Charles Heath. *Life and Works of Michelangelo Buonarroti.* London: J. Murray, 1876.

Wilson, Richard. *The Art of Ogata Kenzan: Persona and Production in Japanese Ceramics.* New York: Weatherhill, 1991.

Wilson, Timothy H. "The Origins of the Maiolica Collections of the British Museum and the Victoria and Albert Museum, 1851–55." *Faenza* 71 (1985): 68–81.

———. "Lustered Maiolica: Gubbio." In *Western Decorative Arts,* edited by Rudolf Distelberger et al. Vol. 1, *Medieval, Renaissance and Historicizing Styles, Including Metalwork, Enamels and Ceramics,* 163–72. Washington, D.C.: National Gallery of Art, 1993.

———. "Saint-Porchaire." In *Western Decorative Arts,* edited by Rudolf Distelberger et al. Vol. 1, *Medieval, Renaissance and Historicizing Styles, Including Metalwork, Enamels and Ceramics,* 242–63. Washington, D.C.: National Gallery of Art, 1993.

———, ed. *Italian Renaissance Pottery: Papers Written in Association with a Colloquium at the British Museum.* London: British Museum Press, 1991.

Wingfield Digby, George, assisted by Wendy Hefford. *The Tapestry Collection: Medieval and Renaissance.* London: HMSO, 1980.

Winter, Carl. *Elizabethan Miniatures.* London: Penguin Books, 1943.

Wood, Christopher. *Victorian Panorama: Paintings of Victorian Life.* London: Faber, 1976.

Woodward, Carla Mathes. "Acquisition, Preservation, and Education: A History of the Museum." In *A Handbook of the Museum of Art, The Rhode Island School of Design,* edited by Carla Mathes Woodward and Franklin W. Robinson, 12–60. Providence: Museum of Art, 1985.

Wulff, Inger. "Den dansen de Siva fra Trankebar." *Jordens Folk: Etnografisk Revy* 2, no. 4 (1966): 326–7.

Yang-Mo, C., ed. *Paekja: Hanguk ui Mi.* Seoul, 1984.

Yetkin, Şerare, translation by Maggie Quigley. *Historical Turkish Carpets.* Ankara: Türkiye İş Bankasi Cultural Publications, 1981.

Acknowledgments

Arnold L. Lehman and Brenda Richardson

A decade ago, in October 1987, we paid a formal call on Dame Elizabeth Esteve-Coll, then recently appointed director of the Victoria and Albert Museum. On that initial visit we put forth a proposal that The Baltimore Museum of Art organize for North American circulation a major exhibition drawn from the collections of the Victoria and Albert Museum. Our suggestion was greeted warmly by Esteve-Coll, who expressed her conviction that such an exhibition was the ideal way to expand awareness of the V&A among a much enlarged public. At the same time, she cautioned us that securing definitive approval for our exhibition would be daunting within the organizationally complex departmental systems that characterized the V&A, systems that would require us to cultivate and negotiate with each separate curatorial and administrative department as if it were an independent museum. (Esteve-Coll would, within a short time after we met her, embark on a daring scheme to reorganize those systems.) This was but the first of what would become our frequent visits to the V&A and, ultimately—once *A Grand Design* had been confirmed—countless more visits by many members of the BMA staff. Now that the project has been realized, it is with the greatest respect and affection that we note with gratitude the pivotal role played by Dame Elizabeth Esteve-Coll. Her personal enthusiasm and directorial commitment to the Baltimore project encouraged us to sustain our efforts in those early years, even as she also demonstrated a firm and positive attitude of leadership toward her own staff in regard to the BMA's exhibition proposal. *A Grand Design* would never have happened without Elizabeth, and we take this opportunity to thank her publicly for her friendship and collegial support.

At the V&A there are quite literally hundreds of staff members who have over this decade extended themselves on behalf of The Baltimore Museum of Art and *A Grand Design*, and it is impractical to attempt to name them individually (some, indeed, have moved on in the interim to positions outside the V&A). In Collections we want to thank all of the curators and support staff of the following departments: Ceramics; Far Eastern; Furniture and Woodwork; Indian and Southeast Asian; Metalwork; Prints, Drawings and Paintings; Sculpture; Textiles and Dress; and the National Art Library and its Special Collections. Each department offered cooperation and active participation in *A Grand Design*, with many staff members writing for this book. We also want to extend our gratitude to the staff of Conservation (and most especially to Nicholas Umney, who has acted as the V&A's conservation liaison for our project); Education (David Anderson, head); Finance (Rosamund Sykes, head); Development; and V&A Enterprises, whose Managing Director, Michael Cass, has been enormously supportive of the BMA effort, as have his associates, notably Mary Butler, head of Publishing.

From the preliminary phases of *A Grand Design* the V&A assigned to the project both a curatorial and a logistical liaison. On the curatorial front we have worked unusually closely with a series of V&A representatives. In the initial project negotiation stage, our liaison was Head of Research Charles Saumarez Smith, who made introductions, eased our way through the physical and organizational maze that constitutes the V&A, and began the process of focusing the V&A staff on an intellectual framework around which we could build the exhibition. When Charles left the V&A (to assume the directorship of London's National Portrait Gallery), he sustained his interest in the project and agreed to write a key text for our book. Curator Craig Clunas of the Far Eastern Collection then took on the liaison assignment and saw us through the most challenging phases of the project as we together forged the detailed thematic structure that would define the nature of the exhibition and went through the laborious and sensitive process of strategizing and selecting the exhibition's contents with each department. When Craig left the V&A (to go to the University of Sussex, Brighton, as a Reader in the History of Art at the School of Cultural and Community Studies), he too sustained his interest in *A Grand Design* and also has written an important text for our book.

In September 1994 Malcolm Baker, Deputy Head of Research and a specialist in eighteenth-century English sculpture, was assigned as project liaison. Malcolm worked closely with us as we completed the final selection of exhibition contents, prepared major grant applications for project support, and conceptualized and produced the monographic book that accompanies *A Grand Design*. We are deeply indebted to Charles Saumarez Smith, Craig Clunas, and Malcolm Baker for their extraordinary commitment and eagerness to share the abundance of their intellectual gifts, personal energies, and diplomatic skills, as well as for the perceptive essays they contributed to this book. *A Grand Design* could not have been realized without them.

On the logistical front we have been dependent on the expertise and generosity of the staff of Special Projects, most especially the department's head, Gwyn Miles, who has taken the lead in implementation of the exhibition from the London side. The Special Projects managers, first Susan McCormack and then Jane Drew, have overseen the project's myriad details and gathered information from throughout the institution for centralized communication with the BMA. It has been a pleasure to work in concert with Special Projects, whose staff has treated us as family from the beginning of our extended relationship. Also closely involved at the V&A on logistical aspects of the project were Mark Hunt and the packers; Peter Riley and the object handlers; Helen Downing and Peter Ellis in the Transit Room; Bill Johnston and the joiners; and David Wright and his staff in the Loans Unit.

On the administrative level, we have worked with an entirely supportive network of professionals, notably Jim Close, Assistant Director (Administration), and

Timothy Stevens, Assistant Director (Collections)—as well as with his immediate predecessor John Murdoch, now director at the Courtauld Institute Galleries—and their staffs. For the past several years we have worked especially closely with Public Affairs, whose head, Robin Cole-Hamilton, has been a forceful advocate for *A Grand Design,* as has his associate, Tracy Williamson.

As the book for *A Grand Design* took form, we were fortunate to have the active involvement of many V&A staff members, including Anthony Burton, who permitted authors of essays for this book to have access to a draft text of his own forthcoming book on the V&A's institutional history, and Richard Dunn, who gave valuable editorial assistance. We are extremely grateful to those essay authors not already mentioned: Rafael Cardoso Denis, who teaches at the Escolo Superior de Desenho Industrial in Rio de Janeiro and wrote a telling piece on the origins of the South Kensington education philosophy and social politics; Partha Mitter, distinguished scholar of Indian art and history and Reader in the History of Art at the School of English and American Studies, University of Sussex, Brighton, who contributed an insightful overview of English attitudes toward India and Indian art from the mid-nineteenth century; and Peter Trippi, Consultant Curator of Nineteenth-Century British Art at The Baltimore Museum of Art. Peter wrote two essays for the book, the first on the influence of the great international exhibitions and the second (coauthored with the V&A's Timothy Stevens) on the South Kensington Museum's concerted effort to acquire major treasures of Italian Renaissance art and to write the canon of Western fine and applied arts based on its own acquisitions. Peter also contributed his expertise and energetic support at every stage of the project, whether writing grant applications or the audiotour script—his role in *A Grand Design* has been absolutely central. We also want to thank Serena Kelly and her colleagues in the V&A Archives and Registry. Altogether, seventy-three writers prepared texts and/or catalogue entries for *A Grand Design,* greatly expanding the points of view we bring to the diverse and magnificent objects in the exhibition. We are grateful to all of them.

We want to make special acknowledgment of Elisa Urbanelli, our book's editor at Harry N. Abrams, Inc., who worked as an intimate member of the BMA editorial team to assure a publication of the highest possible quality. Her expertise as an editor was matched at all times by her intelligence and her sensitivity to the subject. Alex Castro of Castro/Arts, Baltimore, designed the book, with the assistance of Ingrid Castro; its visual eloquence and sympathetic layout reflect their unique and finely tuned sensibilities. We are also grateful to Lisa Pupa, the BMA's Publications Assistant, who did the demanding disk preparation for the book.

From the inception of the project we knew that we wanted the guidance of Michael Conforti, Director of the Sterling and Francine Clark Art Institute in Williamstown, Massachusetts, and the leading American scholar on the history and sociocultural implications of applied arts museums and, specifically, of the Victoria and Albert Museum. Not only did he serve as an integral member of the BMA team in forging the conceptual basis of the exhibition and selecting its contents, but he also agreed to write the lead introductory essay for our book. We are much in his debt for both his expertise and his diplomatic skills. At a somewhat later date we invited Anne Poulet, Curator of European Decorative Arts and Sculpture at the

Museum of Fine Arts, Boston, to join us as the fourth member of our BMA team for purposes of determining the final contents of the exhibition. She too became a supportive partner whose contribution to *A Grand Design* was significant.

We were very fortunate in having early input from a group of humanists we assembled for a round-table discussion of issues that helped to focus the exhibition's thematic structure and presentation. It is a pleasure to express our sincere thanks to David Cannadine, Moore Collegiate Professor of History, Columbia University, New York; Linda Colley, Richard M. Colgate Professor of History, Yale University, New Haven, Connecticut; Ludmilla Jordanova, Professor of Visual Arts, School of World Art Studies and Museology, University of East Anglia, Norwich, U.K.; and Susan Stewart, Professor of English, Temple University, Philadelphia. David Lowenthal, Professor Emeritus of Geography and Honorary Research Fellow at University College, London, also offered his experienced counsel as an informal consultant to the project.

At the BMA there is simply no member of the staff who has not contributed to this enormously demanding effort. Even when stretched to extraordinary limits by what was for our Museum the unprecedented scope of the project, this staff has given fully of its time and talents with awesome commitment, stamina, and professionalism. We cannot thank them all by name but wish to extend our congratulations on their exceptional achievement to all of the staff members of the following departments: Administrative Office (James Huebler, Jr., Director); Conservation (Mary Sebera, Senior Conservator); Design & Installation (Karen Nielsen, Director); Education & Community (Brigid Globensky, Director); Exhibitions (David Penney, Manager); External Affairs (Peter Trippi, Director, Major Gifts, and Roger Marquis, Director, Development Operations); Facilities (Alan Dirican, Director); Library (Wendy Thompson, Librarian); Programs & Special Events (Deborah Tunney, Director); Publications (Audrey Frantz, Director); Public Relations & Marketing (Becca Seitz, Director); Retail Operations (Steven Rostkowski, Director); Registration (Melanie Harwood, Senior Registrar); Rights & Reproductions (Nancy Press, Director, and Duane Suter, Photographer); and Security (Ron Haddaway, Director). Kathleen Basham, Deputy Director for Administration, and Georgeanna Linthicum Bishop, Administrative Assistant to Brenda Richardson, have also contributed essentially to the successful realization of *A Grand Design*. We also had the foresight to include on our BMA team from an early date the New York firm of Resnicow Schroeder Associates to support our major promotional efforts for the exhibition. Principal Frederick C. Schroeder provided experienced counsel on many fronts, always with intelligence, wit, and acute awareness of the sensitivities inherent to complex cultural endeavors.

For a decade the Trustees of The Baltimore Museum of Art have supported us in this ambitious effort despite the magnitude of the staff commitment and the financial underwriting required to realize *A Grand Design*. We want to express our most sincere gratitude especially to current Board Chairman Anthony W. Deering and immediately preceding Board Chairs Constance R. Caplan (1994–97) and James S. Riepe (1992–94) whose lay leadership has assured a position of both stature and stability for the Museum within our own community as well as nationally and internationally. Without the confidence and active engagement of our

Trustees, it would not be possible to initiate and maintain such a high level of exhibition and publication programming as is exemplified by *A Grand Design.*

We are extremely fortunate to have secured a group of sponsors whose enthusiasm for our project was matched by their philanthropy and commitment. Above all, we wish to extend our profound gratitude to the two lead corporate sponsors whose support made it possible to bring *A Grand Design* to North America: Visa U.S.A. and Lockheed Martin.

We are deeply indebted to Carl F. Pascarella, President and Chief Executive Officer of Visa U.S.A., Inc., for his company's magnanimous sponsorship of *A Grand Design,* marking Visa's first national sponsorship of an art exhibition. We have experienced extraordinarily creative involvement on the part of Visa U.S.A., and we want to thank especially Janet L. Soderstrom, Executive Vice President, International Marketing; Michael O'Hara Lynch, Vice President, U.S. Event Marketing; Gerry Sweeney, Director, Marketing Services; and Susan B. Forman, Director, Marketing Communications. Visa not only gave its generous underwriting to the exhibition but also launched an enormous marketing campaign that assured a high profile for the V&A and *A Grand Design.*

We are equally indebted to Norman R. Augustine, Chairman of the Board and Chief Executive Officer, and Vance D. Coffman, President and Chief Operating Officer, of Lockheed Martin Corporation, Maryland's largest company, with 190,000 employees worldwide, as well as to former Chairman of the Board Daniel M. Tellep. Lockheed Martin has demonstrated itself to be a leader in the philanthropic community, committing financial and personnel resources of exceptional magnitude. The company is a major patron of arts and education in the state of Maryland, contributing generously to improve the quality of life for young people and adults alike. We are especially grateful to Buzz Bartlett, Director, Corporate Affairs, whose early convictions about the excitement and importance of *A Grand Design* provided the impetus for Lockheed Martin's support and who has offered his intelligent and sensitive guidance to the BMA on this project for more than six years. We also want to thank Barbara Reinike, Manager of Community Relations.

Additional support for *A Grand Design* was generously provided by Ryland, and we are grateful to R. Chad Dreier, Chairman, President and Chief Executive Officer. Chad Dreier, an active Trustee of the BMA, is a strong advocate for the arts whose commitment is evident in the major sponsorship he extended to this project.

Grants of supplemental support for *A Grand Design* have come from T. Rowe Price Associates, to whose principals James S. Riepe, George A. Roche, and M. David Testa we express our appreciation for their instrumental roles in securing this sponsorship for the Museum; The Baltimore Sun, for whose generous support we thank Publisher Mary Junck; Dresdner Kleinwort Benson North America LLC, with thanks to Executive Vice President Patrick Donelan; and The Rouse Company, whose Chairman and Chief Executive Officer Anthony W. Deering has sustained the tradition of civic leadership in our community for which company founder James Rouse is warmly remembered.

Additional support for the exhibition has been provided by Sotheby's USA (we extend our gratitude to Diana D. Brooks, President and Chief Executive Officer; Richard E. Oldenburg, Chairman of Sotheby's American Division; and Katherine

Ross, Vice President and Director of Museum Services); the Samuel H. Kress Foundation (Marilyn Perry, President); and the Andrew W. Mellon Foundation for its support of the BMA's Publications Endowment Fund. *A Grand Design* has also benefited from grants from the National Endowment for the Humanities and the National Endowment for the Arts, as well as from an indemnity from the Federal Council on the Arts and the Humanities (to whose administrator, Alice Whelihan, we extend our warm appreciation). The Maryland Humanities Council committed funds to the project as well. And we want to add a personal note of acknowledgment to BMA Trustee James Dale and to the Museum's National Trustee Christopher Forbes for their crucial advice and support.

A Grand Design will be seen by audiences throughout the United States and in Canada. The Baltimore Museum of Art is extremely proud to have as partners in this presentation such distinguished colleague museums. It is a pleasure to extend warm thanks to our friends and colleagues at the Museum of Fine Arts, Boston (Malcolm Rogers, Ann and Graham Gund Director; Katherine Getchell, Director of Exhibitions and Design; Anne Poulet, Curator, European Decorative Arts and Sculpture); The Museum of Fine Arts, Houston (Peter C. Marzio, Director; Katherine S. Howe, Curator, Decorative Arts); Fine Arts Museums of San Francisco (Harry S. Parker III, Director; Kathe Hodgson, Coordinator of Exhibitions; Lee Hunt Miller, Curator, European Decorative Arts); Royal Ontario Museum, Toronto (Lindsay Sharp, Director and President; John McNeill, Director Emeritus; Margo Welch, Head of Exhibit Programming; and Dan Rahimi, Head of Exhibit Development).

There are many others who have extended their guidance and support over these many years in ways both logistical and scholarly. We especially want to thank BMA curators James Abbott, Susan Dackerman, Jay Fisher, Jan Howard, Sona Johnston, Anita Jones, Frances Klapthor, and Fred Lamp, each of whom offered expertise and assistance on behalf of *A Grand Design*. Among others whose support has been given generously over the years are Tim Ayers, Stephen Bann, Tim Barringer, Mogens Bencart, the late artist Scott Burton (an informed and passionate devotee of the V&A and the earliest enthusiast for this exhibition), Martin Chapman, Michael Clapper, David Crowley, Carol Duncan, Betsy Fishman, Sophie Forgan, Christopher Frayling, Thomas Gaehtgens, Ivan Gaskell, Paul Greenhalgh, Wendy Kaplan, Ivan Karp, Andrew McClellan, Susan Pearce, Michael Podro, J. F. Heibrok, Hermione Hobhouse, John Physick, Louise Purbrick, Anthony Radcliffe, Margaret Rose, John Steer, Nancy Troy, Clive Wainwright, and Giles Waterfield.

Finally, we want to express our gratitude to Alan Borg who assured us of his support for *A Grand Design* even before he formally assumed his new position as director of the Victoria and Albert Museum in 1995. His commitment to the project has been amply demonstrated since then, and we are proud to have achieved our ambitious goals by working together with such mutual respect.

Index

Note: **Boldface** references indicate principal discussions. *Italic* references indicate illustrations. "V&A" means "Victoria and Albert Museum."

Adam, Robert, 281
  Adam/Chippendale suite, in Sir Lawrence Dundas House, 321, *321*; fig. 117
  armchair, *320*, **321**, 323; cat. 149
  The Kimbolton Cabinet, 322, **323**; cat. 150
Adams, John, 23, 38
African art, 230, 257
Alari-Bonacolsi, Pier Jacopo. *See* Antico
Albert, Prince, 26, 28, 34, 80, 85, 89
Album Book: Plans, Elevations, Sections, and Details of the Alhambra (Jones, with Goury), 95, 117, **118–19**, *118*, 165; cat. 15
Alcock, Sir Rutherford, 101
Alexander, William Cleverly, collection, 272
Alexander Morton & Co. (manufacturer):
  Omar, tapestry, 345, **354**, *354*; cat. 164
  Owl, furnishing fabric, **340**, *341*; cat. 162
Alhambra vase (Deck, with Davillier), *94*, **95**, 137; cat. 6
"Alhambresque" furnishing silk, 93, 115, *119*, **120–22**; cat. 17
Alice in Wonderland, roller-printed cotton (Voysey, designer; Morton Sundour Fabrics, manufacturer), 234, **366–67**, *366*; cat. 175
Allen, Thomas, 98
  Prometheus or *Captive* vase, **97–98**, *97*, 137, 183; cat. 8
Alma-Tadema, Sir Lawrence (designer), armchair, **343**, *343*; cat. 163
Altes Museum (Berlin), 26
American museum movement, 24
Ampthill, Lord, collection, 228, 239
Angeli, Heinrich von, *Portrait of Queen Victoria,* tapestry adapted, after painting by, **103**, *103*, 137; cat. 12
Animal Products Register, 122
Antico, *Meleager,* 98, *148*, **183–85**, *184*, 186; cat. 59; fig. 80
Apex (manufacturer), Radio in a Bag, **373–77**, *374*, 390; cat. 182.5
Apollo and Daphne Candlesticks (after design by Moser), **318–21**, *319*; cat. 148
applied arts, 23–47; education in, in England, 26–28, 107–16; vs. fine arts, 34–36; museums for, 29, 33–37; problems in collecting, 20–21
Apsley House, 77
Archer, W. G., 228–29, 246
architectural ornament, casts of, **127–30**, *127*; fig. 74
Arita porcelain manufacturing center (Japan), 101
armchairs:
  Adam, designer; Chippendale, manufacturer, *320*, **321**, 323; cat. 149
  Alma-Tadema, designer; Johnstone, Norman and Company, manufacturer, **343**, *343*; cat. 163
  Kuramata, designer; Vitra, manufacturer ("*How High The Moon*"), *388*, **389**; cat. 195
  Rietveld, with van der Groenekan, 350, **363–65**, *364*; cat. 173
Armitage, Margaret, collection, 347
Arms and Armor collection (India Museum), **135**, *135*; fig. 79
Arnold, Tom, *Homemaker Tableware,* **380**; cat. 187
Arnoux, Léon, 98

Art and Design Galleries, 72
Art Deco, 390
Art Institute of Chicago, 39
Art Museum, interior, 53, *53*, 130, 150; fig. 23
Art Nouveau, 345, **354–57**, 358
arts, vs. crafts, 231
Arts and Crafts movement, 136, 252, 276, 282, 339, 340, 354, 358, 365
Ashbee, C. R., 277
Ashburnham Centerpiece, The (Sprimont, with Crespin), **317–18**, *317*; cat. 147
Ashmolean Museum (Oxford), 19
Ashton, Leigh, 44, **70–71**, 77, 156, 190, 236, *236*, 280; fig. 106
Aslin, Elizabeth, 349
Aston Webb building, 77
  Central Court, display of English decorative art, 278, *279*; fig. 111
  facade, with figures of English artists, 155, 277, *278*; fig. 110
Autumn Leaves, tapestry (Calder, designer; Pinton Frères, manufacturer), **380–81**, *381*; cat. 188

Bacon, John, 278
Badminton House, Chinese Bed from, 280
Bailey, David, 381
Bailey & Neale, 104
Banks, Thomas, 278
Barberini Vase. *See* Portland Vase
Barker, Alexander, 206
Barlow, Francis, 315
Barman, Christian, electric fan heater, **372**, *372*; cat. 181
Batlis, Thomas, 292
Baudouin, Christopher, textile design for woven silk, 137, **308**, *308*; cat. 139
Baulez, Christian, 216
beaker and cover, **194**, *194*; cat. 67
Beauvais factory, 103
Beckford, William, 197
Beckwith, John, 162
Bel Geddes, Norman, Patriot Midget radio, **373–77**, *374*; cat. 182.2
Bell, Vanessa, 350
  Maud, printed linen pattern, 350, **360–62**, *362*, 369; cat. 171
Bellano, Bartolommeo, *Lamentation over the Dead Christ,* **180–82**, *181*; cat. 57
Benjamin Warner (manufacturer), 120
Berain, Jean, I, 136
  book with etchings and engravings after, **136**, *136*; cat. 31
Berenson, Bernard, 43
Berghof, Norbert, with M. Landes and W. Rang (designers), *Frankfurt Cabinet,* **389–90**, *389*; cat. 196
Bernal, Ralph, 51
  collection, 115, 173, 209
Bernini, 159
Bethnal Green, 45, 76, 77, 93, 97, 104, 159, 346
Bibliothèque Nationale (Paris), 223
Bickford Family (royal locksmiths), *Queen Mary's Jewel Casket,* **300**, *301*; cat. 133

Biedermeier, 360, 390

Bing, Samuel, 358

Birdwood, George, 156, 222, 227

Birkenhead pottery, 180

Bizen ware (Japan), 269
> jar with handles, 87, 233, **269**, *270*, *271*, *272*; cat. 114

Bock, Dr. Franz, 297

Bode, Wilhelm von, 37, 43, 156

Bodhisattva Avalokiteśvara (Sanchi Torso), 228, *228*; fig. 99

Böhler, Julius, 212

Boilerhouse Project, 34, 53, 352
> model (Studio Libeskind), *14, 74, 75*; fig. 3, *54, 55*

Bologna, Giovanni (Giambologna), 198

Bolton, Arthur, 321

boots:
> Dr. Martens (*Vegetarian Shoes* ["Air Wair"]), **392**, *393*; cat. 199.5
> Egeli, **392**, *392*; cat. 199.3
> Quant, **392**, *393*; cat. 199.2

Borg, Alan, 77

Boson, John, console table, *274, 325,* **326**; cat. 152; fig. 109

Boston Athenaeum, 37

bottle (Rie), **385–87**, *385*; cat. 192

Boucher, François, 314
> *Portrait of Madame de Pompadour*, 66, 185, *218*, *219*, 289; cat. 86

boudoir, of Marquise de Serilly, 155, *155*; fig. 86

Boulton and Fothergill, *The Kimbolton Cabinet,* **322**, **323**; cat. 150

Bourne, Baker & Bourne of Fenton, jug, **104**, *105*, 137; cat. 13

Bowes, John, 216

bowls:
> De Morgan, designer; Passenger, painter; De Morgan Pottery, manufacturer, *338*, **339**; cat. 160
> Ottoman fritware, **252**, *253*; cat. 100

box (Nubian), **257**, *257*; cat. 104

Boyle, Robert, 292

Brandt collection, 357

Brinckmann, Justus, 36–37

British art: attitudes toward, 275–83; position of, at V&A, 155, 277–78

British Institute of Industrial Art, 346, 347, 369

British Museum, 17, 18, 27, 45, 84, 224
> Xanthian Room, 27, *27*; fig. 8

Brooklyn Institute (New York), 37

Brown, Ford Madox, 337

Brucciani, Domenico, 129

Brucciani & Co., 127
> fig leaf for *David*, plaster, 53, 58, *106*, 108, **130–32**, *130*; cat. 26; fig. 65

Bryant, William Cullen, 40

Buddha, installation in South Kensington Museum, main entrance, *60*, 61, 160; fig. 33

Buddhist art, 224, 228

Bulley, Margaret, collection, 369

Burges, William (designer):
> decanter, **332**, *333*; cat. 156
> *The Yatman Cabinet,* 282, **332–35**, *334*, 343; cat. 157

Burnap, Frank P. and Harriet C., collection, 296

Burne-Jones, Sir Edward, 185, 335, 337, 339
> *Pomona*, with John Henry Dearle (designers), **337–39**, *337*; cat. 159
> *The Works of Geoffrey Chaucer,* 337, **339–40**, *340*; cat. 161

Bury, Shirley, 282, 349

Bushell, Stephen Wooton, 233

"cabinet" of Francesco Calzolari (engraving of), 25, *25*; fig. 7

cabinet on stand:
> French or Italian, from Rothschild collection, 71, 95, 155, **206–9**, *207*; cat. 77
> Hilaire and Pasti, with Néville, designers; Fourdinois, manufacturer,

87, **95–97**, *96*, 137, 209; cat. 7

cabinets:
> Adam, designer; Ince and Mayhew, with Boulton and Fothergill, manufacturers (*The Kimbolton Cabinet*), **322, 323**; cat. 150
> Berghof, with Landes and Rang, designers; Draenert Collection, manufacturer (*Frankfurt Cabinet*), **389–90**, *389*; cat. 196
> Burges, designer; Poynter, painter; Harland and Fisher, manufacturer (*The Yatman Cabinet*), 282, **332–35**, *334*, 343; cat. 157
> Majorelle, 88, 345, **354–57**, *355*; cat. 165
> South German, *The Holbein Cabinet,* 155, **197**, *197*; cat. 68
> Talbert, designer; Holland and Sons, manufacturer, **98**, *99*, 137, 335, 343; cat. 9
> Walpole, with Kent (*Walpole Cabinet*), 216, 280, **302**, *302*, *303*, 305; cat. 134; fig. 114

Cadogan, Lord, collection, 206

Calder, Alexander, *Autumn Leaves,* tapestry, **380–81**, *381*; cat. 188

calligraphy, Mughal (India), 92, **244–45**, *244*, 246; cat. 92

Calloway, Stephen, 283

Calzolari, Francesco, "cabinet" of (engraving of), 25, *25*; fig. 7

cameo cutting process, display showing (Ronca), 116, **137**, *137*; cat. 32

Cameron, Julia Margaret, *Saint Agnes,* photograph, **137–39**, *138*, 387; cat. 33

Campi, Bartolommeo (?), stirrups, pair of, 65, **199**, *199*; cat. 70

candlesticks:
> *Apollo and Daphne Candlesticks* (after design by Moser), **318–21**, *319*; cat. 148
> Gloucester, 194
> Saint-Porchaire ware, 95, **201**, *201*; cat. 72
> sampler of Western and Southeastern European, 116, **134–36**, *135*; cat. 30

Canova, Antonio, *The Three Graces, 158, 159*; fig. 88

Caradosso del Mundo (Caradosso Foppa) (?), *Martelli Mirror,* 155, 159, 160, 174, **177–78**, *178*; cat. 54; fig. 89

Carnegie, Andrew, 38

Carrier-Belleuse, Albert, 151

Carter, Thomas, *Chaloner Chute,* 137, **305–6**, *305*; cat. 136

Casablanca Sideboard (Sottsass, designer; Memphis, manufacturer), *386,* **387**; cat. 193

Casey, W. L., Marlborough House, watercolor rendering, 153, *153*; fig. 84

caskets:
> *Casket of the Daughter of Abd al-Rahman III,* Hispano-Arabic ivory carving, Madinat al-Zahra, Cordoba, **164–65**, *164*; cat. 43
> *The Medici Casket* (Mola or Master Guglielmo), 155, **205–6**, *205*; cat. 76
> *Queen Mary's Jewel Casket* (Bickford Family royal locksmiths), **300**, *301*; cat. 133
> Saint Thomas à Becket casket (Limoges), 159

Cast Courts, *22, 48,* 58, 72, *72*, 76, 128, 130, 154; figs. 6, 18, 52

cast-making workshop, 127, *128*; fig. 75

casts, 119; of architectural ornaments, **127–30**, *127*; fig. 74; of Indian architectural elements, 226, *226, 227*; fig. 97, 98; as museum exhibition tool, 129–30

Cellini, Benvenuto, 177
> *Head of Medusa,* **186**, *187*; cat. 61
> *Perseus,* detail, 186, *186*; fig. 91

Centennial Exposition (Philadelphia, 1876), 38, 40, 87, *87,* 232, 269, 271, 272; fig. 63

Central Training School of Art, 110, 112

ceramics display, traveling, 349, *349*; fig. 122

Ceramics Gallery, 61, *61,* 95, 155; fig. 34

Chadwick, Helen, *One Flesh,* collage, **387–89**, *387*; cat. 194

Chaffer, William, 292

chairs:
> Mackintosh, **358–60**, *359*; cat. 169
> Maclaren, *344, 370,* **371**; cat. 179; fig. 119

Rietveld (Crate and Zig-Zag), 365

chalice, Pugin, designer; John Hardman and Co., manufacturer, **91**, *91*, 108, 137; cat. 3

Chaloner Chute (Carter), 137, **305–6**, *305*; cat. 136

Chamot, Mary, 299

Channon, John, 324, 326

Charleston, Robert, 311

Charpentier, François, of Orion, 201

Chasuble, Clare, 276

Chelsea porcelain factory, 318

Chermayeff, Serge, 377

Chesterfield Vase (English), *313*, **314**; cat. 144

Chinese art, 230–36
    displayed in North Court, 230, *230*; fig. 102

Chippendale, Thomas:
    armchair, *320*, **321**, 323; cat. 149
    (with Robert Adam) suite in Sir Lawrence Dundas House, 321, *321*; fig. 117

Chiswick House, 326

Choate, Joseph, 24, 40

chocolate or coffee pot (English), **315–17**, *316*; cat. 146

"Choiseul" pair of vases, 66, 185, *215*, **216**, 289; cat. 84

Chola dynasty (India), *Sambandar, the Child Saint*, 92, 228, **239**, *239*; cat. 88

Choson dynasty (Korea), jar, 234, *265*, **267**; cat. 111

Christ Child (Labenwolf, attrib.), **193–94**, *193*; cat. 66

Christie, A. G. I., 297

chromolithography, 118

Chute, John, 216

Cincinnati Art Museum, 24, 39, *39*; fig. 12

Cioli, Valerio, *Narcissus*, 70, 71, **182–83**, *182*, 190; cat. 58

Cizhou ware, 263

Clark, Kenneth, 91

Clarke, Caspar Purdon, 44, 76, 209, 225–26

Clarke, Joseph T., 347

Coates, Wells (designer):
    Ekco Model AD-65 radio, **373–77**, *375*; cat. 182.1
    Ekco Princess Portable Model P63 radio, **373–77**, *374*; cat. 182.3

Codex Forster, notebook page (Leonardo da Vinci), **189–90**, *189*; cat. 63

Codrington, K. de B., 228

Coffin, Edmund, *The Islington Cup*, 326, *327*; cat. 153

Cokayne family, 297

Cole, Henry, 24, 26, 27, 28–32, 33–34, 41, 45, 49, *49*, 71, 76, 80, 83, 85, 108–9, 112, 117, 122, 139, 150–51, 152, 153–54, 157, 159, 177, 294, 351; fig. 17

Cole, Henry Hardy, 225

Coleridge, Anthony, 321

collecting, 19–21, 24–25, 30, 32–33, 43–44, 112–16, 221

"Collection of Animal Products," textile samples from, South Kensington Museum, 53, **120–22**, *121*, 122, 123; cat. 18

Colonial Williamsburg (Virginia), 296

Colonna, Edward (?), curtain, **358**, *358*; cat. 168

Committee on Re-arrangement for the Art Division of the Victoria and Albert Museum, *77*, 114–15, 346

commode (English), **324–26**, *324*; cat. 151

Connecticut Museum of Industrial Art, 38

Conran Foundation, 352

Conservatoire des Arts et Métiers, 26

console table (Kent, designer; Boson, manufacturer?), *274*, *325*, **326**; cat. 152; fig. 109

Constable, John, *Salisbury Cathedral from the Bishop's Grounds*, 276, *284*, **285**; cat. 118

Cook, Thomas, 81

Coomaraswamy, Ananda, 227, 228, 246

Cooper, Peter, 38

Cooper, Susan Vera, 372
    "Kestrel" Coffee Set, 371, **372**; cat. 180

Cooper-Hewitt Museum (New York), 38

Cooper Union for the Advancement of Science and Art (New York), 38

Cope, Syon, 276

Corcoran Gallery (Washington, D. C.), 39–40

Cornille Frères, 358
    curtain, **358**, *358*; cat. 168

cotton, block-printed furnishing, 86, 91, 108, 120, **122–23**, *123*, 124; cat. 19

Country Life, 276

Courtaulds Ltd., 354

Cox, Trenchard, 77, 211

cravat, carving (Gibbons), 216, 280, 302, *304*, **305**; cat. 135

Crawford, Lord, 183–85

Crespin, Paul. *See under* Sprimont, Nicholas

cresting from a gate (German), 108, 110, *110*, **125**, *125*; cat. 22; fig. 69

Crichton, Lionel, 294

Crivelli, Carlo:
    Demidoff altarpiece, 185
    Virgin and Child, 66, **185**, *185*, 218; cat. 60

Cross Gallery (South Kensington), 77, 224

Crown Princess Victoria, 36

Crucified Christ, The (G. Pisano), 156, **165**, *165*; cat. 44

Cruelty in Perfection from *The Four Stages of Cruelty* (Hogarth), 137, **143–44**, *143*; cat. 37

Crystal Palace (Sydenham, England), 76, 79, 84
    postcard image, *83*, 84; fig. 60

cups:
    English, *The Sterne Cup, 293*, **294**; cat. 127
    Flemish (covered), **292–93**, *292*; cat. 126
    German, *195*, **195**; cat. 67.1
    Mughal, 92, 222, **248**, *248*; cat. 96
    Thurston, designer; Coffin, modeler (*The Islington Cup*), 326, *327*; cat. 153

Currie, David, collection, 188

curtain (Colonna, designer?; Cornille Frères, weaver?), **358**, *358*; cat. 168

Curzon, Lord, 227

dagger and scabbard, Mughal, India, 92, 222, **246–47**, *246*; cat. 94

Daniel Keith & Co., 120

Daniels, Harvey, 385

Darby, Michael, 283

Daucher, Hans, *Saint John the Evangelist*, **190**, *191*, 193; cat. 64

Daugny collection, 164

David (Michelangelo), *48*, 130–32
    art student sketching, 130, *130*; fig. 77
    fig leaf for, plaster (Brucciani & Co.?), 53, 58, *106*, 108, **130–32**, *130*; cat. 26; fig. 65

Davillier, Baron Jean-Charles (with Joseph-Théodore Deck), Alhambra vase, *94*, **95**, 137; cat. 6

Day, Lucienne, textile designs, 137, **378–79**, *378*, *379*; cat. 186

Day Dream, The (Rossetti), *335*, **336**; cat. 158

Dearle, John Henry, with Sir Edward Burne-Jones (designers), *Pomona*, **337–39**, *337*; cat. 159

Decaix, Alexis, 329
    vase, *328*, **329**; cat. 154

decanter (Burges, designer; Mendelson, manufacturer), **332**, *333*; cat. 156

Deccan (India), *Nandi, Shiva's Sacred Bull*, 92, 243, *243*; cat. 91

Deck, Joseph-Théodore (with Baron Jean-Charles Davillier), Alhambra vase, *94*, **95**, 137; cat. 6

decorative object, *The Girl-in-a-Swing*, 156, *310*, **311**; cat. 141

De La Rue, Warren, 90

Delaunay, Sonia, 381

della Robbia, Andrea, *Virgin and Child*, 156, **180**, *180*; cat. 56

della Robbia, Luca, 180

De Morgan, William Frend, bowl, *338*, **339**; cat. 160

Department of Industrial Relations, 44

Department of Practical Art, 49, 50, 76

Department of Science and Art (DSA), 27, 76, 108–16

Design for a Candlestick in the Rococo Style Incorporating the Figure of Daphne Turning into a Laurel Tree (Moser), *318*, 321; fig. 116

Design for the Memorial to Sir Isaac Newton Erected in 1731 in Westminster Abbey (Kent), *306*, 307; fig. 115

de Stijl, group, 363, 369

Devonshire collections (Chatsworth), 326

Dickens, Charles:
    manuscript page, *400*; fig. 127
    pages from books of, 144, 190, **329–32**, *329–33*, *400*; cat. 155; fig. 127

dishes:
    Kajiwara Rikichi of the Koransha Company) (Japan, Arita), **101**, *102*, 137, 231, 267; cat. 11
    Palissy, 30, 57, 115, 155, **200–201**, *200*; cat. 71
    Portuguese, **202**, *202*; cat. 73

Doccia porcelain factory (Italy), 315–16

Donaldson, George, 77, 345, 354, 357

Donatello, 159, 179
    Ascension, 174, 177

Donatello (attrib.), *Winged Putto with a Fantastic Fish*, 174, **178–79**, *179*, 183; cat. 55

Donatello (Redgrave), 30, 49, 56, 155, **174–77**, *175*, *177*; cat. 52

Don Raphael Contreras (manufacturer), 119

Doucet, Jacques, collection, 368, 369

Doulton's manufactory, 111

Draenert Collection (manufacturer), *Frankfurt Cabinet*, **389–90**, *389*; cat. 196

Drais, Robert Arnould, *The Five Orders of Architecture*, columns mounted, 66, 185, **216**, *217*, 218, 289; cat. 85

Dresden, royal collection, 25

Dresser, Christopher, 36

dresses:
    Lacroix (evening), **394**, *395*; cat. 200
    Willats (*Variable Sheets*), **382–83**, *383*; cat. 190

dress fabric (English, Spitalfields), **307–8**, *307*; cat. 138

Dr. Martens, *Vegetarian Shoes* ("Air Wair"), boots, **392**, *393*; cat. 199.5

Drunk Punch, studio pottery (Slee), **391**, *391*; cat. 198

Dulac, Edmund, 146

Dumesnil, Debruge, collection, 206

Dundas House, interior, *321*, *321*; fig. 117

Duquesnoy, François, 302

Durlacher, Henry, 197

Duveen firm (art dealers), 43

Dwight, John, 292

Dwight, Lydia, personal memorial sculpture of (Fulham Pottery), **290–92**, *291*; cat. 125

Dyce, William, 108

Eagle: Symbol of St. John the Evangelist, plaque, **161–62**, *161*, 164, 165, 168; cat. 40

East Asian art, 221, 230–36

East Cloister, 232

East Hall, *62*, *62*; fig. 35
    sculptures by Rodin and woodwork display, *348*, *349*; fig. 121

East India Company, 239, 251

Eastlake, Charles Locke, 27, 153, 318

Ecole des Arts Décoratifs, 26

Edgar J. Kaufmann Office (Wright), 350, *351*; fig. 124

Edlin, Martha, 299

Educational Museum, *52*, *53*, 130; fig. 22

Edwards, Ralph, 281

Egeli, M. K., boots, **392**, *392*; cat. 199.3

Egyptian mosque lamp, 62, **255–56**, *255*, *257*; cat. 102

Eitelberger, Rudolf von, 34–35

E. K. Cole Ltd. (manufacturer):
    Ekco Model AD-65 radio, **373–77**, *375*; cat. 182.1
    Ekco Princess Portable Model P63 radio, **373–77**, *374*; cat. 182.3

Ekco Model AD-65 radio (Coates, designer; E. K. Cole Ltd., manufacturer), **373–77**, *375*; cat. 182.1

Ekco Princess Portable Model P63 radio (Coates, designer); E. K. Cole Ltd., manufacturer), **373–77**, *374*; cat. 182.3

electric fan heater (Barman, designer; HMV, manufacturer), **372**, *372*; cat. 181

electrolyte copies, 132, 293

Elkington and Co. (manufacturer), Rosenborg Castle Lions, electrolyte copies of, 108, **132–34**, *133*; cat. 28

Ellis, F. S., *The Works of Geoffrey Chaucer*, 337, **339–40**, *340*; cat. 161

Ellison, collection, 276

embroidered picture, *Susanna and the Elders*, **298**, *299*; cat. 131

Emerson (manufacturer), Patriot Midget radio, **373–77**, *374*; cat. 182.2

Emperor Rudolf II (de Vries), 152, **198**, *198*; cat. 69

Encyclopedia of Ornament (Shaw):
    circulation log from, 113, *113*; fig. 71
    goldsmiths' designs from (Holbein), 108, *109*; fig. 66

Engel, Carl, 290

English art. *See* British art

English folk life, 276–77

English Primary Galleries, 280

Entombment, The (Permoser), 157, **212**, *213*, 215; cat. 82

Esdaile, Katherine, 307

Esteve-Coll, Elizabeth, 77, 352

Esther Hearing of Haman's Plot, tapestry, 30, **209**, *210*; cat. 79

Eumorfopoulos, George, collection, 234, 235–36, 263

ewer, *Griffin Aquamanile*, *167*, **168**; cat. 46

Exhibition of Industrial Art (Paris, 1844), 93

exhibitions at V&A, 122–24
    "Age of Neo-Classicism" (1972), 329
    Anglo-Jewish art commemorating the tercentenary of the Resettlement of the Jews in England (1956), 209
    Anglo-Jewish silver (1978), 209
    "Appearances: Fashion Photography since 1945" (1991), 382
    "Britain Can Make It" (1946), 71, 280, *280*; fig. 112
    "British Art & Design 1900–1960" (1983), 352
    "Brunswick Art Treasures" (1952), 215
    Cartier-Bresson retrospective (1966), 350
    "Collecting for the Future: A Decade of Contemporary Acquisitions" (1990), 352
    Susie Cooper exhibition (1987), 372
    "The Destruction of the Country House" (1974), 71, *71*, 282; fig. 50
    "English Medieval Arts" (1930), 299
    "Examples of False Principles in Decoration" (Marlborough House) (1852), 122–24
    "Exhibition of British and Foreign Posters" (1931), 347, *348*; fig. 120
    "The Fabric of Pop" (1973), 385
    "Finlandia" (1961), 350
    "40 Years of Modern Design" (Bethnal Green), 350
    Gray retrospective (1973), 369
    "Ivory Carvings in Early Medieval England 700–1200" (1974), 162
    "John Channon and Brass-Inlaid Furniture," 326
    "Manchester Art Treasures" (1857), 153, 206
    "Pugin: A Gothic Passion" (1994), 71, *71*; fig. 51
    Rie retrospective (1982), 385
    Special Loan Exhibition at South Kensington (1862), 292
    "Special Loan Exhibition of Spanish and Portuguese Ornamental Art" (1881), 202
    "Specimens of British Manufactures and Decorative Art" (1847–49), 82–83

"Staffordshire Blue & White" (1976), 104
"Style in Sculpture" (1946), *70, 71*, 183, 190, 307; fig. 49
"Thirties," 371
"Towards a Bigger Picture: Contemporary British Photography"
    (1987), 387–89
"Victorian and Edwardian Decorative Arts" (1952), 91, 98, 282, 349,
    358, 366
exhibitions in other venues:
    "Anglo-Jewish Historical Exhibition" (Albert Hall) (1887), 209
    "Chinese Applied Art" (City of Manchester Art Gallery) (1913), 263
    de Stijl retrospective (Stedelijk Museum, Amsterdam) (1951), 365
    Indian Art (Royal Academy) (1947), 228
    "Modern Chairs" (Whitechapel Art Gallery) (1970), 350, *350*, 366;
        fig. 123
    Vienna Secession (1900), 358
Exposition Internationale des Arts Décoratifs et Industriels Modernes
    (Paris, 1925), 377
Exposition Universelle (Paris, 1867), 86, 95, 98, 246
Exposition Universelle (Paris, 1900), 88, *88*, 345, 354, 357, 358; fig. 64

Ferstal, Heinrich von, 34–35
Festival of Britain (1951), 379
fig leaf for *David*, plaster (Brucciani & Co.?), 53, 58, *106*, 108, **130–32**,
    130; cat. 26; fig. 65
Figure of Lydia Dwight, Half-Length Recumbent, personal memorial
    sculpture (Fulham Pottery), **290–92**, *291*; cat. 125
Fildes, Luke, 112
firescreen (Gallé), 88, 354, *356*, **357**; cat. 166
Five Orders of Architecture, The, miniature columns (Drais), 66, 185, **216**,
    217, 218, 289; cat. 85
flagon (Fox), **90–91**, *90*, 92, 108, 137; cat. 2
Floud, Peter, 282, 349
Forster, John, collection, 76, 144, 332
Fortnum, C. D., 156, 171, 174, 177, 193, 204, 252
Foundling Vase (English), *312*, **314**; cat. 143
Fourdinois, Henri-Auguste, cabinet on stand, 87, **95–97**, *96*, 137, 209;
    cat. 7
Fowke, Francis, 57
Fox, Charles Thomas and George, 90
    flagon, 90–91, **90–91**, *90*, 92, 108, 137; cat. 2
Frankfurt Cabinet (Berghof, with Landes and Rang, designers; Draenert
    Collection, manufacturer), **389–90**, *389*; cat. 196
Franklin Institute (Philadelphia), 38
Franks, Augustus W., 151, 233
Fremlin, William, 228
Fremlin Carpet, carpet (Lahore?, India), 92, 228, *250*, **251**; cat. 98
Frith, Francis, *The Great Pyramid, and the Great Sphinx*, photograph,
    140–41, *141*; cat. 35
fritware:
    Islamic frieze tiles, **251–52**, *252*; cat. 99
    Ottoman bowl, **252**, *253*; cat. 100
Fry, Roger, 44, 234, 350, 360
Frye, Thomas, 141
Fulham Pottery, *Figure of Lydia Dwight, Half-Length Recumbent*, per-
    sonal memorial sculpture, **290–92**, *291*; cat. 125
furnishing fabric:
    English, printed cotton, 86, 91, 108, 120, **122–23**, *123*, 124; cat. 19
    English, silk ("Alhambresque"), 93, 115, *119*, **120–22**; cat. 17
    Grant ("*Haircut? Yes Please*"), **383–85**, *384*; cat. 191
    Voysey, designer; Alexander Morton & Co., manufacturer (*The Owl*),
        340, *341*; cat. 162

Gallé, Emile, 354
    firescreen, 88, 354, *356*, **357**; cat. 166
    vase, 88, 354, **357–58**, *357*; cat. 167

Gallery of English Decorative Art, 281, *281*; fig. 113
Gallery 7, Jones collection, 66, *67*, 156, 216; fig. 44
Gamble, James, 180
Gandharan sculpture, 241
    Head of the Buddha, 92, **241**, *242*; cat. 90
Garthwaite, Anna Maria, 308
gas jet (Winfield, manufacturer), 86, 91, 108, **123–24**, *124*; cat. 20
gate, cresting from (German), 108, 110, *110*, **125**, *125*; cat. 22; fig. 69
Germanisches Nationalmuseum (Nuremburg), 19
Gherardini collection, 153
Gibbons, Grinling, 305
    cravat, carving, 216, 280, 302, *304*, **305**; cat. 135
Gigli-Campana collection, 180, 182–83
Gill, Eric, 278
Gillow & Co., 103
Gilman, Benjamin Ives, 44
Giorgio di Pietro Andreoli (attrib.), vase and cover, 115, 155, 174, *176*, **177**;
    cat. 53
Girdlers Company, 251
Girl Aged Five, Holding a Carnation (Oliver), cat. 121B
Girl Aged Four, Holding an Apple (Oliver), cat. 121A
Girl-in-a-Swing, The, porcelain decorative object, 156, *310*, **311**; cat. 141
Glaisher, Dr. James Whitbread Lee, collection, 294
Glasgow School of Art, 358
Glass Gallery (V&A), 20, *72*, *73*; fig. 5, 53
Gloucester Candlestick, 194
Gobelins factory, 103
Goldschmidt, Adolph, 161
goldsmiths' designs (Holbein), from *Encyclopedia of Ornament* (Shaw),
    108, 109; fig. 66
Goury, Jules (with Owen Jones), *Album Book: Plans, Elevations,
    Sections, and Details of the Alhambra*, publication, 95, 117, **118–19**,
    118, 165; cat. 15
Gouyn, Charles, 311
Grammar of Ornament, The, publication (Jones), 109, **117**, *117*, 119, 120,
    165, 188; cat. 14
Grant, Duncan, 360
Grant, Marc Foster, "*Haircut? Yes Please*," furnishing fabric, **383–85**, *384*;
    cat. 191
Gray, Eileen, screen, 350, **368–69**, *368*; cat. 177
Gray's, various ceramic items on display, 349, *349*; fig. 122
Great Buddhist Stupa at Sanchi, Eastern Gateway, cast of, 225, *225*;
    fig. 96
Great Exhibition of 1851, 17, 26, 33, 53, 76, 79–88, 89–90, 98, 108, 222, 231
    Medieval Court (Pugin, designer), 80, *81*, 91; fig. 58
    Prize Medal (Wyon, designer), 80, *80*; fig. 57
Great Pyramid, and the Great Sphinx, The, photograph (Frith), **140–41**,
    141; cat. 35
Greeff Fabrics Inc., 379
Green, Richard A., 332
Green, Valentine (after Joseph Wright of Derby), *Philosopher Shewing
    an Experiment on an Air Pump*, 137, **141–42**, *142*; cat. 36
Green Dining Room (Morris & Co.), 337
Greg, Thomas, 294
Greiffenstein, Hans Lamparter von, 190
Griffin Aquamanile ewer, *167*, **168**; cat. 46
Groenekan, G. van der, armchair, 350, **363–65**, *364*; cat. 173
Gropius, Walter, 36, 371, 377
Guelph collection, 300
Gunnis, Rupert, 306
Guthrie, Charles Seton, collection, 222–23, 239, 246–47

Habgood, Arthur, 216
"*Haircut? Yes Please*," furnishing fabric design (Grant), **383–85**, *384*;
    cat. 191

Hamzanama, "Hamsa's Son, Rustam, with His Mistress, in a Garden Pavilion" from, 229, *229;* fig. 101

Handley-Read collection, 369

hand reliquary (Flemish), *170,* **171;** cat. 48

Han dynasty (China), head and partial torso of horse, *221,* 234, **263,** *263;* cat. 109; fig. 93

Hardie, Martin, 124, 277, 347

Hardman, John, Jr., 91

Harland and Fisher (manufacturer), *The Yatman Cabinet,* 282, **332-35,** *334,* 343; cat. 157

Hart, Solomon Alexander, *Maestro Giorgio of Gubbio,* 56, 155, **174,** *175,* 177; cat. 51

Havell, E. B., 227, 228

Hawkins, J. Heywood, collection, 239

Hayward, John, 215, 281

Hazelius, Arthurs, 35

Head of Medusa (Cellini), **186,** *187;* cat. 61

Head of the Buddha (Gandharan sculpture, India/Afghanistan), 92, **241,** *242;* cat. 90

Heal's Wholesale and Export Ltd. (manufacturer), screenprinted linen, **378-79,** *379;* cat. 186.2

Hencke, Peter, *Saint John Nepomuk,* **211-12,** *212,* 215; cat. 81

Henri II ware, 95

Henry, H. C. J., 103

Herbert, John Rogers, 85

Herkomer, Hubert von, 112

Herman, R. W., student drawing, 109, *109;* fig. 67

Hiernle, F. M., 212

Hilaire and Pasti (designers, with Néville), cabinet on stand, 87, **95-97,** *96,* 137, 209; cat. 7

Hildburgh, Dr. W. L., *77,* 157, 171, 209, 211, 212, 307

Hilliard, Nicholas, *Queen Elizabeth,* **288-89,** *289;* cat. 122

Hindu temple architecture, Tirumala Nayak's Pudu Mandapa, model of, 92, 137, 222, **238-39,** *238,* 308; cat. 87; fig. 108

Hispano-Arabic ivory carvings (Madinat al-Zahra, Cordoba), *Casket of the Daughter of Abd al-Rahman III,* **164-65,** *164;* cat. 43

Hispano-Moresque "ship bowls," 339

HMV (manufacturer), electric fan heater, **372,** *372;* cat. 181

Hobson, R. L., *Chinese Pottery and Porcelain,* 263

Hockney, David, *The Sexton Disguised as a Ghost, from Six Fairy Tales from the Brothers Grimm,* 137, **146-47,** *147;* cat. 39

Hogarth, William, 311

    Cruelty in Perfection from *The Four Stages of Cruelty,* 137, **143-44,** *143;* cat. 37

Hogarth's Dog, Trump (after Roubiliac), **311-14,** *311;* cat. 142

Hogben, Carol, 350

Holbein, Hans, 197, 302

    goldsmiths' designs, from *Encyclopedia of Ornament* (Shaw), *108,* 109; fig. 66

Holbein Cabinet (South German), 155, **197,** *197;* cat. 68

Holland and Sons, cabinet, **98,** *99,* 137, 335, 343; cat. 9

Homemaker Tableware (Seeney, decoration designer; Arnold, shape designer; Ridgway Potteries Ltd., manufacturer), **380,** *380;* cat. 187

Hon'ami Kōetsu (attrib.), teabowl, 87, 233, 269, **271,** *271;* cat. 115

Honey, William B., 234, 267

Honoré, Edouard-D., vase, *78,* **93,** *93,* 137; cat. 5; fig. 56

Hope, Thomas:

    pattern book of, 329

    vase, *328,* **329;** cat. 154

Horniman Museum, 354

horse, head and partial torso, Han dynasty, China, *221,* 234, **263,** *263;* cat. 109; fig. 93

Hôtel de Cluny (Paris), assemblage of contents, by Alexandre Du Sommerard, *30, 31;* fig. 9

"*How High The Moon,*" armchair (Kuramata, designer; Vitra, manufac-

turer), *388,* **389;** cat. 195

Hrazdil, Caspar, writing desk and armchair, 350, **360,** *360, 361;* cat. 170

Hudson, Octavius, *St. Luke,* **134,** *134;* cat. 29

Hunt, Richard Morris, 40

illuminated manuscript, *The Leuville Epistles,* 144, **188,** *188;* cat. 62

Imperial Institute (South Kensington), 63, 76, 225

Imperial Museum (Tokyo), 36

Ince and Mayhew, with Boulton and Fothergill (manufacturers), *The Kimbolton Cabinet,* 322, **323;** cat. 150

incense burner:

    in form of conch shell (Nonomura Ninsei), 87, 233, 269, **272,** *272;* cat. 116

    in form of eagle (Myōchin Muneharu, attrib.), 232, *232,* **267-69,** *268;* cat. 113; fig. 103

India Museum, 63, *63,* 76, 223-27, 228-29; fig. 37

    Arms and Armor collection, 135, *135;* fig. 79

Indian architecture, casts, *226, 227;* fig. 97, 98

Indian art, 86, 92, 222-29

Indian Museum, 224, *224;* fig. 95

industrial arts, 79-88

industrial design, professionalism in, 85

Industrial Museum of Scotland (Royal Scottish Museum) (Edinburgh), 35

Institut Minutoli (Berlin), 36

International Exhibition (London, 1862), 34, 86, *86,* 95, 154; fig. 62

International Exhibition (London, 1872), 101

International Exhibition (Paris, 1878), 101, 103

Ionides, Constantine, 20, *77,* 335

Ionides, Mrs. Basil, 305

Ironwork Gallery, 45, *46;* fig. 16

Irving, Washington:

    The Alhambra, 118

    The Sketch Book, 287

Irwin, John, 229

Islamic art, 164, 251-52

Islington Cup (Thurston, designer; Coffin, modeler), **326,** *327;* cat. 153

Isokon Company, 373

Ives, Halsey Cooley, 39

ivory carvings, 161-65

Iznik ware, 252, 339

    bowl, **252,** *253;* cat. 100

    table, *254,* **255,** 256; cat. 101

Japanese art, 230-36

Japanese national display, Philadelphia Centennial Exposition (1876), 87, *87;* fig. 63

Japonisme, 358

jar:

    Bizen ware, Japan, 87, 233, **269,** *270, 271, 272;* cat. 114

    Choson dynasty, Korea, 234, *265,* **267;** cat. 111

Jean Désert shop, 369

Jeanne-Marc Co., 383

Jewish ritual art, 209

Jin dynasty (China), vase, 234, *262,* **263,** 366, 368, 377; cat. 108

John Hardman and Co., chalice, **91,** *91,* 108, 137; cat. 3

Johnson, Richard, 223

Johnstone, Norman and Company, armchair, **343,** *343;* cat. 163

Jones, Inigo, 302

Jones, John, collection, 66, *66, 67,* 76, 135, 156, 216, 218, 288-89; fig. 42, 43

    dining room at 95 Piccadilly (drawing from handbook), 66, *66,* 156, 216; fig. 41

    in Gallery 7, 66, *67,* 156, 216; fig. 44

Jones, Owen, 20, 27, 79, 85, 86, 90, 115, 122, 151, 222, 232

    (with Jules Goury) *Album Book: Plans, Elevations, Sections, and*

Details of the Alhambra, 95, 117, **118-19,** *118,* 165; cat. 15

The Grammar of Ornament, 86, 92, 109, **117,** *117,* 119, 120, 165, 188, 230; cat. 14

Jourdain, Margaret, 326

Journal of Design and Manufactures, 83

jug (Bourne, Baker & Bourne of Fenton, manufacturer), **104,** *105,* 137; cat. 13

Kaiser Friedrich Museum (Berlin), 37, 43, 44, 156

Kajiwara Rikichi of the Koransha Company, dish, **101,** *102,* 137, 231, 267; cat. 11

Kandler, Charles, Kettle on Stand, 318

Kangra painting (India), *Shiva and His Family at the Burning Ground,* 92, 228, **245-46,** *245;* cat. 93

Kasson (designer), vase, 231, *266,* **267;** cat. 112

Kauffer, Edward McKnight:

carpet, 347, **369,** *369;* cat. 178

Soaring to Success! Daily Herald—The Early Bird, poster, **362-63,** *363;* cat. 172

Kaufmann, Edgar J., office of (Wright), 350, *351;* fig. 124

Kelmscott Press, 337

The Works of Geoffrey Chaucer, 337, **339-40,** *340;* cat. 161

Kendrick, A. F., 277

Kent, William, 307

console table, *274, 325,* **326;** cat. 152; fig. 109

Design for the Memorial to Sir Isaac Newton Erected in 1731 in Westminster Abbey, 306, *307;* fig. 115

"Kestrel" Coffee Set (Cooper, Susie Cooper Pottery), *371,* **372;** cat. 180

kettle, on stand (Kandler), 318

Kimbolton Cabinet (Adam, designer; Ince and Mayhew, with Boulton and Fothergill, manufacturers), *322,* **323;** cat. 150

Kiritsu Kosho Kaisha of Tokyo, 267

Klee, Paul, 379

Klimt, Gustav, 360

Knapp, Ferdinand, 211

Koop, A. J., 233, 234

Koransha Company, dish, **101,** *102,* 137, 231, 267; cat. 11

Korean art, 230-36

Kunstgewerbemuseum (Berlin), 36

Kunstindustrimuseum (Copenhagen), 35

Kunstkammer (Dresden), 25

Kuramata, Shiro, *"How High The Moon",* armchair, *388,* **389;** cat. 195

Kyblich, Ferdinand, 134

labels, "Sunny West" tinned peaches (Richards), 91, 116, 123, **124,** *124;* cat. 21

Labenwolf, Pankraz (attrib.), *Christ Child,* **193-94,** *193;* cat. 66

Laborde, Comte Léon de, 33

Lacroix, Christian, evening dress, **394,** *395;* cat. 200

Lahore (India) (?), *The Fremlin Carpet,* 92, 228, *250,* **251;** cat. 98

Lambert and Rawlings, 90

Lambeth School, 111

Lamentation over the Dead Christ (Bellano), **180-82,** *181;* cat. 57

Landes, Michael. *See under* Berghof, Norbert

Landseer, Sir Edwin Henry, *Lion: A Newfoundland Dog,* 286, **287;** cat. 120

Lane, Arthur, 281, 311

Large Woodcut, The (Le Grand Bois) (Matisse), 137, **144,** *145,* 147; cat. 38

Laver, James, 279

Lawrence Room (painting of, by Enrico Meneghelli), Museum of Fine Arts (Boston), 42, *43;* fig. 15

Leach, Bernard, 234, 263, 296, 387

The Tree of Life, dish, **367-68,** *367,* 385; cat. 176

Le Corbusier, 371

"Lecture on Ironwork" (1870) (illustration), 110, *110,* 125; fig. 69

Lecture Theatre wing, 76, 98

Facade, 57, *57;* fig. 29

Le Gray, Gustave, 140

Leighton, Lord Frederic, *The Industrial Arts of Peace, of War* (frescoes), 56-57

Leonardo da Vinci, *Codex Forster,* notebook page, **189-90,** *189;* cat. 63

Lessing, Julius, 36

Leuville Epistles, The (illuminated manuscript), 144, **188,** *188;* cat. 62

Levin, Phoebus, *Portrait of Queen Victoria,* tapestry adapted by, *103,* **103,** 137; cat. 12

Lewis, J. F., *Sketches and Drawings of the Alhambra,* 118

Libeskind, Daniel, 74. *See also* Studio Libeskind

Lightbown, Ronald, 157

Limoges (France):

enamel work, 168

reliquary chasse, **168,** *169;* cat. 47

Saint Thomas à Becket casket, 159

Lion: A Newfoundland Dog (Landseer), 286, **287;** cat. 120

Little, W. L., 104

Loan Collection of Works of Art, South Kensington Museum, 56; fig. 27

log for circulating books, 113, *113;* fig. 71

Lomax, Charles J., 294

Long, Basil, 279

Longhurst, Margaret, 157, 179, 211, 278

English Ivories, 299

Louvre (Paris), 25-26

Lowell School of Industrial Design, 41

Lucrezia Borgia Mirror, 30, 115, **203,** *203;* cat. 74

Luohan, an Enlightened Holy Man, Yuan dynasty, China, 236, *264,* **265;** cat. 110

lusterware:

Islamic, 251-52

Italian, 177

vase and cover (Giorgio di Pietro Andreoli, attrib.), 115, 155, 174, *176,* **177;** cat. 53

Mackintosh, Charles Rennie, chair, **358-60,** *359,* 360; cat. 169

Maclagan, Eric, 77, 157, 179, 211, 347, 365-66

Maclaren, Denham, chair, *344, 370,* **371;** cat. 179; fig. 119

Macquoid, Percy, 197

Macquoid and Edwards, *Dictionary of English Furniture,* 323

Madonna and Child (Bruges Madonna) (Michelangelo), cast, 108, 130, *130, 131,* **132;** cat. 27; fig. 77

Maestro Giorgio of Gubbio (Hart), 56, 155, *174, 175,* 177; cat. 51

majolica, 171-74, 339

panel, *The Resurrection of Christ,* 156, **171,** *172;* cat. 49

Majolica Painter at Work, plate decoration, 115, 155, **173-74,** *173;* cat. 50

Majorelle, Louis, 354

cabinet, 88, 345, **354-57,** *355;* cat. 165

Mannerism, display in Room 21, 70, *70,* 183; fig. 48

Marimekko, 383

Marlborough House, 27, 31, 50-51, 76, 93, 110, 151, 153; gallery, *51,* 53, 93; fig. 20; Museum of Ornamental Art, 31, *31,* 122, 136, 151; fig. 10; plan, *50;* fig. 19; watercolor rendering (Casey), 153, *153;* fig. 84

Maromme (printer), *Maud,* printed linen pattern, **360-62,** *362;* cat. 171

Marquand, Henry G., 343

Martelli Mirror (Caradosso Foppa, called Caradosso del Mundo), 155, *159,* 160, 174, **177-78,** *178;* cat. 54; fig. 89

Maskell, William, 216

Description of the Ivories Ancient and Modern, 164

Master Guglielmo (?), *The Medici Casket,* 155, **205-6,** *205;* cat. 76

Materials and Techniques Galleries, 72

Matisse, Henri, *The Large Woodcut (Le Grand Bois),* 137, **144,** *145,* 147; cat. 38

Maud (printed linen pattern) (Bell, designer; Maromme, printer), 349,

360–62, *362,* 369; cat. 171

Mecklenburg-Strelitz dinner service, 314

medal, for 1851 Great Exhibition Prize (Wyon, designer), *80;* fig. 57

Medici Casket, The (Mola or Master Guglielmo), 155, **205–6,** *205;* cat. 76

Medici collection, 173

Medici porcelain, 204–5

    pilgrim bottle, 65, 155, 201, **204–5,** *204;* cat. 75

Medieval Court (1851 Great Exhibition) (Pugin, designer), *81;* fig. 58

Meissen porcelain factory (Dresden), 315

Meleager (Antico), 98, *148,* **183–85,** *184,* 186; cat. 59; fig. 80

memento mori jewelry, 290

    The Torre Abbey Jewel, 276, **290,** *290;* cat. 124

Memphis (manufacturer), *Casablanca Sideboard,* 386, **387;** cat. 193

Mendelson, Josiah, decanter, **332,** *333;* cat. 156

Mermaid Dish (Toft), 276, **294–96,** *295,* 367; cat. 128

Merton Abbey, 337, 339

Metropolitan Museum of Art (New York), 24, 40, 43–44, 157

Meynell, Francis, 363

mezzotint, 141–42

Michelangelo:

    Cupid, 182–83

    David. See *David*

    Madonna and Child (Bruges Madonna), cast, 108, 130, *130, 131,* **132;**

        cat. 27; fig. 77

    wax model of slave (Gherardini collection), 154, *154,* 183; fig. 85

Middleton, Sir John, 76, 257

Mies van der Rohe, Ludwig, 377

Milan Triennale, 379

Millais, John Everett, cameo portrait of, 137

Minton, Herbert, 294

Minton & Co., 98, 151, 180, 201

    Prometheus or *Captive* vase, **97–98,** *97,* 137, 183; cat. 8

Miró, Joan, 379

mirrors:

    Lucrezia Borgia Mirror, 30, 115, **203,** *203;* cat. 74

    Martelli Mirror (Caradosso Foppa, called Caradosso del Mundo),

        155, *159,* 160, 174, **177–78,** *178;* cat. 54; fig. 89

    Mughal (India), 92, 222, **248,** *249;* cat. 97

Mitford, A. B., 267

models, 119

    Boilerhouse Project (Studio Libeskind), *14, 74, 75;* fig. 3, 54, 55

    Palace of the Alhambra, Hall of the Comares, 95, **119,** *119,* 137, 252;

        cat. 16

    Tirumala Nayak's Pudu Mandapa, 92, 137, 222, **238–39,** *238;* cat. 87

Moholy-Nagy, László, 377

Mola, Gasparo (?), *The Medici Casket,* 155, **205–6,** *205;* cat. 76

Molesworth, H. Delves, 157, 211

Morant, Robert, 60

Morgan, J. Pierpont, 43–44, 156, 166

Morris, Barbara, 282, 349

Morris, Jane Burden, photograph of (Parsons), **335,** *335;* fig. 118

Morris, William, 103, 155, 252, *278,* 282, 337–40, 354; fig. 110

Morris & Company:

    Green Dining Room, 337

    Pomona, **337–39,** *337;* cat. 159

Morton, Jocelyn, 354, 367

Morton Sundour Fabrics (manufacturer), *Alice in Wonderland,* roller-

    printed cotton, 234, **366–67,** *366;* cat. 175

mosaic pediment, facade (1869), 84, *84;* fig. 61

Moser, George Michael:

    Design for a Candlestick in the Rococo Style Incorporating the Figure

        of Daphne Turning into a Laurel Tree, 318, *321;* fig. 116

    (after) *Apollo and Daphne Candlesticks,* **318–21,** *319;* cat. 148

Moser, Koloman (designer), writing desk and armchair, 350, **360,** *360,*

    361; cat. 170

mosque lamp (Egyptian), 62, **255–56,** *255,* 257; cat. 102

Mughal art:

    calligraphy panel, 92, **244–45,** *244,* 246; cat. 92

    cup, 92, 222, **248,** *248;* cat. 96

    dagger and scabbard, 92, 222, **246–47,** *246;* cat. 94

    The Fremlin Carpet, 92, 228, **250,** *251;* cat. 98

    "Hamsa's Son, Rustam, with His Mistress, in a Garden Pavilion"

        (from *Hamzanama*), 229, *229;* fig. 101

    mirror, 92, 222, **248,** *249;* cat. 97

    pen box and utensils, 92, 222, **247,** *247;* cat. 95

    Portrait of Mirza Abu'l Hasan 'Itiqad Khan, 92, **244–45,** *244,* 246;

        cat. 92

Mughal Room, 228, *229;* fig. 100

Murray, Keith:

    various ceramic items on display, *349;* fig. 122

    vases, **376,** *377;* cat. 183, 184

Murray, William Staite, 350

    Wheel of Life, vase, 350, **377–78,** *378;* cat. 185

Murray and Heath, 139, 140

Musée de Cluny (Paris), 31

Musée des Arts Décoratifs (Paris), 33

Musée d'Orsay (Paris), 19

museology: and collecting, 17–21; and politics, 221

Museum für Kunst und Gewerbe (Hamburg), 36

Museum of Fine Arts (Boston), 24, 37, 40–42, *41,* 44; fig. 13

    entrance, 42, *42;* fig. 14

    Lawrence Room (painting of, by Enrico Meneghelli), 42, *43;* fig. 15

Museum of Manufactures (of V&A), 50, 76, 83, 108, 151

Museum of Modern Art (New York), 44, 365, 369

Museum of Ornamental Art (Marlborough House), 31, *31,* 51, 122, 136,

    151; fig. 10

Museum of Practical Geology, 294, 310, 314

museums: educational goals of, 23, 25–28; history of, 19; and politics,

    221; value systems, changes in, 42–44

Myōchin Muneharu (attrib.), incense burner, in form of eagle, 232, *232,*

    267–69, *268;* cat. 113; fig. 103

Nandi, Shiva's Sacred Bull, (Deccan, India), 92, **243,** *243;* cat. 91

Narcissus (Cioli), 70, *71,* **182–83,** *182,* 190; cat. 58

National Academy of Design (New York), 37

National Course of Art Instruction (NCAI), 76, 108–12

National Gallery (London), 17, 18, 27

national heritage, English idea of, 275–83

National Heritage Act of 1983, 216

National Heritage Memorial Fund, 159

Nationalmuseum, 35

National Portrait Gallery, 276

National Trust (British) (1895), 276

Neale, J. P., 104, 297

Nehru Gallery of Indian Art, 239

Nelham, John, 299

Névillé (with Hilaire and Pasti), cabinet on stand, 87, **95–97,** *96,* 137, 209;

    cat. 7

Newton, Sir Isaac, monument to, preliminary model for, 307

New York Historical Society, 37

Nineteenth-Century Arts of Europe and North America Gallery, 95, 97

Nonomura Ninsei, incense burner, in form of conch shell, 87, 233, 269,

    272, *272;* cat. 116

Nordiska Museet (Stockholm), 35

Norman, Samuel, 321

North Court, 55, 57, 58, 76, 150; fig. 26

    Chinese objects, 230, *230;* fig. 102

    ground plan, *54;* fig. 24

Nubian art, 257

Octagon Court (as Loan Court, 1920), *64, 65*; fig. 38
    English art display in, *64, 65,* 280; fig. 39
Odaschalchi, Prince Baldassare, 36
Ogata Kenzan, 368
Oliver, Isaac, 302
    Girl Aged Five, Holding a Carnation, cat. 121B
    Girl Aged Four, Holding an Apple, cat. 121A
    Pair of Miniatures, 65, **287–88**, *288*; cat. 121
Oman, Charles, 156, 202
    English Domestic Silver, 318
Omar, tapestry (Townsend, designer; Alexander Morton & Co., manu-
    facturer), 345, **354**, *354*; cat. 164
One Flesh, collage (Chadwick), **387–89**, *387;* cat. 194
Opening of the Great Exhibition by Queen Victoria on 1st May 1851
    (Selous), 81, **89–90**, *89,* 231; cat. 1
ornamental panels, cast (from Santa Maria de' Miracoli, Venice), 108,
    127–28, *128;* cat. 24
Ornemens Inventéz par Jean Berain (book with etchings and engravings
    after Jean Berain), **136**, *136;* cat. 31
Oslo, applied arts museum of, 35
Österreichisches Museum für Kunst und Industrie (Museum für ange-
    wandte Kunst) (Vienna), 34, *35;* fig. 11
Ottoman art:
    fritware bowl, **252**, *253;* cat. 100
    table carpet, **256**, *256,* 257; cat. 103
Owen, Philip Cunliffe, 76, 269
Owen, Samuel, 104
Owl, The, furnishing fabric (Voysey, designer; Alexander Morton & Co.,
    manufacturer), **340**, *341;* cat. 162

Padmapani, the Lotus Bearer (Nepalese), 92, 228, **241**, *241;* cat. 89
Pahari (Punjab Hills, India) painting, 245–46
    Shiva and His Family at the Burning Ground, 92, 228, **245–46**, *245;*
    cat. 93
Pair of Miniatures (Oliver), 65, **287–88**, *288;* cat. 121
Palace of the Alhambra, Hall of the Comares (Spain), model of large
    lateral arch, 95, **119**, *119,* 137, 252; cat. 16
Palissy, Bernard, 98
    dish, 30, 57, 115, 155, **200–201**, *200;* cat. 71
Pallas y Puig, D. Francisco, 165
Parker, Richard, 311
parochet (ark curtain) (Italian), *208,* **209**; cat. 78
Parsons, John, photograph of Jane Burden Morris, 335, *335;* fig. 118
Passenger, Fred, bowls, 337, *338,* **339–40**, *340;* cat. 160, 161
Patriot Midget radio (Bel Geddes, designer; Emerson, manufacturer),
    373–77, *374;* cat. 182.2
Paxton, Joseph, 79
Payne, Roger, *278;* fig. 110
Peabody Museum (Salem), 37
pen box and utensils, Mughal (India), 92, 222, **247**, *247;* cat. 95
Pennsylvania Academy (Philadelphia), 37
Pennsylvania Museum and School of Industrial Art, 40
period room displays, 155–56
Perkins, Charles C., 24, 37, 38, 40–42
Perls, Frank, 144
Permoser, Balthasar, *The Entombment,* 157, *212, 213,* 215; cat. 82
Perseus (Cellini), detail, 186, *186;* fig. 91
"Persian" wares, 339
Peterson, Frederick A., 38
Pevsner, Nikolaus, 282
Philosopher Shewing an Experiment on an Air Pump (Green, after
    Joseph Wright of Derby), 137, **141–42**, *142;* cat. 36
Phiz (Hablot Knight Browne), 332
photography, 350; in museum exhibitions, 129, 137–40
Piccolpasso, Cipriano, 174

Piffetti, Pietro, stand, ornamental, 157, *214,* **215**; cat. 83
pilaster capitals, 108, **127**, *127;* cat. 23
pilgrim bottle, 65, 155, 201, **204–5**, *204;* cat. 75
Pink Jelly XK200 Twinphone (Swatch, designer), **390**, *390;* cat. 197
Pinto, Edward, 297
Pinton Frères, *Autumn Leaves,* tapestry, **380–81**, *381;* cat. 188
Piot, Eugène, collection, 178
Pisano, Giovanni, *The Crucified Christ,* 156, **165**, *165;* cat. 44
plaque, Carolingian, *Eagle: Symbol of St. John the Evangelist,* **161–62**, *161,*
    164, 165, 168; cat. 40
Pollen, John Hungerford, 97, 156, 197
Pomona (Burne-Jones with Dearle, designers; Morris & Company,
    manufacturer), **337–39**, *337;* cat. 159
Poole, Mrs. Reginald Stuart, 140
Pop Art, 385
Pope-Hennessy, Sir John, 77, 149, 157, *157,* 165, 179, 183–85, 186, 345, 381;
    fig. 87
Portland Vase (Barberini Vase), copy of (Wedgwood), **309–10**, *309;*
    cat. 140
Portrait of Madame de Pompadour (Boucher), 66, 185, **218**, *219,* 289;
    cat. 86
Portrait of Mirza Abu'l Hasan 'Itiqad Khan (Mughal), 92, **244–45**, *244,*
    246; cat. 92
Portrait of Queen Victoria tapestry (adapted by Levin; after painting by
    Angeli; Royal Windsor Tapestry Manufactory, manufacturer), 103,
    103, 137; cat. 12
postcard image, Crystal Palace (Sydenham), *83, 84;* fig. 60
Pountney & Co., various ceramic items on display, 349, *349;* fig. 122
Powell, Alfred Hoare (designer and painter), vase, **365**, *365;* cat. 174
Poynter, E. J., 182
    The Yatman Cabinet, 282, **332–35**, *334,* 343; cat. 157
Pozzo, Andrea, 302
Pre-Raphaelite Brotherhood, 335
"Presentation of Prizes by Prince Teck at the South Kensington
    Museum" (illustration), 111, *111;* fig. 70
Primary Gallery of Far Eastern Art, 235, 236, 259; fig. 105
Prince Albert of Saxe-Coburg-Gotha (Winterhalter), 82, *82;* fig. 59
Prince Consort Gallery, *161,* 162; fig. 90
Princeton Art Museum, 19
Prometheus or *Captive* vase (Simyan, designer; Allen, painter; Minton &
    Co., manufacturer), **97–98**, *97,* 137, 183; cat. 8
Pudu Mandapa of Tirumala Nayak:
    drawing of, *238,* 308; fig. 108
    model of, 92, 137, 222, **238–39**, *238;* cat. 87
Pugin, A. W. N., 32, 80, 85, 90, 91, 151
    chalice, **91**, *91,* 108, 137; cat. 3
    Medieval Court (1851 Great Exhibition), *81;* fig. 58
Punch, cartoons from:
    "The School of Bad Designs," 116, *116;* fig. 73
    "The Sunday Question," *56,* 57, 155, 201; fig. 28

Qing dynasty (China), 234
    robe, Imperial Dragon, 234, 235, 259, **260**, *260;* cat. 106
    throne, Imperial, 234, 235–36, *235, 258,* 259; cat. 105; fig. 105
    vase, 65, 232, 234, 259, **261**, *261,* 263; cat. 107
Quant, Mary, ankle boots, **392**, *393;* cat. 199.2
Queen Elizabeth (Hilliard), **288–89**, *289;* cat. 122
Queen Elizabeth Virginal, The, 277, **289–90**, *289;* cat. 123
Queen Mary's Jewel Casket (Bickford Family royal locksmiths), **300**, *301;*
    cat. 133

Rackham, Arthur, 146
Rackham, Bernard, 98, 156, 166, 171, 267, 277, 278, 294–96, 339, 365, 366
Radcliffe, Anthony, 178–79

Radio in a Bag (Weil, designer; Apex, manufacturer), **373–77,** *374,* 390; cat. 182.5

radios, **373–77,** *374–76,* 377; cat. 182

Rajput painting, 246

Raku ware, 271

Rang, Wolfgang. *See under* Berghof, Norbert

Raphael, 149–50
  lunettes from Vatican Loggia, 53, 57, 150
  Sistine Chapel tapestry cartoons, 57, 76, 150, *150;* fig. 81

Read, Herbert, 234, 278, 294–96

Redgrave, Richard, 27, 49, *49,* 85, 86, 92, 108–9, 117, 122, 157, 171, 174–77, 222, 275–76; fig. 17
  Donatello, 30, 49, 56, 155, *174–77, 175;* cat. 52

reliquary, hand (Flemish), *170, 171;* cat. 48

reliquary chasse (Limoges), *168, 169;* cat. 47

reproductions. *See* casts; electrolyte copies; models

Resurrection of Christ, The, panel, 156, *171, 172;* cat. 49

Reynolds, C. W., 292

Reynolds, Graham, 281–82

Rhode Island School of Design (Providence), 38

Richards, Frederick Charles, label for "Sunny West" tinned peaches, 91, 116, 123, **124,** *124;* cat. 21

Richmond, Sir Frederick, collection, 299

Ridgway Potteries Ltd., Homemaker Tableware, tableware (ceramic), **380,** *380;* cat. 187

Rie, Lucie, bottle, **385–87,** *385;* cat. 192

Riemenschneider, Tilman:
  Mary, Salome, and Zebedee, 193
  Two Angels, 192, **193;** cat. 65; fig. 92

Rietveld, Gerrit:
  armchair, 350, **363–65,** *364;* cat. 173
  Crate Chair, 365
  Zig-Zag Chair, 365

Rijksmuseum (Amsterdam), 19, 35–36

River Scene, photograph (Silvy), **139–40,** *140;* cat. 34

robe, Imperial Dragon, Qing dynasty, China, 234, 235, 259, **260,** *260;* cat. 106

Roberts Model R500 radio (Roberts Radio Co. Ltd., manufacturer), **373–77,** *375;* cat. 182.4

Robinson, John Charles, 27, 30, 31, 32, 76, 129, 132, 149, 151–54, *151,* 157–59, 174, 180, 204, 294; fig. 82
  collection, 127
  publications of, 151

Rodin, Auguste, sculptures of, on display in East Hall, *348,* 349; fig. 121

Roe, Sir Thomas, 251

Rome, industrial arts museum, 36

Ronca, James, display showing shell cameo cutting process, 116, **137,** *137;* cat. 32

Room 21, Mannerism display, *70, 70,* 183; fig. 48

Rosenborg Castle (Copenhagen):
  Lions, electrolyte copies of (Elkington and Co., manufacturer), 108, **132–34,** *133;* cat. 28
  throne room, *133,* 134; fig. 78

Rossetti, Dante Gabriel, 185, 337, 339
  The Day Dream, **335,** *336;* cat. 158

Rothenstein, William, collection, 227, 229, 246

Rothschild, Baron Ferdinand de, 216

Rothschild, Lionel de, collection, 215

Rothschild collection (Mentmore Towers), 71, 206

Rothstein, Natalie, 282

Roubiliac, Louis François (after), *Hogarth's Dog, Trump,* **311–14,** *311;* cat. 142

Roundel with a Saint (English), **297–99,** *297;* cat. 130

Royal Danish Cabinet of Curiosities, 223

Royal Ontario Museum, 35

Royal Windsor Tapestry Manufactory, 103
  Portrait of Queen Victoria, 103, 103, 137; cat. 12

Rubens, Peter Paul, 98

rug (Kauffer, designer; Wilton Royal Carpet Factory, manufacturer), 347, **369,** *369;* cat. 178

Rumohr, Carl Friedrich von, 173

Rysbrack, Michael, 278
  Sir Isaac Newton, 137, 190, *306,* **307;** cat. 137

Saint Agnes, photograph (Cameron), **137–39,** *138,* 387; cat. 33

Saint George and the Dragon (Stainhart), **211–12,** *211,* 215; cat. 80

Saint John Nepomuk (Hencke), **211–12,** *212,* 215; cat. 81

Saint John the Evangelist (Daucher), *190, 191,* 193; cat. 64

Saint John the Evangelist (Thomas of Oxford, workshop of), stained and painted glass, *166, 166;* cat. 45

Saint Louis Art Museum (St. Louis, Mo.), 39

St. Luke (Hudson), **134,** *134;* cat. 29

Saint-Porchaire ware, 201
  candlestick, **202,** *202;* cat. 73

Salisbury Cathedral from the Bishop's Grounds (Constable), 276, *284,* **285;** cat. 118

Salting, George, 20, 65, 77, 156–57, 354; bequest, 65; fig. 40; collection, 135, 165, 168, 204, 232, 234, 261, 263, 287, 288

Sambandar, the Child Saint (Chola dynasty, India), 92, 228, **239,** *239;* cat. 88

Samsung Gallery of Korean Art, 236

Sanchi Torso (*Bodhisattva Avalokiteśvara*), 228, *228;* fig. 99

Sano Tsunetami, 232

Santa Maria de' Miracoli (Venice), ornamental panels, cast, 108, **127–28,** *128;* cat. 24

Santiago Cathedral, illustration of cast of, from *The Builder,* 72, 129, *129;* fig. 76

sari (India, Benares), **92,** *92,* 108, 137, 222; cat. 4

Sassoon, Sir Albert, 103

Scandinavian design, 350

Scandinavian Ethnographical Collection, 35

Scherenberg, Rudolph von, 193

School of Art at Hanley (Staffordshire), 151

School of Design (London), 27, 76

School of Design for Women (Philadelphia), 38

Schools of Design (England), 107–8

Schreiber collection, 20, 76

Schwabe, Hermann, 36

Science Museum at South Kensington, 45, 122

Scott, Henry, 58

screen (Gray), 350, **368–69,** *368;* cat. 177

sculpture gallery, lecture in, *114,* 115; fig. 72

Seeney, Enid (decoration designer), *Homemaker Tableware,* **380,** *380;* cat. 187

Selous, Henry Courtney, 231
  The Opening of the Great Exhibition by Queen Victoria on 1st May 1851, 81, **89–90,** *89,* 231; cat. 1

Semmelmayr, Josef, 193

Semper, Gottfried, 27, 33–35, 37

Serilly, Marquise de, boudoir of, 155, *155;* fig. 86

Sèvres porcelain, 216, 314
  "Choiseul" pair of vases, 66, 185, *215,* **216,** 289; cat. 84

Sexton Disguised as a Ghost, from Six Fairy Tales from the Brothers Grimm, The (Hockney), 137, **146–47,** *147;* cat. 39

Shaftesbury Shoes Ltd., slingback sandals, **392,** *393;* cat. 199.1

Shah Jahan, nephrite wine cup of, 223

Shaw, Henry, 151, 297

Shaw, Simeon, 294

Shearman, John, 201

Sheepshanks, John, collection, 20, 76, 276, 285, 287

Shell-Mex, 347

Shiva and His Family at the Burning Ground (Pahari painting, Kangra, India), 92, 228, **245-46**, *245*; cat. 93

shoes, English, **392**, *392-93*; cat. 199

    Shaftesbury Shoes, slingback sandals, **392**, *393*; cat. 199.1

    Westwood, **392**, *393*; cat. 199.4

Siddal, Elizabeth, 335

sideboard, *Casablanca Sideboard* (Sottsass, designer; Memphis, manufacturer), *386*, **387**; cat. 193

silver cup, presented by Charles II to Lord Almoner (1865), 276

Silver Gallery, *16*; fig. 4

Silvy, Camille, *River Scene*, photograph, **139-40**, *140*; cat. 34

Simyan, Victor Etienne, 98

    Prometheus or *Captive* vase, **97-98**, *97*, 137, 183; cat. 8

Sir Isaac Newton (Rysbrack), 137, 190, *306*, **307**; cat. 137

Sitwell, Sacheverell, 211

Skinner, Arthur Banks, 77

Slee, Richard, *Drunk Punch*, studio pottery, **391**, *391*; cat. 198

slipware, 294-96, 368

S. M. Franke & Co., 267

Smith, Cecil Harcourt, 77, 346-77, 369

Smith, H. Clifford, 277, 282, 297, 329

Smith, Robert Murdoch, 233

    collection, 252

Smith, Walter, 41

Soaring to Success! Daily Herald—The Early Bird (Kauffer), **362-63**, *363*; cat. 172

Society for the Encouragement and Preservation of Indian Art, 63, 225

Society for the Encouragement of Arts, Manufactures and Commerce (England), 26

Society of Arts (Royal Society of Arts), 82

Solon, Louis Marc Emmanuel, 294

Sommerard, Alexandre Du, 31

    assemblage of contents of Hôtel de Cluny (Paris) by, *30*, 31; fig. 9

Sottsass, Ettore (designer), *Casablanca Sideboard*, *386*, **387**; cat. 193

Soulages, Jules, 51, 177; collection, 30, 93, 115, *152*, *153*, 155, 200, 203, 209; fig. 83

South Court, *55*, 56, 76, 174; fig. 25; ground plan, *54*; fig. 24; ink drawing of, by John Watkins, *232*, *232*, 269; fig. 103; as wartime canteen, 68, *69*; fig. 47

South Kensington (London district), 83-84

South Kensington Museum, 17, 53, 76, 84, 224; becoming the Victoria and Albert Museum, 44-47; collecting philosophy of, 30-31, 32-33; criticism of, 42-43, 45; and education, 107-16; general view, *52*, 53; fig. 21; influence in United States, 37-44; 1862 International Exhibition, *86*, *86*; fig. 62; international influence of, 33-37; Loan Collection of Works of Art, *56*; fig. 27; origins of, 25-28; "Presentation of Prizes by Prince Teck," *111*, *111*; fig. 70; reinstallation project, 44-46; royal inauguration of, 112; social and educational goals of, 28-33. See also Victoria and Albert Museum

South Kensington Museum Art Handbooks, 156

Sparkes, John, 111

Spindler (designer), 354

Spink & Son, 259

Spode, 104

    various ceramic items on display, *349*, *349*; fig. 122

Sprimont, Nicholas, 311-14

    (with Paul Crespin) *The Ashburnham Centerpiece*, **317-18**, *317*; cat. 147

Stable, Harald, various ceramic items on display, *349*, *349*; fig. 122

stained glass, 166

Stainhart, Dominik, *Saint George and the Dragon*, **211-12**, *211*, *212*, 215; cat. 80

stand, ornamental (Piffetti), *157*, *214*, **215**; cat. 83

standing cup and cover (English or Flemish), **292-93**, *292*; cat. 126

Sterne Cup (English), *293*, **294**; cat. 127

Stevens & Williams (manufacturer), vase, *376*, **377**; cat. 184

stirrups, pair (Campi?), 65, **199**, *199*; cat. 70

Stone, R. E., 347

Strange, Edward Fairbrother, 259

Strawberry Hill (Walpole), interior, *302*, *302*, 305; fig. 114

Street, George Edmund, 130

Strong, Roy, 77, 282, 345, 351, 352

Studio Libeskind, Boilerhouse Project (model), *14*, *74*, *75*; fig. 3, 54, 55

Stuers, Victor de, 35

Sugawara (Japanese lacquer master), 368

Susanna and the Elders, embroidered picture, *298*, **299**; cat. 131

Susie Cooper Pottery, 372

    "Kestrel" Coffee Set, *371*, **372**; cat. 180

Suzuki Chōkichi (cast by), vase, 231, *266*, **267**; cat. 112

Swatch (designer), *Pink Jelly XK200 Twinphone*, **390**, *390*; cat. 197

Swift, George, 259

sword fitting, Japanese, 233, *233*; fig. 104

Sykes, Godfrey, 139

Syrlin, Jörg, 193

table carpet (Ottoman), **256**, *256*, 257; cat. 103

tables:

    English, wassail table and furnishings, **296-97**, *296*; cat. 129

    Iznik, **254**, **255**, 256; cat. 101

tableware, Seeney and Arnold, designers; Ridgway Potteries Ltd., manufacturer (*Homemaker Tableware*), **380**, *380*; cat. 187

Taft, Charles P., 23-24, 39

Tagore, Rabindranath, 227

Talbert, Bruce James, 98

    cabinet, **98**, *99*, 137, 335, 343; cat. 9

tapestry, *Esther Hearing of Haman's Plot* (Flemish), 30, **209**, *210*; cat. 79

Tate Gallery, 276

tau-cross, head of (English), **162**, *162*, 165; cat. 41

teabowl (Hon'ami Kôetsu, attrib.), 87, 233, 269, **271**, *271*; cat. 115

telephone, *Pink Jelly XK200 Twinphone* (Swatch, designer), **390**, *390*; cat. 197

Tempesta, Antonio, 211

Tenniel, John, 366-67

textile designs:

    Baudouin, 137, **308**, *308*; cat. 139

    Day, 137, **378-79**, *378*, *379*; cat. 186

textile samples, from "Collection of Animal Products," South Kensington Museum, 53, **120-22**, *121*, *122*, *123*; cat. 18

Theatre Museum, 77

Thomas of Oxford, workshop of, *Saint John the Evangelist,* stained and painted glass, **166**, *166*; cat. 45

Thompson, Charles Thurston, 139, 154

    Soulages collection, photograph, *152*, *153*; fig. 83

    The West Front of Santiago Cathedral, photograph, 58, 108, 127, **129-30**, *129*, 139; cat. 25

Thornton, Peter, 215, 282, 307-8

Thorpe, William, 278-79

Three Graces, The (Canova), *158*, *159*; fig. 88

throne, Imperial, Qing dynasty, Qianlong reign (China), 234, **235-36**, *235*, *258*, **259**; cat. 105; fig. 105

Thurston, John, *The Islington Cup*, **326**, *327*; cat. 153

Tiffany's, 358

tiles, Islamic, 233, **251-52**, *252*; cat. 99

Tipoo's Tiger, 223, *223*; fig. 94

Tipping, H. Avray, 305, 306, 326

Tirumala Nayak. *See* Pudu Mandapa

Toby jug, 391

Toft, Thomas, *Mermaid Dish*, 276, **294-96**, *295*, 367; cat. 128

Torre Abbey Jewel (memento mori jewelry), 276, **290**, *290*; cat. 124

Toshiba Gallery of Japanese Art, 236

Townsend, Charles Harrison (designer), *Omar,* tapestry, 345, **354,** *354;* cat. 164

Townshend, Reverend C. H., 139, 140

Traeger, Ronald, *Twiggy,* photograph, **381–82,** *382;* cat. 189

Trajan's Column, cast of, 58

tray, in the form of Mount Fuji (Nagasaki, Japan?), **101,** *101,* 137, 231, 267; cat. 10

Tree of Life, The, dish (Leach), **367–68,** *367,* 385; cat. 176

T. T. Tsui Gallery of Chinese Art, 236, *237;* fig. 107

tureen, cover and stand in form of chicken (English), 281, *281,* **314–15,** *315;* cat. 145; fig. 113

twentieth-century art, collecting of, 345–53

Twentieth-Century Gallery, 352, *353;* fig. 125, 126

Twiggy, photograph (Traeger), **381–82,** *382;* cat. 189

Two Angels (Riemenschneider), *192,* **193;** cat. 65

Union Centrale des Beaux-Arts Appliqués à l'Industrie, L', 33

valence, with garden scene (English or French), **299–300,** *300–301;* cat. 132

Valentiner, Wilhelm, 44

Variable Sheets dress designs (Willats), **382–83,** *383;* cat. 190.1, 190.2

Vasari, Giorgio, 149

vase and cover (Giorgio di Pietro Andreoli, attrib.), 115, 155, 174, *176,* **177;** cat. 53

vases:

"Choiseul" pair, 66, 185, *215,* **216,** 289; cat. 84

Deck, with Davillier ("Alhambra"), **94, 95,** 137; cat. 6

English (*Chesterfield Vase*), 313, **314;** cat. 144

English (*Foundling Vase*), *312,* **314;** cat. 143

Gallé, 88, 354, **357–58,** *357;* cat. 167

Honoré, *78,* **93,** *93,* 137; cat. 5; fig. 56

Hope, designer; Decaix, manufacturer, 328, **329;** cat. 154

Jin dynasty, China, 234, 262, *263,* 366, 368, 377; cat. 108

Kasson, designer; cast by Suzuki, 231, 266, **267;** cat. 112

Murray, designer; Josiah Wedgwood & Sons, manufacturer, *376,* **377;** cat. 183

Murray, designer; Stevens & Williams, manufacturer, *376,* **377;** cat. 184

Murray (*Wheel of Life*), 349, **377–78,** *378;* cat. 185

Powell, designer and painter; Josiah Wedgwood & Sons, manufacturer, *365,* **365;** cat. 174

Qing dynasty, China, 65, 232, 234, 259, **261,** *261,* 263; cat. 107

Simyan, designer; Allen, painter; Minton & Co., manufacturer (*Prometheus* or *Captive*), **97–98,** *97,* 137, 183; cat. 8

Wedgwood, copy of *Portland Vase,* **309–10,** *309;* cat. 140

Vechte, Antoine, 151

Vegetarian Shoes ("Air Wair"), boots (Dr. Martens), **392,** *393;* cat. 199.5

Verskovis (carver), 302

Victoria, Queen, 77, 89

Victoria and Albert Museum: collecting philosophy, 24–25, 149–60, 221; collections of, 17–18; exhibition philosophy, 45–46, 50–51, 58–60, 70–71; facade (1869), 84, *84;* fig. 61; facade (1909), *59;* fig. 31; ground floor, plan (1905), *58;* fig. 30; ground floor, plan (1918), *60;* fig. 32; history, 17–18; illustrated chronology of, 49–77; newspaper article about acquisitions, "Gems among Gems," *159,* 160, 177; fig. 89; viewing of collections of, 18–19. *See also* exhibitions at V&A; South Kensington Museum; *specific buildings and galleries*

Victorian Primary Gallery, 282

Vienna, royal collection, 25

Vienna Secession group, 358, 360

Village Choir, A (Webster), 276, *285,* **287;** cat. 119

virginal, *The Queen Elizabeth Virginal,* 277, **289–90,** *289;* cat. 123

Virgin and Child (Crivelli), 66, *185,* **185,** 218; cat. 60

Virgin and Child (della Robbia), 156, *180,* **180;** cat. 56

Virgin and Child, ivory carving (French), *163,* **164,** 165; cat. 42

Vitra (manufacturer), *"How High The Moon,"* armchair, *388,* **389;** cat. 195

Volbach, W. F., 257

Vollard, Ambroise, 144

Voysey, C. F. A. (designer):

Alice in Wonderland, roller-printed cotton, 234, **366–67,** *366;* cat. 175

The Owl, furnishing fabric, **340,** *341;* cat. 162

Vries, Adrian de, *Emperor Rudolf II,* 152, **198,** *198;* cat. 69

Vuilleumier, Bernard, collection, 236, 260

Waagen, Gustav, 26, 30

Wainwright, Clive, 283

Wakefield, Hugh, 350

Wallace, Richard, 216

Wallis, George, 104

Walpole, Horace, 216, 288, 302, 305, 314

Walpole Cabinet (Walpole, with Kent, designers), 216, 280, 302, **302,** *302, 303,* 305; cat. 134; fig. 114

Walters, William T., 24

Walters Art Gallery (Baltimore), 24

Wantage collection, 244–45

Warner, Marina, 387

wassail table and furnishings (English), **296–97,** *296;* cat. 129

Watkins, John, ink drawing of South Court, 232, *232,* 269; fig. 103

Watson, Oliver, 278

Webb, Aston, 60

Webb, John, 164, 165, 178; collection, 161–62

Webster, Thomas, *A Village Choir,* 276, *285,* **287;** cat. 119

Wedgwood, Josiah, 104, *278;* fig. 110

Portland Vase, copy of, **309–10,** *309;* cat. 140

and Sons, vases, *365,* 365, *376,* **377;** cat. 174, 183

Weil, Daniel, Radio in a Bag, **373–77,** *374,* 390; cat. 182.5

Wen Zhengming, 234

West, Charles W., 39

West Front of Santiago Cathedral, The, photograph (Thompson), 58, 108, 127, **129–30,** *129,* 139; cat. 25

West Hall, 62, *62,* 256; fig. 36

Westwood, Vivienne, "mock-croc" shoes, **392,** *393;* cat. 199.4

Wheel of Life, vase (Murray), 349, **377–78,** *378;* cat. 185

Whistler, James Abbott McNeill, 335

Whitechapel Art Gallery, 354

Willats, Stephen, *Variable Sheets* dress designs, **382–83,** *383;* cat. 190

Wilson, C. H., 150

Wilton Royal Carpet Factory, rug, 347, *369,* **369;** cat. 178

Winfield, R. W., gas jet, 86, 91, 108, **123–24,** *124;* cat. 20

Winged Putto with a Fantastic Fish (Donatello, attrib.), 174, **178–79,** *179,* 183; cat. 55

Winterhalter, Francis Xavier, *Prince Albert of Saxe-Coburg-Gotha,* 82, *82;* fig. 59

Wittkower, Rudolf, 326

Women's Art Museum Association of Cincinnati, 23–24, 39

Women's Centennial Commission of Rhode Island, 38

Wood, Enoch, 294

Woollard, Dorothy E. G., design series, study of apples, 109, *109;* fig. 68

Works of Geoffrey Chaucer, The (Kelmscott Press; Burne-Jones, illustrator; Ellis, editor), 337, **339–40,** *340;* cat. 161

World War II, 68, 77, 349; bomb damage to west end of Victoria and Albert Museum, 68, *68;* fig. 46; packing objects prior to, 68, *68,* 180; fig. 45; South Court as wartime canteen, 68, *69;* fig. 47

Wornum, Ralph Nicholson, 127

Wright, Frank Lloyd, Edgar J. Kaufmann Office, 350, *351;* fig. 124

Wright, Joseph, of Derby:

Experiment with the Air Pump, 142

Philosopher Shewing an Experiment on an Air Pump, mezzotint after picture by (Green), 137, **141–42,** *142;* cat. 36

writing desk and armchair (Moser, designer; Hrazdil, manufacturer), 350, **360**, *360, 361*; cat. 170

writing table (Japan), **272,** *273*; cat. 117

Wyatt, Matthew Digby, 117, 168, 197

Wylde, Charles, 278

Wyon, William (designer), 1851 Great Exhibition Prize Medal, 80, *80*; fig. 57

Xanthian Room, British Museum, 27, *27*; fig. 8

Yatman, H. G., 332

Yatman Cabinet (Burges, designer; Poynter, painter; Harland and Fisher, manufacturer), 282, **332–35,** *334,* 343; cat. 157

Yriarte, Charles, 33

Yuan dynasty (China), *Luohan, an Enlightened Holy Man,* 236, *264,* **265**; cat. 110

The American and International Friends of the Victoria and Albert Museum, Inc., is incorporated under the laws of Delaware and is a tax-exempt organization as described in section 501(c)3 of the Internal Revenue Code. For further information, please contact the Office of the American and International Friends of the Victoria and Albert Museum, Cromwell Road, South Kensington, London SW7 2RL, United Kingdom.